Launching
New
Ventures

An Entrepreneurial Approach

Launching New Ventures

An Entrepreneurial Approach

Second Edition

Kathleen R. Allen
University of Southern California

Houghton Mifflin Company   Boston New York

To the students and alumni of the Lloyd Greif Center for Entrepre-neurial Studies at the University of Southern California—the finest students I have ever had the pleasure of working with

Sponsoring Editor: Kathy Hunter
Senior Associate Editor: Susan M. Kahn
Project Editor: Tamela C. Ambush
Senior Production/Design Coordinator: Sarah Ambrose
Senior Designer: Henry Rachlin
Senior Manufacturing Coordinator: Marie Barnes
Marketing Manager: Juli Bliss

Cover Design: Minko Dimov

Printed in the U.S.A.

Library of Congress Catalog Card Number: 98-71974

ISBN: 0-395-91845-6

3456789-DC-02 01 00 99

Contents in Brief

Contents

All chapters include an Overview, Terms to Know, New Venture Checklist, Issues to Consider, Experiencing Entrepreneurship, Additional Sources of Information, Internet Resources, and Relevant Case Studies.

Preface

Entrepreneurship is not about money, and it's not just about starting businesses. At the personal level *it's about passion*—doing what you feel passionate about. Talk to most of the truly successful entrepreneurs in this world, and you will probably find that the common denominator is that they are doing something they really love. Of course, there are no guarantees that passion alone will bring success, but it is passion that drives the entrepreneur to succeed. **Entrepreneurship is about passion, about doing what you love.**

Every semester students attend classes searching for the rules they need to follow in order to be successful in business. Everyone wants to learn the "keys to success." Unfortunately, there are no keys—there are no rules. What may appear to be rules change from week to week and from situation to situation. Entrepreneurs make their own rules. And thank goodness they do, because if they had all followed the same rules when starting their businesses, we would never have seen the industry-creating innovations of companies such as software giant Microsoft, biotechnology leader Genentech, and category-killer Wal-Mart. It's only what hasn't been done before that excites the world—that leap into the unknown that shakes us up and makes us take notice. That is the excitement and challenge of entrepreneurship today. **Entrepreneurship is about creativity, innovation, and change.**

For the dynamic entrepreneur the path to success is usually not the path of least resistance, for the path of least resistance tends not to lead to the largest returns. The opportunities that present the greatest challenge also bring the greatest rewards. Entrepreneurs seek out opportunities that are innovative and show potential for growth. The challenge of turning such an opportunity into a business is their passion, which leads them forward with no thought of failure. Failure does not exist in the vocabulary of the entrepreneur. What others judge as failure—a business that didn't survive, a product that didn't find sufficient demand, the inability to secure growth capital—is but a mere pause on the continual journey to success.

Entrepreneurs calculate the risk they take, but they plan for success. For them, success is not measured by how many times their business fails but by how many times they get up, learn from their mistakes, and try again. Each pause in their progress prepares them for the next step ahead. Planning the new venture is a critical component of entrepreneurship. It gives the entrepreneur a fighting chance in a chaotic marketplace. **Entrepreneurship is about challenge, persistence, and planning.**

Launching New Ventures, Second Edition, was written to help entrepreneurs and would-be entrepreneurs understand the nature of the entrepreneurial environment and how to deal with it. It purposely focuses on starting growth-oriented ventures that will potentially have an impact on the economy.

But even those who wish to start small, community businesses or nonprofit organizations can learn much from seeing how an entrepreneurial venture is created, for small business owners are also facing an increasingly competitive environment and need to strive for excellence in their businesses as well. By the end of this book you will have a good sense of what it takes to build a world-class venture and will understand the competitive advantage that can be gained by doing so. You will realize also that world-class status is not synonymous with big business. On the contrary, one of the key aspects of a world-class venture is that it can remain relatively small and flexible while still exerting a major impact on the marketplace. **Entrepreneurship for the twenty-first century is about creating flexible, customer-driven, world-class companies.**

The passion of the entrepreneur is like energy. It can change, but it can never be destroyed—it will simply take on another form. When an entrepreneur's business venture fails, the entrepreneur's passion doesn't die, too; rather, it sustains him or her in the effort to start again. The joy of working with entrepreneurs is that they are willing to make mistakes in order to learn. Because they are willing to make mistakes, they learn that such setbacks are a healthy—in fact, necessary—part of success. Finally, I can teach you the tools of entrepreneurship, but the spirit and passion cannot be taught. No one has a monopoly on passion. Some of the most successful entrepreneurs I know have been teachers, engineers, psychologists, musicians, and filmmakers. Many have had no college education at all, but they were all lifelong learners. They built world-class businesses out of a passion for what they believed in, and what they believed in first and foremost was *themselves*. Will Rogers once said:

> *Know what you are doing.*
> *Love what you are doing.*
> *Believe in what you are doing.*

He must have been talking about entrepreneurs.

Content, Organization, and Unique Coverage

Like the first edition of *Launching New Ventures*, this edition is organized around the process of founding a new venture. If readers follow the process from beginning to end they will learn about all the activities that must take place prior to opening the doors on a new business. These activities include opportunity recognition, developing a business concept, conducting feasibility analysis, writing a business plan, and gathering resources for start-up. In addition, the book looks at issues of growth and harvesting the value of the venture at some point in the future.

Because the focus of *Launching New Ventures* is on the pre-start-up and start-up stages only, it goes into greater depth than the typical entrepreneurship text. For topics related to operating, managing, and growing an entrepreneurial venture, see the follow-up text *Growing and Managing an Entrepreneurial Business*.

Part I introduces the entrepreneurial mindset and the entrepreneurial venture. In Chapter 1, students will learn about the great diversity in entrepreneurial characteristics and behaviors and the book will dispel some myths about entrepreneurs. Chapter 2 deals with the topic of opportunity recognition and how to enhance creativity so that prospective entrepreneurs can more easily find opportunity in the marketplace. Chapter 3 presents a unique discussion of business concept development. The basic premise is that an idea cannot be tested, but a business concept can be through feasibility analysis. The results of this analysis will reveal the conditions under which the entrepreneur can go forward as well as the potential lack of a sufficient market to build a successful business. This book is the only book on the market to treat the issue of feasibility in detail. Most books deal only with the business plan, which is potentially misleading. You cannot write a workable business plan until you know you have a feasible venture. Part I concludes with a discussion of the business plan, which is used to execute the business concept, and how to put together an effective founding team using professional advisers and independent contractors (Chapter 4).

Part II addresses the essence of feasibility analysis: analyzing risks and benefits as they relate to the industry, the customer, the product/service, and the financial and legal aspects of the business concept. Starting with the importance of understanding an industry, not only to identify opportunity but also to know how the industry works, the student learns how to analyze an industry effectively. The feasibility study then shifts to the analysis of the target market and customers as well as competitors. Techniques for estimating demand for a product or service are also presented. Then Chapter 7 considers risks and benefits inherent in the product or service. It is here that another unique feature of this book is played out. Product development for entrepreneurs is a topic that has not been treated in other texts; yet it is a critical part of a product start-up venture. This chapter also considers ways to protect new business concepts through legal means. The next feasibility chapter deals with financial risks and benefits and how to test the financial feasibility of the business concept, including how to forecast sales and calculate how much start-up capital is required (Chapter 8). The final chapter in Part II addresses the legal form of organization of a business. A unique feature of this book is its thorough discussion of limited liability companies and the legal environment of the Internet.

Part III addresses infrastructure issues, starting with Chapter 10, dealing with the virtual enterprise and other start-up processes. This book also includes a chapter on manufacturing processes for entrepreneurs, another topic that is neglected in other texts, while Chapter 12 looks at distribution channels and distribution as a competitive strategy. The final two chapters in this part deal with management and organization and the marketing plan.

Part IV focuses on the finances of the new business by considering sources of capital and the preparation of the financial plan, including pro forma financial statements.

Part V introduces the issue of planning for growth and change in the new venture. Such things as growth strategies, laws and regulations that affect new businesses, and contingency planning are included. Chapter 19 also deals with ways to harvest the wealth of the business and ways to exit when things don't go well.

The final chapter addresses the value system of the new business by looking at ethics and social responsibility, issues that are of increasing importance to businesses dealing in a global market.

Special Features and Additions to the Second Edition

For classroom use, *Launching New Ventures* includes several pedagogical features of value to professors and students. Also noted are features new to the second edition.

Overviews outline key topics for each of the twenty chapters.

Terms to Know, highlighted in color in the chapters and listed at the start of the chapter, give students the key terms relevant to the topic.

NEW! Entrepreneur *Profiles* at the start of each chapter give a real-life scenario related to the topic of the chapter. These profiles provide the basis for discussion of the subject at hand.

NEW! *Profiles* throughout the chapter give real-life examples to help illustrate the application of chapter concepts. We hope that students will be able to identify with the individuals and business ventures that are highlighted, and perhaps even be inspired by them.

NEW! Several *boxed inserts* in each chapter highlight additional examples, stategies, and entrepreneurial tips.

The *New Venture Checklist* at the end of each chapter helps organize the start-up process and directs the entrepreneur's plan of action.

Issues to Consider are questions at the end of each chapter that provoke interesting discussions in class.

NEW! *Experiencing Entrepreneurship* are activities at the end of each chapter that give students a chance to learn about entrepreneurship firsthand by getting them out in the marketplace to find information and interact with entrepreneurs.

Additional Sources of Information are listed at the end of each chapter for more in-depth reading on the topic.

NEW! *Internet Resources* are listed at the end of each chapter to provide another critical source of information on chapter topics.

NEW! *Relevant Case Studies* at the end of the book are designed to illustrate key entrepreneurial issues and include discussion questions for classroom use. New cases have been added to those in the first edition.

Supplemental Materials

An *Instructor's Resource Manual* features lecture outlines, instructor's notes for the case studies, answers to end-of-chapter questions, supplementary lecture material, and a test bank.

An *interactive web site* at the address http://www.hmco.com/college, under "Business," contains resources for both students and instructors. It provides updates of text materials, links to other useful sites on the web, as well as additional examples of feasibility studies and business plans. It also contains additional tips and information to enhance the learning experience.

Acknowledgments

Many people helped make this second edition happen—entrepreneurs, university students, professors, and, of course, the publishing staff at Houghton Mifflin. In particular I would like to thank senior associate editor Susan Kahn whose tireless efforts and unfailing sense of humor got me through a tough production schedule. In addition, appreciation is due to Tamela Ambush, Sarah Ambrose, Ryan Jones, and Marcy Kagan.

I want to thank the instructors who used the first edition and gave me feedback and my colleagues at the Lloyd Greif Center for Entrepreneurial Studies at the University of Southern California who willingly share their ideas, comments, and writings with me. I also want to thank those instructors who provided formal manuscript reviews at various stages of the revision process:

Steven C. Harper
University of North Carolina at Wilmington

Timothy Hill
Central Oregon Community College

Sandra Honig-Haftel
Wichita State University

Tom Lumpkin
University of Illinois at Chicago

Robert Novota
Lincoln University

Charles N. Toftoy
The George Washington University

And finally, I would like to thank my husband, John; and my children, Rob, Jaime, and Greg, who put up with my writing schedule and help me maintain my sense of humor.

K. R. A.

Opportunity and the Entrepreneur

I

1

1

Develop a vision, and never lose sight of that vision.
Sandy Gooch
Sandy Gooch Enterprises

Understanding Entrepreneurship

Overview

▶ The entrepreneur and a changing world market

▶ Who is the entrepreneur?

▶ How can we describe the entrepreneur?

▶ Why do entrepreneurs start businesses?

▶ Entrepreneur myths

▶ The entrepreneurial venture

▶ Entrepreneurial ventures vs. small businesses

▶ The role of the entrepreneur in the marketplace

▶ Trends for the new millennium

▶ The plan of the book

Terms to Know

Profile 1.1

Two Friends, Two Choices

The decisions people make and the reasons for those decisions are always an interesting study. But when two friends with similar backgrounds and interests attend the same university, join the same fraternity, take the same degree program—entrepreneurship—and then make completely different deci-sions about what to do when they graduate, the rea-sons become more interesting. Jon Weisner and Bryan Rosencrantz met at the University of Southern California in 1992. Rosencrantz came to the university from Portland, Oregon, knowing from the beginning that he wanted to major in business. He had grown up

2

in an entrepreneurial family: his uncle founded a major chain of discount stores; his grandfather founded the largest steel company in the western United States; his father was a successful real estate developer. The family generally expected that Rosencrantz would graduate from college and enter one of the family businesses. It seemed only natural, since he had been involved in them since childhood and wouldn't have to make a difficult transition. But the entrepreneurial spirit that infused his family also burned in Rosencrantz, and he became determined to start his own business and make it on his own.

Naturally impatient to make things happen, Bryan Rosencrantz didn't wait until graduation to start his business. By the end of the first semester of his senior year, in 1995, he had gotten Fit-Net off the ground. At that time, the World Wide Web was relatively young, and there were countless opportunities for someone with vision and the ability to pull together the right resources. Rosencrantz, who had a great interest in the fitness industry, decided to become the biggest online clearinghouse for information, equipment, and resources for fitness enthusiasts. He readily admits that although he didn't have unlimited funds, he did have the advantage of significant resources from wise investments in the stock market. He knew that it would be a while before this Internet-based business would make money, and he was aware that he was risking his savings.

As the business grew, he established Fitscape, an umbrella company offering total Internet Service Provider services, which includes Web page design for clients' own web sites. In an alliance with a major company, Fitscape is developing software for the fitness industry. Rosencrantz takes a philosophical approach to the new business. He knows that if the business fails, he can always fall back on the family businesses. Knowing this gave him the cushion he needed to try. His conclusion: "I think I've accomplished something . . . if everything fell apart tomorrow, I'd know I did something."

Jon Weisner had a completely different perspective as he approached business and his impending graduation. He had chosen entrepreneurship to learn how to create a business and how to write a business plan. He recalls his first day in class with 140 majors in entrepreneurship as an overwhelming experience: "I was in this room with all these very serious people who were going to start businesses, and I was there to learn about business plans." At that point, he wondered what he was doing there. Weisner suspected that he wanted to own his own business someday, but—unlike his friend Bryan Rosencrantz—he knew he had much to learn about how to do it. He always saw himself as the type of person who "thinks a lot about something" before he does it.

Jon Weisner had also grown up in an entrepreneurial environment, but in the entertainment industry. His father, a highly respected personal manager in the recording industry, has represented some of the great artists of our time. So Weisner grew up surrounded by entertainers, and his family, like Rosencrantz's, naturally expected him to go into business with his father. That certainly would have been the easy choice, and he knew he could handle the work well. But Weisner had interests that went beyond music to encompass his hobbies: computers and electronics. Fortunately, in his senior year, 1994–95, the entertainment industry and technology were beginning to converge. A new industry was emerging, one that satisfied both his interests. In the realm of technology he recognized an opportunity he could pursue for his business plan.

One day as he was playing with his calculator in class, he began contemplating the liquid crystal display (LCD) and the way the light reflecting on it affected the visibility of the numbers. He wondered whether it was possible to control the visual display in more ways than just on and off. Curiosity moved him to investigate the technology behind LCDs, talking with key people in the industry in an effort to find some clue to the answer. Throughout the first semester of his senior year and after hours of research, he developed a primitive prototype of a system he would eventually call Weisner Windows. This innovative system allowed the user to control the opacity of windows electronically in a manner similar to the way a dimmer controls the degree of light from a light bulb. Almost immediately he saw a market niche for the product: using it on car windows to control the level of tint. As he began to improve on his prototype and it began looking more and more like a feasible product, Weisner filed a notice of disclosure with the U.S. Patent Office to protect his efforts.

As his senior year progressed, Weisner was fast reaching a crossroads. He had to make a decision about his future. Even though he found the Weisner Windows concept fascinating and people appeared interested in helping him do it, Weisner knew he wasn't ready to start his own business and be responsible to investors for its success. The decision to work for someone else was not difficult even though people thought he was crazy for not starting the business. The difficult decision was where to work. The easy route would have been a job in the entertainment industry, where he knew a great many people and could make money quickly. The more difficult choice was to find a type of work that might make a difference in his life—that would mean something. Toward the end of his senior year, an opportunity presented itself to work with technology at the Survivors of the Shoah Visual History Foundation. Shoah (the Hebrew translation for the Holocaust) was founded by producer/director Steven Spielberg. This nonprofit foundation is developing archives of the testimonies of survivors and storing these records in a digital library system so that future generations can learn from them. The pay for this position was certainly not what he could have earned in the for-profit world, but Weisner saw this as an opportunity to learn levels of technology that he could not have learned in school and to meet some very fascinating people. It was also a chance to learn enough so that when he did start his own business, he might not make the same mistakes.

The decision was made more difficult by his awareness that his friend Bryan Rosencrantz was deeply involved in his own business, and several other friends had taken high-paying positions in the entertainment industry. For a student coming out of school ready to earn some real money for a change, the temptation was great. Yet the more Weisner learned about the Shoah Foundation, the more he became convinced that he needed to work there.

In taking the position, Weisner's strategy from the very beginning was to learn everything he could about the whole business, not just his particular position at the foundation. The strategy worked. Within two years, he became the system administrator for the foundation's global network and was working with state-of-the-art technology. He still has dreams of owning his own business, but there's still so much more to learn. . . .

The choice to become an entrepreneur is a difficult one, and a person reaches it in his or her own way. For some, like Bryan Rosencrantz, there is no option but to "just do it"; they have no intention of working for someone else, at least not before trying it on their own. For others, like Jon Weisner, a more conservative approach is called for. No one approach is better than others. Just as there are many types of entrepreneurs, there are many routes to entrepreneurship. The important thing to remember is that becoming an entrepreneur is a personal decision that should be made after careful consideration of who you are and what you want in your life.

SOURCE: Reprinted by permission.

What are some other ways that people approach entrepreneurship?

The Entrepreneur and a Changing World Market

Today there are no safe companies, no sure customers, no secure jobs, and no such thing as an established market share. Yet today entrepreneurship is a mainstream phenomenon because the marketplace has demanded it. The global economy has opened up heretofore-unknown opportunities and with them a new network of suppliers, distributors, and outsourcing resources that will compete with and for American goods and services. Electronic highways like the Internet give virtually anyone instant access to people and information throughout the entire world, providing small businesses the chance to compete with large companies on a more level playing field. With the price of money in the global marketplace changing daily, it is nothing short of a miracle to forecast accurately costs, prices, and interest rates for anything except the immediate future. Many of the products and services businesses will offer ten years from now cannot even be conceived of today. The bottom line is that technology is constantly changing the business of business, from manufacturing to distribution to customer service.

Tom Peters predicted the dynamic nature of the world today and the consequent need to redefine "excellence" in business in his prophetic 1987 book *Thriving on Chaos*. Now, years later, the truth of what he said is being felt. ". . . Excellent firms of tomorrow will cherish impermanence—and thrive on chaos," as Peters stated, or they will not survive. The volatile world market cannot be ignored, and no one is better prepared than entrepreneurs to face the dynamics of the new millennium. For entrepreneurs, uncertainty is the ubiquitous companion of any new venture. Therefore, start-ups must be flexible in nature, and able to change in response to changing needs and requirements. Joseph Schumpeter, a classical economist who often took off that hat when he spoke of entrepreneurs, declared that the job of the entrepreneur is "creative destruction." Entrepreneurs disrupt the economic equilibrium—and from that disequilibrium come new ideas, new businesses, and even new industries.

Dealing with the new global and technological environment requires a different vision and a different mindset today than it did even a decade ago. Whereas in the past, new businesses often started with a narrow geographic focus, purchased equipment and technology to last for the long term, designed products and services before finding customers to purchase them, and built large bureaucratic organizations, today the rules have changed. Today's intrepid entrepreneurs have the distinct advantage of starting with flexible, dynamic organizations poised to respond to change and even to create change as well. Certainly it's easier to start a venture with the expectation of change than to attempt to downsize a monolithic giant and re-educate employees to new ways of doing things.

Accordingly, this book often refers to the new types of entrepreneurial ventures as *world-class ventures*, created by entrepreneurs who have learned much from witnessing the foibles, failures, and frantic downsizing of big business. World-class ventures for the next decade will come from a learning curve that says bigger is *not* more efficient and the largest firms are *not* always the greatest sources of innovation. While world-class ventures take advantage of current technology for product development and manufacturing, they are not necessarily "high-tech ventures" in the strictest sense of the term. Typically, high-tech companies include firms involved with such things as computer software and hardware manufacturing and biomedical technology. Instead, **world-class** as used in this book is a quality term applied to firms that have certain characteristics. Achievement of world-class status begins at start-up with a vision, strategy, and infrastructure that models them. It is likely that start-ups for the new millennium will:

▶ Be smaller and more responsive

▶ Look for niche markets at a global level

▶ Put the customer at the center of the business

- ▶ Innovate with teams and fast-paced product development
- ▶ Be oriented toward quality and customer service
- ▶ Have a less hierarchical organizational structure
- ▶ Rely on outsourcing, the virtual corporation
- ▶ Create value by giving employees a major stake in the organization

Who Is the Entrepreneur?

The term **entrepreneur** has existed in our vocabulary for more than 250 years. The United States was founded on the principle of free enterprise, which encouraged entrepreneurs to freely assume the risk of developing businesses that would make the economy strong. However, it was not the 1980s that the word *entrepreneur* came into popular use in the United States and an almost folkloric aura began to grow around men and women who started rapidly growing businesses. These formerly quiet, low-profile people suddenly became legends in their own time, with the appeal and publicity typically accorded movie stars or rock musicians. Extraordinarily creative and enterprising business people in the 1980s like Bill Gates, who created Microsoft, Anita Roddick, who founded Body Shop International, and Steven Jobs and Steven Wozniak, who started Apple Computer, suddenly found that the whole world was interested not only in their businesses but in their personal lives as well, because they captured the essence of the American pioneering spirit.

At the same time, academic researchers began attempting to define what made these entrepreneurs so successful and so different from other business owners, and to look at the new venture process as something quite distinct from starting a small business or managing an established company. In the early stages of the study of entrepreneurship, researchers, with little success, attempted to identify psychological characteristics or traits associated with entrepreneurs in order to differentiate them from managers. What they discovered was that many of the characteristics normally encountered in entrepreneurs also exist in some managers.

What characteristics are typically found in entrepreneurs and in people who have the entrepreneurial mindset? Research points to the entrepreneur's ability to take calculated risks, to have an achievement orientation or intense drive to succeed, a sense of independence, an internal locus of control, and a tolerance for ambiguity. Recall the profile of Bryan Rosencrantz and Jon Weisner. Did you see these characteristics in both men? (Remember that not all entrepreneurs have all these characteristics. They were derived from statistical averages.)

Risk-Taking

The consensus of the research on risk-taking in entrepreneurs is that they are not big risk-takers.[1] They are, instead, moderate, calculated risk-takers who define the risks inherent in any venture and attempt to minimize them or manage them while remaining focused on opportunity. Not being a big risk-taker is certainly not a deterrent to entrepreneurship.

Need for Achievement

Entrepreneurs tend to have a high desire to be personally responsible for solving problems and setting and reaching goals—in other words, a need for achievement.[2] This need for achievement has often been referred to as "the burning gut," "fire in the belly," or simply "passion." Entrepreneurs are innately driven to make things happen. They are not generally daunted by failure but tend to keep trying until they succeed.

A Sense of Independence

Entrepreneurs also seem to purposely seek independence—to be their own boss in situations that allow them to assume a higher degree of personal responsibility for their decisions and achievements. This need for independence, however, often makes it difficult for entrepreneurs to delegate authority.

Internal Locus of Control

Locus of control means the degree to which people believe events in their lives are within their control. Those who believe they have control over aspects of their environment and destiny are said to have an internal locus of control, whereas those who feel controlled by their environment are said to have an external locus of control. Many studies have determined that entrepreneurs have a strong internal locus of control.[3] In fact, the issue of the entrepreneur's need for control has even been referred to as the dark side of the

---

Profile 1.2

Turning Failure into Success

No one knows more about how it feels to fail than Wally Amos, founder of Famous Amos Cookies. After building an $80 million business as "the face that launched 1,000 chips," he lost his fortune, his business, and even the right to use his name in a new business. He says that failure came because he was irresponsible and didn't take on professional management to grow the company. Instead, he moved to Hawaii, 2,500 miles away from the corporate headquarters, to enjoy the good life.

By the 1980s he was on the verge of losing the company. Out of fear, he took on investors who ultimately seized control of the company and left him out in the cold. Taking full responsibility for the loss of his company, Amos set out to start another, Wally Amos Presents: Chip and Cookie, in 1991. It was not to be. Within eighteen months, the owners of Famous Amos enjoined him against using his own name. On the verge of bankruptcy, Amos, ever persistent, started yet another cookie company in 1993, the Uncle Noname (no-nahm-ay) Cookie Co., which he is promoting nationwide. This time, however, he is donating 1 percent of net sales to an organization called Cities in Schools, which offers a dropout prevention program. On every bag of cookies is a recipe for lemonade, reflecting Amos's "philosophy of life": If life hands you a lemon, turn it into lemonade.

entrepreneur, since entrepreneurs often have difficulty delegating authority or giving up control in any way.

Tolerance for Ambiguity

The start-up process is by its very nature dynamic, uncertain, complex, and ambiguous. Entrepreneurs, however, seem to work well in this type of environment, possibly because it is challenging and exciting and offers more opportunity than a more structured environment.

How Can We Describe the Entrepreneur?

If psychological characteristics are not a good measure of who the entrepreneur is, how, then, do we describe the entrepreneur? Not by who the entrepreneur is, but by what the entrepreneur does. It is the behaviors of entrepreneurs that distinguish them.[4]

The act of creating a business—perceiving an opportunity, assessing and risking resources to exploit the opportunity, managing the process of building a venture from an idea, and creating value—is the entrepreneurial act. Those who have the passion to build innovative businesses from the idea stage and who continue to act entrepreneurially, making strategic decisions that engage the business in risk-oriented activity, growth, and consequent high performance, are considered entrepreneurs.

In line with the behavioral approach, recent research has proposed that entrepreneurship is about the process of organizing,[5] which includes but is not limited to:

‣ Committing resources to an opportunity[6]

‣ Establishing procedures for the use of resources[7]

‣ Identification, assembly, and configuration of resources

‣ Interaction among people[8]

‣ Coordination and establishment of routines[9]

Why Do Entrepreneurs Start Businesses?

Entrepreneurs start businesses for a variety of reasons. Sometimes they are blocked at their achievement at the company for which they work. Such was the case of Ruth Owades, who founded Gardeners' Eden, sold it, and then started Calyx and Corolla, both successful mail-order catalogs. She was working for a large mail-order company when she saw a need for a catalog that catered to upscale gardeners, offering interesting and unusual tools and other gardening paraphernalia. Unfortunately, she could not win the support of her employers, who were nervous about investing in an idea that strayed from what they were currently doing. She decided to leave that company and start one of her own.

Should You Start a Business?

No quiz can really tell you if you are the kind of person who should start a business. This little quiz and its discussion at the end of the chapter will simply help you learn if you may have some of the characteristics typical of many entrepreneurs and people who think like entrepreneurs. Answer the following questions without spending a lot of time thinking about them. You are looking for a spontaneous reaction. There are no right or wrong answers, but when you have finished, look at the end of the chapter to see what research has found to be the typical responses made by entrepreneurs.

1. Which are you?
   a. married   c. widowed
   b. single   d. divorced

2. Which are you?
   a. a man   b. a woman

3. What is your primary reason for wanting to start a business?
   a. to make money   d. to give yourself a job
   b. to be independent   e. to be famous
   c. to gain power

4. How comfortable are you with uncertainty and ambiguity?
   a. very comfortable   c. not at all comfortable
   b. somewhat comfortable

5. To be successful in an entrepreneurial venture, what do you believe you will need?
   a. money   d. good idea
   b. luck   e. all of these
   c. hard work

6. In terms of taking risk, which are you?
   a. high risk-taker (gambler) c. small risk-taker
   b. moderate risk-taker   d. not relevant

7. Have you ever been fired?
   a. at least once   b. never

8. Did you start any businesses before you were twenty?
   a. many   c. none
   b. one or two

Some entrepreneurs have started their businesses after taking a course in entrepreneurship at a community college or university. For Tyler Conrad, taking a course in entrepreneurship at the University of St. Thomas in Minnesota, coupled with the fact that his parents are entrepreneurs, opened his eyes to opportunity. He saw a niche in the market for Polar Fleece mittens that were more fashionable and colorful than those then on the market. This opportunity led to the founding of Colorblock Corporation, a Minnesota-based manufacturer, which produces a full line of fashionable outerwear.

Others start businesses for very personal reasons. This was the case for Sandy Gooch, who suffered from severe reactions to artificial additives in food. They actually became toxins in her body. Learning that many others also suffered in this way, she decided to become an expert on natural foods, and in 1977 she founded her first Mrs. Gooch's Natural Foods Market in the Los Angeles area. By 1993 the company had seven stores, was doing about $80 million in annual revenues, and had over 800 employees. In 1996, Gooch sold her company to Whole Foods and went on to found several other companies. (See Case Studies at the end of the book.)

Still others simply want to own their own businesses. After World War II, Masaru Ibuka started a company in a rented room of a bombed-out department store in Tokyo with $1,600 of his own savings and seven employees, but no idea what the business should be. After weeks of brainstorming, he and his workers decided to produce a rice cooker. Unfortunately, it didn't work the way it was supposed to. However, Ibuka and his team persisted in spite of failure. Their company is known today as Sony Corporation.

Whatever the reason, most entrepreneurs have the intense desire—the passion—to start a business long before they know what that business will be. It is that internal need to be independent and create something, "the burning gut," that drives entrepreneurs.

Entrepreneur Myths

Before leaving the topic of what defines entrepreneurs, some of the myths that have surrounded them over the years need to be dispelled.

Myth: Entrepreneurs are born, not made. Entrepreneurs come in all ages and backgrounds. Even though research has demonstrated links to role models of previous generations within a family, the entrepreneurial drive has not been shown to be hereditary. Almost anyone who has a vision for a new venture, tremendous drive, and the willingness to risk failure can acquire the technical skills to be an entrepreneur through education and experience. Entrepreneurial drive, however, is something that must exist naturally in a person. It cannot be learned.

Myth: Entrepreneurs are gamblers. Entrepreneurs are not gamblers! In fact, as stated previously, entrepreneurs attempt to minimize the risk of an undertaking by calculating the consequences of their decisions before implementing them. For this reason, they conduct feasibility analyses to determine an idea's potential viability with some degree of accuracy before they expend a lot of time and money on it.

Myth: Money is the most important component of the start-up package. Researchers and venture capitalists will tell you that while sufficiently capitalizing a new business is important to its survivability, the most important component is the founding team. An excellent founding team can take an undercapitalized but feasible opportunity and make it a commercial success. A mediocre team may have a difficult time making even a sufficiently capitalized opportunity a success. What constitutes an excellent management team is discussed in Chapter 4.

Myth: Entrepreneurs are motivated solely by money. As you saw from the stories of Tyler Conrad, Bryan Rosencrantz, Sandy Gooch, and Masaru Ibuka, entrepreneurs are motivated to start businesses for a variety of reasons, many of which are personal and have nothing whatsoever to do with money. For people like Sandy Gooch, for example, money is a means to an end, providing natural foods that people can eat without worrying about toxic consequences.

The Entrepreneurial Venture

The entrepreneur is only one component in the process of new venture creation. (See Figure 1.1.) The behaviors and experience of the entrepreneur interact with all the other components of the new venture process to create a business.

The second component, the environment, is the most comprehensive in the venture creation process. It includes all those factors, apart from the entrepreneur's personal background, that affect the entrepreneur's decision to start a business.

Four categories of environmental variables have a significant impact on a new venture's ability to start and grow. They are depicted in Figure 1.2.

All these environmental characteristics affect the new venture concept that the entrepreneur develops and will vary depending on the specific nature of the industry in which the new business will operate. For example, entrepreneurs who start high-technology companies, such as computer and electronics companies, face an environment at once highly dynamic (changing) and very complex. In contrast, entrepreneurs who start restaurants face a more technologically stable and less complex environment. The more of

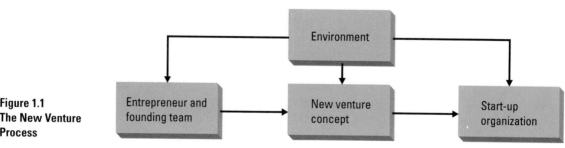

**Figure 1.1
The New Venture
Process**

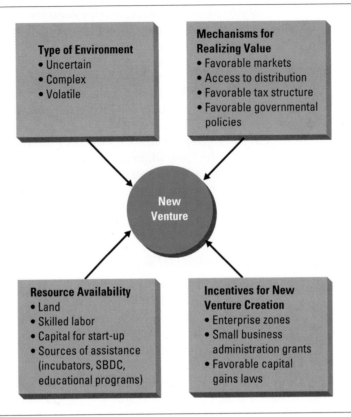

**Figure 1.2
Environmental
Variables**

these environmental components there are in their favorable form in the environment when the entrepreneur starts the business, the better the chance the new venture will grow and become successful.

While the details of the list of environmental variables will be discussed in their appropriate chapters, in general, the environment for starting new ventures in the year 2000 and beyond is characterized by:

1. Global competition

2. Faster product development times

3. Rapidly changing technology

4. Higher expected standards for quality and service

5. The need for strategic alliances

6. A decline in traditional financing sources

Within specific industries and in specific geographic regions, environmental variables and the degree of their impact will differ.

The new venture concept, the third component in the entrepreneurial process, is the development of the initial business idea, taking into consideration the entrepreneur's goals and the environment in which the business will operate. Developing the business concept is the subject of Chapter 3.

Entrepreneurial Ventures vs. Small Businesses

It is important to make a clear distinction between entrepreneurial ventures and small businesses. While many of the venture creation processes discussed in this book are applicable to both types of businesses, in a world-class entrepreneurial venture there is a distinct difference in the vision and mindset of the entrepreneur and the goals for the business from those of the small business owner. Therefore, decisions, resources, and strategies will be different as well.

Recall from the earlier description of the process of entrepreneurship that entrepreneurial ventures are essentially

▶ innovative

▶ value-creating

▶ growth-oriented

An entrepreneurial venture brings something new to the marketplace, whether it be a new product or service (the fax machine or an executive leasing service), a new marketing strategy (the World Wide Web), or a new way to deliver products and services to consumers (Pointcast's push technology on the Web). The entrepreneurial venture creates value through innovation, through bringing new jobs to the economy that don't merely draw from other businesses currently existing, and through finding unserved niches in the market. Moreover, entrepreneurial ventures are growth-oriented. The entrepreneur typically has a vision of where he or she wants the business to go and, generally, that vision is on a regional, national, or more often a global level.

By contrast, small businesses are generally started to generate an income and a lifestyle for the owner or the family. Often referred to as mom-and-pop or "lifestyle" businesses, they tend to remain relatively small and geographically bound. A specific example will illustrate the difference between entrepreneurial ventures and small businesses.

If you were to start a company that remanufactures machine tools for local manufacturers, you would be starting what is termed a small business, in this case a job shop, because the concept in and of itself is not innovative. Your employees would likely come from similar businesses. If, however, you were to specialize in remanufacturing certain types of machinery, using the latest technology or developing proprietary technology, marketing the company on an international level with a plan to go public in seven years, you would have started an entrepreneurial venture. It would be innovative and therefore would create value by offering something that doesn't currently exist and existing apart from its founder; it would create new jobs; and it would have a growth orientation. Logically, many small businesses have the potential to become world-class entrepreneurial ventures. The reason they don't is often a conscious decision on the part of the founder to remain a small, lifestyle business.

Additional characteristics are associated with world-class entrepreneurial ventures. They focus on people—empowering employees, reshaping the traditional hierarchies, providing training and education, and giving employees responsibility, ownership in the company, and opportunity. The result is more loyalty on the part of employees, less turnover, and better performance. These world-class ventures are also customer driven. More often than not, customers and the marketplace dictate the products and services offered by the entrepreneur and even the direction the new venture will take. These ventures are also in constant pursuit of excellence in all aspects of the business. Finally, they are flexible both in organizational structure and in strategy, ready to respond quickly to changes in the environment.

If you understand the differences between world-class entrepreneurial ventures and small businesses, you will realize that knowing what kind of business you are starting is very important, since it affects the decisions you make from the outset and your goals for that business. For example, if your intent is to grow the business to a national level, you will make different decisions along the way than if your intent is to own and operate a thriving

 What Do You Really Feel About Business?

It is important that you seriously examine your feelings on a number of key issues related to the kind of business you might want to own. If your feelings on these issues conflict with the type of business you start, you will in all likelihood be very unhappy and less successful in that business. So, how do you feel about:

1. Using debt or having a highly leveraged business?

2. Unions and the use of union workers?

3. Employees and your ability to manage them?

4. Your religious beliefs and their impact on employees and the business?

5. Government regulation and paperwork?

6. Dealing with people from other areas of the United States or the world?

7. Getting involved in the community?

8. Traveling?

9. Sharing ownership of the business?

restaurant in your local community that competes only with other small businesses in that community. Generally, a small business requires good management skills on the part of the owner, since the owner must perform all tasks associated with the business as it grows. By contrast, entrepreneurs typically do not enjoy or have the skills to handle the management aspects of the business and would prefer to hire experts to carry out that function, leaving the entrepreneurial team free to innovate, raise capital, and get involved in public relations.

The Role of the Entrepreneur in the Marketplace

From the founding of this country, individuals with an entrepreneurial spirit have started the businesses that are the basis of the free enterprise system. With a careful eye on trends and consumer needs, they have supplied us with new technology and new products and services of every conceivable type while also creating jobs. Beyond all this, the most successful entrepreneurs affect our lives, the way we do things, and the choices we make. A legendary example is Steve Jobs and Steve Wozniak, who in 1976 created the personal computer through their company, Apple, and started a revolution that in less than five years resulted in a whole new industry with hundreds of ancillary businesses and thousands of new jobs that had not existed previously. Marc Andreesen, young entrepreneur and cofounder of Netscape Communications, was responsible for bringing the wealth of information on the Internet to the average person through a user-friendly graphical interface. Starbucks Coffee rekindled America's love for coffee and turned coffee drinking into an art form. Entrepreneurs like these shake up the economy. They look for unsatisfied needs and satisfy them. In fact, the most creative entrepreneurs, like these four, invent needs that consumers and businesses never knew they had.

Today **small business**—businesses with fewer than 100 employees—accounts for about 90 percent of all new jobs created. How has this happened? Figure 1.3 summarizes the evolution that has taken place since the 1960s.

In the mid–1960s, large companies were the norm. In fact, all but two of the biggest companies in the world were American. It is estimated that General Motors in the 1960s earned as much as the ten biggest companies of Great Britain, France, and West Germany combined. The reason American companies enjoyed such unrestricted growth was that at that time, they basically had no competition from Europe and Japan. Therefore, job security for employees was high and companies tended to diversify by acquiring other kinds of businesses.

The 1970s saw the beginning of three significant trends that would forever change the face of business: macroeconomic turmoil, international competition, and the technological revolution. A volatile economic climate pervaded the 1970s, the likes of which had not been seen since World War II. The Vietnam War economy brought with it inflation, the dollar was devalued,

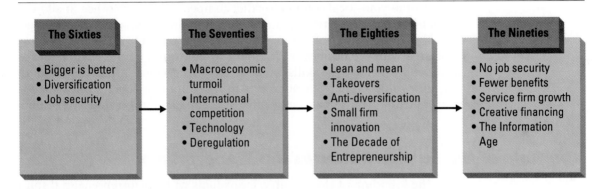

Figure 1.3
The Entrepreneurial Evolution

food prices skyrocketed due to several agricultural disasters, and the formation of OPEC sent gas prices up 50 percent. Furthermore, by the late 1970s the Federal Reserve had let interest rates rise to a prime of 20 percent. The result was no borrowing, no spending, and a recession that spilled into the 1980s, bringing with it an unemployment rate of ten percent.

To compound the effects of the economy on business, by 1980 one-fifth of all American companies faced foreign competition that had far more favorable cost structures. Imports, particularly in the automobile and machine tools industries, were suddenly taking a significant share of the market from American businesses.

The third event affecting business was the technological revolution brought about by the introduction of the microprocessor by Intel in 1971, the Mits Altair personal computer in 1975, and the Apple II computer in 1977. Microprocessors succeeded in rendering whole categories of products obsolete—such things as mechanical cash registers and adding machines, for example—and effectively antiquated the skills of the people who made them.

Increasing the pressure for business, the government ushered in a new era of business regulation with the Environmental Protection Agency, the Occupational Safety and Health Agency, and the Consumer Product Safety Commission, all of which increased costs to businesses. On the opposite front, deregulation forced planes, trucks, and railroads to compete, and in general, big companies no longer had control of the marketplace.

By the early 1980s, business was in terrible shape. The Fortune 500 saw a record 27 percent drop in profits.[10] Large mills and factories were shutting down; manufacturing employment was declining; yet ironically, productivity remained the same or increased. It was found that new, smaller manufacturers were still generating jobs—and not only manufacturing jobs, but service jobs as well. How was this possible? To become competitive, the smaller, more flexible, entrepreneurial manufacturers hired subcontractors who could perform tasks such as bookkeeping and payroll more efficiently. These service firms developed to support the needs of the product sector, but they too inspired the creation of other service firms as well—people who work often need day-care service or maid service, so even more jobs were created.

With the creation of all these jobs, it is no wonder that the 1980s have been called the Decade of Entrepreneurship by many, including the dean of management science, Peter Drucker, who was not alone in asserting that the United States was rapidly and by necessity becoming an entrepreneurial economy.[11]

Responding to this entrepreneurial drive, big business in the 1980s found it necessary to downsize and reverse the trend of diversification it had promulgated for so long. If big companies were going to compete with the dynamic, innovative smaller firms and fend off the takeover bids so prevalent in the 1980s, they would have to restructure and reorganize for a new way of doing business. This restructuring and reorganizing actually resulted in improved performance, increased profits, and higher stock prices. It also meant, however, that many jobs would no longer exist, people would receive fewer benefits, and the only "secure" jobs left would be found in civil service.

All these events moved this country in the 1990s toward a period that required the vision, the resources, and the motivation of the entrepreneur to seek new opportunities and create new jobs in a vastly different global environment electronically linked via the Internet. At the end of the century, small companies are growing, and large ones are not. The number of home-based businesses has grown by one-third during 1991–96.[12] In that same period, the number of business failures declined by 26 percent. The period 1995–97 saw growth of businesses on the Internet surge from approximately 19,000 sites in 1995 to an astounding 740,000 sites in 1997. One measure of the awareness of this entrepreneurial trend is the increasing number of schools worldwide that now offer entrepreneurship courses. Today well over 400 colleges and universities offer at least one course in entrepreneurship. Community colleges and community-based programs are also seeking to give aspiring entrepreneurs the tools they need to succeed.

Trends for the New Millennium

Today potential entrepreneurs thinking about starting a business need to become aware of the trends that will affect global markets into the next century. Understanding societal trends is also a good way to prepare yourself to recognize opportunity. What major trends are currently evolving?

An Emphasis on Social Responsibility

Today an increasing number of businesses are doing more than simply making profits. They are also concerned about **social responsibility**—that is, about giving something back to their community through community-aid programs, by being responsible about the pollutants they create in their

production process, and by demonstrating an awareness of their intercon-
nectedness with society as a whole. Young entrepreneur Melissa Bradley used
the money from the sale of her first company to launch The Entrepreneurial
Development Institute (TEDI) in Washington, D.C. It is a nonprofit organization devoted to teaching entrepreneurship to at-risk youths. She chose the
nonprofit route because the customers she wanted to serve couldn't afford a
fee-based training program.[13]

A Focus on the Environment

Not only are businesses becoming more responsible about not polluting the
environment, many entrepreneurs are starting environmental businesses to
help Americans in their efforts to clean up the environment. A good example
is Gardeners' Supply, a mail-order company located in Burlington, Vermont,
which collects and composts grass clippings, leaves, and food scraps for free.
The compost is then passed on to gardeners. The program has been so successful that Gardeners' Supply is now collecting 3,000 to 4,000 tons a year.
Its goal is to recycle 30 percent of the total waste in the community.

A Global Orientation

The old saying that the world is an increasingly smaller place seems to be
true. Technology has made access to other countries as easy as contacting the
business in the next city. Exporting products and services to other countries
has almost become a necessity for a growing business to remain competitive.
Today it is just as likely you will purchase some of your supplies overseas as
it is that you will purchase them domestically. You may even manufacture in
another country.

Fitness and Health

The business of keeping people healthy and physically fit is a huge industry
that began taking shape in the 1980s. The ubiquitous baby boom generation,
which has just reached its 50s, provides the astute entrepreneur with an enormous customer base of people who want to stay "young" and fit as long as
possible. Bryan Rosencrantz, a southern California young entrepreneur,
started Fit-Net on the World Wide Web to give fitness enthusiasts a one-stop
source of information, equipment, products, and services in the fitness industry. (See Profile 1.1.)

The Aging Population

In less than twenty years, the oldest of the baby boomers will have reached
retirement age. We are facing a major population shift; average age is increasing. Consequently, opportunities abound for product and service businesses
that meet the needs of this enormous consumer group. Bruce Lunsford is an

example of someone who saw this trend and started Vencor, Inc., which specializes in long-term care. Today he runs hospitals in 11 states.

Career Flexibility

Keeping the same job for thirty or more years is a thing of the past. Today adults must be prepared for change, and they must constantly update their skills so that when change comes, they can adapt. Roe Hatlen found himself out of a job at age 40. Fortunately, it was just the jump-start he needed to make the decision to start his own company. He managed to build the very successful Old Country Buffet chain of restaurants, offering home-style entrees.

Information Is Power

You have no doubt heard the terms *information age* and *information super-highway*. With the advent of the computer revolution, information is more readily available and in greater quantity than ever before. In fact, some

Should You Become an Entrepreneur?

Here are some questions to consider before you decide to become an entrepreneur. There are no right or wrong answers, but it is important to acknowledge that these issues affect every entrepreneur to some degree.

1. How do you feel about security? Many new ventures take up to two years to show a profit or permit the entrepreneur to receive a salary.

2. What are your reasons for wanting to own your own business? If money is the goal, you need to consider that there are easier, less risky ways to make money. Most entrepreneurs start businesses for reasons other than money, although they fully intend to create wealth through their companies.

3. Are you in shape to start a business? Launching a new business requires tremendous amounts of time and energy, as well as support from family and friends.

4. What kind of lifestyle are you looking for? Will your business and its location provide the kind you want?

5. In what type of business environment do you like to work? If you prefer the outdoors, don't start a business that keeps you inside at a desk all day long.

would say we are actually suffering from "information overload," too much information and too little time to process it all. Today a company's power—or an individual's power, for that matter—comes from staying on top of new information. We are no longer a society that can educate people through age 21 and claim that they are sufficiently educated. "Life-long learning" is the trend, and as a result, distance learning via the Internet, satellite, and video-conferencing is a growing industry.

Women in Business

Today women are starting businesses at a rate twice that of men. Moreover, women now employ more people than the Fortune 500 worldwide. Why is this? One reason is that women are no longer comfortable in a big business culture dominated by men, which often prevents them from reaching the highest levels of management. Women also start businesses so that they can make the major decisions and create a culture that reflects their different management style. Emyre Robinson, for example, founded Barrios Technologies, an engineering contractor to NASA and major space contractors, to meet a need in the industry but also for the opportunity to create a business culture based on the nuclear family, where people come first. Her door is open to any employee of the company, and all are encouraged to participate in its growth process and its success.

The fact that more women are starting businesses is also important from an economic standpoint; women now require the services they traditionally supplied for their husbands: housecleaning, child care, cooking, and so on. Consequently, some women are starting those very service businesses that help other women move into economic sectors previously dominated by men. While it is true that, in general, women start small businesses in the retail and service sectors, we are now seeing a significant increase in the number of women who start high-growth ventures in industries previously dominated by men.

Staying Home

Faith Popcorn, a noted market consultant to Fortune 500 companies, has observed a trend she calls **cocooning**. Cocooning is simply staying home: entertaining at home or working from home via telecommuting. What this means to entrepreneurs is that people are demanding more delivery services for things such as restaurant food, groceries, dry cleaning, and so forth. They want to entertain themselves at home, so they are purchasing more in-home entertainment systems, renting more videos, and shopping from home via computers.

Consolidation of Industries

One growing trend is that of entrepreneurs who go into their industry and buy up independent mom-and-pop operations or bring them together in a co-op type of arrangement to provide products and services that are more economical to their customers. One of the most famous consolidators is Wayne Huizenga, who consolidated the video industry with Blockbuster, the garbage industry with Waste Management—and is now working on the used cars industry with Auto Nation. On a smaller scale, entrepreneur Todd Smart started Absolute Towing and Trucking in the San Fernando Valley of Southern California to consolidate the towing industry, which consisted of many independent tow truck owners.

The Plan of the Book

Starting a new venture is a process that begins long before the business ever opens its doors. Consequently, this book takes a process approach to starting a world-class venture. It begins with opportunity recognition and the development of a concept for a new business. It then explains how to test that concept in the marketplace through a feasibility study. Finally, it discusses the business plan as a means for documenting the creation of a new company to support the feasible business concept. The topics covered in each chapter give the reader the information needed for preparing to launch a new business. Issues related to the management of a growing business are covered in *Growing and Managing an Entrepreneurial Business* (Boston: Houghton Mifflin Company, 1998).

In the next decade, entrepreneurial skills will be the key not only to economic independence and success, but literally to survival as well. The marketplace places a premium on creativity, initiative, independence, and flexibility, characteristics present in dynamic entrepreneurs.

New Venture Checklist

Have you:

- ❏ **Concluded that you have what it takes to be an entrepreneur?**

- ❏ **Determined why you want to start a business?**

- ❏ **Decided if you will start an entrepreneurial venture or a small business?**

- ❏ **Determined how the trends for the new millennium will affect your search for a business idea?**

Answers to Quiz on page 9: Should You Start a Business?

1. The average entrepreneur is married, probably because most entrepreneurs are older when they initiate their ventures and having a working spouse gives an additional source of income during start-up.

2. Most entrepreneurs today are still men, particularly in high-growth ventures, but women are starting businesses at a rate much higher than that of men. And more and more women are starting high-growth ventures.

3. The primary reason most entrepreneurs give for starting a business is to gain independence—the right to do things the way they want.

4. In general, entrepreneurs tend to be very comfortable with ambiguity and uncertainty. An uncertain environment, which is characteristic of start-up ventures, offers a challenge that entrepreneurs enjoy meeting. Moreover, a dynamic, uncertain environment generally offers more opportunity.

5. Entrepreneurs will need all of these factors. But note that entrepreneurs believe they make their own luck.

6. Entrepreneurs are moderate risk-takers. They calculate risk and take on risks that have a good probability of producing adequate rewards.

7. Entrepreneurs often report having been fired, probably because they don't easily fit into traditional company molds.

8. Most entrepreneurs have started several ventures before age 20.

Issues to Consider

1. Why is it so difficult to assign "typical" characteristics to entrepreneurs in order to describe them?

2. Do you agree with the notion that entrepreneurs start businesses for more than money? Why or why not?

3. What impact does the environment have on your ability to start a business?

4. What does "creating value" mean to you as a potential entrepreneur?

5. Take a typical "small business" in your community and discuss how you could turn that business into an entrepreneurial venture.

6. What evidence do you find for the statement that we are becoming an "entrepreneurial economy"?

7. Which of the trends for the next decade do you believe holds the most promise for business opportunity and why?

Experiencing Entrepreneurship

1. Interview an entrepreneur in an industry or business that interests you. Make the focus of this interview on how and why this entrepreneur started his or her business. Based on your readings in the chapter, what type of entrepreneur is this?

2. Visit an entrepreneurial venture and a small business. Compare and contrast them in terms of the distinctions discussed in the chapter. Which type of business is more suited to your personality and your goals?

Additional Sources of Information

Case, J. (1992). *From the Ground Up*. New York: Simon & Schuster.

Drucker, P.F. (1986). *Innovation and Entrepreneurship*. New York: Harper & Row.

Godfrey, J. (1992). *Our Wildest Dreams*. New York: HarperCollins.

Kushell, J. (1997). *No Experience Necessary*. New York: Random House.

Naisbitt, J., and Aberdene, P. (1990). *Megatrends 2000: Ten New Directions for the 1990s*. New York: Fawcett Columbine.

Peters, T. (1987). *Thriving on Chaos*. New York: Harper & Row.

Vesper, K.H. (1994). *New Venture Experience*. Seattle, WA: Vector Books.

Internet Resources

Entrepreneurial Edge Online
http://www.edgeonline.com/
Resources for entrepreneurs and links to magazines, journals, and trade associations.

An Electronic Guide for the Entrepreneur
http://www.successmagazine.com/info/thesource.html
An easy way to find competitive intelligence from a variety of sources.

Relevant Case Studies

1. Toy Tips, Inc.
2. Mrs. Gooch's Natural Foods Markets
3. Flight Time

2

Few ideas are in themselves practical. It is for want of imagination in applying them, rather than in acquiring them, that they fail. The creative process does not end with an idea—it only starts with an idea.
John Arnold
Massachusetts Institute of Technology
Business Week, December 29, 1956

Recognizing and Testing Opportunity

Overview

▶ **Recognizing opportunity**

▶ **Enhancing your creative skills**

▶ **Sources of new venture ideas**

▶ **Where will the opportunities be in the next decade?**

▶ **Developing a business concept**

Terms to Know

Profile 2.1

If It Looks like a Duck . . .

Ideas for businesses can come out of virtually anywhere. In the case of Andrew Wilson, a Boston investment banker, opportunity hit like a bolt of lightning. In 1992, tired of working 100-hour weeks, he traveled across country to visit family and friends. Along the way he stopped in Memphis to visit the legendary Graceland, estate of Elvis Presley. It was there that he first came upon an amphibious military vehicle from the World War II era known as the "duck," which had been converted to a kind of tour bus. It occurred to him that the amphibious nature of the vehicle was perfect for land and water tours of Boston.

The City of Boston wasn't as sure as Wilson. Part of the problem was that Wilson didn't even own a "duck" that he could show the city leaders. It took him nine months to discover a funeral home director, Manuel Rogers, who happened to be a collector of military vehicles; he owned a duck. Not only did he lend it to Wilson to convince the city officials to let him start his business by giving sample tours, he helped raise start-up capital as well. Wilson painted his ducks bright colors and configured each to carry 32 passengers. In the spring of 1994, Wilson launched his ducks in the Charles River. By fall, 33 investors had placed their faith in Wilson to the tune of $1.25 million. The company was officially in business in October of 1994. By 1996, Boston Duck Tours, sporting 12 boats and 19 Coast Guard licensed "captains," was carrying 250,000 riders and boasted revenues of $3.4 million. Wilson has plans to open tours in other cities that have plenty of history—and water as well.

SOURCE: Michael Barrier, "The Mighty Ducks," *Nation's Business*, October 1997, pp. 78-79.

Which niche in the market did Wilson's opportunity serve?

Recognizing Opportunity

Have you ever wondered where people get those great ideas that turn into extraordinarily successful businesses? Is the ability to recognize opportunity something you're born with? Not necessarily. Can it be learned? Absolutely! Certainly some people have an easier time generating ideas than others, but that's only because they may possess better-developed creative and awareness skills. This is good news, because even if you have never thought of yourself as a creative person, you have the ability to become one.

What does creativity have to do with entrepreneurship? Very simply, **creativity** is that behavior that results in **innovation**, which is finding a new way to do something, a key ingredient in entrepreneurial success. Moving into the new century, entrepreneurs face an exciting but uncertain future. A stable and growing economic climate results in more jobs and thus less incentive to start new businesses. It is a curious fact of life that in the worst of environments—in fact, especially in the worst environments—creative men and women find innovative problems and opportunities as well as ways of adapting to the environment and making it work for them. The worst of times often brings out the best in entrepreneurs. The case of John Wiley and Alan Ackerman is a good example. (See Profile 2.2.) Nevertheless, no matter what the environment throws at entrepreneurs, if they put their creative talents to work, they can find a way to succeed.

Profile 2.2

Making Creativity Work

In 1982 John Wiley and Alan Ackerman started a company called Microbits Peripheral Products, Inc., to produce hardware for the Atari personal computer. Within a year and a half, they were doing $3 million in sales and had 55 employees. Then, in 1985, the Atari market collapsed, Microbits was unable to keep up its loan payments, and its loan was called by the bank. The company could not be sold, so the bank decided to package the assets and auction them through a sealed bid process. Wiley and Ackerman could have given up at that point; instead, they saw a chance to turn a disaster into a creative opportunity by rounding up ten investors who helped them repurchase their assets at auction for 10 cents on the dollar.

With their investors they started Supra, which produces modems and communication devices for a number of different computers. Starting in their garage, Wiley and Ackerman turned a failure into a success within a year.

Enhancing Your Creative Skills

Creative people are curious people who exhibit a strong sense of awareness of their surroundings. They ask questions and aren't afraid to do things differently. They are openly accepting of all ideas, figuring that every idea is worthy of at least initial consideration, and they seem to have a high tolerance for ambiguity.

However, some people resist creativity and ambiguity; they are uncomfortable in uncertain environments and don't know how to use their creative skills to survive. This is not surprising when you consider that many schools do not challenge students to be creative, but instead expect them to follow a structured environment laid out by the teacher, which includes coming up with only the expected correct answers.

Entrepreneurship is a creative, not a scientific, process. From the generation of the business idea to the development of the marketing plan to the management of the growing business, it is creativity in all aspects of the venture that sets the most successful new businesses apart from those that merely survive.

Before considering some specific techniques you can use to generate business ideas, you might want to try a couple of exercises to prepare yourself for thinking creatively.

1. Pick a simple item you have in your home, perhaps a box of granola, and see how many uses or new products based on it you can develop. There are at least 30! Remember, don't limit your thinking. For example, you could glue the granola to a backing, spray it with shellac, and use it as jewelry! As silly as this idea sounds, you will find that the more you do this exercise with different products, the easier it gets and the more ideas you are able to generate. Some of them may actually turn out to be sound business ideas.

2. The next time you say to yourself, "I wish there were a way to . . ." or "I wish I had something that could . . . ," stop yourself and start thinking about how to get from here to there. This is, by the way, how breakthrough products like the fax machine were developed. The question that led to the fax machine was "How can I get a written document to people as quickly as I can phone them?" For the solution, the inventor didn't limit himself by looking only at what was obviously possible. Think of all the inventions and services that are part of life today that wouldn't be here if the inventors had limited themselves to what was "possible."

Sources of New Venture Ideas

It is important to distinguish between an idea and an opportunity. Everyone has ideas; in fact, you probably have hundreds of them every day. Every time you make a decision to do something, it is based on an idea or thought that came to you prior to making the decision. However, opportunity, in a business sense, is an idea that can be turned into a business or commercialized in some manner. In fact, it is the very act of developing a business concept and testing it through feasibility analysis that turns an idea into an opportunity.

One way to understand the difference between an idea and an opportunity is to consider the difference between an inventor and an entrepreneur. An inventor plays with ideas and concepts and may turn them into products, whereas the entrepreneur recognizes the market potential of the idea and sees a way to create value.

Much of creativity and innovation today occurs within the confines of what is already known: planes to spaceships, drive-in restaurants to drive-in banks. It is only when a few very insightful people who think "out of the box" break those boundaries and leap into an untried, unknown universe that products such as the computer, for which there really was no precedent, are created. Even a simple product like Velcro was inspired by going beyond human boundaries and observing the sticky hook spine of the common burr in nature.

What sets off the creative process is a very personal thing. How many times have you come up with an idea while listening to a dry lecture or a boring sermon? Some people find their best ideas come while they are driving, reading, or exercising. Do you get ideas through dreams—or in the shower? If you can identify where and when you seem to get most of your creative thoughts, you may want, if possible, to perform that activity or a similar one more often and actually write down the ideas you get as they occur.

There are several ways you can use your newfound creativity to generate some ideas that may lead to an opportunity and help turn you into an entrepreneur.

Keep an Idea File or Notebook

You have often heard about people who keep a notepad by the bed in case they have a good idea during the night. Why not keep a notepad with you all the time? Who knows when the spark of a great idea will come to you? Don't take a chance that you will remember it later. Chances are you won't because other thoughts and activities will invade your consciousness during the day, leaving you struggling later to recall that great idea you had.

Talk with People—Network

Dr. Naka Mats claims (see Profile 2.3) that networking with people wherever he goes is a prime source of inspiration for new product ideas. In talking with a wide variety of people, you find out more about their needs, and an unmet need is an opportunity. Talk with consumers, suppliers, your potential competition; there is something to be learned from everyone you meet.

Read Voraciously

Read newspapers, business magazines, and trade journals from the industry that interests you. Keep up with current trends in the marketplace, as well as present and potential governmental policies that may affect your type of work. Remember, an idea can come from anywhere. The wealth of new environmental businesses was spawned by awareness of what our business and life practices have been doing to the world we live in and also by the regulations that ensued.

Try Thinking in Opposites

Try thinking about what a product or service will not do or be. Charles Thompson, who wrote an excellent book on creativity, tells of an unusual technique he developed to collect debts.[1] He did it by thinking in opposites. Most people send formal invoices to their customers reminding them of their debt. He sent a cartoon of himself lying on the floor with a giant knife stuck in his back and a bubble saying, "I trusted you." Most people send bills to the client's office. He sent it to the home. Most people send the bill in a business envelope by regular mail; Thompson sent it in a three-foot package by next-day UPS. The technique was extremely successful and even turned into a small business because he thought about a problem from a different perspective; he did the opposite of what everyone else was doing.

Look for New Uses for Old Things

Johann Gutenberg took two unconnected ideas—the wine press and the coin punch—and came up with the printing press and movable type. The mechanism for roll-on deodorant was the inspiration for the ballpoint pen. You might try looking a little closer at the products you use every day and probably take for granted. How many times have you given an item a new use simply because you didn't own the correct tool to do what you wanted to do? Look a little more closely at everything you use; see if there is a way you can

Profile 2.3

A Creative Way to Generate Ideas

Dr. Yoshiro Naka Mats is truly the essence of a creative, innovative person. He holds more than 2,300 patents, more than double the number that prolific American inventor Thomas Edison held. For example, Naka Mats is responsible for the floppy disk, which he licensed to IBM, the compact disk and player, the digital watch, and the water-powered engine. Naka Mats even has a creative way of generating ideas. He starts the creativity process by sitting calmly in a room in his home, which he calls the "static room" because it has only natural things in it, much like the meditation gardens in Kyoto, Japan. It is in this room that he opens his mind to the creative flow of new ideas. He then moves to the "dynamic room," a dark room with the latest audio/video equipment. Here he listens to jazz, easy listening music and Beethoven's Fifth Symphony—one of his favorites. In this room the genesis of new ideas begins to form. Following a period of time in the dynamic room, he heads for the swimming pool, where he swims underwater for extraordinarily long periods of time. It is underwater that he finishes the process of "soft thinking" or playing with the idea and is ready to move on to the more practical phase of considering how to implement the idea.

Naka Mats, by the way, also swears by the brain food he eats: dried shrimp, seaweed, cheese, yogurt, eel, eggs, beef, and chicken livers!

Generating Business Ideas

Here are some exercises you might try to spark some new ideas and new ways of looking at things.

List some geographic areas that are not being serviced by a particular product or service.

1.

2.

3.

List some market segments (populations) that are underserved.

1.

2.

3.

List some big or troublesome problems for which the solution could turn into a potential business.

1.

2.

3.

improve on it or come up with an entirely new tool. 3M scientist Arthur Fry was working on developing bookshelf arranger tape when he came up with the idea for a sticky-backed book marker, which ultimately became Post-it Notes. See the box above for an example of a way to generate new ideas.

Brainstorm Your Way to a New Idea

Brainstorming is a technique whereby you come up with ideas one after the other without stopping to consider if the idea is feasible. The advantage of brainstorming is that it often puts you in a position to come up with ideas as quickly as possible. Brainstorming opens your mind and helps you suspend judgment. Challenging beliefs and assumptions through brainstorming about what might be possible resulted in the computers, fax machines, and space shuttles that exist today.

Team with an Inventor

People often confuse inventors with entrepreneurs, believing that the terms are synonymous. But as with the terms *idea* and *opportunity*, inventors and entrepreneurs are often very different types of people. Inventors normally are involved with implementing ideas; entrepreneurs are involved with implementing opportunity. The reason is that inventors are idea people, representing the essence of creativity. They tend to look at every aspect of life as a problem to be solved or a product to be improved. Sometimes this idea-seeking attitude can serendipitously result in a new product idea. For example, one researcher who was developing an anti-ulcerative drug accidentally licked his fingers and discovered aspartame, which is now sold as Nutrasweet. Whether they are scientists, engineers, mechanics, or just "tinkerers," inventors are continually generating ideas and prototypes for new products. Many of those products will never see the marketplace, though, because inventors often lack the necessary skills to commercialize their inventions—that is, to create a business opportunity by which to bring their products to market.

That's where entrepreneurs come in. Entrepreneurs possess the ability to identify a market for the inventor's product, gather sufficient resources to create a business to market the products, and create value for both the inventor and the entrepreneur. This is not to say inventors and entrepreneurs cannot be one and the same. Don Beaver and Ben Stapelfeld invented a method for cleaning up industrial waste oil and went on as entrepreneurs to found The New Pig Corporation (see Profile 7.3). Nevertheless, many times it is the teaming of an inventor with the right entrepreneur that results in a successful new business venture. Because inventors often don't know how to commercialize their inventions, they can partner with an entrepreneur or license to the entrepreneur the right to commercialize an invention. The entrepreneur then pays the inventor a royalty based on gross sales.

Inventors are found through networking with associations like venture groups and colleges and universities. Schools that focus on invention in the sciences, engineering, computers, and the like often have technology transfer offices that manage the commercialization of any invention developed there.

Look to the Government

The federal government or your state government can be a great source of new venture ideas. New laws and regulations often require the use of a product or service that didn't previously exist. For example, the establishment of the Occupation Safety and Health Administration (OSHA) provided an opportunity for people who could provide training to businesses on everything from how to meet the stringent requirements in the workplace to filling out the incredible amount of paperwork associated with those requirements. City ordinances that require that certain products, such as glass and plastic, be recycled have produced many new businesses that provide new uses for these materials.

Where Will the Opportunities Be in the Next Decade?

Organizations that monitor the growth of industry believe that the sectors of the economy that will attract sales and investment in the coming years are in the health industries, particularly home health care, and computer-related industries, specifically companies working on networking and the Internet as well as **intranets**, which are closed Internets accessible only by the companies that owns them. Next are consumer goods and telecommunications. The most successful firms in these industries, generally high-tech and high-growth firms, flourish in an environment of change. This is not to say that the business opportunity you find must be in these areas to be successful; it is, however, more likely your firm will grow rapidly and have above-average sales if it is. Of course, the way you run your business and the amount of control you exert over its growth will be a function of the type of entrepreneur you are and your goals for yourself and the business.

Developing a Business Concept

An opportunity has to be defined in such a way that it can be tested through a process called **feasibility analysis,** which will be discussed in Chapter 3. The opportunity can be defined by developing a **concept statement** that contains the four elements that will need to be tested. They are the product/ service, customer, benefit, and distribution, as depicted in Figure 2.1.

Assume that your business concept involves developing intranets for businesses in the restaurant industry. By answering the following questions, you can arrive at an effective business concept that can be tested.

Industries That Offer Technical Opportunity for the Next Decade

The following needs will provide opportunity for entrepreneurs in the next decade because they represent important technical challenges that must be met.

▶ Affordable home-based health care

▶ Personalized consumer products

▶ The convergence of technology in the home

▶ Protecting the environment and natural resources

▶ User-friendly interfaces for technology in the home

▶ Nutritional health

▶ Mobile energy—alternative fuels

▶ Micro-security

▶ Renewed infrastructure for cities

▶ Global business competition and the ability to control technology

SOURCE: "Top 10 Challenges for 2007," created by Battelle. *Engineering News,* June 23, 1997 *(http://www.designnews.com).*

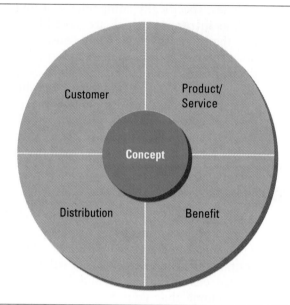

Figure 2.1
The New Venture
Concept

1. *What is the product or service being offered?* In this case it is a service that will link all areas of a restaurant business via an intranet.

2. *Who is the customer?* The customer is the restaurant or restaurant chain.

3. *What are the benefits?* The company (restaurant) will be constantly linked to all its sites; management and employees will be able to share information in real time; it will be easier to plan and conduct meetings and deal with suppliers.

4. *How do we get the product or service to the customer?* We will do on-site planning, installation, and training.

Now we have a concept that is ready for testing.

Testing the Concept Quickly

You know you have a business idea worthy of further consideration when you can't stop thinking about it. When that happens, it's time to develop a concept statement and do a quick test to see if a full-blown feasibility study is warranted. There are several ways to accomplish this task.

1. *Talk with some trusted friends and get initial feedback on the idea.* Don't be discouraged or write off the idea if they tell you it's crazy. People thought Fred Smith was crazy when he said he could deliver a package anywhere in the United States overnight—that is, until he founded Federal Express.

2. *Do a quick checklist of the forces working for your idea and the forces working against it.* How does the idea stack up? Are there more forces in favor of the idea than against it?

3. Ask yourself three very important questions.
   a. *Am I really interested in this business opportunity?* If you develop this concept, it is going to take all the time and energy you can give it, so it's important that you like it.
   b. *Is anyone else interested?* You can't have a business without customers, and you may need investors, so you had better be sure that others are interested in what you plan to offer.
   c. *Will people actually pay for what I am offering?* Often when people hear about a new product or service they express interest, even excitement, over it. But what are they willing to pay for it? If they are not willing to pay what you believe it's worth, you may need to rethink the idea.

If your business concept can pass these tests, it's time for the next level of investigation: the feasibility study. Once you determine that the concept is feasible, you can begin to create a business plan. Feasibility studies and business plans are the subject of Chapter 3.

New Venture Checklist

Have you:

❏ **Tried the creativity-enhancing exercises in this chapter?**

❏ **Started a file to keep track of business ideas?**

❏ **Started networking and reading in your industry?**

❏ **Visited the local Chamber of Commerce and Small Business Administration office to see what information and help are available to small business owners?**

❏ **Defined a concept statement for your new business opportunity?**

❏ **Done a quick test on your concept?**

❏ **Made a list of the information you will need to complete the feasibility study and business plan for the new venture?**

Issues to Consider

1. Give an example to demonstrate that you understand the difference between an idea and an opportunity.
2. Why do you suppose many people shy away from talking about failure?
3. Pick a business in your community and find a creative way to change either the product/service or the way it is delivered to the customers.
4. What are the components of an effective business concept?
5. How can you quickly test a concept for preliminary feasibility?

Experiencing Entrepreneurship

1. Spend an afternoon walking around your community or your university or college campus. Don't look for anything in particular. Observe the things that you don't normally see because you're in a hurry. Watch people—what they do and don't do. At the end of the afternoon, write down all the thoughts that come to you based on your afternoon of observation. Which of these ideas could possibly become a business opportunity and why?

2. Pick one of the trends discussed starting on page 17 of the chapter. Using the Internet, Lexis/Nexis, or your library, develop a report on the current status of that trend using articles and sources no more than two years old.

Additional Sources of Information

Brandt, S.C. (1982). *Entrepreneurship: The Ten Commandments for Building a Growth Company*. Reading, MA: Addison-Wesley Publishing.

Dacey, J.S. (1989). *Fundamentals of Creative Thinking*. New York: Free Press.

Gumpert, D.E. (1990). *How to Really Create a Successful Business Plan*. Boston: The Goldhirsch Group.

Habino, S., and Nadler, G. (1990). *Breakthrough Thinking*. Rocklin, CA: Prima Publishing.

Hall, D., and Wecker, D. (1995). *Jumpstart Your Brain*. New York: Warner Books.

Tichy, N., and Sherman, S. (1994). *Control Your Destiny or Someone Else Will*. New York: Harper Business.

van Oech, R. (1990). *A Whack on the Side of the Head*. New York: Warner Books.

Internet Resources

Association of Collegiate Entrepreneurs
http://www.csupomona.edu/ace/
Information on events of interest to young entrepreneurs, with links to many Internet sites.

Business Opportunities Handbook: Online
http://www.ezines.com/
Features articles about running a small business. Also lists business opportunities.

National SBDC Research Network
http://www.smallbiz.suny.edu/
This site is administered by the State University of New York and is a good source of U.S. small-business development centers and links to many Internet resources.

Relevant Case Studies

1. The Penduline Putter
2. OXO (A)
3. Autopsies-to-Go

I'd rather have a Class A entrepreneur with a Class B idea than a Class B entrepreneur with a Class A idea.

Gifford Pinchot III
The International Institute of Intrapreneurs
Intrapreneuring
(Harper & Row, 1986)

Developing and Testing the Business Concept

Overview

▶ **The feasibility components**

▶ **The genesis or founding team**

▶ **The business plan**

▶ **The business plan components**

▶ **Putting the business plan together**

Terms to Know

Profile 3.1

Follow the Dough

Attorneys have long been associated with dough—the green kind, that is. But entrepreneur Doug Low had been an attorney for twenty-one years in the Central Valley of California when he decided he might prefer cookie dough to the green type. That was in 1993. Over the next four years, he worked on recipes to find the perfect cookie. He was constantly testing his product with potential customers. His plan was to open a shop next to the law firm and put his wife, Marsha Eichholtz, a paralegal, in charge. She agreed on the condition that he come up with a recipe that was "really, really good." He did just that. The market told him he had a product

that people wanted. In February of 1997, Low and Eichholtz opened Doug-Out Cookies and claimed to be "the only law office in town that has four different kinds of coffee."

Opening Doug-Out, a baseball-themed shop, has meant working twelve to fifteen hours a day, six days a week. Eichholtz starts the day at 5:00 a.m., mixing dough for 32 different recipes for a variety of baked goods, including the now-famous baseball cookie. By 8:00 a.m., Low is in the law office or at the Workers' Compensation Appeals Board. By 5:00 p.m., they're both back at the law office, where the work day ends at 7:30. Seven months into the business, they were still testing the waters but breaking even, slowly building up a loyal customer base including several restaurants that purchased what Low calls "season tickets," or the right to regular deliveries of Doug-Out products.

Low and Eichholtz are gradually discovering various ways they can grow the business. Recognizing the popularity of themed food concepts, they have plans to franchise the business nationally and take their concept to baseball stadiums around the country. They hope that eventually they'll be able to make a transition out of the law practice and run their new business full-time. Low believes that "just having the dream is an end in itself."

SOURCE: Greg Ahlstrand, "Doug-Out Lineup Is Big League," *The Fresno Bee,* September 19, 1997.

How do you suppose Low and Eichholtz determined there was sufficient demand for their concept to go ahead and open the business?

In the previous chapter, we talked about how to recognize an opportunity and develop that opportunity into a business concept that can be tested in the marketplace. You learned how to do a quick test to see when a feasibility analysis was warranted. In this chapter, you'll learn how to conduct a feasibility analysis that will tell you

▶ Whether or not there is market acceptance for the concept.

▶ What conditions must be present for you to move into the business planning stage.

A **feasibility study** gives you an indication of whether there is sufficient demand for your product or service. The estimation of demand is a vital step in deciding if you have a viable business concept, for there is no business without enough satisfied customers. Once you have concluded there is adequate demand for the product or service, other issues such as the operational and organizational requirements can be undertaken and a business plan completed. There is no need to spend considerable time and effort on those issues if the feasibility study indicates insufficient interest in your product or service.

Even though the feasibility study is a tool geared primarily toward providing information to the entrepreneur, it's often possible to attract outside interest in your concept at that point if the results are positive. That interest may result in some funding to help you complete a comprehensive business plan, conclude product development, and start the business. The feasibility study may also assist in attracting quality people to the founding team.

The Feasibility Components

In general, the feasibility analysis will answer the following three questions:

1. Are there customers and a market of sufficient size to make the concept viable?

2. Do the capital requirements to start, based on estimates of sales and expenses, make sense?

3. Can an appropriate start-up or genesis team be put together to make the business happen?

To answer these questions requires looking at four broad areas of the business: product/service, industry, market/customer, and finance. Table 3.1 presents some in-depth questions that can be asked about each of these areas.

Product/Service

The first area of analysis is the actual product or service being offered. It is in this section that the unique features will be determined, as well as possibilities

Table 3.1   Feasibility Analysis

Area to Be Analyzed	Questions to Ask
Product/Service	1. What are the features and benefits of the product or service?
	2. What product development tasks must be undertaken and what is the timeline for completion?
	3. Is there potential for intellectual property rights?
	4. How is the product or service differentiated from others in the market?
Industry	5. What are the demographics, trends, life cycle stage of the industry?
	6. Are there any barriers to entry? If so, what are they?
	7. What is the status of technology and R&D expenditures?
	8. What are typical profit margins in the industry?
	9. Have you talked with distributors, competitors, retailers, etc.?
Market/Customer	10. What are the demographics of the target market?
	11. What is the customer profile? Who is the customer?
	12. Have you talked with customers?
	13. Who are your competitors and how are you differentiated from them?
	14. Which distribution channel alternatives are available and which customers will be served by them?
Finance	15. What are your start-up capital requirements?
	16. What are your working capital requirements?
	17. What are your fixed cost requirements?
	18. How long will it take to achieve a positive cash flow?
	19. What is the break-even point for the business?

for spin-offs, which are innovations in the product/service or additional products and services that are complementary to the original.

If a product needs to be designed and a prototype developed, the analysis will look at how this will be accomplished and the timeline for development. Block and Macmillan suggest milestone planning.[1] This process includes ten milestones, or performance points, at which the entrepreneur must make choices that will have a significant impact on the success of the company. See Table 3.2 for these milestones. Product development will be discussed in detail in Chapter 7.

Industry Risks and Benefits

A complete understanding of the nature of the industry in which the business will operate is enormously important, because it enhances your ability to find an effective entry strategy for your product or service. By considering such things as barriers to entry, stage of growth, competitors, market share, and potential for growth, the industry analysis will result in a profile that gives a clear picture of the industry. The profile also includes information on typical sales and gross margin percentages for the industry. A good understanding of the industry also facilitates zeroing in on your target market, the primary purchasers of your product or service. See Chapter 5 for a complete discussion of how to undertake an industry analysis.

Market/Customer Risks and Benefits

The market analysis section of the feasibility study is a critical portion of the analysis because it presents support for the contention that there is a market and a demand for the product or service. An in-depth analysis of the target market includes the size, location, buying habits, and needs of the customer base. A profile of the typical customer is developed. Also accomplished in

Table 3.2   Product Development Milestones

1. Completion of concept and product testing
2. Completion of prototype
3. First financing
4. Completion of initial plant tests (pilot or beta test)
5. Market testing
6. Production start-up
7. Bellwether sale (first substantial sale)
8. First competitive action
9. First redesign or redirection
10. First significant price change

SOURCE: Zenas Block and Ian C. Macmillan, "Milestones for Successful Venture Planning," In *The Entrepreneurial Venture* (Boston, Mass.: Harvard Business School Publishing, 1992), pp. 138–148.

this section is a comprehensive analysis of both direct and indirect competitors. A description of emerging competitors and substitute products demonstrates that the entrepreneur has considered all possible competition. Finally, this section defines those unique competitive advantages the business enjoys. Chapter 6 looks at how to analyze customer and market risks and benefits.

Financial Risks and Requirements

The financial analysis looks at the capital requirements for launching the business. Through forecasts of potential sales and expenses, as well as working capital and equipment requirements, it gives the entrepreneur a sense of whether or not it's financially feasible to move forward with the business concept. This analysis is discussed in Chapter 8.

The Genesis or Founding Team

While not strictly a part of the feasibility analysis, the issue of who is part of the founding team and how this contributes to the potential success of the

College Students Starting Businesses

College students are starting businesses in increasing numbers as they face a job market that is forcing them to invent careers and career paths that have not previously existed. However, the nature of the job market is just one incentive for starting a business. A more positive one is the myriad opportunities available as a result of technology. For college students, technology is like breathing—it's easy, it's readily available, and it allows them to readily create new businesses that can compete with the largest companies on a level playing field: the Internet.

Two Stanford University graduate students, Jerry Yang and David Filo, spent their off-hours compiling a computerized listing of their favorite Internet sites. It became so popular with other students that it was wreaking havoc with the university computer system. Yang and Filo were forced to move their budding venture off campus. A venture capitalist approached them with an offer of an initial $1 million investment. In 1996, Yahoo! went public at $13 a share, making its founders each $132 million richer.

College campuses are fertile ground for new ideas: experimentation is encouraged, and failure is just one step in the learning process. Some of the great companies founded by college students include Cisco Systems, Microsoft, Apple Computer, and Kinko's.

Source: Hal Plotkin, "Student Uprising," *Inc.*, August 1996, pp. 30–38.

venture must be considered. In many cases, it's having a strong team that becomes the deciding factor in whether an entrepreneur takes the risk associated with the new concept or not. Knowing that you have a team with the expertise you need may be enough to push the go/no-go decision to the positive. The issue of what constitutes an effective genesis team is discussed in Chapter 4.

The Business Plan

What is the difference between a feasibility study and a business plan? A feasibility study gives you a way to test a new concept in the marketplace. By contrast, a **business plan** is a more comprehensive analysis that includes, in addition to the market research, a discussion of the operational and financial management and controls of the new business. Simply stated, the feasibility study focuses on the idea; the business plan focuses on the company. The business plan serves three purposes:

▶ It serves as a reality check.

▶ It is a living guide to your business.

▶ It is a statement of intent for interested third parties.

The Reality Check

Usually, by the time the business plan is completed, you will have an excellent idea of whether this business concept has a chance of succeeding. You will also know whether you are still interested in starting the business. Frequently the period of concept development is much like a "honeymoon" phase. The entrepreneur believes completely that this business will be a success and can picture exactly how it will work. In fact, the process of doing the plan helps the entrepreneur understand more clearly the nature of all aspects of the business. Unfortunately, going through the exercise of doing a business plan, researching costs, preparing forecasts, and strategizing about operating procedures sometimes reveals potential problems previously unrecognized. Strong negatives or difficulties can lead to the decision not to proceed. This is not considered a failure for the entrepreneur. It merely indicates the value of doing a business plan in the first place. It is certainly preferable to halt the effort at that point than to go forward and possibly fail farther down the road when significant time and money have been expended.[2]

The Living Guide to the Business

The business plan is a blueprint for the start-up and growth of the new venture. It is a complete and comprehensive picture of the business.[3] It's called a living document because it's subject to a changing environment. The original business plan for a new business contains estimates and assumptions for what the entrepreneur expects will happen when the business starts, and it is often prepared with subjective data. Consequently, the entrepreneur typically re-evaluates the plan and updates it periodically the first year, then annually thereafter. This process compares the goals and projections from the original business plan with the actual achievements of the firm during the period under investigation. If significant differences in figures are observed, the entrepreneur attempts to learn what may have caused the differences and adjust projections for the next period to account for any changes. In this way the business plan always reflects what the business is actually doing, thereby improving and refining projections for the future.

Statement of Intent for Third Parties

In addition to the entrepreneur, it may be necessary to induce others to become interested in the new venture. These third parties include:

▶ Investors

▶ Bankers

▶ Potential management

▶ Strategic partners

▶ Suppliers

▶ Lessors

Each of these groups looks at the business plan from a different perspective.

Investors

Investors review closely both the factors that predict growth and the qualifications and track record of the management team. This is because they want to ensure that their investment increases in value over the period of time during which they are involved in the business and that it is in capable and experienced hands. They look at the deal structure; that is, what their investment will buy them in terms of an equity interest and subsequent ownership rights in the company. They also want to know how they will be able to liquidate their investment at some future date.

Bankers/Lenders

Bankers/lenders are primarily interested in the company's margins and cash flow projections because they are concerned about how their loans or credit lines to the business will be repaid. The margins indicate how much room there is for error between the cost to produce the product or deliver the service and the selling price. If margins are tight and the business finds itself having to lower prices to compete, it may not be able to pay off its loans as consistently and quickly as the bank would like. Similarly, bankers look at cash flow projections to see if the business can pay all its expenses and still have money left over at the end of each month. Bankers also look at the qualifications and track record of the management team and may require personal guarantees of the principals.

Potential Management

At start-up or some later date, the entrepreneur may want to attract qualified personnel to the key management team to fill the gaps in experience. The business plan provides these people with a complete picture of the business and the role they could potentially play in its start-up and growth.

Strategic Partners

Some entrepreneurs, particularly those who intend to manufacture a product, choose to form a strategic alliance with a larger company so that they don't have to incur the tremendous costs of purchasing equipment for a manufacturing plant. They may, for example, license another firm to manufacture and assemble the product and supply it to the entrepreneur to market and distribute. Alternatively, they may enter into an agreement with a supplier to provide necessary raw materials in exchange for an equity interest in the start-up venture.

Strategic partners like this want to review the growth plans of the company and the market strategy, as these plans indicate how much business the strategic partner may get. They are also interested in the new venture's ability to pay them for their work. Knowing in advance what these third parties are looking for will prompt you to address their specific needs in your business plan, facilitating your ability to achieve the goals of the business.

Having considered the value of doing a business plan, note that some successful businesses were started without one—Crate and Barrel, Pizza Hut, and Reebok, to name just a few. It is certainly possible to start a business without a business plan—people do it every day; however, entrepreneurs today operate in an intensely competitive, complex, and dynamic environment. Unless you are starting a very simple, small business or buying an established and successful firm, you will probably not want to rely solely on your talent or luck. A business plan is one way to compensate for knowledge you don't have and gives you credibility in the eyes of others. It reduces risk and helps keep the entrepreneur on target as the business starts operations.

What the business plan is not is a guarantee of success. Businesses have succeeded in spite of poorly done business plans and have failed even when the plan was carefully crafted. The business plan is a tool entrepreneurs use to enhance their chances of success. That is why it is important that both the entrepreneur and the founding team be fully involved in the development of the business plan. There are companies that will write your business plan and do research for you, but you know the business better than anyone else. And you will understand it that much better if you and your team do the necessary work to put together a business plan.

The Business Plan Components

Table 3.3 presents an outline of the business plan. Notice that the first three sections of the business plan are identical to those in the feasibility study. This is a suggested outline; however, any business plan should reflect the personality and goals of the entrepreneur, so no one format works for every business. The sections presented here are those critical to persuading the entrepreneur and other interested parties that the company is viable and has a healthy future. As with the feasibility study, the sections are discussed briefly and you are referred to the chapter in which a more complete discussion takes place. Note also that only those sections not previously discussed under feasibility are discussed here.

Operational Analysis

In this section of the business plan, a detailed description of the product/service process is presented, including engineering specifications and a description of the prototype, should there be a product involved. The status of product/service development is addressed, as well as additional steps that must be taken before the product/service is ready to sell to the public. The time and cost requirements of completing the development tasks are also included. In addition, this section contains a discussion of the distribution channels used to move the product or service from the producer to the end user. A major portion of this section is devoted to a description of how the business will operate, where it will get its raw materials, how they will be manufactured and/or assembled, and what type and quantity of labor is required to operate the business. The outline of the business plan notes where businesses other than manufacturing have the same information requirements as manufacturing. See Chapter 12 for a more detailed discussion on operational analysis.

Organization Plan

The organization plan focuses on issues related to how the company will be structured and includes such things as the philosophy of management and company culture, the legal structure, key management, compensation, and key policies. The issues that need to be addressed in the organization plan are dealt with in Chapter 13.

Marketing Plan

The marketing plan is something quite distinct from market analysis. Market analysis gives the entrepreneur the information about the customer that will be used to create a marketing plan, which is the strategy for making the customer aware of the product/service. The plan includes a discussion of the plan's purpose, the market niche, the business's identity, the tools that will

Table 3.3 Business Plan Outline

EXECUTIVE SUMMARY (2-page summary in plan)

I. BUSINESS CONCEPT
   Business Concept (Product/service, customer, benefit, distribution)
   Purpose of the Business
   Core Values
   Description and Uses, Unique Features/Benefits
   The Primary Customer
   Spin-offs
   Environmental Impact

II. MANAGEMENT TEAM
   Qualifications of Key Management (Founders)
   ▶ Management team needs

III. MARKET ANALYSIS
   Industry Description
   ▶ Industry size
   ▶ Industry status (growing, mature, in decline)
   ▶ Growth potential
   ▶ Geographic locations
   ▶ Trends and entry barriers
   ▶ Profit potential
   ▶ Sales patterns and gross margins
   Target Market
   ▶ Primary target markets
   ▶ Secondary markets
   ▶ Demographics
   ▶ Results of primary research
   ▶ Customer profile
   ▶ Customer needs analysis
   ▶ Distribution channels—customer grid
   ▶ Entry strategy (initial market penetration)
   Competitors—Competitive Grid
   ▶ Direct and indirect
       Market share
       Description
       Strengths and weaknesses
   ▶ Emerging
   ▶ Substitute products

(continued)

Table 3.3   *(continued)*

Product/Service Differentiation & Competitive Advantage
▶ Unique features
▶ Potential for innovation
▶ Proprietary protection
▶ Other competitive advantages

Pricing
▶ Venture v. competitors
▶ Value chain

IV. PROCESS ANALYSIS

Technical Description of Products/Services
▶ Uses, design, prototype
▶ Issues of obsolescence

Status of Development and Related Costs
▶ Current status of development
▶ Tasks to be completed, time and cost to complete
▶ Potential difficulties, resolution
▶ Government approvals

Distribution Channels & Physical Distribution Plan

Manufacturing or Operating Requirements and Associated Costs
▶ Manufacturing cycle or service delivery process
▶ Materials requirements
▶ Inventory requirements (also retail/wholesale business)
▶ Production requirements (also retail/wholesale or service)
▶ Labor requirements (all businesses)
▶ Maintenance and quality control requirements (all businesses)
▶ Financial requirements (all businesses)

V. ORGANIZATION PLAN

Philosophy of Management and Company Culture

Legal Structure of the Company

Organizational Chart
▶ Key management
▶ Duties and responsibilities

Compensation Programs and Incentives
▶ Key management

Key Policies
▶ Orders, billing, paying

Key Benefits

VI. MARKETING PLAN

Purpose of Marketing Plan
▶ Target market

Table 3.3   *(continued)*

> ▶ Unique market niche
> ▶ Business identity
>
> *Marketing Tools*
> ▶ Advertising & promotion
>
> *Media Plan*
> ▶ Uses and costs of specific marketing tools
>
> *Marketing Budget*
> ▶ Individual costs and total costs as a percentage of sales

---

VII. FINANCIAL PLAN

Summary of Key Points and Capital Requirements

Needs Assessment (Fixed costs, working capital, start-up)

Break-even Analysis and Payback Period

Assumptions for Financial Statements

Pro Forma Financial Statements
> ▶ Cash Flow (Monthly Yr 1, Qtr Yrs 2,3), Income (Qtr Yr 1, Annual Yrs 2,3), Balance Sheet (Annual Yrs 1-3), Sources & Uses (Annual Yrs 1-3)

Capital Expenditures

VIII. GROWTH PLAN

Strategy for Growth

Resources

Infrastructure Changes

APPENDIX

CONTINGENCY PLAN

Potential deviations from the original plan and solutions

DEAL STRUCTURE (if relevant)

Debt and/or equity funding amounts

Projected return on investment

Harvest strategy

SUPPORTING DOCUMENTS

Résumés, contracts, maps, etc.

be used to reach the customer, a media plan for specific marketing tools, and a marketing budget. The marketing plan is discussed in Chapter 14.

Financial Plan

The financial plan presents the entrepreneur's forecasts for the future of the business. Generally these forecasts are in the form of financial statements broken out by month in the first year or two, and then annually for the next two to five years. This section demonstrates the financial viability of the venture and the assumptions made by the entrepreneur in doing the forecasts. It is designed to show that all the claims about the product, sales, marketing strategy, and operational strategy can work financially to create a business that can survive and grow over the long term. A complete discussion of financial analysis related to the business plan is found in Chapter 16.

Contingency Plan

The **contingency plan** is simply a way of recognizing that sometimes the "best laid plans" don't work the way you intended. It presents potential scenarios, usually dealing with situations like unexpected high or low growth or changing economic conditions and then suggests a plan to minimize the impact on the new business.

Growth Plan

The growth plan discusses how the entrepreneur plans to take the business from start-up through growth. It looks at the strategy that will be used to ensure that the business continues to grow over its life. This may mean looking at new products and services or acquiring other businesses. It's important that this section reassure an investor or lender that the company has a future. Growth is the subject of Chapter 17.

Deal Structure

The **deal structure** section presents the offering to potential investors, including how much capital is required, in what form (equity, debt, or a combination), return on investment, and a plan for harvesting the investment at a later date. This section should be written from the investor's point of view and present the benefits to the investor of putting money into the new venture.

Undertaking a feasibility study and completing a business plan are certainly daunting tasks, but they are an absolutely essential exercise that helps the entrepreneur understand more clearly every aspect of the new venture and how all the pieces fit together. Even successful entrepreneurs who have started businesses without a written plan have had to write business plans when they needed growth capital or a credit line from the bank. Those starting high-growth global ventures will find they need outside capital and resources fairly quickly.

Executive Summary

The executive summary, although discussed last here, is probably the most important part of the business plan because it is the primary means of interesting an investor, banker, or other interested party in reading the full business plan. The executive summary should be no more than two pages, at a maximum three, and should contain the most important points from all the sections of the business plan.

It is vital that the executive summary capture the reader's attention instantly in the first sentence by using a key selling point or benefit of the business. One way to do this is by introducing a problem and countering with the products and services the company will offer to alleviate the problem. Another way is by using a provocative statement or statistics to entice the reader. In any case, the first paragraph should contain a clear and concise statement of the business concept, including the product/service, customer, benefit, and distribution, so that the reader instantly knows the nature of the business. In addition, you should emphasize the profitability potential of the company and the potential for growth.

Remember, you have only about thirty seconds to capture the attention of an investor, banker, or venture capitalist, who probably sees many business plans a month. Use the checklist in Table 3.4 as a guide to preparing your executive summary.

Putting the Business Plan Together

This book was designed to carry you through the business planning process in a "logical" progression. Following this progression may be the ideal way to go about preparing a business plan, but frankly, business plans aren't often handled in such an orderly fashion. Typically, information for the various parts of the business plan is gathered at various points in time, usually at the convenience of the entrepreneur. The entrepreneur may talk with a distributor in the industry, seeking a sense of market demand for the proposed product—and wind up getting, in addition, an understanding of typical gross margins in the industry, information that will not be needed until after it has been determined that there is a market for the product. From talking with suppliers during market research, the entrepreneur may become concerned that the cost to produce the product is too great, so he or she will quickly calculate the cost to produce and the probable selling price, based on preliminary information, to see if there will be enough money left to pay overhead and eventually make a profit. If it looks as though there isn't enough profit in it to make the effort worthwhile, the entrepreneur may decide to abandon the concept even before finishing the market research.

As you can see, business planning is a fluid and dynamic process. One way to gain a measure of control of the information gathered over time is to set up files for each of the major sections of the business plan. As each piece of information is collected, it is filed in the appropriate folder. When it's time to analyze and prepare that section of the business plan, all the information needed to do it will be there.

You will find people who will proudly proclaim that they never had a business plan and yet were successful. That may be true—there are always

Table 3.4 Business Plan Checklist

1. Did the executive summary grab the reader's attention and highlight the major points of the business plan?
2. Did the business product/service plan clearly describe the purpose of the business, the customer, the benefit to the customer, and the distribution channel?
3. Did the management team section persuade the reader that the team could successfully implement the business concept?
4. Did the market analysis support acceptance for the business concept in the marketplace?
5. Did the process plan prove that the product or service could be produced and distributed efficiently and effectively?
6. Did the management and organization section assure the reader that an effective infrastructure was in place to facilitate the goals and operations of the company?
7. Did the marketing plan successfully demonstrate how the company will effectively create customer awareness in the target market?
8. Did the financial plan convince the reader that the company has long-term growth potential and will provide a superior return on investment for the investor, and sufficient cash flow to repay loans to potential lenders?

exceptions to every rule—but more often than not, these entrepreneurs started small businesses rather than high-growth, world-class ventures, or perhaps never had to seek capital from outside sources. Also, many of the more famous companies that were started without plans—Pizza Hut, Crate and Barrel, Microsoft, and Reebok—were started in the 1970s and early 1980s in a less global, less technologically complex business environment. Moreover, most of these companies eventually had to write business plans when expansion required taking on investors, going public, or being acquired by a major corporation. Then, too, you can't dismiss the luck aspect. Being in the right place at the right time has played a telling role in the early success of many ventures.

Organizing to Write the Plan

No one will deny that writing a business plan is a chore, but if you organize the information in advance and plan for the time it takes to actually do the writing, it can be accomplished with a minimum of pain and frustration. Be realistic. This is not a job that can be completed in a marathon weekend, but is a job that you as the lead entrepreneur and the key members of your founding team must tackle seriously if you are to ensure the best chance for achieving the goals of the business. Plan on it taking several months to do properly.

Too often entrepreneurs approach the writing of the business plan with a "what do I need to know" approach, without considering the reader's interests. It is important to know prior to writing the plan that different readers have different needs, which must be addressed. How is it possible to write one business plan for several different audiences? It isn't. You may need to have more than one version of the plan to appropriately address the specific needs and requirements of various audiences. For example, a business plan written with venture capitalists in mind would focus on growth and high return on investment, but might be considered too risky by a banker, who is more interested in how the bank's loan will be repaid. Likewise, a plan written to meet the needs of the banker will not capture the attention of a venture capitalist, because generally it is too conservative in its projections.

There are several audiences for the business plan, as was discussed briefly earlier in the chapter. This section focuses on those typically encountered by entrepreneurs starting high-growth ventures: investors and venture capitalists, bankers or lenders, strategic alliances, customers and suppliers, and key management. We will look at some specific needs of these parties.

Investors and Venture Capitalists

Anyone investing in the new venture has four principal concerns: rate of growth, return on investment, degree of risk, and protection. Investors are generally betting that the value of their ownership interest in the business will increase over time at a rate greater than that of another type of investment or of a bank account. They want to know how fast the business is projected to grow, when that growth will take place, and what will ensure that the growth actually occurs as predicted. For this reason, they tend to look for market-driven companies as opposed to product or technology-driven companies because they're interested in such things as short payback periods for customers.[4] They expect that predictions will be based on solid evidence in the marketplace and a thorough knowledge of the target market.[5]

Investors are naturally concerned about when and how the principal portion of their investment will be repaid and how much gain on that investment will accrue over the time they are invested in the company. The answers to these concerns are largely a function of the structure of the investment deal, whether that be a limited or general partnership, or preferred or common stock, and so forth. Consequently, investors want to understand what the entrepreneur intends as far as deal structure, knowing full well that the investor will at some point have some input into how the deal is ultimately structured.

Investors want to thoroughly understand the risks they face in investing in the new venture; principally, how their original equity will be protected. They expect the entrepreneur to present the potential dangers facing the new venture, along with a plan for mitigating or dealing with them to protect the investors against loss. Finally, investors want to know how their equity will be protected if the business fails and how the business will protect its assets from seizure by creditors.

There are some typical errors that entrepreneurs frequently make when writing the business plan for investors or venture capitalists:

▶ **Projecting rapid growth beyond the capabilities of the founding team.** This is a common problem. The new venture shows potential for rapidly increasing demand, sales doubling or tripling on an annual basis in the first few years. The entrepreneur believes this will be very attractive to investors. What he or she doesn't realize is that there is no evidence in the business plan to prove that the founding team can manage and control this type of growth, and this is cause for great concern on the part of the investors. Too often they have seen a business fail during rapid growth because management didn't have the systems in place to deal with it. The entrepreneur should be careful to project controlled growth and have a plan for bringing on the necessary personnel at the point at which the company is ready for more rapid growth. The other danger in projecting too high a level of success is that you increase your chances of not being able to achieve it. It is better to project a little more conservatively and try to exceed those projections.

▶ **The three-ring circus with only one ringleader.** Many entrepreneurs pride themselves on being a "jack of all trades." They claim to have expertise in all the functional areas of the new venture. What they really have is general knowledge of all the functional areas and maybe a real expertise in only one. Investors are very nervous about relying on solo entrepreneurs to lead world-class ventures. They much prefer a team of founders with at least one person specializing in each of the functional areas.

▶ **Performance in some or all areas that exceeds industry averages.** While it is possible for a new venture to exceed industry averages in a particular area, it is not likely. Most averages, such as those for receivables turnover and bad debt losses, have come about as a result of economies of scale, which the new venture is not likely to achieve for some time. It is better for the business plan to initially indicate performance measures at or slightly below industry averages with a plan for how to exceed those averages at some point in the future.

▶ **Underestimating the need for capital.** Investors need to know that the business plan projects sufficient capital infusion to grow the company until internal cash flows can carry the load and then provides the plan an additional infusion of capital when the company is ready for rapid expansion. If the entrepreneur underestimates the amount of capital needed, most savvy investors will recognize this and attribute the error to naiveté on the part of the entrepreneur, or, conversely, they will rely on the figures presented in the plan and ultimately suffer the potential loss of their investment as a result. Every estimate for capital should contain an additional amount for contingencies.

▶ **Confusing strategy with tactics.** It is much easier to develop tactics than to develop strategies. Strategies define the overall focus of the business; tactics are the methods by which those strategies will be achieved. When an investor asks what the entrepreneur's strategy is for achieving a projected market share by year three and the entrepreneur responds with "attending trade shows and advertising in trade journals," the entrepreneur loses the confidence of the investor by responding with tactics. This mistake is often made, as many entrepreneurs focus too much attention on tactics, often to the exclusion of identifying the overall strategy those tactics will support. The strategy for achieving the market share may be to become the first mover in a market niche.

▶ **Focusing on price as a market strategy for a product or service.** This is similar to projecting performance above industry averages. It is rarely possible for a new venture with a product or service that currently exists in the marketplace to enter on the basis of a lower price than competitors'. Established companies have achieved economies of scale that the new venture usually cannot, and they will no doubt easily match the price set by a new entrant into the market. Furthermore, this strategy does not impress investors. They are more interested in how the new venture will differentiate itself in terms of product, process, distribution, or service.

▶ **The entrepreneur's investment in the business.** Investors are more comfortable investing in a new venture where the entrepreneur has contributed a substantial amount of the start-up capital. That signals to the investors a level of commitment necessary to achieve the goals of the company.

Bankers or Lenders

Like investors, bankers or lenders want to know they are going to get their money back. When considering a business plan and an entrepreneur for a loan, lenders have several concerns:

▶ **The amount of money the entrepreneur needs.** Lenders are looking for a specific amount that can be justified with accurate calculations and data.

▶ **What positive impact the loan will have on the business.** Lenders would like to know that the money they are lending is not going to pay off old debt or pay salaries, but rather improve the business's financial position, particularly with regard to cash flow.

▶ **What kind of assets the business has for collateral.** Not all assets are created equal. Some assets have no value outside the business because they are custom-made or specific to that business and therefore cannot be sold on the open market. Lenders prefer to see industry-standard equipment and facilities that can easily be converted to another use.

▶ **How the business will repay the loan.** Lenders are interested in the earnings potential of the business over the life of the loan, but more important, they want to know that the business generates sufficient cash flow to service the debt. While fixed expenses are fairly easy to predict, variable expenses—those related to the production of the product or service—present a more difficult problem. That is why lenders are also interested in the market research section of the business plan, which tells them what the demand for the product/service is, and the marketing plan, which tells them how the entrepreneur plans to reach the customer.

▶ **How the bank will be protected if the business doesn't meet its projections.** Lenders want to know that the entrepreneur has a contingency plan for situations where major assumptions prove to be wrong. They want to ensure they are paid out of cash flow, not by liquidating the assets of the business.

▶ **The entrepreneur's stake in the business.** Like investors, lenders feel more confident about lending to a business where the entrepreneur has a substantial monetary investment in the business. That way the entrepreneur is less likely to walk away, leaving the lender stranded.

Strategic Alliances

Strategic alliances may involve formal partnership agreements with major corporations or simply an informal agreement through a large purchase contract. In either case, the larger company that is allying itself with the new venture is usually looking for new products, processes, or technology that complement its current line of products or services. Accordingly, it will search for a new venture management team that has some large corporate experience, so that the relationship will be smoother. Larger companies are also interested in strategic issues like the marketing and growth strategies of the new venture.

Major Customers and Suppliers

Major customers and suppliers are concerned with the new venture's performance record since the company was founded. As it takes some time to establish a stable performance record, these third-party readers of the business plan will probably not be interested in seeing the plan until the business is up and running and beginning to demonstrate that its predictions for sales are fairly accurate.

Key Management

Key management that the founding team wishes to attract during the growth phase of the new venture will also be concerned about how precisely and accurately the entrepreneur has forecasted demand for the product or service. Many of these targeted key management people will leave other jobs to join the new venture, so they will want to feel confident that the business will not fail and has strong potential for growth. More than any other group mentioned, potential key management will be interested in the details of the operations of the company.

At the beginning of this section, it was suggested that various versions of the business plan be developed, depending on the audience. The longest and most detailed version will probably be for internal use and for attracting key personnel. Investors, strategic alliances, and lenders in particular will probably prefer a more concise—perhaps 40-page—version of the plan, focusing on the specific areas of interest they have. It's a good idea to read other companies' business plans to get a sense of what works and what doesn't in terms of impressing the reader. If the style and organization of a particular plan make the business concept seem more appealing, consider adapting them for your business plan. But make sure the content is written in your own unique style—otherwise, it may sound like a "canned" or professionally prepared business plan and will win no points with a potential funder.

What to Include in the Business Plan

While there are no hard and fast rules about all the items to include in a business plan and where to put them, most business plans contain the sections discussed below. The major sections of the business that have already been discussed and outlined in detail in various chapters of the book will only be listed here.

The Cover Page for the Bound Document

Like any other document designed to sell something, the business plan is attempting to convince various third parties—and the entrepreneur—of the viability of the new venture. Therefore, the cover page should convey in an attractive, professional manner the confidence and creativity of the entrepreneur. In the case of venture capitalists and lenders, most have dozens of business plans cross their desks every day, so it is important to make your plan stand out. Appearance may be only skin deep, but positive first impressions go a long way toward attracting the attention of a potential financial source. The typical information to have on the cover page is:

▶ The name of the company

▶ The words *Business Plan*

▶ The name of the contact person for the new venture and the address and phone number of the business

Some ways to make the business plan stand out are to use color on the cover, the business's logo with the name, or a design that reflects the personality of the business.

Between the executive summary and the table of contents for the business plan, it is useful to put another cover page containing the name of the business and the words "Business Plan."

The Body of the Business Plan

The body of the business plan contains all the major sections of information that were presented in the outline on pages 44–46 and discussed throughout the book.

Business plans contain a lot of private information, some of which you may not want to share with everyone who reads the plan. Again, that is the reason for having several versions. A section like "Deal Structure," for example, probably should not be included in a plan being given to a lender or potential management employee, but usually is needed when dealing with investors or venture capitalists.

Be sure that the body of the business plan answers the basic questions:

1. Who are you?

2. What is the company?

3. What do you sell?

4. Who will buy?

5. Why will they buy?

6. How is your financial health?

Supporting Documents—The Appendices

Many items that might be important to the reader but would clog up the body of the business plan and make it more difficult to read quickly can be placed in appendices after the body of the plan. Some items that typically go in an appendix include:

▶ Résumés of the founding team

▶ Job descriptions

▶ Lease agreements

▶ License agreements

▶ Contracts

▶ Letters of intent

▶ Incorporation agreements or partnership agreements

▶ Evidence of patents

▶ Designs, architectural or product

▶ Personal financial statement (only where required, typically by a lender or investor)

Visual Presentation of the Business Plan

By now you know that the appearance of the business plan is the first step in getting the plan read. The trick, however, is to have the plan look professional without being too slick by making it a hard-bound, full-color, textbook-style business plan. Besides, a hard-bound plan suggests it's not subject to change anytime soon, which is not an impression you want to convey. Here are some suggestions for ways to make the business plan stand out from the crowd.

▶ The plan should be bound in such a way that it lies flat when you read it. A spiral-type binding or binder works well.

▶ Use index tabs to separate major sections and make it easier for the reader to find something.

- Use a 12-point type font and an easily read font style like Times Roman, for readability.

- Use bold subheadings and bullets generously, again to facilitate finding information.

- If you have a logo, use it at the top of every page.

- Make sure your writing is focused and concise. Prune excess words with a vengeance.

- Make sure all claims are supported by solid evidence.

- Ask several people to edit the plan.

- Do not use fill-in-the-blanks computer programs to write the plan. The result will not reflect the personality of your business.

- Revise and rewrite several times.

- Number each copy of the business plan and include with it a Statement of Confidentiality that the reader should sign. Keep track of who has which plan.

- Place a statement on the cover page prohibiting copying of the plan.

Oral Presentation of the Business Plan

It is not uncommon, particularly if the plan is being used to seek capital, for the entrepreneur to be asked to do a presentation of the business concept, highlighting the key points of the business plan. Usually this occurs after the potential funders have read the executive summary and perhaps done a cursory reading of the complete business plan. In any case, they feel it is worth their time to hear from the entrepreneur and the founding team to see if they measure up to expectations. While this presentation should not be confused with a formal speech, it does share with a speech many common elements. The presentation of the business plan should

- *Answer the fundamental questions as discussed in the preceding section on the body of the business plan.*

- *Keep the presentation under a half hour.* That is plenty of time to present the key elements. Questions and discussion will probably follow the presentation.

- *Be sure to catch the audience's attention in the first 60 seconds.* Let them know you're happy to be there and immediately get them involved in the presentation by showing concern, for example, about whether or not they can easily see the presentation slides.

- *Stand without using a podium.* It will give you better command of the situation and make it easier to use gestures and visual aids.

▶ *Move around but don't pace.* It is deadly to stand constantly in one place, but it is equally annoying to pace back and forth with no purpose. Moving helps reduce stress and livens up the presentation.

▶ *Maintain eye contact with everyone.* Talk to the audience, not over their heads.

▶ *Use visual aids.* Color slides or overheads help keep the presentation on track and focused on key points. Be careful not to dazzle the audience with too many overheads, however, as the audience may find themselves more interested in the rhythm of the motions you subconsciously develop as you flip through the slides than in what you say. Keep the slides simple—no more than five lines per slide—and professional-looking.

▶ *Make sure the key members of the founding team are involved in the presentation.*

▶ *Do a demonstration of the product or service where possible.* It helps generate excitement for the concept.

▶ *Practice the presentation in advance for a small group of friends or colleagues who will critique it, or videotape the practice session so that the founding team can critique themselves.*

▶ *Anticipate questions that may be asked by funders and determine how they should be answered.*

If the founding team have successfully made it through the presentation, they have cleared the first hurdle. The second hurdle, however, is harder: answering questions from the funders. One thing to learn about funders is that they generally like to ask questions to which they already know the answers; this is a test to see if the founding team know what they're talking about. Furthermore, funders will ask questions that either require an impossibly precise answer or are so broad as to make the entrepreneur wonder what the questioner is looking for.

Another type of question typically asked is "What are the implications of . . . ?" With this question, funders are looking for an answer that addresses their needs and concerns relative to the request for capital. Finally, the type of question that poses the most problems for the founding team is the inordinately complex one that contains several underlying assumptions. For example, "If I were to analyze your new venture in terms of its market share before and after this potential investment, how would the market strategy have changed and how much of the budget should be allotted to changing that strategy?"

The first thing you should do when faced with such a complicated question is to ask that it be repeated, to ensure nothing has been missed that might cause the entrepreneur to make an incorrect assumption. Alternatively, you can restate the question and confirm that it has been understood correctly. Another suggestion is to ask for a few minutes to formulate your answer. With this type of question, you may only feel comfortable answering part of it; for example, you may have evidence you could present to support a change in market share as a result of the capital infusion. On the other hand, you probably don't want to commit to any course of action or any budget amount without having had time to consider it further and gather more facts. Saying this in response to the question will no doubt gain you a measure of respect, for you will have demonstrated that you don't make important decisions precipitously, without considering all the facts.

If you are asked a factual question for which you do not know the answer (usually these are tangential to the business plan and are asked to see how you will respond), admit that you don't have that answer off the top of your head but will be happy to find it after the meeting is completed and get back to the questioner. If the presentation or anything the team has proposed is criticized (a likely possibility), be careful not to be defensive or turn the criticism in any way on the audience, or you will lose your chance with them immediately and may never regain it. Remember, you are playing in their ballpark. They make the rules. If it appears that they will be difficult people to deal with as investors or lenders, you don't have to use them. Chalk up the presentation to practice and go on to the next one.

Preparing and presenting the business plan is the culmination of months of work. The business plan represents the heart and soul of the new venture, and if it has been researched and written well, it can enhance the chances of starting a successful high-growth venture. Entrepreneurs should understand, however, that a business plan is not just for those starting new businesses, but for the growing company as well. The business plan lets you benchmark your progress toward company goals. It establishes the purpose, values, and goals of the company that will guide its decision making throughout its life. No entrepreneur plans to fail, but many fail to plan and end up reacting to situations in the environment instead of proactively dealing with a changing environment. In the next chapter we'll look at how the genesis team sets the stage for a successful new venture.

New Venture Checklist

Have you:

❏ **Done a feasibility analysis to determine if you should go forward with your concept?**

❏ **Gathered all the information necessary to complete the business plan?**

❏ **Determined the focus of the plan and how many versions are needed?**

❏ **Decided the presentation format for the business plan?**

Issues to Consider

1. Why is the business planning process an excellent exercise for any entrepreneur contemplating the start-up of a new venture?
2. What is the difference between a feasibility study and a business plan?
3. How might the business plan change if the reader were an investor versus a potential management hire?
4. What are the key components of the business plan?
5. When might you need to include a personal financial statement in the appendix?
6. What are three key elements of a successful business plan presentation?

Experiencing Entrepreneurship

1. Define a concept for a new venture using the four components discussed in the chapter: product/service, customer, benefit, and distribution. Quick test on some potential customers through either a focus group, interviews, or a survey. Did you get enough information to feel confident to move forward to a feasibility study? Why or why not?
2. Interview an "angel," someone who invests in small businesses, about what they look for in a business plan. Based on your discussion, what will you need to remember when you write your business plan?

Additional Sources of Information

Bangs, D.H., Jr. (1992). *The Business Planning Guide*. Dover, NH: Upstart Publishing Company, Inc.

Detz, J. (1984). *How to Write and Give a Speech*. New York: St. Martin's Press.

Gumpert, D.E. (1990). *How to Really Create a Successful Business Plan*. Boston: Inc. Publishing.

Hoff, R. (1992). *I Can See You Naked*. Kansas City, MO: Andrew and McMeel.

Mancuso, J. (1985). *How to Write a Winning Business Plan*. New York: Simon & Schuster.

Internet Resources

Association of Collegiate Entrepreneurs
http://www.csupomona.edu/ace/
Information on events of interest to young entrepreneurs with links to many internet sites.

BizPlanit
http://www.bizplanit.com
Helps entrepreneurs create, evaluate, and improve business plans.

Business Opportunities Handbook: Online
http://www.ezines.com/
Features articles about running a small business. Also lists business opportunities.

Business Plan Templates
http://www.vfinance.com/
Business plan templates that can be downloaded and viewed in Microsoft Word.

National SBDC Research Network
http://www.smallbiz.suny.edu/
This site is administered by the State University of New York and is a good source of U.S. small-business development centers and links to many Internet resources.

Relevant Case Studies

1. Mrs. Gooch's Natural Foods Markets
2. Flight Time
3. Autopsies-to-Go

The people who get on in this world are the people who get up and look for the circumstances they want,
and, if they can't find them, make them.
George Bernard Shaw
Nobel laureate in literature
Mrs. Warren's Profession

The Founding Team

Overview

▶ **The solo entrepreneur vs. the team**

▶ **The founding team**

▶ **Professional advisers**

▶ **Outsourcing savvy—independent contractors**

▶ **The shadow team**

Terms to Know

Profile 4.1

The Value of Team Vision

One of the new opportunities for entrepreneurs in the coming decade is women's health. Finding ways to prevent typical health problems of women of all ages is becoming big business. Transitions For Health, Inc., a Portland, Oregon–based company that sells health products for women, is bringing positive changes to women's lives through the company vision.

The company's owner and CEO, Sharon MacFarland, believes that all her employees must stay tuned to the core values of the company, which include em-

ployee involvement, learning and personal renewal, environmental protection, and diversity. To help them do this, she has developed something called the Values Game. Managers choose one of the core values, and each employee sets a goal related to that value and vows to attain it in three months. For example, when the core value chosen was psychological health, one employee chose a goal of reading three nonfiction books within the three-month period. Each time the company has played the game, 80 percent of workers have achieved their goals. Crossing the

80 percent mark resulted in everyone receiving a gift certificate to a health food store or a bookstore.

Transitions now has 23 employees and a team environment with a set of values they live by. The firm is an excellent model for entrepreneurs today who recognize that a team effort is what it takes to succeed in a dynamic environment. No one person can do it alone. *Oregon Business Magazine* selected Transitions as one of the 100 Best Companies to Work for in Oregon in 1996–97.

Sources: Transitions For Health, Inc., "About the Company" (*http://www.progest.com/Company.html*); Roberta Maynard, "Staying in Step with the Firm's Mission," *Nation's Business*, October 1997, p. 12.

How does MacFarland create a team atmosphere in her business?

The Solo Entrepreneur vs. the Team

By nature, entrepreneurs in their quest for independence often attempt a new venture as soloists. In this way they can retain sole ownership, make all key decisions, and not have to share the profits. This approach to starting a business is still the most common in small businesses and in the craft or artisan areas. Unfortunately, however, in today's market, it is becoming increasingly difficult to succeed alone, particularly if the goal is to create a world-class company. With more new ventures operating in complex, dynamic environments and requiring more capital, it is highly unlikely that any one person will have enough knowledge and resources to start a world-class company as a soloist.

Collaboration is, therefore, an essential ingredient in most start-ups today. Studies of high technology start-ups in particular have demonstrated that a team effort will provide a better chance for success than a solo effort.[1] Often this is because the technology inventor or creator may not have any business acumen. There are several other important reasons for using a founding team.

▶ The intense effort required of a start-up can be shared.

▶ Should any one team member leave, it is less likely to result in the abandonment of the start-up.

▶ With a founding team that includes major functional areas—marketing, finance, operations—the new venture can proceed further before it will need to hire additional personnel.

▶ A quality founding team lends credibility to the new venture in the eyes of lenders, investors, and others.

▶ The ability to analyze information and make decisions is improved because the lead entrepreneur has the benefit of the varied expertise of his or her team members; in this way ideas may be viewed from several perspectives.

Young entrepreneur Kim Camarella started her new apparel company—Kiyonna Klothing—with two friends. Camarella handles the business and fi-

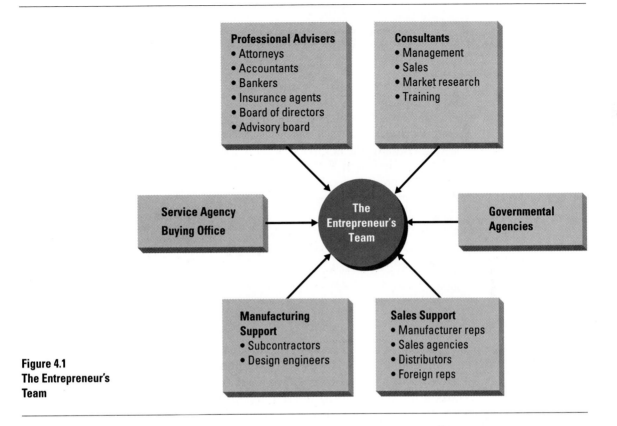

Professional Advisers
• Attorneys
• Accountants
• Bankers
• Insurance agents
• Board of directors
• Advisory board

Consultants
• Management
• Sales
• Market research
• Training

Service Agency
Buying Office

The Entrepreneur's Team

Governmental Agencies

Manufacturing Support
• Subcontractors
• Design engineers

Sales Support
• Manufacturer reps
• Sales agencies
• Distributors
• Foreign reps

Figure 4.1
The Entrepreneur's
Team

nancial tasks, Yvonne Buonouro is the designer, and Donna Maldonado is in charge of sales and marketing. They outsource all their manufacturing. This team effort has made it possible for them to grow their business faster than they would otherwise have been able to, since they share the major functions of the company.

The team approach to starting a business does not stop with the founding members. The founding team, in an effort to ensure a successful start-up, also forms alliances with professionals and industry experts to act as advisers and form what can be called an extended founding team. (See Figure 4.1.)

The Founding Team

When an entrepreneur decides to use a team effort to create the new venture, he or she generally looks for people who have complementary skills. In other words, if the entrepreneur happens to be an engineer, finding a market expert and someone who knows how to raise capital would be advantageous to the new venture. Since the start-up of a new venture is a multifunctional process, the entrepreneur and the venture will benefit greatly from a team comprised

The Technology Entrepreneur

Today's technology start-ups require a different type of entrepreneur to steer a young company through product launch in a chaotic market. Business writers Klimek and Sheehan report that technology entrepreneurs must be "visionary, adaptable, market driven, experienced, and connected." Today's technology entrepreneur must have a clear and strong vision of the company's future, based on a comprehensive knowledge of the industry. Still, he or she cannot plan every move because the market demands a more dynamic, forceful approach—zero market share to 40% as fast as you can. The technology entrepreneur must stay in tune with the customer's needs and that requires in-depth marketing experience. And last, but not least, he or she needs important contacts that result from constant networking.

SOURCE: Mark Klimek and David Sheehan, "What It Takes," *ASAP: The New Tech Elite*, October 7, 1996 (*http://www.forbes.com/asap/100796/66.html*).

of a variety of strengths and disciplines. Another advantage to forming a multifunctional team is that the founding team has a vested interest in the new venture. They invest not only their time but often their money as well. Thus the burden of raising the resources needed to start the venture is distributed among the team members, giving the lead entrepreneur access to the network of contacts of the other members in addition to his or her own. This vastly increases the information and resources available to the new venture and allows the venture to grow more rapidly.

Of course, it isn't always possible to put together the "perfect" team from the start. You may not have yet found the right person to fill a particular need—or you may have found the right person, but he or she is too expensive to bring on board during start-up. No matter. Talk to that person anyway about joining the team at a later date and keep that person up-to-date on what the company is doing. You would be surprised at how many times an aggressive start-up company can woo an experienced person away from a major corporation.

Professional Advisers

When a new venture is in the infancy stage, it generally doesn't have the resources to hire in-house professional help such as an attorney or an accountant. Instead, it must rely on building relationships with professionals on an "as-needed" basis. These professionals provide information and services not normally within the scope of expertise of most entrepreneurs, and they can play devil's advocate for the entrepreneur, pointing out potential flaws in the business concept. They provide the new venture—and the entrepreneurial team in love with its own concept—a reality check that is invaluable.

Attorneys

The first thing an entrepreneur should realize when dealing with attorneys is that for the most part, they are not business people. They are professionals who specialize in one area of the law: tax, real estate, business, patents. Therefore, it is important to select an attorney who specializes in the particular area needed by the entrepreneur. Attorneys can provide a wealth of support for the new venture. Within their particular area of expertise, attorneys can:

▶ Advise the entrepreneur in the selection of the correct legal organizational structure—that is, sole proprietorship, partnership, or corporation.

▶ Advise and prepare documents for intellectual property rights acquisition.

▶ Negotiate and prepare contracts for the entrepreneur, who may be buying, selling, contracting, or leasing.

▶ Advise the entrepreneur on compliance with regulations related to financing and credit.

▶ Keep the entrepreneur apprised of the latest tax reform legislation and help minimize the venture's tax burden.

▶ Assist the entrepreneur in complying with federal, state, or local laws.

▶ Represent the entrepreneur in any legal actions as advocates.

Choosing a good attorney is a time-consuming but vital task that should be accomplished prior to start-up. Decisions made at inception may affect the venture for years to come; hence, the need for good legal advice. A few tips may facilitate the search.

▶ Ask accountants, bankers, and other business people for recommendations of attorneys who are familiar with the challenges facing start-ups.

▶ Retain an experienced attorney who is competent to do what you want.

▶ Look for an attorney who is willing to listen, has time for you, and will be flexible about fees while the business is in the start-up phase.

▶ Check out the firm by phone first. You can learn a lot about the law firm by noting who answers the phone and with what tone of voice.

▶ Confirm that the attorney carries malpractice insurance.

Accountants

Your lawyer is your advocate, but your accountant is bound by rules and ethics that do not permit advocacy. Therefore, where an attorney is bound to represent you no matter what you do, the accountant, who is bound by the **GAAP** (Generally Accepted Accounting Principles), cannot defend you should you choose to do something that violates the GAAP.

Accounting is a fairly complex form of communication that the entrepreneur needs to understand. In the beginning of the business, the accountant may set up the company's books and maintain them on a periodic basis, or—as is often the case—the entrepreneur may hire a bookkeeper to do the day-to-day recording of transactions; the entrepreneur then can go to the accountant only at tax time. The accountant will also set up control systems for operations as well as payroll. A growing business has to do the following:

- Verify and post bills
- Write checks
- Issue invoices
- Make collections
- Get suppliers to cooperate
- Balance the checkbook
- Prepare financial statements

- Establish inventory controls
- File yearly tax returns
- Prepare budgets
- Prepare stockholder reports
- Make payroll tax deposits
- Secure insurance benefits
- Keep employee records

The accountant can assist in all these areas. Once the new venture is beyond the start-up phase and growing consistently, an annual audit is needed to determine whether the accounting and control procedures are adequate. Additionally, the auditors may also require a physical inventory. If everything is in order, they will issue a certified statement, which is important should the entrepreneur ever decide to take the company public on one of the stock exchanges. Accountants are also a rich networking source in the entrepreneur's search for additional members of the new venture team. Like attorneys, accountants tend to specialize, so finding one who is used to working with young, growing businesses will be an advantage. It is highly likely that the accountant who takes your business through start-up and early growth may not be the person to take care of the company's needs when it reaches the next level of growth. As the financial and recordkeeping needs of the business increase and become more complex, the entrepreneur may need to consider a larger firm with expertise in several areas.

Bankers

There is a saying that all banks are alike until you need a loan. Today that phrase is even truer. Having a qualified banker on the advisory team of the new venture is an issue not only when you need a line of credit for operating capital or to purchase equipment but from the moment you open the business account. Bankers offer a variety of valuable services, and you should think of a banker as a business partner who can contribute in these ways:

▶ Be a source of information and networking

▶ Help you make decisions regarding capital needs

▶ Assist you in preparing pro forma operations and cash flow analyses and evaluate projections you have made

▶ Assist you in all facets of procuring financing

Selecting a bank should be as careful a process as that for choosing an attorney or accountant. To narrow the search for a banker, the entrepreneur needs to develop a list of criteria that defines the needs of the new venture with respect to the banking relationship. The entrepreneur should also talk with other entrepreneurs in the same industry to identify a bank that works well with the type of venture planned. Asking an accountant or attorney to suggest the best bank for the new venture is another way to find a good banker.

When choosing a banker, seek out an officer with a rank of assistant vice president or higher, as these officers are trained to work with new and growing businesses and have a sufficient level of authority to quickly make decisions that affect the new venture.

Insurance Agents

Many entrepreneurs overlook the value of a relationship with a competent insurance agent, but a growing venture will require several types of insurance.

▶ Property and casualty   ▶ Unemployment

▶ Medical   ▶ Auto on firm's vehicles

▶ Errors and omissions   ▶ Liability (product and personal)

▶ Life on key management   ▶ Bonding

▶ Workers' compensation

Major insurance firms often can handle all types of insurance vehicles, but many times you will need to seek specialists for certain kinds of protection such as **bonding** (which is common in the construction industry, to protect against a contractor's not completing a project), product liability insurance, and errors and omissions (which protects the business against liability from unintentional mistakes in advertising). The new venture's insurance needs will change over its life, and a good insurance agent will help the entrepreneur determine the needed coverages at the appropriate times.

Board of Directors

The decision to have a **board of directors** is influenced by the legal form of the business. If the new venture is a corporation, a board of directors is required. If the business requires venture capital, a board will be necessary and the venture capitalist will probably demand a seat on it. Boards of directors serve a valuable purpose: if chosen correctly, they provide expertise that will benefit the new venture. In that capacity they act as advisers. They also assist in establishing corporate strategy and philosophy, as well as goals and objectives.

It is important to distinguish between boards of privately owned corporations and those of publicly owned corporations. In a privately owned corporation, the entrepreneurial team owns all or the majority of the stock, so directors serve at the pleasure of the entrepreneur, who has effective control of the company. On the other hand, directors of publicly traded companies have legitimate power to control the activities of the company.

Boards can be comprised of inside or outside members or a combination of the two. An **inside board member** is one who is a founder, employee, family member, or retired management of the firm, while an **outside board member** is someone with no direct connection to the business. Which type of board member is better is a matter of opinion and circumstance, as research has not provided any clear results on this issue. In general, however, outside directors are beneficial for succession planning and capital raising. They can often bring a fresh point of view to the strategic planning process, along with expertise that the founders may not possess.

Insiders have the advantage of complete knowledge about the business; they are generally more available and have demonstrated their effectiveness. They will usually have the necessary technical expertise as well. Yet there are political ramifications when the board members report to the CEO. For that reason they may not always be objective and independent in their thought process. They also may not have the broad expertise necessary to effectively guide the growth of the business.

Consider carefully whether the new venture requires a working board; that is, one that directs the strategy of the business. Most working boards are used for their expertise, for strategic planning, for auditing the actions of the firm, and for arbitrating differences. These activities are not as crucial in the start-up phase, when the entrepreneurial team is gathering resources and raising capital. However, a board of directors can assist the entrepreneurial team in those functions and can network with key people who can help the new venture. At this juncture in the new venture, some potential directors will ask to be included on the board so that they can monitor their investment in the company. This is common with large private investors, bankers, and even accountants. To ensure getting only the best people on the board, standards should be set in advance and strictly adhered to.

During the growth period of the new venture, the entrepreneurial team is normally buried with operational details, the need to generate sales, and the problem of maintaining a positive cash flow. Dealing with a board of directors is not something they will want to do. But the board members can offer the struggling team an objective point of view and the benefit of their considerable experience. The size and complexity of your business will determine how many directors serve on the board. The general recommendation is to have no fewer than five and no more than fifteen board members.[2]

When choosing people to serve on the board of directors, you should consider those who have:

▶ The necessary technical skill related to the business

▶ Significant, successful experience in the industry

▶ Important contacts in the industry

▶ Expertise in finance, capital acquisition, and possibly Initial Public Offerings (IPOs)

▶ A personality compatible with the rest of the board

▶ Good problem-solving skills

▶ Honesty and integrity, to engender a sense of mutual trust

Functions of a Board of Directors

In general most boards of directors perform the following duties and functions:

1. Select and hire or fire the CEO

2. Approve the selection, hiring, and termination of senior management

3. Nominate other directors, who are then voted upon by the shareholders

4. Audit the company's records in accordance with GAAP

5. Review the performance of the company against projections

6. Prepare and monitor the strategic plan for the company

7. Approve the sale of company assets, major acquisitions, and investments

8. Approve major policy changes

9. Monitor compliance on legal, ethical, and environmental issues

10. Declare dividends

11. Step in, in times of crisis

SOURCE: Grant Thornton, "Changing Roles for Boards of Directors in Entrepreneurial Companies," GT Online: *Assurance and Governance*, 1996, (*http://www.gt.com/gtonline/assuranc/changec.html*).

If the entrepreneurial team is not careful, they may learn too late that a director they have appointed to the board considers the position an appointment for life, much like being appointed to the Supreme Court. To prevent such a situation from occurring—you'll want new directors at times, in order to bring new life to the board—ask directors to serve on a rotating basis for a specified period of time.

The board is headed by the Chairman, who, in a new venture, is typically the lead entrepreneur. The entrepreneur will also, most probably, be the President and Chief Executive Officer (CEO). The current trend is to have the CEO and perhaps the Chief Operating Officer (COO) as the only inside members on the board.

Boards normally meet an average of five times a year, depending on the type of business. How often the board meets will be largely a function of how active it is at any point in time. Directors typically spend about nine to ten days a year on duties related to the business and are usually paid a retainer plus a per-meeting fee, with their expenses also reimbursed. The compensation can take the form of cash, stock, or other perquisites.

Today it is more difficult to get people to serve as directors because in some cases they can be held personally liable for the actions of the firm, and the frequency with which boards are being sued is increasing. For this reason, potential directors may require that the business carry directors' and officers' (D & O) liability insurance; however, the expense of this insurance is often prohibitive for a growing company. Additional expenses related to the development of a board of directors include meeting rooms, travel, and food.

Advisory Board

The **advisory board** is an informal panel of experts and other people who are interested in seeing the new venture succeed. Advisory boards can range from those that meet once or twice a year and do not pay advisers to those that meet more regularly and whose members are compensated. Be careful, however, not to choose advisers who serve just for the money. Advisory boards are often used when a board of directors is not required or in the start-up phase when the board of directors consists of the founders only. An effective advisory board can provide the new venture with the needed expertise without the significant costs and loss of control associated with a board of directors. In a wholly owned or closely held corporation there really is no distinction between the functions of a board of directors and those of a board of advisers, as control remains in the hands of the entrepreneurial team.

Entrepreneurs tend to resist the idea of having outside advisers because of the intense desire to be independent and to maintain some secrecy about the business. Also, entrepreneurs tend to believe that an outsider could never understand the business.[3] Although many business owners may reject a formal board, they risk developing tunnel vision unless they consider using an advisory board. An advisory board is a step in the direction of creating a more professional organization that researcher Donald R. Jonovic asserts is comprised of three elements:

1. Shareholder harmony, achieved through shareholder agreements and buy-sell agreements

2. Effective management that has a vision and goals for the company

3. Efficient internal communication through shareholder meetings, advisory board meetings, and management meetings[4]

Mistakes to Avoid

Putting together the extended founding team is a serious undertaking that if unsuccessful, could have severe ramifications for the future of the business. Several common mistakes in forming the team should be avoided:

▶ Forming the team casually or by chance—that is, without careful consideration of the experience and qualifications each person brings to the team.

▶ Putting together a team whose members have different goals; this could impede the growth of the company.

Profile 4.2

How Two Companies Used Boards

While entrepreneurs typically don't like to use outside board members, two companies found that their outside board members actually saved their businesses. Nancy Olsen, the founder of Impostors Copy Jewels, a retailer/franchiser of costume jewelry, experienced one of those moments that makes business owners shudder. Two employees who managed the technology side of the business left without explanation. Her dealers were panicking because they couldn't get their point-of-sale computers to work properly. On top of that, six boxes of glass display cases for stores about to open arrived damaged. In serious financial trouble, Olsen was preparing company reports for her newly formed outside advisory board. She had no idea how important that board would be to the success of her business.

As things turned out, one board member, president of a financial services firm, became her temporary CFO, while another created a new ad campaign. Over time, the board helped her solve all her problems and reach annual revenues of $17 million.

Don Beaver and Ben Stapelfeld wanted a board that not only had expertise they needed but also bought into their philosophy of business. Beaver and Stapelfeld are the founders of New Pig Corp., a Pennsylvania-based company that produces devices to clean up waste in factories. Their first product was the Pig sock, a long hose that laps up oil from leaky machinery. When the company was founded in 1985, the board was involved in everything from pricing to suppliers to packaging. When Beaver and his partner disagreed about the way to capitalize the company, the board served as mediator and came up with a third way, a private stock offering, which resolved the impasse. One of the board members even leased out part of his own plant to New Pig for a year until its founders could get one of their own. Today New Pig is as large as most of the companies of its board members and sometimes even advises *them*.

SOURCE: Elizabeth Conlin, "Unlimited Partners," *Inc.*, April 1990, p. 71.

▶ Using only insiders for the board of directors—that is, friends and family members instead of the people most qualified to advise the business.

▶ Using family members or friends as attorney and accountant for the business. As these professional advisers must remain objective at all times to best represent and assist the entrepreneur, choosing relatives can cause unnecessary problems.

▶ Giving the founding team stock in lieu of salary. The lead entrepreneur does not want significant shares of stock in the hands of people who may later leave the company. Furthermore, loose stock could land in the hands of the firm's competitors. In a later chapter, the issue of a buy-sell agreement to prevent this problem will be discussed.

Outsourcing Savvy—Independent Contractors

New ventures typically do not have the resources to hire all the management staff they might need to run the business. In fact, most entrepreneurs "bootstrap" in the early stages of growing a business. **Bootstrapping** in this context means "begging, borrowing, or renting everything" to get the business off the ground. Bootstrapping represents collectively all the creative techniques employed by entrepreneurs in the start-up phase. Here are some of the general rules of thumb for bootstrapping:

▶ Hiring as few employees as possible (employees are usually the single largest expense of a business)

▶ Leasing rather than buying, so as not to tie up limited funds in equipment and facilities. With a lease, there is often no down payment, and the cost is spread over time

▶ Arranging longer terms with suppliers

▶ Where possible, getting customers to pay in advance

The first rule of thumb just stated above is relevant to this chapter. How does a new venture survive with as few employees as possible and still grow? One solution is to hire workers from a temporary service; another is **outsourcing**, using independent contractors. **Independent contractors** own their own businesses and are hired by the entrepreneur to do a specific job. They are under the control of the entrepreneur only for the result of the work they do and not for the means by which that result is accomplished. There are several advantages to the entrepreneur in using independent contractors.

▶ Independent contractors usually are specialists in their field.

▶ Hiring an independent contractor often costs less than hiring an employee because the entrepreneur does not supply the contractor's medical and retirement benefits, unemployment insurance, and Social Security tax, or withhold income tax. These benefits can amount to as much as 32 percent or more of the base salary.

If, however, the entrepreneur does not follow the rules regulating classification of workers as independent contractors, the entrepreneur can be held liable for all back taxes plus penalties and interest, which can result in a substantial sum. Entrepreneurs using independent contractors should

▶ Consult an attorney.

▶ Draw up a contract with each independent contractor, specifying that the contractor will not be treated as an employee for state and federal tax purposes.

▶ Be careful not to indicate the time or manner in which the work will be performed.

▶ Verify that the independent contractor carries workers' compensation insurance.

▶ Verify that the independent contractor possesses the necessary licenses.

More specifically, the IRS uses a 20-point test for classifying workers. (See Table 4.1.) Even if you follow all the IRS rules, however, there is no

Table 4.1 The 20-Point Test for Independent Contractors

A worker is an employee if he or she

1. Must follow the employer's instructions about how to do the work.
2. Receives training from the employer.
3. Provides services that are integrated into the business.
4. Provides services that must be rendered personally.
5. Cannot hire, supervise, and pay his or her own assistants.
6. Has a continuing relationship with the employer.
7. Must follow set hours of work.
8. Works full-time for an employer.
9. Does the work on the employer's premises.
10. Must do the work in a sequence set by the employer.
11. Must submit regular reports to the employer.
12. Is paid regularly for time worked.
13. Receives reimbursements for expenses.
14. Relies on the tools and materials of the employer.
15. Has no major investment in facilities to perform the service.
16. Cannot make a profit or suffer a loss.
17. Works for one employer at a time.
18. Does not offer his or her services to the general public.
19. Can be fired at will by the employer.
20. May quit work at any time without incurring liability.

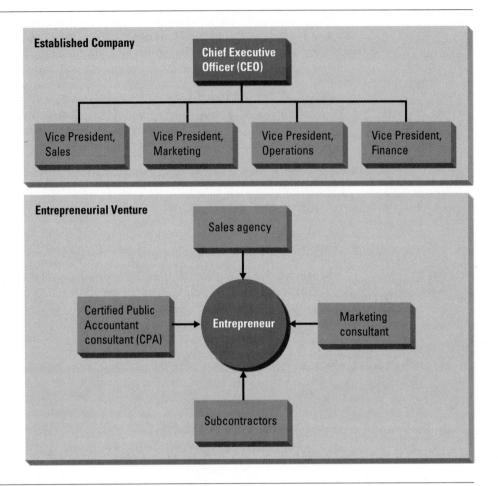

**Figure 4.2
The Virtual
Entrepreneurial
Company**

guarantee that the IRS won't challenge your position. Therefore, it is important to document the relationship with an independent contractor through a legal agreement that explicitly demonstrates that the independent contractor owns his or her own business. The IRS can decide that a worker is an employee if even one of the 20 points is true.

If all the IRS rules are followed, independent contractors can make the very small start-up venture look like an established corporation to anyone on the outside. A large corporation will generally have vice presidents for departments of operations, sales, marketing, and finance. It is possible for you to replicate the larger corporate functions by using independent contractors, thereby lowering costs and remaining more flexible. Figure 4.2 shows how a growing entrepreneurial venture can imitate the strength, stability, and expertise of a much larger, more established company through the use of independent contractors. The concept is called the "virtual corporation" and will be discussed at length in Chapter 10.

Caveats for Leasing

Leasing employees has become big business. Both small and large companies have discovered that they can "rent" anyone from a receptionist to a Chief Financial Officer as easily as they can rent equipment. Employee-leasing companies, also known as **professional employer organizations** (PEOs), are essentially co-employers. PEOs provide a diverse range of benefits and services such as payroll, workers' compensation insurance, retirement plans, and so forth. The client is charged an administration fee that can range from 2% to 8% of the total payroll. The advantage of this system is that several small businesses can enroll under the same PEO and take advantage of lower insurance costs because the total volume of business increases.

Because some PEOs end up going out of business, it's important to choose wisely. Here are some things to consider.

▶ The audited financial statements of the company. Be sure to have your accountant check them.

▶ Ask for a substantial list of the PEO's clients. Then call some of them and ask questions about their experiences. This will also tell you if the PEO has experience in your industry.

▶ Consider the PEO a strategic partner and apply the same rules you would for any other partnership.

▶ Choose a PEO that will customize its services to meet your needs.

▶ Negotiate the contract and be sure that the PEO hasn't absolved itself of all liability.

▶ Check with the Institute for the Accreditation of Professional Employer Organizations in Bethesda, Maryland, to find one of the 15+ PEOs accredited to date.

SOURCE: Jay Finegan, "Look Before You Lease,"*Inc.*, February 1997, p. 106.

The Shadow Team

Many types of independent contractors operate behind the scenes of the new venture but make a valuable contribution nonetheless.

Consultants

The consulting industry is one of the fastest growing industries in the United States, and it can provide a variety of services for the new venture.

- Train the sales staff and/or management
- Conduct market research
- Prepare policy manuals
- Solve problems
- Act as temporary key management
- Recommend market strategy
- Design and engineer product
- Design a plant layout and equipment
- Conduct research and development
- Recommend operational and financial controls

Since they tend to be fairly expensive, consultants are best used for critical one-time advice or problem solving. However, this is a matter of perspective, as a quality consultant can accomplish a mission or job more efficiently and effectively than an employee because these consultants' greatest strengths usually are problem solving and working quickly within a strict budget.

Outsourcing Your Staff

Leasing the staff is a way for a new business to enjoy the advantages of major corporations without incurring the expense. The way it works is that a leasing company assumes the payroll and human resource functions for the business for a fee that generally ranges from three to five percent of gross payroll. Each pay period the new venture pays the leasing company a lump sum to cover payroll plus the fee. The National Staff Leasing Association reports that there are about one million leased employees in the United States and that the industry is growing at an annual rate of 30 percent.

Manufacturing Support

Even those new ventures that involve manufacturing a product can avail themselves of the benefits of independent contractors. Because the cost of building and equipping a new manufacturing plant is immense by any standards, many entrepreneurs choose to subcontract the work to an established manufacturer. In fact, it is possible for the entrepreneur with a new-product idea to subcontract the design of the product to an engineering firm, the production of components to various manufacturing firms, the assembly of the product to another firm, and the distribution to yet another.

Sales Support

Hiring a sales staff can be an expensive proposition for any new venture, not only from the standpoint of benefits but because they must be trained as well.

As new high-growth ventures seek a geographically broad market, even global, it is vital to consider manufacturer's representatives (reps) and foreign reps who know those markets and can act as the entrepreneur's representative. Using distributors allows the entrepreneur to reach the target market without having to deal with the complex retail market. In addition, sales agencies can provide fully trained sales persons to the new venture in much the same manner as temporary services supply clerical help. Some can also provide advertising and public relations.

Service Agencies

With many established firms downsizing and contracting out for services, some entrepreneurs have seen an opportunity to provide those services and have built highly successful, high-growth businesses. As a result, it is now possible for a new venture to subcontract for payroll services, computer services, and temporary help, to name a few. The service firm employs the individual and provides the benefits while the entrepreneur pays a fee for the services.

Buying Offices

When the entrepreneur is ready to consider a global market, he or she may opt to use either an import/export agency or broker or the international department of a major bank. These people understand the laws, customs, and currency exchange rules in the countries with which the entrepreneur will deal.

Governmental Agencies

There are many agencies at the federal, state, and local levels that offer various services to new ventures. Notable among them are the Small Business Administration, which provides education, loans, and grants to small business; the Department of Commerce, which can assist the entrepreneur on issues of trade; and state and local economic development corporations.

By taking advantage of the many services available, the entrepreneur can literally start a business from home to reduce start-up capital requirements, yet still operate like a major corporation. This is not to suggest that a company can always avoid hiring employees and still grow. That will depend on the type of business started. However, it does suggest that in the start-up, bootstrapping phase of a new venture, the use of independent contractors can help ensure that the business survives long enough and generates enough revenues to hire employees.

New Venture Checklist

Have you:

❏ **Identified the members of the founding team or at least the expertise needed to start the venture?**

❏ **Begun asking questions about potential professional advisers such as an attorney or accountant?**

❏ **Determined if you will need a board of directors, advisory board, or both?**

❏ **Identified at least one type of independent contractor the new venture could use?**

❏ **Determined what expertise is missing from the management team and how you will take care of it?**

Issues to Consider

1. What are the advantages of starting a new venture with a team, rather than as a solo entrepreneur?
2. At what point in the growth of a new venture should an entrepreneur consider creating a board of directors or an advisory board?
3. Attorneys are considered advocates; accountants are not. Why is this important for the entrepreneur to know?
4. How can you ensure that you are using independent contractors correctly and in accordance with the law?
5. Suppose you are starting a computer service company that does custom programming. What kinds of independent contractors can help you start this venture?

Experiencing Entrepreneurship

1. Interview an entrepreneur who started a venture as a soloist; then visit an entrepreneurial venture started by a team (two or more). Based on your interviews, what are the advantages and disadvantages of each approach?
2. Choose a lawyer, accountant, or banker to interview as a potential professional adviser to your business. What information will you need to get from him or her to make your decision?

Additional Sources of Information

Covey, S.R. (1989). *The 7 Habits of Highly Effective People.* New York: Simon and Schuster Trade.

Ford, R.H. (1992). *Boards of Directors and the Privately Owned Firm.* New York: Quorum Books.

Ward, J. (1991). *Creating Effective Boards for Private Enterprise.* San Francisco: Jossey-Bass.

Internet Resources

Advanced Consulting Group
http://www.advgroup.com
Free articles that help home-based entrepreneurs with management concerns. Good links to other sites.

EntreWorld
http://www.entreworld.com
Excellent source of information on team building as well as other start-up topics.

Relevant Case Studies

1. Flight Time
2. OXO (A)
3. Simtek, Inc.

Analyzing and Testing Opportunity

5

The man with a new idea is a crank—until the idea succeeds.
Mark Twain

Analyzing Industry Risks and Benefits

Overview

▶ **Defining the industry**

▶ **Industry evolution**

▶ **Competitive entry strategies**

▶ **Competitive analysis**

▶ **Industry analysis**

▶ **The ideal industry**

▶ **Presenting the industry data in the feasibility study or business plan**

Terms to Know

Carrying capacity 84
Dynamism 84
Complexity 84

Economies of scale 85
Cost superiority 90

Differentiation 90
Niche strategy 90

Standard Industrial
Classification 94

Profile 5.1

In Handcuffs in a Tough Industry

The apparel industry has never been particularly friendly to new entrants. For the most part, it's difficult if not impossible to protect an idea, and beginners often are at the mercy of the big retailers. But that didn't thwart Bob Mellon and his brothers, Chuck and Mark, who had no previous experience in either the apparel or retail industries. A motorcycle accident in which Mark fell and tore a thumb-size hole in his sweatshirt precipitated the design of a unique sweatshirt with extendable cuffs that create fingerless gloves with thumbholes.

The brothers decided that there might be a market for this innovative product. Certainly, others might have a need to protect their hands from the elements. Initially, the Mellons ignored the industry, focusing on the market in their hometown of Fresno, California. The first year they sold 1,000 "Handcuffs;" the second, 4,000. In 1997, they estimated selling between

75,000 and 100,000. Without a doubt, they had discovered a niche in an unforgiving industry, a way to enter the market quickly before their product was "knocked off" by another manufacturer.

In the third season "Handcuffs" began to grab national attention with a two-page layout in J.C. Penney's *Cold Weather Remedies* catalog. The Mellon brothers had sent a sample sweatshirt to Penney's national buyer, who invited them to corporate headquarters in Texas. The result was a sale of 21,000 sweatshirts in eight colors, three styles, and a variety of sizes. More national exposure was achieved when motorcycle manufacturer Harley-Davidson bought 800 of the sweatshirts and featured them in its catalog. The brothers have also made a deal with California Lifestyle, a wholesaler who distributes to resorts and airport gift shops, and expect to close a deal with a similar company in Canada.

The Mellon brothers may have entered the industry ignorant of the barriers, but they quickly learned how to get around them and how to make themselves known. They've made partners of potential competitors and are planning to introduce a children's clothing line with their distinctive "thumbs-up" logo. As long as they keep moving forward, they may well stay ahead of any competition that's sure to come.

SOURCE: Sanford Nax, "No Sweat, This Shirt Is Red Hot," *The Fresno Bee,* October 6, 1997.

What was the Mellon brothers' strategy for penetrating a difficult industry?

Defining the Industry

One of the factors that affects both the creation and the strategy of new ventures is the environment in which they will operate. This environment includes:

1. The industry in which a business operates

2. The market the business serves

3. The state of the national—and perhaps the international—economy

4. The people and businesses with which the business will interact

A strategic position in a growing, dynamic, healthy industry can go a long way toward ensuring a successful venture. However, a weak position in a mature industry may sound a death knell for the business before it even opens its doors. A young, growing industry with many new entrants will present at once a highly competitive environment for the new venture and a chance to gain significant market share if entry is early. This was the case in the software industry in the 1980s. A more mature industry, by contrast, may have already passed through the period of "survival of the fittest" and will now consist of a few firms with large market shares, as in the automobile, semiconductor, and airline industries, to name a few.[1]

Research has identified three dimensions of the industry environment that help the entrepreneur evaluate the new venture's potential in the industry: carrying capacity, dynamism, and complexity.[2]

Carrying Capacity or Degree of Saturation

Carrying capacity is the extent to which the industry can support growth. Entrepreneurs will typically seek out an industry that can support expansion, thus allowing the new venture to grow and to obtain the resources it needs. Difficulty in entering a specific industry suggests that the industry may be approaching saturation—that is, the production capability of the existing firms equals or exceeds the demand by customers for industry products. The only way to enter such an industry then is through the introduction of new technology or by discovering a niche where a need has not been met. This was certainly the strategy of Vidal Herrera (see case study: Autopsies-to-Go) who, through his in-depth understanding of the industry and experience in it, saw an opportunity to provide private autopsy services.

Uncertainty

Dynamism, another often-used term for this dimension, is the degree of certainty or uncertainty in the industry, as well as stability or instability; in other words, a dynamic environment is one that is difficult to predict because it is in constant flux. Industries that operate in volatile environments, like the computer industry, contain higher degrees of uncertainty or risk. Consequently, the rewards are usually higher as well. Dynamic, even chaotic, environments also provide a fertile growing ground for new opportunities and have given birth to such successful companies as Amazon, Netscape, and Pixar Animation Studios.

Complexity

Complexity is the number and diversity of inputs and outputs facing an organization. Firms that operate in complex industries usually have to deal with more suppliers, customers, and competitors than other industries, and they usually produce a greater number of dissimilar products for global markets. Industries with a high degree of complexity by their very nature make it difficult for new businesses to enter. They are also extremely competitive; therefore, new ventures often find a great deal of hostility rather than collaboration in those industries. Telecommunications and biotechnology are both industries with a high degree of competition and government regulation and have very short product life cycles.

Industry Structure

In studying the industry in which the new venture will operate, you need to develop a broad picture of how the industry works, how friendly it is to new entrants, and where it is headed. The work of Michael Porter provides a framework for looking at the nature of your industry's environment. Porter asserts that there are five forces in any industry that affect the ultimate profit potential of a venture in terms of long run return on investment. If we look at these forces from the point of view of the entrepreneur with a new business, they are:

1. Barriers to new business in the industry

2. The power of suppliers to affect your strategy

3. Threat of substitute products

4. The power of buyers to affect your strategy

5. The degree of rivalry among competitors in the industry[3]

These are the forces that drive competition and affect the long run profitability of the new venture as well as of other firms in the industry. Short run profitability, by contrast, is affected by such things as economic forces, changes in demand, material shortages, and so forth. Let's look at each of these forces in more detail.

Threat of New Entrants

In some industries barriers to entry are high and will discourage a potential entrepreneur from attempting to enter. These barriers may include:

Economies of Scale

Many industries have achieved **economies of scale** in marketing, production, and distribution. This means that their costs to produce have declined relative to the price of their goods and services. A new venture cannot easily achieve these same economies, so it is forced into a "Catch-22" situation. If it enters the industry on a large scale, it risks retaliation from those established firms in the industry. If it enters on a small scale, it may not be able to compete because of high costs relative to everyone else. Another version of this dilemma is an industry where the major players are vertically integrated; that is, they own their suppliers and/or distribution channels, which effectively locks out the new venture. What most new ventures attempt to do when faced with economies of scale is to form alliances with other small firms to share resources and compete on a more level playing field.

Brand Loyalty

New entrants to an industry face products and services that have loyal customers, so an extensive marketing campaign focused on making the customer aware of the benefits of the new venture's products will be required. The cost of undertaking this strategy can be a significant barrier to entry unless customers are dissatisfied with the competing brands.

Enormous Capital Requirements

The cost of entering many industries is prohibitive for a new venture. These costs may include up-front advertising, R&D, and expenditures for plant and equipment to compete on par with established firms in the industry. Entrepreneurs often overcome this barrier by outsourcing to established companies.

Switching Costs for the Buyer

Buyers in most industries don't readily switch from one supplier to another unless there is a demonstrated reason to do so. Switching costs the buyer money and time to retrain staff and potentially learn a new technology. For example, users of the Microsoft Windows graphical interface will not readily switch to a different system because they have spent a lot of time learning the Windows environment and are used to it. As a new entrant, you will need to spend considerable time and money convincing customers that your product is worth switching to.

Access to Distribution Channels

The new venture must persuade established distribution channel members to accept the new product or service and must prove that it will be beneficial to distributors to do so. This persuasion process can be costly for the new venture. One solution is distributing via the Internet, which is a direct method of reaching the customer.

Proprietary Factors

Barriers to entry also include proprietary technology, products, and processes. Where established firms hold patents on products and processes that the new venture requires, they have the ability to either keep the new venture out of the industry or make it very expensive to enter. Most favorable location is another form of proprietary barrier. Often entrepreneurs will discover that existing firms in the industry own the most advantageous business sites, forcing the new venture to locate in a less competitive site. The Internet diminishes such location advantages. Moreover, established firms, being further along on the learning/experience curve, are probably more cost efficient in their operations—something that will take time for the new venture to achieve. These proprietary factors are all substantial barriers to entry for a new venture.

Government Regulations

The government can prevent a new venture from entering an industry through strict licensing requirements and by limiting access to raw materials through laws or high taxes and to certain locations via zoning restrictions. Food products and biochemicals must obtain FDA approval.

Industry Hostility

Some industries are extremely retaliatory toward new businesses that attempt to compete in the industry. This typically occurs where there are many well-established firms that have sufficient resources to spend the time and money going after a new entrant. It is also common in mature industries where growth has slowed, so rivalry for market share intensifies as profits decline. Weaker firms ultimately exit the industry.

Threat from Substitute Products

A new venture must compete not only with products and services in its own industry but also with those that are logical substitutes in other industries as well. Generally, these substitute products and services accomplish the same basic function in a different way or at a different price. For example, restaurants regularly compete with other forms of entertainment for the consumer's disposable dollars. The threat from substitute products is more likely to occur where firms in other industries are earning high profits at better prices than can be achieved in the new venture's industry.

Threat from Buyers' Bargaining Power

Buyers of products and services can force down prices in the industry through volume purchases. This is particularly true where the industry products comprise a significant portion of the buyers' requirements. Under this scenario, the buyer is more likely to seek the lowest possible price. The largest buyers also pose a threat of backward integration, where they actually purchase their suppliers, thus better controlling costs and affecting price throughout the industry. The more buyers understand the nature of the industry and the more the products are standardized, the greater the likelihood that these buyers will have significant bargaining power. In industries where buyers have bargaining power, it is more difficult for a new entrant to gain a foothold and grow. Examples of buyers that have this type of bargaining power are Price/Costco, Target, and Toys 'R' Us.

Threat from Suppliers' Bargaining Power

In some industries suppliers exert enormous power through the threat of raising prices or changing the quality of the products that they supply to manufacturers and distributors. If the number of these suppliers is few relative to the size of the industry, or the industry is not the primary customer of the suppliers, that power is magnified. Moreover, if these suppliers are the primary source of materials and components for the new venture, the ability to compete on cost may be negatively affected. A further threat from suppliers is that they will forward integrate—that is, they will purchase the outlets for their goods and services, thus controlling the prices at which they are ultimately sold.

It is interesting to consider that labor is really a source of supply. In certain industries where highly technical skills are required or where unions are strong, labor as a supplier has enormous bargaining power and can significantly impact costs for the new venture. Key employees who have highly marketable skills and are mobile can demand higher salaries and perks than the new venture can afford. This situation is seen frequently in the hi-tech arena.

Rivalry Among Existing Industry Firms

In general, it can be said that a highly competitive industry will drive down profits and ultimately the rate of return on investment. To position themselves in a competitive market, firms often will resort to price wars, advertising skirmishes, and enhanced service. Once one firm decides to make such a strategic move in the industry, others will follow. The clearest example is the airline industry; when one airline discounts its prices significantly, most of the others immediately follow. The problem with this tactic is that it ultimately hurts everyone in the industry and may even result in forcing some smaller firms out because competitive prices drop below cost. Most new ventures can't compete on price and can't afford costly advertising battles to build an image. To compete in an industry that is highly competitive, they must find a market niche they can dominate that has not been served by the major industry rivals and enter the industry without causing movement on the part of the major players.

The Special Case of Emerging Industries

Emerging industries are those that are just coming into being. Some examples are interactive television and telecommunications. In these types of industries, there are no rules initially. Instead, technical uncertainty exists until the major technology developers enter the industry and it becomes apparent which technology is the best. Consequently, there is no standardization of products and processes in the industry for some time, and as a result costs to produce are high. Securing sufficient raw materials may also be difficult.

Buyers in an emerging industry are, for the most part, considered first-time buyers. They will pay a premium for the product at its introduction but will usually see that price decline significantly as competition increases and standardization of technology occurs.

For entrepreneurs, an emerging industry is at once exciting, challenging, and extremely risky. Certainly the strongest position is to own the technology being introduced and be able to enter the market with sufficient resources to establish a firm market share and brand identity. If, however, others are also entering the market at the same time with similar proprietary technology, resources will have to be directed toward promoting the benefits and superiority of the entrepreneur's technology. This was the case for Microsoft's Windows, which ultimately overcame the threat of IBM's OS/2 technology. If major companies from other compatible industries are entering the new industry, the task is that much harder. That is the situation for new ventures hoping to garner a piece of the action in the telecommunications industry, where they are competing for market share against the likes of AT&T and Microsoft.

Industry Evolution

Industries do not remain static or stable over time. In fact, they are in an almost constant state of evolution. Like a business, an industry moves through

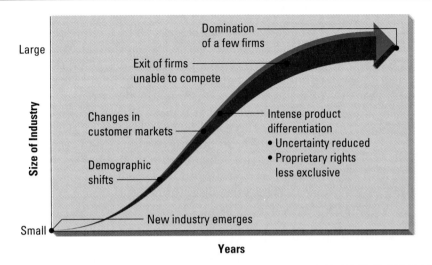

**Figure 5.1
Industry Growth
Cycle**

a life cycle that includes birth, growth, maturity, and ultimately decline. Of course, for every industry the life cycle stages occur at different rates and last for varying lengths of time. The video rental industry presents a classic example of an industry in transition. In the early stages it was comprised of small independent (mom-and-pop) owners when Wayne Huizenga sought to consolidate the industry by developing Blockbuster Video, a video megastore. In just a few years, independents were disappearing in favor of large-volume chain outlets. Yet in a few more years the megastores will likely give way to video available on demand over cable television.

As an industry grows, it sees demographic shifts, changes in costs of materials and labor, product and process innovations, and changes in its customer markets. Industry products tend to become commodities over time, so the competitive tendency to differentiate products is enhanced. With time, uncertainty is reduced and proprietary rights become less exclusive, which may result in larger, risk-averse firms entering the industry. These larger firms have the resources to integrate vertically, gaining control of suppliers and distribution channels and instituting product and process innovations that can result in larger volumes of goods being produced and sold. These actions can cause a change in the cost structure of the industry and the exit of firms unable to compete in the new industry structure. A few firms will finally dominate. Figure 5.1 displays this evolution.

Competitive Entry Strategies

The new venture's entry strategy will be largely a function of the structure of the industry into which it seeks entry. In general, three broad strategies are available to the new venture: cost superiority, product/process/service differentiation, and niche.

Cost Superiority

Essentially, **cost superiority** entails entering the industry with an organizational structure that is lean and mean, with tight controls on costs. To accomplish this usually requires designing the production process and distribution mechanisms to operate under strict controls, meeting stringent quantity targets. Consequently, this strategy is very difficult for a new venture to achieve in that it most often results from being further along on the experience curve and from producing in high volumes. It is rare that a new venture will have the infrastructure and resources in place, and sufficient product/service demand from the beginning to allow it to use cost superiority as an entry strategy. One exception is an emerging industry where everyone is at the same disadvantage.

Differentiation

Differentiation is a strategy that involves distinguishing the new venture from others in the industry through product/process innovation, or a unique marketing or distribution strategy. Differentiation often creates brand loyalty among customers, thereby making the product or service less sensitive to price. Consequently, margins are usually increased, which better insulates the company against supplier and buyer bargaining power, and moves the focus away from the cost to produce. Additionally, substitute products are less likely to be a threat where differentiation is the strategy. When Marianne Szymanski created Toy Tips, Inc. (see case study), she refused to accept money from toy manufacturers and thereby differentiated herself from other companies that were evaluating toys. With this strategy, she made her firm the only independent toy research company in the United States.

If your business is competing in the mainstream market, as opposed to focusing on a niche (see the next section), it will be vitally important to differentiate yourself from others in the market. Otherwise, how will you answer the crucial question "Why will they buy from my company?"

Niche Strategy

The third strategy is often referred to as a **niche strategy**, which simply means that the new venture focuses on a particular customer group or specific geographic region not currently served by the industry effectively. This was the strategy of the Mellon Brothers with "Handcuffs." By selecting a segment of a market, niche entrepreneurs attempt to insulate themselves from market forces such as competitors and the barriers to entry in an industry. A niche may be created by using any of the key elements of the business: customer, product design, price, service, packaging, geographic focus, and distribution.

Many a new venture has entered an established industry via a niche by finding a gap in the market that allows the company to compete without going head to head with the major companies in the industry. Where competition is weak and exposure to substitute products is a minor issue, the niche strategy offers a safer route to establishing a foothold in the industry. Uri Budnik entered the cluttered telecommunications industry via a niche. His company, Telebuzón, provides voice mail service between people in the United States and Mexico, even if subscribers don't have a phone. This particular service was not available to this niche customer prior to Budnik's entry into the market; he created a niche that he intends to dominate and for which he sets the standards.

It is not necessary, however, to create a niche and offer something completely new. In fact, often the cost of creating customer awareness for a radically different product or service cannot be justified.[4] Alan Reed found a niche in the greeting card industry by targeting children and others who want to use their creativity to create a unique pop-up greeting card. These cards were distributed through craft outlets and toy stores rather than the usual greeting card outlet.

The important thing to remember about niche marketing is that it allows a small company to define and target a segment of a large market and own that segment. Working in a niche gives the company time to develop, to become stronger and better able to compete against companies in the mainstream market.

Competing on a Global Level

Michael Porter, in *Competitive Strategy* (1980), contends that while there are many differences when competing in an industry on an international basis, structural factors and general market forces are essentially the same. Entrepreneurs can go global through licensing products and services to international firms, exporting, strategic alliances, marketing and distributing on the Internet, or investing in plant and equipment in another country. Many resources are available to the entrepreneur who chooses to compete in the global marketplace.

While the advantages of competing on a global level include increased potential for growth, there are a number of difficulties that often impede the process. Transportation and storage of product in other countries is often difficult. Many times products made in the United States must be modified to meet the specifications and demands of customers in other countries. For example, sizes of clothing vary from country to country, and electrical current, which is 110v in the United States, is 240v in many other countries. Distribution channels inside the borders of other countries usually operate differently. Sometimes the problem is a matter of political clout or government regulation. Finally, the legal protections, such as patent laws, that are enjoyed by entrepreneurs in the United States are not always respected in the same manner in other countries. The complexity of investigating an industry on a global level is exacerbated by the fact that not only must you grasp how the industry works in that country, you also must have a good understanding of the culture and political process.

Competitive Analysis

Within any industry, it is important to hypothesize about the competitive strategy of the competition—in other words, to know the competition as well as you know your own business. Studying the history and management style of your major competitors will give insight into what motivates them and how they may potentially react to your strategy. You need to identify their current strategy to learn how they have positioned themselves in the industry. In the same way that you would analyze your strategy's strengths, weaknesses, opportunities, and threats, you should also study theirs.

Not all of your competitors will exhibit the same strategy, so it is useful to categorize them to get a handle on what the new venture is facing. Using a competitive grid (Figure 5.2 displays an example) will make it easier to see differences and recognize opportunities.

Once the competitors have been categorized, you will more readily see in what strategic grouping the new venture lies; that is, who your key competitors are. From there the new venture's position in that group will be determined as well as the strategic group's position in the industry as a whole. To have the best chance for success, the new venture should be positioned in the strategic group that offers the best profit potential, yet a reasonable cost of entry.

Identifying the Competition

There are three types of competitors for your product or service: direct, indirect, and emerging. Identifying specifically who these companies are—their strengths, weaknesses, and market share—will put the new venture in a better position to be a contender in the industry and particularly in the target market.

Direct Competitors

Those businesses that supply products or services that are the same as or similar to yours, or are a reasonably good substitute for yours, are direct competitors to the new venture. However, be careful: the term *competition* is not quite that simple. Suppose you are going to open an entertainment center that offers virtual reality computer games in a shopping mall. One possible direct competitor that comes to mind is a video arcade. But if you consider your venture to be in the entertainment business, you will see that other direct competitors for the consumer dollars you are seeking are movie theaters, miniature golf courses, bowling alleys, and video rental stores. That certainly complicates the picture, and it's not the only source of competition for the new venture.

Indirect Competitors

Indirect competitors may not even be in the same industry as the new venture but do compete alongside it for consumer dollars. To refer to the example just cited: consumers may choose to spend their limited dollars at restaurants rather than on entertainment, or perhaps on a weekend vacation. Indirect

	Ranking by size	Product	Unique Benefits and Features	Price	Place	Promotion	Weaknesses/Threats
Koidra-Tek	4th	*Asia Business Suite*™ • CD-ROM package covers 10 growing Asian countries • Directory of resources • Interactive language learning • Addresses travel options (hotel, restaurants, etc.)	• Reduces the need for cross-referencing • User friendly • Compact • Transportable • Inexpensive	*Direct:* $39.99 *Retail:* $49.99	• Airport shops • Bookstores • Catalogues • Travel agencies • Direct sales • Internet • Computer retail outlets	• Trade shows • Direct mail • Press releases • Internet • Ads in trade journals and publications • Personal selling • Brochures • Guerilla marketing	• Lack of brand recognition • Individuals may not have a laptop with CD-ROM • Potential "copycat" products • Possible buyout of company • Technological changes
Culture Shock Series	2nd	• 12 country book series • Focuses on customs, culture, and etiquette	• Covers almost every Asian country • Analyzes each culture thoroughly	$156.00 (total for 12 books)	• Retail book stores • Internet	• Internet	• Does not focus on doing business in Asia • Numerous competitors
Boye Lafayette De Mente (Author)	3rd	• 3 country book series • Deals with etiquette and ethics	• In-depth analysis of customs and etiquette relating to business	$51.00 (total for 3 books)	• Retail book stores • Internet	• Internet	• Covers Japan, China, and Korea only • Numerous competitors
Price Waterhouse LLP	1st Largest	• Consulting service	• Personal consultation	Varies with size of firm	• Personnel • Direct marketing channel	• Business-to-business advertising • Referrals • Press releases	• Expensive • Technology-based consulting programs

Figure 5.2
Competitive Grid

Source: Brian Wong and Esther Nguyen, *Koidra-Tek Business Plan*, March 26, 1998. Used with permission.

competitors, therefore, are often substitutes outside the entrepreneur's industry or target market.

Emerging Competitors

When entering a market as a new business, it is vital to assess not only the existing competition but also the potential for new competition—emerging competitors—at some time in the future. In many industries today, technology and information are changing at such a rapid pace that the window of opportunity to successfully start a new venture has been closing. Consequently the entrepreneur must be ever-vigilant as to new trends and new technology, both in the industry in general and in the specific target market.

Competitive Advantage

Understanding who your competitors are is one step in learning what the new venture's competitive advantages are. If your product or service has intellectual property rights—patent, trademark, copyright—that is a significant competitive advantage. Other advantages may be found in the market strategy, the distribution strategy, and the operations strategy. The bottom line in competitive advantage is innovation in all aspects of the business. What this suggests is that knowing your competitors as well as you know your new venture allows you to seek more ways in which the new venture can innovate, can distinguish itself from its competitors, and can attain an important level of competitive advantage in the marketplace.

Industry Analysis

The importance of understanding the industry in which the new venture will operate cannot be overstated because the industry environment has a direct impact on how the new venture does business and on its potential for success. The nature of the industry certainly must be taken into consideration when establishing the competitive strategy for accomplishing the goals of the venture.

An industry analysis requires a plan of attack to avoid wasting time hunting for inadequate information and not knowing what to do with it once it is collected. The analysis will include:

▶ Identifying the industry

▶ Examining secondary resources

▶ Talking with people in the industry

▶ Analyzing the data and drawing conclusions

Standard Industrial Classifications

It is possible to determine the specific industry in which the new venture will operate by identifying the **Standard Industrial Classification** (SIC) for

Table 5.1   Manufacturing Industrial Classifications

2400	Food & Kindered Products
2600	Paper & Allied Products
2700	Printing, Publishing & Allied Industries
2800	Chemicals & Allied Products
3000	Rubber & Miscellaneous Plastic Products
3200	Stone, Clay, Glass & Concrete Products
3300	Primary Metal Industries
3400	Fabricated Metal Products, except machinery & transportation equipment
3500	Machinery, except electrical
3900	Miscellaneous Manufacturing Industries

the product or service. Knowing the four-digit SIC code for the business allows the entrepreneur access to a wealth of information typically categorized by SIC code. Standard Industrial Classification Codes were developed by the U.S. Bureau of the Budget in 1972. The major classifications include such industries as agriculture, mining, construction, manufacturing, and wholesale. For example, under the major classification of manufacturing, the types of businesses and their respective codes can be found listed in Table 5.1. Table 5.2 presents the categories of data to be included in the industry analysis.

Sources of Industry Information

An industry analysis usually begins with a search of secondary data sources— journals, trade magazines, reference books, government publications, and annual reports of public corporations—sources normally available in a university or community library. Historical data, such as annual reports over a ten- to fifteen-year period, can often help the entrepreneur spot trends, cycles, and seasonal variations in the industry. Trade magazines provide a good sense of which are the key firms and of the directions the industry may be taking. Table 5.2 provides a listing of some of the essential raw data on the

Table 5.2   Categories of Data for Industry Analysis

▶ Growth	▶ Technology of production
▶ Complementary/substitute products	▶ Distribution channels
▶ Competitors	▶ Innovation
▶ Market strategies	▶ Suppliers
▶ Economic environment	▶ Product lines
▶ Regulatory environment	▶ Buyer behavior
▶ Socio-political environment	

industry, data that should be collected. Some of this information will also be useful later for the market analysis.

After the secondary data are collected, they must be organized and analyzed. In general, the key questions about the industry that should be answered are:

▶ *Is the industry growing?* Growth is measured by sales volume, number of employees, units produced, number of new companies entering the industry, and so forth.

▶ *Where are the opportunities?* Does the industry provide opportunities for new businesses with strategies involving new products and/or processes, innovative distribution, or new marketing strategies?

▶ *What is the status of any new technology?* How quickly does the industry adopt new technology, and does technology play a significant role in the competitive strategy of firms in the industry?

▶ *How much does the industry spend on research and development?* Expenditures on R&D will tell you how important technology is, how much you will need to spend, and how rapid the product development cycle is.

▶ *Who are the major competitors?* Which firms dominate the industry?

▶ *Are there young, successful firms in the industry?* This will give you an indication of how formidable the entry barriers are and whether or not the industry is growing rapidly.

▶ *What does the future look like?* What appears likely to happen in the next five years? What are the trends?

▶ *Are there any threats to the industry?* Is there any chance that new technology will render obsolete either the industry or that segment of the industry in which you're doing business?

▶ *What are the typical margins in the industry?* Looking at gross margins in the industry gives you an indication of how much room there is to make mistakes. If the industry typically has 2% margins or less, like the grocery industry, you will have to sell in large volumes and keep overhead costs to a minimum. Where margins run at 70% or more, there is a lot more room to play, but generally these industries (like software) have relatively short product life cycles, so R&D costs are high.

The Importance of Primary Data

Secondary research paints the broad picture of the industry; however, given the lead time from data gathering to print, it is rarely the most current information available. Therefore, to access the most timely information, it is extremely important to gather primary field data on the industry. (See Figure 5.3.) In other words, you need to talk with people in the industry—"pound the pavement," so to speak. Some of the sources to tap are as follows:

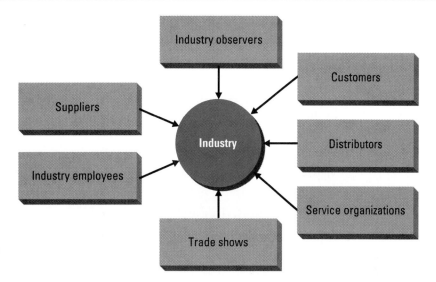

**Figure 5.3
Sources of Field Data
for Industry Analysis**

▶ *Industry observers*, those who study particular industries and regularly report on them in newspapers or newsletters or through the media.

▶ *Suppliers and distributors*, who are in an excellent position to comment on the health of the industry in terms of demand for products and services, as well as on the financial strength and market practices of major firms.

▶ *Customers*, who can be a clue to satisfaction with the industry and the product or service supplied.

▶ *Employees of key firms in the industry*, who are a good source of information about potential competitors.

▶ *Professionals from service organizations*, such as lawyers and accountants, who regularly work with a particular industry.

▶ *Trade shows*, which give a good indication of who the biggest competitors are and who has the strongest market strategy.

Tactics for Talking with Key Industry People

Field research is usually accomplished via interviews or casual discussions with people in the industry. Getting them to open up and talk will be easier if you follow a few simple rules.

▶ Where possible, secure an introduction from someone who knows the interviewee. You will find that once you talk with the first person, that person will recommend someone else, and you'll be on your way to gathering more information than you could ever use.

▶ Seek out individuals who regularly deal with the media, since they are easier to approach; however, be aware that they also are accustomed to being very careful about what they say.

▶ Allow sufficient lead time for the meeting, since you probably are dealing with very busy people on tight schedules.

▶ Offer something that might be of value to interviewees, such as a summary of the results of the industry analysis, a popular book in the field, or a subscription to a business magazine—or take interviewees to lunch.

▶ Be honest about your affiliation with a university or a business. Interviewees want to know that you understand the value of their time.

▶ To give yourself credibility, demonstrate your knowledge of an interviewee's business. (Research the business before the meeting.)

▶ If possible, take a colleague or business partner along to ensure that you obtain all the needed information and catch all visual cues. This is particularly true when talking with potential competitors.

▶ Carefully observe the surroundings. Physical clues and nonverbal communication are often excellent indicators of the nature of the industry.

▶ Be sure your opening questions are easy and nonthreatening and show a genuine interest in your interviewee's business.

The Ideal Industry

While no industry is perfect, an industry comprised of the following features offers more opportunity for a new venture.

▶ An industry with over $50 billion in sales will probably have niche markets of sufficient size to allow for the attainment of an adequate market share.

▶ An industry that is generally growing at a rate greater than the GNP offers more potential for growth of the new venture.

▶ An industry that allows for after-tax profits of greater than 5 percent of sales within three to five years will enhance the new venture's chances for success.

▶ An industry that is socially and environmentally responsible will be compatible with current societal and political trends and consequently may be eligible for special grants and other types of funding.

New ventures entering an emerging industry will not have the luxury of a track record that can indicate potential for growth and profits. They can, however, look to the experiences of other recently formed industries similar to their own, to predict patterns and potential market demand. These characteristics are merely benchmarks. With so many variables involved, no one can guarantee that a new venture will survive or become a success, even if the industry possesses all the requisite characteristics. However, the more information the entrepreneur has, the better his or her chances are of not making costly mistakes.

Presenting the Industry Data in the Feasibility Study or Business Plan

The industry analysis provides the entrepreneur and others with the information necessary for determining if the industry in which the business will be started appears conducive to new ventures. The data collected should be presented in the feasibility study or business plan in a way that highlights the key points and answers the major questions addressed in this chapter. Often this can be accomplished best through the use of tables and graphs. These can display data efficiently and should be used where appropriate; however, the entrepreneur must never assume that readers will pick out the most salient points from tables and graphics or even from the narrative text, for that matter. It is important to point out key trends and patterns in the data as the entrepreneur sees them.

A comprehensive industry analysis will include:

▶ *The current size* of the industry as measured by total sales volume, total number of firms, and total number of employees. You may divide the industry into major segments to approximate more closely the environment in which your business will be operating.

▶ *Profile of key players in the industry.*

▶ The *growth potential*, based on historical trends in size. Is the industry growing, shrinking, or remaining stable?

▶ *Geographic location*, where the industry seems to cluster (e.g., Silicon Valley, California; Route 128 in Massachusetts, and so forth).

▶ *Industry trends* in terms of products, services, innovation, and technology.

▶ *Seasonality* of demand for products and services, based on days of week, months, or seasons of the year.

▶ *Profit potential*, based on performance of existing firms in the industry.

▶ *Sales patterns* as measured by frequency and quantity of purchase.

▶ *Gross margins on products* as an indicator of how easy or difficult it will be to cover overhead.

▶ *Technology*, both process and product, as an indicator of barriers to entry and potential for innovation.

▶ *Government regulation* of aspects of the industry that may affect the new venture's growth potential.

Knowing your industry well can mean the difference between succeeding over the long term and missing an opportunity that might have kept your business alive. Being able to convey that industry knowledge to others will help you raise capital, bring aboard key team members, and continually find opportunities for growth. Both the entrepreneur and other interested parties will want to know that the industry is healthy and growing and that it provides an excellent window of opportunity for the new venture.

New Venture Checklist

Have you:

❏ **Identified the SIC code for the industry in which your new venture will operate?**

❏ **Collected secondary data on the industry?**

❏ **Conducted field research by interviewing suppliers, distributors, customers, and others?**

❏ **Developed an industry profile that will tell you and others if the industry is growing, who the major competitors are, and what the profit potential is?**

Issues to Consider

1. How does your industry measure up in terms of uncertainty and complexity?
2. Which primary and secondary information will tell you if the industry is growing and favorable to new entrants?
3. What kinds of information can suppliers and distributors give you?
4. What information about the industry can trade shows provide?
5. How should tables and graphs be used in the industry profile?

Experiencing Entrepreneurship

1. Choose an industry that interests you. Create a status report using the Internet, Lexis/Nexis, current periodicals, and interviews with people in the industry. In your estimation, is this an industry that has a great potential for new business opportunities? If so, where do those opportunities lie?
2. Interview a producer, a supplier, and a retailer or wholesaler in an industry that interests you. What is their role in the industry? Compare and contrast how they view the status of the industry.

Additional Sources of Information

Cornwall, J.R., and Perlman, B. (1990). *Organizational Entrepreneurship*. Homewood, IL: Irwin.

Darnay, A.J. (Ed.) (1994). *Manufacturing USA: Industry Analyses, Statistics, and Leading Companies*. Detroit: Gale Research Inc.

Elster, R.J. (Ed.) (1998). *Small Business Sourcebook*, 12th edition. Detroit: Gale Research Inc.

Jasinowski, J., and Hamrin, R. (1995). *Making It in America: Proven Paths to Success from 50 Top Companies*. New York: Simon & Schuster.

Porter, M. (1980). *Competitive Strategy: Techniques for Analyzing Industries and Competitors*. New York: Free Press.

Porter, M. (1985). *Competitive Advantage.* New York: Free Press.

Thomas Register of American Manufacturers

U.S. Census Data: State and County Business Patterns

Internet Resources

CNNfn
http://www.cnnfn.com/index.html
This site covers a broad range of topics. You can get headlines, in-depth reports, and other business information (e.g., Hoover's Online Business Profiles).

Department of Commerce
http://www.doc.gov
Links to many sites of interest to business owners.

IndustryLink
http://www.industrylink.com/
Offers links to sites of interest to people in a number of industries.

PR Newswire
http://www.prnewswire.com/
Good source of immediate news from corporations worldwide.

Securities and Exchange Commission
http://www.sec.gov/
Good source for researching specific industries.

SEC Edgar Database
http://www.sec.gov/edgarhp.htm
Contains documents that publicly traded companies must submit to the SEC.

Thomas Register
http://www.thomasregister.com:8000/
This is the online version of the Thomas Register of American Manufacturers. Contains information about products, services, and companies.

Wall Street Journal Interactive
http://www.wsj.com/
There is a charge for this site, but it may be worth paying, for the latest news from around the world. Also good information about the economy and specific companies and industries.

Relevant Case Studies

1. Toy Tips, Inc.
2. The Penduline Putter
3. Autopsies-to-Go

6

Because its purpose is to create a customer, the business enterprise has two—and only these two—basic functions: marketing and innovation. Marketing and innovation produce results; all the rest are "costs."
Peter F. Drucker
Management consultant, writer
People and Performance
(Harper & Row, 1977)

Analyzing Customer Risks and Benefits

Overview

▶ **Defining the target market**

▶ **Forecasting new product/service demand**

▶ **Getting the product/service to the customer**

▶ **Preliminary conclusions as to feasibility**

Terms to Know

Profile 6.1

Build a Business by Knowing the Customer

When Richard Foos and Harold Bronson set out to start a company in a very difficult industry, they decided to do it by breaking all the traditional rules. In the recording industry, everything is driven by market research, which essentially looks at the past. The goal is to replicate hits. Foos and Bronson took a different approach; they decided to create products that they would buy: CDs, videos, and books creatively packaged in collections of material from the past. In other words, they thought like customers. To make it work, they hired employees who felt the same way they did. If they found an artist they used to like who had never produced a "best of" album, Rhino Records took on the task with gusto and pros-

pered. In fact, the name Rhino Records came from the fact that Foos started the business with no business plan, no financing; he just opened the doors and charged ahead.

The business started as a small shop in Westwood in 1973, an area of Los Angeles next to the UCLA campus, and it became known for its crazy promotions and crazier record collectors who came there looking for their favorite "oldies." In 1978, Foos sold the store to go into the recording business on a full-time basis. With his new partner, Bronson, they achieved their first hit, an all-kazoo version of Led Zeppelin's "Whole Lotta Love." It was a novelty tune, and the company grossed $60,000 in 1978 alone.

As the company grew, Foos and Bronson kept the overhead down and continued to focus on thinking like the customer. It was fortunate they did, for the market for the novelty tunes they were creating died in 1979. As part of the baby-boom generation, the undaunted pair saw demand increasing for compilations of past records. At the time, these songs, called reissues, were about at the bottom of the food chain in the recording industry. But the partners took a fresh approach by creatively packaging these songs in themed collections. Their customer-focus strategy worked: 90 percent of their products today are profitable in an industry where only 10 percent of the records produced make a profit.

Today, it seems as if everyone is interested in the reissue business, but Foos and Bronson aren't worried. Their customers like them and *are* like them, and Rhino Records isn't likely to go away.

SOURCE: Michael Warshaw, "Master the Future," *Success*, October 1996, pp. 28–30.

How did Foos and Bronson figure out who the customers were for their business and how do they keep them coming back?

Defining the Target Market

One of the most important tasks the entrepreneur must undertake is the identification of the primary customer for the product or service being offered by the new venture. The **target market** is that segment of the marketplace that will most likely purchase the product or service. It is referred to as the **primary market**. The **secondary market**, by contrast, consists of those customers outside the target market for whom a different market strategy will be required.

The ability to identify the target market is based on an analysis of customer need, which usually begins at the earliest stages of business concept development. In fact, often the idea for an innovative product or service springs from a need observed by the entrepreneur (e.g., Bob Kearns and the intermittent wiper blade). The preliminary needs analysis is then refined through target market research and eventually becomes the focal point for many of the decisions and strategies of the new venture. Unfortunately, most entrepreneurs don't place enough emphasis on in-depth market analysis. Instead they assume levels of need and demand without any evidence to support them. As a result, they tend to overestimate their market forecasts for demand by as much as 60 percent.[1]

The Market

No matter what the size of the target market, it is crucial that the entrepreneur know as much as possible about the customer. Heidi VanArnem knew her customers' needs because she matched their profile herself. VanArnem is paralyzed from the waist down. After college she had trouble finding a job, so in 1991, she started her own business in the travel industry. Her niche? Making travel easier for people with disabilities. A significant portion of her customer base is comprised of people who want to know which hotels have wheelchair ramps and showers that accommodate wheelchairs, among other things. Because she understands her customers' needs, she is able to provide exactly what they want. Sales reached $2 million in 1996 in this niche market.[2]

Defining the target market really means describing the primary customer for your product or service—that customer who will help your business grow and succeed. In the beginning stages of market analysis, you will probably have a fairly loose description of the target market. This description will be refined and may even change as you talk to the target customers during the field research. The key questions you will be attempting to answer are:

▶ Who are my customers?

▶ What do they typically buy and how do they hear about it?

▶ How often do they buy?

▶ How can my new venture meet the customers' needs?

Researching the Target Market

The research conducted on the target market will provide some of the most important data needed by the entrepreneur to decide if the new venture is feasible. To ensure that useful and correct conclusions can be drawn, the research methods must be sound. A four-step process will ensure that the information needed to make this crucial decision is gathered and used correctly. (See Figure 6.1.)

Assessing Information Needs

Before you can begin to collect market data, you must determine how that data will be used in the market analysis section of the feasibility study and the business plan. Will it demonstrate a demand for the product or service? Will it describe the target customer? You may be wondering how you can decide how data will be used and analyzed when it hasn't yet been collected. Precisely the point. A good researcher will decide first what he or she is attempting to accomplish with the research, so that the correct type of data

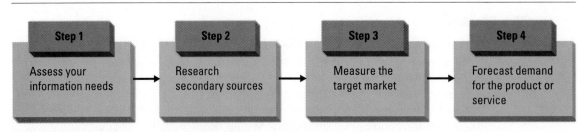

Figure 6.1
Steps to Market Research

Table 6.1 Sample Demographics of the Target Market

Average age of customer:	32
Average income level:	$35,000
Average number of years of education:	14
Marital status:	Married

needed for the analysis will be gathered. Nothing is more discouraging to a researcher than finding out after all the data are collected that a crucial piece of information is missing.

Also, once you know what you want to determine with the data, it will be easier to choose a particular type of analysis that will lead to the desired result. For example, if one of your research goals is to refine the description of the target market, you may decide to seek the most common characteristics or demographics (the statistical mode) of the customer—in other words, indicate the most common age, education level, income, and so on. To do this, you will need to gather numerical data. Granted, this is a rather simple and obvious example; however, others are not so apparent.

Suppose, for example, you wish to calculate demand for the product or service by using a statistical forecasting technique. The type of technique you choose will dictate the kind of data you must collect. For example, if the technique requires continuous numerical data (i.e., all values for an answer are possible), you would not gather data or design a questionnaire that would give you "yes-no" answers. Fortunately, the market research most entrepreneurs do involves simple, descriptive statistics as seen in Table 6.1.

Recall that the entrepreneur collects both primary and secondary market data. It is important, however, to gather the secondary data first, so that you have a better understanding of the market prior to designing a sampling plan and doing the field research.

Researching Secondary Sources

Secondary data on the target market give the entrepreneur an understanding of the market before going into the field to talk directly with customers, suppliers, distributors, and others. The library is an excellent starting point. The government publications section will contain Federal Census Bureau data that allow you to define your market by region of the country, major metropolitan area, city, or even neighborhood. The *1990 Census Basics* provides demographic information such as age, education, income, and workers per household. It permits you to determine if the geographic area you have defined is growing or declining, aging or getting younger, or if the available work force is mostly skilled or unskilled, along with other trends.

Some groups of **demographics** (age, income, race, occupation, and education) help identify the likelihood that a person will choose to buy a product.[3] This is true even for industrial products. Demographic data also allow you to segment the target market into subgroups that are estimably different from one another. For example, if your target market is retired people over the age of 60, you may find that buying habits (requirements and quantity of purchase) vary by geographic region or by income level.

Finally, census data can be used to arrive at an estimate of how many target customers are within the geographic boundaries of the target market. Then, within any geographic area, those who meet the particular demographic requirements of the product/service can be segmented out.

Most communities have economic development departments or Chambers of Commerce that keep statistics on local population trends and other economic issues. Some communities have Small Business Development Centers (SBDCs), branches of the Small Business Administration that contain a wealth of useful information, as well as services, for small and growing businesses. Other sources available in the library are reference books and trade journals on all types of industries. Apart from the library, useful information can be found from trade associations like the National Association of Manufacturers, commercial research firms, financial institutions, and the Internet. These resources will assist you in determining the size and characteristics of the target market.

Measuring the Market with Primary Data

There are many ways to collect primary data in the target market. Among them are mail surveys, phone surveys, interviews, focus groups, and product clinics. Each has advantages and disadvantages over the other, and a decision to use one or more of them is usually based on time and money. The first three require drawing a representative sample from the population of customers you're interested in. Selecting a sample should be done with great care, for it will determine the validity of the results achieved. In general, you want to attempt to choose a random sample, that is, one in which you have as little control as possible over who will be selected to participate in the sample. Most entrepreneurs, because of cost and time, choose to use what is called a **convenience sample.** This means that not everyone in the defined target market has a chance of being chosen to participate. Instead, the entrepreneur may, for example, choose to select the sample from people who happen to be at a particular shopping mall on a particular day. Clearly, the entrepreneur will not be reaching all possible customers at that mall, but if the target customer typically shops at malls, there's a good chance of achieving at least a representative sample from which results can be derived fairly confidently.

Even if a convenience sample is used, there are ways to ensure the randomness of selection of the participants. Using the mall example, the entrepreneur can decide in advance to survey every fifth person who walks by. In this way, the person is not chosen on the basis of attractiveness or lack of it—nor for or any other reason, for that matter. A random number generator on a computer can select names from a telephone book. Whatever system is employed, the key point is to make an effort not to bias the selection.

Often you will hear potential entrepreneurs say that they took a sample of friends and relatives who loved the new product idea. Friends and relatives may be able to give you some initial feedback, but they are not the best source of unbiased information. Remember, one of the reasons you are doing a feasibility study and ultimately a business plan is to convince others about the viability of the new venture concept. The credibility of your market research results will be measured by the quality of the sample you select.

The following are some of the research techniques you can use to study your customers:

Mail Surveys   Doing a mail survey entails designing a survey instrument, usually a questionnaire, that provides the entrepreneur with the desired information. Questionnaire design is not a simple matter of putting some questions on a piece of paper. There are, in fact, proven methods of constructing questionnaires to help ensure unbiased responses. It is not within the scope of this text to present all the techniques for questionnaire construction; however, a few key points should be remembered.

▶ Keep the questionnaire short, with lots of white space, so that the respondent is not intimidated at the outset.

▶ Be careful not to ask leading, biased questions.

▶ Ask easy questions first, leading up to the more complex ones.

▶ Ask demographic questions (age, sex, income) last, when the respondent's attention span has waned. These questions can be answered very quickly.

▶ For questions people generally hesitate to answer (age, income), group possible responses in ranges (25–35 for age, $35,000–$45,000 for income) so the respondent doesn't feel he or she is disclosing very private information.

▶ Keep in mind that people generally increase their income classification one class and decrease their age one class.

▶ Mail surveys are a relatively easy way to reach a great many people in the target market, and they take less time than many other methods. However, mail surveys do have a few weaknesses.
   a. The response rate is generally very low, usually around 15 percent, which means that about 85 of every 100 persons sampled do not respond. Consequently, the potential for nonresponse bias makes it difficult for the entrepreneur to feel very comfortable about the reliability of the results.
   b. The entrepreneur does not have the benefit of the nonverbal communication that would be available from an interview. This is significant, when you consider that at least 85 percent of all communication is nonverbal.
   c. The entrepreneur has no way of questioning or clarifying a response.
   d. There is no control over the accuracy of the information given.
   e. Normally, a second, follow-up mailing is necessary to achieve the desired response rate.

Phone Surveys   Like mail surveys, phone surveys use questionnaires so that consistency in the questions asked can be achieved. Phone surveys have two particular advantages over mail surveys: they allow for explanation and clarification of questions and responses, and the response rate is higher. However, phone surveys take more time to accomplish and are more prone to surveyor bias; that is, there is more opportunity for the person conducting the survey to bias the results by the tone in his or her voice or by unscripted comments. In addition, phone surveys do not offer the advantage of being able to observe nonverbal communication.

Interviews   Although more costly and time-consuming than mail or phone surveys, interviews have many advantages.

▶ They provide more opportunity for clarification and discussion.

▶ They offer the advantages of nonverbal communication. The entrepreneur will be better able to discern the veracity of what the interviewee is saying.

▶ The response rate is high.

▶ Interviews permit open-ended questions that can lead to more in-depth information.

▶ They provide an opportunity to network and develop valuable contacts in the industry.

Where time and money permit, interviews are probably the best source of valuable information from customers, suppliers, distributors, and anyone else who can help the new venture. It is also possible, however, to use a combination of techniques. For example, the entrepreneur may start with phone surveys to obtain basic information and follow up with interviews with the most useful sources.

Focus Groups   One more efficient way to gain valuable information before investing substantial capital in production and marketing is to conduct a **focus group**. The entrepreneur brings together a representative sample of potential customers for a presentation and discussion session. Assuming that the new venture involves a consumer product, the entrepreneur may choose to introduce the new product in concert with other products to test the unsolicited response to the product when presented with its competition. For example, suppose your product is a new type of nonalcoholic beverage. You might serve the new beverage along with several competitors' beverages in glasses labeled with numbers, and then solicit feedback on taste, aftertaste, and so on.

Some products and services do not easily lend themselves to blind studies like the one just described. In those instances, the product can simply be presented to the focus group and their opinions and feedback solicited. It is important that the person leading the focus group have some knowledge of group dynamics and be able to keep the group on track. Many times these focus group sessions are videotaped so that the entrepreneur can spend more time analyzing the nuances of what occurred. Thus, in many ways, focus groups often can prevent the entrepreneur from making the costly error of offering a product or service in which there is little or no interest.

Clinical Studies   **Clinical studies** are one of the more expensive routes to gathering market data and, in general, are used by large corporations introducing new products. A clinical study takes place in a controlled setting and is most often used for consumer products. Consumers are asked to visit a test center, which may be set up as a small store. They are given a certain amount of money and asked to choose among a variety of new products available in the test store. This helps the company learn which products are most attractive to customers. In another type of study, consumers may be asked to do blind testing of products such as shampoos or food products to compare tastes and preferences.

Forecasting New Product/Service Demand

One of the most difficult tasks facing the entrepreneur is forecasting the demand for the new product or service, particularly if that product/service has never existed previously in the marketplace. Adding to this difficulty is the fact that most entrepreneurs do their own research because they generally don't have sufficient resources prior to start-up to hire professional market research firms. However, doing your own market research does have the advantage of giving you a clearer sense of your target market and its needs. A number of different techniques can assist you in arriving at a realistic forecast of demand.

Use Historical Analogy or Substitute Products

If the new product is an extension of a previously existing product, it may be possible to extrapolate from that product's demand to yours. For example, the demand for compact disks was derived from the historical demand for cassette tapes and records. In other cases it may be possible to substitute another product in the same industry to give an indication of demand potential, assuming the same target market.

Interview Prospective End-Users and Intermediaries

No one knows the market better than the men and women who work in it every day. They are typically very astute at predicting trends and patterns of buyer behavior. Spending time in the field talking with customers, **intermediaries** (distributors or wholesalers, sometimes referred to as "middlemen"), retailers, and the like can provide a fairly good estimate of demand.

Go into Limited Production

Sometimes the only way to test the reaction of potential customers is to produce a small number of products and put them in the hands of people to test. This is also an appropriate next step if the first two techniques have produced positive results. Not only will limited testing of the product gauge customer satisfaction; it may suggest possible modifications to improve the product. These samples of the product are called **prototypes**. Prototypes are generally associated with product companies, but in fact, service businesses must also develop a prototype of the operation or procedures involved in delivering the service. Prototyping permits the testing of a product or service in the actual environment in which it will be used. It is difficult to conduct meaningful market research without a working prototype, as most potential customers need to see and use the actual product before they can become enthusiastic about it. Construction of a prototype will also facilitate estimating costs to actually produce the product later on.

Do a Formal Test Market

When a product is fairly complex and expensive to produce, doing a formal test market in a selected geographic area can provide valuable information on demand and acceptance of the product, prior to spending substantial capital for a major product roll-out. The movie industry regularly introduces new movies with a "limited release" in a few strategic theaters. In this way, film companies can gauge audiences' reactions and make changes based on them before releasing the film on a national basis. Major product companies like Procter and Gamble will put a new product into certain geographic test markets like Denver, Colorado, to get feedback from customers.

Profile 6.2

Let Me Entertain You

When Junki Yoshida arrived in the United States 28 years ago, he had only $500 in his pocket. Today his company, The Yoshida Group of Portland, Oregon, a diverse collection of companies doing everything from snowboards to board games, boasts revenues of over $50 million annually. Yoshida attributes that success to karate, which teaches you to understand your weaknesses so that others can't take advantage of you.

Yoshida's most famous business is Yoshida's Original Gourmet Sauce. The idea for this product came in 1982 at Christmas time, when he and his wife were trying to figure out what to give his karate students as gifts. As they had no money for gifts, they decided to bottle marinade made from a secret family recipe and give that. Students liked it so much that they wanted more, so Yoshida would spend his nights making marinade. It appeared that he was about to go into business. By pledging his car and his life insurance policy as collateral, he managed to obtain a loan from the bank, but on learning that he was

giving away as much marinade as he was selling, the bank officials made an immediate call on the loan. Starting over again, he raised $150,000 that included both his wife's life insurance policy and his father-in-law's pension.

Then Price/Costco agreed to stock his sauce in that company's Seattle warehouse. Realizing that he had to get the customers' attention, he soon became known for his showmanship. His entertaining style was so contagious that customers decided to try his product. As he acquired more accounts with businesses like Safeway, Albertson's, Wal-Mart, and Sam's Club, he expanded his product line and began training demonstrators in his style. His approach to testing the customer was so successful that between 1988 and 1991, the company grew 52% a year. Since that time he has purchased an average of two businesses a year. Yoshida understands what makes customers happy, and happy customers buy his products.

SOURCE: Carla Goodman, "Enterprise with a Kick," *Nation's Business,* September 1997, p. 77.

(Many a new product has met an untimely death as a result of these test market studies.)

The Cost/Benefit of Market Research

Market research is undoubtedly one of the more expensive aspects of starting a business, and it is time-consuming as well. For these reasons, and because many entrepreneurs don't know how to conduct market research or believe their product or service is so good that customers will automatically desire it, the market analysis section is probably the least well-researched and least well-written section of the business plan. Yet good market research answers the question "Is there a demand for my product or service?" Surely that is the most crucial question an entrepreneur can answer.

Despite the importance of market research, the entrepreneur needs to weigh the cost of doing certain types of market research against the benefits of getting the product/service into the market quickly. In today's dynamic business environment, this is a real concern. Spending too much time on market research can result in losing a window of opportunity for entering the market. Some basic market research techniques can provide excellent information at very little cost and relatively quickly.

▶ Use focus groups to gauge potential customer reaction.

▶ Observe buyer behavior at random times in outlets where the product may be offered.

▶ Use small, representative segments of the target market to test the product/service.

▶ Examine case studies of similar companies.

▶ Study census data for demographic information.

Getting the Product/Service to the Customer

With a target market well defined and sufficient demand estimated to exist, the entrepreneur faces the important task of deciding how to get the product or service to the customer. A distribution channel is, quite simply, the route a product takes from the manufacturer to the customer or end-user. Depending on the type of new venture, there are many choices available. Each choice will have distinct advantages, disadvantages, and consequences, and will to some extent dictate the kind of organization the new venture becomes. Today your distribution strategy is as important as every other aspect of your business. Many new businesses today are using distribution strategy as their competitive advantage. Domino's Pizza was the first to capitalize on home delivery to differentiate itself in a crowded market.

Each of the different methods of getting the product to the customer, channels of distribution, involves the development of a different type of business: retail, mail order, licensing, and so forth. Furthermore, the channel of distribution determines to some extent your product's cost, the potential for

Table 6.2   Customer Grid for Rhino Records

Customer	Benefit	Distribution
Baby boomers	Convenience and economy: can find compilations of their favorite songs without having to buy entire albums of one artist	Retail outlet
Record stores	Provides unique compilations of hard-to-find great hits of the past to satisfy the baby-boomer segment of their market	Wholesale to record store
The busy professional with no time to shop	Convenience of shopping any time of the day or night and having all the information at one's fingertips	Internet store for online purchasing

loss or damage through transit, and how quickly the product reaches the customer. Finding the most efficient and effective channel can provide a new venture with a distinct competitive advantage.

The subject of distribution channels is discussed in detail in Chapter 12, but for now we'll simply consider the distribution channel as the method for getting the product or service to the customer. One useful way to summarize and analyze the different customers and distribution channels available to you is to create a customer grid. The customer grid (see Table 6.2) outlines the customer, the benefit, and the distribution strategy. This is one way of making sure that you're differentiating among customers and giving them exactly what they need in the way they need it.

Profile 6.3

Direct to Your Home

Wisconsin businesswoman Mary Adashek is one of a growing number of people selling products at home parties. Adashek is an independent rep for Pampered Chef, the Illinois-based kitchen implements company that relies on multilevel marketing (MLM) to reach customers. About ten times a month, Adashek travels to customers' homes to demonstrate products and socialize with the attendees. In addition to receiving a percentage of the sales, she shares commissions with the people who recruited her and with the people she recruits.

According to the Direct Selling Association, MLM sales reached $18 billion in 1995, up from $13 billion in 1991, and today more than 1,000 legitimate companies use MLM as their primary distribution method. The products sold range from personal-care products to home and family-care products to services and health products. Companies are choosing this route because it relies on personal selling one-to-one with the customer. Lane Nemeth, who founded Discovery Toys, boasted sales of $85 million in 1996 in the United States, with more than 30,000 reps.

The secret to success with MLM? Have a passion for your product, believe in what you're doing, focus on the customer, and build a reputable company.

Source: Dale D. Buss, "A Direct Route to Customers," *Nation's Business*, September 1997, p. 46.

The grid in Table 6.2 highlights three potential customers for Rhino Records. The next step is to decide which of these three customers to go after first. Notice the different benefits and distribution strategies for each customer. In effect, we have three different businesses here: a retail outlet, a wholesale distributorship, and an Internet business. The choice as to where to go first is a function of the size of the market, customer demand, and resources. For example, owning a retail outlet is potentially the most costly in terms of facility, inventory, and marketing expenses, while the Internet may be the least costly.

You can make a customer grid as simple or as complex as you like, but it's an important tool for looking at your customer options.

Preliminary Conclusions as to Feasibility

Once the market study is completed, you are in a good position to answer this question: Is there sufficient demand for the product or service the new venture will offer?

If you have personally conducted the research and done all the work to this point, you not only will have important information to help make the decision but also will have an intuitive or "gut" feeling as to whether or not the new venture concept is viable. If market indicators are positive, it is time to consider other aspects of feasibility and proceed to test the business concept further.

Nevertheless, many entrepreneurs will find it difficult to abandon an idea with which they have fallen in love, even in the face of market data indicating that demand for the new product or service is weak. When this happens, it is important to remember that without customers there is no business. It is far better to abandon a business concept at this point than to venture ahead to the more costly aspects of a business start-up and ultimately fail.

New Venture Checklist

Have you:

❏ **Defined the target market for your product or service?**

❏ **Identified direct, indirect, and emerging competitors?**

❏ **Described your product or service's competitive advantage?**

❏ **Listed the information you will need in order to do the market analysis?**

❏ **Researched secondary data sources such as census data on demographics?**

❏ **Determined the most effective method for gathering primary data on your target market?**

❏ **Estimated demand for the product or service?**

❏ **Organized, analyzed, and presented the data to answer the key question: Is there sufficient demand for the product or service?**

Issues to Consider

1. What is the value of defining a market niche?

2. Why is it important to do secondary market research before primary market research?

3. What advantages do interviews have over other data collection methods?

4. Suppose you want to determine the demand for your new product, a special type of fast-food dessert. What methods would you use to forecast demand?

5. Market research can be an expensive, time-consuming process. What can you do to minimize the costs while still achieving your goals?

Experiencing Entrepreneurship

1. For a business concept that you've developed, create a customer grid similar to that on page 112. Feel free to add more information than what is given. Which customer would you seek out first and why?

2. Pick a product or service and formulate a plan for estimating the demand for it using the triangulation technique discussed in the chapter. Justify your plan.

Additional Sources of Information

Andreason, A.R. (1988). *Cheap But Good Marketing Research*. Burr Ridge, IL: Irwin.

Breen, G., and A.B. Blankenship. (1989). *Do-It-Yourself Marketing Research*. New York: McGraw-Hill.

Crispell, Diane. (1990). *The Insider's Guide to Demographic Know-How*. Chicago: Probus.

Findex: The Directory of Market Research Reports, Studies and Surveys. (1990). Gaithersburg, MD: Cambridge Information Group Directories.

Levinson, J.C. (1984). *Guerrilla Marketing*. Boston: Houghton Mifflin.

Internet Resources

American Demographics/Marketing Tools
http://www.demographics.com/directory
This site will help you learn how to target your marketing efforts.

American Marketing Association
http://www.ama.org
Focuses on the services of this organization.

Electric Library
http://www.elibrary.com
Archive of 150 newspapers, 800 magazines and journals and 30,000 photos, images, and maps. It costs $9.95/month.

Understanding Your Market
http://www.sbaonline.sba.gov
From the Small Business Administration; helps you go through the process of under-standing your customers.

Relevant Case Studies

1. Toy Tips, Inc.
2. Mrs. Gooch's Natural Foods Markets
3. OXO (A)

7

Innovation . . . endows resources with a new capacity to create wealth.
Peter F. Drucker
Management consultant, writer
Harvard Business Review, *May/June 1986*

Analyzing Product/Service Risks and Benefits

Overview

▶ **The nature of product/process development today**

▶ **Product development the entrepreneur's way**

▶ **Protecting your business concept**

Terms to Know

Profile 7.1

Proprietary but Not Patentable

What do you do when you've developed an important proprietary process that is the essence of your business—but can't patent it? How do you protect it? That was precisely the problem facing Matt Livingston, one of three brothers who co-founded Arion Water Processing in Hyannis, Massachusetts. Arion develops water processing and purification systems for industrial sites with companies principally in the biotech and semiconductor industries.

Livingston is a trained chemist whose job it is to stay on top of the latest technologies, which are essential to his clients, so that his company can be competitive. His clients rely on him for accurate test results and methods. Until 1997, the business was

small and family-owned, and Livingston found himself so entrenched in its day-to-day struggles that he didn't have time for what he most loves doing—designing and developing new technologies. The company was perceived as small, and this was limiting the Livingston brothers' ability to contract with new clients. Matt Livingston knew he had a proprietary process that made Arion's system far more attractive than others in the market, but he also knew that since it didn't fall into any of the Patent and Trademark Office (PTO) guidelines for what is patentable, he had no way to protect it. As the company grew and more people knew about the process, it would be only a matter of time before someone "reverse-engineered" it for their own competitive advantage. Livingston was in a quandary.

What he didn't realize was that although a patented process certainly does give a growing company some protections, it doesn't really prevent someone from copying and modifying the process and getting away with doing so. After all, a patent merely gives you the right to sue an infringer; it doesn't prevent anyone from infringing on your rights. A small company with very limited resources would find it difficult to successfully sue a larger, infringing company over any protracted period of time.

With the help of a consultant, Livingston learned that smallness is an advantage because it allows him and his brothers to be more flexible and more produc-tive and to change with their customers' needs without passing along the costs of a large overhead. They needed to begin to define their company more broadly, as a proactive strategy against a potential infringer. The Livingstons saw this as a new beginning. They would define their firm as an information resource—a solution provider. In this way, they would build close learning relationships with their customers, who would remain their customers because of that relationship—even if someone were to steal their proprietary process. That is the essence of competitive advantage.

SOURCE: This profile was compiled by the author based on a personal interview she conducted with the subject and an article entitled, "Transform Your Business," by Don Wallace which appeared in *Success Magazine,* September 1997, p. 59.

What are some other legal protections that Arion can take advantage of?

Putting the customer at the center of the business has been a constant theme throughout this book. Never is this philosophy more important than when the product or service is first conceived. This chapter will look at the risks and benefits associated with the new product or service and at how to test it in order to ensure its feasibility in the marketplace.

The Nature of Product/Process Development Today

The processes, techniques, and timelines—in fact, the whole area of product development in the United States—have undergone profound change brought about by three factors:

▶ International competition

▶ Sophisticated customers in fragmented markets

▶ Widely diversified and changing technologies[1]

International Competition

Since the 1980s the number of companies competing in the global market-place has increased enormously. Couple that with the fact that similarity in product concepts has expanded, and you have the makings of an intensely competitive arena for product development. An American company finds it is no longer competing simply with other American companies; now, it must also compete with companies from diverse regions of the world who put their own stamp on processes and products. This volatile environment actually is good news for entrepreneurs who realize that the most innovative new products emerge from environments where there is high uncertainty, risk, and ambiguity.[2] In these environments small companies often shine because of their high degree of flexibility, which lets them respond quickly.

Sophisticated Customers in Fragmented Markets

The ability of today's customer to differentiate products on a very subtle level, along with customers' demands for products that reflect their lifestyles and value systems, make it incumbent upon product developers to create products that differentiate themselves on many levels in the marketplace. Whereas formerly product performance and price were the main competitive measures, today these two factors are givens. Superior performance and value-based pricing must be present for a company to even begin to be competitive. This means that a manufacturing company can never stop improving its design and manufacturing processes if it wishes to remain competitive, and a service company must continually find ways to improve its delivery methods.

Widely Diversified and Changing Technologies

Certainly, technology is essential to product development, and today the marginal cost of added technological capability is small. Yet a growing business cannot build its competitive advantage around technology alone. Customers are primarily interested in a product that will meet a need or desire; they are not necessarily interested in the technology or technological processes that produced it. Often a customer is not willing to pay for extra technology just because it's easily available.

A company operating in a technology-based industry like electronics must keep up with changing consumer demand as well as with the technological innovations of its competitors. Competitive advantage can be built around a line of market-differentiated products, but it must be enhanced by proprietary processes. A new product must not only create value for the customer but also must be difficult for someone else to produce at the same quality level and for the same cost.

Technology has also shortened product life cycles. Whereas 50 years ago a new tool product or a game or toy had life cycles of 18 and 16 years respectively, today those life cycles have shrunk to five years.[3] Consequently, today companies must constantly be researching and developing new products and improving existing ones to stay ahead of the competition.

Product Development the Entrepreneur's Way

Most large corporations have separate departments responsible for research and development, engineering, and testing. In many cases, the budgets for these particular departments are astronomical, since new-product development, as well as the continual improvement of existing products and processes, is considered one of the most important and challenging tasks of high-performing, world-class businesses.

In the case of start-up ventures, the task is equally challenging; however, most new ventures, unlike large corporations, have very limited or nonexistent budgets. Funding research and development, engineering, and testing for a new company is considered the highest-risk stage by most investors; consequently, this type of funding is difficult, if not impossible, for entrepreneurs to secure. They are left with a dilemma: how to perform the R&D that will result in a factory-quality, engineered prototype as quickly as possible yet as inexpensively as possible. It is not surprising, then, that many good product ideas fail to achieve market introduction.

Designing Right the First Time

Today, more than ever before, it's important to design the new product, process, or service right the first time. Redesign, which involves re-engineering, new drawings, and a reworking of the prototype, can be more costly than the original design in terms of actual costs and the costs of missing a window of opportunity if you are working in a dynamic market. Product design accounts for only about 8 percent of the product budget but determines fully 80 percent of the cost of the product. Design also determines the marketability of the product as well as quality, reliability, and serviceability. The length of time to launch and the cost to produce are also determined by product design.

Time-to-Market

One of the most critical aspects of effective product development today is **time-to-market.** If an entrepreneur takes too long to introduce a new product, the market may have changed just enough to force a redesign, which will not only lengthen the process but cost the company in lost opportunities and higher costs. By contrast, the closer the designing of the product is to market introduction, the more likely the product will meet customers' needs at that moment. Moreover, it is estimated that a six-month jump on competitors in a market accustomed to 18- to 24-month design lives can translate into as much as three times the profit over the market life of the design.[4] Still, the only real measure of time-to-market is the time to trouble-free production, which depends on getting the design right the first time.

The biggest gains in shortening the time to market come from:

1. Reducing wait time between design and production tasks

2. Using off-the-shelf components where possible

3. Overlapping tasks where possible

4. Avoiding redesign by designing right the first time

Outsourcing Product Development

Other difficulties faced by entrepreneurs at this pre–start-up stage include finding the right consultants to do the engineering, material and parts sourcing, and model building. This effort can be expensive and time-consuming, so choosing the wrong consulting firms can be devastating. As engineers tend to specialize (mechanical, electrical, civil), it is possible that one product may require the services of more than one type of engineer. Some of the areas of product development that require engineering analysis, design, and expertise include:

▶ Component design

▶ Materials specifications

▶ Machinery to process

▶ Ergonomic design

▶ Packaging design

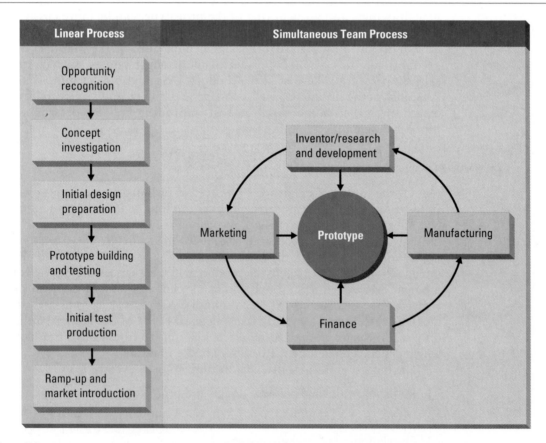

Figure 7.1
The Product Development Cycle

> Assembly drawings and specifications

> Parts and material sourcing (suppliers)

> Operator's and owner's manuals

The Product Development Cycle

Entrepreneurs who develop products usually go through a process much like that shown in Figure 7.1. The **product development cycle** consists of a series of tasks leading to introduction of the product in the marketplace. It should be noted, however, that product development is no longer a linear process, but rather a team effort where many tasks go on simultaneously.

Opportunity Recognition

Recall from Chapter 2 that the first stage in the development of a business concept is opportunity recognition: identifying a niche that has not been served, detecting an improvement in an existing product, or seeing an opportunity for a breakthrough product. Once the opportunity has been identified, it is critical to move forward with the next stage, concept investigation, to shorten the product development cycle as much as possible.

Concept Investigation

Concept investigation is simply doing some investigation to determine if the idea currently exists, if there is a potential market, how much it will cost to produce the product, and how much time will it take. This last piece of information is crucial, since an enforced shorter development cycle allows the company to have a first-mover advantage, better meet its customers' needs, lower the costs of production, and cut off the tendency by the entrepreneur or inventor to keep "improving the product" instead of getting it out into the market.

Initial Design Preparation

The first stages of design preparation go hand in hand with concept investigation because an entrepreneur normally needs some preliminary working drawings of the product to estimate costs and manufacturing processes. These preliminary drawings are also used to apply for a patent if the product is patentable. However, once it has been determined that the product has real potential, it is time to bring in the design engineers and the other members of the functional team—marketing, operations, and finance—to put together accurate drawings of the product and initial specifications.

Prototype Building and Field Testing

From the initial engineered drawings will come the **prototype** or model of the product. Often the first prototype does not closely resemble the final product in appearance, but usually does in function. In fact, today it's important to reach the physical stage of prototyping as quickly as possible because involving key functional team members is much less expensive at this early stage. The importance of involving key functional players in the development of the prototype cannot be overstated. It is far less costly to discover at this stage from the marketing expert that the customer will not like the ergonomics of the product, or from the operations and finance experts that the equipment to produce the product is beyond the current budget. With little money invested, team members are free to simulate the use of the product and make mistakes while finding the best version of the prototype.

Technology has even entered the prototyping stage of product development in the form of "rapid prototyping." Today you can purchase a device that, working from information in your computer, will cut and shape metal or other raw materials into three-dimensional parts. In this way, you can design a part on the computer screen and then cut it into a real prototype virtually instantly in your office. The obvious advantage of this is avoiding the shipping of two-dimensional drawings to a parts manufacturer and waiting for the part to be made.

With a prototype it is also easier to acquire more accurate target-market-demand information, more accurate cost estimates, and a clearer sense of whether the product will work as proposed in the design phase. The added benefit is that eliminating features that do not create value in the mind of the customer can reduce manufacturing costs 25–40 percent. Moreover, through field testing the prototype, adjustments and modifications can be made, leading to a production-quality prototype: in essence, the final product.

Various engineers can be employed to take the crude prototype and determine the best assembly design, the types of materials to use, the most effective components, the required suppliers, and which other subcontractors might be needed to make the product ready for production. From the engineered assembly drawings, parts lists, and specifications, the production-quality prototype can be assembled. Small engineering firms or solo engineers who support entrepreneurs and inventors; small job shops; and machine shops or model builders may be used to complete the prototype. These sources are normally quicker and less expensive than the larger, better-known firms. When seeking an engineer or a model builder, the entrepreneur must use caution. Careful analysis of qualifications, experience, and references relative to the task are essential. A good source of referrals is a major university engineering department; so are other engineers.

Businesses that do not manufacture products—service, retail, wholesale, and so forth—still need to design a prototype, but the prototype in this case will not be physical. Instead it will be a design for how the business will provide a service or product to its customer, maintain and control inventories, hire employees, and guarantee quality and satisfaction. Entrepreneurs who intend to start nonmanufacturing businesses should read this chapter substituting the design for their service as the product where appropriate.

One of the time-consuming aspects of this stage of product development is sourcing the components and raw materials for the product. Deciding which switch to use, who should mold the plastic, or which vendors provide the best materials at the lowest prices requires a lot of legwork. Of course, the entrepreneur could leave these decisions to the design engineers, but at $150 an hour, it doesn't make sense to have the engineer searching for and comparing all the parts and materials. The engineer may offer suggestions based on experience, but the actual legwork is usually done by the entrepreneur and the founding team. What the engineer does is ensure that the product meets **OSHA standards** (assuming that it needs to) and suggest warning labels that may be required on the product.

Initial Test Production Run

The number of prototypes used in the field testing stage is limited. Usually the entrepreneur has not yet met the supplier's volume level for discounts, so the cost to produce at this stage is very high. After conducting a small initial test production run in a limited market, the product is honed to completion and market-ready status. It is also the first opportunity for the entrepreneur to test the manufacturing and assembly processes and determine accurate costs of production at varying levels of volume.

Product Market Introduction and Ramp-Up

At this stage the product is ready for introduction into the market, and the manufacturing processes are in place to meet projected demand.

Today it is simply not enough to produce a high-quality product at a fair price. To become and remain competitive, the new business must strive for a product development cycle that achieves low cost and high quality as quickly as possible.

Quality Function Deployment

The team-based approach to product development referred to previously is known as **Quality Function Deployment** (QFD). QFD was developed in 1972 at Mitsubishi's Kobe shipyards and was later adopted by Toyota because it was thought to reduce design costs by 60 percent and design time by 40 percent. QFD was introduced in the United States in 1986 at Ford and Xerox.

Profile 7.2

Shortening Development Time Through Teams: The 3M Experience

While 3M manufactures a variety of consumer and industrial products, it is probably best known for its adhesives; namely, Scotch Tape and Post-it Notes. Because it focuses on unpatentable products whose origins lie in customer needs, it is crucial that 3M be able to identify and solve problems quickly to get new products to market. Using the traditional engineering development cycle would put 3M at a disadvantage, as it would be fairly easy for a competitor to replicate the production process and come out with a competing product shortly after 3M's introduction of its own.

To solve this problem, 3M built a research and design center in Austin, Texas, and housed its engineers and its marketing staff there. The Austin group found that they could work from physical prototypes almost immediately, without needing detailed drawings. In fact, it made more sense to customize and modify the design using a physical prototype, resulting in the right version's being reached much more quickly. This was true, for example, with 3M's mechanical splicing device for optical cables; it was possible to go into full production without detailed blueprints, and the product worked. Interestingly enough, when the group ultimately did create the blueprints according to the original design, the product didn't work!

The purpose of QFD is to insert customer input throughout the design, manufacturing, and service delivery phases of product development. The market research done for QFD addresses strategic decisions such as performance versus comfort, and functional or ergonomic decisions such as where to place a handle. It does this through customer input known as **voice of the customer**, which is a prioritized, hierarchical set of "customer needs."

Customer Needs

Customer needs is a description in customers' own words of what their needs are with regard to the product. For example, in the case of a new portable computer, the typical customer may say, "It must be easily carried in a briefcase." A list of several hundred needs may be developed, but they generally fall into three categories: basic needs or assumptions about the product (e.g., that it must be small); desired functions (e.g., what they want it to do); and unusual or unexpected desires (e.g., needs that may surprise or excite the customer).

Hierarchy of Needs

Customer needs are structured into three categories: primary, secondary, and tertiary. Primary needs are strategic and consist of the top five to ten customer needs. These direct the engineers as to whether—using a laptop computer as an example—the size, weight, or functions of the computer should be the focus of their efforts. Each primary need then is expanded into three to ten secondary or tactical needs—in other words, what the product development team must do to satisfy that primary need. For example, how is the desired size achieved, or what is the optimal shape? Tertiary or operational needs provide the engineers and R&D personnel with details needed for developing the solutions to the tactical requirements. For example, how to know when the desired size is achieved.

Importances

Importances are the priorities customers place on certain features like size, weight, and so forth. These priorities are then weighed against the cost and feasibility of satisfying a particular need.

Customer Perceptions of Performance

Customer perception is a measure of how customers perceive other products in the market that are currently satisfying a particular need. Where no such product exists, it measures the way that customers attempt to satisfy the need.

Using QFD, the team identifies those design attributes that will affect customers' perceptions of the product if modified to meet their needs. The team also considers the realities of engineering and the costs. What has been presented here is merely an overview of the QFD process. What has not been covered are the possibilities for mathematical operations to develop indices and scales for enhancing decision making. Check "Additional Sources of Information" at the end of the chapter for more on this subject. The key point to remember about QFD is that it represents a philosophy of product devel-

Table 7.1   New Product Checklist

The Market	Yes	No	Perhaps
Is there an existing need for this product in the marketplace?	___	___	___
Will I be first in the marketplace with this product?	___	___	___
Can I protect the product legally?	___	___	___
Can I erect entry barriers?	___	___	___
SWOT Analysis (Strengths, Weaknesses, Opportunities, and Threats)			
Do the strengths of this product exceed any weaknesses?	___	___	___
Are there various opportunities for commercializing this product?	___	___	___
Do any significant threats exist to the development of this product?	___	___	___
Design/Development/Manufacturing			
Is the product innovative?	___	___	___
Can it be developed quickly to market-ready state?	___	___	___
Can it be easily manufactured?	___	___	___
Do I have the resources to manufacture the product?	___	___	___
Is it more practical to subcontract the manufacturing?	___	___	___
Is there a possibility for spin-off products?	___	___	___
Financial			
Is the return on this investment sufficient to justify the effort?	___	___	___
Are the development costs within reason?	___	___	___
Can the manufacturing investment be minimized while still maintaining quality and control through outsourcing?	___	___	___
Is the money needed to produce the product available?	___	___	___

opment that brings all members of the team in at the beginning of the design phase, including the most important member of the team—the customer. Many entrepreneurs have used this team approach successfully without implementing the complete QFD process, a fairly complex method that usually requires the assistance of an outside consultant with experience in QFD.

Protecting Your Business Concept

One of the competitive advantages enjoyed by many new ventures falls under the heading of **intellectual property** rights, or proprietary rights. These apply to patents, trademarks, copyrights, and trade secrets. You don't have to manufacture a product to take advantage of these rights. Even if your business is a service, retail, or wholesale business, you may be able to protect the use of your name, a logo, or a written document against its being used by someone else.

Patents

If the new venture opportunity involves a product, it is especially important that the inventor, the entrepreneur, or both investigate the potential for acquiring intellectual property rights—that is, determine if there are legal ways to protect the product idea from competitor duplication until after it has gone to market.

The issue of who owns an idea is a crucial one as it could mean the difference between having a successful business and not having one. The primary legal means of protecting an original idea is through a **patent**.

The U.S. patent system was designed 200 years ago by Thomas Jefferson to protect the inventions of the independent inventor. Today, although most inventors work in the research departments of large corporations, the basic legal tenets of patent law still remain true to the independent inventor. Since the first patent was issued in 1790, more than five million U.S. patents have been granted.

A patent grants an inventor the exclusive right to an invention for a period of years, depending on the type of patent. It also prevents others from manufacturing and selling the invention during the period of the patent. At the end of this time, the patent is placed in public domain. Two types of patents concern most inventors: utility patents and design patents. Utility patents are the most common type. They protect the functional part of machines or processes, in addition to computer programs associated with hardware. Some examples are toys, film processing, protective coatings, tools, and cleaning implements. A utility patent is valid for 20 years from the date of application.

Profile 7.3

Making Pigs of Themselves: Inventors Turned Entrepreneurs

For years factories have struggled with the problem of how to clean up greasy spills and leaks on their floors. The method most commonly used was cat litter, but it tended to be messy and get into the machinery. Don Beaver and Ben Stapelfeld, owners of an industrial cleaning business, began playing around with absorbent materials, putting them in everything from athletic socks to pantyhose, and throwing the concoction away when it became saturated. At one point, facing financial disaster with their business, they decided to push ahead and develop their absorbent-sock concept into a real product.

They tried every type of absorbent material and finally hit upon ground-up corncobs. With an investment of $500,000 from banks and private investors, they began to build the company. Going through the traditional industrial distribution channels was unsuccessful because their product provided relatively small commissions to distributors in comparison with commissions on large hydraulic systems. So they developed a unique market strategy that involved giving the company an unusual name—The New Pig Corporation—using promotional items such as pig coffee mugs and pig hats, and spending 40 percent of revenues on advertising.

The most important thing they did, however, was to define their business not as a one-product business but as a problem-solving business. They encouraged their customers to make suggestions, and from these suggestions sprang numerous new products. The company now employs over 140 people.

Design patents protect new, original ornamental designs for manufactured articles. The design patent protects only the appearance of an article, not its structure or utilitarian features.[5] The design must be nonfunctional and part of the tangible item for which it is designed. Some examples are a gilding, an item of apparel, or jewelry. Design patents are valid for 14 years from date of issuance.

Ever vigilant to changing technology, in 1980 the Patent Office created a new category of protection: life forms. It covers such controversial things as altered human genes and microbes that break down crude oil. Another special category is the plant patent, which protects any new variety of a sexually or asexually reproduced plant.

Computer programs present some special problems requiring several methods of protection. For example, they may be protected by a trade secret contract if the developer/owner merely licenses the program for distribution by someone else to a narrow market. If wide dissemination is the goal, a patent offers more protection and is available if the program contains at least one

---

Profile 7.4

The Importance of Proprietary Rights

Bob Kearns was tired of windshield wipers that operated either too slowly or too fast. He wondered why they couldn't function like an eyelid and literally blink. Kearns had a damaged eye, the result of being hit with a champagne cork on his wedding night, and had great difficulty seeing while driving one night in a severe rainstorm. That's when the inspiration for intermittent windshield wipers came to him.

For Kearns, generating ideas for products that solved problems was a way of life. His first invention was a comb that distributed hair tonic; then came an amplifier for people who had undergone laryngectomies, followed by an innovative type of weather balloon. Most of the ideas never went beyond the model stage, which is not atypical for inventors. Kearns, who had a master's degree in mechanical engineering, began working on the prototype of the intermittent wiper blade in 1963. When he had a working prototype, which he installed in his car, he arranged to show it to engineers at Ford. They encouraged him to field test it to see if it would achieve three million cycles. When it did, he again approached Ford—which suddenly didn't seem interested anymore. He then went to a friend who owned a mid-sized manufacturing firm that supplied parts to the auto industry. Kearns assigned the rights to the patent to his friend in exchange for his friend's paying the costs of getting the patents and paying Kearns royalties plus $1,000 a month to continue research and development.

Then, surprisingly, in 1969, Ford came out with an intermittent wiper blade that used the Kearns design. GM followed suit in 1974 and Chrysler in 1977, along with several foreign car companies. Kearns, who by that time had reacquired his patent rights, filed suit against Ford in 1978 for patent infringement and later against Chrysler. It took 12 years of intense work (Kearns represented himself) for the first case to come to trial. In the first suit, Ford agreed to settle for $30 million after the jury found in Kearns's favor, but he turned that down (he was seeking $1.6 billion). In a second trial, Kearns was awarded $5.2 million. Ultimately Ford and Kearns settled for $10.2 million. The Chrysler case, which concluded in June 1992, gave Kearns an additional $11.5 million, but he was still unhappy because the jury didn't find that the automaker had been willful in the infringement. Still, Kearns stands as a role model to other inventors who regularly face patent infringement by large corporations.

unique algorithm that is part of the machine or physical process. Copyrights are commonly used for programs that don't qualify for a patent. In addition, the name of the program can be trademarked and the instructions copyrighted.

Is the Invention Patentable?

Before deciding to file for a patent, it is important to first determine the patentability of the invention. There are four basic criteria:

1. It must fit into one of the five classes established by Congress:
   - Machine (fax, rocket, electronic circuits)
   - Process (chemical reactions, methods for producing products)
   - Articles of manufacture (furniture, diskettes)
   - Composition (gasoline, food additives)
   - A new use for one of the above

   Many inventions can be classified into more than one category. That does not present a problem, however, since the inventor does not have to decide which category the invention fits.

2. It must have utility; in other words, be useful. This is not usually a problem unless you have invented something like an unsafe drug or something purely "whimsical." The Patent Trademark Office (PTO) has been known to issue patents on some fairly strange inventions, such as a male chastity device (#587,994).

3. It must not contain prior art. **Prior art** is knowledge that is publicly available or published prior to the date of the invention—that is, a date before the filing of the patent application. Accordingly, it is important to document everything that is done in the creation of the invention. Also, you must follow the "one-year rule," which says the invention must not become public or available for sale more than one year prior to filing the patent application. This rule is meant to ensure that the invention is still novel at the time of application. Novelty consists of physical differences, new combinations of components, or new uses.

4. It must be **unobvious**. The invention must not be obvious to someone with ordinary skills in the field. This is a tricky definition but has been further explained by the PTO as an invention that contains "new and unexpected results." If your invention is rejected on the first pass as not being "unobvious," it probably means that the patent examiner wants you to demonstrate its unobviousness.

The Patent Process

The process for obtaining a patent is well defined; however, it is advisable to use the services of a patent attorney, especially when applying for foreign patents. Attorneys understand the complicated system at the Patent Office in Washington, D.C., and can do a better job of expediting the process. The Patent Office is staffed by attorneys and engineers, so a patent attorney may have more success communicating with them than an inventor would.

Understanding the requirements for patents in other countries is a fairly complex specialty, given that the laws vary from country to country. An attorney with experience in filing foreign patents can ensure that you receive all the rights to which you are entitled. The bottom line is that the patent should be applied for correctly to avoid costly problems later on. Here is the process.

▶ *File a disclosure document.* The inventor will normally file a disclosure statement that documents the date of conception of the invention. This statement is crucial in the event that two inventors are working on the same idea at the same time. The one who files the disclosure document first has the right to file for a patent. However, filing a disclosure statement does not in any way "diminish the value of the conventional, witnessed, permanently bound, and page-numbered laboratory notebook or notarized records as evidence of conception of an invention."[6] The disclosure document is a detailed description of the invention and its uses and may include photos; however, it is not a patent application. The inventor has a two-year period in which to file a patent application but must demonstrate diligence in completing the invention and filing the application to maintain the right to first filing for a patent. If the inventor publicly uses or sells the invention more than a year prior to filing the patent application, he or she will be prohibited from gaining a patent. To file a disclosure statement, send

— a cover letter requesting that the PTO accept the disclosure statement,
— a check for the required fee,
— a copy of the disclosure statement, and
— a stamped, self-addressed, return envelope.

Do not use the tactic of mailing a dated description of the invention to yourself by certified mail. It has no value to the Patent Office.

▶ *File a formal patent application.* The patent application contains a complete description of the invention, what it does, and how it is uniquely different from anything currently existing (prior art). It also includes detailed drawings, explanations, and engineering specifications. The claims section of the application specifies the parts of the invention on which the inventor wants patents. The description of these claims must be specific enough to demonstrate the invention's uniqueness but broad enough to make it difficult for others to circumvent the patent; that is, modifying it slightly and duplicating the product without violating the patent. Be sure you file the patent application no more than one year after offering the product for sale or using it commercially. It is infinitely preferable to file before any public disclosures are made.

The cost, on average, of filing a disclosure statement and patent application is between $1,500 and $2,000. However, the more complex the application, the higher the patent attorney fees. These figures do not include the costs of engineered designs and drawings, which must accompany the application and vary significantly from product to product.

Once the application is received, the Patent Office will conduct a search of its patent records. During this period the invention is said to be "patent applied for," which establishes the inventor's claim and dates relative to prior art. An invention can stay in the patent-applied-for stage for up to two years, the primary advantage of this being that the public does not have access to the patent application and drawings, which might allow someone else the chance to design around the patent.

The Patent Office contacts the inventor and states that it either accepts the claims in the application or denies the application and gives the inventor a period of time to appeal or modify the claims. It is not uncommon for the original claims to be rejected in their entirety by the PTO, usually because of prior art. If and when the Patent Office accepts the modified claims, the invention is in the patent-pending stage; that is, awaiting the issuance of the patent. The inventor may market and sell the product during this period, but must clearly label it "patent pending." Once the patent is issued, however, it becomes public record.

If the patent examiner rejects the modified claims, the inventor has the right to appeal to a Board of Patent Appeals within the Patent Office. Failing to find agreement at this point, the inventor may appeal to the U.S. Court of Appeals for the Federal Circuit. This appeals process may take years.

Be aware that the patent, once issued, is a powerful document that gives the holder the right to enforce the patent against infringers in a court of law. Under the law, the patent holder is entitled to a reasonable royalty from the infringer; if the infringer refuses to pay, the patent holder can enjoin or close down the operation of the infringer. If the entrepreneur is planning to export products, patent applications should be filed in the countries in which the product will be sold. This can be a costly process if the entrepreneur is dealing with a number of countries. Furthermore, entrepreneurs have often found their patents violated in countries that do not have as stringent patent laws as the United States.

Provisional Patent

Since June 8, 1995, the PTO has offered the option of filing a provisional patent application, which is much less expensive and puts U.S. applicants in parity with foreign applicants. This application does not require claims or an oath, but it does give the applicant the right to use the term *patent pending* in conjunction with the product. Provisional patents may not be filed for design patents. The provisional patent expires 12 months from the date of filing, but that period is not counted in the 20-year term for a nonprovisional patent. Since the 20-year clock starts with the filing of the formal patent application, the provisional patent effectively extends patent protection by one year.

Trademarks

A **trademark** is a symbol, word or design that is used to identify a business or a product. For example, Apple Computers uses a picture of an apple with a bite out of it followed by the symbol ®, which means "registered trademark." A trademark has a longer life than a patent, with certain conditions. A business has the exclusive right to a trademark for as long as it is actively using it. However, if the trademark becomes part of the generic language, like aspirin and thermos, it can no longer be trademarked. Furthermore, a trademark cannot be registered until it is actually in use. Before that time the entrepreneur should use ^{TM} (or ^{SM} for services) after the name until the trademark is registered.

To register a trademark, an applicant can use one of three methods:

1. If the mark has already been in use, the applicant can file a use application requesting registration and ownership of the mark. You will also have to submit three specimens showing actual use of the mark.

2. If the mark has not yet been in use, you can file an intent-to-use application. After the mark is in use, you must submit the three specimens showing actual use before receiving registration.

3. Depending on international agreements with a specific country, an applicant can file on the basis of having a trademark in another country.

To apply, you need to submit PTO Form 1478 with a drawing of the mark and the appropriate fee. The PTO does not require a search for potentially conflicting marks prior to filing the application. However, it is probably wise to do a search, since it isn't difficult. You can conduct a search in the PTO public search library or in a patent and depository library, or you can hire a specialist to search for you. The PTO determines whether your mark may be registered and notifies you. If the PTO rejects the application, you have six months to respond.

Marks that cannot be trademarked include:

▶ Anything immoral or deceptive

▶ Anything that uses official symbols of the United States or any state or municipality, like the flag

▶ Anything that uses a person's name or likeness without permission

---

Profile 7.5

A Cop on the Trail of Infringers

In Hollywood he's known as a "dead-celebrity cop." It's definitely an unusual niche in the market, representing dead celebrities and protecting their rights. If you decide to use Albert Einstein's image in an unflattering manner, for example, you may receive a stern warning from Roger Richman to which you had better reply promptly or he'll take you to court. If your company wants to use Judy Garland or Mae West in an ad, you'd better check with Richman first.

Roger Richman has been running this very unusual business for over 20 years. He not only seeks out abusers of a celebrity's image but also licenses that image in appropriate settings for a fee of about 35 percent. His Beverly Hills office represents 45 deceased people in 19 countries, including the Wright Brothers. In fact, he was instrumental in the passage of the California Celebrity Rights Act, which forbids the unauthorized use of celebrity images (name, voice, signature, photograph, or likeness) without permission of the family for 50 years after death.

SOURCE: John M. Glionna, "Dead-Celebrity Cop Polices Trademark Infringements," *Los Angeles Times*, October 6, 1997, Monday, Home Edition, Metro; Part B; p. 1.

Trade Secrets

Trade secrets are whatever aspects of the business you wish to protect from disclosure by employees or others involved with the business. The only way to protect trade secrets is through an employment contract that specifically details any trade secrets. Then, should a former employee use a specified trade secret, the company can use legal remedies, such as an injunction or suing for damages.

Aspects of the business that may be considered trade secrets are recipes or ingredients (Mrs. Fields Cookies), source codes for computer chips, customer discounts, manufacturer costs, and so forth.

 ## The Savvy Entrepreneur: Are Your Secrets Really Safe?

The Cold War was over long ago; open book management is in. Does this mean that keeping secrets is taboo? Not at all, but it does mean that protecting them is much harder. The FBI has reported that 23 foreign governments are pulling trade secrets from major U.S. corporations on a regular basis; the victims include Intel, GM, Hughes, and Lockheed-Martin.

Congress has responded with the Economic Espionage Act of 1996, which makes the theft of trade secrets a federal offense. Although the original goal was to put a dent in foreign espionage, the reality is that such theft also hits close to home. Under EEA, you may actually be asked to protect competitors from their own stupidity. For example, suppose you're at a party and overhear your competitors talking about their latest marketing strategy. You might be wise to warn them that you can hear what they're saying; otherwise, you may become liable should you attempt to thwart their marketing efforts with similar ones of your own.

You may also have a problem if you hire someone who arrives with her Rolodex from the previous job, because those contacts may be considered trade secrets. Previously, the term *trade secret* was defined quite broadly, but under the new provisions, it includes all types of business and financial information. The important point to remember is that if you suspect your trade secrets have been stolen, and you have taken reasonable care to protect them, you must take legal measures immediately. The best way to ensure that your secrets are kept is to earn the loyalty and respect of those who work with you.

Source: Alan Farnham, "How Safe Are Your Secrets?" *Fortune*, September 8, 1997, pp. 114–120.

Copyrights

Copyrights protect original works of authors, composers, screenwriters, and computer programmers. A copyright does not protect the idea itself but only the form in which it appears. For example, a computer programmer can copyright the written program for a particular type of word processing software but cannot copyright the idea of word processing. This is why several companies can produce word processing software without violating a copyright. They really are protecting the unique programming code of their software. A copyright lasts for the life of the holder plus 50 years, after which it goes into public domain. Copyrighted works cannot be copied without permission of the copyright holder.

To obtain federal copyright protection, the work must be in a fixed and tangible form—that is, you must be able to see or hear it. It should contain a copyright notice (although this is no longer required by law) so that a potential violator cannot claim innocence because there was no notice. The notice should use the word *copyright* or the symbol © and should provide the year and the complete name of the person responsible for the work.

Though it is not required, registration at the Copyright Office at the Library of Congress in Washington, D.C., is important in order to obtain full protection under the law. Along with the application and fee, you must submit a complete copy of an unpublished work or two complete copies of a published work.

The key point to remember about intellectual property rights is that they can't stop someone from infringing on your rights. What they can do is provide you with offensive rights—that is, the right to sue in a court of law, a long and costly process. Consequently, intellectual property rights should never be the sole competitive advantage a business possesses.

There are risks and benefits associated with the products and services you develop. Part of the goal of feasibility analysis is to address those risks and benefits so that you will be able to make an informed decision as to whether or not you want to go forward with a new business concept.

New Venture Checklist

Have you:

- ❏ **Found ways to incorporate customer input into the design of your products, processes, and services?**

- ❏ **Found independent contractors who can help you build your prototype?**

- ❏ **Determined which aspects of your product, service, or business can be protected from infringement?**

- ❏ **Filed a notice of disclosure if your product is patentable?**

Issues to Consider

1. How has the environment for product development changed today?
2. What is the difference between a disclosure document and a patent application?
3. What is the difference between patent-pending status and patent-applied-for status?
4. Why is it important to file a disclosure document immediately?
5. Suppose you have an idea for a new type of sunless tanning lotion. What procedures would you follow to protect your idea?

Experiencing Entrepreneurship

1. Interview an entrepreneur who has developed a product. Which product development strategy did they use, outsourcing or doing everything in-house, and why?
2. Visit your local patent office or the U.S. Patent Office on the Internet, *http://www.uspto.gov*. Pick a patented product that interests you and do a search to find the patent for the product.

Additional Sources of Information

Cohen, L. (1995). *Quality Function Deployment: How to Make QFD Work for You.*

Mosely, Jr., T.E. (1992). *Marketing Your Invention.* Dover, NH: Upstart Publishing.

Pine, J. II. (1993). *Mass Customization.* Boston: Harvard Business School Press.

Wheelwright, S.C., and K.B. Clark. (1992). *Revolutionizing Product Development.* New York: The Free Press.

Internet Resources

ANSI Online
http://www.ansi.org
The American National Standards Institute site, which also provides links to many other sites.

European Patent Office
http://www.epo.co.at/epo

Japan Patent Office
http://patent-jp.com

The National Technology Transfer Center
http://www.nttc.edu
This organization helps companies work with federal laboratories to turn their work into technology that businesses can use and sell.

Patent Laws—United States Code
http://www.kuesterlaw.com/lawrule/lawdex.htm

SBA Office of Technology (SBIR)
http://www.sbaonline.sba.gov/sbir

U.S. Copyright Office
http://lcweb.loc.gov/copyright

U.S. Patent and Trademark Office
http://www.uspto.gov

Relevant Case Studies

1. The Penduline Putter
2. OXO (B)
3. Simtek, Inc.

No great deed is done
By falterers who ask for certainty.
George Eliot (Marian Evans) English novelist, essayist, editor, The Spanish Gypsy

Analyzing Financial Risks and Benefits

Overview

▶ **Finding the right numbers**

▶ **Estimating sales and capital expenditures**

▶ **Forecasting expenditures**

▶ **Preparing the pro forma income statement**

▶ **How much start-up money is needed?**

Terms to Know

Profile 8.1

How Do You Explain a "No-Profit" Strategy?

Investors expect that most new ventures will not show a profit for a time. What they don't expect to see is a strategy stating explicitly that the company doesn't expect to make money for a long time. Yet that's exactly the tactic Jeffrey Bezos has used with investors in his online bookstore, Amazon.com. Bezos blatantly insists that unprofitability is his strategy for the foreseeable future—maybe five years—and that, in fact, the company will incur substantial losses.

Bezos is not crazy. His publicly held company saw its stock rise from $18 to $23.50 at close on the first day of trading in May 1997, so his investors appear to have confidence in his strategy. Venture capitalists Kleiner Perkins Caufield & Byer placed $10 million in Amazon, the biggest single placement ever, and received less than 15% of the company. Maybe it's because in 1994, Bezos was a rising senior vice president with a successful Wall Street hedge fund when he saw a huge opportunity in online commerce. He considered a number of different types of businesses to start, and various products to sell online, finally setting on books because there are so many of them, and unlike the music industry (his other choice), there are no "800-pound gorillas" in book publishing and distribution. Even the Goliath-sized Barnes & Noble holds less than 12% of the market. From a garage in the Seattle area, he built a multimillion dollar virtual company that employs over 110 people. Amazon sold its first book in July 1995. Today over 44% of its sales are to repeat customers, and Bezos has developed over 1,800 associates, partners online who have linked their sites with Amazon to share information and encourage sales.

It appears from the current success of Amazon that Bezos' no-profit strategy is working. He's invest-ing in the parts of the business that count, while keeping overhead to the bare bones. Revenues are increasing, and he fully expects they will someday make the business profitable.

SOURCE: Michael H. Martin, "The Next Big Thing: A Bookstore?" *Fortune*, December 9, 1996, p. 169.

What are some ways you can keep overhead costs down so that your new business achieves profitability sooner?

Once you have determined that a market exists for your new venture concept, you must ask yourself this question: "Under what financial conditions will I be willing to go forward to start this venture?" and does it appear to you that this new concept can be profitable?

No matter how many financial tools entrepreneurs use or how many complex analyses are constructed, the bottom line for any new venture is cash. Income statements and balance sheets can make a company look good on paper—these are accounting measures—but cash pays the bills and allows the company to grow. Cash is the lifeblood of the business and certainly the nourishment a potential new business needs to survive. So in making the decision to go forward with a new venture concept, you will want to estimate your cash needs for starting and operating the business until it can produce a positive cash flow from the revenues it generates. To do this requires a cash flow projection, a profit and loss projection, and a break-even analysis. Other types of financial analyses are more appropriate at the business plan stage and will be considered at that point. Before we consider how to do a cash needs assessment, however, let's look at how we gather the data needed to accomplish it.

Finding the Right Numbers

Estimating revenues, expenses, and start-up costs at the feasibility stage is a daunting task at best for an entrepreneur with a new business concept. At this stage the concept is still fluid, and in the case of a new product that is still in the design phase, the numbers you gather relative to the cost of producing that product may be quite different from the final numbers you achieve when the business plan is complete. We should say at this point that even the numbers you arrive at for the business plan will change when the business is in operation and the real world throws unexpected curves your way. There are many reasons why the numbers you use to determine feasibility will probably change when you move to the business plan.

1. If you are a manufacturer or are outsourcing to a manufacturer, it will be nearly impossible for you to estimate parts and manufacturing costs accurately without a production-quality product in place. For this reason it's important to get to a physical prototype stage early, so as to have a better idea of the parts, components, and types of materials you'll need, as well as labor.

2. For many new-product companies, product development may take several months to several years, depending on the nature of the product—and the costs for prototyping are always substantially higher than the ultimate production cost will be. Therefore, it's difficult to determine true feasibility before you reach a physical prototype. Moreover, your potential customers may have a difficult time deciding whether they're interested in a product if they can't see it.

3. For service companies, the actual costs to deliver a service must be based initially on information gathered from other companies in the industry. This is difficult to achieve without "inside information"; that is, without the benefit of knowing someone who works in that type of company. Your estimates for the cost of delivery of the service will achieve a higher accuracy rate if you do an "alpha" test or prototype the service under a variety of the most common scenarios. For example, a restaurant might want to calculate how long it takes to completely serve a customer from the time of arrival to the time of departure. Next to be looked at would be the number of tables planned, hours of operation, and number of servers and cooks needed. Peak and slow periods, and other aspects of serving customers, also would be factored in. The more variables you can account for, the better your estimates will be.

4. As you grow in knowledge of your industry, the information you receive becomes better and better because you know whom to talk with and where to find the best information. Since getting inside an industry is a difficult and time-consuming task, many entrepreneurs choose to start ventures in industries with which they're familiar or in which they have experience.

With an understanding of the inherent difficulties in forecasting numbers for a potential new business, let's consider an overall strategy that will at the very least give you a higher probability of arriving at some numbers that make sense. The process is called **triangulation**, which means that you will attack the problem from three angles: the industry, the market/customer, and your own knowledge.

The Industry

The importance of understanding how your industry works cannot be overstressed. You need to get out in the industry and talk with suppliers, vendors, manufacturers, distributors, industry experts. You also need to read industry trade journals and other periodicals written by experts in the field. Merely going to a similar or even a competing business to ask how they forecast sales is not going to work. For the most part, private business owners consider these figures to be proprietary and part of their competitive strategy, so they're unlikely to reveal them to you. However, you may find others in the industry, such as distributors, to be more forthcoming. Go shopping and talk to wholesalers and retailers of products similar to yours to get a feel for how much volume they're doing on a monthly basis. If you're in a service business, find out how many clients they can reasonably serve in a month or over a specific period of time. Remember, this is just one source in the triangle, but it's an important one.

The Market/Customer

Another critical source is the customer. Customers are far more likely than a competing business to give you good information. From customers you will learn what they buy, how often, and in what quantities, and what terms are expected. You can also extrapolate from their numbers to your other customers if they are similar in nature. The customer should be at the core of every aspect of your business, and predicting sales is certainly no exception to that rule. Don't rely on what others say about customers. Get out and talk to them yourself.

Your Knowledge

The knowledge and experience you bring to the business will also be helpful in forecasting sales. If you've worked in the industry for a while before starting a business, you may already have a sense of the volume of sales you can expect. Remember, though, that since your venture is new, it probably won't be able to achieve the level of sales of others in the industry for a time. One good technique is using field observation of your customers in their "normal habitat." That is, go to a place where they're likely to purchase what you have to offer and observe the buying ritual. Notice how many customers come into a location over a specific period of time and determine how many of them actually purchase something. What did they buy and how much did it cost? You can gain considerable valuable information by spending time away from your desk and out in the field.

By using all three sources of information—industry, market/customer, and your own knowledge—you should be able to arrive at some reasonable estimates of what sales over the first year will be. This will allow you to at least calculate the financial feasibility of the venture and how much money you'll need to start.

Estimating Sales and Capital Expenditures

The sales forecast should be calculated first because sales affect the other expenditures of the business. We know that with a new product that is either a line extension or the next generation of an established product, we can rely on historical data that will help ensure a more accurate estimate. With a brand new or breakthrough product, however, we are left to rely on market data, comparison of similar products, and the opinions of market experts. Therefore, to improve the estimate, we will use the triangulation method discussed previously, in addition to calculating best case, worst case, and most likely case scenarios that will cover about 90 percent of all the possible sales results.

Forecasting Sales with Consumer Products and Services

If the product or service being offered does not currently exist in the market, you must find a competing product or service that is similar or is a substitute product to study. The information needed includes the volume of "sell-in" to the retailer and the volume of "sell-through" to the customer—that is, the amount of product that is sold by the manufacturer or distributor to the retailer and the amount of that product that is ultimately sold to the customer. Naturally, since a service business generally operates with direct channels of distribution, it concerns itself only with the sell-through volume. In addition, you'll want to determine if there is any seasonality in the market that would affect the volume of sales during any particular period of time.

The mistake made by many companies who sell to retailers is focusing on how much product they are selling to the retailer and structuring their production and/or inventory accordingly. They do not carefully monitor retail sales to the customer. Consequently, when consumer buying slows and the retailer cannot move sufficient product, the manufacturer or producer is left with excess inventory. The entrepreneur with a new product or service, therefore, should monitor retail sales of competing products to consumers in the same category to arrive at an estimate of sales demand. Best case and worst case scenarios should also be calculated.

One word of caution: when choosing competing companies for comparison purposes, be aware that if the company is publicly held or well-established, your new venture probably will not achieve the same level of sales for some time. Therefore, the sales figures you gather serve merely as an upper limit benchmark as you determine how much below that figure your sales level will be. The percentage increase in your sales over a three- to five-year period will depend on these factors:

▸ Growth rates in the market segment of the product or service

▸ The innovations offered that will make your product/service more attractive to the consumer, even at a higher price

▸ The technological innovations employed that permit you to produce the product or service at a lower cost than your competitors, thus making it more accessible and enticing to the consumer

Forecasting Sales with Industrial Products

With industrial products, which are generally sold business to business, it is important to understand the needs of the customer and the buying cycles of the industry. Again, talking with experts (e.g., distributors) in the field, getting sales figures from noncompeting product manufacturers in the same industry, and generally determining the size of the market niches you intend to enter all help in arriving at an estimate of sales demand. As with the consumer market, in the industrial market it is vital to bracket the estimate with best case/worst case benchmark figures so that you are prepared for the most likely contingencies. The rate at which sales increase is a function of the same three factors listed for consumer products and services.

Forecasting Expenditures

Once sales have been forecast, predicting expenditures becomes a much easier task, particularly if they vary with sales. In wholesale businesses, for example, after the sales forecast has been determined, you can apply the figures for inventory purchases as a percentage of sales and forecast from that. So if inventory cost is 25 percent of sales, you can apply that percentage to sales as they increase to forecast changes in the volume of inventory. In manufacturing businesses, it is a bit more complex because you must first derive the Cost of Goods Sold (COGS), which usually consists of direct labor, cost of materials, and factory overhead. Looking at the sales forecast in terms of units produced to arrive at a dollar figure for COGS and then applying costs of goods sold as a percentage of sales will probably suffice for purposes of pro forma statements (see pp. 142–143) for the feasibility stage. Month-by-month analysis of outcomes and use of a cost accounting model that considers raw materials inventory, work-in-process inventory, finished-goods inventory, total inventory, factory overhead, work-in-process flow in units, and weighted-average cost per unit will give a more accurate estimate as the business grows.

In service businesses, the COGS is equivalent to the time expended for the service. The rate at which you bill the service, say $100 an hour, is comprised of the actual expenses incurred in providing the service, a contribution to overhead, and a reasonable profit. The actual expenses incurred are the cost of goods sold equivalent.

General and Administrative Expenses

The expenses of running the business, or general and administrative expenses, are considered fixed but must be forecast separately in a detailed breakout statement. This is because some of these items may vary over a 12-month period, while others remain stable. Therefore, do not use a percentage of sales figure for G&A expenses. Only the totals of G&A expenses for each month will be used in the financial statements, with a footnote directing the reader to the G&A breakout statement. Selling expenses, which include advertising, travel, sales salaries, commissions, and promotional supplies, should be handled in the same manner, with a breakout statement, and totals only in the financial statements. Sample lists of manufacturing or construction expenses, distribution and warehouse expenses, and selling expenses are shown in Table 8.1. Keep your financial spreadsheets as clean as possible—that is, avoid cluttering them with minute details that are better attached as a breakout statement.

Table 8.1   Sample Lists

Sample Manufacturing or Construction Expenses List

Manager's Salary	Paid Employees' Salaries
Payroll Taxes	Vehicle Lease and Maintenance
Related Travel	Packaging Costs
Supplies	Depreciation on Owned Equipment

Sample Distribution and Warehouse Expenses List

Manager's Salary	Employees' Salaries
Drivers' Salaries	Payroll Taxes
Vehicle Lease & Maintenance	Warehouse Loading Vehicles
Lease/Maintenance	Depreciation on Owned Equipment
Freight Expenses	Supplies

Sample List of Selling Expenses

Sales Manager's Salary	Inside Sales Salaries
Inside Sales Commissions	Telephone Sales Salaries
Telephone Sales Commissions	Field Sales Salaries
Field Sales Commissions	Payroll Taxes for Sales Employees
Sales Vehicles Lease & Maintenance	Sales-Related Travel
Advertising and Promotion	Depreciation on Owned Equipment

Sample List of General & Administrative Expenses

Advertising	Rent
Salaries & Wages	Utilities
Office Supplies	Insurance
Office Equipment	Business Taxes
Payroll Taxes	

Taxes

The last item to forecast is taxes. Though many businesses may be able to take advantage of a tax-loss carry-forward for losses during R&D, ultimately the business will have to account for state, federal, and possibly local taxes that are paid at varying times of the year. To calculate your business tax liability, you will need to do a **pro forma income statement**, a discussion of which follows.

Preparing the Pro Forma Income Statement

The income statement, also known as a profit and loss statement, gives information regarding the profit or loss status of the business for a specified period of time. It is normally calculated first so that income tax liability can be determined. The taxes owed on the basis of the profit made by the company appear on the cash flow statement (which will be calculated next) when they are paid. As income taxes vary from state to state, the financial statements presented here are not indicative of tax rates in every state. Figure 8.1 displays an example of an income statement for a corporation. Note that should the business be structured as a sole proprietorship, partnership, or in some cases limited liability company (LLC), the reference to taxes will be deleted, as taxes are at the personal tax rates of the owners. The legal form of organizations is discussed in Chapter 9.

The income statement should also contain footnotes for each item to refer the reader to supporting material in the "Notes to Financial Statements." Any unusual major expenses, such as the cost of participating in a trade show, should be footnoted separately and explained.

It is not uncommon for a new business to not show a profit in the first year. It is really a function of the type of business and the cost of start-up. Recall the no-profit strategy of Jeff Bezos with Amazon.com. (See Profile 8.1.) In particular, high technology and manufacturing start-ups are capital intensive and generally take longer to realize a profit than service businesses. In the hypothetical example of Mega Burrito (see Figure 8.1), the company projected ending the year with a cumulative net profit before taxes of $20,744. This represents its tax liability for the year. If a 40 percent tax rate, including federal and state income taxes, is used for illustration purposes, the company will owe approximately $8,297.60 in taxes for the year.

How Much Start-Up Money Is Needed?

Probably the key question to be answered when you're developing the financial plan for the new business is how much money will be needed to start the business and keep it operating until a positive cash flow is achieved. The first thing to understand is that the best estimates of the start-up total are just that—estimates. There is no way to guarantee that you have figured correctly. You can, however, achieve figures that will prevent the business from dying before it has a chance to succeed through the careful collection of information on both potential revenues and expenses.

This section starts with a summary of start-up costs, then moves to the pro forma cash flow statement. At that point there will be enough information, including the income statement information, to calculate the total start-up funds needed to keep the business running for a year.

Summary of Start-Up Costs

The bulk of expenses in the first year of a new business probably occur prior to the business's opening its doors for the first time. Purchasing furniture, equipment, start-up inventory, and supplies can quickly add up to a substantial amount. Add to that deposits for leases and utilities and you may have used up the first year's profits, assuming there would have been profits. See Figure 8.2 on page 145 for typical expenses to start up the business.

Mega Burrito — Income Statement, 1st Year

	Premise	Month 0	Month 1	Month 2	Month 3	Month 4	Month 5	Month 6	Month 7	Month 8	Month 9	Month 10	Month 11	Month 12	Total
Number of days open for business			17	30	31	30	31	31	28	31	30	31	30	31	351
Sales Forecast															
Food			10,816	20,533	22,712	23,425	19,723	25,700	24,563	30,482	32,101	24,804	19,666	20,321	274,846
Beverages			404	767	848	875	737	960	917	1,138	1,199	926	734	759	10,264
Total Sales Forecast			11,220	21,300	23,560	24,300	20,460	26,660	25,480	31,620	33,300	25,730	20,400	21,080	285,110
Variable Costs															
COGS	33% of sales		3,703	7,029	7,775	8,019	6,752	8,798	8,408	10,435	10,989	8,491	6,732	6,956	94,086
Labor Cost	2 employees in months 1, 2, 5, 11, 12; 3 employees in months 3, 4, and 6–10		4,960	4,800	7,440	7,200	4,960	7,440	6,720	7,440	7,200	7,440	4,800	4,960	75,360
Total Variable Cost			8,663	11,829	15,215	15,219	11,712	16,238	15,128	17,875	18,189	15,931	11,532	11,916	169,446
Fixed Cost															
Salaries — Principals	1,500 per month each		3,000	3,000	3,000	3,000	3,000	3,000	3,000	3,000	3,000	3,000	3,000	3,000	36,000
Gen. & Adm. Expenses			600	600	600	600	600	600	600	600	600	600	600	600	7,200
Building Rent	Per 1 year lease		1,800	1,800	1,800	1,800	1,800	1,800	1,800	1,800	1,800	1,800	1,800	1,800	21,600
Equipment			2,200	2,200	2,200	2,200	2,200	2,200	2,200	2,200	2,200	2,200	2,200	2,200	26,400
Advertising			1,200	1,200	1,200	1,200	1,200	1,200	1,200	1,200	1,200	1,200	1,200	1,200	14,400
Insurance			1,600	1,600	1,600	1,600	1,600	1,600	1,600	1,600	1,600	1,600	1,600	1,600	19,200
Utilities			510	510	510	510	510	510	510	510	510	510	510	510	6,120
Total Fixed Cost			7,910	7,910	7,910	7,910	7,910	7,910	7,910	7,910	7,910	7,910	7,910	7,910	94,920
Total Cost			16,573	19,739	23,125	23,129	19,622	24,148	23,038	25,785	26,099	23,841	19,442	19,826	264,366
Net Profit or (Loss)			(5,353)	1,561	435	1,171	838	2,512	2,442	5,835	7,201	1,889	958	1,254	20,744
Cumulative P&L		(5,353)	(5,353)	(3,792)	(3,356)	(2,185)	(1,347)	1,165	3,607	9,442	16,643	18,532	19,490	20,744	20,744

Figure 8.1
Mega Burrito*
Income Statement, 1st year

*All financial statements for this chapter come from a feasibility study prepared by Jason Hodder and Santiago Gonzalez as students in the Entrepreneur Program of the Marshall School of Business, University of Southern California, Fall Semester, 1997. Reprinted by permission.

Office lease—deposit				$ 2,000
Furniture and fixtures				25,000
Equipment (computer, plant equipment, etc.)				50,000
Business cards and brochures				2,500
Office supplies				1,000
Fees and licenses				500
Legal and accounting				2,000
Initial inventory				15,000
Employee training and wages				8,000
Pre–start-up marketing/promotion				10,000
Signage				1,000
Utility deposits and installation				3,000
				$120,000

**Figure 8.2
Summary of Typical
Start-Up Cost
Categories**

A manufacturing start-up might also include product development costs, a plant lease deposit, and raw materials costs. Start-ups with new products typically accrue heavy pre–start-up development costs that include engineering, prototyping, and patent work. These are one-time expenses to get the business started. For accounting purposes, some of these initial costs like equipment must be depreciated over a period of time on the income statement; others, such as organizational and formation expenses, must be amortized as start-up costs. For determining start-up funding requirements, however, these costs are treated as a lump sum. Your accountant can advise as to the correct disposition of all start-up costs when your business is in operation.

Forecasting Cash Flow

The **cash flow statement** is the most important financial statement to the entrepreneur because it depicts the cash position of the company at specified points of time and lets the entrepreneur know when the company is expected to generate a positive cash flow based on sales—in other words, the company's liquidity position. It is important to others (bankers and investors) because it reflects the company's ability to generate future positive cash flow, meet its obligations, and pay dividends (assuming a corporate structure).

To begin to forecast cash flow in an effort to determine how much start-up capital is needed, you must have a good estimate of potential sales. This is no easy task, as you learned in an earlier discussion. Certainly, the market research you conducted has given you a sense of the demand for your product or service. That research probably included discussions with suppliers, competitors, and customers as well as studying industry trends.

Figure 8.3 gives an example of a cash flow statement for Mega Burrito, which is a food service business that has inventory to sell and is structured as a corporation. As with all financial statements, each item on the statement should be footnoted in the "Notes to Financial Statements" to explain what the assumptions were and how the figures were derived.

The first section of the statement, cash inflows or receipts, records all the sources of cash that come into the business when they are received. This is an important point to remember about a cash flow statement: it records cash inflows and outflows when they occur. Therefore, if a sale is made in March, for example, but payment is not received until April, the sale is counted in April on the statement. This explains the differences in figures on the income statement and the cash flow statement.

The next section records operating cash outflows or disbursements. Notice that since this is a start-up venture, we have included a Month 0 to account for up-front expenses that occur before the business is in operation. Other expenses include such things as Cost of Goods Sold (COGS), general and administrative expenses, selling expenses, and other expenses of running the business. Recall that only the totals of G&A and selling expenses should be reported on the cash flow statement unless the list is quite short, as in the Mega Burrito example. Longer lists of expenses should be reported in a separate, detailed breakout statement prepared to present the individual expenditures.

The final section gives crucial information to the entrepreneur: the net change in cash flow—in other words, whether the business had a positive or a negative cash flow in that month. Note that in each month, the net cash flow reflects only the cash inflows and outflows for that month, assuming no start-up capital. With the net change computed for each month of Year One, it is now possible to calculate how much total cash is needed to start the business. There are several ways to do this. One simple approach is to use the ending balance for the year and add to that the start-up costs. This amount will take you to a positive cash flow. You can verify this by inserting the total capital requirements you have calculated in the spreadsheet and seeing the effect on cash flow.

Probably a better and more entrepreneurial way to estimate cash needs is to start by finding the highest negative cash balance on the cash flow statement. This amount ($35,276 in Figure 8.3 on the Cash Flow Statement) is the minimum amount it would take for you to feel confident that you could go forward with the venture. Looking at what comprises that figure gives us a way to, perhaps, leverage or manipulate the amount of cash required. Figure 8.4 on page 148 presents a breakout of the start-up capital requirements of $35,276.

Mega Burrito — Pro Forma Cash Flow Statement														
	Premise	Month 0	Month 1	Month 2	Month 3	Month 4	Month 5	Month 6	Month 7	Month 8	Month 9	Month 10	Month 11	Month 12	Total
Number of days open for business			17	30	31	30	31	31	28	31	30	31	30	31	351
Sales Forecast															
Food			10,816	20,533	22,712	23,425	19,723	25,700	24,563	30,482	32,101	24,804	19,666	20,321	274,846
Beverages			404	767	848	875	737	960	917	1,138	1,199	926	734	759	10,264
Total Sales Forecast			11,220	21,300	23,560	24,300	20,460	26,660	25,480	31,620	33,300	25,730	20,400	21,080	285,110
Cash Inflows	70% COD		7,854	14,910	16,492	17,010	14,322	18,662	17,836	22,134	23,310	18,011	14,280	14,756	
	30% collection of 7 days		1,980	6,285	6,963	7,185	6,453	7,578	7,539	9,255	9,801	8,307	6,435	6,324	
Total Cash Receipts			9,834	21,195	23,455	24,195	20,775	26,240	25,375	31,389	33,111	26,318	20,715	21,080	283,682
Cash Outflows															
Upfront Cash															
Deposit—Rent	1 month in advance	1,800													1,800
Equipment Down Pymt.		2,200													2,200
Permits		1,737													1,737
Property Improvement		15,000													15,000
Initial Supplies		1,200													1,200
Insurance Down Pymt.		1,600													
Computer		0													0
Advertising		2,000													2,000
Misc.		3,000													3,000
Total Upfront Cash		28,537													28,537
Variable Costs															
COGS	33% of Sales		3,703	7,029	7,775	8,019	6,752	8,798	8,408	10,435	10,989	8,491	6,732	6,956	94,086
Labor Cost	2 employees in months 1, 2, 5, 11, 12 3 employees in months 3, 4, and 6 – 10		4,960	4,800	7,440	7,200	4,960	7,440	6,720	7,440	7,200	7,440	4,800	4,960	75,360
Total Variable Costs			8,663	11,829	15,215	15,219	11,712	16,238	15,128	17,875	18,189	15,931	11,532	11,916	169,446
Fixed Cost															
Salaries — Principals	1,500 per month each		3,000	3,000	3,000	3,000	3,000	3,000	3,000	3,000	3,000	3,000	3,000	3,000	36,000
Gen. & Adm. Expenses			600	600	600	600	600	600	600	600	600	600	600	600	7,200
Building Rent	Per 1 year lease		1,800	1,800	1,800	1,800	1,800	1,800	1,800	1,800	1,800	1,800	1,800	1,800	21,600
Equipment			2,200	2,200	2,200	2,200	2,200	2,200	2,200	2,200	2,200	2,200	2,200	2,200	26,400
Advertising			1,200	1,200	1,200	1,200	1,200	1,200	1,200	1,200	1,200	1,200	1,200	1,200	14,400
Insurance			1,600	1,600	1,600	1,600	1,600	1,600	1,600	1,600	1,600	1,600	1,600	1,600	19,200
Utilities			510	510	510	510	510	510	510	510	510	510	510	510	6,120
Total Fixed Cost			7,910	7,910	7,910	7,910	7,910	7,910	7,910	7,910	7,910	7,910	7,910	7,910	94,920
Total Cash Expenditures			45,110	19,739	23,125	23,129	19,622	24,148	23,038	25,785	26,099	23,841	19,442	19,826	292,903
Net Cash In/Out per Month			(35,276)	1,456	330	1,066	1,153	2,092	2,337	5,604	7,012	2,477	1,273	1,254	(9,221)
Cash Balance—Beg. of Month		0	0	(35,276)	(33,820)	(33,489)	(32,423)	(31,270)	(29,178)	(26,841)	(21,237)	(14,225)	(11,748)	(10,475)	(9,221)
Cash Balance—End of Month		(28,537)	(35,276)	(33,820)	(33,489)	(32,423)	(31,270)	(29,178)	(26,841)	(21,237)	(14,225)	(11,748)	(10,475)	(9,221)	

Figure 8.3
Mega Burrito Pro Forma Cash Flow Statement

Notice that the total of these items is equal to the total capital requirements of $35,276. Working capital covers such things as accounts receivable, inventory, and materials and is the difference between the highest cash need from the cash flow statement and the sum of the up-front cash and start-up loss from Month One on the Income Statement. If Month One had shown a profit, you would have deducted that amount from the total requirements because you wouldn't have needed cash to cover that amount.

It's important to also calculate a **safety factor**. Remember, these capital requirements are estimates and minimums. Any unexpected deviation from them could cause real problems for the new business, so adding a cushion to at least make sure your fixed costs are covered is necessary. Since every industry is different and every business is different, deciding on a safety factor

Capital Cost					
Equipment	2,200				
Property Improvement	15,000				
		17,200			
Soft Cost					
Deposits	1,800				
Permits	1,737				
Insurance	1,600				
Advertising	2,000				
Misc.	3,000				
Initial Supplies	1,200				
		11,337			
Up-front Cash			28,537		
Start-up Loss			5,353		
Working Capital			1,386		
Total					$35,276

**Figure 8.4
Breakout of Start-Up
Capital
Requirements**

requires understanding the nature of the business. You might decide you need an additional amount to cover two months of fixed costs in case of changes in your estimates; if your business has significant seasonal fluctuations, you may need a greater amount. In any case, it's essential to look ahead and predict any possible deviations from your original estimates as carefully as you can.

From doing this cash needs assessment, you now know that you will need a minimum of $35,276 to start and operate this business until it generates a positive cash flow and makes a profit on its own. By breaking out this amount in hard, soft, and working capital categories, we may find ways to lower that amount, at least initially. For example, instead of investing $2,200 in cash up front for equipment, you may be able to lease the equipment, thereby reducing your initial cash outlay significantly. Your accounts receivable is determined by when you are able to collect on sales. If you're in a business where you can collect COD, your working capital needs will decline significantly. If, on the other hand, your customers typically pay in 60 days, you'll need working capital to cover your expenses during that period.

Use a spreadsheet program to set up the cash flow statement as well as the other financial statements. If you have set it up correctly with the appropriate formulas and links, when you make a change in one item, the computer will recalculate all the relevant figures to give you a new net cash flow figure. Because it is relatively easy to produce very detailed analyses, however, there is a tendency to overwhelm the potential reader with page after page of financial statements. This will hurt rather than help. Instead, be concise and to the point, and be sure to understand and document how figures were calculated so you can explain them if asked.

Break-Even Analysis

The **break-even analysis** is a useful tool the entrepreneur can use to calculate when the business will make a profit in terms of either units sold or total sales dollars. In order for a business to break even and begin to make a profit, it must be able to generate a volume of sales that will cover both fixed and variable costs of running the business.

Mathematically speaking, the break-even point is reached when total revenue (TR) equals total costs (TC). Total revenue is comprised of the quantity of units (Q) produced times the price (SP) per unit. Total costs are comprised of fixed costs (FC) plus variable costs (VC) per unit times the quantity of units (Q). Variable costs are associated with the production of the product— materials, selling expenses, direct labor, and so forth. Figure 8.5 displays a break-even analysis for Mega Burrito.

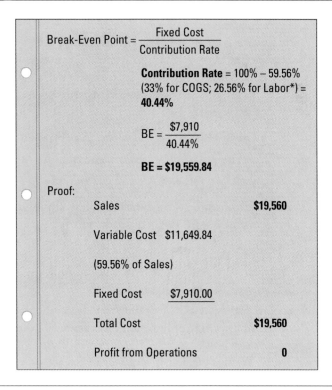

$$\text{Break-Even Point} = \frac{\text{Fixed Cost}}{\text{Contribution Rate}}$$

Contribution Rate = 100% − 59.56%
(33% for COGS; 26.56% for Labor*) =
40.44%

$$BE = \frac{\$7,910}{40.44\%}$$

BE = \$19,559.84

Proof:

Sales	\$19,560
Variable Cost \$11,649.84	
(59.56% of Sales)	
Fixed Cost \$7,910.00	
Total Cost	\$19,560
Profit from Operations	0

**Figure 8.5
Break-Even Analysis
for Mega Burrito**

* Mega Burrito is assuming that Labor is 26.56% of the gross sales. This number was derived by dividing the total labor for the first twelve months by the gross sales for the first twelve months. \$75,360 / \$283,682 = 26.56%. This number makes sense because it is very close to the industry average of 27.1% given by the National Restaurant Association.

We now know that once start-up costs have been covered, at sales of $19,560, we will break even and cover all the fixed costs.

Analyzing the financial risks and benefits of a new venture is a difficult and challenging exercise, but it must be done so that two fundamental questions can be answered:

1. Do the start-up capital requirements make sense? (In other words, is the business doable?)

2. If we look at the capital investment and the profit possibilities, is there enough money in this opportunity to make the effort worthwhile?

Unfortunately, many businesses are feasible—they can be made to work financially—but the return on the initial investment is so low that the entrepreneur would be better off putting that investment in the stock market. New businesses take an extraordinary amount of work, which entrepreneurs frequently fail to put a value on. All too often the business is running and making a profit, but the entrepreneur is making less than he or she would have made working for someone else. The feasibility stage, when the investment has been minimal, is the time to look seriously at the financial feasibility and potential of the venture to ascertain exactly what the risks and benefits are.

New Venture Checklist

Have you:

- ❏ Gathered the numbers you need for performing your financial analysis?

- ❏ Gathered sales forecast data through triangulation?

- ❏ Calculated an income statement for year 1?

- ❏ Created a cash flow statement for year 1?

- ❏ Performed a cash needs assessment to determine how much capital you'll need to start the business?

Issues to Consider

1. Why is the cash flow statement the most important statement for the entrepreneur?

2. What kinds of information must be collected to complete pro forma financial statements?

3. What is the best strategy for forecasting sales?

4. How is forecasting sales for consumer products different from forecasting sales for industrial products?

5. What are the three basic types of money found in the cash needs assessment?

Experiencing Entrepreneurship

1. Interview a banker and an accountant about the key financial statements that entrepreneurs need to understand to run their businesses. Ask about the biggest mistakes business owners make in preparing their financial statements. Compare and contrast the responses of the banker and the accountant.

2. Interview an entrepreneur to find out how he or she calculated how much money was needed to start the venture. Did it turn out to be enough? Why or why not? What would you have advised the entrepreneur?

Additional Sources of Information

Kolb, R.W., and R.J. Rodriguez. (1996). *Financial Management.* Second Edition. Cambridge, MA: Blackwell Publishers.

Financial record keeping for small stores. *SBA Small Business Management Series.* Stock No. 045-000-00142-3.

Frankston, F.M. (1981). "A Simplified Approach to Financial Planning." *Journal of Small Business Management,* January.

Stickney, C.P. (1997). *Financial Reporting and Statement Analysis: A Strategic Perspective.* New York: Dryden Press.

Internet Resources

AccountingNet
http://www.accountingnet.com
A general source of accounting information for business owners.

Browse the Federal Tax Code—Tax Regs in Plain English
http://www.irs.gov/tax_regs/
Here you can search for specific words and phrases.

Glossary of Insurance and Financial Planning Terms
http://www.ucalgary.ca/MG/inrm/glossary/index.htm
A handy site that is simple to use.

Internal Revenue Service—The Digital Daily
http://www.irs.ustreas.gov/prod/
This site is full of free information about the IRS and tax-related issues.

The World Bank
http://www.worldbank.org/
Offers the latest news from the World Bank, including research studies and publications.

Relevant Case Studies

1. Flight Time
2. Simtek, Inc.

9

It will not injure you to know enough of law to keep out of it.
The Old Farmer's Almanac (1851)

Analyzing Legal Risks and Benefits

Overview

▶ **The legal form of the new venture**

▶ **Sole proprietorship**

▶ **Partnership**

▶ **Corporation**

▶ **S-corporation**

▶ **Limited liability company**

▶ **The nonprofit corporation**

▶ **The legal environment of the Internet**

Terms to Know

Profile 9.1

Which Form Is Best?

Deciding on the best legal form for your business is no longer a simple task; yet many new business owners are making the decision without adequate expert advice. Mark Kalish is the co-owner and vice president of EnviroTech Coating Systems Inc. of Eau Claire, Wisconsin. His company paints products ranging from motorcycles to musical instruments, using an electrostatic process known as powder coating.

In trying to determine which legal form made sense, Kalish and his business partner John Berthold focused on three key issues: legal liability, tax ramifications, and cost of creation. Kalish and his partner didn't want and couldn't afford the personal liability for any potential losses or problems occurring from the operation of the business. This meant that they could not consider the sole proprietor and partnership forms, as both result in personal liability for the owners.

The next consideration was the ability to minimize tax liability. Corporations have more options in this regard but are subject to "double taxation"; that is, income is taxed at the corporate level and again when dividends are distributed. However, Kalish learned that his problem can often be solved with an S-corporation form. In addition, the losses that businesses typically face in the early years can be used to reduce their personal tax liability.

The next issue was the cost of formation and maintenance of the chosen form. Kalish learned about the high cost in time and money of recordkeeping and paperwork associated with a corporation, as well as the higher initial costs of incorporating.

His conclusion was that the sole proprietorship certainly was the best option, assuming that the business owner had a substantial umbrella insurance policy for protection against liability. Unfortunately, Kalish could not avail himself of that option, for several reasons. He had intentions of growing the business by issuing and selling additional shares of stock. The corporate form makes this relatively easy to do. He also wanted to ensure that the business survived his death, and the corporation would do that.

The decision about the legal form of the business should be made with careful consideration of the type of business you have and your personal goals for that business. Most important, get legal advice from a competent attorney before making the final decision.

SOURCE: Lin Grensing-Pophal, "Choose Your Vehicle." *Business Start-Ups Online, Entrepreneur Magazine Online* (http://www.EntrepreneurMag.com/), December 1996.

Should Kalish have considered the limited liability company form? What advantages might he have gained from that?

O nce you know you have a feasible business, it's time to focus on how to create a company that will implement that business concept. As with all other aspects of business, there are risks and benefits associated with the legal form of business you ultimately choose, so understanding them all is critical to making an informed decision. This chapter will look at the major forms of organization as well as at some legal issues related to putting your business in the environment of the Internet.

The Legal Form of the New Venture

All businesses operate under one of four broad legal structures—sole proprietorship, partnership, limited liability company, or corporation—with variations on each. The legal structure of a new venture has both legal and tax ramifications for the entrepreneur and any investors; consequently, entrepreneurs must carefully consider the advantages and disadvantages of each form. Also, since businesses change over time, it's quite possible a business might change its legal form sometime during its lifetime, usually for financial, tax, or liability reasons. These situations will be discussed as each legal form is considered. A summary comparison chart on legal forms is found in Table 9.1.

Table 9.1   Comparative Forms of Legal Ownership

Issues	Sole Proprietorship	Partnership	Limited Liability Company	C-Corporation
Number of owners	One	No limit	No limit	No limit on shareholders
Start-Up Costs	Filing fees for DBA and business license	Filing fees for DBA Attorney fees for partnership agreement	Attorney fees for organization, documents, filing fees	Attorney fees for incorporation documents, filing fees
Liability	Owner liable for all claims against business	General partners liable for all claims Limited partners only to amount of investment	Members liable as in partnerships	Shareholders liable to amount invested Officers may be personally liable
Life of Business	Dissolution on the death of the owner	Dissolution on the death or separation of a partner unless otherwise specified in the agreement Not so in the case of limiteds	Continuity of life	No effect
Transfer of Interest	Owner free to sell	General partner requires consent of other generals to sell interest Limiteds' ability subject to agreement	Free transferability of interests	Shareholders free to sell unless restricted by agreement
Distribution of Profits	Profits go to owner	Profits shared based on partnership agreement	Profits shared based on member agreement	Paid to shareholders as dividends according to agreement and shareholder status
Management Control	Owner has full control	Shared by general partners according to partnership agreement	Rests with management committee	Rests with the board of directors appointed by the shareholders

Before examining the various legal forms, consider the following questions related to you as the entrepreneur, since they affect your ability to select certain legal structures:

1. Do you have all the skills needed to run this venture?

2. Do you have the capital required to start the business alone or can you raise it through cash or credit?

3. Will you be able to run the business and cover your living expenses for the first year?

4. Are you willing and able to assume personal liability for any claims against your business?

5. Do you wish to have complete control over the operation of the business?

If you answered "yes" to all these questions, you may be able to use the sole proprietor form of organization for the new venture.

Sole Proprietorship

Nearly 76 percent of all businesses in the United States are **sole proprietorships,** most probably because it is the easiest form to create. In a sole proprietorship, the owner is the only person responsible for the activities of the business. Likewise, the owner is the only one to enjoy the profits and suffer the losses.

To operate as a sole proprietor requires nothing more than a **DBA** if the entrepreneur does not use his or her name as the name for the business. A DBA is a "Certificate of Doing Business Under An Assumed Name" and can be obtained by filing an application with the appropriate local government agency. The certificate, sometimes referred to as a "fictitious business name statement," ensures that yours is the only business in the area (usually a county) using the name you have chosen and provides a public record of business ownership for liability purposes. For example, Anthony Jackson and Associates does not require a DBA if the entrepreneur's name is Anthony Jackson, but Corporate Consultants does.

Advantages of the Sole Proprietorship Form

Sole proprietorships have several advantages.

▶ They are easy and inexpensive to create.

▶ They give the owner complete authority.

▶ The income from the business is taxed only once, at the owner's personal income tax rate.

Disadvantages of the Sole Proprietorship Form

There are, however, some distinct disadvantages that deserve serious consideration.

▶ The sole proprietor has unlimited liability for all claims against the business; that is, any debts incurred must be paid from the owner's assets. Therefore, the sole proprietor puts at risk his or her home, bank accounts, and any other assets. In the current litigious environment, exposure to lawsuits is substantial. To help mitigate this liability, a sole proprietor should obtain business liability insurance, including errors and omissions coverage.

Sole Proprietors and the Hobby Rule

Sole proprietors come under the **Hobby Rule** of the Internal Revenue Code, which says that if a company makes no profit in three out of five years, it can be judged to be a hobby rather than a going concern. The result will be that it will not be able to deduct losses from gross income to reduce its taxable income. One way to avoid scrutiny under this rule is to conduct your business in a businesslike manner; that is, keeping personal and business accounts completely separate, and maintaining formal accounting records.

▶ It is more difficult to raise debt capital because the owner's financial statement alone often may not qualify for the amount needed.

▶ The sole proprietor usually relies on his or her skills alone to manage the business. Of course, employees with specific skills can be hired to complement the skills of the owner.

▶ The business's ability to survive is dependent on the owner, and therefore, the death or incapacitation of the owner can be catastrophic for the business.

Often small businesses such as shoe repair shops and boutiques are run as sole proprietorships. This is not to say that a high-growth venture cannot be started as a sole proprietorship—many are; it just will in all likelihood not remain a sole proprietorship for long, as the entrepreneur will typically want the protections and prestige a corporation affords. If you know your business will need to take a corporate form, it's probably better to start that way because your recordkeeping will be more consistent, and you'll probably get more respect in the industry.

Partnership

When two or more people share the assets, liabilities, and profits of a business, the legal structure is termed a **partnership**. The partnership form is an improvement over the sole proprietorship from the standpoint that the business can draw on the skills, knowledge, and financial resources of more than one person. This is an advantage not only in operating the business, but in seeking bank loans and the like. Like the sole proprietorship, however, the partnership requires a DBA when the last names of the partners are not used in naming the business. Professionals like lawyers, doctors, and accountants frequently employ this legal structure.

A partnership is essentially a sole proprietorship involving more than one person in terms of its advantages and its treatment of income, expenses, and taxes. However, where liability is concerned, there is a significant difference. In a partnership, each partner is liable for the obligations another partner incurs in the course of doing business. For example, if one partner signs a contract with a supplier in the name of the partnership, the other partners are also bound by the terms of the contract. However, creditors of an individual partner can attach only the assets of that individual partner, including his or her interest in the partnership.

Partners also have specific property rights. For example, each partner owns and has use of the property acquired by the partnership unless otherwise stated in the Partnership Agreement. Each partner has a right to share in the profits and losses, and each may participate in the management of the partnership. Furthermore, all elections such as depreciation and accounting methods are made at the partnership level and apply to all partners.

Partnership Agreement

Though the law does not require it, it is extremely wise for a partnership to draw up a written partnership agreement, based on the Uniform Partnership Act, that spells out business responsibilities, profit sharing, and transfer of interest. This is because partnerships are inherently fraught with problems that arise from the different personalities and goals of the people involved. A written document executed at the beginning of the partnership will reduce the eventual disagreements and provide for an orderly dissolution should

 Structuring an Effective Partnership Agreement

An effective partnership agreement, formal or informal, between individuals or companies, should address several critical issues.

▶ The legal name of the partnership

▶ The nature of the business

▶ The duration of the partnership

▶ Contributions of the partners

▶ Sales, loans, and leases to the partnership

▶ Withdrawals and salaries

▶ Responsibility and authority of the partners

▶ Dissolution of the partnership

▶ Arbitration

Remember that in the absence of a partnership agreement, all partners are considered equal. In any case, an attorney should oversee the development of the partnership agreement.

irreconcilable differences arise. Partnerships are burdened by the same disadvantages as sole proprietorships, with the additional encumbrance of personal conflicts, usually over power and authority, which can result in the dissolution of the partnership. Many partnerships have solved much of this problem by assigning specific responsibilities to each of the partners in the Partnership Agreement.

Types of Partnerships

There are two types of partnerships: general and limited. In a general partnership, all the partners assume unlimited personal liability and responsibility for the management of the business. In a limited partnership, by contrast, the general partners seek investors whose liability is limited to their monetary investment; that is, if a limited partner invests $25,000 in the business, the most he or she can lose if the business fails is $25,000. It is important to note, however, that limited partners have no say in the management of the business. In fact, they are restricted by law from imposing their will on the business. The penalty for participating in the management of the business is the loss of their limited liability status.

Protective Measures in Partnerships

Issues arise when one or more of the partners in a partnership leave, either voluntarily or through death. To protect the remaining partners, the partnership should have in place a buy/sell agreement and key person life insurance.

A buy/sell agreement spells out how the value of the departing partner's interest will be calculated and purchased by the partnership. Having this in place from the beginning prevents disagreements and legal battles with the departing partner or with the estate of a deceased partner.

Key person life insurance is a policy on the life of principal members of the partnership, usually the senior partners. Upon the death of a partner, the insurance proceeds can be used to keep the business going or to buy out the deceased partner's interest under a buy/sell agreement.

Corporation

Only about 17 percent of all businesses are **corporations,** but they account for 87 percent of all sales. A corporation is different from the preceding two forms in that it is a legal entity in and of itself. The U.S. Supreme Court has defined the corporation as "an artificial being, invisible, intangible, and existing only in contemplation of the law." It is chartered or registered by a state and can survive the death or separation of the owner(s) from the business. Therefore, it can sue, be sued, acquire and sell real property, and lend money. The owners of the corporation are its stockholders who invest capital in the corporation in exchange for shares of ownership. Like limited partners, stockholders are not liable for the debts of the corporation and can lose only the money they have invested.

Most businesses form what is known as a **closely held corporation**; that is, the corporate stock is owned privately by a few individuals and is not traded publicly on a securities exchange such as the New York Stock Exchange. This chapter will focus on private corporations. The issue of "going public" typically arises after the business is established and desires to raise substantial capital for growth by issuing stock through an **initial public offering** (IPO). The IPO and public corporations in general are the subject of Chapter 15.

A corporation is created by filing a certificate of incorporation with the state in which the company will do business and issue stock. This is called a **domestic corporation**. A **foreign corporation**, by contrast, is one that is chartered in a state other than in the one in which it will do business. It also requires the establishment of a board of directors, which meets periodically to make strategic policy decisions for the business. The regular documentation of these meetings is crucial to maintaining the corporation's limited liability status. The board also hires the officers who will run the business on a day-to-day basis.

C-Corporation

The C-corporate form is the most common and has several important advantages. It enjoys limited liability in that its owners are liable for its debts and obligations only to the limit of their investment. The only exception to this protection is payroll taxes that may have been withheld from employees' paychecks but not paid to the Internal Revenue Service. Capital can be raised through the sale of stock up to the amount authorized in the corporate charter; however, the sale of stock is heavily regulated by federal and state governments. A corporation can create different classes of stock to meet the various needs of its investors. For example, it may issue **non-voting preferred stock** to conservative investors who, in the event the corporation must liquidate its assets, will be first in line to recoup their investment. **Common stock** is more risky because holders of it are paid only after the preferred stockholders. Common stockholders are entitled to vote at stockholders' meetings and divide the profits remaining after the preferred holders are paid their dividends, assuming that these profits are not retained by the corporation to fund growth.

Ownership is easily transferred. This is at once an advantage and a disadvantage, as the entrepreneur will want to be careful, particularly in the start-up phase, that stock does not land in the hands of undesirable parties such as competitors. This problem is normally handled through a buy-sell clause in the stockholders' agreement that states that stock must first be offered to the corporation at a specified price before being offered to someone outside the corporation.

Because it is a legal entity, the corporation can enter into contracts, sue, and be sued without the signature of the owners. In a start-up or young company, bankers, creditors, and such will likely require that majority stockholders or officers personally guarantee loans. This is because often a new corporation will be wholly owned by the entrepreneur; that is, the entrepreneur or the founding team holds all the issued stock. As the company does not have a track record and is in a high-risk phase of development, creditors protect themselves against the potential failure of the corporation by requiring the signatures, thus giving them the ability to pursue the assets of the owners.

Corporations often enjoy more status and deference than do other legal forms, principally because they are a legal entity that cannot be destroyed by the death of one or all of the principal shareholders. Moreover, to enter the public equity markets, a business must be incorporated. Also, the perception is that corporations probably keep better records than do other forms of ownership because corporations tend to be under greater scrutiny from governmental agencies. The reason for this scrutiny is the fact that the assets of the corporation are separate from the assets of the individual owner/shareholders.

Corporations can take advantage of the benefits of retirement funds, Keogh and defined-contribution plans, profit sharing, and stock option plans. These fringe benefits are deductible to the corporation as an expense and not taxable to the employee.

Finally, the entrepreneur can hold certain assets such as real estate in his or her own name and lease the use of the assets to the corporation.

Risks and Disadvantages of Corporations

Corporations do, however, have disadvantages that must be carefully considered. They are certainly more complex, subject to more governmental regulation, and cost more to create. While it is possible to incorporate without the aid of an attorney, it is not recommended. Too many cases can be cited of businesses that ultimately failed or endured significant financial hardship because they did not incorporate properly at the start of the business.

A more cumbersome disadvantage derives from the fact that the corporation is literally a person for tax purposes. Consequently, if it makes a profit, it must pay a tax whether or not those profits were distributed as dividends to the stockholders. And unlike the partnership or sole proprietorship, stockholders of C-corporations do not receive the benefit of losses (the S-corporation does enjoy these benefits and will be discussed in the next section). In a C-corporation those losses, if they can't be applied in the year they are incurred, must be saved to be applied against future profits. Accordingly, C-corporations pay taxes on the profits they earn, and their owners (stockholders) pay taxes on the dividends they receive; hence, the drawback of "double taxation." It is principally for this reason that many entrepreneurs who operate alone or with a partner do not employ this form. However, if the entrepreneur draws a salary from the corporation, that salary is expensed by the corporation, effectively reducing its net income subject to taxes, and is taxed instead only at the entrepreneur's personal income tax rate.

By creating a corporation and issuing stock, the entrepreneur is giving up a measure of control to the board of directors. Many an entrepreneur has found himself or herself "out of a job" because he or she did not retain sufficient stock to prevent this type of occurrence. It is not always necessary, however, that the entrepreneur retain 51 percent of the stock to maintain control. As long as the entrepreneur's skills and vision are vital to the success of the venture, and as long as most of the shareholders share that vision, the entrepreneur will have effective control of the organization, no matter how much stock has been given up. Nevertheless, with a corporate form, unlike the sole proprietorship or partnership, the entrepreneur is accountable principally to the stockholders and secondarily to anyone else. In reality, however, if the corporation is privately held, the board usually serves at the pleasure of the entrepreneur, who is accountable to himself or herself and any investors.

A corporation must endeavor in all ways to act as an entity separate from its owners. It must keep personal finances completely separate from corporate finances, hold directors' meetings, maintain minutes, and not take on any financial liability without sufficient resources to back it up. Failing to do any of these things can result in what is known as "piercing the corporate veil," which leaves the officers and owners open to personal liability.

Where to Incorporate

Apart from legal considerations, where to incorporate is also an important issue. It is normally advantageous to incorporate in the state in which the entrepreneur intends to locate the business, so that it is not under the regulatory powers of two states (the state in which it is incorporated and the state in which it must file an application to do business as an out-of-state corporation).

Normally, however, a corporation will not have to qualify as a "foreign" corporation doing business in another state if it is simply holding directors'/shareholders' meetings in the state, or holding bank accounts, using independent contractors, or marketing to potential customers whose transactions will be completed in the corporation's home state. It has often been said that you should incorporate in Delaware because it has laws favorable toward corporations. If you don't intend to do a substantial amount of business in Delaware, however, the cost and hassle of qualifying in another state may overcome the benefit of a Delaware incorporation. The entrepreneur should also consider the favorableness of the laws governing corporations in the state chosen. Some states, like California, have a required, minimum annual corporate income tax, whether or not the business has a taxable income.

S-Corporation

An **S-corporation**, unlike the C-corporation, is not a tax-paying entity. It is merely a financial vehicle that passes the profits and losses of the corporation to the stockholders. It is treated much like the sole proprietorship and the partnership in the sense that if the business earns a profit, that profit becomes the income of the owners/stockholders, and it is the owners who pay the tax on that profit at their individual tax rates.

The rules for election of the S-corporation option are very specific.

Incorporation Checklist

1. Determine in which state to incorporate.

2. Select the name of the corporation.

3. Find a registered agent who will receive legal service for the business in another state, if necessary.

4. Fill out a certificate of incorporation and file with the Secretary of State with filing fees.

5. Hold a meeting to elect directors and transact necessary business.

6. During the first organizational meeting of the board of directors, select the corporate seal and stock certificates, issue shares, elect corporate officers (Chief Executive Officer, President, etc., as necessary).

7. Open bank accounts and apply for an Employer Identification Number.

8. Choose the corporation's fiscal year.

9. If necessary, file a DBA certificate.

10. Fill out applications to do business in other states if necessary.

11. Apply for required state and local licenses or permits.

12. If appropriate, elect an S-corporation status.

▶ The business must first be incorporated.

▶ It can have no more than 75 stockholders.

▶ Shareholders must be U.S. citizens or residents (partnerships and corporations cannot be shareholders). It is important that the shareholder agreement protect shareholders against termination of the S-corporation election through transference of shares to an unqualified person or entity.

▶ It can have only one class of stock issued and outstanding; that is, either preferred or common.

▶ No more than 25 percent of the corporate income can be derived from passive investments, such as dividends, rent, and capital gains.

The S-corporation cannot be a financial institution, a foreign corporation, or a subsidiary of a parent corporation.

It is always wise to check with an attorney to make certain the election of S-corporation status is valid. If a C-corporation elects to become an S-corporation and then reverts back to C-corporation status, it cannot re-elect S-corporation status for five years.

The S-corporation is different from the C-corporation in several ways.

▶ The entrepreneur is taxed on corporate earnings whether they are distributed as dividends or retained in the corporation.

▶ Any losses incurred by the S-corporation can be used as a deduction on the entrepreneur's personal income tax up to the amount invested in the corporation. If there is more than one shareholder, the loss is shared according to the percentage of ownership.

▶ If the entrepreneur sells the assets of the business, the shareholder pays a tax on the amount of appreciation. With a C-corporation, the gain is taxable to the corporation, and the balance paid to the stockholder is also taxed.

Risks and Benefits

The businesses that benefit most from an S-corporation structure are those that don't have a need to retain earnings. In an S-corporation, if the entrepreneur decides to retain, say, $100,000 of profit to invest in new equipment, the stockholders must still pay taxes on that profit as if it had been distributed. Furthermore, while most deductions and expenses are allowed, S-corporations cannot take advantage of deductions based on medical reimbursements or health insurance plans. Another consideration is that unless the business has regular positive cash flow, it could face a situation where the business makes a profit that is passed through to the owners to be taxed at their personal rate, but generates insufficient cash to pay those taxes.

The S-corporation was a valuable financial tool under the 1986 Tax Reform Act because personal tax rates were significantly lower than corporate rates. However, there is some question about the tax advantages under the 1993 Tax Code and beyond, as top personal rates have increased and surcharges have been imposed, so a C-corporation might be preferable at higher profit levels. For some small businesses, however, the S-corporation may still be less costly in the long run because it avoids double taxation of income. A good tax attorney or CPA should advise the entrepreneur on the best course of action.

Ventures that typically benefit from election of the S-corporation status include service businesses with low capital asset requirements, real estate investment firms during times when property values are increasing, and start-ups that are projecting a loss in the early years. Entrepreneurs should probably not elect the S-corporation option if they want to retain earnings for expansion or diversification, or if there are significant passive losses from investments such as real estate.

Limited Liability Company

A new corporate form has recently emerged and is now available in most states. It is known as a **Limited Liability Company** (LLC) and like the S-corporation, enjoys the pass-through tax benefits of partnerships in addition to the limited liability of a C-corporation. It is, however, far more flexible in its treatment of certain ownership issues, income tax, and in its implementation. Only privately held companies can become LLCs, and they must be formed in accordance with very strict guidelines.

The owners of an LLC are called "members" and their interests are known as "interests." An LLC will have two or more members and is formed via filing articles of organization, which resemble a limited partnership agreement. The management of the company can be undertaken by the members or by people they have elected to manage it. Managers, officers, and members are not personally liable for the company's debts or liabilities except as they have personally guaranteed these debts or liabilities. The members create an "operating agreement," which is very similar to a partnership agreement that spells out rights and obligations of the members.

Risks and Benefits

Most LLCs will be organized for tax purposes like partnerships, so that income tax benefits and liabilities will pass through to the members. In New York and California, however, the LLCs will also be subject to state franchise taxes or fees. A rule, as of January 1997, under the Internal Revenue Code now allows LLCs to maintain all four characteristics of a corporation—limited liability, continuity of life, centralized management, and free transferability of interests—and still be treated as a partner for tax purposes without fear of being reclassified as a corporation. This enhances the attractiveness of the LLC, already the fastest growing legal form. The 1997 rule makes it possible for sole proprietors to operate as single-member LLCs, giving them a liability shield they have never had before.

The LLC is most often compared to the limited partnership and the S-corporation. However, there are differences. In a limited partnership, one or more people (the general partners) agree to assume personal liability for the actions of the partnership; this is not the case with an LLC. Unlike a limited partnership, in an LLC a member does not have to forfeit the right to participate in the management of the organization in order to retain his or her limited liability status.

In an LLC, unlike in an S-corporation, there are no limitations on the number of members or on their status. LLCs permit corporations, pension plans, and nonresident aliens. Also, while S-corporations can't own 80 percent or more of the stock of another corporation, an LLC may actually possess wholly owned subsidiary corporations. LLCs are not limited to one class of stock, and in some ways they receive more favorable tax treatment. For example, unlike an S-corporation shareholder, the LLC member can deduct losses in amounts that reflect the member's allocable share of the debt of the company.

If at a later date the entrepreneur decides to go public, the LLC can become a C-corporation by transferring the LLC assets to the new corporation. It is, however, a bit more difficult to go the other way, as you must pay capital gains tax on the appreciation.

LLCs are also becoming a popular vehicle for companies that may have global investors, as the S-corporation does not permit foreign ownership. As this is still a fairly new legal structure, an attorney should be consulted to find out if this form is available in the entrepreneur's state. The attorney can help the entrepreneur understand and abide by the requirements associated with it.

The Nonprofit Corporation

It is not outside the realm of possibility for a nonprofit corporation to be a high-growth, world-class company; however, it is not generally started with that goal in mind. A nonprofit corporation is a corporation established for charitable, public (i.e., scientific, literary, or educational), religious, or mutual benefit (i.e., trade associations, tennis clubs) purposes as recognized by federal and state laws. Like the C-corporation, the nonprofit corporation is a legal entity and offers its shareholders and officers the benefit of limited liability. There is a common misconception that nonprofit corporations are not allowed to make a profit. As long as the business is not set up to benefit a single person and is organized for a nonprofit purpose, it can make a profit on which it is not taxed if it has also met the IRS test for a tax-exempt status. However, income derived from for-profit activities is subject to income tax.

There are two distinct hurdles that nonprofit corporations must overcome if they want to operate as a nonprofit corporation and have tax-exempt status:

1. Meeting the state requirements for being designated a nonprofit corporation that can operate as such in a given state, and

2. Meeting the federal and state requirements for exemption from paying taxes **(IRS 501(c)(3))** by forming a corporation that falls within the IRS's narrowly defined categories.

In forming the nonprofit corporation, the entrepreneur gives up proprietary interest in the corporation and dedicates all the assets and resources of the corporation to tax-exempt activities. If a nonprofit corporation is ever dissolved, its assets must be distributed to another tax-exempt organization.

Choosing the legal structure of the new venture is one of the most important decisions an entrepreneur can make, for it affects the tax strategy of the company for years to come. The correct selection depends on the type of venture the entrepreneur is starting, the profits the venture generates, the personal tax bracket of the entrepreneur, the assets used by the business, its potential for growth, and state incorporation laws. Again, particularly in the case of incorporation, it is important that an attorney review the documents to ensure that the entrepreneur has followed the rules and will receive all of the benefits to which the business is entitled.

The Legal Environment of the Internet

Internet law is one of the newest frontiers of the legal field. With more and more companies conducting business over the Internet, lawyers are finding that the "the rules that govern conventional situations are sometimes difficult to apply in cyberspace."[1] It is these situations where technology has created issues that have never been addressed in a court of law or by the legislature that put companies operating on the Internet on very slippery ground. Two such issues will be examined in this section: copyright infringement and contract issues.

Copyright Infringement

Downloading and uploading copyrighted materials is one of the most common activities on the Internet. Soon it will be possible to download and upload digital copies of music CDs and motion pictures as well. The growing concern by producers of these artistic works is the ability of infringers to use them without permission. It is the relative anonymity of the Internet that makes it easy for infringers to succeed in their efforts.[2] The current copyright law was discussed in an earlier section of this chapter. The question with regard to the Internet is whether or not a **BBS** (bulletin board system) operator can be held liable for violating copyright laws when users of the BBS download copyrighted materials.* The precedent-setting case discussed in the footnote *(Sega v. MAPHIA)* holds BBS operators directly liable for reproducing video games without authorization. The law is still forming on this issue; but clearly, BBS operators should be aware that the potential is great that they will be held liable if infringement is occurring on their system, with or without their knowledge.

Electronic Contracts

Many business people are unaware that legal contracts under the UCC can be formed without paper and signatures or human interaction of any kind.[3] These situations can occur when a user purchases something from a company on the Internet. The very act of agreeing to buy something and giving the information online can create a contractual situation. Those studying this area of the law believe that any symbol contained in the computer message that is put there to

---

*The case that currently establishes precedent for holding BBS operators directly liable for unauthorized reproduction is *Sega Enterprises Inc. v. MAPHIA 857 F. Supp. 679 (N.D. Cal. 1994)*. In this case the MAPHIA BBS encouraged users to upload unauthorized copies of Sega video games which MAPHIA would then charge other users to download, clearly aiding and abetting its users in infringing on the copyright.

Another case, *Religious Technology Center v. Netcom Inc., 1995 U.S. Dist. LEXIS 18173 (N.D. Cal. 1995)*, found that there is no liability for direct infringement under certain circumstances; that is, when the BBS *automatically* stores materials for a brief time and then retransmits them. This is not considered making unauthorized copies. This situation occurs when a user uploads copyrighted material to the BBS, which happens to be connected to a Usenet system, and the BBS transmits the materials to other Usenet groups. However, yet another case, *Playboy v. Frena*, held a BBS liable for directly infringing on *Playboy*'s right to distribute photographs. Apparently, Playboy photographs were being uploaded and downloaded on the defendant's BBS without his knowledge. The court held, "It does not matter that Defendant Frena may have been unaware of the copyright infringement. Intent to infringe is not needed to find copyright infringement." Intent or knowledge is not an element of infringement, and thus even an innocent infringer is liable for infringement.

authenticate the message and indicate assent should satisfy the signature requirement.[4] Previously, letterheads and telegrams have been accepted as signatures. For a symbol to satisfy the **Statute of Frauds** concerning computer messages, the contract should be sent using reasonably secure methods that document a forensic trail back to the signer.[5] It is recommended that businesses that deal in electronic commerce use the model agreement of the American Bar Association, whose contract contains clauses that address these issues and requires computer messages to state their legal intent and whether the message is binding without formal acceptance (i.e., purchase orders).

Companies doing business on the Internet need to be mindful of the rapidly changing environment of Internet law. As more and more attorneys become familiar with the Internet, it will be easier for growing companies to obtain the advice they need.

Understanding the laws related to starting and growing a business is paramount to avoiding issues and mistakes that could not only be costly in terms of time and money, but could even result in business failure.

New Venture Checklist

Have you:

❏ **Decided on the legal form that will best suit your business?**

❏ **Completed the necessary agreements for the legal form you have chosen (partnership agreement, articles of incorporation, and so forth)?**

❏ **Met the test for tax exemptions under IRC 501(c)(3) if you own a nonprofit corporation?**

❏ **Checked with an attorney conversant in Internet law if you intend to do business on the Internet?**

Issues to Consider

1. Assuming you were running a successful business as a sole proprietorship, what would induce you to change the legal form to a corporation?
2. Compare the pros and cons of a partnership versus an LLC.
3. Can your company make a profit as a nonprofit corporation? Why? or why not?
4. What two key issues regarding electronic contracts should you be aware of?

Experiencing Entrepreneurship

1. Interview an attorney about the various forms of legal ownership. Using a business that you might want to start, get his or her advice about the best form to use for your type of business.

2. Visit an entrepreneur whose business is set up as a partnership. What kind of experience has it been for the entrepreneur? How have they divided up the duties and responsibilities? What key issues have they covered in their partnership agreement?

Additional Sources of Information

Corporate Agents, Inc. (1995). *The Essential Limited Liability Company Handbook.* Grants Pass, OR: The Oasis Press.

Friedman, R. (1993). *The Complete Small Business Legal Guide.* Chicago: Dearborn Enterprises.

Hedglon, M. (1992). *How to Get the Best Legal Help for Your Business (at the Lowest Possible Cost).* New York: McGraw-Hill.

Jennings, M.M. (1994). *Business: Its Legal, Ethical, and Global Environment.* (Wadsworth Series in Business Law). Belmont, CA: Wadsworth Publishing.

Kurz, R.A., B.G. Newland, S. Lieberman, and C. Jimenez. (1996). *Internet and the Law: Legal Fundamentals for the Internet User.* Government Institutes, ASIN: 0865875065.

Nicholas, T. (1993). *The Complete Guide to "S" Corporations.* Chicago: Dearborn Publishing Group, Inc.

Internet Resources

Advertising Law Internet Site
http://www.webcom.com/~lewrose/home.html
This site is maintained by a law firm and contains information about advertising law, choosing a name for your business, and business opportunities.

Small Business Law Center
http://www.courttv.com/legalhelp/
This site is sponsored by CourtTV and has links to legal resources for entrepreneurs.

Relevant Case Studies

1. Toy Tips, Inc.
2. Flight Time
3. Autopsies-to-Go

New Venture Processes

169

10

Until someone has a small business, they have no comprehension of how hard it is. People who start businesses from scratch, if they survive, are the toughest people on the face of the earth.
Sue Szymczak
Safeway Sling

New Venture Processes

Overview

▶ **The virtual enterprise**

▶ **The business site**

▶ **The business process**

Terms to Know

Profile 10.1

idealab!: Spinning Off New Technology Ventures

Bill Gross, the brains behind the educational software company Knowledge Adventure, is a fountain of ideas that he regularly dispenses to his employees and anyone else who'll listen. This is his core competency. He's admired as a "mad genius" by people such as Steven Spielberg who, along with others like Michael Douglas and Ben Rosen, backed him financially on a new company—idealab!—designed to fit Gross's style of creativity and to serve as an incubator for Internet-based start-up companies. idealab! is literally a start-up factory.

idealab! was born in March of 1996. Since that time, it has given birth to 19 independent companies, and it employs about 400 people. Since creativity is what matters above all else to Gross, he wanted to make sure his fledgling entrepreneurs didn't get bogged down in the operations of the business. So he provided what he calls an "Internet start-up in a box," essentially a boilerplate company structure that includes such things as stock options, benefits, and a system for using open-book management. In addition to start-up capital for an equity stake in the company, idealab! even provides each new company with a temporary CEO.

Gross firmly believes that the Internet world is not so much about money as it is about creativity, execution, and speed. To execute his plan, Gross imports CEO-caliber executives and hands them an idea. Then his staff of 15 begin to work with the new CEO to develop a business around the idea. He follows this with seed money of up to $250,000. He is betting on getting a couple of strong IPOs from his portfolio of new ventures that will fund idealab! into the future.

The key to success, Gross believes, is freeing the entrepreneur from management duties to focus on ideas because today intelligence and speed are more important than money. You can always find more money, but you cannot find more time. The virtual operations he creates support a team of creative talent that can execute a plan without making mistakes, and because the environment of idealab! fosters shared knowledge among the companies, they are better able to avoid the operational mistakes that start-up entrepreneurs typically make.

SOURCES: Useem, Jerryl, "The Start-up Factory," *Inc.* February 1997, p. 40; idealab! (http://www.idealab.com); Michael Krantz, "Million Dollar Brain," *Time,* September 23, 1996; Eric Matson, "He Turns Ideas into Companies–at Net Speed," *Fast Company,* January 6, 1997.

What is the philosophy behind the process strategy at idealab!?

If you have concluded that there is a need or market for the new business concept and that the concept makes financial sense, the test of feasibility has been passed, at least to the degree that you feel comfortable going forward with the venture idea and developing a full-blown business plan. Recall that the business plan is about the creation of a company: the infrastructure, processes, and systems by which you will take your business from idea to reality. Now it becomes important to consider how to operate the business effectively and profitably.

Doing this section of the business plan will also force you to consider seriously how the business will work. It's one thing to come up with a great idea that people love. It's quite another to turn that idea into an operating business. Bill Gross knew that when he founded idealab!, the incubator for start-up Internet companies (see Profile 10.1). To ensure successful execution of ideas, he put systems and infrastructure in place.

This chapter will look at the processes involved in both product and service companies, ways for entrepreneurs to develop their operations with limited resources, and what to consider when choosing a site for your business. This chapter will also look at the specific process needs of retail/wholesale and service businesses. Chapter 11 will examine the unique requirements of manufacturing ventures.

The Virtual Enterprise

When entrepreneurs contemplate starting businesses, perhaps they picture a traditional office, manufacturing plant, or retail outlet with employees. But that vision is changing. Out of necessity, the 1990s ushered in a new type of business—the "virtual enterprise" or virtual company. The term **virtual company** comes from the computer industry's latest offering in entertainment—virtual reality—which essentially allows the player to be an integral part of a video game's environment without leaving the safety of the real world.

In business, a "virtual enterprise" has much the same purpose. It permits the owner to actively build a company in an industry without incurring the risk of employees, costly equipment, and enormous overhead. A virtual company makes it possible to operate the business from virtually anywhere—your home, car, or vacation cabin. The goal of the virtual enterprise is to deliver to the customer the highest-quality product at the lowest possible cost in a timely manner. To do this requires the participation and management of the entire distribution channel from producer to customer through a series of strategic alliances. Traditionally this was accomplished by building the business to the point where it could afford to buy out its suppliers and/or distributors, giving the company more control over quality and delivery. This strategy is known as **vertical integration**.

Virtual Companies Outsource

Today it is much more difficult for a new venture to accomplish total in-house control of its value chain. The global marketplace is more complex, time-to-market has decreased, and it is difficult for any one company to have the necessary expertise for mastering all the functional levels of the distribution channel. Today a growing company is more likely to increase its flexibility by choosing one function, its core competency, to concentrate on and subcontracting functions it does not want to handle. The general rule is, if the resources to manufacture, assemble, and distribute the product effectively already exist in the market in which you wish to do business, don't duplicate the effort. Outsource it. Besides streamlining the operation, using independent contractors has the added benefit of establishing peer-to-peer relationships rather than hierarchical ones as is seen in a vertically integrated channel. It becomes more of a team effort, with everyone having the ultimate goal of producing a successful product.

For example, a new equipment manufacturer, Gentech Corporation, decided that the only way to get off the ground and succeed in a very competitive market was to purchase existing components from established manufacturers so it wouldn't have to incur the heavy costs of tooling up a manufacturing plant. Gentech chose to establish an assembly operation and distribute its product initially through an established channel of equipment rental outlets. Gentech also formed alliances with its suppliers, so the parts it received were made to their specifications, saving time and money.

Often a business whose competitive advantage lies in proprietary rights on its product will choose to maintain control of strategic functions and outsource such things as warehousing, transportation, and some aspects of marketing. A retailer may outsource administrative functions like payroll, accounting, and inventory management and may even lease its employees from an employee leasing company. Some retail operations like bookseller Amazon.com have gone online to become virtual companies without the enormous expense of a retail site. Becoming a virtual company lets the new venture

Check Out Your Virtual Partners Carefully

To avoid problems when working with other companies in strategic alliances or in independent contractor relationships, be sure to do the following:

▶ Investigate the company's track record and assure yourself that it is trustworthy. This can be accomplished by checking with its customers, vendors, and distributors.

▶ Always remember that the contracting company doesn't know your customers' needs the way you do, and it is more worried about keeping all its own customers happy than about yours. Let contractors know specifically what your customers need.

▶ Make sure your subcontractors and partners understand the big picture. Otherwise, outsourcing all of your business's activities can be a coordination nightmare. Explain how the whole process works.

▶ Educate subcontractors and partners as to how your business works and what you must do to satisfy your customers.

▶ Create a situation where contractors have a vested interest in seeing your business succeed. Usually this will happen if you can demonstrate to them that your company holds the potential to provide them with a new, untapped market.

SOURCE: Courtney H. Price and Kathleen Allen, *Tips and Traps for Entrepreneurs; Real-Life Ideas and Solutions for the Toughest Problems Facing Entrepreneurs*, © 1998 McGraw-Hill Publishing. Reprinted by permission of The McGraw-Hill Companies.

be more innovative, closer to the customer, and quicker to market. Of course, the ultimate in virtual enterprises is one where the entrepreneur literally outsources all business functions and acts as the ringmaster in a three-ring circus.

Virtual Companies Form Strategic Alliances

Yet another way that virtual companies become more flexible and responsive is by forming **strategic alliances** or teams of businesses to share resources and reduce costs. These alliances accomplish more than simple outsourcing. They are more like true partnerships. They may purchase major equipment jointly, or share the costs of research and development and of training. Particularly in the area of R&D, it is very difficult for any one small company to manage the expense alone. For example, the Massachusetts Metalforming Network put together $25,000 of its own money, which gave it the ability to secure $40,000 in grants. That $65,000 allowed the network to collaborate on research to find a good solvent to clean metal parts. This example demonstrates that even competing companies can enjoy the benefits of networking.

Small manufacturers like Erie Bolt Company were instrumental in starting a network of 16 suppliers in their industry. The network operates like a "virtual enterprise" that subcontracts jobs to the network members who can do them most efficiently. The fact that they also share resources and facilities has given them an economy of scale that has produced a savings of 30 percent to the customers and more than doubled their business.

Networking and business alliances allow smaller businesses to bid successfully against large companies. They offer the convenience and savings of one source for everything, shared quality standards, and coordination of vendors. The key to success with a small-business alliance is being willing to share internal information such as manufacturing processes, quality control practices, and product information for the good of all. Strategic alliances are discussed again in Chapter 15.

Profile 10.2

Taking the Virtual Concept to the Limit

Walden Paddlers of Acton, Massachusetts, is the classic model for the virtual company. Its purpose is to design, produce, and market a technically advanced kayak made from recycled plastic that outperforms and underprices the competition. Walden Paddlers' founder, Paul Farrow, comes out of the corporate world, having lost his job to restructuring. Not wanting to build his way back up the corporate ladder, he sought to start a business that would allow him to work in the environment he enjoyed most—outdoors—and provide him with plenty of exercise. It took a vacation with his sons, kayaking on a lake, for him to come up with the perfect idea. Farrow quickly realized that the kayak they were using, which was fairly basic, probably cost all of $17.50 to make (it was plastic), yet it retailed for $400. An opportunity was presenting itself.

Upon returning home, he dove into the world of kayaks, talking to anyone who knew anything about them and learning everything he could about design, products, manufacturing, and distribution. As a result of his research, he believed he could carve out a niche in the entry-level kayak market—which was not being well served by the three major manufacturers of kayaks—with a boat that was cheaper than others yet performed better. He identified his target market as a middle-aged person just learning to kayak who would probably use the boat in fairly calm waters.

Farrow knew he didn't have the resources to do it all himself. He wanted to get into the market very quickly, so he set out to form a series of alliances with established companies. The first alliance was with Hardigg Industries, a Massachusetts rotomolder of plastics. Farrow persuaded Hardigg to put to use some of that firm's unused capacity molding kayaks. This was a fortunate relationship, as Hardigg not only believed in what Farrow was trying to do but also held the key to his business's getting off the ground. Hardigg Industries also saw this as an opportunity to develop a new customer and another profit center for the business.

Farrow also needed a designer. Through a series of contacts with various people, he finally found the one he was looking for in Jeff Allott. They agreed to spread the payments for his work over the stages of development of the prototype.

The third alliance was with boat dealers. Farrow decided to provide prospective dealers with demo boats they could use for 30 days. His only stipulation was that at the end of 30 days, they would either pay him or return the boat. The plan worked; soon he had sold his first 100 boats. Farrow's operational strategy is to outsource as long as he can and ultimately create a deal with a major national distributor to reach a mass audience.

Source: Edward O. Welles, "Virtual Realities," *Inc.* August 1993, p. 50; John Case, "The Wonderland Economy," *Inc.: The State of Small Business,* 1995.

Building a virtual corporation and dealing with strategic alliances is not without problems. For the entrepreneurial team that wants to maintain control of every aspect of the growing venture, it is frustrating to have to give up some of that control to other companies. Getting virtual partners to meet entrepreneurs' demands for quality, timeliness, and efficiency can also be a long and difficult process. Consequently, it is important that the entrepreneur and the virtual partner come to written agreement on their duties and responsibilities and that the relationship be beneficial to both parties. Many entrepreneurs have found that the benefits of virtual partners far outweigh the problems and that the virtual corporation is the most efficient and effective way to get the venture off the ground.

Technology has also contributed to helping start-up ventures perform like major corporations for relatively little money. Desktop computers and software such as computer-aided design allow new ventures to do things that previously required experts. Electronic networks make it easier to communicate with strategic alliance partners and to access commercial information databases around the world. Computerizing control systems on machine tools permits growing entrepreneurial manufacturers to compete with major companies. But don't make the mistake of thinking that becoming a virtual company is as easy as purchasing the right technology. On the contrary, there are management issues unique to this type of business, and they must be understood. Look at Profile 10.3 to learn what these management challenges are and how to solve them.

One of the biggest requirements for the success of a virtual company is a complete understanding of how the business works. To achieve this, it's important to look at the business from the customer's point of view.

The Fantasy Tour of the Business

To make the job of defining the operations and requirements of the business easier, take an imaginary tour of the business. In this way you can begin to list all the functions, people, equipment, supplies, and space required to run the business. As you enter the imaginary door of the business, ask yourself three questions:

1. Who does the work in this business?

2. Where do they work?

3. What do they need to do the work?

Then begin making lists of tasks, equipment, and people needed to run the business. This information will also be useful when you need to figure expenses for financial projections later on. For example, suppose you have a packaging solutions business. When a customer approaches the site, what is the first thing he or she will see? The sign for business? A display window? When customers enter, is there a counter with someone who will answer their questions? What equipment do they see? As you can see, you've already amassed quite a list of purchases—and you haven't yet begun to consider the type of work that's being done, who's doing it, and what they need to do it. The fantasy tour is one of the best ways to begin to look at the process needs of your business.

The Business Site

You may already be familiar with the three key factors for determining value in real estate: "location, location, location." The location of the business has a serious impact on its success. Location determines who will see the business, how easily they can access it, and whether or not they will want to access it. Even businesses like manufacturing, where the customer doesn't come to the site, benefit from a location near major sources of transportation. Since many business owners view their business site as permanent, selecting the best site becomes one of the most crucial decisions to make, one that will need to be justified to the readers of the business plan. Site decisions begin at a macro level with the state or region of the country and work their way down to the parcel on which the facility is located.

Choosing the Region or State

Locating a site for a new business normally begins with identifying the area of the country that seems best suited to the type of business being started. "Best

---

Profile 10.3

How VeriFone Makes a Virtual Operation Work

Operating virtually results in a new set of management challenges that don't necessarily face entrepreneurs with more traditional organizations. The problems arise from the very nature of the virtual form—no employees, people doing their work from a variety of locations, lack of informal communication.

VeriFone, the market leader in the manufacture of credit card terminals, finds that operating virtually by putting staff and resources near customers or centers of technological know-how has allowed the company to grow much faster. Over time, their staff has discovered ways to overcome the loss of synergy from daily personal contact. Here are some of the successful tactics VeriFone has used that any entrepreneur considering a virtual company should consider.

▶ All senior managers should work virtually at least some of the time so as to have a complete understanding of the needs of their "remote" people.

▶ The entrepreneur needs to visit remote offices frequently and meet face-to-face with his or her re-

mote staff. That way, the vision of the company is reinforced in a positive and personal manner.

▶ Make certain that remote work spaces, whether in the person's home or another remote office, are set up for productivity and are separate from any other activities going on at the location.

▶ Promote strong ties with people working at the main office. Encourage face-to-face meetings often.

▶ Create ways to maintain casual conversation and interaction. Videoconferencing and e-mail are two ways to do this.

▶ Make sure that remote workers receive frequent updates on what's going on everywhere in the business.

SOURCE: William R. Pape, "Remote Control," *Inc. Technology*, No. 3, 1996, p. 25.

suited" may mean that firms in your industry tend to congregate in a particular region, such as the high-tech firms that gravitate to Route 128 in Massachusetts or to Silicon Valley in California. For some businesses "best suited" may mean that a state is offering special financial and other incentives for businesses to locate there. In other cases, "best suited" means a manufacturer's choosing to locate near major suppliers. Often the entrepreneur starts the business in a particular region because that's where he or she happens to live. This may be fine during the incubation period, but the area must be considered carefully for what it contributes to the potential success of the business.

Of course, there is another important factor that must be included in the decision mix, and that is the entrepreneur's desire for a certain lifestyle. Sometimes the desire to maintain a particular lifestyle in a particular location far outweighs the potential negative effects of locating the business in a less than optimal location. Mo Siegal, founder of Celestial Seasonings, was one such entrepreneur. He was adamant about remaining in his beloved Colorado when he started his now enormously successful venture. Doing business there may have cost more and may not have been as convenient for shipping purposes, but the ability to run his business from his hometown was more important. In fact, as it turns out, the image of Colorado with its Rockies, cool streams, and beautiful blue skies actually enhanced the perception of his herbal teas.

Choosing a Community

The community in which you currently reside may not necessarily be the best place in which to start the business. Certainly it is always easier to deal with something you know well, particularly when starting something as risky as a new business, but don't assume that the location factor applies only to decisions within your own neighborhood. Many potentially successful new ventures have failed because they were not located in a region or community that supported that type of business.

To start, it is important to examine the major competitors in the industry to see where they tend to locate: is it in particular areas of the city, in specific regions of the country, or near major transportation routes? Doing this will give the first clue to a potentially successful location with the required infrastructure and a skilled work force. You also want to define your business's specific needs in terms of labor (skilled/unskilled), land (amount and type), and transportation (highways, ports, international airports). Three key factors about any area under consideration should be examined: economic base, financial incentives, and demographics.

Economic Base

The **economic base** of a region or community is simply the major source of income for the area. Communities are viewed as primarily industrial, agricultural, or service-oriented. In general, industrial communities export more goods out of the community than they import into it. For example, suppose the community's principal income is derived from farming and the associated products it ships to other communities. This activity brings money into the community. Now suppose the citizens of the community must travel to another community to do major shopping. This activity takes money out of the community. The important thing to learn about the community is whether the money brought in from farming exceeds the money leaving for shopping. If it does, the community appears to have a growing economic base, which is a favorable factor for new businesses.

You can learn more about the economic base of any community in which you are interested by contacting the state or regional economic development agency in the area. These organizations exist to bring new business into the region, so they have to stay on top of what is going on. They can give you all the statistics you will need on the economic condition of the region as well as estimate the cost of doing business there.

Financial Incentives

Most community governments are faced with cash needs that go well beyond the tax tolerance level of its citizens; consequently, they work diligently with economic development agencies to attract new businesses and the accompanying tax revenues into the community. One of the ways they attract businesses is by offering incentives such as lower taxes, cheaper land, and employee training programs. Some communities have enterprise zones, which give the businesses that locate in them favorable tax treatment from the state based on the number of jobs created, as well as lower land costs and rental rates. They also expedite permit processes and help in any way they can to make the move easier.

Look carefully, however, at communities that offer up-front cash in compensation for the community's lack of up-to-date infrastructure. They may be hiding a high corporate tax rate or some other disincentive that could hurt your business's chances of success. In general, the larger the incentives, the more careful you should be in doing your homework.

Demographics

In addition to studying the economic base and the community's attitude toward new business, look carefully at the population base. Is it growing or shrinking? Is it aging or getting younger? Is it culturally diverse? The level and quantity of disposable income in the community will indicate whether there is enough money to purchase whatever you are offering. Demographic information is usually based on the U.S. Census, which tracks changes in population size and characteristics. The United States is divided into Standard Metropolitan Statistical Areas (SMSAs), which are geographic areas that include a major metropolitan area like Los Angeles or Houston. These are further divided into census tracts, which contain approximately 4,000–5,000 people, and neighborhood blocks. With this information you can readily determine, for example, if the city in which you want to locate a new software development firm has enough people with sufficient technical and educational skills to support it. Population data also indicate the number of people available to work. Demographic data is easily obtained from the economic development agency, the public library, or the post office, which tracks populations by zip code.

Choosing a Retail Site

With a retail business, the entrepreneur is dealing directly with the consumer, so naturally, one of the first considerations is being near the customers. Since a retail business lives or dies based on the number of consumers who have access to the business, it is important to locate where there are suitable concentrations of consumers.

The Trade Area

The **trade area** is the region from which the entrepreneur expects to draw customers. The type of business will determine to a large extent the size of the trade area. For example, if the business sells general merchandise that can be found almost anywhere, the trade area is much smaller, as customers will not travel great distances to purchase common goods. Yet a specialty outlet—for example, a clothing boutique with unusual apparel—may draw people from other communities as well.

Once the location within the community is identified, the trade area can be calculated. With a map of the community, designate the site for the business; then, using a compass, place the epicenter on the proposed site and draw a circle that represents the distance (the radius) you expect people to drive to reach the site. Within the circle is the trade area, which can now be studied in more detail. Using the demographics and a census tract map, identify census tracts within the trade area and look at the census data to determine how many people reside within the boundaries of the trade area. The demographic information will also describe these people in terms of education level, income level, average number of children, and so forth.

Competition

Within the trade area, you can also identify the competition. To do this, drive through the area (assuming it is not too large) and spot competing businesses. Note their size and number, and also gauge how busy they are at various times of the day by observing their parking lots or actually entering the business. If competitors are located in shopping malls or strip centers, look for clusters of stores similar to yours and low vacancy rates. This would indicate a strong attraction for the site. Look at the stores near your proposed site to check for compatibility. Often, locating near a competitor is a wise choice because it encourages comparison shopping. Observe the character of the area. Does it appear to be successful and well maintained?

Accessibility

It is important to identify the routes your customers might take to reach the proposed site: highways, streets, and public transportation routes. If the site is difficult to locate and hard to reach, you can be certain potential customers will not expend the effort to find you. Also check the parking situation. Most communities require a sufficient amount of parking space for new construction, through either lots or garages; however, in some older areas, street parking is the only available option. If parking is hard to find or too expensive, you will lose customers.

Do a foot and car traffic count for your proposed site to determine how busy the area is. Remember, retail businesses rely heavily on traffic for customers. Whether or not you need a high volume of foot traffic is a function of the type of business. Obviously, a coffee house benefits immensely from a high volume of foot traffic, whereas for a warehouse hardware store it may not be as vital. A traffic count is easily accomplished by positioning yourself near the targeted site and tallying the customers going by and into the business. City planning departments and transportation departments maintain auto traffic counts for major arterials in the city.

Choosing the Service/Wholesale Site

If a service or wholesale business has customers who come to the place of business, the needs for a site will parallel those of the retailer in some respects. Accessibility, attractiveness, and a trade area of sufficient size are all key factors in the selection of a site. The entrepreneur does not, however, need to choose from the more expensive commercial sites, as the expectations of the customers may not be as great for a wholesale outlet that sells to the public, for example. Customers going to these types of businesses usually want to save money, so they don't expect the Cadillac version of a business site. Some service businesses, on the other hand, require attractive office space that is easily accessible. These are usually professional businesses—lawyers, accountants, consultants, and so forth. The image they present through the location and appearance of their offices is crucial to the success of the business.

Many service and wholesale businesses do not have customers coming to their places of business. Some examples are distributors, contractors, and certain types of consultants. In these cases, it is more prudent for the business to be located in less expensive, less high-profile areas of town where they are near the customers they serve but can take advantage of savings in rent or land costs.

Choosing the Manufacturing Site

For the manufacturer, the location choices narrow significantly. Communities have zoning laws that limit manufacturing companies to certain designated areas away from residential, retail, and office commercial sites so as to reduce the chance of noise, odor, and pollutants affecting the citizens. Often these areas are known as industrial parks, and they usually are equipped with electrical power and sewage plants appropriate to manufacturing. By locating in one of these parks, the new business may also benefit from the synergy of other manufacturing nearby. Opportunities for networking and sharing resources and costs are enhanced.

Another common location for manufacturing is **enterprise zones**, which are public-private partnerships designed to bring jobs to inner cities, downtown areas, and rural areas suffering from the shift of jobs and population to the suburbs. There are thirty-five states (as well as the District of Columbia) with authorized enterprise zones. The draw for businesses is tax incentives, regulatory relief, and employee training programs. However, the enterprise zone program is not without its critics. The principal criticism is that there is no net economic gain for the community. Since businesses often move from one area of town to the enterprise zone simply to take advantage of tax

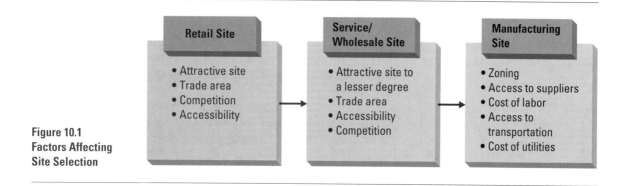

Figure 10.1 Factors Affecting Site Selection

breaks, no new jobs are created. Still another criticism comes from established businesses in the area that complain that the zones are nothing but incubators for competitors. In spite of these criticisms, enterprise zones are likely to continue as one method for creating jobs and rebuilding decaying inner cities.

Wherever an entrepreneur looks for a manufacturing site, he or she is concerned with four key factors: access to suppliers, cost of labor, access to transportation, and cost of utilities. These factors may not be equally weighted. Depending on the type of manufacturer, one or more factors may have greater importance in evaluating a site.

Access to Suppliers

Manufacturers and processors usually try to locate within a reasonable distance from their major suppliers to cut shipping time and save transportation costs. Certainly a food processor attempts to set up business near the growing fields, so that the food is as fresh as possible when it arrives at the processing plant. Similarly, a manufacturer that uses steel as one of its main raw materials might want to locate in the same region of the country as the steel mills to save the high costs of trucking heavy steel great distances.

Cost of Labor

Today many manufacturers choose a location on the basis of the cost of labor, rather than proximity to suppliers, since labor is generally the single highest cost in the production of goods. Wages and laws relating to workers, such as workers' compensation, vary from state to state, and sometimes from city to city. For example, California laws and cost of living tend to make it a more expensive place to hire employees than those same employees might cost in Missouri. Some labor-intensive businesses have found that the only way they can compete is by having plants in Mexico or China, where labor costs are a fraction of those in the United States, and where laborers are not protected by as many laws. Mattel Toy Company, for example, has a plant in China to produce the hundreds of different toys it markets every year. The bottom line is that the entrepreneur must weigh carefully the costs in terms of access to labor when considering a particular location for a manufacturing plant.

Access to Transportation

Most manufacturers prefer to locate near major transportation networks: railways, major highways, airports, and ports of call. The reasoning is obvious: the greater the distance between the plant and a major transportation network, the higher the cost to the company and ultimately, to the customer. Also, the more transportation people who handle the product, the greater the cost. Thus, in terms of simple economics, to remain competitive, manufacturers must consider the cost benefit of locating away from a major transportation network. The higher transportation costs will result in a smaller profit margin for the company or higher costs for the customers. Either way, you lose.

Cost of Utilities

Utility rates vary from state to state, and usually from city to city within a given state. If the new venture is heavily dependent on electricity, gas, or coal, this factor could be a significant variable in the cost of producing a product and therefore should be examined carefully.

The Building: The Lease-Buy-Build Decision

To this point, only the site itself has been considered. Naturally, there is a building or facility involved as well, which makes the site decision that much more complex. If the site contains an existing building, the question becomes whether to lease or buy. If the site is bare land, building a facility is the only choice. As a significant portion of a new venture's start-up costs is contained in a facility, each of these scenarios is looked at in more detail.

The Existing Building

Any existing building on a potential site must be examined carefully with consideration given to the following questions:

▶ Is the building of sufficient size to meet current and reasonable future needs?

▶ Do the building and site allow for future expansion?

▶ Is there sufficient parking?

▶ Is there space for customers, storage, inventory, office space, and rest rooms?

Allowing for future growth is essential. The initial higher cost of a larger building is often offset by avoiding the extraordinarily high costs of moving and the potential for lost sales and time away from the fundamental work of the business while the business is in transition.

When examining an existing building, begin with the exterior and ask the following questions:

1. Does the building have curbside appeal, assuming customers will come to the site?

2. Is the building compatible with its surroundings?

3. Does it have enough windows of sufficient size?

4. Is the entrance inviting?

5. Is the signage attractive, and does it satisfy the local regulations?

6. Is the parking adequate to meet customer and employee demand and satisfy local building codes?

7. Does the interior of the building meet your needs in terms of walls, floors, and ceilings?

8. Are there sufficient lighting fixtures and outlets, and enough power to run equipment?

These are just a few of the questions to ask before finalizing a decision on a building. Most entrepreneurs can answer these eight questions to their own satisfaction, but to be certain the building is not hiding anything that could come back to haunt the entrepreneur and be costly for the business, it is wise to hire a licensed contractor or inspector to examine the building for structural soundness.

Leasing a Building

The speed of change, innovation, and technological advancement has shortened and will continue to shorten product and service life cycles, and this has an impact on the facilities in which businesses operate. Also, buildings have long physical lives and typically are very expensive to refurbish and remodel. Consequently, in many communities factories and retail outlets can be seen lying vacant for long periods of time, even years. Ultimately they sell for or are leased at an amount far below what it cost to build them.

It has been suggested that one solution to the problem is for businesses to hold short leases of five years or less. In this way the company does not tie up precious capital that it may not be able to recover, and it has the ability to move on when a product or service is deemed technologically antiquated and no longer in demand. There are, however, some serious disadvantages to short-term leasing.

▶ *Rents are escalated more frequently, due to short-term renewal.* Many a business has found itself in this awkward position. Demand for the product or service has been successful beyond initial predictions, so the business needs to remain in its current location beyond the term of the lease. When the entrepreneur goes to renegotiate the lease terms, he or she inevitably finds that the landlord intends to raise the rents for a new lease. This is usually justified by increasing market rents; however, at the same time, the landlord is aware that it would be costly for the tenant to relocate. The business would have little time to do so and still maintain its current production rate. Furthermore, the potential for having to replace employees and create new logistics for suppliers and buyers is daunting. All these factors put the entrepreneur in a very weak position to negotiate a new lease.

To strengthen your position, negotiate up front a clause that permits the option to renew at a specified rate, and an escape clause in case the business must be closed. These two clauses may cost a bit more initially, but can yield long-term savings.

▶ *It will be more difficult to remodel mid-term.* If you have a short-term lease, the landlord will be less likely to approve any substantial tenant improvements if they do not increase the value of the building to future tenants.

When the lease is first negotiated, come prepared with a five-year plan for the facility and be able to demonstrate the benefits to the landlord of allowing the remodeling of the building.

▶ *You will not be able to show a substantial asset on the balance sheet.* Therefore, it will not be a good vehicle for raising capital.

If you own the building, by contrast, you can later sell it to raise needed capital and lease it back, thereby avoiding moving costs and providing the new landlord with an instant tenant, a factor that increases the value of the building to the new owner.

The cost of leasing a building is a function of the demand in the marketplace for rentals as well as a number of other factors.

▶ Buildings that are newer, suitable for a variety of uses, and well located generally enjoy higher lease rates, as do buildings in short supply.

▶ Since rent is normally based on square footage of space, the larger the space, the more costly the lease.

▶ Retail and service business sites are generally more expensive than industrial sites.

▶ A retail site in a regional mall will likely be the most expensive.

Be aware, though, that while manufacturing sites enjoy low rental rates, manufacturers usually pay higher amounts for water, power, and sewerage. That is why it is worthwhile to consider all the costs related to leasing a facility. Not including the cost of expensive utilities or a common use area fee could spell disaster to the business's cash flow.

Businesses face three basic types of leases.

1. **Gross lease.** This lease allows the entrepreneur to pay a fixed rate per month, with the landlord covering the cost (and getting the benefit) of insurance, taxes, and building operating expenses such as outdoor lighting, security, and so forth.

2. **Net lease** (also known as triple net). This lease has the entrepreneur paying a fixed monthly rate plus taxes, operating expenses, essentially everything but the mortgage and the building insurance, which the landlord pays. What the entrepreneur actually rents is a shell with stipulated improvements.

3. **Percentage lease.** This is the most complicated of all the lease types because it has several variations. It can be written as a percentage of the net income of the tenant or as a flat rate plus a percentage of the gross revenues. The latter is very common in retail operations.

Fortunately for businesses seeking lease facilities, for the most part it's still a renters' market and will probably remain so for the foreseeable future as demand lags behind the oversupply created in the 1980s. Moreover, savvy customers expect businesses to reflect the trend toward "less is more" by controlling costs and simplifying operations. In a renters' market, businesses can expect to negotiate leases that provide a certain period of free rent, free parking, allowances for tenant improvements, and greater flexibility to extend or shorten the lease. For instance, one Chicago-based company renegotiated its high-rent lease, reducing its obligation from $36 per square foot to $22. In addition, the landlord agreed to cover the $1 million tenant improvements, which would be recovered over the term of the new ten-year lease.

Even more savings in a lease can be achieved by reading it carefully.

▶ Make sure there is a provision for examining the books of the landlord to view the costs related to the building. In this way you may discover **pass-throughs,** or costs in the form of capital improvements that should not be passed on to the tenants, such as the cost of a new security system. You may also find charges to the tenants for expenses that are rightfully the owner's, such as personal services to the owner who is also a tenant of the building.

▶ Check carefully for clerical mistakes, particularly the easily overlooked simple items like addresses, suite numbers, square footage, and rental amounts.

▶ Talk with other tenants of a building to find out common needs that may be achieved through a unified effort.

▶ Ask for a breakdown of taxes and operating expenses for the previous three years and projections for the next five years.

▶ Ask for a work letter that explains all improvements the landlord will make for the tenant as well as work the tenant must complete and all costs associated with the completion of these improvements.

▶ Make certain the building meets requirements and safety levels prescribed by the Environmental Protection Agency.

Remember first and foremost that leases are written from the landlord's point of view and are, therefore, negotiable. The fact that something appears in printed form does not mean it is true or that you have to agree to it. A lease represents a significant portion of a business's overhead, and you will most likely have to live with it for a long time, so make sure it's what you really want. Leases are a great way for start-up businesses to get into the marketplace, but don't let your enthusiasm for starting the business blind you to the potentially disastrous terms of a poorly written lease. The best advice is to seek the assistance of an attorney who can represent your interests.

Buying a Building

If the entrepreneur has the resources, buying a building has some advantages. A valuable asset is immediately created on the balance sheet, which can be leveraged later on when growth capital is needed. For example, the building could be sold and leased back (called a **sale-leaseback**), withdrawing equity for other uses and negotiating favorable long-term lease terms. Sale-leasebacks are attractive options for investors, so these buildings generally sell quickly. Of course when you sell the building, you effectively lose control of it, so be certain to negotiate terms that allow you to remodel and extend the lease should you wish to do so.

One advantage of owning a building is that it can be traded in a **tax-deferred exchange** for other property you need. For example, suppose you owned an office building but needed a distribution warehouse to support a new direction your business was taking. You might take advantage of a tax-deferred exchange by trading the office building for the warehouse. The exchange would defer capital gains tax on the sale of the office, and you would have the warehouse you need.

One other option to consider is a joint venture between you, the entrepreneur, and a real estate developer on a building in which you will be one of the tenants. If you are able to occupy a substantial portion of the building, it is easier for the developer to acquire a mortgage and additional tenants. Of course, this type of arrangement has the inherent problems of any partnership and should be considered carefully with the advice of an attorney before any agreement is executed.

Buying a building requires a contract, much like a lease agreement. It spells out the terms of the purchase and the items included and excluded from the purchase agreement. As always, read it carefully to make sure that what you agreed to verbally has been translated correctly on paper. It would be wise to hire a due diligence team (inspector, contractor, CPA, attorney) to inspect the building and the agreement so that your interests are protected.

Building the Facility

When you can't find the type of building in the location you want, building the facility from the ground up becomes the only option. This will entail an architect, permits, possibly zoning variances, a construction bidding process, **off-site improvements** (curbs, gutters, water and power lines, roads), and a lengthy building and inspection process. This option should not be undertaken without the aid of a licensed general contractor. Be sure to check the reputation of any contractor you are considering. This is important should the contractor have a dispute with any of the subcontractors hired for the various aspects of the job. The subcontractors have a right to lien the property you own. You will then have to sue the contractor to resolve the issue and remove the lien (you cannot receive a Certificate of Occupancy if any liens are present), and this is a time-consuming and costly process.

Also, as you are most probably responsible to the lender for the construction loan, you can ensure that any subcontractors are paid by 1) using a **voucher system**, which is a cumbersome method whereby the subcontractor receives a voucher for work completed and must take it to the lending bank for payment and release of liens, or 2) by paying the subcontractors directly and receiving lien releases. The latter is known as "jointing a check."

It prevents the general contractor from using the funds for other purposes and potentially not having the money to pay the subcontractor.

Constructing a building is no doubt the most complex option; however, you will end up with a building that completely meets your needs. This option is most suitable when the needs for the building and/or the location are unique, when you have the time to wait, and when you intend to remain in the facility long term.

Starting the Business from Home

Almost 20 percent of the 92 million households in America have home offices that produce an income for the owner. It is estimated that more than 1,200 new home businesses begin every day. Add to that the increasing number of people employed in traditional offices who work at least part of the week from home as telecommuters and you have approximately 38 million people who work from home!

Some of the largest, most successful companies in the world today started from home, including Apple Computers, to name just one. The biggest reason so many new ventures start from home is cost, as one of the biggest line items in the budget of a start-up is rent or the cost of buying a building. Consequently, many new companies choose to start with minimal overhead until their product or service gets off the ground, to better ensure that the company survives the risky start-up phase. Once orders or clients start coming in regularly, the business can move to a more permanent location.

For some entrepreneurs, however, the goal is to never leave home, but to subcontract all activities that cannot be accomplished from home. This new type of business is a phenomenon that started in the 1990s and is likely to continue in popularity as people seek to acquire more control over their lives, to reduce stress, and to avoid interruptions and traffic jams. With a phone, fax, copier, and computer, technology has made possible the era of the telecommuter and the virtual enterprise.

Anyone considering working from home, even for the short term, should consult with local government agencies to see what the zoning ordinances are. In general, most communities frown on home-based businesses in residential areas, especially if the business receives a lot of auto traffic. For example, Los Angeles prohibits home-based businesses, even those of typical home-office users like consultants, free-lance writers, and artists. However, in spite of the ban, it is estimated that more than 2.2 million households in the Los Angeles area contain a full- or part-time home business. To avoid potential penalties, check the laws and restrictions regarding home-based businesses in your local community.

Alternatives to Conventional Facilities

Today business owners have a variety of alternatives to conventional business locations. These alternatives lower the cost of overhead and make it easier for a business to change its mind should the location not work out. We'll consider four of these alternative sites: incubators, shared space, mobile locations, and temporary tenant agreements.

Incubators

Some entrepreneurs find it helpful to start their new venture's life in a business **incubator**, which has the same purpose as an incubator for an infant— to create a controlled environment that will enhance the chances of the business's surviving the start-up phase. Private and state-sponsored incubators can be found in nearly every region of the country for almost any type of business. They offer space at a lower than market rate to several businesses, which may then share common support functions like receptionist, copy machine, and conference room. The incubator may even offer business courses and training to help new entrepreneurs with the myriad details involved in running the business. After about three to five years, depending on the incubator, the young business is helped to move into its own site elsewhere in the community.

Some incubators cater only to high-tech firms or to service firms. Others, like the Entrepreneur Partnership Program at the Mall of America in Bloomington, Minnesota, help entrepreneurs determine if their retail or service businesses are suited to the demands of a major mall. This particular program helps the entrepreneur formulate a business plan and open a store. It also provides incentives such as waiving the costs of improving the store space and consulting in marketing and operations. Some incubators like idealab! in Pasadena, California (see Profile 10.1) focus on particular types of businesses—in this case, Internet companies. Others focus on manufacturing companies, while many accept a variety of types of businesses.

Shared Space

Another choice is to locate the company within the facilities of a larger company. As the largest of the chain stores continue to downsize, opportunities to take excess space arise. This was the case for Toys 'R' Us, which rents space in ten of Montgomery Ward's stores. A variation on this theme is to lease a location that has enough space to sublease to a complementary business. For example, a copy service might lease excess space to a computer graphics company. If you decide on a location that's good for your business, approach a complementary business in the area to see if a shared arrangement can be made.

Mobile Locations

One of the more interesting ways to introduce new businesses and new products/services to the marketplace is through the use of **pushcarts and kiosks**. This was the strategy of Bill Sanderson, president of CalCorn, Inc., which owns Popcorn Palace, a chain of boutique-type gourmet popcorn stores. Their typical location is a high-traffic site in an upscale regional mall. This space is one of the more expensive in the mall; therefore, to test the potential viability of a new site, Sanderson often starts with a pushcart location on that site before making a commitment to a long-term lease. Pushcarts and their more fixed alternative, the kiosk—a small booth—also allow a company to expand to many new locations without the high overhead of a conventional retail storefront.

Temporary Tenant Agreements

Some landlords have found that rather than sit on an empty space until the new tenant moves in, they can rent the space on a temporary basis so that their cash flow is not interrupted. In fact, the concept of the temporary tenant has grown so rapidly that there are now leasing agents who specialize in that area. The most successful of these temporary tenants have the following characteristics:

▶ Personalized merchandise

▶ Opportunities to sample the product

▶ Products that can be demonstrated

▶ Products that can be used for entertaining the customers.[1]

For the temporary concept to work, significant foot traffic and high customer turnover is required. This is an excellent alternative for retail businesses that want to test a location before making a major commitment.

Relying on experts to select a site is probably the best way to ensure a good decision. There are consultants specializing in all types of business site locations. The advantage to using consultants is that they have a duty of confidentiality, they generally are unbiased and take an objective view, and they take a broader view of the needs of the business than say, a real estate broker who is representing specific properties.

The Business Process

Every business has a basic process that repeats itself every day for every customer, and that process is different for every type of business. The rest of this chapter will look at some of the process issues related to retail/wholesale and service businesses. To properly analyze any business process, you would need to create a flowchart of all the activities undertaken during a typical business day in the order in which they're accomplished. It would be important to look for areas of duplication as well as for activities that may require controls to avoid shrinkage through either employee or customer theft. The goal is continual improvement of the process so that the most effective system is achieved. Even in the retail business, it takes more than sales to create profits; it also requires good systems and processes.

Purchasing and Inventory

Wholesalers purchase goods to resell to retailers, who purchase an inventory of goods to sell to the consumer. Purchasing decisions, to be effective, must be based on current information rather than on intelligent guesses. Significant amounts of money can be saved by keeping track of prices and new products and by purchasing in a timely manner.

Purchasing

Effective purchasing begins with a purchasing strategy that takes into consideration quality, service, and price. In this sense, *quality* means that the product suits the purpose for which it was intended. *Service* means that it will be delivered when needed and corrected if defective. *Price* means a competitive price, but not necessarily the lowest price. In other words, all three must be considered before selecting a product and a supplier (vendor).

For entrepreneurs who are outsourcing much of their work, the ability to rely on a competent vendor becomes critical. Here are some things you should consider when selecting a vendor.

1. Do due diligence on a potential vendor. Get to know everyone from the president on down, and visit the vendor's facility. By inspecting its site, you can learn a great deal about how a firm does business.

2. Design a vendor survey form, a type of questionnaire or checklist, that will ensure that you gather all the information you need for making a decision.

3. Verify a vendor's claims with at least three other customers of the vendor.

The following profile gives an example of the value of selecting vendors carefully.

Profile 10.4

The Importance of Great Vendors

Many entrepreneurs bet on one vendor for their needs in a particular area. Because it has taken so long to find that vendor, they often don't take additional time to locate a backup vendor in case the main one doesn't work out. This is a huge mistake. One bad vendor can end the life of a growing small business.

Softub is a $15 million-a-year builder of hot tubs in Chatsworth, California. Like most other entrepreneurs, Softub relies on materials purchased from about 200 vendors. It also outsources the assembly of its motor, pump, and control unit. Softub's president chose the vendor for this task after a successful meeting and from talking with some of the vendor's customers. Everything looked fine until Softub started experiencing equipment failures in customers' homes. Not long after, the vendor went out of business, leaving Softub to take care of the bad tubs. That vendor cost Softub $500,000.

Gary Anderson, the purchasing agent for Softub, lost no time in designing a vendor survey form hitting key issues like on-time delivery, quality control, oper-

ations, and so forth. Softub now checks out such things as how busy vendors are relative to their size. If they're not using all their capacity, Anderson asks why. Softub looks at a Dun & Bradstreet report to find out if a company owes more than it's worth. How is their facility run? Is it clean and organized and are people following safety rules? After all, an accident and a subsequent lawsuit can put a company out of business.

The payoff for Softub has been lower vendor turnover and fewer product defects. The new relationships with vendors have also resulted in new ideas for Softub. One vendor taught Softub employees how to handle electronic parts that are sensitive to static electricity. Another vendor that used illustrated work instructions in front of every station on its assembly line helped Softub develop a similar system. Being careful about how you choose vendors can pay off in the long run.

Source: Stephanie Gruner, "The Smart Vendor-Audit Checklist," *Inc.*, April, 1995, p. 93.

Inventory

Inventory is basically assets purchased and held for sale. With the possible exception of some service companies, all businesses have some type of inventory. Inventories carry inherent costs—insurance, storage, shrinkage, and so forth—so it's vital that a growing company have a system in place to manage its inventory. To reduce some of the costs of inventory, many firms are moving toward a **just-in-time system,** where they are linked electronically with their suppliers, who then know when the company reaches a trigger point where its inventory of a particular product must be replenished.

There are basically three types of inventory: finished goods, raw materials, and work-in-process. The latter two relate to manufacturing operations, which will be discussed in Chapter 11. **Finished goods inventory** refers to items ready for sale, and this is the type of inventory that retailers hold to ensure that they have enough on hand to meet their customers' needs. Certainly, customer demand fluctuates, so retailers must have a keen sense of when to carry above-average levels of inventory. Too much inventory means high carrying costs; too little inventory results in lost sales.

There are many costs associated with inventories, and such costs can add as much as 25 percent to the base cost of the inventory. They include:

▶ *Financing Costs.* The interest paid on money borrowed to purchase the inventory.

▶ *Opportunity Cost.* The loss of use of the money tied up in inventory.

▶ *Storage Costs.* The amount spent on warehouse space to store the inventory.

▶ *Insurance Costs.* The cost of insuring the inventory.

▶ *Shrinkage Costs.* The money lost from inventory that is broken, stolen, or damaged.

▶ *Obsolescence.* The cost associated with inventory that has become obsolete.

Informal Inventory Tracking Methods

When a company is small and its suppliers are close, it can reorder inventory on an "as-needed" basis. One method used by smaller companies is to divide the inventory into expensive and inexpensive items, then track more frequently the status of the expensive items, since they account for a larger portion of the inventory as a whole. Larger retailers, by contrast, typically use a bar code system to track inventory and establish trigger points with their suppliers to know when to reorder. With this system, when a sale occurs, it is recorded electronically and the inventory is simultaneously updated.

Hardware stores and wholesale businesses typically use a version of kanban to track inventory. It is essentially a **two-bin system,** suitable for small items, where two containers of the item are carried at all times. The open container/display is placed on top of the closed container. When the open container is empty, it's time to reorder and open the bottom container. Bookstores that shelve books "cover forward" use a variation of this system by placing a reorder card in the last book at the back of the stack.

Yet another method involves dividing inventory into three groups, based on price. Then each group is analyzed to determine the best tracking method for that group. Usually one group will require more frequent reordering than another.

Formal Inventory Tracking Systems

The following systems are more elaborate and sophisticated than those previously discussed, and they require computers and specialty software.

Point-of-Purchase Systems.   POP systems exist for virtually every type of retail or wholesale business and ensure a more accurate tracking of inventory in "real time." When an item is purchased, its code is entered into the terminal and the inventory is immediately reduced by that item. This makes it very easy to know when to reorder.

Bar Coding.   Bar coding actually facilitates POP systems by relieving the salesperson from having to enter code. Consequently, one potential point of data entry error is eliminated, which can be a significant saving to the company. The bar code is a label containing black-and-white parallel bars encoded with information. To use a bar code system requires a computer, a laser scanner, a decoder, and the bar code symbols.

Electronic Data Interchange (EDI).   EDI takes electronic data entry one step further by linking the retailer with the supplier so that reordering essentially becomes automatic. Linking directly or through a third party such as America Online (AOL) or another Internet provider means that inventory is shipped when needed, resulting in higher inventory turnover and the elimination of the need for demand forecasting or other traditional inventory tracking devices.

Inventory Turnover

Inventory turnover is an important indicator of the effectiveness with which the company is managing its inventory. Inventory turnover is the average number of times an inventory for a particular product line is sold out during the year. The rate of turnover is different for each industry (e.g., men's clothing is 3; restaurants, 22; and some chemical manufacturers, 100), but knowing the average rate for the industry in which the company is competing is an important benchmark against which to measure the company's effectiveness. For example, if it is known that a particular industry has an inventory turnover rate of 5, the following equation represents how much inventory must be kept on hand.

$$\frac{12 \text{ months}}{5 \text{ turnover rate}} = 2.4\text{-months' supply}$$

On average, then, a 2.4-months' supply of inventory will need to be on hand. Once the quantity required to be on hand is known, the cost of the inventory can be calculated by using the company's forecasted sales for the upcoming year and the cost of goods sold (inventory) percentage. For example, if the company is forecasting $200,000 in sales and the COGS is 50% of sales,

$$\frac{\$200,000 \times .50}{5 \text{ turnover rate}} = \$20,000$$

It will cost $20,000 to maintain a 2.4-months' supply in inventory, not including carrying costs. Naturally, if the company deals in several product lines, calculations for each of them will need to be done, as they may have varying turnover rates.

Using a variation of the preceding formula, a company can calculate its inventory turnover rate to compare itself against the industry average. This is done by dividing the cost of sales by the average inventory:

$$\frac{\$100,000}{\$20,000} = 5$$

This means that the company turned over its inventory an average of five times during the year, or every 73 days (365/5).

It's important to look not only at total inventory turnover but also at turnover of individual items, in order to find the slow-moving ones. A simple analysis of the number of any item on hand against the number sold in, say, the past 60 days will point up which products need inventory on hand decreased and which need it increased.

Shrinkage

Shrinkage is loss due to theft and due to shoplifting by both customers and employees. It is by all accounts a significant problem in the retail industry because so many people pass through a retail establishment's doors. To illustrate the impact of theft on a company's profitability, consider a case where a software retailer loses a $39.95 software program every day for a year. If the store operates at a 10 percent profit margin, for example, it would have to sell an additional $145,817.50 of merchandise to compensate for the loss.

Shoplifting, the most common crime in the retail business, accounts for about 3 percent of the selling price of an item. While it may seem that expensive items are shoplifted more often, the fact is that most stolen items range in price from $1 to $5. Only a small percentage of shoplifters are professionals: the vast majority are juveniles (50%) and substance abusers. To combat shoplifting requires that sales personnel be aware of the habits of shoplifters. They may appear nervous and may spend a considerable amount of time just looking around. They may carry large bags or wear bulky clothing. The more successful thieves arrive when the store is understaffed and travel in groups so that one or two can cause a distraction while the others steal merchandise. Some tactics to help deter shoplifting include:

▶ Keeping the store well lit and display cases low to maintain a clear view

▶ Using two-way mirrors or closed-circuit TV

▶ Using electronic tamper-proof tags on articles of clothing

▶ Hiring a uniformed security guard

To ensure a clear-cut case against a shoplifter, the salesperson or security guard must see the person take the merchandise, be able to prove that the merchandise belongs to the store, prove that it was taken with intent to steal, and prove that it was not paid for. In addition, it is important to apprehend the shoplifter outside the store to strengthen the intent argument.

While shoplifting is a frustrating problem for retailers, about 75–80 percent of all retail crime is committed by employees, who add 15% to the cost of consumer goods. Employees have an advantage: they normally have access to the business in a way that no outsider does. There are several things a company can do to minimize the opportunity for employee theft.

1. Keep all nonentry or exit doors locked when not in use.

2. Control who has access to keys to the business and change the locks if theft is suspected.

3. Periodically check the trash bins, as they are a typical hiding place for stolen items.

4. Watch for a large number of voided or no-sale transactions.

5. Don't let one person control a transaction from beginning to end. For example, one transaction could involve a salesperson, a register clerk, and a bookkeeper.

6. Be careful about hiring and check references.

A few precautions taken consistently will go a long way toward protecting the business and its customers.

The importance of understanding how your business operates cannot be stressed too much. In dynamic environments that are highly competitive, the company that executes its concept well wins.

New Venture Checklist

Have you:

❏ **Determined how your business will operate?**

❏ **Found ways to operate like a virtual enterprise?**

❏ **Located a site for the business?**

❏ **Examined the economic base, incentives, demographics, and trade area?**

❏ **Decided whether to lease, buy, or build the facility?**

❏ **Determined how your business operates, by taking a fantasy tour?**

Issues to Consider

1. What are the advantages and the disadvantages of a virtual company?
2. What is the purpose of the fantasy tour of the business?
3. Which important factors in choosing a retail site would not be relevant to a manufacturing site—and vice versa?
4. Explain two disadvantages of short-term leasing.
5. Compare and contrast buying an existing building with building a new facility.
6. Discuss two informal and two formal inventory tracking methods.

Experiencing Entrepreneurship

1. Choose an industry in which you have an interest. Find a business in that industry and do a flowchart of the business process, based on visiting the site and talking with key personnel.
2. You are going to open a new restaurant in your city that requires 100,000 people within a 2.5 mile radius of the site. Identify a site for the restaurant on a map; draw a 2.5 mile radius around the site; then determine through census tract maps and driving the trade area how many people reside within the area and who the competition is.

Additional Sources of Information

Bar, V., and C.E. Broudy. (1986). *Designing to Sell*. New York: McGraw-Hill.

Choosing a Retail Location. SBA Pub. No. MP10.

Locating or Relocating Your Business. SBA Pub. No. MP2.

Practical Business Use of Government Statistics. SBA Small Business Management Series, Stock No. 045-000-00131-8.

"The Survey of Buying Power." *Sales and Marketing Management* (Annual).

Using Census Data to Select a Store Site. SBA Pub. No. MA2.023.

Internet Resources

Barcode Server
http://www.milk.com/barcode/
Find out how bar codes work and generate your own.

Census Bureau
http://www.census.gov
Demographic information useful for identifying and analyzing the trade area.

Liszt
http://www.liszt.com/
Searchable directory of mailing list topics.

U.S. Census Bureau Tiger Map Service
http://tiger.census.gov
Source of census tract maps.

Relevant Case Studies

1. Toy Tips, Inc.
2. OXO (B)
3. Simtek, Inc.
4. Flight Time

11

*It is probably not love that makes the world go around, but rather those
mutually supportive alliances through which partners recognize their
dependence on each other for the achievement of shared and private goals.*

Fred Allen
Chairman, Pitney-Bowes Inc.
Leaders (1979)

Manufacturing Processes
for Entrepreneurs

Overview

▶ **The nature of world-class manufacturing for entrepreneurs**

▶ **The product manufacturing process**

▶ **Total quality control**

▶ **Product/process maintenance requirements and warranties**

▶ **Financial requirements**

Terms to Know

Continuous
  improvement 199
Total quality
  control 200

Self-managed
  teams 200
Product-focused
  organizations 202

Process-focused
  organizations 202
Just-in-time system 205
Gannt Charts 206

PERT 206
Quality circles 209
ISO 9000 212

Profile 11.1

Keeping America's Companies Clean

Most people might think that a company producing industrial detergent would be pretty mundane. (After all, how difficult is it to produce a cleaning agent?) To ChemStation in Dayton, Ohio, industrial cleaners are as varied and unique as the customers, and the company mass-customizes its products to the specific needs of each customer.

    The fifteen-year-old company's customers range from car wash companies to the U.S. Air Force. In 1983 ChemStation was delivering its industrial detergent in its own 55-gallon drum, but at about that time, the costs of plastic, gasoline, and drivers went up drastically.

CEO George Homan soon found himself spending more for packaging than for making the detergent. In a moment of creativity and daring, he began a new delivery system based on permanent reusable containers, tanks half the size of the originals. They were half-sized because he was now delivering concentrate, letting the customer add the water on site. During the process of installing permanent tanks at customer sites, he discovered that his detergent reacted differently in different environments. In other words, it cleaned better in some environments than in others. Homan was determined to meet his customers' cleaning needs, but accomplishing this would require adopting the latest technology and training his salespeople to collect the required information from the customer.

The process of collecting it became very important. ChemStation's salespeople go out to the customer sites to learn firsthand what kind of dirt, grease, or grime a customer is dealing with and what type of cleaner is needed. Information collected in the field is stored in a database called the Tank Management System, or TMS, which is linked to the ChemStation main lab and each of the 40 plants nationwide by modem. The plants contain the computer-driven machines that mix the customer's formula, machines that George Homan developed. When the plant receives a request for a particular type of detergent, the worker simply touches the number of the correct detergent formula; the machine then adds the selected raw materials and mixes the formula. Then a driver takes the mixture to the customer's site and fills the reusable tank. This process is based on the just-in-time system, so ChemStation monitors the usage of detergent at each site. In the beginning the salesperson will check the site periodically and call in an order when the tank is low. Over time, however, usage patterns develop and the salesperson doesn't have to check the tank. Homan is working on a device attached to the customer's tank that will dial the TMS when the tank is low and order a new batch.

Homan claims that using the mass customization technique has saved the company a tremendous amount of money. Since 1985, his gross profit margin per customer has jumped about 50 percent, while the cost per customer has dropped 25 percent. In fact, because of technology, ChemStation now can manufacture the custom product as cheaply as the company was able to manufacture a standardized product.

SOURCE: Sarah Schafer, "Have It Your Way," *Inc. Technology*, November 1997, p. 56.

How does ChemStation use mass customization and just-in-time to satisfy its customers?

Many high-growth ventures involve new, innovative products. For these product manufacturing or assembly ventures, the operational plan for the business consists of a fairly complex analysis that includes product development, prototyping, production processes, and inventory control mechanisms. The depth of analysis is a function of the type of product or service being offered, the technological newness of the product, and the number of different ways the product can be produced. Generally speaking, product companies must undergo more in-depth, thorough technical analysis than service companies, although a lack of thoroughness in either case can spell disaster for a new venture. Certainly ChemStation's development of a sophisticated process to serve customer needs resulted in enormous growth and substantially higher gross margins.

This chapter will look at the product manufacturing process. Recall that the product development aspect of the process was discussed in Chapter 7.

The Nature of World-Class Manufacturing for Entrepreneurs

World-class manufacturing process strategy is comprised of four primary components: the customer, state-of-the-art technology, superior resources and processes, and continuous improvement. The absence of any one of them will result in a reduction in the overall productivity and effectiveness of the company.

The Customer

The customer is considered the driving force and the foundation on which all the other functions are based. You can achieve superior performance as a manufacturer only when the customer is involved in the manufacturing process. Today, when customers expect superior levels of quality, service, and response time, manufacturers cannot afford to be rigidly structured, cumbersome in size, and bureaucratic in their decision making. Instead, they must be small, flexible, fast, organizationally flat, and simple in design. This is good news for entrepreneurs whose businesses generally reflect these characteristics.

The Impact of Technology on Manufacturing

Probably no single factor has had more of an impact on manufacturing processes for entrepreneurs than technology. Technology has made it possible for entrepreneurs to focus on their core competencies—what they do best—and outsource to other manufacturers those tasks that the other manufacturers do best. Network technology enables entrepreneurs to stay in touch with the companies to which they outsource and to decrease their set-up and wait times. In fact, in some industries, small companies are elaborately linked to provide a type of "one-stop shopping" experience for a much larger company. Certainly this is the case in the film industry, where many smaller companies work together on a single project.

The Importance of Total Quality Management to Manufacturing

Total Quality Management (TQM) refers to a framework or system for integrating superior quality into all aspects of a business. For manufacturers this means designing processes that include continuous improvement, total quality control, self-directed teams, automation, computer-integrated manufacturing, and just-in-time production and inventory control introduced in Chapter 10.

Continuous Improvement

Under the principle of **continuous improvement**, everything that a company does is a process, and every element of that process is held under a microscope to see if it can be improved upon. This can be accomplished through a process known as PDCA, which stands for *plan, do, check, act.* It is a way of analyzing a process problem (for example, a problem in judging quality against a standard), then planning for a change in the current process and monitoring the results of that change.*

---

*An expanded discussion of PDCA can be found in Kathleen Allen's *Growing and Managing an Entrepreneurial Business* (1999). Boston: Houghton Mifflin.

Total Quality Control

The goal of **total quality control** (TQC) is to eliminate all defects at all stages of the process; in other words, to achieve perfection. The basic principles of TQC include (1) customer satisfaction as the fundamental goal of any organization; (2) the use of quality circles or some process by which employees are brought together frequently to discuss issues and plans; (3) policy deployment or a planning and review tool that consists of annual objectives and strategies; and (4) foolproof solutions to problems, so that they don't occur again. TQC is discussed in more detail on page 208.

Self-Managed Teams

Like quality circles, **self-managed teams** (SMTs) give employees more input into what they do for the company and result in higher levels of productivity and quality. They also improve flexibility and responsiveness to changing market conditions because decisions are made more quickly and changes are implemented with fewer problems. In manufacturing, this may mean putting a team in charge of the production of a particular product or a particular portion of a more complex product. They have responsibility and authority to make decisions related to quality issues.

Automation

One of the most far-reaching effects of technology is automation in the various forms of robotics, machinery, computers, and so forth. Today automation is used not just for cost reduction but for gains in productivity, flexibility, and quality. A few of the automation techniques in use include:

1. *Bar coding.* This procedure was first used in the retail industry to track inventories of products, but it's also an excellent tracking device for manufacturers. Each part or product is inscribed with a bar code that contains all the relevant information about the part and relieves the company of the necessity of entering this information into a computer, where the chance for entry error is high.

2. *Computer-generated instruction, fabrication, and assembly.* The most technologically advanced manufacturers have put computer screens on the factory floor at work areas so that workers can easily access designs, do instantaneous modification, and program parts for fabrication or assembly. They can all access essential information on purchase orders, such as new orders, the status of orders in process, and the final disposition of an order.

3. *Electronic data interchange (EDI).* This technology makes it possible for companies to transfer designs and other graphical data between remote sites virtually in real time. It has also made it possible for retailers and wholesalers to be online with their manufacturers so that reorders are triggered electronically. This is important for companies that want to maintain minimal inventories and to ensure that high-demand items are rapidly replaced on store shelves.

The Product Manufacturing Process

A typical manufacturing plant has five functional areas, as depicted in Figure 11.1.

The *purchasing* function is responsible for the purchase of raw materials or components. Its effectiveness is judged by the quality of the raw materials, by their cost, and by the timeliness of their delivery. The *materials management/production scheduling* section is responsible for moving the raw materials through the production process and storing them. Its effectiveness is judged by both the cost of inventory and ability to meet demand for raw materials. *Production* converts raw materials into finished goods. Its effectiveness is judged by the quality of the goods produced, by their cost, and by the timeliness of production. These effectiveness factors also apply to assembly plants. The *quality* function is responsible for the quality of the finished product and is judged by its ability to detect defective goods before they leave the factory and to develop methods for reducing the number of defects during production. The *maintenance* function maintains and upgrades the manufacturing equipment. Its effectiveness is judged on the basis of cost, as well as on the percentage of unscheduled downtime that the equipment experiences.

Profile 11.2

Bringing Your Competitor into the Business

Small manufacturers today have learned that it's often difficult to compete in a market unless they do some once-radical things like working with their direct competitors. Consider the case of a plastics-molding company facing the opportunity to work with a very large customer. The small plastics manufacturer can handle, up to a point, the molding job the larger company wants, but not the decorating work required. To keep the customer, this manufacturer has to align itself with a competitor who has the capability to do both.

It's a great risk for the tiny manufacturer, but it's a risk that must be taken in order to survive. The risk is threefold, as it involves sharing information, potentially exposing one's own company's weaknesses, and possibly losing the customer to the competitor.

Microbrewers in Oregon have put together a network of 40 brewers under the marketing label of Full Sail Brewing in an effort to gain clout in an industry where the behemoths Miller and Anheuser-Busch dominate. In the beginning, Microbrewers used the network to lobby for common causes such as excise taxes and advertising limits, but it soon became apparent that they had marketing clout as well against the "pseudo craft brews" coming out of the giant breweries. Their network has also achieved marketing power in overseas markets where individually, they wouldn't have been noticed.

One important thing to remember about using networks is that in a changing marketplace, you must expect that the network will change over time. Partners will come and go, and a mechanism must be set up to deal with that contingency. The fundamental basis for success in a network is trust. You must create a team environment built on the knowledge that you and your competitors will all be better off for having worked together than any of you would have been working against each other. And the market will decide who has the best product.

Source: Donna Fenn, "Sleeping with the Enemy," *Inc.*, November 1997, p. 78.

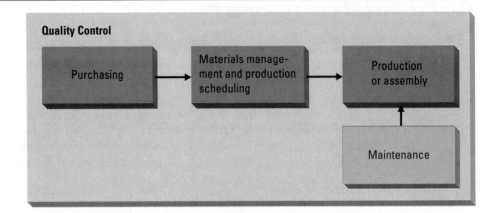

Figure 11.1
The Product
Manufacturing
Process

Manufacturing firms are typically organized as product-focused or process-focused organizations. **Product-focused organizations** generally are highly decentralized, so that they can respond better to market demands. Therefore, each product group acts essentially like a separate company, a profit center. This type of organization is well suited to products that don't require huge economies of scale or capital-intensive manufacturing technologies. **Process-focused organizations,** on the other hand, are common among manufacturers with capital-intensive processes such as those seen in the semiconductor industry. These organizations are highly centralized in order to control all the functions of the organization. Whether the company is product- or process-focused, it must be able to extend its control beyond the five functional areas, so that it is not at the mercy of its suppliers at one end and its distributors at the other. This control is usually accomplished through strategic alliances.

As was discussed in Chapter 10, the virtual enterprise, consisting of strategic alliances between all links in the value chain, is one way to achieve control of the entire process from raw materials to distribution, while still remaining small and flexible enough to meet changing needs and demands. This model is similar to that of the Japanese *keiretsu,* which links banks, suppliers, electronics, and auto firms together through a series of cross-ownerships. The United States model, however, leaves ownership in the hands of the individual owners but links the organizations into a virtual entity that acts as a team with a common goal. Wal-Mart is probably the best example of this type of partnership and integration. It has established point-of-sale linkups with its suppliers and has given its manufacturers the responsibility for handling inventory. The ultimate goal is to construct one organization with a common purpose that encompasses the entire supply chain from raw materials supplier to retailer, with each link along the chain performing the task that it does best. Establishing this type of network takes time. A start-up company can't expect to quickly achieve the level of integration and control that a Wal-Mart has taken years to accomplish. Instead, start-up companies need to build relationships slowly, starting with key independent contractors to whom they may be outsourcing some tasks.

Materials Requirements

Any business that purchases raw materials or parts for production of goods for resale must carefully consider the quality, quantity, and timing of those purchases. Quality goods are those that meet specific needs. Quality varies considerably among vendors, so if you've established certain quality standards for your products, you must find vendors who will consistently supply that precise level of quality. The quantity purchased is a function of demand, manufacturing capability, and storage capability. Planning purchases so that capital and warehouse space are not tied up any longer than necessary is the result of good timing. As materials account for approximately 50 percent of total manufacturing cost, it is crucial to balance these three factors carefully.

Vendor Issues

Locating vendors to sell you raw materials or goods for resale is not difficult, but finding the best vendors for your purposes is another matter entirely, as you learned in Chapter 10. The first decision is whether to buy from one vendor or more than one. Obviously, if a single vendor cannot supply all your needs, that decision is made. There are several advantages to using a single vendor where possible:

▶ You will probably get more individual attention and better service.

▶ Your orders will be consolidated, so you may be able to get a discount based on quantity purchased.

However, the principal disadvantage of using just one vendor is that should that vendor suffer a catastrophe (its facility burns to the ground, like the Japanese company that was the prime supplier of RAM chips), it may be difficult or impossible to find an alternate source in a short period of time. To guard against this contingency, you may want to follow the general rule of using one supplier for about 70 to 80 percent of your needs, and one or more additional suppliers for the rest.

When considering a specific vendor as your source, ask yourself several questions:

1. Can the vendor deliver enough of what you need when you need it?

2. What is the cost of transportation using the vendor you are considering? If the vendor is located far away, costs will be higher and it may be more difficult to get the service you require.

3. What services is the vendor offering you? For example, how often will sales representatives call on you?

4. Is the vendor knowledgeable about the product line?

5. What are the vendor's maintenance and return policies?

It is also important to shop vendors to compare prices, just as you would if you were purchasing equipment. Check for trade discounts and quantity discounts that may make a particular vendor's deal more enticing.

Computer technology has made materials planning more of a science than ever before. Information systems can now provide you or the person doing your purchasing with detailed feedback on supplier performance, delivery reliability, and quality control results, which facilitates supplier comparisons. Comparing results across suppliers gives you more leverage when it's time to renegotiate the annual contracts with suppliers. Check Profile 11.3 to see how one company built vendor relationships.

Inventory Requirements

Today, businesses that hold inventories of raw materials or goods for resale have found that they must reduce these inventories significantly to remain competitive. Instead of purchasing large quantities and receiving them on a monthly basis, businesses are purchasing daily or weekly in an effort to avoid costly inventories. Of course, some inventory of finished goods must be maintained to meet delivery deadlines; therefore, a delicate balance must be achieved between goods coming into the business, work in progress, and goods leaving the business to be sold.

In the past, inventories were built up on the basis of the state of the economy or in reaction to problems in an inventory control system. If times were

---

Profile 11.3

A Quick Lesson in Vendor Relationships

In 1994, David Brent took over as president of The Nutty Bavarian, a snack retailer in Lake Mary, Florida, and got a fast lesson in vendor relationships. The company operates kiosks where its cinnamon-glazed almonds and pecans are sold. At the time when Brent took over operations, about a third of the kiosk locations were unprofitable, causing a cash crunch for the company. It wasn't long before Brent found that The Nutty Bavarian owed more than $100,000 to suppliers with whom the previous management had not maintained very good relations.

Brent decided that being direct with his suppliers would be the best approach. He then mapped out a course to work out payment plans with suppliers and to close some of the unprofitable kiosks. He found that his suppliers liked his honesty and were willing to give him extended terms as long as he paid the agreed-upon amounts on time and continued to order nuts. By the end of his first year, all the overdue debts were paid.

Brent believes that it makes sense to call suppliers when there's a problem—rather than wait until they call you. "When you actually do what you say you will," he points out, "that separates you from 90 percent of the others they work with." In 1997, revenues were expected to reach $4 million.

SOURCE: "The Nuts and Bolts of Supplier Relations," *Nation's Business,* August 1997, p. 11.

good, producers increased stocks of inventory to meet expected demand. Then, when the economy slowed, they usually had shelves of leftover stock. Reductions in inventory succeeded in exposing typical problems: equipment imbalances, paperwork backlog, excessively long setups, vendor problems, and problems with purchase lead time.

Newer systems, like just-in-time (JIT), help manufacturers maintain better control of their inventories by eliminating production and inventory problems, then reducing inventory to only that which is needed.

Just-in-Time

The **just-in-time system** of materials and inventory management deserves its own heading, as it is fundamentally different from other inventory systems. Coming originally from Japan, JIT has taken hold in the United States. The philosophy behind JIT is "to produce the minimum number of units in the smallest possible quantities at the latest possible time."[1] A well-devised and implemented JIT system can do the following things.

▶ Increase direct and indirect labor productivity

▶ Increase equipment capacity

▶ Reduce manufacturing lead time

▶ Reduce the cost of failure

▶ Reduce the cost of purchased materials

▶ Reduce inventories

▶ Reduce space requirements

In essence, the goal is to eliminate waste in the manufacturing process. Consequently, to implement JIT it is necessary to look beyond mere inventory to all other aspects of the manufacturing process as well. Starting with the last operation, which is usually the customer requirement, work backward through the manufacturing process. Customer demand determines how many products are produced. The number of products to be produced determines the production capability requirements, which in turn determine the amount of raw materials needed. In general, a firm maintains an inventory no larger than needed to support one day of production. To do this, it has to have the cooperation of its suppliers and its distributors, with severe penalties for not being on time—that is, for being either too early or late. This, of necessity, reduces the number of suppliers a JIT firm typically deals with. JIT also requires strict quality control because with minimal inventories, there is no excess inventory to cover rejects.

A traditional factory is laid out by functional department, usually based on a particular process or technology. The result is that products are produced in batches. This is the antithesis of JIT, which specifies that the plant be laid out by product. With JIT the equipment is positioned in the order in which it is used to produce a particular product or family of related products.

It is also important to plan production so as to produce only enough to meet demand. For example, suppose you expect to sell a total of 100 units of your product next month. Then:

$$100/20 \text{ work days} = 5 \text{ units a day}$$

$$5/8 \text{ work hours} = .63 \text{ unit per hour}$$

$$\text{or 1 unit every hour and a half}$$

This calculation must be reworked every month as demand changes.

One way suppliers are meeting the needs of a company using JIT is by involving independent contractors specializing in "time-sensitive" deliveries. For example, one company has installed two-way satellite communication on its trucks so that shipments can be tracked in real time. Other businesses, like American Distribution Systems, Inc., help businesses that need to ship to retailers. They stock merchandise in their warehouses, process orders, make deliveries, and handle billing. In that way retailers don't incur the costs associated with a backup supply of items. Avoiding too much inventory seems to be a continuing trend for the next decade. However, to work effectively, it requires careful coordination and cooperation of all members of the supply chain.

Production Requirements

The production function of a manufacturing business is its lifeblood. Decisions made in this area directly impact output level, product quality, and costs. Planning for production, therefore, is key to manufacturing efficiency and effectiveness. Most manufacturers begin by scheduling; that is, by identifying and describing each activity that must be completed to produce the product, and the amount of time it takes to complete each activity. Two methods traditionally used to aid the scheduling process are Gannt Charts and PERT Diagrams.

Gannt Charts

Gannt Charts are a way to depict the tasks to be performed and the time required for each. Consider Figure 11.2. The task to be completed is outlined (in this case, fulfilling customer orders) on the vertical axis, with the time to completion on the horizontal. Notice that the solid line represents your plan for completion, while the dashed line depicts where you are in the process toward completion. Gannt Charts are best for simple projects that are independent of each other.

PERT Diagrams

PERT is an acronym for Program Evaluation and Review Technique. This method is helpful when the production being scheduled is more complex and subject to the interdependence of several activities going on either simultaneously or in sequence. In other words, some tasks cannot be started until others have been completed. To begin, you must identify the major activities involved in producing the product and arrange them in the order in which

Scheduled time — — — — Actual progress

Order	Order	September				October				November			
Number	Quantity	6-9	12-16	19-23	26-30	3-7	10-14	17-21	24-28	1-5	7-11	14-18	21-25
5348	1,000												
5349	1,500												
5350	500												

Figure 11.2
Gannt Chart

they occur. Be sure to identify any activities that must occur in sequence; that is, one activity cannot occur until another is finished. Construct a pictorial network that describes the process. Then estimate the time to complete each activity and note it on the chart. This is usually calculated as most optimistic, most likely, and most pessimistic. The statistics involved in analyzing the network are beyond the scope of this book but essentially consist of 1) identifying the critical path, which is the longest path and is important because a delay in any of the activities along the critical path can delay the entire project; 2) computing slack time on all events and activities (difference between latest and earliest times); and 3) calculating the probability of completion within the time allotted.

Profile 11.4

The Virtual Distribution Channel: The Case of Lee Apparel Company, Inc.

Based in Merriam, Kansas, the Lee Apparel Company learned that creating strategic alliances up and down its distribution channel would allow it to fine-tune its production and better meet the demands of its retailers. Using Point-of-Sale (POS) data transmitted electronically from the retailer to Lee on a daily or weekly basis, the retailer is able to replenish high-demand products within a matter of days instead of weeks. In some cases Lee has agreements with retailers to ship automatically when POS data indicate stock has reached a critical level based on demand.

To accomplish this, Lee sends every item from its factory with a Universal Product Code (UPC) bar code attached. When the bar code is scanned, the retailer's computer records the item number, color, and size. This information then helps Lee adjust its manufacturing process to meet demand. The success of this program is ultimately dependent on businesses' willingness to share information. In the end, everyone benefits.

The numbered nodes on the diagram (Figure 11.3) refer to the start and completion points for each event. The dummy line was placed in the diagram to account for the completion of event e's being preceded by events b and d. Both must be completed before event g can start.

There are several popular software products on the market, such as Micro Planner X-Pert and Microsoft Project, that can help entrepreneurs schedule their production capacity. Tracking production from the outset of the business allows you to make more realistic strategic decisions about growth and expansion.

Identifying all the tasks in the production process makes it easier to determine what equipment and supplies are needed for completing the tasks. If it is determined that the equipment necessary to produce the product is beyond the start-up resources of the entrepreneur, it may be time to consider outsourcing part or all of production to a manufacturer who has excess capacity with the needed equipment.

After the production tasks are identified, a preliminary layout of the plant to estimate floor space requirements for production, offices, and services can be made. It may be beneficial to consult with an expert in plant layout to ensure that you make the most efficient use of the limited space you have.

Total Quality Control

Total quality control is the process of reconciling product output with the standards set for that product. More specifically, it is "an effective system for integrating the quality-development, quality-maintenance, and quality-improvement efforts of the various groups in an organization so as to enable marketing, engineering, production, and service at the most economical levels, which allow for full customer satisfaction."[2] In this sense quality does not necessarily mean "best"; it means "best for certain customer requirements," which are the actual use and selling price of the product.[3] It has been

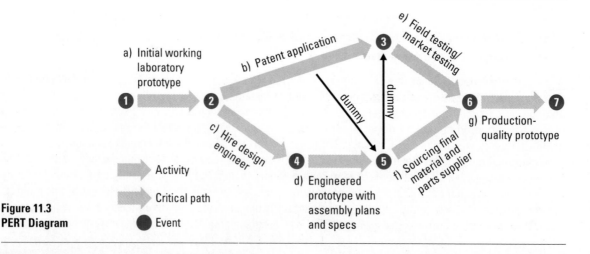

Figure 11.3
PERT Diagram

said that one thing manufacturers have learned from history is that "the primary objective of the company is to put the quality of the product ahead of every other consideration. A profit or loss notwithstanding, the emphasis will always be on quality."[4] Today thousands of manufacturers have embraced the philosophy of quality first but have focused principally on equipment and processes rather than on the human element. Both must be done, as total quality control must permeate every aspect of the organization.

Quality is a strategic issue that is designed to bring about business profitability and positive cash flow. Effective total quality programs result in "improved levels of customer satisfaction, reduced operating costs, reduced operating losses and field service costs, and improved utilization of resources."[5]

The Inspection Process

One way manufacturers control quality is through implementing a regular inspection process that takes place during several stages of the manufacturing operation. Often, primarily due to cost, a random sample of products is chosen for the inspection. This method catches potential defects early in the process, before the products become finished goods. Whether each item produced is checked or a random sampling is conducted is a function of what is being produced, the cost, and whether the item will be destroyed by the inspection process. For example, if you are producing an expensive piece of machinery, it may be prudent to subject each item to the inspection process, as the cost of inspection is more than offset by the price of the item. But if you are producing a food product, once it is inspected it cannot be sold, so you can't afford to inspect more than a representative random sample of each batch.

Entrepreneurs who want to achieve total quality will probably set a no-defect goal for product manufacturing. In Chapter 7 we discussed the importance of designing right the first time and designing for manufacturability. Superior design is the first step in achieving defect-free production. Another step is giving work teams the power to stop production for a quality issue.

Pelco, a California-based manufacturer of video surveillance equipment, has achieved a virtually defect-free manufacturing environment based on this philosophy.* It has been so successful that rather than needing to inspect at the end of the process, Pelco has built inspection for quality into every step of the process so that it is every worker's responsibility to catch a defect before the product is passed on to the next worker.

Quality Circles

Quality circles are groups of employees who regularly work together on some aspect of the production process. They meet several times a month with the help of an outside facilitator to discuss problems and ideas related to

---

*A case study on Pelco, Inc., written by the author is available in *Growing and Managing an Entrepreneurial Business* (1999). Boston: Houghton Mifflin.

their work environment. They often come up with new solutions to problems, solutions that are then put into effect, thus improving the efficiency and effectiveness of the manufacturing process and the product as well. Using quality circles gives employees a vested interest in what they are producing; consequently, they are more likely to pay close attention to improving the way their task is completed.

In reality, the real success or failure of the quality control effort is dependent on the human element in the process: customers, employees, and management. Quality begins with satisfying the needs of the customers, and that cannot be accomplished unless those needs and requirements are communicated to management and employees. An entrepreneur with a new venture has a unique opportunity to create a philosophy of quality from the very birth of the business, in the way the business is run and in the employees hired. In this sense entrepreneurs have the advantage of creating new habits and patterns of behavior instead of having to change old ones.

Using Customers for Quality Control

Recall the discussion of Quality Function Deployment from Chapter 7. At its core is the philosophy that a company produces what the customer needs, when he or she needs it. How does this translate into quality control? Customers, by their demands for reliability and performance in a highly competitive market, establish the standards that must be met when the product is designed and produced. If customers perceive that the product does not meet their needs or does not meet them as well as another product could, lost sales result.

Using Employees for Quality Control

If you want employees to buy into the notion of quality control at every level, they must be given the responsibility and authority to make changes that will improve the process and product at every level. If you are going to install new technology to improve the process, the employees need to be trained not only in how to use it but also in how to look for potential problems that would affect quality. The continual use of awareness and training programs will help employees understand their importance in the whole manufacturing process.

Using Management for Quality Control

For total quality management to work, key management must be "on the floor," learning every aspect of production and supporting the efforts of employees. It is their job to bring the requirements of customers to the people who will satisfy those requirements. It is also management's job to establish company-wide, measurable quality goals. Too often management focuses more on productivity goals than on quality goals. Ultimately it is quality, not productivity, that will sell the product.

The Baldrige Award Criteria

The Malcolm Baldrige National Quality Award is the United States' highest quality honor. Competition is tough and the selection process daunting, but the award creates a standard to which small companies can compare themselves. Following is a list of the Baldrige criteria.

1. *Leadership.* Demonstrate evidence that senior management promotes quality values, and that those values influence day-to-day management.

2. *Information and analysis.* How effectively is the company using competitive comparisons and does it support quality objectives through data analysis?

3. *Strategic quality planning.* Does the business plan incorporate quality requirements?

4. *Human resources development and management.* What are the systems and practices that involve employees in education, training, assessment, and recognition?

5. *Management of process quality.* Check for quality in product and service design, process control, quality assessment and documentation, and assurance of the quality of supplies.

6. *Quality and operational results.* Examine trends and levels in improvement of products and services, business services, and suppliers' quality.

7. *Customer focus and satisfaction.* Evaluate customer service standards, customer satisfaction ratings, and the use of customer complaints and suggestions.[6]

For a small, growing firm, however, it is a fairly costly process that includes, among other things, writing a quality control manual. The cost of achieving the standards is not as great as the cost of obtaining certification, which is subject to audit semiannually and must be renewed annually. However, these costs must be weighed against the advantages. With certification, the companies with which the entrepreneur does business don't have to inspect to know the company's standards for quality, and it makes it much easier to enter the export market. Here are three ways to reduce the costs involved:

▸ Compare fees charged by ISO consultants to find the best rate.

▸ Check with major customers to see if they will help subsidize the cost of certification.

▸ Determine whether you really need certification. Perhaps just meeting the standards is sufficient in your business.

In an increasingly global market, it is not surprising that the need for international quality standards has arisen. **ISO 9000**, developed by the International Organization for Standardization in Geneva, is a series of international quality standards and certification that makes it easier for a product to enter the export market. Approved by 95 countries, the standards apply to both manufacturing and service businesses and certify quality control procedures.

Product/Process Maintenance Requirements and Warranties

Maintenance, in the manufacturing process, refers both to the maintenance of plant and equipment used to produce the product and the maintenance or servicing of the product after it is sold.

Process Maintenance

At some point any machine will break down, which can mean lost sales and costly repairs. There are three ways to prevent unexpected breakdowns from disrupting the production process. The process can be organized so that when one machine is down, the work can be shifted to another. Another way is to build up inventories at each stage of the production process so that machines can keep working as long as the inventory lasts. (This method, however, will probably not work in a company that has chosen a JIT system of inventory management.) The third, and perhaps the best, approach is to regularly undertake preventative maintenance by checking and fixing the machines before they break down. The advantage of this approach is that you control when the downtime occurs.

Product Maintenance

The entrepreneur who subscribes to total quality management will likely wish to provide warranties with products, so as to protect against potential liability and to demonstrate that the company stands behind the product. Today product warranties have also become a marketing tool.

Some of the decisions to be made regarding warranties include:

▶ *Length of warranty.* This depends on industry standards.

▶ *Covered components.* Some components may come from other manufacturers who have their own warranties. In this case, it is important to have your use of that component on the product certified by the OEM (Original Equipment Manufacturer) so that you don't invalidate the warranty. Then, if a warranted component from that manufacturer becomes defective, it can be sent back. However, it is probably good business practice to have customers return the product to you or your distributors for service, repair, or exchange under your warranty, which covers the whole product.

◗ *Product scope.* Will the warranty cover one or all products in a line or will there be separate warranties?

◗ *Market scope.* Will the same warranty apply in all markets? This will be a function of state and foreign laws.

◗ *Conditions of the warranty that the customer must fulfill.* Is there anything the customer must do to keep the warranty in force, such as servicing or replacing disposable parts? These conditions should not include registering the product via a postcard. Today a product is covered by warranty from the moment it is purchased, whether or not the purchaser returns a postcard stating when and where it was purchased and answering a short, informational questionnaire. What many companies do to get the postcard information is offer update notification and potential discounts on future products.

◗ *Who executes the warranty?* The entrepreneur must decide who will handle warranty claims (manufacturer, dealers, distributors), recognizing that customers do not like to mail products back to the manufacturer.

◗ *How the public will be educated about the warranty.*

◗ *Policies for refunds and returns, and shipping and handling costs.* This is a function of the entrepreneur's philosophy about doing business. A customer-oriented company would probably offer a generous return policy and pay for the cost of returns.

Providing a warranty involves a cost to the manufacturer; however, that cost must be weighed against the potential loss of business if no warranty is provided. In the case of a new business with a new product, it is difficult to anticipate the number of problems that might occur as the product gets into the marketplace. Careful and adequate field testing of the product prior to market entry will go a long way toward eliminating many potential problems and the possibility of a recall, which is very costly for any firm, let alone a growing new business.

Financial Requirements

Once the raw materials and parts list has been developed and the manufacturing or assembly process defined, including labor requirements, it is possible to calculate the total investment required to start the business and the per unit cost of manufacturing the product. To be sure, the initial units produced will cost significantly more to manufacture and assemble because the volume will usually not be sufficient to achieve industry discounts on raw materials and parts, and the plant and equipment will not be used to full capacity. Consequently, gross margins may be extremely small in the early stages until a sufficient increase in volume allows an economy of scale that reduces the per unit cost.

The calculation of the up-front investment in plant and equipment, coupled with the high per unit cost of production, has resulted in many entrepreneurs' deciding to outsource manufacturing to an established manufacturing firm. Some products that consist of off-the-shelf components from OEMs can give the entrepreneur the option to set up an assembly operation, which is far less costly than a manufacturing plant. In any case, the process of outlining all the costs of setting up a product company is invaluable in making the final decisions about how the business will operate.

Table 11.1   Technical/Operational Plan

Product Specifications
Design and performance specifications
Level of quality
Service requirements
Status of development

Materials Requirements
Raw materials and parts required
Availability of raw materials and parts
Source of supply for raw materials and parts
Delivery lead time for suppliers

Inventory Requirements
Description of inventory system
Raw materials and purchased parts in inventory
Work in process inventory
Finished goods inventory

Production Requirements
Explanation of production process
Equipment needed, costs and alternatives
Output capacity from production
Materials handling equipment

Labor Requirements
Skills required
Availability of labor and cost
Support staff required

Maintenance Requirements
Plant equipment maintenance and repair
After sale service and warranties on product

Financial Requirements
Start-up investment in equipment and inventory
Manufacturing costs—raw materials, labor, equipment usage

Check Table 11.1 for an outline of a technical/operational plan to help you look at this aspect of your manufacturing business. Entrepreneurs who wish to manufacture products have many options today. It is still possible in most industries to manufacture domestically and be able to compete if you refine your processes and build quality into every step. If it is too costly to do all your manufacturing in-house, consider outsourcing the capabilities that are not your strengths, or outsource everything and play a coordination role until the company is producing a healthy cash flow. In some industries, particularly labor-intensive ones, the only way to achieve competitive costs is to manufacture in a country where labor costs are low; Mexico and China are two examples. Look at what other firms in your industry are doing. Be aware, though, that customers are not always looking for the lowest cost; rather, they're looking for the highest quality at a competitive price. If the products you produce are innovative and meet the specific needs of your target customer, you should be able to manufacture domestically in a successful way.

New Venture Checklist

Have you:

❑ **Outlined the production process?**

❑ **Found suppliers for your material requirements?**

❑ **Determined how inventory will be handled?**

❑ **Developed quality control measures?**

❑ **Determined the product/process maintenance requirements?**

Issues to Consider

1. What is the difference between product-focused and process-focused companies?
2. What are three factors that should be taken into consideration when choosing vendors to meet materials requirement?
3. How can PERT diagrams aid the entrepreneur in production scheduling?
4. In what ways can the human resources of the business help control quality in all areas of the organization?

Experiencing Entrepreneurship

1. Visit a manufacturing facility that is using technology and develop a flow chart of the manufacturing process.
2. Interview an entrepreneur about quality and what system is being used to maintain it.

Additional Sources of Information

Clark, K., & T. Fujimoto. (1991). *Product Development Performance*. Boston: Harvard Business School Press.

Dobler, D.W. and D.N. Burt. (1995). *Purchasing and Supply Management*. New York: McGraw-Hill.

Griffin, A., and J.R. Hauser. (1993). "The Voice of the Customer." *Marketing Science*, Vol. 12, No. 1, p. 1.

Hay, E.J. (1988). *The Just-in-Time Breakthrough*. New York: John Wiley.

Hayes, R.H., S.C. Wheelwright, and K.B. Clark. (1988). *Dynamic Manufacturing*. New York: The Free Press.

Hopper, K. (1982). "Creating Japan's New Industrial Management: The Americans as Teachers." *Human Resource Management*, pp. 13–34.

Juran, J.M. (1988). *Juran on Planning for Quality*. New York: Free Press, pp. 4–5.

Manufacturing Assistance Program, Oak Ridge, TN. Tel. (800) 356-4USA. Technical assistance from U.S. Department of Energy scientists and engineers.

Mizuno S. (1988). *Management for Quality Improvement: The 7 New QC Tools*. Cambridge, MA: Productivity Press.

Shores, R. (1994). *Reengineering the Factory: A Primer for World-Class Manufacturing*. Milwaukee, WI: ASQC Quality Press.

Internet Resources

ISO Online
http://www.iso.ch
The International Organization for Standardization site, which explains their work and the standards for quality management and assurance.

Technology Transfer Information Center
http://www.nal.usda.gov/ttic
A good site to help turn federally funded research into profits.

Relevant Case Studies

1. The Penduline Putter
2. OXO (B)
3. Simtek, Inc.

Distribution Channels

Overview

▶ **Distribution as a competitive strategy**

▶ **Distribution channels**

▶ **Creating a distribution strategy**

Terms to Know

Category killers 218
Value-added business
 solutions 219
Value chain 219

Direct channel of
 distribution 220
Indirect channel of
 distribution 220

Intermediaries 220
Consumer market
 channels 221
Wholesalers 222

Agents/manufacturer's
 reps 223
Industrial channels 223
Logistics firms 228

Profile 12.1

Facing the Music

Would you say there might be a market for your product if distribution increased 300 percent in one year? Shirley Halperin thought so in February 1995, when she launched *Smug,* an alternative-music magazine based in Gramercy Park, New York. It took the music world by storm, growing from a dozen pages to fifty after just four issues.

Of course, when she decided to leave college just three units shy of graduation, Halperin had no idea she would be publishing a magazine. At that time she was working both at a small Manhattan record label and as an arts editor of the *Rutgers Review.* After being fired from the paper, she decided to start her own magazine with just $1,700 in personal

savings, and she brought with her a following from the staff of the paper. Though she was not prepared in the traditional sense to start a business, she did have a good handle on her competition. The *Village Voice* focused too much on politics; the *Aquarian Weekly* was targeted toward aging hippies. Both were expensive to subscribe to. Halperin saw a niche in providing a free magazine covering music that people her age would care about. She offered a new distribution channel for up-and-coming bands who couldn't afford to advertise in her competitors' magazines. For example, *Spin* charges $29,700 for a four-color full-page ad; *Smug* charges just $1,000. Her concept and distribution channel seem to be effective: huge companies like Polygram Group Distribution in Queens often use *Smug* to test or break in a new group.

Halperin has a staff of 30 writers, photographers, editors, and designers who work for free. Why? Because they're certain the magazine will make it big in the near future, and they want to be there when it does. Halperin runs the business from her Gramercy Park home. Most of the articles and artwork are delivered via modem, and her father handles the books. Totally lacking in business sophistication, she survives on creativity.

When *Smug* was a year old, Halperin finally wrote a business plan to raise capital. She needs $500,000 to grow to the next stage. Her goal is to become "the primary source of music information for every college student, concertgoer, and record buyer interested in New York's eclectic and hard-driving music scene." The magazine is available in 169 outlets in New York City, New Jersey, and Philadelphia, but is not carried by large music retailers. (She's working on that.) Still, Halperin is optimistic because the writing in *Smug* is considered very high caliber in the industry; in fact, it's been called "almost literary."

SOURCE: Alessandra Bianchi, "What's Love Got to Do with It?" *Inc.*, May 1996, p. 76.

What was the unique distribution strategy Halperin employed to penetrate her market in the publishing industry?

Distribution has traditionally been part of the marketing process—how do we get the product or service to the customer?—and looked at as a physical strategy of delivering the benefit to the customers when and where they need it. This usually entails a system of intermediaries (middlemen), a series of activities known as logistics, and relationships with the intermediaries, called channels of distribution.

Today, however, distribution has become a significant competitive strategy as well, in two major arenas. First, the new paradigm of mass customization requires a different distribution strategy, one that allows a company to compete successfully in a dynamic marketplace by satisfying *individual* customer needs. Shirley Halperin found a distribution niche in music industry publishing by providing her magazine, *Smug*, for free, something her 16–30-year-old customers appreciated. Some early examples of these new distribution strategies are direct marketing, cable TV shopping, and Internet shopping.

Second, low-cost distribution is a powerful tool for value creation in a market with sophisticated customers and with products and services that are less differentiated. In such a situation, price becomes the defining factor. Wal-Mart is probably the best example of successful low-cost distribution strategies that can force manufacturers to lower prices or modify their operations in order to deliver on price and a minimum level of quality. In commodity-type industries, such as food, manufacturers are often obliged to become their own low-cost distributors in order to survive. Even service industries are affected by these **category killers**. For example, information is fast becoming a commodity, with hundreds of companies positioning themselves as the low-cost provider of Internet services.

This chapter will look at distribution as a competitive strategy for marketing as well as the physical movement of products and services to the customer.

Distribution as a Competitive Strategy

In his book *Value Migration*, Adrian J. Slywotzky identified four new distribution patterns that entrepreneurs should be aware of.[1]

1. *The collapse of the middle.* In many industries a shift from routine product sales to a customized bundling of price, distribution, support, and information has occurred. Therefore, many products and services are being converted to **value-added business solutions**. For example, in the forms industry, for every dollar spent on business forms, customers spend $20 on the system for handling forms—labor, routing, storage, revisions, and so forth. Consequently, the physical product itself is not what contains the value, but the system for handling it. Companies that create value by improving systems or outsourcing the process will have greater success.

2. *Emergence of new customer sets.* As important as it is to identify current customers, it is equally important to recognize emerging customers. These emerging customers represent new niches in the market and potentially, new distribution strategies. For example, in the airline industry, deregulation resulted in a whole new class of leisure travelers who were price conscious, so airlines began to offer packages that delivered this benefit.

3. *Migration within the value chain.* The most successful companies are aware of the differing importance of individual steps in the **value chain** and concentrate on particular activities that allow them to capture maximum value at a particular step. The value chain is essentially the points in the distribution channel where value is added to the product or service. On the computer value chain, for example, suppliers Microsoft and Intel followed a strategy to dominate key upstream activities—operating systems and processors—while companies like EDS and Hewlett-Packard captured key downstream activities—the delivery of computing solutions to end-users.

4. *Redefinition of the product/service offering.* Value migration has occurred in many products and services. Starbucks, for instance, changed the way customers thought about coffee. The company transformed the product from a daily grind to an affordable luxury, from a beverage to an experience.

The Importance of a Distribution Strategy

Distributors, retailers, and other outlets are one way that businesses communicate to the customer, so they are very much partners in the organization, particularly in a virtual company. Their goal is to gather information from the customer so that the manufacturer or producer can revise and improve its offerings, and they are so important to the virtual company that finding good, loyal outlets is competitively difficult. In fact, distribution, once a mundane, routine occupation, has become the glamour stock of the business world with "channel surfer" entrepreneurs who are constantly seeking the most productive channel.[2]

The following are just a few examples from *Inc.* magazine of how some entrepreneurs are successfully making distribution strategy their competitive advantage.

- *Millstone Coffee.* Provides coffee beans to supermarket shoppers; selling direct to the supermarket. The normal channel is food brokers.

- *Design Basics.* A catalog of residential building plans geared toward professional residential builders and developers; uses direct mail. The usual channel is classified ads in builders' magazines.

- *Counterpoint Publishing.* Produces customized collections of state and federal rules and regulations for corporate-regulatory-compliance officers; uses an online route via the Internet. The normal route is direct mail.

- *IQ Software.* Wanted to focus on creating report-writing software and let other software developers who wrote for specialized industries license IQ's basic product to customize for accountants, pharmacists, and a variety of other end-users. It was cheaper and easier for these developers to license IQ's software than to write their own.[3]

Distribution Channels

Recall from Chapter 6 that a distribution channel is, quite simply, the route a product takes from the manufacturer to the customer or end-user (p. 111). We mentioned there are a number of choices available, depending on the nature of a venture, and noted that each choice will offer advantages, disadvantages, and consequences and will determine the type of organization the new venture becomes.

There are two basic types of distribution channels: direct and indirect.

Direct Channel

In a **direct channel of distribution**, the product or service moves from the manufacturer or producer directly to the customer. Service businesses generally operate in this fashion. For example, when you call a plumber to fix a pipe, or call your accountant to do your taxes, the work is handled directly by the company you called; no one else is involved. Selling through mail order is another way of using a direct channel. When manufacturers sell to the customer through one of their manufacturer's outlets, they are also using a direct channel. Newer examples of direct channels include the Internet and cable TV.

Indirect Channel

An **indirect channel of distribution** involves one or more **intermediaries** (middlemen), people who move products from the manufacturer or producer to the end-user. They include wholesalers, retailers, distributors, and agents. For example, suppose you are producing paper products such as cups and plates and so on. When the product leaves the production facility, it may go to a wholesaler who will then secure retailers. The retailer's job is to advertise so as to find customers who will buy the product.

Depending on the kind of business you plan to start, you will be dealing with either consumer channels or industrial channels of distribution.

Consumer Market Channels

Consumer market channels are used by businesses that sell to people who purchase consumer goods at the wholesale or retail level. There are several routes by which manufacturers can reach their target customers. (See Figure 12.1.) These routes include direct selling, retailers, wholesale distributors, and agents, to name just a few.

Direct Selling

The most direct channel in the consumer market is to sell to the customer, using no intermediaries. As discussed earlier, service businesses usually fall into this category. However, in the past few years a number of manufacturers have also begun bypassing intermediaries and selling directly to their customers. Clothing, household, and furniture manufacturers, among others, have opened outlets in special factory outlet malls located away from major metropolitan areas. Generally, however, manufacturers sell direct after they have established a following through their normal channels, as name recognition is present and little marketing effort is necessary. The outlets are a good way to get rid of excess inventory and slightly defective merchandise that can't be sold in the manufacturers' normal retail outlets. The substantial discounts attract customers from considerable distances.

Retailers

The most common way for manufacturers to get their products to customers is through retail stores, which are responsible for sales and advertising of the products. Using this channel, the manufacturer does not have to incur the

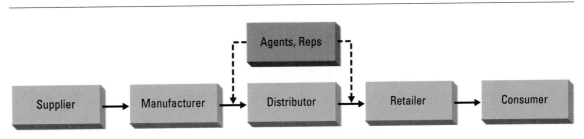

Figure 12.1
Indirect Consumer Channel

expense of maintaining a sales staff or stores. However, without a distributor, the manufacturer needs manufacturer's reps or in-house salespeople to locate potential retail customers and arrange for product distribution.

Wholesalers/Distributors

Wholesalers, or distributors (the terms are interchangeable in common usage), buy products in bulk from manufacturers and then seek retail outlets to reach the consumer. The wholesaler removes from the manufacturer the responsibility of finding suitable retail outlets for the products. A wholesale distributor can mean the difference between success and failure for a business. When you realize you are entrusting your most valuable assets—your customers—to the distributor, it becomes clear that selecting a distributor is a crucial part of the start-up process. Not only will good distributors contribute to increased sales; they also will help with product planning for the future. The specifics of what a distributor may do depend on the distributor. Some of the tasks performed by them are:

◗ Warehousing products

◗ Advertising and promotion

◗ Packaging and displays

◗ Training retail sales personnel

◗ Assisting with transportation to retailers

◗ Providing service backup

◗ Restocking retailers' shelves

The key to finding a good distributor is knowing whom to ask. Some of the sources of information on distributors are:

◗ Customers

◗ Suppliers

Profile 12.2

A New Source of Distribution

You've probably never considered the Houston Ballet's Nutcracker Market as a distribution channel for consumer products. Or how about a Junior League event?

Many consumer product merchants are finding that fund-raising events can be a profitable distribution channel for a small, growing company. Jazz It Up is a marketer of detachable sequin appliqués that distributes exclusively through fund-raising boutiques. They pay about $500 for space at an event and 10% of sales. Jazz It Up can gross $40,000 at a good show.

Chiasso, a Chicago-based retailer-cataloger of upscale toys and desk items, launched a retail site in Los Angeles after having a very profitable exhibit at a Junior League event in Newport Beach, California. Keven Wilder, Chiasso's founder, calls such events an excellent way to test market a new product.

Source: Susan Greco, "Distribution: Cash in with a Cause," *Inc.,* February 1995, p. 107.

- Lawyers

- Business consultants

- Bankers (they have knowledge of a distributor's payment record)

Look for a distributor who provides good service, prices competitively to retail outlets, and is trustworthy. When that distributor is chosen, execute a written contract with the distributor and monitor performance on a regular basis by sampling retail customers to determine whether they are satisfied with the product and the service the distributor provides.

Agents/Manufacturer's Reps

Often manufacturers/producers retain **agents**, brokers, or **manufacturer's reps** to find suitable outlets for their products. These agents arrange agreements with wholesalers and retailers for the manufacturer. Agents usually do not buy or hold an inventory of goods from the manufacturer; instead, they bring together manufacturers and distributors or retailers to establish the most efficient distribution channel. The manufacturer or producer shares the cost with other manufacturers represented by the agent and pays a commission on only what the agent sells.

Manufacturer's representatives are essentially independent salespeople who handle the manufacturer's business in specific territories and are paid on commission. Unlike agents who bring buyers and sellers together for individual transactions, reps work with a specific manufacturer on a continuing basis, receiving a commission per product sold. Reps may also provide warehousing in a territory and handle shipping the product to the retailer.

Industrial Channels of Distribution

Industrial channels consist of customers who purchase goods for use in their businesses. In these markets, the manufacturer is targeting another business,

---

Profile 12.3

Try Distributing Electronically

Today, virtually any product can be distributed electronically, even wine—in fact, especially wine, when you're a very small vintner who can't capture the attention of the major distributors. Long Vineyards of Napa Valley, California, a micro $750,000 producer of high-priced, award-winning chardonnays, sauvignon blancs, pinot grigios, and cabernets, decided to test the virtual method of distribution—to see if people would buy wine they had never tasted or smelled. Long Vineyards linked up with Virtual Vineyards, a retail site on the Internet, in hopes of reaching his target market: educated, high-income, curious customers. He saw the Internet as a way to reach a larger audience and increase pretax profits by 25% by letting Virtual Vineyards act as both distributor and retailer. Approximately 2,000 potential customers visit the Internet site daily to learn about wine. Though revenues to date have been nominal, the great benefit has been finding out who and where these unique customers are.

SOURCE: Stephanie Gruner, "Distribution: Pursuing the Electronic Channel," *Inc.,* March 1996, p. 91.

perhaps even another manufacturer, for the sale of its products. The options for industrial markets are similar to those in the consumer market. The manufacturer can choose to sell directly to the industrial user, using no intermediaries, or can use distributors or manufacturer's reps, who market to end-users. Another alternative is to work with agents, who act as a sales force for the manufacturer and either go through a distributor or go directly to the industrial user. (See Figure 12.2.)

Creating a Distribution Strategy

It's a good idea to depict your distribution options graphically. Apart from the obvious value of seeing the various options for getting the product or

---

Profile 12.4

Calyx & Corolla Innovation in Distribution

Jumping from a catalog called *Gardener's Eden*, which sold specialty gardening tools, to a fresh-flowers catalog may not seem a tremendous feat, but for Ruth Owades it was a true leap of faith. Her goal in starting Calyx & Corolla was to give customers the ability to see the fresh flowers they were buying in the catalog one day and receive them the next. How was this idea different from sending flowers through FTD?

Most flowers are cut (often in South America) and then shipped to a wholesaler (equivalent to a manufacturer/producer), then to a distributor, and finally to a retailer. Before they reach the customer, the flowers are six to ten days old. Owades wanted to streamline this complicated distribution system, to get the flowers to the customer more quickly.

To accomplish her dream, Owades had to convince growers that they should be in the gift business and send smaller quantities than usual. She needed grower partners who focused on quality, specialized in a particular flower variety, and had a commitment to service. She also had to find an overnight shipper used to dealing with perishable items and multi-shaped boxes, and a way of shipping the flowers undamaged. After negotiating a volume-pricing schedule and taking on legal liability for packages left at the door, Owades got Federal Express to work with her on the project.

By Valentine's Day after the first catalog went out, Calyx & Corolla had logged 5,000 orders. Yet things didn't go totally smoothly. Owades quickly learned, for instance, that she had to confirm a particular style of bouquet with a grower or face a situation where the grower didn't have what she specified. She also ended up dropping one of her six growers because the quality was not consistent. And then there were the natural disasters—the snowstorm that delayed shipping of flowers for Valentine's Day, the 1989 San Francisco earthquake that destroyed a warehouse and hurt some of her growers, and a freak cold spell in California in December that froze some stems.

Still, Ruth Owades ultimately succeeded by making the people in her distribution channel part of her start-up team, having them give input during each phase of the start-up process. The strategic alliances were formed to be mutually beneficial to all parties. As a result, Calyx & Corolla completed the start-up phase of the business more quickly than most new companies. In 1992, the company posted profits greater than 5% on sales of $10 million. Today the $20 million company has put its catalog online at web site http://www.calyxandcorolla.com, and is going global.

SOURCE: Leslie Brokaw, "Twenty-eight Steps to a Strategic Alliance," *Inc.*, April 1993, p. 96.

**Figure 12.2
Indirect Industrial
Channel**

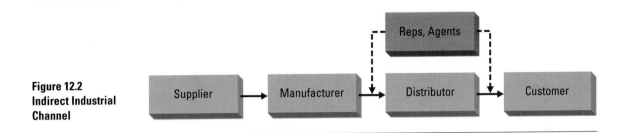

service to the customer, graphing the distribution channel will help you do the following:

▶ Judge the time from manufacturing to purchase by the customer on the basis of the lead time needed by each channel member

▶ Determine the ultimate retail price, based on the required markups by the intermediaries

▶ Figure the total costs of marketing the product

All these issues are a function of the distribution channel chosen.

Factors Affecting the Choice of Strategy

The usual factors should be considered when attempting to determine the most effective distribution strategy: costs, market coverage, and level of control.

Costs

Costs include all the various expenses related to marketing and distributing the product to the customer or end-user. Suppose you are manufacturing a consumer product in the sporting goods industry. Here is how you might compare the distribution options available to you. The most common route to the customer is:

$$Manufacturer \rightarrow Wholesaler \rightarrow Retailer \rightarrow Customer$$

At each stage, the channel member adds value to the product by performing a service that increases the chances of the product's reaching its intended customer (see Figure 12.3). The wholesaler seeks appropriate retail outlets, and the retailer advertises and promotes the product to its customers. The value created allows each channel member to increase the price of the product to the next channel member. For example, the manufacturer charges the wholesaler a price that covers the costs of producing the product plus an amount for overhead and profit. The wholesaler, in turn, adds an amount to cover the cost of the goods purchased and his or her overhead and profit. The retailer does the same and charges the final price to the customer. That price can typically be 4 to 5 times what it cost to manufacture the product (labor and materials).

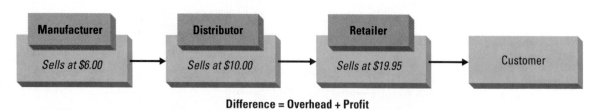

Difference = Overhead + Profit

Figure 12.3
Example of a Value Chain

Suppose you decide to bypass the wholesaler and sell directly to retailers:

Manufacturer→Retailer

It appears on the surface that the final retail price could be substantially lower, perhaps even priced at the rate at which the wholesaler sold to the retailer in the first example. However, there is a flaw in this reasoning. The wholesaler performed a valuable service. He or she made it possible for the manufacturer to focus on producing the product and not incur the cost of maintaining a larger marketing department, a sales force, additional warehouses, and a more complex shipping department. All these activities now become a cost to the manufacturer of doing business with retailers and must be factored into the decision to choose this distribution channel. This is not to say that it never makes sense for manufacturers to sell direct to retailers. However, it is important for the entrepreneur to consider all the costs, advantages, disadvantages, and consequences of choosing a particular market channel to reach the customer.

Other aspects of starting the new venture can be examined by studying the distribution channel options. For example, location and transportation decisions will be affected by the method chosen to reach the customer. Suppose you have chosen the following channel:

Manufacturer→Retailer

In this instance it may be advantageous to locate the manufacturing plant near major transportation networks to hold down shipping costs. Now consider the following channel:

Manufacturer→Wholesaler→Retailer→Customer

Here it is not important for the manufacturer to be located conveniently near the retailer. Having a location that minimizes shipping costs to the wholesaler becomes a more relevant issue.

If the entrepreneur is a retailer (or wholesaler), he or she looks at the distribution channel from both directions. The customer will be reached directly, but looking back down the distribution channel, the retailer is also concerned with finding a good distributor who represents quality manufacturers.

Market Coverage

If you're a start-up company, it's often advantageous to use intermediaries because it allows you to enter a larger market more quickly. Selling your product to just five distributors can give you access to hundreds of wholesale and retail outlets without increasing your marketing efforts or sales staff. This is important when you have very limited resources.

Control of Distribution

The choice of distribution strategy will affect the level of control you exert over what happens to your product once it leaves your hands. If your product is such that it requires unique or unusual marketing tactics to entice the customer, you may not want to put it with an intermediary that is carrying competing lines or a variety of other products, as your product may not get the attention it requires to achieve the sales level you need. In this case, a direct channel may be more appropriate.

The Functions of Intermediaries

Recall that intermediaries are available in most channels of distribution to take on some of the activities that aren't part of the core competency of the producer or the manufacturer. Intermediaries serve both the producing end of the channel and the end-user end because they make it easier for customers to find products where they expect to find them. In general, intermediaries perform four basic functions:

1. **Assume some of the risk of distribution.** Some intermediaries, like wholesalers and distributors, actually purchase a product from the manufacturer and hold it as inventory in their warehouses. This relieves the manufacturer of further obligation beyond that established in the warranty agreement.

2. **Aggregate heterogeneous goods into a line of goods under a single retail or wholesale category.** For example, a small producer of a sports accessory like Gregg Levin's Perfectcurve™, which maintains the curve in baseball caps, would look for a distributor of sports equipment and accessories so that potential retailers could find everything they need from one distributor.

3. **Break bulk.** Some distributors buy from manufacturers in huge volume and then break that bulk into quantities that their customers typically purchase. That way they can get the cost advantage of a bulk purchase but customize it to their customers' needs.

4. **Provide customer/market information to the producer/manufacturer.** This information will help the producer/manufacturer price products more effectively and also better control production so as to not overproduce or fail to anticipate an increase in demand.

Logistics

It takes a long time before a new venture can justify having its own distribution center. Consequently many growing companies are outsourcing their packaging, warehousing, inventory control, and trucking requirements to third-party **logistics firms**. In distribution terminology, logistics is the timely movement of goods from the producer to the consumer. It includes transportation, storage, and materials handling. In addition to other services, logistics firms can negotiate the best deals and the most efficient carriers, potentially saving the growing venture thousands of dollars.

In the next chapter, we'll look at issues related to the management of a new venture.

New Venture Checklist

Have you:

❏ **Decided whether your new venture will operate in a consumer or an industrial distribution channel?**

❏ **Determined the most effective channel of distribution to get your product or service to the customer?**

❏ **Planned how you will get information on the members of your distribution channel so you can choose the best people to serve your business?**

❏ **Figured the costs associated with the distribution channel you have chosen?**

❏ **Determined the length of time it will take to get your product to the customer?**

❏ **Organized the distribution channel section of the business plan?**

Issues to Consider

1. What are three trends in distribution?
2. How does direct selling in the consumer and industrial channels of distribution differ?
3. What kinds of companies may be involved in both consumer and industrial channels?
4. What are the advantages of using wholesalers?
5. How does a distribution channel affect the price of the product or service?

Experiencing Entrepreneurship

1. Surf the Internet and come up with five products or services that are using the Internet as a new distribution channel, not just as an advertising medium.

2. Pick a product in the consumer marketplace and trace it back through the value chain to its origins. Show where value is added at each point.

Additional Sources of Information

American Logistics Management Association, 2000 Santa Cruz Street, Anaheim, CA 92805. Tel. (714) 937-8970; fax (714) 937-0402.

Davidson, J.P. (1989). *Marketing Sourcebook for Small Business.* New York: John Wylie.

_____ (1991). *Selling to the Giants.* Blue Ridge Summit, PA: Liberty Hall.

Inbound Logistics, 5 Penn Plaza, Eighth Floor, NY 10001.

Lele, M.M. (1988). *The Customer Is Key.* New York: John Wiley.

Levinson, J.C. (1989). *Guerrilla Marketing Attack: New Strategies, Tactics and Weapons for Winning Big Profits for Your Small Business.* Boston: Houghton Mifflin.

North American Logistics Association, 1300 W. Higgins Road, Suite 111, Park Ridge, IL 60068. Tel. (708) 292–1891; fax (708) 292-1896.

Transportation and Distribution Magazine. 100 Superior Avenue, Cleveland, OH 44114. Tel. (216) 696-7000; fax (216) 696-4135.

Internet Resource

EXPOguide
http://www.expoguide.com
A large list of trade shows and conferences.

Relevant Case Studies

1. Mrs. Gooch's Natural Foods Markets
2. Flight Time
3. Autopsies-to-Go

13

People are the key to success in any undertaking, including business. The foremost distinguishing feature of effective managers seems to be their ability to recognize talent and to surround themselves with able colleagues.

Norman R. Augustine
President and CEO, Martin Marietta Corp.
Augustine's Laws *(Penguin, 1987)*

The Management and Organization Plan

Overview

▶ The entrepreneurial approach to organizational structure

▶ Total quality management

▶ Ownership and compensation in a corporation

▶ Hiring—job descriptions and specifications

▶ The employee handbook

▶ Other policies

Terms to Know

Profile 13.1

You Won't Find This Fender on a Car

If your company and its products achieve the enviable position of being *the brand* in the industry, be prepared for an uproar if you ever make major changes. Fender Musical Instruments can attest to that fact. Their clients, who range from Bruce Springsteen to Eric Clapton and Travis Tritt, love their Fender guitars because "they're as close to perfection as anything gets.

. . ." And that has been true for fifty years. Actually, in the 1950s Leo Fender revolutionized the music industry when he introduced his solid-body electric guitars— the Telecaster and the Stratocaster—to the music industry in a market niche and soon set the standard.

In the late 1970s, however, a recession hit, interest rates soared, and Fender's famous quality began to take a precipitous slide. William Schultz, then an executive for CBS, organized a buyout and in 1985 acquired the name and distribution, taking the company private. At that point Fender was manufacturing only twelve guitars a day, as musicians were becoming entranced with music synthesizers. Schultz, however, succeeded in implementing a total quality management plan that would make Fender profitable every year from 1985 on. Fender now produces more than 335,000 guitars annually, all presold.

Schultz's plan focused on five areas that needed improvement.

1. **The management team.** Schultz put together a group of people who had musical backgrounds and were as passionate about Fender as he. As a team, they would carry the vision.

2. **Overhead.** He moved the guitar factory from Orange County, California, eastward to less pricey Corona in Riverside County. This allowed the company to focus its resources on production and quality.

3. **Quality.** Schultz invested in state-of-the-art woodworking machines, so that quality would be consistent. He also trained every worker in quality control procedures and efficiency and incorporated inspecting for quality into the manufacturing process, so that every guitar would be defect-free.

4. **Customization.** Schultz created a separate custom shop to meet the needs of customers requesting guitars designed and hand-built to their exact specifications. These customers have a wait of up to one year and pay between $1,500 and $50,000.

5. **Core competency.** One of the outstanding things Schultz did was return Fender to what it had been doing best when it was the industry leader in the late 1950s and '60s. To win back loyal customers, he reissued some of the original designs and updated 1940s low-tech vacuum-tube amps that were preferred by professional musicians.

Today, Fender Musical Instruments has come of age and is creating the best guitars possible, using Silicon Graphics Indy workstations; blending science, music, and computer technology; and reducing time-to-market and material costs.

From this company that has successfully reinvented itself, the lesson for entrepreneurs is to maintain the vision at all costs, make sure your employees hold the vision as well, focus on what you do best, and do it the best way you can.

Sources: Bob Spitz, "And on the Lead Guitar ...," *Sky*, August 1996, p. 55; *Fender Musical Instruments Corporation*, "SiliconWorks Success Stories" (http://www.sgi.com/Works/SuccessStories/fender.html).

How did Fender Musical Instruments use Total Quality Management to turn its business around?

How to manage and organize the business is a fundamental decision every entrepreneur must make, one that has an impact on all aspects of the business, from product design to customer service. You could see clearly in the case of Fender Musical Instruments that ineffective management and organization of the company was the source of its problems in the early 1980s. The way a business is organized and staffed can also affect communications, morale, and performance in ways the entrepreneur never expected. Many business owners have traditionally resorted to the ubiquitous line and staff organizational charts as shown in Figure 13.1 to formulate a structure for their businesses. This chart depicts a company that is established, so it is more hierarchical than a typical entrepreneurial venture.

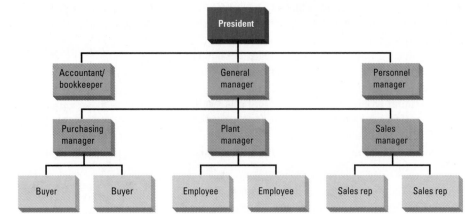

**Figure 13.1
Traditional Line and
Staff Organizational
Chart for a Simple
Manufacturing Plant**

The Entrepreneurial Approach to Organizational Structure

Compare the traditional organizational chart with the typical entrepreneurial start-up, which is very flat structurally. The entrepreneur and the founding team often perform all the functions when the business is just starting. What is not depicted by the traditional, hierarchical chart in Figure 13.1 is the informal organization or network of relationships that account for a significant portion of the daily work. **Informal networks** of people consist of those who tend to gravitate toward each other in an effort to accomplish tasks in a more efficient and effective manner than may be dictated by the chart. These networks form the shadow organizational structure that brings the business through an unexpected crisis, an impossible deadline, or a formidable impasse. They are social links that form the real power base in the organization. Metaphorically speaking, the organizational chart may be thought of as the skeleton of the body, while the informal network constitutes the arteries and veins that push information and activity throughout the organization—in other words, the lifeblood of the organization.

Research has found three types of informal networks: the **advice network,** which includes those people who are the problem solvers in the organization; the **trust network** where political information is shared; and the **communication network,** which consists of employees who discuss work-related issues on a frequent basis.[1] Often the people in these networks come from various functional areas in the organization that don't typically deal with each other on a daily basis. For example, the political/trust network might include the bookkeeper, a sales rep, and a plant employee.

Entrepreneurs seem to have recognized intuitively the value of informal networks in the organizational structure and often the most successful new ventures adopt a team-based approach with a flatter structure. Figure 13.2 depicts the nature of this structure. The lead entrepreneur is the driving force

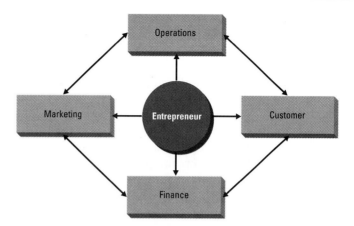

**Figure 13.2
An Entrepreneurial
Organization**

for the entrepreneurial team, which normally consists of people with expertise in at least one of the three functional areas of a new venture: marketing, operations, and finance. The organization consists of interactive, integrated teams. In the new venture, these are rarely "departments" in the traditional sense, but rather functions, tasks, or activities. The statistics reflect this pattern. Fifty-one percent of the growing companies that have made it to the *Inc. 500* list do not have a marketing director, while 61 percent have neither a COO nor a personnel director. Thirty-two percent do not have a CFO, and an astounding 67 percent have no one to manage information systems in their companies.[2]

What is the explanation for this? For one thing, entrepreneurs are usually too creative and flexible to be bound by the strictures of a formal organizational structure. They are more comfortable bringing together resources and people as a team and making decisions on the spot without having to go through layers of management. Another reason is that growing new ventures must be able to adapt quickly as they muscle their way into the market. Uncertainty and instability are a way of life for young ventures, and a rigid, formalized, bureaucratic structure would unduly burden a new venture both financially and operationally.

Three components make up the entrepreneurial organizational structure: formal processes, people, and culture. Formal processes include the planning system, control mechanisms, compensation and reward policies, and other processes that make the organization run more efficiently and effectively. These processes are not independent units, but rather are linked to all functions of the organization that require them. For example, quality control mechanisms are not solely the purview of a single department, but flow from product development through manufacturing, to distribution, and throughout all the support functions needed to facilitate the process of getting the product to the customer.

People who work in market-oriented, entrepreneurial companies must think not only of their individual tasks but of the product and company as a whole. People required to make the business work need to have team-building skills as well as the ability to make decisions and implement them with very little input from top management or the CEO. In new ventures those teams may consist of independent contractors whose skills are being "rented" on an as-needed basis.

Informal networks create flexibility and speed up operations. They also have the advantage of managing the personal issues not easily handled through policies and structure.

Entrepreneurs have always recognized the value of an integrated, team-based approach to management and organization because they have learned that one of the greatest benefits of the entrepreneurial or market-oriented style of management is that relationships with customers improve. Teams come in many varieties: self-directed work teams, problem-solving teams, quality teams, cross-functional teams. Essentially they serve the same underlying purpose: "A team is a small number of people with complementary skills who are committed to a common purpose, set of performance goals, and approach for which they hold themselves mutually accountable.[3]

What makes the entrepreneur's situation unique is that—at least when the venture is in the start-up or initial growing phases and capital resources are limited—the team the entrepreneur develops will most likely consist of several people outside the organization: namely, independent contractors. For example, you may decide to subcontract the manufacturing of a product to an established company. This means that you need to understand how that subcontractor works and will, of necessity, become a part of that company's team in the production of the product. Your marketing, sales, operations, and finance people must also be able to work with the manufacturing subcontractor to ensure that the goals of the new venture are met with the timeliness and level of quality desired. This requires the team to have skills not normally learned in school, skills such as diplomacy in the management of intra- and inter-team relationships, problem-solving skills, and the ability to take responsibility for innovative changes on the spot, often without your direct approval.

Total Quality Management

Total Quality Management, or TQM, became the buzzword of the early 1980s. As a management plan, it requires businesses to become flexible and more responsive to their internal and external environments. TQM is an integrated, systematic, organization-wide management philosophy that helps build customer-driven businesses. It strives to improve product and service quality in all aspects of the business by empowering employees to change processes. It demands systematic changes in management practice, the redesign of tasks, and the redefinition of managerial roles.[4]

Eventually TQM came under attack because despite its popularity, only 20 percent of those companies that instituted TQM could identify significant improvement in their performance.[5] There appear to be two reasons for many companies' failed attempts to successfully execute the TQM principles. First, to effect change in the organization, its structure and culture must be amenable to change, and most established companies are well entrenched in their structures and cultures. Second, most of the new change literature (re-engineering) focuses on one segment of the company without necessarily considering the company as a whole.[6]

Start-up ventures have a singular advantage with regard to implementing TQM. From the very beginning, entrepreneurs can establish for the company a vision that embodies the TQM principles, and they can hire people who understand and believe in that vision. It's always easier to implement a major program from the beginning, when the team is being put together, than it is to change an already existing and entrenched structure. We'll now turn to discussing the TQM model.

A Model of TQM

Bill Creech, a four-star general who applied TQM to the Tactical Air Command to prepare the Air Force for the Gulf War in 1990 and is probably the most successful practitioner of TQM since its inception, writes that the basics of TQM are supported by five pillars of the organization: product, process, organization, leadership, and commitment, as depicted in Figure 13.3.

The management system embodied in Creech's five pillars is designed to meet the requirements of a dynamic new market environment. The five pillars are integrated in the following way:

▶ Commitment by everyone in the organization from the bottom up supports the other four pillars. If total commitment is not possible or is weak, the other four cannot stand.

▶ The product focuses the organization on purpose and achievement. Everyone in the organization produces a product or service, from the production people to the billing staff. Quality certainly begins with the product/service, but it is totally dependent on quality in the process as well.

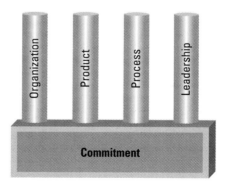

Figure 13.3
The Five Pillars of TQM

▶ The process for producing the product or service is integrated with the actual product/service and dependent on the organization as a whole for its ultimate quality.

▶ The organization must allow for quality throughout by encouraging employee learning and empowerment through a decentralized structure that is flexible and supportive. The success of the organization depends directly on its leadership—the entrepreneur.

▶ The entrepreneur serves as a model of spirit, energy, and vision for the company and sees to it that the company remains on the path it set. The entrepreneur must be obsessed with the idea of creating a people-oriented company and in that regard, must be willing to listen to the employees and adopt suggestions wherever possible.

Adding the Customer to the Model

We would add one more element to the TQM model, and that is the customer. If commitment is the foundation on which TQM rests, the customer is the roof that helps keep the pillars from falling. Without the customer, there can be no company, no business to conduct, and no organization to manage. We depict this new model in Figure 13.4.

Customer input into product/service and process has a strong impact on the way the company is organized to meet the customer's needs. Likewise, leadership makes it possible for everyone in the organization to know the customer and deal with the customer at some level. The commitment of everyone to achieving customer satisfaction in all areas of the business is what will assure the ultimate success of the company.

Figure 13.4
The Five TQM Pillars
Plus the Customer

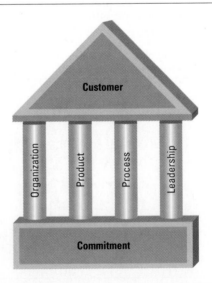

Ownership and Compensation in a Corporation

Two of the most perplexing management issues facing an entrepreneur with a new corporation are how much of the company to sell to potential stockholders and how much to pay key management. There is a tendency on the part of small, privately held companies to use minority shares as an incentive to entice investors and to pay key management, primarily because new companies do not have the cash flow to provide attractive compensation packages. The prevailing wisdom is that providing stock in the new company will increase commitment, cause management to be more cost conscious, reduce cash outlay for salaries, and induce loyalty to the company in the long term. But recent studies have found this is not always the case.[7] More often than

Profile 13.2

Implementing TQM in a Small Company

Tudor Handle Corp. is a small manufacturer in Queens, New York, producing hardwood handles for the paintbrush industry. In 1992 it employed 55 people, of which 50 were production workers. At that time Tudor Handle was experiencing poor performance. Sales in 1991 had decreased by 15% from the previous year's sales, customer returns had increased to 8% of sales and material costs for wood had increased by 17%. Cash flow was at a critically low level, and customers were demanding higher-quality products.

To add to the dilemma, 1992 would bring a labor contract renegotiation that would result in substantial increases in medical benefits. In an effort to correct the situation, the company President and the general manager, who had read about TQM, conferred with a TQM consultant and decided to implement a program.

Implementation involved:

▶ Getting the cooperation of the union

▶ Drafting a mission statement

▶ Educating everyone on the benefits, culture, and process of TQM

▶ Selecting quality leaders from among the workers

▶ Collecting and analyzing data from production, inspection, machine downtime, scrap, and rework

▶ Examining every process in the company for quality issues

▶ Designating time for cleanup every day

▶ Getting input from customers on their needs

▶ Benchmarking with competitors' products

▶ Including the new TQM approach in company promotional materials

At the end of one year, sales had increased by 12%; customer returns were down from 8% to 1.6%; productivity had increased by 35.7%; and the wood yield had increased from 50% to 75%. The company had also decreased its losses due to inspection, scrap, and rework, and gross profit had increased from 21% to 32.9%. The return-on-investment ratio was calculated at 6/1 for the year.

An interesting side note is that with the death of the company's president in 1993, the TQM program was terminated by the new management, who didn't understand it. By the end of 1993, the company was in Chapter 11 bankruptcy. Finally, when the new President permitted the general manager, who had been a part of the original TQM program, to re-implement TQM, the performance of the company rose enough to take it out of Chapter 11 reorganization.

SOURCE: Moreno Taliapietra, "Implementation of TQM in a Small Manufacturer," (http:www.lagcc.cuny.edu/cqc/moreno.htm).

not, the person to whom you have given stock in good faith will ultimately leave the company, taking the stock with him with the potential for future harm to the business.

In the initial growth stage of a new venture, it is difficult to determine with any degree of accuracy what long-term role a particular person may play in the organization. Often the entrepreneur, due to limited resources, is not able to attract the best person to take the company beyond the start-up phase, so a person with fewer qualifications will be hired for little salary plus a minority ownership in the company. The entrepreneur is literally betting on the potential contribution of this person, an eventuality that usually doesn't pay off. Later, when the company can afford to hire the person it needs, the entrepreneur has to deal with a minority shareholder who has developed territorial "rights." When minority ownership is an important issue to a potential employee, it is important to make clear to that person what it means. There are few legal and managerial rights associated with a minority position; thus, for all practical purposes, **minority ownership** is simply the unmarketable right to appreciated stock value that has no defined payoff period and certainly no guarantee of value.

Founder's Stock

Founder's stock (144 stock) is stock issued to the first shareholders of the corporation or assigned to key management as part of a compensation package. The payoff on this stock comes when the company goes public or is sold. Assuming the company is successful, founder's stock at issuance is probably valued at the lowest level it will ever be, relative to an investor's stock value. Consequently, one tax problem that arises as a result occurs when private investors provide seed or working capital to the new venture. Often the value of the stock the investors hold makes it very obvious that the founder's stock was a bargain and not the true value of the stock. According to IRC 83, the amount of the difference between the founder's price and the investor's price would be taxable as compensation income.

One way to avoid this problem is to issue common stock to founders and key management, and convertible preferred stock to investors. The preference upon liquidation should be high enough to cover the book value of the corporation so the common stockholders would receive nothing. This action would effectively decrease the value of the common stock so it would no longer appear to be a bargain for IRS purposes and subject the founders to an immediate tax liability.

Founder's stock is restricted, and the SEC rules (Rule 144) state that the restriction refers to stock that has not been registered with the SEC (private placement) and stock owned by the controlling officers and shareholders of the company (those with at least 10 percent ownership). If a stockholder has owned the stock for at least three years, and public information about the company exists, Rule 144 can be avoided in the sale of the stock. If the stockholder has held the stock for less than three years, the rules must be strictly complied with. It is not the intent of this chapter to discuss the details of Rule

144. Suffice it to say that the rule is complex and the appropriate attorney or tax specialist should be consulted.

Compensating with Stock

Giving someone ownership rights in the company is a serious decision that should receive very careful consideration. There are several things to contemplate before taking on an equity partner, whether an investor or key management.

1. Anyone brought in as an investor/shareholder or partner with the entrepreneur does not have to be an equal partner. An investor can hold whatever share of stock you have determined is warranted based on what that partner will contribute to the business.

2. Never bring someone in as a partner/investor if you can hire that person to provide the same service, no matter what you may feel the urgency of the situation is. The most advantageous way to hire someone for a new venture is to hire the person as an independent contractor.

3. Do not lock yourself into future compensation promises like stock options. Use cash as bonuses whenever possible.

4. Establish the company as yours before taking on partners, unless, of course, you have founded the company as a team.

5. Consider having employees work for the company at least two years before they are vested and given stock or stock options.

Issuing Stock When the Company Is Capitalized

The number of shares you authorize when you form the corporation is purely arbitrary. Suppose you decide there will be one million **authorized shares** in the new venture. This means you have one million shares available to be issued to potential stockholders. If you value each share of stock at $1 and capitalize $100,000, you will have 100,000 **issued shares;** if each share is valued at $10, you will have 10,000 issued shares. The value you place on each share is arbitrary; for psychological reasons you may wish to value a share at $1, so a shareholder who contributes $10,000 to the business can say that he or she owns 10,000 shares of stock as opposed to 1,000 shares at $10/share. In short, the number of shares issued depends on the initial capitalization and the price per share.

Now suppose that you, the entrepreneur, will be initially contributing $250,000 in cash and $300,000 in assets (equipment, furniture, etc.) to the company. At $1 a share, you issue yourself 550,000 shares of stock and own a 100% interest in the company because you have issued only 550,000 shares total. At a later date you issue 29,000 additional shares at $5 a share to an investor. Your minority shareholder has therefore contributed $145,000 to the company and owns a five percent interest in the company (29,000/579,000 issued stock). The investor will require that the current value or future additional income of the company be sufficient to justify the increase in price per share. You can see that as additional shares are issued, the original stockholder's percentage ownership in the company declines. However, the founder's shares will not go below 55 percent (550,000/1 million) unless the company authorizes additional shares and issues a portion or all of those additional shares.

The type of stock you will be issuing is **common stock**, which is a basic ownership interest in the company. This means that holders of common stock share in both the successes and the failures of the business and benefit through dividends and the appreciating value of the company. Once common stock is issued, a company can issue **preferred stock**, whose holders are paid first if the company is liquidated. Preferred stockholders, however, must accept a fixed dividend amount, no matter how much profit the company makes. If you form a sub-chapter S corporation, you may issue only one type of stock.

One form of stock you may want to offer investors as an inducement is called IRC Sec. 1244 stock, which permits a shareholder of a corporation with capital and paid-in surplus of $1 million or less to treat a portion of any loss on the disposition of the stock as an ordinary loss, rather than a capital loss. The amount the shareholder can take as a loss is limited to the shareholder's original investment.

Buy-Sell Agreements

One of the real concerns entrepreneurs with privately held corporations face is what to do when a stockholder wants to sell stock or an employee with stock decides to leave the company to work for a competitor. A **buy-sell agreement** spells out the terms and conditions for the sale of stock to people outside the organization. It is a way to maintain control of the company. Usually a buy-sell agreement provides for a right of first refusal to the company to buy the stock before it is sold to someone else. To determine the value of the stock at that point in time, it's a good idea to call for an appraisal of the company. Then the stock can be purchased using savings, insurance, or asset sales. All investor, stockholder, and employment contracts involving stock should contain buy-sell clauses.

Prenuptial Agreements

Entrepreneurs with family businesses face the additional threat of divorce from their spouses or the divorces of their children from spouses. One way entrepreneurs protect themselves from losing a significant ownership interest in the company to a divorcing spouse, whether theirs or their children's, is to have a **prenuptial agreement**. If the "prenup" is properly structured, the couple would not be allowed to hold company stock jointly. This is particularly important where a son or daughter who is a minority shareholder marries and subsequently divorces. The entrepreneur does not want to have to deal with an ex–in-law. A prenuptial agreement, while not foolproof, will probably be upheld in a court of law if it is not vague and is reasonable in its terms.

Trusts

An **irrevocable trust** offers the greatest protection for the ownership of stock. For example, you may set up a trust for your child that contains his or her stock in the family corporation. The trust will stipulate that creditors have no rights to the trust. This also includes a potential spouse that your child might divorce. The important thing to remember is that you, the entrepreneur, must set up the trust using an attorney specializing in that area of the law.

Alternatives to Equity Incentives

There are other ways to compensate key management that will not require the entrepreneur to give up equity in the company.

Deferred Compensation Plans

In a **deferred compensation plan,** the entrepreneur can specify that awards and bonuses be linked to profits and performance of both the individual and the company, with the lion's share being on the individual's performance. The employee does not pay taxes on this award until it is actually paid out at some specified date.

Bonus Plans

With a **bonus plan,** a series of goals are set by the company with input from the employee, and as the employee reaches each goal, the bonus is given. This

---

Profile 13.3

Perks for Entrepreneurial Ventures

Most entrepreneurs can't afford to provide their management and employees with expensive perks. Yet there are many other ways to show appreciation and provide incentives for employees. Firmani and Associates, a small Seattle-based public relations firm, shuts down four times a year and takes its employees to a film matinée. Like a number of other companies in a fast-changing world, Firmani wants to make its workplace a more enjoyable environment.

Here are some ways you can provide valuable benefits at very little cost.

1. Provide flexible schedules so that employees who commute don't have to come in every day.

2. Offer a casual dress code as long as the employee can quickly switch to business attire if necessary.

3. Share the perks of your industry. For example, Hot Topic, a chain of music-related apparel and accessories based in Pomona, California, reimburses its employees for tickets to rock concerts. In return the employees must report on the apparel of the artists and offer some merchandising ideas.

4. Do the unexpected. One entrepreneur periodically rents a bus and takes his staff to a Mariners baseball game or to play laser tag.

5. Feed your employees.

Of course, the most effective benefit of all is recognition for a job well done.

Source: Christopher Caggiano, "Perks You Can Afford," *Inc.,* November 1997, p. 107.

method is often used with sales personnel and others who have a direct impact on the profitability of the company. The key to success with bonus plans is to specify measurable objectives.

Capital Appreciation Rights

Capital appreciation rights give employees the right to participate in the profits of the company at a specified percentage, while not being full shareholders with voting rights. Capital appreciation rights, or **"phantom stock,"** provide for long-term compensation incentives whose value is based on the increase in the value of the business. The phantom stock will look, act, and reward like real stock, but will have no voting rights and will limit the employee's obligation should the business fail. Typically the employee has to be with the company for a period of three to five years to be considered vested, but otherwise employees do not have to pay for these rights.

Profit-Sharing Plans

Profit-sharing plans are distinct from the previously discussed plans in that they are subject to the ERISA rules for employee retirement programs. These plans must include all employees without regard to individual contribution to profit or performance. They are different from pensions in that owners are not required to contribute in any year and employees are not "entitled" to them.

Whatever plan you choose for compensating and rewarding key management, understand that these rewards may not produce the desired performance. You should carefully consider alternative plans before granting

---

Profile 13.4

Attitude Is More Important Than Skill

You can learn a lot about how to hire for your new company by following the lead of some very successful companies who have built renowned cultures. When Southwest Airlines looks for flight attendants, it's seeking just the right combination of energy, team spirit, humor, and self-confidence. Anyone without these characteristics will definitely not fit into Southwest's quirky culture. In fact, the vice president of Southwest's People Department says that becoming an employee of Southwest is a little like joining a cult.

Like Southwest, Silicon Graphics Inc. (SGI), manufacturer of computer workstations, servers, and supercomputers, cultivates an extremely informal environment for its very technical employees. On any given day you may see someone skateboarding between office cubicles. The culture works because SGI spends considerable time on the hiring process and gets great people.

Here are four suggestions for "smart hiring."

1. Hire people with the right mind-set.
2. Look for what you want. The best way to get the best people is to know what type of personality you're looking for.
3. Evaluate people by watching them work.
4. Don't wait for people to come to you. Start your recruiting with your own people and their referrals. Who understands your culture better than your current employees?

SOURCE: Peter Carbonara, "Hire for Attitude, Train for Skill," *Fast Company,* August/September 1996, p. 73.

minority ownership status, as you may be able to achieve the results you are looking for without having to give up a portion of ownership.

Hiring—Job Descriptions and Specifications

One of the most important decisions made by any business is the hiring decision; yet more often than not, those doing the hiring don't know what they're doing. They hire quickly, on the basis of instinct, and then have to worry about how to get rid of the person. Today, with more employees suing their bosses for wrongful discharge, sexual harassment, and racial/gender/age discrimination, it is increasingly important that the entrepreneur understand how to hire. Hiring, however, is not a simple matter of placing a help-wanted ad in the newspaper, receiving résumés, and then holding interviews to select the best candidate. The bulk of the work of hiring comes before the person is actually needed.

Job Profiles

Part of organizing the business is determining what positions are needed for the required tasks of the business. Naturally, in the start-up phase most entrepreneurs do the biggest share of the work themselves, but they know that at some point they will have to hire employees, even if just a receptionist or administrative assistant. Preparing profiles and job descriptions for all the functions of the business ensures that you have them when you need them. Typically when entrepreneurs (and managers) develop job descriptions, they focus entirely on the duties and responsibilities of a particular job. While this is important, it is equally important to develop behavioral profiles of these jobs; in other words, what behavioral traits are typical of and vital to a particular position. An effective bookkeeper, for example, may require the following attributes: has detail orientation, is focused, can work alone, is responsible and organized.

In addition to looking at the best behavioral traits for each position, the entrepreneur must have a good sense of the business culture. Even though a job candidate may have the education and experience required by the job description and display some of the behavioral traits necessary for success in the position, the candidate's chemistry may not fit in well with the culture of the organization. This is an important distinction because education and experience can be achieved, behaviors can in most cases be taught, but chemistry—fitting in with the company culture—must already be present in the job candidate.

The Employee Search

The first and best place to look for an employee is among your current employees, subcontractors, or professional advisers. Referrals from people you know and trust who know the business have a greater likelihood of producing a successful hire. That is why if you can induce a key management person to leave an organization and join your business, that person will probably induce someone else you need later on to come as well. Even during start-up, be constantly on the lookout for good people who might come on board as the business grows.

Help-wanted ads are another source. An estimated 75 percent of those who read the ads are employed and have no intention of seeking another job—unless they see an opportunity that interests them. Consequently, you must make certain your ad stands out and presents to a qualified person an opportunity that he or she can't pass up. You may also consider executive search firms for key management positions.

Résumés

The most important thing to know about a résumé is that it is a selling document. The person is attempting to convince you to give him or her an interview. Therefore, expect most résumés to exaggerate a person's importance somewhat. If a résumé indicates that a person has had a number of jobs in a relatively short period of time or a number of "very important" positions— vice president of this company and president of that company—it may mean that this person truly is in demand and has been wooed away from several companies, or it may mean that this person can't hold a job. Consequently, you need to think of the résumé as a screening tool to see if the candidate has the requisite skills and experience. The more important information will be gained in the interview.

Interviews

Most entrepreneurs dread interviewing job candidates, primarily because they don't know what to say and don't understand that they should ask questions that get at the person's personality—how he or she might react in certain situations. This can be accomplished in part by asking open-ended questions, questions that call for more than "yes-no" answers. For example,

▶ What is your greatest strength?

▶ How would you handle the following hypothetical situation?

While the person is answering the questions, be careful to note the nonverbal communication being sent through body language. Does the person appear confident, at ease with what is being discussed? Does the person look at you directly? Does the person sit with a very closed posture (arms crossed as if to protect) or in a more open, relaxed manner? It is said that 90 percent of communication is nonverbal, so if you don't trust what a person is saying verbally, check to see if the nonverbal signals match the verbal ones.

Entrepreneurs should know that certain questions may never be asked in an interview situation because they are illegal and leave you open to potential lawsuits. Under the laws administered by the EEOC (Equal Employment Opportunity Commission), before the point of hire, you may not ask about a person's

- Religion or religious background

- Nation of origin

- Living arrangements or lifestyle choice

- Plans for pregnancy

- Age (to avoid discrimination against people over 40 or under 21. You may ask a young person who must be 21 to hold the job if proof of the required age can be shown after hiring.)

- Criminal arrest record (You may ask only "Have you ever been convicted of a crime?")

- Military record

Screening Potential Employees

In an effort to screen potential employees for drugs, criminal records, false information, and workers' compensation history, some entrepreneurs are resorting to hiring firms that do background checks. Whether or not you need to run a background check is a function of the type of job for which you are hiring. A receptionist position probably does not require more than contacting previous employers to verify information on the résumé. But hiring a bookkeeper or a Chief Financial Officer may call for checking for a criminal record. Likewise, a truck driver position may require verifying a clean driving record.

Some companies are requiring drug tests as well, and those jobs with physical requirements may call for medical exams. In addition, many companies are using integrity tests, which are psychological tests that measure whether a candidate is more or less likely to steal, take drugs, or be violent. Still others use personality assessment tests to see how a person matches a job profile or fits in with the company culture. Since psychological tests can be wrong, however, it is important to give them as only one part of a comprehensive interview and hiring process. To avoid the possibility of a discrimination suit, all these tests should be given *only after a job offer has been made*.

The recent surge in sexual harassment, wrongful termination, and discrimination suits against employers has prompted a new form of business insurance called employment-practices liability insurance. It came about after many businesses found to their dismay that their standard business liability insurance did not include, or specifically excluded, employment practices suits. These new policies generally have limits from $50,000 to $10 million and are not inexpensive, averaging about $150 per employee annually.

Employee Contracts

Once you have decided to hire someone, it is crucial to put the terms of the agreement in writing to avoid misunderstandings about salary, benefits, duties, and responsibilities. What is *not* included in the agreement should be spelled out clearly as well. Include in the contract a clause that calls for mandatory arbitration in the event of a dispute and a **non-compete clause** if it's legal in your state to prevent someone from leaving your business to start a competing business with your confidential information and customer/supplier lists.

Protecting the Company Against Lawsuits

Fighting a lawsuit filed by an angry employee is a costly expense for any company, but especially for a growing, small business with limited resources. Part of the problem is that employees can sue without putting up any money, as they can seek out attorneys who work on a contingency basis and may collect over 50 percent of the award if they win. If they lose, there is no cost to the client. Consequently, it's often a win/win situation for the employee. And unaware entrepreneurs, focusing on acquiring customers and meeting market demands, often forget to carefully document issues related to employment and are shocked at how badly a disgruntled employee can hurt their already struggling business. A little effort up front can prevent costly litigation. There are several things a company can do to at least minimize the chances of being sued.

1. **Be very careful about whom the company hires.** All expectations should be spelled out *before* the person is hired and documented for future reference. Every effort should be made to assess the person's character and trustworthiness accurately, and references should be carefully checked.

2. **Keep a file on each employee.** The file should contain documentation of all events of importance in terms of promotion, raises, training, performance evaluations, and potential for termination, written in a style that is factual and suitable as evidence in a court of law. It is also wise to have more than one person contributing to this file.

3. **Any communications with an employee regarding performance should always be in writing.** The dates on which any violations of expectations have occurred and the specific nature of those violations should be stated very clearly. *It is very important that written confirmation of receipt be obtained from the employee.*

4. **Before terminating any employee, seek counsel from an attorney.** An attorney experienced in labor law can check the company's documentation to look for potential problems or openings for the employee to sue.

The Employee Handbook

Every new business should have an employee handbook that spells out the company policies and procedures, the mission, the expectations for employees, and the company philosophy. It is at once a legal document that protects both owners and employees and an enthusiastic rendition of the company culture. The handbook serves as documentation of everything from compensation and promotion to vacations and health care. It also lets employees know under what circumstances their employment can be terminated and what that process is. If a dispute arises, you may find your state court will bind you to the handbook as written, not as intended; therefore, state all policies and procedures clearly without leaving room for ambiguity. Any vague provisions will likely go in favor of the employee, since the handbook was written by you, the employer.

The Company History

Relating the story of how the company was founded should definitely be the first entry in the handbook, because it sets the tone and gives the employees a sense of history, of belonging to something potentially great. Tell the story like a story; in other words, make it personal, entertaining, and readable (you never know when this portion of your handbook will end up in some magazine!). Remember that honesty about some of the troubles you faced in starting the business will make your employees feel that they are part of a human effort rather than a serendipitous occurrence in a moment of extraordinary luck.

The Company Philosophy

The company philosophy is essentially a statement of the identity of your company—who you are and what you stand for. If the history section describes the birth of the company's culture, the philosophy section ingrains that culture in the minds of the employees. After reading this section, the employees should have a good sense of what you believe in, where the company is going, and how they fit into the picture. If your philosophy is that employees should be creative, assertive, productive, self-motivated problem-solvers who aren't afraid to be wrong, let them know that at the outset. Remember that most employees' experiences with company cultures has been quite the opposite. Shake them up a bit and help them see clearly that their experience with your company will be positive.

What Goes into the Handbook?

The best way to determine what to put into the handbook is to first consider what your employees want to know about the business; then take a look at the handbooks of other companies for comparison purposes to see what you like and don't like. In general, include the following information in the handbook:

▸ A section stating that the handbook is not a contract and is subject to changes. This is necessary because business conditions may force work hours or vacation times to change, and employees should be forewarned of this possibility. State also that the employment relationship may be terminated at any time, for any reason, with or without cause or notice. Have the employee sign a copy of this statement, acknowledging receipt of the handbook and agreement with its terms.

▶ Employment policies on such things as opportunity, work hours, pay, performance reviews, vacations, sick leave, jury duty, and so forth.

▶ Benefits such as health, dental, insurance, disability, workers' compensation, and retirement. Include something on the Family and Medical Leave Act as required by law.

▶ Guidelines for employee conduct, including a written sexual harassment policy and dispute resolution procedures. State clearly that included are merely examples of unacceptable conduct and not a comprehensive list.

▶ An organizational chart so that the employees know who is who and where they themselves fit in the big picture.

▶ Phone numbers of key people.

▶ Table of contents, question/answer sections, and an index. The handbook should not be too cumbersome; 20–30 pages is plenty for a young company. It should be designed so that information can be easily accessed.

The Problem with Employee Handbooks

Employers, in their exuberance as they convey the corporate culture, often make statements that later can cause legal problems. Sloppy language and broad statements of policy are often worse than no handbook at all. In the 1980s, a storm of wrongful-termination suits put companies on notice about employee handbooks. In particular, the court in the landmark case *Toussaint v. Blue Cross and Blue Shield, 1980,* ruled that an employer who reassured workers verbally and in the handbook that termination would come about only for "good cause" could not later dismiss them "at will."

Handbooks should avoid language that suggests any of the following:

▶ Employees can expect a long and enjoyable relationship with the company.

▶ Managers and supervisors can solve all employee problems.

▶ The handbook establishes the rights of the employees.

▶ The handbook tells employees what is expected of them.

▶ Certain absolute disciplinary steps will always be taken prior to termination. This allows no freedom for quick termination when necessary.

▶ There are only certain specific violations for which people will be fired. It limits the company to foreseen problems.

Other Policies

Besides policies relating to employees, create policies and procedures for the routine tasks that are accomplished each day in the business. For example, procedures for order taking, shipping, handling invoices, billing, and all the other administrative functions the business undertakes will be needed. One way to figure out what procedures may be required is to take the business through a hypothetical, typical day or week and list all the activities that occur from the point at which an order is received until it is shipped, or from the point at which a sale is solicited until the sale is closed. Activities that take place over and over again require established procedures to promote efficiency and effectiveness. Naturally, many of the procedures you develop when you start the company will be modified as you bring on employees and receive their input. But it's still a good idea to start with something.

New Venture Checklist

Have you:

- ❏ Determined the personnel required to run the business at start-up and over the next three to five years?

- ❏ Written a mission statement for the new venture?

- ❏ Determined the ownership and compensation requirements of the business?

- ❏ Created job profiles for positions in the business?

- ❏ Formulated a plan to find the best candidates for positions in the company?

- ❏ Established policies and procedures for the business?

- ❏ Drafted an employee handbook?

Issues to Consider

1. In what ways can the new venture assume a market orientation?
2. Why might the traditional line and staff organizational chart not be suitable for a new entrepreneurial venture?
3. What are the advantages and disadvantages of using stock as compensation and incentives?
4. Compare and contrast common and preferred stock and the tax implications of each.
5. Discuss three ways the entrepreneur can prevent stock from being sold to outsiders?
6. List three alternatives to equity incentives for key management.
7. How can the entrepreneur improve the chances of choosing the best job candidate?
8. What is the purpose and value of the employee handbook?

Experiencing Entrepreneurship

1. Interview an entrepreneur about his or her hiring practices. How successful have those practices been in getting and retaining good employees?

2. Interview two entrepreneurs in the same industry about the incentive systems they use to reward both management and employees. Compare and contrast.

Additional Sources of Information

Alexander Hamilton Institute. *The Employee Handbook Audit*. Tel. (201) 587-7050.

Balkin, D.B. (1988). "Compensation Strategy for Firms in Emerging and Rapidly Growing Industries." *Human Resource Planning*, Vol. 11 (3).

Bruce, S.D. (1993). *How to Write Your Employee Handbook*. Madison, CT: Business & Legal Reports.

Nobile, R.J. (1995). *Guide to Employee Handbooks*. Boston: Warren Gorham Lamont.

Sack, S.M. (1990). *The Hiring and Firing Book: A Complete Legal Guide for Employers*. New York: Facts on File.

Tibbetts, J. S., Jr., and E. T. Donovan. (1989). "Compensation and Benefits for Start-Up Companies." *Harvard Business Review* (January/February).

Internet Resources

EntreWorld
http://www.Entreworld.org
A source of information and articles on all aspects of starting and building a company.

Institute of Management & Administration Business Pages
http://www.ioma.com/
Sample articles about things like employee benefits and handling receivables. Hundreds of links to other sites.

Relevant Case Studies

1. Toy Tips, Inc.
2. Mrs. Gooch's Natural Foods Markets
3. Flight Time

14

Don't forget that it [your product or service] is not differentiated until the customer understands the difference.

Tom Peters
Business writer
Thriving on Chaos (Knopf, 1987)

The Marketing Plan

Overview

▶ **Relationship marketing**

▶ **Guerrilla marketing**

▶ **The marketing plan**

▶ **The product**

▶ **Price**

▶ **Place**

▶ **Promotion**

▶ **Marketing to industrial customers**

▶ **Online market research**

Terms to Know

Profile 14.1

Doing All the Right Things

What company can boast that its stock over the three years from 1995 to 1997 far outpaced in growth the stock of industry giants Intel, Microsoft, Cisco Systems, and Compaq? Only Dell Computer Corporation can; its stock went from a split-adjusted low of $.39/share in 1990 to $80/share in 1997—not bad for

251

a company started in 1983 in Michael Dell's dorm room at the University of Texas at Austin. The secret of Dell's success? Superior execution and low-cost, direct-sales, not just to consumers but to businesses like Ford, Boeing, and the mammoth Deutsche Bank. Dell's very successful web site now accounts for $2 million in daily sales, or about 5 percent of the company's business. Dell has learned that some of its sales are made completely online and that customers who first go online, and then call, are twice as likely to buy.

Dell's success cannot be attributed solely to its products—state-of-the-art computers that have virtually become commodities in an industry where to the customer, price is everything. Instead, it's a result of superior execution of its founder's production and marketing strategies, along with a very clear understanding of how the business should work. Michael Dell personally spends an inordinate amount of time with customers and has even been known to participate in sales presentations to senior executives. He believes that it's vital to stay in touch with the market and that talking directly with customers is the best way to do that. He created a web site that allows customers to configure their own computers and see the price on the spot. His business customers such as Boeing, which buys about 160 computers a day, have a dedicated Dell sales rep working inside their company.

In the computer industry, no market position is ever guaranteed, since the environment is so dynamic. In the early 1990s Dell Computer was growing so fast—that's where the focus was—that it was in danger of falling apart for lack of systems and controls. On the management side, Dell brought in experienced Motorola executive Mort Topfer to contribute maturity to the decision making. In addition, the company implemented some very controversial strategies that run counter to industry trends. First, instead of instigating a price war to increase sales, Dell Computer focused on high-margin customers like Boeing. Second, it used direct marketing to these customers, bypassing retail and the burgeoning home PC market. Dell began to concentrate on what it does best—achieving on-time, rapid delivery of customized PCs to a market that orders via phone and fax. Today the mission of the company includes not only growth but liquidity and profitability, and competitors such as Compaq are considering imitating Michael Dell's strategy.

Intel and Microsoft technologies dominate the industry. For Dell, this is a positive, because their customers will get those technologies via Dell computers in the most effective and least costly way possible.

Michael Dell learned some important lessons about growth: focus on what you do best and give the customers what they want. Those lessons seem to have paid off.

SOURCES: Andrew E. Serwer, "Michael Dell Turns the PC World Inside Out," *Fortune*, September 9, 1997, p. 76; Michael Dell, "Michael Dell's Plan for the Rest of the Decade," *Fortune Techno* file, June 9, 1997 (http://pathfinder.com/fortune/digitalwatch/0609dig2.html); Rahul Jacob and Rajiv M. Rao, "The Resurrection of Michael Dell," *Fortune*, September 18, 1995.

How did Michael Dell's understanding of the customer affect the marketing strategy for his company?

Marketing includes all the strategies, tactics, and techniques used to raise customer awareness and to promote a product, service, or business. Traditionally, marketing has consisted of a *push strategy*, where a customer who has not necessarily expressed a need for or interest in the product or service is persuaded to purchase it, through selling techniques. In other words, the focus was on the product, not the customer. In relationship marketing, by contrast, the primary focus is on the customer. If the product or service is designed with the customer's needs in mind, much of the "selling" that would otherwise have to be done has been taken care of by giving the customers what they want. As you saw in Profile 14.1, Michael Dell learned early the value of knowing the customer, which accounts in large part for the success of Dell Computer. This chapter will explore the issue of relationship marketing for entrepreneurs and will discuss how to create a marketing plan that will help you build long-term relationships with your customers.

Relationship Marketing

The essence of **relationship marketing** is building trust, satisfying customers, producing shared customer and company goals, communicating with customers, and making customers part of the team. Don Peppers and Martha Rogers, in their book *The One to One Future,* call this trend "share of customer."[1] Relationship marketing is about developing a learning environment where customer and company learn from each other with the goal of achieving a mutually beneficial life-long relationship. What remains is to make customers aware of a product's or service's availability and how and where they can purchase it. Table 14.1 displays the differences between traditional transaction marketing and relationship marketing.

Relationship or **one-to-one marketing** can involve changing not only the company's philosophy but the very way the company does business. Using interactive databases, companies can effectively focus on one customer at a time, with the goal of supplying as many as possible of their needs as are congruent with the company's capabilities. However, one-to-one marketing is not just about collecting information from the customer. For example, merely asking customers where and how they bought the product doesn't produce an answer to the question "How do customers *want* to buy the product?" The customers' answers tell only the purchasing method the company made available to them. By asking the right questions and dialoguing with customers, Apple, for example, learned that its MacIntosh users preferred to purchase products by mail. Relationship marketing is about carrying on a dialogue with the customer over time. Moreover, if the focus is on one customer at a time, market share is no longer an issue or a relevant goal. The goal becomes to create life-long customers who have a vested interest in the company, because the company sincerely wants to meet their needs.

There is a side benefit to the creation of customer relationships. If a problem occurs, a customer who has spent time building a relationship with the

Table 14.1   Transaction v. Relationship Marketing

Transaction Marketing	Relationship Marketing
Concerned with the single sale	Concerned with a long-term relationship
Focus on product/service features	Focus on benefits to customer
Customer service an afterthought	Customer service paramount
Limited commitment to customer	Total commitment to customer
Moderate customer contact	Continual customer contact
Quality the province of production	Quality everyone's business

company won't automatically shift loyalty to a competitor. Often that loyalty is actually strengthened after a problem-solving session with the company results in a satisfying conclusion. All too often, customers have had negative experiences with companies whenever a problem has arisen. If a problem is not resolved satisfactorily, the customer never forgets. Today, customers have a multitude of platforms from which to air their grievances, and one problem aired on national television can cause a public relations nightmare from which the company may never recover. A case in point is what happened to the Cunard cruise line when, in what could only be described as a moment of insanity on the part of management, it decided to launch its Christmas cruise of the renovated *Queen Elizabeth II* despite a ship full of builders who hadn't yet finished their work. Apparently Cunard believed the customers would overlook the mess!

Perhaps the most important benefit to a company of establishing lifelong customer relationships is that over time, the full value of customers is revealed. Customers no longer are viewed as a series of transactions but as bonafide, contributing members of the team who bring value to the bottom line. The more the company learns from its customers, the better the company becomes, and the more difficult it will be for a competitor to adversely affect the business.

Identifying and Rewarding the Best Customers

It is totally unrealistic to think that a company will be able to build long-term relationships with all of its customers, especially if the number of those customers starts heading into the thousands and beyond. What *is* realistic is to search the company's customer base for the most valuable customers, those who warrant in-depth relationships, the customers who account for the biggest percentage of the company's revenues. It is not uncommon for a company to find that as few as 24 percent of its customers account for 95 percent of its revenues. These, therefore, are the customers the company needs to know well, and these are the ones it needs to keep happy. (By the same token, the company should also identify and jettison the worst customers, the ones who have a bad-debt history with the company and buy so infrequently and in such little volume as to cost the company money to retain them.)

After a company has been in business for a while, it becomes easier to identify the most valuable customers. One way to do this is by calculating the lifetime customer value on the basis of viewing the customer as a series of transactions over the life of the relationship.[2] A statistical method for doing this involves calculating the present value of future purchases, using an appropriate discount rate and period of time for the relationship. Add to that the value of customer referrals and subtract the cost of maintaining the relationship (advertising, promotions, letters, questionnaires, 800 numbers). The result will be the customer's lifetime value. Another, nonstatistical, method is to simply dialogue with the customers and ask what their intentions are. The better the company knows the customer, the more valuable and reliable the information will be.

There are a variety of things that companies can do to provide special programs, incentives, and rewards for its best customers.

Frequency Programs

The airlines have used **frequency programs** with great success. The people who fly the most frequently with the airlines receive the most benefits in terms of free tickets, VIP service, and upgrades. Rewards increase with use; therefore, the customer has a vested interest in using a particular airline.

Frequency programs have been used successfully with all types of businesses. Cosmetics companies, for instance, have issued to customers cards that give them a free product after a certain number of product purchases. Similarly, small entertainment centers like miniature golf and water parks often offer discounts for season passes purchased by customers who use the service the most.

Setting up a club or membership makes customers feel special, as if they have input into the company and receive special privileges for being a member; examples include informational newsletters, discounts, and other special programs. Young upstart auto manufacturer Saturn invites its customers to pick up their new cars at the factory and meet the people who made them. Some companies offer their best customers next-day delivery as well as access to a special unlisted toll-free number.[3]

Frequency programs derive their benefit from repeat purchases. The more a customer buys from a company (assuming satisfaction), the higher the probability that he or she will buy repeatedly and the lower the cost to the company of each repeat purchase. In establishing one-to-one relationships, it's essential to single out the best customers for special treatment.

Just-in-Time Marketing

Keeping track of important dates on customers gives the company an opportunity to contact the customer on a special occasion such as a birthday, to remind the customer of the need to repurchase something, or to notify a customer of an impending sale of an item he or she typically buys. This is known as **just-in-time marketing**. Chris Zane of Zane's Cycles in New Haven, Connecticut, made his bicycle shop the most successful in the area by using one-to-one techniques. He availed himself of just-in-time marketing when he heard that another local shop was going out of business and the owner would be leaving the area. He arranged for the phone company, for a small fee, to forward to his shop all calls made to the defunct business. In that way the customers of the defunct business were directed to a new source for their cycling needs. He also bets on customer relationships by offering lifetime service on every bicycle he sells.[4]

Complaint Marketing

You may recall our statement earlier that a dissatisfied customer will probably tell at least nine other people about the problem he or she faced with a company. (And of course those nine people will tell their friends as well!) It's easy to see how quickly a company's reputation can be damaged by even one dissatisfied customer. Consequently, the company ought to think of complaints not as something to avoid dealing with, but as opportunities for continual improvement. It should be made easy for the customer to make a complaint, and he or she should find it possible to carry on a dialogue with a human being who listens and attempts to understand. Nothing is more frustrating than to have to leave a complaint on a voice mail message. Pizza Hut provides a toll-free number for customers. When one calls to complain, the caller talks with a trained rep (Pizza Hut contracts this service out) who then communicates the nature of the complaint via computer to the manager of the appropriate store. The manager is then required to call the customer within forty-eight hours and resolve the issue.[5]

Some companies have used bulletin board services on the Internet to let customers communicate complaints, but this method, though effective attracts more complaints than other methods. Companies using bulletin boards have found, in fact, that this system works almost too well, since customers communicating by computer feel free to vent their frustrations more angrily than when they are hearing a soothing, caring voice at the other end of a phone line. Moreover, since anyone with access to the Internet can read the angry diatribes, a strong complaint can build momentum and create more problems than necessary.

One way to stem complaints at the source is to provide satisfaction surveys at every point of contact with the customer, so that the company can cope with problems quickly, at the outset, before the customer becomes so angry that resolution and satisfaction will be nearly impossible. Following are several suggestions for effective complaint-handling.

▶ Recognize that the customer is a human being and treat him or her as such, never as a number, never as someone without a name or feelings.

▶ Let the customer completely explain the complaint without interruption. In this way, the company is acknowledging that the complaint is viewed as important and worthy of attention.

▶ To find out what the customer really wants, ask the most important question: *"What is one thing we can do to make this better?"*

▶ Defuse the anger of the customer by sincerely taking his or her side on the issue; then move the customer from a problem focus to a solution focus. Get the customer to agree on a solution.

▶ Contact the customer one week later to find out whether he or she is still satisfied with the solution and express the company's desire for a continued relationship.

The most important message you can send to your customers through your marketing efforts is that the customer is the most important part of the organization and you will do whatever it takes to keep good customers satisfied. While it's certainly true that a young, growing company needs to build a customer base by continually adding new customers, it will reap the greatest returns from investing in the customers it currently has.

Guerrilla Marketing

Entrepreneurs approach marketing from a point of view distinctly different from that of the traditional marketer. While they may employ some of the same techniques as a large corporate marketer, they also will take advantage of many other marketing opportunities, ones that the corporate marketer may ignore. Jay Conrad Levinson has called the entrepreneurial marketing approach **guerrilla marketing,** which is an alternative to traditional, expensive marketing tactics.[6] Given that entrepreneurs don't have the time or money for elaborate, high-profile marketing strategies, they essentially mimic what the big companies do, but do it for much less money and for a shorter period of time.

Guerrilla marketing is distinguished from relationship marketing in that relationship marketing is a way of looking at building long-term customer relationships, whereas guerrilla marketing is a set of strategies and tactics to get the most return in marketing success from limited dollars and resources. This chapter now presents some suggestions for creating an entrepreneurial marketing plan that provides the best results for the least amount of money possible. It will look at the marketing plan in general and then consider the traditional "4 P's" of marketing—product, price, place, promotion—in more detail and from an entrepreneurial point of view.

The Marketing Plan

For any company, an effective marketing strategy begins with a marketing plan. The **marketing plan** for an entrepreneurial company is a living guide to how the company plans to build customer relationships over its life in order to fulfill the mission statement in the business plan. It details the strategies and tactics that will create awareness on the part of the customer and build a loyal customer base over time. Marketing plans are written at many points in the life of a business. The original business plan will contain a marketing plan for introducing the company and its products and services to the marketplace. Later you may develop a marketing plan to create market awareness for your company, to introduce new products and services, and to grow the business, perhaps in a new direction.

A few steps taken before the actual writing of the marketing plan ensures that the plan is on target and is one you can live with for a long time. Saying you must live with the plan for a long time probably sounds inconsistent with the need of the entrepreneur to remain flexible and adapt to change in the marketplace, but one of the biggest problems with most marketing plans is that they are not followed long enough to achieve the desired results.

Typically, the business owner does not see immediate results from the marketing effort and decides it must not be working—so he or she changes it and starts the cycle all over again. Changing the plan precipitously is precisely the wrong thing to do. It takes time to make customers aware of the product or service. It takes time for a particular marketing strategy to take hold and build confidence in the customer. From the first time a customer sees an ad, for example, to the point at which the customer actually buys the product may be weeks or even months. On average, the customer will see the ad 15 to 20 times before the product actually is purchased. Therefore, just like a good stock market investor, you must think of the marketing plan as an investment in the future of the business, and any investment takes time to mature. Reaping the benefits of a well-structured marketing plan requires persistence and unwavering dedication until the plan has an opportunity to perform.

There are several steps to take prior to writing a marketing plan.

1. *Make a list of the options.* To even begin to know which marketing options should be considered, you need to talk to other business owners, customers, and suppliers. Read some books and articles on marketing strategies for entrepreneurs, like those suggested at the end of this chapter. This process will produce a list of possibilities that may range from sponsoring a business conference to advertising in a national trade publication. Determining which strategies are the most effective, or even feasible, can be left for later.

2. *Think like a customer.* Imagine the business from the customer's point of view. What would entice you to enter that store, buy that product, avail yourself of that service?

3. *Study the competition.* Take a look at the businesses that will be competing with yours and determine what makes them successful or unsuccessful. What marketing strategies do they seem to employ, and are those effective? How could you improve on what your competitors are doing?

4. *Analyze the options and rank them.* Eliminate first those that either don't meet the needs of the target market or simply are not feasible at this time (usually for budgetary reasons). Then rank the top ten choices. You are now ready to begin writing the marketing plan.

The Marketing Plan in One Paragraph

Many experienced marketers suggest that the first step in creating the marketing plan is to condense all the ideas about marketing strategy into a single paragraph that says it all. Impossible? Not at all. A single well-written paragraph will force you to focus carefully on the central point of the overall marketing strategy. The paragraph should include:

▶ The purpose of the marketing plan.

　What will the marketing plan accomplish?

▶ The benefits of the product/service.

　How will the product/service help the customer or satisfy a need?

▶ The target market.

　Who is the primary buyer?

▶ The market niche.

> *Where do you fit in the industry or market? How do you differentiate yourself?*

▶ The marketing tactics to be used.

> *What specific marketing tools will be employed?*

▶ The company's convictions, its identity.

> *How will the customers define the company?*

▶ The percentage of sales the marketing budget will represent.

> *How much money will you be allocating to the marketing plan?*

Here is an example of an effective one-paragraph statement of the marketing plan for a product business.

The purpose of the marketing plan is to create brand awareness for *ABC Corporation.*

> *ABC* will sell innovative, portable power source equipment at the highest quality and the lowest possible cost. *ABC* will accomplish this by positioning itself as the leader in providing reliable, dual power source products that reduce the number of pieces of equipment a user must own. The target market is the construction industry, and more specifically, those who use power tools in areas where no power is available. The niche *ABC* will enter is that of construction companies that own or lease power equipment. Initial marketing tactics will include direct sales to equipment rental outlets, advertisements in trade publications, and trade shows. *ABC's* customers will see the company as service-oriented with a quick response to customer needs both in service and in product design. Twelve percent of sales will be applied to the marketing strategy.

With your paragraph in hand and the focus established, a more detailed marketing plan can now be created. Every marketing plan incorporates the "4 P's" of marketing: product, price, place, and promotion. Once these aspects of the plan have been dealt with, the creative aspects such as the advertising

What's in a Name?

Even the name of your business should be part of the overall marketing plan because it's the first point of identity you establish with the customer. It should be easily remembered and should relate to what you are selling. A name like "Useful Products," the name of one California company, would not win any prizes for originality and style, but "Higher Ground," an Oregon coffee company, might.

goals can be addressed. You will also develop a media plan that details what media will be used, when they will be used, and how much it will cost.

The Product

There are a number of considerations, relative to the product or products, that must be addressed in the marketing plan. They include product features and benefits—identity, branding, packaging, and labeling—product positioning, and product mix.

Product Features and Benefits

For marketing purposes, think of the product as a bundle of benefits to the customer. These benefits include a wide variety of things: attractiveness, distinctive characteristics, quality, options, warranties, service contracts, delivery, and so forth. But more important to the customer, the product offers intangible benefits like convenience, savings in time and money, or improved health. This bundle of benefits is the information the customer must have about the product/service in order to feel comfortable about buying it.

Merely offering these benefits is not enough, however. They must be offered consistently. In other words, the benefits the customer derives from using the product/service must be received time and time again. Often, for example, a company will focus on a high level of quality without concerning itself with minor fluctuations in that quality. The only way to build confidence in customers and thereby increase the chance of return customers is by providing consistency in all the product benefits.

Product Branding, Packaging, and Labeling

Product hype via mass marketing seems to have been the strategy of the 1990s, seen in everything from Coca-Cola versus Pepsi ads to the auto manufacturers who told us, "It just feels right!" Creating an image through branding, packaging, labeling, and advertising is pervasive because it works. While an ad featuring a young, athletically slim woman drinking a "lite" beer seems to be an oxymoron, subliminally it hits the mark. Drinking lite beer is sexy, healthy, youthful, and low in calories. Whether it is true or not is irrelevant; the image remains.

For companies that participate in the war of the images, the battle is everything. They will do anything to win. What is important is the brand name, keeping it in the public eye. Most times we don't even know what company is promoting the brand. Often the name appears only briefly at the end of the ad. This is the strategy of Calvin Klein and Nike. Image and reality are frequently separated by an enormous gap. The belief is that if you repeat a slogan—for example, "We're number one"—often enough, people (including the company) will believe it, even if it's not true. Eventually, however, the lie catches up and customers begin to lose faith in the product (not necessarily in the company, however, because its name was never used).

A counter movement, however, has begun to occur among world-class entrepreneurial ventures. A number of very successful businesses like Ben and Jerry's, Pelco, Smith and Hawkens, and Starbucks Coffee are resisting image positioning as the way to communicate their message. Instead of promoting brand names, they choose to communicate the philosophy of their business, which is at the core of all their products, and which by its very nature differentiates these companies from others in the market. They do not go head to head with their competitors in a war of images; they create their own niche in marketing strategy by seeking ways to increase pride and loyalty not only in their customers but in their employees as well. They break with tradition to make themselves stand out.

For example, Starbucks Coffee places great importance on its employees. In an industry that regularly experiences high employee turnover and low wages, Starbucks sees the employees as its competitive advantage. The comprehensive compensation package, health care, and stock options it offers all employees gives them a vested interest in the company and a desire to see it succeed. This philosophy is communicated to customers in a more personal manner than through mass marketing. It is communicated in the way Starbucks employees treat their customers.

The differences in products that these new marketing strategists promote are real and can be measured. These real differences not only distinguish them from the false reality of their competitors' images, but expose those images for what they are. Of course, developing a sound company philosophy or culture is not an overnight achievement. It takes time, and while you are working at building that philosophy, the image builders will probably receive the bulk of the attention. Nevertheless, persistence will pay off when you are able to deliver precisely what you said you would.

Packaging

The way a product is packaged reflects the philosophy of the business. If you are producing a consumer product, attractive packaging will grab the consumer's attention as that product sits among many competing ones on the shelf. In global marketing, packaging can often be as important as the product itself. In Japan, for example, consumers value products that come in artistically beautiful boxes and will pay more for such packaging.

In general, packaging should depict

▶ What the product is

▶ Its key product benefits

▶ The company philosophy

▶ The level of quality

When Jan Davidson of Davidson, Inc., a leading educational software manufacturer, first studied the packaging of software back in 1979, she noted that most of it was in plastic bags hanging on hooks in the stores. Since she was an educator herself, she wanted her software to be more associated with books and education, so to differentiate her product at the retail level, she packaged it in binders that looked like colorful books on the shelf.

Labeling

Today many companies are promoting products they call environmentally friendly, but they often stretch the limits of that term. In an effort to protect consumers, the Federal Trade Commission has issued guidelines for the use of environmental terms in advertising and product labeling. For example, a product can be labeled **recyclable** only if the entire product can be collected or separated from solid waste and used in the manufacture of other products. A product may be labeled **recycled content** if the recycled materials in the product came from solid waste stream. You also have to distinguish between materials recycled from manufacturing and those from consumer waste by weight. To use the terms *degradable, biodegradable*, and *photodegradable*, there must be evidence that the product will completely break down and return to nature in a relatively short period of time. Otherwise you have to qualify just how degradable it really is.

Product Positioning

Product positioning is the way customers view the product in relation to competitors' products. Is the product more luxurious, of higher quality, less expensive, more attractive, and so forth? In other words, product positioning really defines the product by its benefits to the target customer. Consequently, any product will probably be repositioned several times during the course of its product life cycle as customer tastes and preferences change. And this is precisely why a small company that is flexible and can move more quickly can take on a giant in a market niche that the giant has not yet tackled.

It is also important to note that you will position not only the product but the company, distribution channel, and technology as well. Savvy customers today are concerned more and more about the reputation of the company they are dealing with, so if, for example, a company associates with distributors whose level of service is not up to the company's standards, that will ultimately reflect on the company. Realistically, a product's position in the market will be a function of the customers' perception of where it should be. That is, you may have designed your product to replace another established product, whereas the customers see it as a product they would like to have, once they have already bought the existing product. Precious marketing dollars will be wasted if you don't respond to the customers' perceptions.

In positioning the new product, refer to the customer profile developed when you did your market research. However, be aware that you must constantly receive feedback from customers to stay on top of changes in tastes and preferences that may call for a repositioning of the product later on. Most products will have primary market segments and then sub-sets of those segments. *Sub-sets* are other markets or uses for the product. Just as you studied the primary market, you must also understand the sub-sets to correctly position the product in those markets.

It is also important to study your competitors carefully to determine their strengths and weaknesses and how they might respond to your entry into the market. If a competitor is a publicly traded company, annual reports are available. In the event they are not, talking with distributors, customers, and advertisers can provide valuable information to help in planning a strategy. If you find out that a competitor holds the position you wish to occupy, you have three choices: 1) find another opportunity; 2) try to overtake the competitor in the position; or 3) attempt to reposition the competitor. Overtaking the competitor is very difficult to achieve and is rarely accomplished. If you have positioned the business in an emerging niche, there may be an opportunity to re-educate the customers about the competitor's product as well as introduce them to the different benefits of yours.

Studying the market carefully can produce niches that may not have been considered or vulnerabilities in competitors not previously apparent. It may also result in positioning the product a little differently than originally planned. Remember, however, to look not only for evidence to support a particular positioning but also for evidence to refute it.

Once you have determined the position you wish to occupy and have written the positioning statement, it needs to be tested in the marketplace. There are several methods that can be used, and they vary in the time and cost involved. In all cases, however, news of the product will be shared prior to market entry, so have anyone who participates in the testing sign a **Statement of Nondisclosure**.

▶ **Peer Review**. Ask anyone and everyone you know to give an opinion on the positioning statement. Ask for their impressions and perceptions of how the product will do in this position.

▶ **Distribution Channel Review.** Ask salespeople, distributors, and retailers what they think of the position statement. These are people who understand the industry and will have a pretty good sense of where you and your product might fit in.

▶ **Focus Groups**. Bring together a representative sample of the customer base and get their opinions.

▶ **Test Marketing.** This involves producing a limited amount of product and selling it in a defined geographic region to determine if the product positioning is correct. For most start-up companies, test marketing isn't economically feasible, so the cost of this approach must be weighed against getting out in the market as quickly as possible.

As discussed in Chapter 6, entrepreneurs need to consider the costs versus benefits of expensive market research. With most markets far more volatile than ever before, it usually pays to shorten the development and test time to get into the market quickly, particularly where a company can gain a first-mover advantage. When you have a good positioning statement that will produce the desired results, communicate this statement to everyone involved in the production and distribution of the product, so that the company and everyone involved with it will share a common philosophy and communicate a consistent message to the customer.

Product Mix

Product mix refers to all the products the business will produce and/or sell. If the business will offer multiple products, you must consider how these products relate to one another and whether they all serve to communicate your company's identity and product positioning message. The products that comprise the product mix will be determined by the markets to be served; for example, a more diversified product mix may be needed when several markets are being served.

Catherine White, founder of Financial Architects, a financial services firm in Lexington, Massachusetts, offers social screening of potential investments as an additional service in her "product mix." Clients who wish to invest in companies that have certain social goals can use her services, as can clients whose investing is based on purely financial criteria. In this way, she is serving a larger market with a more diverse product mix.

Price

Price is one of the most important features of a product. As a marketing tool, price more than any other factor affects customer acceptance of the product, the business's cash flow, and in general the profitability. Price is determined by many factors:

▶ The demand for the product is strong relative to the supply. Where demand is greater than supply, a higher price may be commanded.

▶ The demand for the product is inelastic; that is, people will buy no matter what the price because they need the product. This is typically true for commodities with no viable substitute, like milk.

▶ Intense competition may force the price of the product down.

▶ Additional features may warrant a higher price.

▶ New technology may call for a higher price.

▶ Product positioning may be associated with a certain price level. For example, positioning a product among luxury items commands a higher price.

Strategies for Pricing

Pricing becomes a feature of the product when it is the central selling point. The product that is considered a commodity or the product that faces intense competition will often be marketed on the basis of lower price for the same quality. How a product is priced is a function of a company's goals. Is the goal to

▶ *Increase sales?* This may entail lowering prices to raise the volume sold.

▶ *Increase market share?* Again, lowering prices may increase volume, thus increasing market share.

▶ *Maximize cash flow?* Increasing cash flow can be achieved several ways, including raising prices and reducing direct costs and overhead.

▶ *Maximize profit?* Similar to maximizing cash flow, this can be accomplished several ways, including raising prices, lowering prices and increasing volume, or decreasing overhead.

▶ *Set up entry barriers to competition?* Lowering prices on the basis of using efficient production methods, achieving economies of scale, and keeping overhead low can often set up entry barriers to companies that can't compete on that scale.

▶ *Define an image?* Setting a higher price based on higher perceived and/or actual quality is one way of establishing a particular image in an industry.

▶ *Control demand?* Where a company does not have the resources to meet demand, prices can be set at a level that discourages sales to a particular degree.

Knowing what a pricing strategy is supposed to accomplish in advance of setting a price will ensure compatibility with the company's goals.

There are several components of a pricing strategy.

1. **Cost-based pricing.** This component adds the cost of producing the product, the related costs of running the business, and a profit margin to arrive at a market price.

2. **Demand-based pricing.** This component is based on finding out what customers are willing to pay for the product, then pricing it accordingly. For new products with no direct comparison, a combination of this approach and cost-based pricing is often used to arrive at a satisfactory price. In general, customers recognize several prices for any one product: the standard price, which is the price normally paid for the item; the sale price; the price paid for specials; and the relative price, which is the price of the item compared to a substitute product. For some products, customers may have to add to the normal cost of shipping, handling, or installation in their comparison with other like products.

3. **Competition-based pricing.** Where the product has direct competition, the entrepreneur can look at competitors' pricing strategy and price the product in line with theirs, higher if it is determined that the product has added value, or lower if competing on price.

4. **Psychological pricing.** Using an odd-even strategy can suggest a pricing position in the market, an odd number ($12.99) to suggest a bargain, an even number ($40.00) to suggest quality, or higher than average pricing to suggest exclusivity.

5. **Distribution channel pricing.** The channel of distribution through which the entrepreneur chooses to move the product will affect the ultimate price to the customer, as allowance for each intermediary in the channel must be made to make a certain percentage of profit.

6. **Extrapolating from other industries.** It is important to look at the pricing strategies of businesses in other industries. The fact that your industry does not seem to employ a particular strategy does not mean that the strategy won't work. Staying competitive on price means always looking for new methods of pricing products.

Place

The place strategy will dictate how products get to the customers. This is essentially the distribution strategy, which was discussed in detail in Chapter 12. In this section, however, the scope of distribution and some issues related to transportation are addressed. As in any aspect of marketing, consistency is important. Naturally, the location of the business is a relatively stable feature, so customers always know where to find it. It is equally important to establish stable distribution channels so that customers don't have to think about how to find your products. Once a customer associates your product with a particular outlet, whether wholesale or retail, a major change—such as moving to a mail order channel—may cause frustration and lead the customer to seek a substitute product. On the other hand, some commodity products gain new life from an innovative distribution channel. Take coffee, which became an experience rather than just a drink, due to the creative genius of the founder of the Starbucks coffee chain.

The distribution strategy dictates how broadly your products are distributed. Choosing to distribute to all possible outlets involves using an intensive distribution strategy. Limiting distribution to select outlets is a selective strategy. With an exclusive distribution strategy, distribution is limited to one outlet per geographic area. The strategy you choose will be a function of your growth strategy.

Dealing with Multiple Channels of Distribution

More often than not, as a company grows and the diversity of its customer base increases, it develops more than one channel of distribution. It may, for example, use direct sales to service the largest customers and intermediary channels of resellers and manufacturer's reps to bring in new customers. It is often not easy to determine which channel is the most effective. Indirect channels are generally associated with a lower level of marketing and sales expense because this task is taken on by the reseller. However, indirect channels are also associated with lower net margins because of the discounts given to resellers so they can make a profit as well; hence the source of the oft-stated "The cost is in the middleman."

What is rarely recognized, however, is that resellers often deal in competing products or several products from one manufacturer and can therefore usually achieve economies of scale, thus reducing their selling costs. Direct sellers, on the other hand, are less able to compete on price with a variety of accounts and typically incur the highest cost per sales call of the two methods. In addition, they are not generally equipped to economically provide products to multiple receiving points in the same way a distributor with regional warehouses can.

The advent of distribution computer software has encouraged the development of major distributors who can, more efficiently than a manufacturer, handle orders, shipping, invoicing, inventory management, and receivables. Today distributors are more than simply transfer agents or bulk breakers for smaller companies; they actually add value through services provided to both their suppliers and their customers.

Transportation Is the Link in the Chain

Transportation is potentially the weakest link in the distribution chain because it usually receives the least amount of attention from manufacturers. However, when you consider that raw materials as well as finished goods spend a good part of their time in transit or in inventory, incurring costs at both stages, any savings in logistical functions bring more to the bottom line for everyone in the chain. Even where price differentiation is not feasible, value can be added through differentiation in logistical strategy. The goals of an effective logistics system include:

- Increasing information
- Reducing inventories
- Increasing cycle times
- Reducing variable costs
- Improving customer service

Information is the key. The company that has a communications system that lets it stay in touch with its distributors and sales force wherever they are will be a more efficient and effective company. Some trucking companies, for example, use two-way satellite communication and track shipments via computer, so they are never out of touch. Thus, logistics is a significant aspect of any marketing plan.

Promotion

The promotion function of the marketing strategy is the creative one, for this is where advertising, publicity, sales promotion, and personal selling tactics—in short, your promotional mix—is decided. Not every business has the same promotional mix; it is a function of the type of business, the target market, and, of course, the budget. For entrepreneurs with new ventures, the last item—the budget—usually dictates a creative approach.

Creativity begins with a clear understanding of the customer, the economy, current trends, and even the daily news. You never know where a creative idea will come from or what current event will trigger an idea for an ad campaign. In the 1990s, for example, social responsibility became a big issue; hence the proliferation of ads like those of The Body Shop depicting a company that cares about people and natural resources. In fact, the ad may never mention the product being offered for sale. Tying a marketing strategy to current trends like social responsibility means you must remain flexible and willing to change the strategy, should the current trend change. Customers are fickle, and no matter how sound or beneficial a trend may be, they will eventually tire of it, and a new tactic must be employed.

A new business requires two promotional plans: one for opening the business and making customers aware of its existence; the other, for growing the business. The opening plan establishes the identity or philosophy of the business. Remember that identity and philosophy are quite different from image. An *image* is what you may aspire to be, whereas your business character and philosophy define who you are in reality. The marketing plan for growing the business is the one you will implement and use consistently for the long term. It is the plan you invest in to build a customer base. It will define the target market and market share you wish to achieve, what people and resources it will take to reach that share, and which services will be needed.

There are many ways to effectively promote your company. We'll look at several of them.

Advertising

Advertising media generally fall into two categories: print and broadcast. The following sections examine the various types of media and their uses. It is not the purpose of this book to provide all the information needed to use each medium presented, only to create awareness of how and when each is used, so that a decision can be made about which media will best serve the business.

Print Media

The Newspaper   The purpose of a newspaper is to distribute the news in a direct, to-the-point fashion. Today that doesn't mean just the town gazette. Most cities have one or more major newspapers in addition to business newspapers, shopper newspapers, ethnic newspapers, and national newspapers. How does an entrepreneur know which is most appropriate for the product or service being sold? With businesses spending nearly one-third of their advertising dollars on newspaper ads, this question becomes crucial.

Newspaper advertising offers these advantages:

▶ Broad coverage in a selected geographic area

▶ Flexibility and speed in bringing an ad to print and changing it along the way

▶ Quickness in generating sales

▶ Relatively little cost

Newspapers have disadvantages as well. Broad coverage means you are paying to reach people who may not be part of the target market. Furthermore, since newspapers carry hundreds of ads every day, it is not easy (short of taking a full page) to attract the attention of the reader. Then, too, a newspaper has a very short life. A person may read it with breakfast and throw it out before leaving for work. Even an ad that was noticed may be forgotten by the end of the day. Therefore, you may want to consider a specialized newspaper that will better reach the customer you want. Here are some tips for using newspaper advertising.

▶ Determine which newspaper is best for your business by placing ads in all of the ones in your target region the first time. If appropriate for your business, include in the ad a coupon or toll-free number so that the potential customer will either bring the coupon into your place of business or call on a special line. In either case, ask the person who responds where he or she heard about the business. Ads in the papers with the highest response rates should be continued and all others dropped. Once this has been done in one or two geographic regions, you can safely assume that a similar type of newspaper in another part of the country will give similar results.

▶ Be sure you or someone you have paid designs the ad so that it doesn't look like every other one on the page. Often a distinctive border will make the ad stand out.

▶ Create a basic design for advertising that reflects the philosophy of the business and use that design consistently in all advertising. Customers will eventually recognize that the ad is for your company before they even read it.

▶ The best location for the ad is a right-hand page, above the fold of the newspaper, but it is probably the most costly.

▶ Keep track of the results of your ads, particularly if you are experimenting with size and design.

▶ A national newspaper like *USA Today* offers a good opportunity to do national advertising for less money and a broader reach than a magazine.

Magazines   A number of national magazines offer businesses the opportunity to advertise to certain broad-based target markets. Magazines like *People, Newsweek, Business Week,* and *Time* reach hundreds of thousands of people every week. In addition, there are specialty magazines like *Sports Illustrated, Modern Maturity, Rolling Stone,* and *Road & Track* that focus on specific interests. These magazines are useful for businesses that are targeting a particular interest like cars and car accessories or senior citizen issues. There are also a great number of trade magazines that reflect the needs of specific trade organizations, like *Advertising Age* and *Variety*. Magazine advertising, however, is more costly and the time lag for printing is generally 6–8 weeks, so it lacks the flexibility of newspapers. These things must be weighed against the fact that you may be doing a better job of reaching the target market.

Magazines also offer the entrepreneur one thing newspapers can't: credibility. According to Jay Levinson, "A properly produced magazine ad, preferably of the full-page variety, gives a small business more credibility than any other mass marketing medium."[7] Obviously, you would want to run the ad more than once; but it is possible to run the ad one time and order reprints at a fraction of the original cost to use in direct mail campaigns and in brochures.

Here are some tips for magazine advertising.

▶ If the magazine has a regional edition, run the ad in the region you are targeting.

▶ Use a media buying service to gain real cost advantages.

▶ Ask the magazine if you can run a split-run ad; that is, run one headline in half the magazines and another in the other half. Be sure to code them so you can keep track of responses.

▶ Code all ads to reflect publication, date, run, and ad size.

▶ Use color effectively and take advantage of the fact that you can provide more information in a magazine ad than in a newspaper ad because the reader generally spends more time with a magazine ad.

▶ Always give a phone number or mail-in coupon in the ad to encourage people to contact you for a full brochure or a video.

▶ Check on "remnant space," leftover space that must be filled before the magazine goes to print. It will be a fraction of the original cost of an ad.

Profile 14.2

Laughing All the Way to the Bank

When was the last time you flew one of the top three airlines and applauded the flight attendant's rap rendition of the emergency-exits and oxygen-mask instructions, or had the president of a $3 billion airline serve you the in-flight meal? It can happen on maverick Southwest Airlines, where making the customers happy is the primary goal. And Southwest succeeds in doing so, despite the fact that it's a no-frills airline with no reserved seats. What Southwest does best is have the fewest customer complaints of any airline, and the best baggage handling and on-time flight performance record. Here's what Southwest does to stay on top.

1. Define a corporate culture on the basis of company-wide values and stick to it.

2. Keep costs low and manage growth.

3. By keeping costs low, you can also keep prices low for your customers.

4. Do what you do better than anyone else.

5. Always keep your promises to customers.

6. Hire for attitude and train for skills.

7. Cross-train your employees so they will feel they know the company inside and out.

8. Celebrate everything and encourage an environment where failures turn into successes.

9. Set your company apart from the crowd and keep the corporate culture at the forefront of everything you do.

10. Never stop thinking like an entrepreneur.

SOURCE: Kristin Dunlop Godsey, "Slow Climb to New Heights," *Success*, October 1996, p. 20.

The Yellow Pages   Many businesses can benefit from placing ads in the Yellow Pages of their telephone directory. If you are in the retail business or offer a service not considered a professional service (consultant, lawyer, accountant), there is a good chance people will look in the Yellow Pages for what you offer. However, remember that the Yellow Pages is fairly expensive advertising space and targets only the local market for your product or service, so it should not be considered a major source of advertising, particularly if you market nationally or globally.

Signs   Signs are a relatively inexpensive way to expose a lot of people to the business. They also encourage impulse buying of consumer products. Naturally, signs play the most important role in retail businesses where they become part of the total advertising campaign. In other types of businesses, the sign is merely a feature to help someone locate the business. Signs do, however, outlive their usefulness fairly quickly. If a sale sign is left in a window too long, people will tune it out; they will no longer see it, and it will have lost its value.

Database Marketing

Database marketing (DBM) is a system for gathering and using information on customers and prospects with the goal of increasing profitability. A well-constructed database will contain names, addresses, and attributes of people who are likely to purchase what the company has to offer. It will help the entrepreneur define a trading area, reach new customers in the marketplace, select specific target audiences, and survey current customers. DBM is not merely a way to reach customers by mail more easily. Today retaining and maintaining current customers is more important than spending money to find new customers. It has been reported that 65 percent of a company's business comes from current customers. In fact, it costs five to ten times more to go after a new customer than to serve an existing one.[8] With good customer profiles, an entrepreneur can match demographic information on current customers with demographic data in the geographic area of interest to find prospects more effectively. Information contained in the database can be used in advertising, sales promotion, public relations, direct mail, and personal selling.

The competitive advantages to DBM are many. It helps entrepreneurs increase their response rates, aids in the development of new products, helps in the forecasting of sales, and improves mass marketing decisions. Database marketing also allows the company to personalize advertising, cross-sell related products, and increase customer loyalty.

Database marketing is really an overall approach to doing business, an approach that requires the total commitment of everyone in the organization. The payoff to this approach takes time—many frustrated entrepreneurs will give up before seeing the results of the efforts. To successfully implement DBM, there must be measurement standards in place to ensure that the efforts are producing the desired results.

Dealing with Information Overload

One of the biggest problems entrepreneurs have when using databases to keep track of customer information is how to control the massive amounts of information they amass. Here are a few tips for dealing with information overload.

1. Be careful about what you choose to store in your database. Make sure it's really useful, not just another piece of minutiae you'll have cluttering up the file.

2. Rank your customers as to their importance to the company so that as you enter more information, you can make better decisions about whether or not to keep it.

3. Think carefully about how to enter names and key words so that you can easily find things again. If, for example, a company is known by its corporate initials as in AAA, don't file it under American Automobile Association.

4. Keep only your best customers in the main database. Archive older or lost customers for future reference if needed.

5. To make a database work, you must regularly enter data; in other words, keep it current.

SOURCE: Susan Greco, "Good Cheap Data," *Inc.*, August 1997, p. 94.

Direct Marketing

Direct marketing includes direct mail, mail order, coupons, telemarketing, door-to-door, and TV shopping networks. The essence of direct marketing is that the entrepreneur attempts to close a sale at the moment the advertising takes place. Direct marketing also permits coverage of a wide geographic area while, at the same time, targeting specific customers; therefore, more sales can be generated with fewer dollars. Much more information can be provided in a direct-response brochure; in other words, it can answer all the customer's potential questions so that he or she can make an immediate decision. Consequently, direct mail has the highest response rate of any type of advertising, and the responses received from a purchased mailing list become the business's personal direct mailing list. Another way to create a personalized mailing list is to have people who "walk in" to the place of business fill out a database card and suggest other people who may be interested in the product or service.

The average response rate for direct mail is two percent. That rate can be increased 50 to 100 percent if you include a toll-free number in the advertising, which is easier than filling out an order form. That response rate can be

Telemarketing Law

Be sure you understand the Telephone Consumer Protection Act, which says you must maintain a "do-not-call" list and bans unsolicited advertising via fax machines. You can find out more about this law by writing for "Marketing by Telephone," to the Direct Marketing Association's Ethics and Consumer Affairs Department, 1101 17th St. NW, Suite 705, Washington, DC 20036-4704.

increased from 100 to 700 percent by following up the mailing with a phone call—telemarketing—within 72 hours. As a small, growing company, it is important to consider the staff resources you have and to control mailings to the number you can reasonably follow up on within the 72 hours.

To get the highest possible response rate, you have to do several repeat mailings. For catalogs, four times a year is typical. Also, since most customers have a tendency to throw out direct, unsolicited mail before reading it, it is important to put the central selling point on the envelope as well. Customers must be enticed to open the envelope. A tag line that suggests that what is contained in the envelope will bring the customer money, health, love, or success will certainly encourage people to see what you have to offer. Be sure to continuously update the mailing list and refine it so that the number of nonresponses declines.

More than half of any success with direct mail is attributable to using a good mailing list, followed by offering something the customer wants, and being creative in the marketing of the product or service. If you use a targeted mailing list, offer a real benefit to the customer, and send that offer in a business envelope with no return address, the chances of getting a response climb significantly. Not all products are suitable for direct mail, however. Those that are not consumable (requiring repeat orders), or not easily shipped, or are short-lived as in a fad, too seasonal, or too easily available in stores are not good bets for direct mail advertising.

If you are dealing in a consumer item, you may also want to consider interactive TV shopping shows or infomercials to sell the product. The interactive version where the viewer can see the product and order it immediately is in place in several test markets and will eventually be accessible by anyone who wishes it. Interactive TV allows you access to the consumer you seek by sex, age, special interests, occupation, and so forth. It is estimated that 70 million people watch Home Shopping Network; 28 million watch Cable Value Network; and 18 million watch QVC. This is definitely a growing market for direct market sales, and as soon as interactive TV becomes a reality for anyone who wants it, those numbers will increase. Computer online services like Prodigy and Compuserve also provide an outlet for consumer products and will be something to look at carefully in the future.

Broadcast Media

Radio   Radio is an excellent medium for local or regional advertising, as the audience can be targeted geographically and generally by age group. Radio stations keep extensive records on the demographics of their listening audience to help determine if this audience will be interested in a particular product or service. It is useful to advertise on more than one station to saturate your market. Recently many companies have been able to gain a national presence by sponsoring a national radio program. This was the case with Snapple Beverage Company, which bought time on the Rush Limbaugh radio talk show and immediately gained access to 20 million listeners a week. Sales for the company soared as a result.

When dealing in radio advertising it is important to understand that the ad can't be a one-shot ad. As radio listeners are fickle and tend to change stations often, the ad needs to be played several times a day, several days a week to achieve an impact. Keeping track of the responses received from the ad indicates where the greatest impact has been made. A general rule of thumb is that prime radio time is during commuting hours in the morning and late afternoon. The cost will be higher at those times, but you will reach the most people. Be sure to provide finished recorded commercials to the station so you can maintain quality and consistency in your advertising. Don't rely on the radio station personnel to give your ad the energy and professionalism it needs. Here are a few more tips for radio advertising.

▸ Stick to shorter spots. You can usually achieve just as much in a well-designed 30-second ad as you can in a one-minute ad.

▸ Use music and sound effects to set the tone for the commercial. Both can be rented from most radio stations for a modest amount.

▸ Be sure to design the commercial to catch the listener's attention in the first few seconds.

▸ Run your ads three weeks out of every four for good coverage at less cost.

Profile 14.3

Your Mailing List Has Great Value

Financial types like CPAs and bankers have a difficult time measuring the value of a mailing list—you can't borrow against it; yet when you want to place a value on your business to a potential buyer, it can be a gold mine. It has been said that a good list is worth at least 40 percent of the entire mailing effort. John Storey of Storey Communications knows this to be true. In his first year without generating any other promotion, his list of previous customers generated $250,000 in revenues.

Storey asserts that some of the benefits of mailing lists include:

▸ The ability to control your marketing efforts more precisely.

▸ The ability to build value and equity for your business.

▸ The ability to tap a new channel of distribution in your industry.

SOURCE: M. John Storey, "Hidden Value," *Success*, April 1997, p. 28.

Television   Many businesses spend one quarter of their advertising dollars on television; consequently, it is the second-most-popular form of advertising after newspapers for consumer products. With television, people can see as well as hear about the product or service, and the audience can be targeted at the national, regional, or even local level as well as by interest group by using cable channels. However, television advertising is expensive, not only for the actual on-air time but for the preparation and filming of the commercial.

Television time is based on the **gross rating point** (GRP), which, put very simply, means that you will pay per GRP, a rate that differs depending on whether you are in a small town or a large city. The range is about $5 to $500 per GRP. A rule of thumb for deciding whether or not to use television as an advertising medium is to calculate whether you can purchase 150 GRPs per month for three months. If this level of advertising is not within the budget, forget TV; you will probably be wasting your money. When using television seek the help of a media buying service. These services are the equivalent of buying health insurance through group pools, and they can get your media time much more cheaply than you can because they buy millions of dollars' worth every month.

While learning how to produce a television spot is a book by itself, here are two pieces of advice: 1) Write the script yourself and let the television studio provide the product equipment and expertise; and 2) do not appear in the commercial yourself unless you are a professional actor.

Miscellaneous Advertising   Many simple advertising tactics have been very successful for new and growing consumer products or service businesses. Offering for sale (or as a giveaway) T-shirts and baseball caps with the company's name emblazoned on them has been a very successful tactic. Using searchlights to attract people to your business site is an attention getter. Couponing has certainly been an advertising staple, and there are many coupon magazines in which you can buy space. These magazines are distributed to households across the country and have been an excellent source of new customers for businesses. Look for any and all opportunities to demonstrate the product free to potential customers. One young entrepreneur who developed a successful, easy-to-use cleaner for silk plants reports his sales always increase when he does demonstrations in stores. Creating a videotape of the product in action is another useful technique, especially where the product is not easily transported. Many firms like PictureTel Corp. of Massachusetts have incorporated videos into free seminars. An outstanding 80 percent of people who attend these seminars end up purchasing one of their products.

This section has provided just a few of the hundreds of tips and techniques available to entrepreneurs who wish to advertise products or services in the most efficient and effective ways while the new venture is growing. The series of books on guerrilla marketing by Jay Conrad Levinson is highly recommended for its marketing suggestions geared specifically to young, growing companies.

Publicity and Public Relations

Publicity is essentially free advertising for a product or business, through newspaper articles, radio and television stories, and talk shows. Public relations, on the other hand, is the way a marketing campaign is structured so as to present the desired perception to the public.

The key to publicity is having a unique or newsworthy product or business. For example, your product may be environmentally friendly, where your competitor's is not. Or the way your business was founded may be an interesting story. If the business or product is newsworthy, there are several ways to get some publicity. Write to a reporter or editor to tease him or her with an idea, and follow up with a phone call. Issue a press release answering the who, what, where, when, and why of the business and include a press kit containing the press release, bios and photos of the key people in the story, any necessary background information, and copies of any other articles written about the company. The idea is to make it as easy as possible for the reporter to write or tell the story. When an article is written about the business, use reprints in future advertising and brochures to get even more value for the effort.

Whenever possible, get to know people in the media on a first-name basis; even take them to lunch. This gives you instant clout when you need free publicity. The media are always looking for news and appreciate the effort to give them something newsworthy. An effective news release should contain the following:

▸ The date, your name, and a phone number

▸ The release date (for immediate release, or after a certain date)

▸ An appropriate headline

▸ The release information typed double-spaced with wide margins

▸ The who, what, where, when, and why

▸ A photo if appropriate

▸ A note explaining briefly why you sent the release

There are also several publishing services that can be used to distribute information on the business. The *Contact Sheet*, a monthly publication, prints news releases written and paid for by companies. It is sent to over 1,800 editors and reporters nationally who have free use of the material. Another publication is the *PR Newsletter*, which is a membership electronic service that also assists a company in writing a message targeted to a specific media audience.

Personal Selling

Traditional selling techniques just don't meet the needs of today's customers. Today, people expect a quality product at a fair price with good service. That's a given. If you start with this in mind, you will find that the way you sell your products and your business is quite different from the traditional approach. Today, a business distinguishes itself in the marketplace by identifying and meeting specific customer needs. So even if you are "selling" a commodity, you need to figure out some way to add value to the product.

A good example of this is a small manufacturer of molded plastic parts in Massachusetts. Its largest account is a major acoustic speaker manufacturer, also in Massachusetts. The speaker company asked the plastics company to assign a full-time salesperson to their plant, which would help them eliminate some of the costs of buyers and planners and at the same time let the plastics plant concentrate on service rather than on trying to acquire new accounts. As a result, the plastic company's sales have increased nearly 40 percent per year.

Becoming a value-added company, tailoring products to meet customers' needs, requires that everyone in the company become service oriented, a time-consuming task that necessitates training and educating employees. It also demands an opportunity mindset, rather than a selling mindset. And as this type of selling is usually accomplished at higher levels in an organization, it is a more lengthy process; however, the returns are potentially greater. Working more closely with customers can translate into reduced selling and marketing costs.

One of the most difficult issues an entrepreneur faces with regard to selling is that of compensation—what and how to pay sales representatives. The possibilities are endless: incentives can be tied to profit or gross margins, contract size, the number of new accounts acquired, company goals, and so on. One of the latest techniques is to pay salespeople a salary plus a percentage of the profits. Yet another issue is how to compensate those who provide service to customers. Service is the key to customer retention, and the people who provide that service are becoming increasingly more important to a firm's success. Studying the compensation practices in your industry as well as those of other industries will help you decide which method is best for your business.

Trade Shows and Exhibits

For some entrepreneurs trade shows, fairs, and exhibits are a primary way to expose their products. Trade shows are a good way to find out who the competitors are and what marketing techniques they are using. It is also the place to meet and negotiate with sales reps and to get names for a mailing list. But the primary reason to display your products at a trade show is to eventually sell more product. To accomplish this, you should do the following:

1. Rent booth space. Hire a display designer to design and produce a quality display booth that will attract attention. Visiting several trade shows prior to doing your own will give you some ideas as to what works and what doesn't. You may also be able to work out a deal with a company that has compatible products to share a booth and combine resources.

2. Hire a model to distribute to as many people as possible at the trade show an information sheet that invites people to stop by the booth. Save the expensive brochures to hand out at the booth to potential customers. Also be sure to ask for business cards so you can follow up with people who took the brochure.

3. Have enough knowledgeable, personable people in the booth that potential customers are not kept waiting to talk with someone. Stagger breaks to keep the booth staffed at all times.

4. Consider renting a hospitality suite in the hotel where the trade show is located, to entertain key people in your industry.

5. Offer something free at your booth: a sample or a contest.

6. Follow up with letters to anyone whose business card was collected and phone calls to all serious prospects.

Marketing to Industrial Customers

When the target market you are trying to reach is other businesses, the marketing strategy is somewhat different in terms of advertising and promotion. Consumer products and services require a considerable amount of high-profile advertising and promotion to entice customers away from numerous other possible choices. With industrial products and services, the focus is on letting the targeted businesses know that the product or service is available and what it can do for the business.

In general, industrial products and services do not use broadcast media or most popular print media. Instead, they rely heavily on direct mail, personal selling, trade shows, and articles and advertisements in trade journals. As most industrial product manufacturers distribute their products through wholesalers, it becomes the wholesalers' job to market to and locate retail outlets. If you are dealing with industrial customers, investigate how products and services are marketed in your particular industry.

Online Market Research

With the addition of so many new electronic databases to the "information superhighway," it is now possible to do at least some of the needed market research online. Electronic bulletin boards catering to special interests, U.S. Census data, real-time stock quotes, financial and product information on foreign companies, Dun & Bradstreet's *Financial Profiles and Company Reports*, demographics, active trademark listings, and analysts' reports are but a few of the information sources now available.

Yet the information superhighway may even be too much of a good thing. So many options and so much information can boggle the mind. In addition, the convenience of online information must be weighed against the cost of retrieving it. Most database services charge either a monthly service fee, a per-search fee, an hourly rate, a print charge, or all four. This can add up to a considerable amount of money. Table 14.2 presents a summary of just a few of the services available from the most common database sources. Before signing up for any, arrange for a demonstration of several at once so that you can compare them for speed, ease of use, and information provided.

Table 14.2   Online Sources for Market Research

COMPUSERVE: Business Demographics **Iquest** (gateway to more than 850 databases) **Magazine Database Plus:** Full text articles **Marketing/Management Research Center:** Full texts of major business magazines **Neighborhood Report:** Demographics by zip code	**DIALOG: ABI/INFORM:** Business Publications **Arthur D. Little/Online:** Industry forecasts **Business Software Database** **D&B Donnelley Demographics** **D&B-Dun's Electronic Business Directory** **Employee Benefits Inforsource** **Moody's Corporate Files** **PTS Newsletter Database**
DOW JONES NEWS RETRIEVAL: Comprehensive Company Reports **Business Newswires** **Text Library:** Full text articles from over 500 publications **Dun & Bradstreet Financial Profiles & Company Reports** **Japanese Business News:** Same-day coverage Statistical Comparisons of Companies & Industries **Standard & Poor's Profiles & Earnings Estimates:** Company reports **Top Business, Financial & Economic News**	**NEXIS: Analyst Research:** Brokerage Houses **Computers and Communications:** Full text sources **Company:** Company and industry research reports **Consumer Goods:** Trade publications **LEXPAT®:** Full text of U.S. patents **Marketing:** Trade publications and general sources on marketing information **PROMT/PLUS:** Trends in markets and technology

The marketing plan, like the rest of the business plan, is a living document subject to change based on new information. However, a marketing plan should not be changed often. It takes time to implement an effective plan, and it takes time to see the results. The plan you create should be the best one achievable, given the resources available.

New Venture Checklist

Have you:

❑ Analyzed the marketing options and ranked them?

❑ Written a clear, concise, one-paragraph statement of the marketing plan?

❑ Written a position statement for the product/service?

❑ Determined the distribution channels for the product/service?

❑ Developed an advertising, publicity, and promotion strategy?

Issues to Consider

1. What is the difference between an entrepreneurial marketing strategy and a large corporation's market strategy?
2. Why is it important to stick with your marketing plan even if it isn't returning immediate results?
3. What does the marketing plan do for the business?
4. Why should an entrepreneurial venture not engage in image positioning like large corporations?
5. How can a position statement be tested?
6. How is price for a product or service determined?
7. How does the promotion strategy for consumer-oriented businesses differ from that of industrial businesses?

Experiencing Entrepreneurship

1. Compare and contrast the marketing strategies of two companies in the same industry in terms of the points in the marketing plan on pages 258–259.
2. Find a company that is using relationship marketing strategies and discuss their effectiveness.

Additional Sources of Information

Advertising Age. 740 N. Rush St., Chicago, IL 60611.

Adweek. 5757 Wilshire Boulevard, Los Angeles, CA 90036.

Albrecht, K., and Bradford. (1989). *The Service Advantage: How to Identify and Fulfill Customer Needs.* New York: Dow Jones-Irwin.

Bangs, D.H. (1995). *The Market Planning Guide.* 4th ed. Dover, NH: Upstart Publishing.

Benson, R.V. (1987). *Secrets of Successful Direct Mail.* Savannah, GA: Benson Organization.

Cohen, W.A. (1987). *Develop a Winning Marketing Plan.* New York: John Wiley.

Debelak, D. (1989). *Total Marketing: Capturing Customers with Marketing Plans That Work.* New York: Irwin.

Electronic Retailing. Creative Age Publishing. Tel. (800) 624-4196.

Hoyer, W.D., and D.J. MacInnis. (1997). *Consumer Behavior.* Boston: Houghton Mifflin.

Levinson, J.C. (1993). *Guerrilla Marketing.* Boston: Houghton Mifflin.

———. (1993). *Guerrilla Marketing Excellence.* Boston: Houghton Mifflin.

National Infomercial Marketing Association. (NIM). Will refer to both ad agencies and direct marketers. Tel. (202) 962-8342.

Response TV. Advanstart Communications. Provides details of pitching products on home shopping networks. Tel. (800) 346-0085, ext. 477.

Reynolds, D. (1993). *Crackerjack Positioning: Niche Marketing Strategy for the Entrepreneur.* Tulsa, OK: Atwood Publishing.

Sewell, Carl. (1992). *Customers for Life: How to Turn that One-Time Buyer into a Lifetime Customer.* New York: Simon & Schuster Pocket Books.

The Standard Directory of Advertising Agencies. National Register Publishing. Available in the reference section of the library.

Tradeshow and Convention Guide. Order from Budd Publications, P.O. Box 7, New York, NY 10004.

Treacy, M., and F. Wiersema. (1995). *The Discipline of Market Leaders: Choose Your Customers, Narrow Your Focus, Dominate Your Market.* Reading, MA: Addison-Wesley.

Internet Resources

AdvertisingAge
http://www.adage.com
This is the online version of the magazine that focuses on the advertising industry.

American Demographics/Marketing Tools
http://www.marketingtools.com
This site will help you learn how to target your marketing efforts.

American Marketing Association
http://www.ama.org
Focuses on the services of this organization.

How to Price Your Products and Services
gopher://www.sbaonline.sab.gov/00/business-development/general-information-and-publicat
This page comes from the Small Business Administration and offers advice regarding pricing strategies.

Understanding Your Market
gopher://www.sbaonline.sba.gov/00/business-development/general-information-and-publicat
From the Small Business Administration; helps you go through the process of understanding your customers.

Relevant Case Studies

1. Toy Tips, Inc.
2. OXO (B)
3. Autopsies to Go

New Venture Financing

Money is the seed of money, and the first guinea is sometimes more difficult to acquire than the second million.
Jean Jacques Rousseau

Financing Start-Up and Growth

Overview

▶ **Financing start-ups**

▶ **Financing growth**

▶ **Valuing the business**

Terms to Know

Profile 15.1

Making Money on Bad Debts

Many entrepreneurs starting new ventures come from ground zero. They have a great idea but no capital. What could be worse than that? Well, how about starting a new business $1 million in debt, essentially at sub-zero? That was the situation in which Bill Bartmann of Muskogee, Oklahoma found himself in 1985 as he watched his pipe manufacturing business (it supplied pipes for oil rigs) die a rapid death. OPEC's oil cartel had crumbled and drilling had come to a standstill. Bartmann had to say good-bye to 71 employees. Not only did he lose the business; he also lost friends and business associates, who now considered him a pariah. Owing more than a million dollars to creditors, he knew he had to come up with an outrageous plan for making money, so that he could pay them back and avoid bankruptcy.

Bartmann and his former COO, Jay Jones, put their heads together. They happened to notice in the newspaper that the Federal Deposit Insurance Corporation (FDIC) was auctioning off the delinquent loans it had taken back from a failed bank in Tulsa. At first they thought the idea of buying someone's bad loans was hilarious, but they decided to investigate the matter in person. In doing so, Bartmann realized he knew how these debtors felt. Maybe there was a business there. Maybe if he treated these people like customers, he might find a way to collect what they owed. His plan was to buy the loans for two cents on the dollar and then attempt to collect on them.

The first bank he approached for money was the very same bank to which he owed $1 million. In a moment of pure "just do it," he asked for $13,000 to buy bad loans. Apparently his performance was stellar; he walked out of the bank with the money. Using the telephone in his kitchen and working alone, he managed to collect $64,000 on the loans, which translated to a 400% return.

On the next trip to the bank, Bartmann asked for $100,000 to buy more loans. From this he planned to use $20,000 for expenses and the rest of what he collected to pay down this new loan. A few months later he returned to the bank with $204,000 to pay down the loan. This pattern continued, and by 1990, Bartmann's new company, which he dubbed Commercial Financial Services (CFS) had 71 employees. In that year there was a tidal wave of bank failures throughout the country, and Bartmann knew that this was his chance to make it big. However, he would need to move to Tulsa, where capital sources were better and the work force more plentiful.

In his new location, he began with 17 people that he had brought with him from his Muskogee office and set about establishing a mission statement: "Achieve net earnings each year equal to at least 200% of the previous year." Bartmann knew that to accomplish this he would have to collect debts at a rate higher than anyone ever had before. And to do that, he had to set up rigid procedures and provide his collectors with the best training possible. He also knew that to get the best people, he would have to pay them 150% above the industry average and give them plenty of incentives because such work is grueling and repetitive. (The company culture, in fact, is reminiscent of the Marines.)

The strategy worked. The company was growing very rapidly, but there was still one problem, and it derived from the nature of the collection industry. The time lag between purchasing the bad loans and collecting on them was such that it required bank financing to cover the gap. Once again Bartmann came up with a creative financing solution. He proposed taking thousands of nonperforming debts, bundling them together, and offering them to the Wall Street bond market. This would generate the cash to purchase more bad debts. But Wall Street was not buying, being used to bundles of performing loans that were collateralized. Bartmann went to six banks and finally, at the seventh, Banc One Capital Corp. understood the collection miracle that Bartmann had performed in the industry and took a chance on him. One year later CFS had completed its first bond offering. Since then it has completed ten A-rated bond issues totaling over $1 billion. CFS's cash standing in 1997 was over $147 million.

Today CFS has over 2,500 employees and is the world's largest repository of bad consumer debt, nearly $7 billion. Their net profit margin is 48%—thanks to an entrepreneur who started out $1 million in the hole.

Source: Jerry Useem, "The Richest Man You've Never Heard Of," *Inc.,* September 1997, p. 43.

What was the financial strategy Bartmann used to finance the start-up of CFS?

"How can I fund my new business?" Probably no question is more on the minds of entrepreneurs with new venture ideas. Alternatively, you may hear "Where can I find venture capital?" These questions spring from lack of understanding of start-up ventures and the nature of financial markets.

Because start-up companies are inherently risky investments, the number of sources for financing them is more limited than would be the case for a company that has reached critical mass—that is, has reached the point where it is surviving on its own and needs additional funds only to support a new growth spurt. This chapter will look at sources of financing for both start-up and growing companies.

Financing Start-Ups

Bootstrapping means using techniques for creative financing, getting by on as few resources as possible and using other peoples' resources whenever feasible. It involves begging, borrowing, or leasing everything needed to start a venture and is the antithesis of the "big money model" espoused by many when they talk about entrepreneurial ventures.[1] More often than not, bootstrapping is a model for starting a business without money—or at least without any money beyond that provided by the entrepreneur's personal resources. Bootstrapping encompasses more than money, though. It also includes tactics such as hiring as few employees as possible, leasing and bartering, and sharing other people's resources. See Figure 15.1 for a characterization of bootstrapping entrepreneurs.

Entrepreneur Resources

Most entrepreneurs start their ventures with their own resources. These resources include savings, credit cards, mortgages, and friends and family. The Department of Commerce reports that 67 percent of all businesses were started without borrowed money. Enita Nordick liquidated her stocks and sold her home to contribute the required capital to start Unity Forest Products, which remanufactures lumber blanks into such things as siding and paneling and sells them to retailers. Calzone & Co., a Washington-based manufacturer of frozen food, did $2.8 million in revenues in 1997 on $5,000 of start-up capital.[2] Fawcette Technical Publications was started in 1991 in Palo Alto on no capital. By 1997 it was doing $24 million a year in revenues.[3] These entrepreneurs comprise the rule, not the exception; typically, only close friends and family will fund the risk of a new venture. The added benefit is that you may not have to give up as much of the company as you would with an outside investor.

Hire as Few Employees as Possible

Normally the greatest single expense a business has is its payroll (including taxes and benefits). Subcontracting work to other firms, using temporary help, or hiring independent contractors can help keep the number of employees and their consequent costs down. This was the tactic taken by Mike

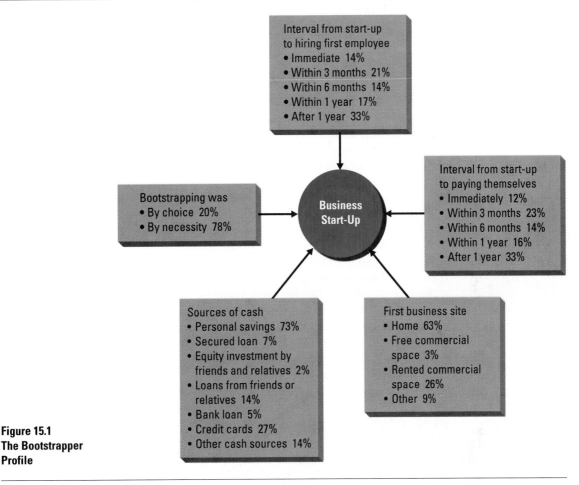

**Figure 15.1
The Bootstrapper
Profile**

SOURCE: Joshua Hyatt and Robert A. Mamis, "Profile of a Bootstrapper," *Inc.*, August 1997, p. 61.

Milliorn, who founded Daydots Label Inc., a Fort Worth, Texas manufacturer of custom labels. He and his wife run the $22 million company, having formed a strategic alliance with a key raw-materials vendor. Similarly, Marianne Szymanski founded Toy Tips Inc., a nationally recognized, independent product testing and research firm in Milwaukee, using student interns from Marquette University and bartering for office space. The interns received university credit for working with her, and she didn't have to deal with payroll. The issue of using independent contractors and leasing employees was discussed in Chapter 4.

Lease, Share, or Barter Everything

Virtually all new ventures at some point need to acquire equipment, furnishings, and facilities. Through leasing rather than purchasing major equipment and facilities, precious capital is not tied up at a time when it is badly needed to keep the new venture afloat. With a lease, there usually is no down payment, and the payments are spread over time. A word of caution, however. Be careful about leasing new and rapidly changing technology for long periods of time or you may soon find yourself with obsolete equipment but a continuing obligation.

Some entrepreneurs have shared space with established companies not only to save money on overhead but to give their fledgling ventures the aura of a successful, established company. This was the strategy used by Michael Kempner of Strategic Communications, Inc., a public relations firm. Kempner moved in rent-free to space in a friend's elegant advertising offices with the agreement that he would refer clients to his friend's business in exchange for the space. Others have gotten established companies to barter. When Marianne Szymanski of Toy Tips, Inc., found she needed a professional wardrobe for her media tour, she went to JH Collectibles and explained her situation. As a young businesswoman with a start-up company, she didn't have much money to spend, but she wanted their clothes to wear on the tour. JH Collectibles gave her a wardrobe of clothes she could promote on the tour while also promoting her business.

Bartering is a well-established tradition among entrepreneurs with new ventures. It is a way to conserve cash, reduce payables, collect on old receivables, and get rid of excess inventory. In fact, it is even used by large corporations going into global markets. In Russia, for example, Pepsico traded its surplus cola for vodka, which could be sold in the United States. Similarly, New Zealand traded dairy products for Russian coal. These barter arrangements are known as "one-to-one trades." There are also barter exchange groups where a member can earn credits by providing products or services, then use those credits to "buy" products or services from another company when needed. The start-up fee for barter exchanges runs from $50 to $750 in addition to a fee of 10 to 15 percent of the value of each transaction.[4] At the end of the tax year, the exchange provides the participating company with a Form 1099 and sends a copy to the IRS. Barter should always be considered a cash transaction.

Other People's Money

Another key to bootstrapping success is getting customers to pay quickly and suppliers to allow more time for payment. Entrepreneurs must be willing to stay on top of receivables. Sometimes that means walking an invoice through the channels of a major corporation in person or locating the person who can adjust the computer code that determines when a government agency pays its bills.

Suppliers are an important asset of the business and should be taken care of. If you establish a good relationship with your major suppliers, you may be able to arrange favorable payment terms. After all, the supplier also has an interest in seeing the new venture succeed. Use several suppliers to establish credit. Often a young company can't get sufficient credit from one supplier, so it is a good idea to seek smaller amounts of credit from several reputable suppliers. In this way, when you can qualify for a larger credit line, you will know which supplier is the best source.

If possible, sell wholesale rather than retail. By dealing with wholesale distributors, you make your life easier because they are the experts at working with the customers. They have already set up the consumer and industrial channels you may need for expanding your market.

Bootstrapping Ethics

Whenever bootstrapping tactics are employed to let a new venture survive long enough to use other sources of financing, the issue of ethics arises. This occurs because when an entrepreneur bootstraps, by definition he or she is making the new venture appear much more successful than it is to gain some credibility in the market. But the entrepreneur must be careful, because credibility, if it is ill-gotten, comes at a tremendous price to the business. Lying to survive will return to haunt the business at some future time. Intuit, a very successful software manufacturer, spent several start-up years bootstrapping, during which it quickly became clear to the company that trust is an essential element to long-term success. (See Profile 15.2.)

Financing with Equity

When someone invests money in your venture, it is normally for an ownership share in the business. This ownership share is termed **equity**. It is distinguished from debt in that the equity investor puts his or her capital at risk; usually there is no guaranteed return and no protection against loss. For this reason, most entrepreneurs with start-up ventures seek investment capital from people they know who believe in them. There are a variety of sources of equity financing, including personal resources, "angels," private placement, and venture capital.

Profile 15.2

The Importance of Ethics

Scott Cook, founder of Intuit, the software developer known for its product Quicken, reported in *Inc.* magazine that "being truthful is good business."[5] A common practice in the software industry is to use promotional schemes to "load" the dealers with excess product in the belief that the dealer will then push that product to get rid of it before taking on a competitor's product. The practice also involves overstating demand.

Intuit refused to participate in this scheme and preferred to communicate expectations for sales honestly to the dealers. In this way the dealers were not burdened with excess inventory, and Intuit kept its manufacturing facilities operating at an even keel rather than in costly boom-and-bust cycles.

Personal Resources

As stated earlier, the number one source of start-up money is the entrepreneur's personal resources: savings, credit cards, parents, and friends and family. The reasons are many:

1. New ventures by definition have no track record, so all the estimates of sales and profits are pure speculation.

2. An enormous number of new ventures fail, so the risk for an outside investor is usually too high.

3. Many new ventures have no proprietary rights that would give them a competitive advantage.

4. The founders often do not have a significant track record of success.

5. Too many new ventures are "me too" versions of something that already exists, so they have no competitive advantages.

In addition to the personal resources already mentioned, entrepreneurs can tap the equity in their brokerage accounts. Margin is, in effect, another source of credit, and when interest rates fall below those of the typical credit card, this source of funds becomes very attractive. With a margin loan, the security in your brokerage account is pledged as collateral for the money borrowed, just like pledging the equity in your home against a second mortgage. You can still trade the collateralized security (buy or sell), but cannot take possession of it until the loan is repaid.

Private Investors—Angels

The next source usually investigated for funding is private investors, typically people the entrepreneur knows or has met through business acquaintances. These investors, called **angels**, are part of the informal risk-capital market—the largest pool of risk capital in the United States, over $50 billion. They can't be found in a phone book, and they don't advertise. In fact, their intentions as investors are often well hidden until they decide to make themselves known. They do, however, have several definable characteristics:

▶ They normally invest between $10,000 and $500,000 and usually focus on first-stage financing; that is, start-up funding or funding of firms younger than five years.

▶ They are well educated, often entrepreneurs themselves, and tend to invest within a relatively short distance from home, as they like to be involved in their investment.

▶ They tend to prefer manufacturing, energy and resources, and service businesses. Retail ventures are less desirable because of their inordinately high rate of failure. Today angels are also investing in high technology firms.[6]

▶ They typically look to reap the rewards of their investment within three to seven years. The risk/reward ratio is a function of the age of the firm at the time of investment. They may want to earn as much as ten times

Some Money Terms

Angel: Business jargon for a private investor who holds an equity interest in the venture.

Asset-Based Loan: A loan collateralized by accounts receivable, inventory, or other assets. If the entrepreneur defaults on the loan, the lender can seize the assets.

Equity: An ownership interest in a company based on an investment of capital.

Factor: A lender who purchases a company's accounts receivable and then advances cash at a certain percentage of the value of the receivables.

Securities: The interest of a creditor or investor in the property or business of a debtor or owner, pledged to secure repayment of the debt or investment.

Seed Money: Money needed to complete research and development prior to starting the business.

Senior Debt: Usually a bank loan that has seniority over all other financial interest should the business fail.

Subordinated Debt: Nonbank debt that is repaid after senior debt in the event of business failure. Can often contain rights to convert to equity.

Venture Capital: Professional groups of individual investors whose purpose is to invest money in new and growing businesses. They typically supply second-stage or buyout financing.

their original investment if the venture is a start-up; as much as five times their investment, if the venture has been up and running for a couple of years.

▶ They find their deals principally through referrals from business associates.

▶ They tend to make an investment decision more quickly than other capital sources, and their requirements as to documentation, business plan, and due diligence may be lower. Due diligence is discussed on page 304.

In general, angels are an excellent source of seed or start-up capital. The secret to finding these elusive investors is networking—getting involved in the business community—so you come into contact with sources of private capital or people who know these sources—lawyers, bankers, accountants, and other business people. Developing these contacts takes time; you can't wait until you need the capital to look for it. Of course, taking on an investor means giving up some of the ownership of the company. Therefore, it is

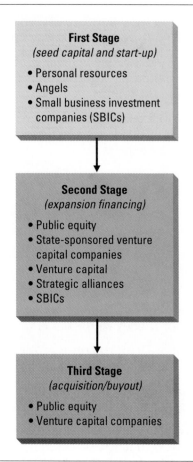

Figure 15.2
Stages of Financing
for Ventures

probably wise to plan at the outset for a way for the investor to exit. Including a buyout provision in the investment contract with a no-fault separation agreement will ensure that the entrepreneur doesn't have to wait for a criminal act like fraud to end the relationship. Structuring the buyout to be paid out of earnings over time will avoid jeopardizing the financial health of the business. Above all, avoid using personal assets as collateral to protect an angel's investment.

Private Placement

Private placement is a way of raising capital from private investors by selling securities in a private corporation or partnership. Securities are common and preferred stock, notes, bonds, debentures, voting-trust certificates, certificates of deposit, warrants, options, subscription rights, limited partnership shares, and undivided oil or gas interests. The investors you solicit via a private placement memorandum must be "sophisticated" in terms of the rules of private placement, which are stated in the Security & Exchange Commission's **Regulation D**. Regulation D was designed to simplify the private offering process and allow the entrepreneur to seek funding from private investors who met the Regulation D requirements. Doing a private placement memorandum involves the completion of a business plan and a prospectus detailing the risks of the investment.

As with any complex legal document, it is crucial to consult an attorney well versed in the preparation of the private placement memorandum and disclosure of information about the company and its principals. Problems don't usually arise if the business is successful; however, if the venture fails and the investors uncover a security violation, you and other principal equity holders may lose your protection under the corporate shield and become personally liable in the event of a lawsuit. Security violations have been dealt with severely by the courts, and there is no statute of limitations on the filing of such a suit.

Private placement is a less costly, less time-consuming process than a public offering, and many states now offer standardized, easy-to-fill-out disclosure statements and offering documents.

The advantages of a private offering are many. The growing venture is not required to have a great many assets or credit references, which it would need for bank financing, or a lengthy track record. The entrepreneurs also don't have to file with the Securities and Exchange Commission (SEC). They do, however, have to qualify under the rules of Federal Regulation D, which makes it easier and less expensive for smaller companies to sell stock. Not all states recognize the exemptions under Regulation D in their "Blue Sky" laws (laws that protect investors from fraud), so the issuer of a private placement memorandum may have to register with the state. Essentially, Regulation D says:

▶ The entrepreneur must file five copies of Form D with the SEC within 15 days after the first sale of securities, then every six months thereafter, and 30 days after the final sale.

▶ The entrepreneur must follow the rules for notices of sale and payment of commissions.

▶ Rule 504a permits placements of up to $500,000 with no disclosure/information requirements and no limits on the kind or type of purchasers.

▶ Rule 504 permits the entrepreneur to sell up to $1 million worth of securities to any number of investors, whether they are sophisticated or not, during a 12-month period. *Sophisticated* in this context refers to people who invest on a regular basis and have a net worth of at least $1 million.

▶ Rule 505 allows the founders to sell $5 million of unregistered securities in a 12-month period to up to 35 investors of any type in addition to an unlimited number of accredited investors. **Accredited investors** include institutional investors such as banks and insurance companies, investors who purchase at least $150,000 of securities in the entrepreneur's venture, investors with a net worth over $1 million or annual income of over $200,000 in each of the previous two years, and directors, officers, and general partners of the company.

▶ Rule 506 treats placements in excess of $5 million. It allows the founders to sell to 35 nonaccredited purchasers and an unlimited number of accredited purchasers and relatives of the founders but without general solicitation through advertising. An issuer under this rule can sell securities to accredited investors without any disclosures whatsoever. An example might be selling securities to someone with whom you have an ongoing business relationship who qualifies as an accredited investor.

The burden is on the issuer to document that the exemption from registration requirements has been met. Therefore, the "sophistication" of all offerees should be examined closely and the reasons why they qualify carefully documented. The issuer should also number each private placement memorandum and keep a record of who has looked at the memorandum or discussed the offering with the issuer. The memorandum should have a qualifying statement on it that the contents must not be copied or disclosed to anyone other than the offeree. If an offeree becomes an investor, the issuer should document when and where the offeree examined the books and records of the company. When the offering is complete, the issuer should place in the offering log a memo stating that only those persons listed in the log have been approached regarding the offering.

Even if the offering qualifies as exempt from registration, it is still subject to the antifraud and civil liability provisions of federal securities laws and state Blue Sky securities laws. Many states have adopted the Small Corporate Offering Registration Form, also called SCOR U-7, which makes the registration process much simpler by providing 50 fill-in-the-blank questions that ask for the basic financial, management, and marketing information for the company. Your lawyer should be consulted, as some of the adopting states have restrictions as to who can use Form U-7.

Within the structure of the corporate private placement, the entrepreneur can sell preferred and common stock, convertible debentures, and debt securities with warrants. Recall that preferred stock has dividend and liquidation preference over common stock, in addition to antidilution protection and other rights as may be specified in a stockholder agreement. Common stock, on the other hand, carries with it voting rights and preserves the right of the corporation to elect S-corporation status. **Convertible debentures** are secured or unsecured debt instruments that can be converted to equity at a later date as specified in the agreement. In its debenture form, however, it provides for a fixed rate of return (interest), which can be deducted by the corporation. Debt securities with warrants give the holder the right to purchase stock at a fixed price for a specified term. Purchasing common stock under this instrument does not invalidate the preferred position of the debt holder as creditor.

Venture Capital

In general, **venture capital companies** are professional pools of managed funds that often operate in the form of a limited partnership. Equity venture capital funds are the most common type. While some venture capitalists invest in start-up companies, it is probably prudent not to attempt to seek venture capital funding at this stage for several reasons. Venture capitalists recognize that start-up is the riskiest time for a business, and as there are many growing young companies with a track record of performance (however short) available, their funds are probably better placed with these companies. Venture capitalists require substantial returns on their investments, generally in the 60 to 70 percent annual return range, and a significant ownership interest, which may force the entrepreneur to give up controlling interest in the new venture before the company gets off the ground.

In general, for most types of businesses funds are not as prolific as they were in the 1980s, and almost 60 percent of available venture capital funds are held by megafunds, usually institutional investors who prefer to invest in increments of $2 million and up. For this reason venture capital is more commonly a second-stage financing strategy. As such, it will be discussed in more detail in the section on growth capital.

Strategic Alliances

A partnership—whether formal or informal—with another business is a **strategic alliance**. Through strategic alliances, entrepreneurs can structure deals with suppliers or customers that will help reduce expenditures for marketing, raw materials, or R&D. By reducing expenditures, cash flow is increased, providing capital that wouldn't have otherwise been available.

One type of strategic alliance is the **R&D limited partnership**. This vehicle is useful for entrepreneurs starting hi-tech ventures that carry significant risk due to the expense of research and development. The limited partnership contracts with the new venture to provide the funding for the R&D to develop a market technology that will ultimately be profitable for the partnership. This is advantageous for both the limited partner and the new venture. Limited partners are able to deduct their investment in the R&D contract and enjoy the tax advantages of losses in the early years on their personal tax returns; they also share in any future profits. In the R&D limited partnership, the new venture acts as a general partner to develop the technology, then structures a license agreement with the R&D partner whereby the venture can use the technology to develop other products. Often the limited partnership's interest becomes stock in a new corporation formed to commercialize the new technology.

An alternative to this arrangement is an agreement to pay royalties to the partnership. Yet another vehicle is the formation of a joint venture, which allows the entrepreneur to purchase the joint venture interest after a specific period of time or when the company reaches a certain volume in sales. As with the private placement, strategic alliances should involve an attorney. The new venture may incur significant costs in creating the partnership, a process that could drag on for up to a year. In addition, giving up the ownership of the technology may be too high a price if the partnership does not survive.

Small Business Investment Company (SBIC)

Small Business Investment Companies are actually privately managed venture capital firms licensed by the Small Business Administration. They get financing in partnership with the federal government to invest through equity (generally preferred stock or debt with warrants) and long-term debt in small and growing businesses.

Companies that qualify for SBIC financing should have a net worth under $18 million and average after-tax earnings of less than $6 million during the past two years. The typical deal involves a loan with options to buy equity, a convertible debenture. Preferred stock is sometimes used for first-round financing. See the end-of-chapter resources for contact information.

Grants

The Small Business Innovation Development Act of 1982 was designed to stimulate technological innovation by small businesses in the United States. It requires that all federal agencies with research and development budgets in excess of $100 million give a portion of their budgets to technology-based small businesses in the form of grants. Small businesses find out about these grants by checking the published solicitations by the agencies (see Table 15.1) to see if they can provide what the agency needs.

The grants have three phases:

1. Phase I is the concept stage and feasibility phase, which provides up to $50,000 for an initial feasibility study to determine the scientific merit of the proposed idea. This amount is for six months. If results are promising, the company is eligible for Phase II funding.

2. Phase II provides up to an additional $500,000 for two years to pursue the innovation and develop a well-defined product or process.

3. Phase III brings in private sector funds to commercialize the new technology.

To qualify for an SBIR grant, the company must employ fewer than 500 people, be independently owned at least 51% by a U.S. citizen, be technology-based, be organized for profit, and not be dominant in its field. The proposer must perform two-thirds of the Phase I effort and one-half of the Phase II effort. At least half of the principal investigator's time must be spent working in the small business.

On an annual basis, each agency publishes the topics of interest to it. To be a part of the mailing list for presolicitation announcements, contact the Office of Innovation, Research and Technology, SBA, 409 Third Street, S.W., Washington, DC 20416.

Table 15.1   Small Business IR Agencies

▶ Department of Defense	▶ Nuclear Regulatory Commission
▶ Department of Energy	▶ Environmental Protection Agency
▶ Department of Transportation	▶ Health and Human Services
▶ Department of the Interior	▶ National Science Foundation
▶ Department of Education	▶ U.S. Department of Agriculture
▶ National Aeronautics & Space Administration (NASA)	

Venture Capital Institutes and Networks

Many areas of the country offer access to venture capital networks through institutes established on the campuses of major universities. The university acts as a conduit through which the entrepreneurs and investors are matched and assumes no liability for or has no ownership interest in either the new venture or the investor's company. The entrepreneur typically pays a fee, in the $200 to $500 range, and submits a business plan to the institute. The plan is then matched to the needs of private investors in the database who subscribe to the service. If an investor is interested in the business concept, he or she contacts the entrepreneur. In general, venture capital networks are a way for entrepreneurs to gain access to investors they may not be able to find through other channels. Furthermore, the investors in the database are there voluntarily, so they are actually looking for potential investments.

Financing with Debt

When an entrepreneur chooses a debt instrument to finance a portion of the start-up expenses, he or she provides a business or personal asset as collateral in exchange for a loan bearing a market rate of interest. The asset could be equipment, inventory, real estate, or the entrepreneur's house or car. There are several sources of debt financing.

Commercial Banks

Banks are not normally a readily available source of either working capital or seed capital to fund a start-up venture. Banks are highly regulated; their loan portfolios are scrutinized carefully, and they are told in no uncertain

---

Profile 15.3

How Two Partners Creatively Financed Their Company

How would you feel if you faithfully made payments on your bank line of credit and carefully managed your resources—only to be told by your banker that your $1 million line of credit was due in 90 days? This is exactly what happened in 1991 to Timothy Rashleger, co-owner of Minnesota-based Milltronics Manufacturing. Milltronics designs and builds computer numerical-control systems for metal-cutting equipment. At the time, Rashleger and his partner, Gary Welch, were in the process of designing a new product that they hoped would increase their sales, but they needed cash to launch it. Without the bank line of credit, they were stuck.

Putting their heads together, the partners found three solutions to the problem:

1. They visited their vendors and negotiated extended-payment plans.

2. They found a new bank that gave them the credit they needed.

3. They persuaded their employees to take a 20 percent pay cut for a year. They repaid that cut at the end of the year.

What Rashleger and Welch learned from this experience was the importance of relationships with bankers, employees, and vendors. The strategy was successful and in 1995, Milltronics revenues were at $26 million, more than a 270% increase over three years.

Source: Sharon Nelson, "Capital Ideas for Financing," *Nation's Business,* September 1996, p. 19.

terms not to make loans that have any significant degree of risk. Banks like to see a track record of positive cash flow because this is how their loan will be repaid. Unfortunately, new ventures don't have a track record, so an unsecured loan is probably not possible.

Generally, banks make loans on the basis of what is termed **"the five C's"**: character, capacity, capital, collateral, and condition. In the case of the entrepreneur, the first two—character and capacity—become the leading consideration because the new business's performance is based purely on forecasts. Therefore, the bank will probably consider the entrepreneur's personal history carefully. However difficult, it is important for the new venture to establish a lending relationship with a bank. This may mean starting with a very small secured loan and demonstrating the ability to repay in a timely fashion. Bankers also look more favorably on ventures with hard assets that are readily convertible to cash.

Commercial Finance Companies

As banks have tightened their lending requirements, commercial finance companies have stepped in to fill the gap. They are able to do this because they are not as heavily regulated and they base their decisions on the quality of the assets of the business. Thus, they are often termed **asset-based lenders**. They do, however, charge more than banks by as much as five percent over prime. Therefore, the entrepreneur must weigh the cost-benefit of taking on such an expensive loan. Of course, if it means the difference between starting the business or not starting it, or surviving in the short term, the cost may not seem so great.

Profile 15.4

What's in a Covenant?

In 1995, when Allen Systems Group Inc., a computer software manufacturer, was about to sign a credit agreement with its bank, the chief financial officer wisely decided to examine carefully the loan covenants the bank wanted to include. To his dismay, he found that they were so restrictive as to prevent the business from growing. By negotiating with the bank, using short- and long-term financial projections, he was able to get more reasonable terms.

Here are some tips for looking at loan covenants *before* you sign that agreement.

1. Ask your bank officers whether they intend to sell the loan or retain it themselves. If they intend to sell it, you may not have much negotiating room with regard to covenants.

2. Check on your bank's experience in your particular industry. You need to know that the bankers understand how your business works.

3. Ask for a sample list of covenants before closing the deal.

4. Look at your company's track record if you've been in business for a while and see if you would have met the loan covenants in terms of such things as key ratios.

5. If you determine that you could not have met the covenants, consider negotiating better terms with the bank.

SOURCE: Jill Andresky Fraser, "The Art of the Covenant," *Inc.,* August 97, p. 99.

Small Business Administration

When a commercial bank loan does not appear to be a viable option, the entrepreneur may want to consider an SBA guaranteed loan. Between 1980 and 1991, the SBA guaranteed $31 billion in loans, principally for start-up and expansion. In 1993 alone, the SBA backed $6.4 billion in loans, which was a 40 percent increase since 1991. The SBA guarantees to repay up to 90 percent of the loan to the commercial lender should the business default. A further incentive to banks is that SBA-funded ventures tend to be growth-oriented and have a higher survival rate than other start-ups. In a study conducted by Price-Waterhouse, SBA-funded businesses versus non-SBA businesses were compared during the period between 1984 and 1989.[7] The results were astounding.

	SBA Funded	Non–SBA Funded
Employee Growth	167%	0%
Revenue Growth	300%	37%
Survival after 4 years	75%	<65%

Of course, since these loans are backed by the government, the documentation and paperwork are extensive, and interest rates are usually no different than with a conventional loan.

The Small Business Administration also has a new program, the micro loan, that makes it easier for entrepreneurs with limited access to capital to borrow small amounts (up to $25,000). Instead of using banks as in their guarantee program, they use nonprofit community development corporations. The Answer Desk at the SBA, 800-827-5722, can provide information on micro lenders in a particular area of the country.

State-Funded Venture Capital

Many states provide a range of services to help new and growing ventures. From venture capital funds to tax incentives, states such as Massachusetts, New York, and Oregon are seeing the value of establishing business development programs. They usually receive their funding from the state government, which enables them to seek larger investment amounts from private sources. In states where equity funding is not available, there is typically a loan program aimed at new ventures. For example, in Massachusetts, favorable debt financing is often exchanged for warrants to purchase stock in the new company. Pennsylvania was the first to create a funding program aimed at minority-owned businesses.

The next round of financing required by entrepreneurs is that needed to fund the growth of the business beyond the start-up stage.

Financing Growth

The natural by-product of a successful start-up is growth. But growth is costly and often puts an enormous strain on the already tight resources of the young venture. Typically, to meet significant demand, the new company will need additional capital beyond any internal cash flows. Growth capital, or second-round financing, refers to those funds needed to take the venture out of the start-up phase and move it toward becoming a market presence. To the extent that the entrepreneur has met the sales and earnings targets estimated in the start-up business plan, the choices available increase substantially when growth financing, or second-round financing, is sought. The fact that more choices are available is important because normally, the amount of money needed to grow the business is significantly larger than that required to start the business. One exception is high-tech companies that incur considerable R&D costs prior to start-up. These types of companies may spend millions of dollars and accrue several years of negative income before their first sale.

Most professional venture capital today is still going to the biotechnology, software, and computer ventures, but in general, the best companies in any industry have the easiest time finding capital from any source. Being one of the "best" companies requires an excellent track record (however short), a sound management team, a potential for high growth, and a plan for investor exit with an excellent rate of return on the money invested. Investors in growth companies typically will not go into a situation where their new money is paying off old debt, or where a company has poor cash flow. They want to know that the infrastructure is in place, sales are increasing, and the growing venture needs capital only to take it to the next stage.

The Process of Raising Capital

Make no mistake about it, raising growth capital is a time-consuming and costly process. For this reason, many entrepreneurs opt instead for growing slowly, depending exclusively on internal cash flow to fund growth. They have a basic fear of debt and of giving up any control or equity of the company to investors. Unfortunately, they may act so conservatively as to actually stifle growth.

If you've decided to raise growth capital, it's important to understand the nature of raising money so that your expectations will not be unreasonable. The first thing to understand about raising growth capital (or any capital, for that matter) is that it will invariably take at least twice as long as you thought to actually have the money in the company's bank account. If you are attempting to raise a substantial amount of money—several million dollars, for instance—you can expect to spend up to several months finding the financing, to wait several more months for the potential investor or lender to do due diligence and say yes, and then to wait up to six more months to receive the money. In other words, if you don't look for funding until you need it, it will be too late. Moreover, as this search for capital can take you away from the business when you are needed most, it is helpful to use financial advisers who have experience in raising money, and to have a good management team in place so that you don't have to worry about the business while you're out raising capital.

The second thing to understand about raising growth capital is that your chosen financial source may not complete the deal, even after months of courting and negotiations. It's essential, therefore, to continue to look for investors who may become backups if your original investor fails to materialize.

Another thing to realize about second-round investors is that they often request a buy-out of the first-round funding sources, who could be friends or family, because they feel the first round has nothing more to contribute to the business and they no longer want to deal with them. This can be a very awkward situation, since the second-round funder has nothing to lose by demanding the buy-out. They can certainly walk away from the deal; there are thousands more out there.

It truly does take money to make money. The costs incurred before the money is received must be paid up front by the entrepreneur, while the costs of maintaining the capital can often be paid from the proceeds of the loan, or in the case of investment capital, from the proceeds of a sale or internally generated cash flow.

If the business plan and financial statements have been kept up-to-date after the start of the business, you have taken the first step in preparing the company for presentation to a funding source and saved some money in the process. If you are seeking capital in the millions, however, growth capital funding sources prefer that your financials have the approval of a financial consultant or investment banker, someone who regularly works with investors. This person is expert in preparing loan and investment packages that are attractive to potential funding sources. Your CPA will prepare the business's financial statements and work closely with the financial consultant. All these activities result in costs to the entrepreneur. In addition, if you are seeking equity capital, you need a prospectus or offering document, which requires legal expertise and often has significant printing costs. Then there are the expenses of marketing the offering; such things as advertising, travel, and brochures can become quite costly.

In addition to the up-front costs of seeking growth capital, there are "back-end" costs when the entrepreneur seeks capital by selling securities (shares of stock in the corporation). These can include investment banking fees, legal fees, marketing costs, brokerage fees, and various other fees charged by state and federal authorities. The total cost of raising equity capital can go as high as 25 percent of the total amount of money sought. Add that to the interest or return on investment paid to the funding source(s) and you can see why it definitely costs money to raise money.

The Venture Capital Market

Private venture capital companies have been the bedrock of many high-growth ventures, particularly in the computer, software, biotechnology, and telecommunications industries. As venture capitalists rarely invest in start-up ventures outside the high-tech arena, the growth stage of a new venture is where most entrepreneurs consider approaching them. Waiting until this stage is advantageous to the entrepreneur because using venture capital in the start-up phase can mean giving up significant control. Private venture capital is, quite simply, a pool of money managed by professionals. These professionals usually assume the role of general partner and are paid a management fee plus a percentage of the gain from the investment by their investors. The venture capital firm takes an equity position through ownership of stock in the company. It also normally requires a seat on the board of directors and brings its professional management skills to the new venture in an advisory capacity.

In 1995, the total amount of funds raised by venture capital firms was $3.8 billion, a 51 percent increase over 1993.[8] Two experts on venture capital markets, Bill Bygrave and Jeff Timmons, suggested the venture capital system was at a "crossroads," with the need for a new vision.[9] Others have agreed, calling venture capital the "incredibly shrinking venture capital industry."[10] Yet the possibility of global venture capital is now very attractive. Europe, for example, has 342 million inhabitants, making it arguably the richest market in the world.

The Venture Capital Sequence of Events

To determine whether venture capital is the right type of funding for the growing venture, the entrepreneur must understand the goals and motivations of venture capitalists, for they dictate the potential success or failure of the attempt. The venture capital company invests in a growing business through the use of debt and equity instruments to gain long-term appreciation on the investment within a specified period of time, typically five years. By definition, this goal is often different from that of the entrepreneur, who usually looks at the business in a much longer frame of reference. The venture capitalist (VC) also seeks varying rates of return, depending on the risk involved. An early-stage investment, for example, characteristically demands a higher rate of return, as much as 50 percent or more, whereas a later-stage investment demands a lower rate of return, perhaps 30 percent. Very simply, as the level of risk increases, so does the demand for a higher rate of return, as depicted in Figure 15.3. This relationship is not surprising. Older, more established companies have a longer track record on which to make predictions about the future, so normal business cycles and sales patterns have been identified, and the company is usually in a better position to respond through experience to a dynamic environment. Consequently, investing in a mature firm does not command the high rate of return that investing in a high-growth start-up does.

Usually the first thing venture capitalists look at when scrutinizing a potential investment candidate is the management team to see if experienced people with a good track record are in place and able to take the company to the next level of growth. In addition to experience, they are looking for commitment to the company and to growth because they recognize that growing a company requires an enormous amount of time and effort on the part of the management team. Once they have determined that the management team is solid, they look at the product and the market to see if the opportunity is substantial and if the product holds a unique or innovative position in the marketplace. Product uniqueness, especially if protected through intellec-

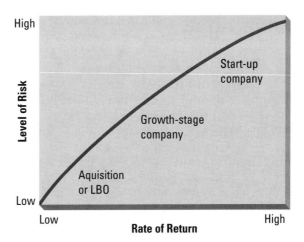

**Figure 15.3
Risk Versus Rate of
Return**

tual property rights, helps create entry barriers in the market, commands higher prices, and adds value to the business.

The other major factor is the potential for significant growth and the amount of growth possible, because it is from the consequent appreciation in the value of the business that the venture capitalist will derive the required return on investment. The venture capitalist weighs that potential for growth against the risk of failure and the cost of achieving the growth projected. Therefore, when negotiating with venture capitalists, the entrepreneur should have a good sense of the value of the business, a topic discussed at the end of this chapter.

Armed with an understanding of what venture capitalists are looking for, you are prepared to begin the search for the company that meets your needs. As the venture capital community is fairly close-knit, at least within regions of the country, it is wise not to "shop" the business plan around looking for the best deal. First do some research on the venture capital firms in your state to see if any specialize in your particular industry or type of business. Get recommendations from attorneys and accountants who regularly deal with business investments. In fact, the best way to approach venture capitalists is through a referral from someone who knows the VC. Once a venture capital company has been chosen, it is preferable to stay with that company until you are certain the deal will not work. Under no circumstances should you be talking with two companies at once.

The venture capital company will no doubt ask for a copy of the business plan with an executive summary. The executive summary is a screening device—if it can't be immediately determined that the entrepreneurial team's qualifications are outstanding, the product concept innovative, and the projections of growth and return on investment realistic, the company officials will not bother to read the entire business plan.

If, on the other hand, after studying the plan they like what they see, they will probably call for a meeting to determine whether the entrepreneurial team can deliver what they project. This may or may not call for a formal presentation of the business by the entrepreneur. During this meeting, the initial terms of an agreement may also be discussed; however, you should not be too eager to discuss issues like owner compensation until the venture capitalist indicates a deal is imminent. It is also very important that you not hype the business concept or make claims that cannot be substantiated. Venture capitalists have literally seen it all and readily recognize when an entrepreneur is puffing. You should, however, disclose any potential negative aspects of the business and propose ways to deal with them.

If the meeting goes well, the next step is due diligence—that is, the venture capital firm has its own team of experts check out the entrepreneurial team and the business thoroughly. If the venture capitalists are still sold on the business, they draw up legal documents to detail the nature and terms of the investment and declare that "the check is in the mail." Don't spend the money, however, as it may take some time to receive it. Some venture capitalists wait until they know they have a satisfactory investment before putting together a partnership to actually fund the investment. Others just have a lengthy process for releasing money from the firm.

You should not be surprised if the money is released in stages based on meeting agreed-upon goals. Also realize that the venture capital firm will continue to monitor the progress of the new venture and probably will want a seat on the board of directors, to have a say in the direction the new venture takes.

Capital Structure

It may seem that the entrepreneur is totally at the mercy of the venture capitalist. That, unfortunately, is true if the entrepreneur enters the negotiation from a weak position, desperately needing the money to keep the business alive. A better approach is to go into the negotiation from a position of strength. True, venture capitalists have hundreds of deals presented to them on a regular basis, but most of those deals are not big hits; in other words, the return on the investment is not worth their effort. They are always looking for that one business that will achieve high growth and return them enough gain on their investment to make up for all the average- or mediocre-performing investments in their portfolio. If the entrepreneur enters the negotiation with a business that has a solid record of growth and performance, he or she is in a good position to call many of the shots.

Any investment deal has four components:

‣ The amount of money to be invested

‣ The timing and use of the investment moneys

‣ The return on investment to investors

‣ The level of risk involved

How these components are defined will affect the venture for a long time, not only in constructing its growth strategy but in formulating an exit strategy.

Venture capitalists often want both equity and debt—equity because it gives them an ownership interest in the business, and debt because they will be paid back more quickly. Consequently, they tend to want redeemable preferred stock or debentures so that if the company does well, they can convert to common stock, and if the company does poorly or fails, they will be the first to be repaid their investment because they have preferred stock. If you have entered the negotiation from a position of strength, you will more likely be able to convince them to take common stock, which makes things much easier for you. In another scenario, the venture capitalists may want a combination of debentures (debt) and warrants, which allows them to purchase common stock at a nominal rate later on. If this strategy is carried out correctly, they can conceivably receive their entire investment back when the debt portion is repaid and still enjoy the appreciation in the value of the business as stockholders.

There are several other provisions venture capitalists often request to protect their investment. One is an **antidilution** provision, which ensures that the selling of stock at a later date will not decrease the economic value of the venture capitalist's investment. In other words, the price of stock sold at a later date should be equal to or greater than the price at which the venture capitalist could buy the common stock on a conversion from a warrant or debenture. One way for them to ensure that dilution does not occur is to have a **full ratchet clause** that allows the venture capitalist to buy common stock at the lowest rate at which it has been sold. For example, if the lowest price at which the stock has been sold to this point is $1, that is the conversion rate for the VC. However, if subsequently the stock is sold at $.50, then all the VC's convertible shares can be purchased at the new lowest rate. Where a $1 million investment would have bought 1 million shares at

---

Profile 15.5

Use a PIG to Grow Your Business

When you've considered all the options for financing the growth of your business, don't forget to think about a PIG. A PIG is a private investment group that pools capital from pension funds, endowments, institutions, private investors, and entrepreneurs who have cashed out of their businesses. In 1996, PIGs raised almost $23 billion. Compare that with the $10 billion raised by venture capitalists in the same year.

PIGs typically invest in mature companies with consistent profits for three to five years that also have a strong potential for growth. They look for manufacturing or distribution companies with deals starting at about $1 million. In general a PIG deal will cash out the owner but keep him or her on board to help expand the business. The PIG will then cash itself out in five to seven years through a merger or an initial public offering.

To use a PIG, you should engage the services of a lawyer experienced in mergers-and-acquisitions to negotiate the deal, as well as a national accounting firm. It's also important to select key advisers who have completed many transactions in your industry.

SOURCE: Juan Hovey, "A Source of Funds in Search of Work," *Nation's Business,* September 1997, p. 37.

$1/share, the VC now can buy 2 million shares at $.50 a share, effectively reducing the equity holding of the founders.

You should negotiate to use a **weighted ratchet approach**, which uses the weighted price per share of all the stock issued after the founder's stock and before the lowest stock price that will cause dilution. This is certainly fairer to the founders and prevents them from losing control of the company should the value of the stock decrease substantially.

In addition, to guard against having paid too much for an interest in the company, the VC may often request a **forfeiture provision**. This means that if the company does not achieve its projected performance goals, the founders may be required to give up some of their stock as a penalty to the VC. The forfeited stock increases the VC's equity in the company and may even be given to new management that the VC brings on board to steer the company in a new direction. One way to mitigate this situation is for the entrepreneur to request stock bonuses as a reward for meeting or exceeding performance projections.

Using venture capital is certainly an important source for the entrepreneur with a high-growth venture. It is, however, only one source, and with the advice of experts, the entrepreneur should consider all other possible avenues. The best choice is one that gives the new venture the chance to reach its potential and the investors or financial backers an excellent return on investment.

The Initial Public Offering (IPO)

The initial public offering, or "going public," is the goal in many companies because it is an exciting way to raise money for growth. However, deciding whether or not to do a public offering is difficult at best, because once the decision has been made to go ahead with the offering, a series of events is set in motion that will change the business and the relationship of the entrepreneur to the business forever. Moreover, returning to private status once the company has been a public company is an almost insurmountable task. An **initial public offering** is simply a more complex version of a private offering, in which the founders and equity shareholders of the company agree to sell a portion of the company (via previously unissued stocks and bonds) to the public by filing with the Securities and Exchange Commission and listing their stock on one of the stock exchanges. All the proceeds of the IPO go to the company in a primary offering. If the owners of the company subsequently sell their shares of stock, the proceeds go to the owners in what is termed a *secondary distribution*. Often there is a combination of the two events; however, an offering is far less attractive when a large percentage of the proceeds is destined for the owners, as that clearly signals a lack of commitment on the part of the owners to the future success of the business.

Advantages and Disadvantages of Going Public

The principal advantage of a public offering is that it provides the offering company with a tremendous source of interest-free capital for growth and expansion, paying off debt, or product development. With the IPO comes the future option of additional offerings once the company is well known and has a positive track record. A public company has more prestige and clout in the marketplace, so it becomes easier to form alliances and negotiate deals with suppliers, customers, and creditors. It is also easier for the founders to harvest the rewards of their efforts by selling off a portion of their stock as needed or borrowing against it. In addition, public stock and stock options can be used to attract new employees and reward existing employees.

There are, however, some serious disadvantages to the public offering. Of the 3,186 firms that went public in the 1980s, only 58 percent are still listed on one of the three major exchanges. Moreover, in 1993 the stock of only one-third of these firms was selling above its issue price.[11] A public offering is a very expensive process. Whereas a private offering can cost about $100,000, a public offering can run well over $300,000, a figure that does not include a seven to ten percent commission to the underwriter, which compensates the investment bank that sells the securities. One way to prevent a financial disaster should the offering fail is to ask for stop-loss statements from lawyers, accountants, consultants, and investment bankers. The stop-loss statement is essentially a promise not to charge the full fee if the offering fails.

Going public is an enormously time-consuming process. Entrepreneurs report that they spend the better part of every week on issues related to the offering over a four- to six-month period. Part of this time is devoted to learning about the process, which is much more complex than this chapter can express. One way many entrepreneurs deal with the knowledge gap is by spending the year prior to the offering preparing for it by talking with others who have gone through the process, reading, and putting together the team that will see the company through it. Another way to speed up the process is to start running the private corporation like a public corporation from the beginning; that is, doing audited financial statements and keeping good records.

A public offering means that everything the company does or has becomes public information subject to the scrutiny of anyone interested in the company. The CEO of a public company is now responsible primarily to the shareholders and only secondarily to anyone else. The entrepreneur, who before the offering probably owned the lion's share of the stock, may no longer have the controlling stock (if the entrepreneur agreed to an offering that resulted in the loss of control), and the stock that he or she does own can lose value if the company's value on the stock exchange drops, an event that can occur through no fault of the company's performance. World events and domestic economic policy can adversely (or positively) affect a company's stock regardless of what the company does.

A public company faces intense pressure to perform in the short term. Though an entrepreneur in a wholly owned corporation can afford the luxury of long-term goals and controlled growth, the CEO of a public company is pressured by stockholders to show almost immediate gains in revenues and earnings, which will translate into higher stock prices and dividends to the stockholders. Last but not least of the disadvantages, the SEC reporting requirements for public companies are very strict, time-consuming, and therefore costly.

The Public Offering Process

There are several steps in the IPO process, as depicted in Figure 15.4. The first is to choose an *underwriter,* or *investment banker.* This is the firm that sells the securities and guides the corporation through the IPO process. Some of the most prestigious investment banking firms handle only well-established companies because they feel smaller companies will not attract sufficient attention among major institutional investors. Consequently, you should contact anyone you know who either has gone public or has a connection with an investment bank to gain entry.

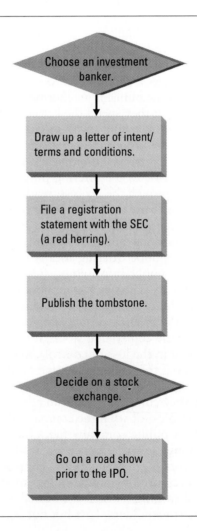

**Figure 15.4
The IPO Process
Simplified**

The importance of investigating the reputation and track record of any underwriter cannot be stressed enough, as investment banking has become a very competitive industry, with the lure of large fees from IPOs attracting some firms of questionable character. The entrepreneur should also examine the investment mix of the bank. Some underwriters focus solely on institutional investors, others on retail customers or private investors. It is often useful to have a mix of shareholders, as private investors tend to be less fickle and more stable than institutional investors. The investment bank should also be able to provide the IPO support after the offering by way of financial advice, buying and selling stock, and helping to create and maintain interest in the stock over the long term.

Once chosen, the underwriter draws up a *letter of intent,* which outlines the terms and conditions of the agreement between the underwriter and the entrepreneur/selling stockholder. It normally specifies a price range for the stock, which is a tricky issue at best. Typically, underwriters estimate the price at which the stock will be sold by using a price/earnings multiple that is common for companies within the same industry as the IPO. That multiple is then applied to the IPO's earnings per share. It should be emphasized that this is only a rough estimate. The actual going out price will not be determined until the night before the offering. If the entrepreneur is unhappy with the final price, the only choice is to cancel the offering, an action that is highly unpalatable after months of work and expense.

A **registration statement** must be filed with the SEC. This document is known as a "**red herring**," or prospectus, because it discusses all the potential risks of investing in the IPO. This prospectus is given to anyone interested in investing in the IPO. Following the registration statement, an advertisement, called a "**tombstone**," in the financial press announces the offering. The prospectus is valid for nine months; after that the information becomes outdated and cannot be used except by officially amending the registration statement.

Another major decision to make is where to list the offering—that is, on which exchange. In the past, smaller IPOs automatically listed on the American Stock Exchange (AMEX) or National Association of Securities Dealers Automated Quotation (NASDAQ) only because they couldn't meet the qualifications of the New York Stock Exchange (NYSE). Today, however, the NASDAQ, with companies like Microsoft and Netscape, is the fastest growing exchange in the nation.

There is a difference between the way the NASDAQ and the other exchanges operate. The NYSE and AMEX are auction markets with securities traded on the floor of the exchange, enabling investors to trade directly with one another. The NASDAQ, on the other hand, is a floorless exchange that trades on the National Market System through a system of broker-dealers from respected securities firms who compete for orders. In addition to these three, there are regional exchanges like the Pacific and Boston stock exchanges that are less costly alternatives for a small, growing company.

The high point of the IPO process is the *road show,* a two-week whirl-wind tour of all the major institutional investors by the entrepreneur and the IPO team to market the offering. This is done so that once the registration statement has met all the SEC requirements and the stock is priced, the offering can virtually be sold in a day. The coming-out price determines the amount of proceeds to the IPO company, but those holding stock prior to the IPO often see the value of their stock increase substantially immediately after the IPO.

An IPO can help a company grow much faster than it otherwise might, but you should weigh very carefully the pros and cons of becoming a public company.

Strategic Alliances to Grow

Earlier in the chapter we discussed how to use strategic alliances to create the virtual company or grow the business. Strategic alliances with larger companies are also an excellent source of growth capital for young companies. Sometimes the partnership results in major financial and equity investments in the growing venture. Such was the case of United Parcel Service of America, which acquired a 9.5 percent ownership interest in Mail Boxes Etc. for $11.3 million. This gave Mail Boxes Etc. capital to grow and UPS additional pickup and drop-off outlets. Growing companies that link with established companies usually get a better deal than they would have gotten from a venture capitalist. In addition, they derive some associated benefits that give them more credibility in the marketplace. The large investing partner is, at a minimum, looking for a return of the cost of capital, but in general a return of at least ten percent on the investment.

Strategic alliances are every bit as tricky as partnerships, so you must evaluate the potential partner carefully as well as do "due diligence" on the company. It is also crucial to not focus on one partner but instead consider several before making a final decision. For the partnership to really work, the benefits should flow in both directions; that is, both partners should derive cost savings and/or revenue enhancement from the relationship. It probably is best not to form a partnership that requires one of the partners (usually the smaller company) to be too heavily dependent on the other for a substantial portion of their revenue-generating capability. It is a dangerous position to be in, should the partnership dissolve for any reason.

Valuing the Business

A key component of any growth strategy is determining the value of the company, as a realistic value figure is needed no matter which financial strategy is undertaken to raise growth capital. However, understand at the outset that *value* is a subjective term with many meanings. In fact, at least six different definitions of value are in common use. Summarized, they are as follows:

- *Fair Market Value.* This is the price at which a willing seller would sell and a willing buyer would buy in an arm's length transaction. By this definition, every sale would ultimately constitute a fair market value sale.

- *Intrinsic Value.* This is perceived value arrived at by interpreting balance sheet and income statements through the use of ratios, discounting cash flow projections, and calculating liquidated asset value.

- *Investment Value.* This is the worth of the business to an investor and is based on the individual requirements of the investor as to risk, return, tax benefits, and so forth.

- *Going Concern Value.* This is the current status of the business as measured by financial statements, debt load, and economic environmental factors such as government regulation that may affect the long-term continuation of the business.

- *Liquidation Value.* This value assumes the selling off of all assets and calculating the amount that could be recovered from doing so.

- *Book Value.* This is an accounting measure of value and refers to the difference between total assets and total liability. It is essentially equivalent to shareholders' or owners' equity.

Methods for Valuing a Business

While there are numerous ways to value a business, this book will focus on three methods that are used frequently: 1) adjusted book value, 2) multiple of earnings, and 3) discounted cash flow.

Adjusted Book Value

The **book value** of a going concern is simply the owners' equity; that is, the value of the assets less the outstanding debts. Adjusted book value is based on balance sheet items. The difficulty with this method of valuing a business comes in the way assets are valued—as realizable value or as liquidation value.[12] Cash and near-cash items are easily valued, but in the case of accounts receivable, not all are readily collectible. You will need to know what your bad debt rate is so that you can deduct it and provide a better estimate. But there will also be costs associated with collecting that have to be taken into account. Land and facilities have real estate market value that would have to be estimated by an appraiser. In short, both inflation and depreciation affect the value of all assets to some degree. Therefore, balance sheet items are adjusted upward or downward to reflect their fair market value.

It should be noted that since many entrepreneurial companies in the early stages tend to have few assets relative to firms at later stages of development, this approach may not reflect the true value of the company.

Multiple of Earnings

Using a **price/earnings ratio** (P/E) to value a business is a common method with publicly owned companies because it's simple and direct. It consists of dividing the market price of the common stock by the earnings per share. For example, if a company has 200,000 shares of common stock and its net income is $250,000, the earnings per share would be 200,000/$250,000, or $.80 per share. If the price per share rises to $3.00, the price/earnings ratio is $3/$.80, or 3.75. The business would now be valued at $750,000 (200,000 shares × 3.75).

Another method, which typically results in a higher valuation, is using a year's worth of after-tax earnings and multiplying it by the industry average multiple based on the P/E ratio of public companies in the industry. This method must be considered with care. To say that a young private company with earnings of $250,000 in an industry where the average P/E is 12 should be valued at $3 million is probably overstating the case. It has been suggested that public firms have a premium value of about 25% to 35% over a closely held company and therefore any P/E multiple used should be discounted to reflect that premium.[13] That would mean that our private company now has a value of $2,250,000 ($250,000 × 9). Even with discounting, the variation in ways a company can calculate earnings and the difficulty in finding a public company that is comparable often make this a dubious measure at best for purposes of valuation.

Discounting Cash Flows

If valuing the business by its potential earning power is the goal, the most common measure—and the one that gives more accurate results—is future cash flows because only cash or cash equivalents are used in the calculations. The method is called **discounted cash flow analysis**, or *capitalization of future cash flows to the present value*. This simply means calculating how much an investor would pay today to have a cash flow stream of X dollars for X number of years into the future.

For this analysis, the entrepreneur uses pro forma cash flow statements for the business and determines a forecast period. Refer to Chapters 8 and 16 for discussions of pro forma cash flows and methods for forecasting sales and expenses. The length and nature of business cycles in the industry must also be understood in order for a forecast period that goes either from trough to trough or peak to peak in a cycle to be chosen. In other words, there needs to be at least one complete business cycle within the forecast period to give a fair representation of the effect on cash flow. (See Figure 15.5.)

Once the forecast period has been defined and the cash flow projections prepared, a discount rate must be chosen. This is not a purely arbitrary exercise. The buyer's or investor's point of view must be considered, and that viewpoint will often involve the opportunity cost to the investor/buyer of investing in or buying this business. It has been suggested that the decision should be based on three factors:

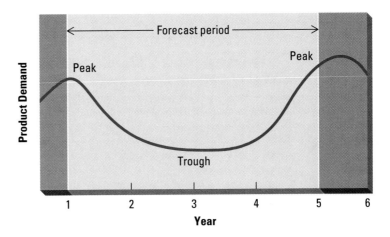

Figure 15.5
Business Cycles and
the Forecast Period

1. The rate achievable in a risk-free investment such as U.S. Treasury notes over a comparable time period. For example, for a five-year forecast, the current rate on a five-year note is appropriate.

2. A risk factor based on the type of business and the industry should be added to the interest rate in #1. Several precedents for determining what these factors are have been established over years of study. One accepted standard is that offered by James H. Schilt[14] in the form of six categories of business. Note that even within each category there is room for degrees of risk.

   a. Category 1: Established businesses with good market share, excellent management, and a stable history of earnings: *6–10%*

   b. Category 2: Established businesses in more competitive industries, still with good market share, excellent management, and a stable earnings history: *11–15%*

   c. Category 3: Growing businesses in very competitive industries, with little capital investment, average management team, and a stable earnings history: *16–20%*

   d. Category 4: Small businesses dependent on the entrepreneur or larger businesses in very volatile industries; also the lack of a predictable earnings picture: *21–25%*

   e. Category 5: Small service businesses operating as sole proprietorships: *26–30%*

3. The life expectancy of the business—since typically, discounting is based on this factor.

The example in Table 15.2 will illustrate this valuation method:

Table 15.2   One Method for Discounting Cash Flows

Assume: 6% risk-free rate
          +14% risk factor (Category 2 business)
            20% discount rate
Discount the Cash Flow

End of Year	Cash Flow ($000)	Factor (20%)	Present Value
1	200	.8333	166.7
2	250	.6944	173.6
3	300	.5787	173.6
4	375	.4823	180.9
5	450	.4019	180.9
Totals	$1,575		$875.7

Assuming that the current rate on a ten-year treasury note is 6 percent and the business is a Category 2 business at a 14 percent risk factor, the adjusted discount rate becomes 20 percent. Using a calculator or a present value table, the present value of the five-year cash flow stream can be calculated. What this example shows is that this hypothetical business will throw off $1,575,000 of positive cash flow over five years. Hence, a buyer would be willing to pay $875,000 today for that business, given the discount rate.

If three scenarios have been created—best, worst, and most likely cases or success, survival, and liquidation—there will be three values for the business. The entrepreneur then assigns a probability of occurrence to each scenario and multiplies the discounted cash flow by that probability to arrive at an adjusted present value.

A variation of the discounting cash flows method is the **excess earnings method,** which combines the estimate of future earnings with the value of the business's existing assets minus liabilities. The advantage of this approach is that it accounts for **goodwill,** which is an intangible asset that represents the difference between an unproven business and an established, successful one. In brief, this method has the following steps:

1. Compute the adjusted tangible net worth of the business. Tangible assets such as equipment are adjusted up or down for market value; then liabilities are subtracted.

2. Compute the opportunity cost of this investment. How much would the investor/buyer earn investing the same amount in another, comparable, investment?

3. Forecast net earnings. Earnings from previous income statements can provide a basis for the forecast, which is made before subtracting the owner's salary.

4. Calculate the extra earning power, which is the difference between forecasted earnings and opportunity costs.

5. Estimate the value of intangible assets or goodwill. If your business has extra earning power (some small businesses and family businesses do not), you can multiply that figure by what is known as **years-of-profit figure** (YOP). An average business will have a YOP of 3–4; a high risk business may have a YOP of 1, while an established business may have a YOP of 7.[15]

6. Calculate the value of the business by adding up the figures.

Once a mathematical estimate of value has been achieved, other factors will come into play that are difficult to put into the equation and are more rightly points of negotiation. All the projections used in the valuation of the business are based on assumptions, and the buyer/investor will likely question them and perhaps discount the value of the business even further. Another factor affecting the final valuation is the degree of legitimate control the owner has in the business. This is typically measured by the amount of stock the owner holds. Buying out an owner who holds the majority of the stock is more valuable than buying out one who does not. Finally, intangibles like a loyal customer list, intellectual property, and the like will also create additional value for the business. The "real" value or market value of the business will ultimately be determined through negotiation with investors, lenders, or underwriters. However, doing the calculations just discussed provides an excellent jumping-off point for the negotiations.

Valuation is by its very nature an incremental process that involves bringing together key pieces of information that it is hoped give some insight into the health and future of the business. In all discussions of value, the entrepreneur should be clear as to whose definition of value is being used.

The entrepreneur with a new venture has many options. However, crafting a capital structure that works for the new venture depends in large part on the creativity and persistence of the entrepreneur in securing the capital needed at the right price to successfully launch the venture. Recall from Chapter 1 that entrepreneurs work with a vision of where they see their companies going and what they will look like when they get there. That vision sustains them through the ups and downs of start-up and the breathless speed of growth when the company finally takes off. It also supports them in the difficult search for capital to feed that growth and ensure that the business will remain successful. The growth period of a world-class venture can be an extraordinarily exciting time for everyone involved if the entrepreneurial team has prepared for growth by doing the following:

▶ Networking, researching, and lining up potential capital sources well in advance of need

▶ Determining at least three years in advance whether the company will go public at the most appropriate window of opportunity. This is so the company can begin, if it hasn't already, to regularly prepare audited financial statements, using a nationally recognized accounting firm, and to put in place the financial and control systems required of a public company.

▶ Updating the comprehensive business plan

New Venture Checklist

Have you:

❏ **Considered how many personal resources you have to help fund the new venture?**

❏ **Determined ways to bootstrap the start-up of the new venture?**

❏ **Networked to come in contact with potential "angels"?**

❏ **Identified an attorney who can help structure a private placement agreement if needed?**

❏ **Investigated the sources of debt financing in the community?**

❏ **Determined how much growth capital will be needed?**

❏ **Developed a strategy for seeking growth capital?**

❏ **Established a value for the business?**

Issues to Consider

1. What are some ways a new venture can bootstrap to conserve capital?
2. What are some of the pitfalls of bootstrap financing?
3. What is the role of angels as a source of new venture funding?
4. At what stage of venture development do venture capitalists typically become involved, and why?
5. What is the purpose of a private offering?
6. Why are commercial banks not usually a reliable source of new venture financing?
7. What are three additional sources of debt financing?
8. Why should a private offering be used as a capital-raising vehicle before a public offering is used?
9. For what kind of business would private venture capital be a logical financial strategy for growth? Why?
10. How can strategic alliances be used to help grow the business?
11. What are some things that should be done to prepare for a public offering before the year of "going public"?

12. In approaching a venture capitalist, how can the entrepreneurial team deal from a position of strength?

13. What are the key components in valuing a new or growing venture?

Experiencing Entrepreneurship

1. Visit an SBA office in your area or visit the SBA web site and gather a portfolio of information that answers your questions about raising money to start your new venture.

2. Interview a venture capitalist or an angel (preferably both) to learn their expectations when they are reviewing business plans for new ventures.

Additional Sources of Information

Blechman, B., and J.C. Levinson (1991). *Guerrilla Financing*. Boston: Houghton Mifflin.

Bygrave, W.D., and J.A. Timmons (1992). *Venture Capital at the Crossroads*. Cambridge, MA: Harvard Business School Press.

Gladstone, D. (1988). *Venture Capital Handbook*. Englewood Cliffs, NJ: Prentice-Hall.

Latus, J. (1992). *Cashing in on Free State Government Money*. San Diego, CA: Lion Publishing Co.

National Association of Small Business Investment Companies, 1199 N. Fairfax Street, Suite 200, Alexandria, VA 22314. Tel. (703) 683-1601.

National Association of Trade Exchanges, 9790 Southwest Pembrook St., Portland, OR 97224.

O'Hara, P.D. (1989). *SBA Loans: A Step-by-Step Guide*. New York: John Wiley.

Pratt's 1993 Guide to Venture Capital Sources. Venture Economics. Tel. (800) 455-5844.

Tuller, L.W. (1994). *Small Business Valuation Book*. Holbrook, MA: Bob Adams, Inc.

Wilmeth, J.R. (Ed.) (Semiannual: June and December). *Directory of Operating Small Business Investment Companies*. Washington, DC: Small Business Administration.

Internet Resources

FinanceHub: Venture Capital on the Web
http://www.financehub.com/
This site contains a database of 11,000 investors and links to many venture firms.

Foundation Center
http://fdncenter.org
A nonprofit organization designed to help individuals and organizations find funding from foundations and philanthropists.

PricewaterhouseCoopers National Venture Capital Survey
http://www.pwcvc.com/
This site contains a quarterly survey of venture capital trends and results from around the nation.

Financing
http://www.morebusiness.com/financing
This site will help you determine whether or not venture capital is right for your business.

Relevant Case Studies

1. Toy Tips, Inc.
2. Mrs. Gooch's Natural Foods Markets
3. Simtek, Inc.
4. Flight Time

If you would know the value of money, go and try to borrow some.
Benjamin Franklin, 1706–1790
American printer and statesman
The Way to Wealth

Preparing the Financial Plan

Overview

▶ **Estimating sales and capital expenditures**

▶ **Preparing the pro forma income statement**

▶ **Preparing the pro forma cash flow statement**

▶ **Preparing the pro forma balance sheet**

▶ **Preparing the pro forma sources and applications of funds statement**

▶ **Ratios to describe the business**

Terms to Know

Profile 16.1

What Can Happen When Passion Runs the Business

Sue Mackarness had had eighteen years of experience teaching English in fourteen different countries. So in 1989, when colleague Christopher Notley suggested that they create a school that used her imaginative approach to teaching English as a second language, she thought, Why not! With money borrowed from friends and family, they set up their school, Transworld Teachers, in San Francisco. The first year was characterized by long hours and limited cash flow, but during that time enrollment doubled to 390 students, 80% of whom successfully found jobs overseas. It seemed as though Mackarness and Notley were on track; 40% of their new students came from referrals. That year the two married.

The school was known for Mackarness's teaching methods, which were based on the American style of learning and class participation. It was run more like a family than a business. Located in a Victorian house in an area of cafés and pubs, the atmosphere was one of casual friendliness. Everything seemed to be working. In 1992, revenues were at more than $300,000; by 1993, they had reached $550,000.

The troubles began in 1992 when Notley and Mackarness began having marital problems and Mackarness's father died. Soon the business began running short of cash. Neither of the two founders had any idea whether they were making a profit; their chief concern was meeting the payroll for their employees. Often they would hire people without knowing whether or not they could afford to. In 1991, they made a critical mistake when they acquired, very cheaply, another language school. It took nine months to receive certification and in the meantime, Transworld was paying the rent and salaries of the teachers at the newer school, even though they only had eight students.

Notley's casual attitude toward finances proved disastrous. Expenses were rarely recorded, and he failed to distinguish between corporate and personal funds. To get people to invest, Notley would promise outrageous returns; one person who invested $5,000 got a return of 300%! He was also careless about collecting tuition, telling students they could pay when they were able. Many times students never did pay.

One fateful day in 1994, a consultant named Neville Fridge, who had been referred by one of Transworld's investors, came to the school to observe a session. Afterward he sat down with Mackarness and Notley and suggested that they consider him for their business manager. His goal was to focus on profits and create a business plan for the growth of Transworld. The first thing he did was fire the bookkeeper and send the books out to be audited. Then he asked for equity in the company instead of pay, and for the position of president. Mackarness and Notley were only too happy to oblige this "savior" of their business; they gave him full voting shares without any shareholder agreement along with 20% of the company. They were confident in Fridge's ability and too tired to think about anything but their passion for the business, that they stopped paying any attention to financial matters. At one point, Fridge advised them that they had too many shareholders and suggested that he buy out the minority holders. Fridge paid $7,000 to raise his stock holdings to 29.6% and became the single largest shareholder.

When Mackarness and Notley separated in 1994, Fridge gave them and himself $2,000 bonuses. With his bonus he bought additional shares of stock. It wasn't long before Fridge began to see the potential in the business and decided it was time to get rid of Notley. He went to another investor and reported that Notley was diverting funds from the company. He then persuaded that investor to sell his shares to him. Fridge now had a controlling interest in the company and immediately locked Notley out of the business. Then he called an emergency shareholder meeting, appointed a board of directors, and fired Mackarness, who froze the company's accounts. This was followed by lawsuits, but because Notley and Mackarness couldn't afford a protracted legal battle, they settled out of court and bought Fridge's shares back. Though they tried to rebuild the school, Transworld ended up filing for Chapter 7 bankruptcy in September 1996.

Fridge, meanwhile, went back into business under the title New World Teachers and took several of Transworld's staff with him.

SOURCE: Stephanie Gruner, "The Takeover," *Inc.*, April 1997, p. 72.

How could Notley and Mackarness have avoided the financial problems that Fridge caused?

No matter how many financial tools entrepreneurs use or how many complex analyses are constructed, the bottom line for any new venture is cash. Income statements and balance sheets can make a company look good—these are accounting measures—but cash pays the bills and allows the company to grow. Cash is the lifeblood of the business. We cannot stress enough the importance of doing your own financials in the beginning. There is no better way to gain an understanding of how your business works. Even if you're able to hire a bookkeeper or accountant, don't just turn the books over to that person; you must monitor them yourself. (Remember the profile on Transworld Teachers to remind yourself of how true this is.)

In Chapter 8 you learned how to create pro forma cash flow and income statements for a new venture in order to calculate the start-up capital requirements. In this chapter we look at the financial statements that are found in the typical business plan. The financial plan for the new business is based on growth strategies you establish, as well as on the market research you've done to determine demand.

While this book has promoted creativity in all aspects of developing the business concept, this creativity should not be reflected in the financial statements. Financial statements must follow **GAAP**, "generally accepted accounting principles," so that the reader of the business plan recognizes standard terms and sees items in their normal order of presentation. This familiarity instills confidence that the numbers are genuine.

Furthermore, every assumption made in constructing the statements must be justified with supporting evidence—because with a new venture, you are forecasting not on the basis of historical performance but on your belief as to how the new venture will perform. Industry expertise, test marketing, and/or experience with a similar business goes a long way toward imbuing the reader with a sense of trust. In addition, having your accountant prepare and/or review the financials also adds credibility.

Estimating Sales and Capital Expenditures

Now might be a good time to refer back to Chapter 8 for an in-depth discussion of how to estimate sales and capital expenditures for a new business with no track record. As you recall, forecasting with a new venture is a difficult task at best. An example will make the challenge clear. Gentech Corporation is a new company manufacturing a technology-based industrial machine. It had to purchase motors and other parts from its suppliers. In the start-up phase, the company did not have enough sales to buy parts in sufficient volume to warrant the maximum discount from the supplier, so initially material costs were high. To compensate, the founders subcontracted some of the work, performed the assembly themselves, and sold products with little or no gross margin. The question then became "When will the business generate enough sales to buy in adequate volume, thereby reducing costs and increasing profit?" At the same time, once the volume was attained, the business would likely need to purchase additional equipment, perhaps expand facilities, and add employees. At what point should the founders do this, and how much should they spend?

This is the dilemma of the new venture. To answer these difficult questions, the entrepreneur must gain a great deal of knowledge about the industry and how similar businesses operate within it, then extrapolate from that until the business has been in operation for a while and has developed some patterns of its own that better define it.

Figure 16.1 depicts the process of creating the financial plan for the new venture and also reviews the steps already discussed in Chapter 8.

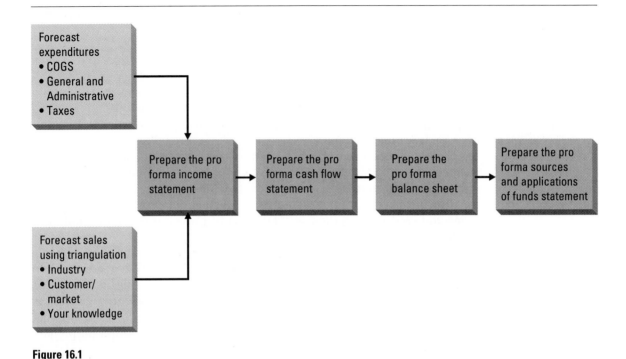

Figure 16.1
Steps in Preparing the Financial Plan

The information needed for completing the pro forma financial statements includes demand, cost, and operating figures. The goal is to forecast the financial condition of the new venture for the next three to five years on the basis of the information collected. These pro forma statements reflect the entrepreneur's best estimate of how the company will perform and what the associated expenses will be. The entrepreneur probably will also assume the ability to acquire credit and take on debt at some time. It is necessary, then, to understand that since these pro forma statements are estimates, they are subject to change based on the more accurate information gained when the business actually begins operating. This is why entrepreneurs typically reevaluate the financial statements on a monthly basis for the first year.

Preparing the Pro Forma Income Statement

Recall from Chapter 8 that the income statement reflects the profit and loss status of the business at the end of a specified period, normally one fiscal year. The income statement should also contain footnotes for each item to refer the reader to supporting material in the "Notes to Financial Statements." Any unusual major expenses like the cost of participating in a trade show should be footnoted separately and explained.

In the hypothetical example of NEW VENTURE INC. (see Figure 16.2), the company ended the year with a net profit before taxes of $15,250 on

New Venture Inc.
Pro Forma Income Statement — Year 1 by Month (000s)

	Month 1	Month 2	Month 3	Month 4	Month 5	Month 6	Month 7	Month 8	Month 9	Month 10	Month 11	Month 12	Totals
Sales — 1	15.00	19.50	25.35	32.96	42.84	55.69	72.40	94.12	122.36	159.07	206.79	268.82	1114.90
Less: COGS — 2	9.00	11.70	15.21	19.77	25.70	33.42	43.44	56.47	73.42	95.44	124.07	161.29	668.94
Gross Profit	6.00	7.80	10.14	13.18	17.14	22.28	28.96	37.65	48.94	63.63	82.72	107.53	445.96
Operating Expenses													
General and Administrative	3.75	4.88	6.34	8.24	10.71	13.92	18.10	23.53	30.59	39.77	51.70	67.21	278.73
Selling Expenses	5.00	2.34	3.04	3.95	5.14	6.68	8.69	11.29	14.68	19.09	24.81	32.26	136.99
Depreciation	1.25	1.25	1.25	1.25	1.25	1.25	1.25	1.25	1.25	1.25	1.25	1.25	15.00
Total Operating Expenses	10.00	8.47	10.63	13.44	17.10	21.86	28.04	36.08	46.52	60.10	77.76	100.71	430.71
Profit (Loss) Before Taxes	(4.00)	(0.66)	(0.49)	(0.26)	0.04	0.42	0.92	1.57	2.42	3.52	4.95	6.81	15.25
Taxes	0.00	0.00	0.00	0.00	0.00	0.00	0.00	0.00	0.00	0.00	0.00	4.41	4.41
Net Profit (Loss)	(4.00)	(0.66)	(0.49)	(0.26)	0.04	0.42	0.92	1.57	2.42	3.52	4.95	2.40	10.84

1 — Sales are expected to increase at 30% per month for the first year, a pattern in the industry.
2 — COGS amounts to 60% of sales.

Figure 16.2
NEW VENTURE INC.

which it must pay taxes. For purposes of illustration, a 40 percent tax rate was used to include federal and state income taxes.

Preparing the Pro Forma Cash Flow Statement

Recall from Chapter 8 that the cash flow statement gives a picture of the financial health of the company. It records all the cash inflows and outflows of the business. Figure 16.3 gives an example of a cash flow statement for a business that has inventory to sell and is structured as a corporation. As with all other financial statements, each item on the statement should be footnoted in the "Notes to Financial Statements" to explain what the assumptions were and how the figures were derived.

Notice that this cash flow statement includes the amount by which the new venture was capitalized, $280,000. By doing this analysis you learned that with an infusion of $280,000 in investment capital, the company maintains a positive cash flow and finishes the first year with an ending cash balance of $6,660, which will be recorded on the end-of-year pro forma balance sheet as cash available.

Use a spreadsheet program to set up the cash flow statement as well as the other financial statements. When you make a change in one item, the computer recalculates all the relevant figures to give you a new net cash flow

Profile 16.2

Finding Capital with an Effective Financial Plan

Recall that in Chapter 15 we emphasized that banks are not reliable sources of start-up capital. Still, it never hurts to try. That's what David Cupp learned when he dared to approach a bank in Columbus, Ohio, for start-up capital. Actually, he approached not just one bank but five different banks, over a period of seven months. Each time he was turned down, he refined his business plan to make it more appealing. Cupp asserts that he never would have gotten Banc One in Columbus to fund his company if he hadn't had a first-rate business plan.

Cupp started his company, Photos Online, Inc., in 1994. A prize-winning professional photographer for such notable publications as *National Geographic*, Cupp owns thousands of photographs from his hundreds of freelance assignments. What he saw was an opportunity to meld stock photography and the Internet to deliver high-quality photographs to customers online, but he needed $25,000 for equipment to start. He sought the help of his brother, a renowned golf-course designer, who invested $10,000 in the fledgling company. Then Cupp took a

seminar on business plan writing and went through the excruciating experience of trying to figure out his financial plan. With the additional help of an SBA volunteer tax accountant, Cupp went on to translate his ideas into dollars and cents. Banc One was the fifth bank he approached, and there he found a banker who understood what he wanted to do. Of course, by then his business plan had been refined to the point that it included everything the banker needed to make a decision.

In addition to the standard pro forma financial statements, Cupp was asked to provide equipment lists with costs and collateral used. Here he learned not to use his house or personal property as collateral, but to use savings, bank accounts, and vehicles instead. He also was advised to use notes to his financial statements to explain questionable figures.

Cupp's gamble paid off and in 1996 his revenues totaled $50,000. In 1997 they were expected to exceed $100,000.

Source: Susan Hodges, "One Giant Step Toward a Loan," *Nation's Business*, August 1997, p. 34.

New Venture Inc.
Pro Forma Cash Flow — Year 1 by Month (000s)

	Start-Up	Month 1	Month 2	Month 3	Month 4	Month 5	Month 6	Month 7	Month 8	Month 9	Month 10	Month 11	Month 12
Cash Inflows													
Sales		0.00	9.25	12.95	18.13	25.38	35.53	49.75	69.65	97.51	136.51	191.11	267.56
Capitalization	280.00	0.00	0.00	0.00	0.00	0.00	0.00	0.00	0.00	0.00	0.00	0.00	0.00
Total Cash Inflows	280.00	0.00	9.25	12.95	18.13	25.38	35.53	49.75	69.65	97.51	136.51	191.11	267.56
Cash Outflows													
Cost of Goods Sold	15.00	9.00	11.70	15.21	19.77	25.70	33.42	43.44	56.47	73.42	95.44	124.07	161.29
General and Administrative	94.00	3.75	4.88	6.34	8.24	10.71	13.92	18.10	23.53	30.59	39.77	51.70	67.21
Selling Expenses	11.00	5.00	1.11	1.55	2.18	3.05	4.26	5.97	8.36	11.70	16.38	22.93	32.11
Total Cash Outflows	120.00	17.75	17.69	23.10	30.19	39.46	51.60	67.51	88.36	115.71	151.59	198.70	260.61
Net CF Before Taxes	160.00	(17.75)	(8.44)	(10.15)	(12.06)	(14.07)	(16.07)	(17.76)	(18.71)	(18.20)	(15.08)	(7.59)	6.95
Taxes	0.00	0.00	0.00	0.00	0.00	0.00	0.00	0.00	0.00	0.00	0.00	0.00	4.41
Net Cash Flow	160.00	(17.75)	(8.44)	(10.15)	(12.06)	(14.07)	(16.07)	(17.76)	(18.71)	(18.20)	(15.08)	(7.59)	2.54
Beginning Balance	280.00	160.00	142.25	133.81	123.66	111.60	97.53	81.46	63.70	44.99	26.78	11.70	4.11
Ending Balance	160.00	142.25	133.81	123.66	111.60	97.53	81.46	63.70	44.99	26.78	11.70	4.11	6.66

Figure 16.3
NEW VENTURE INC.

figure. Because it is relatively easy to produce very detailed analyses, however, there is a tendency to overwhelm the potential reader with page after page of financial statements. This will hurt rather than help. Instead, be concise and to the point, and be sure to understand and document how figures were calculated, so that you can explain them if asked.

Spreadsheets make it easier to forecast best and worst case scenarios for your financial statements. Doing these **sensitivity analyses** is extremely valuable because they provide a range of capital needs based on different economic scenarios. For example, what effect will a sudden decrease in sales have on the overall picture? What would be the impact of a change in the tax law? To attempt to reconcile the various scenarios, it is often suggested that you calculate a **contingency factor**.[1] Take the annual cash flow figures for the most optimistic and most pessimistic scenarios and calculate the difference between them and the conservative cash flow figure (most likely). You will now have a range of values. The greatest negative difference becomes the contingency factor. The calculations using hypothetical best and worst case figures would be as follows:

Best case or most optimistic cash flow	$ 50,000
Worst case or most pessimistic cash flow	($300,000)
Most likely or conservative cash flow	($153,000)

Pessimistic	Optimistic
$(300,000)	$ 50,000
− (153,000)	− (153,000)
$(147,000)	$203,000

In this example, the most optimistic case produces a positive cash flow of $50,000, which means that $203,000 less capital would be needed to fund the start-up. In the most pessimistic case, however, $147,000 more capital is

Profile 16.3

Keeping Track of Cash

Steve Simon had no intention of losing control of his financial situation. As the CEO of AutoLend Group Inc., a used-car-financing company based in Miami Beach, Florida, he was watching his business grow at a cosmic rate. At the end of its first fiscal year in 1995, the company had earned revenues of $24 million. The growth was funded out of internal cash flows, so it was vitally important for Simon to know every day where the company stood.

He decided to call in his senior staffers to help him devise a sheet that would give them the critical information they needed each day. What they conceived became known as the "Daily Flash Report." By 7:00 A.M. every day, Simon and the chief operating

officer, chief financial officer, controller, collection manager, and other key people receive the Flash Report, which they look over and are prepared to discuss at the daily 9 A.M. meeting.

The report compares the current day with the previous day, and month or year as appropriate on such numbers as cash on hand, payroll expense, applications approved, and accounts in delinqency or default. While some business owners might balk at daily meetings, Simon believes that holding them lets him catch negative trends early before they become financial disasters.

SOURCE: Jill Andresky Fraser, "The No-Surprises Daily Money Watcher," *Inc.*, August 1995, p. 73.

required for start-up. This is the amount that should become the contingency factor, bringing the total investment to $420,000 ($153,000 plus the contingency factor of $147,000—the greatest difference—plus the start-up capital requirement of $120,000). Rather than capitalizing the business with only the $280,000 as calculated using simply the conservative cash flow statement, it is probably more prudent to seek an investment of at least $420,000 so that the probability of covering all possible contingent situations is higher. Besides, the company ends the first year with a positive cash balance of only $6,660, which is a very weak position, leaving little room for error heading into the second year.

Using the cash flow statement to determine the amount of capital needed to start and run the business is certainly not its only use. Particularly during the first year of operation, compare the monthly cash flow statement against actual inflows and outflows of cash to the business to determine where estimates deviated. Making adjustments to the remaining projections avoids any surprises later on. Essentially the cash flow statement becomes a budget for the business. As the business grows, it is also a good idea to put someone in charge of monitoring cash flow throughout all functions of the organization. That person should be familiar with all the operations of the business; consequently, the accountant is often not the best choice for someone to manage cash flow at the operational level.

Preparing the Pro Forma Balance Sheet

The balance sheet shows the condition of the business in terms of its assets and liabilities and the net worth of its owners at a specific point in time. Unlike the cash flow and income statements, the balance sheet is usually prepared to reflect the condition of the business at the end of each of the first five years of a new business. Figure 16.4 displays a sample balance sheet for a new business.

Forecasting Assets

The first section of the balance sheet is the assets, everything of value the business owns. **Assets** are valued in terms of actual cost for the item. **Current assets** are those consumed in the operation of the business during the year, while fixed assets are tangible assets used over the long term. Accounts receivable must be **forecast** based on the seasonality experienced by the business. If the business experiences no pronounced seasonality, you may be able to assume a certain percentage of sales that will not be paid in cash each month, based on industry averages or an accounts receivable turnover rate. Once the business is established, however, it develops its own pattern of receivables, and a more accurate turnover rate can be calculated. To account for the fact that some accounts receivable will not be collected, some entrepreneurs choose to subtract from receivables an **allowance for bad debt**, a small percentage (two to five percent) based on typical bad debt figures for the industry. Again, your business will develop its own unique pattern over time, and it will be easier to predict more accurately what the bad debt rate will be.

Inventory turnover must also be forecasted. Again, if the business experiences seasonality, it is not feasible to employ a constant turnover rate based

New Venture Inc. Pro Forma Balance Sheet — End of First Year	
ASSETS	
Current Assets	
Cash	$6,660
Accounts Receivable	201, 560
Inventory	23,000
Supplies	1,000
Total Current Assets	**232,220**
Fixed Assets	
Equipment	75,000
Less Depreciation	15,000
Total Fixed Assets	**60,000**
Total Assets	**$292,220**
LIABILITIES AND OWNER'S EQUITY	
Current Liabilities	
Accounts Payable	2,000
Current portion of long-term debt	0
Total Current Liabilities	**2,000**
Long-Term Liabilities	
Notes Payable	0
Total Long-Term Liabilities	**0**
Owner's Equity	
G. Brown, Capital	137,500
P. Smith, Capital	137,500
Retained Earnings	15,220
Total Owner's Equity	**290,220**
Total Liabilities and Owner's Equity	**$292,220**

Figure 16.4
NEW VENTURE INC.

on cost of goods sold. Inventory is a more complex issue for a manufacturing firm than accounts receivable, because at any time, a business may have raw materials, work in process, and finished goods. In the beginning stages of the business, you will probably estimate the amount for each of these stages and then use the total of the three for each month as the estimate for the year-end balance sheet. As the business grows, however, using a cost accounting model in which the three totals are shown separately on the balance sheet is a preferred method.

Forecasting Liabilities

Liabilities are everything the business owes to its creditors. Those that are due within one period are called **current liabilities**. New ventures generally have to pay for materials and inventory with cash until they have established a line of credit with suppliers, so you need to show a separate schedule that depicts when you expect to begin to use credit. Indicate only the total of materials and inventory for the year on the balance sheet, however. If the business paid cash for the entire year, which is not uncommon for a start-up, there will be no accounts payable. The current portion of long-term debt is that portion owed in the coming year.

Owner's or Stockholder's Equity

Owner's equity, also known as stockholder's equity in the corporate form, represents the excess after liabilities have been subtracted from assets and is the net worth of the business. Note that the individual investment contributions of the owners are also stated in this section. **Retained earnings** means the profit (loss) from the business that was not distributed as dividends.

When the balance sheet is completed, the total of the assets must equal the sum of the liabilities plus owners' equity. In other words, the balance sheet must balance! Understand that should you decide to use venture capital, private investors, or bank financing, the party involved may want a say in your debt-to-equity ratio; therefore, as capital is raised, the balance sheet is subject to adjustment.

Preparing the Pro Forma Sources and Applications of Funds Statement

To demonstrate how net operating income and other sources of funds to the business were used to increase assets or pay off debt and what effect this had on working capital, the **sources and applications of funds statement** is created. Figure 16.5 displays such a statement.

New Venture Inc. earned an after-tax profit of $10,840 during the year, which becomes a source of funds for the business. Depreciation, which is not a cash expense, is added back into the equation. Typical uses of funds include paying dividends, increasing assets like equipment, paying off long-term debt, and decreasing owners' equity. The net increase in working capital is the difference between total funds received (sources) and total funds applied. Notice that the statement must balance, with the balance item being working capital.

Ratios to Describe the Business

Many tools are needed to completely analyze a company's financial picture. No one tool or technique can provide all the answers to a very complex situation. Ratios are a particularly good way to begin to interpret the information contained in the financial statements from a lender's or investor's perspective. What ratios do is to make comparisons of items in the financial statements and put

New Venture Inc.	
Pro Forma Sources and Applications of Funds	
End of First Year	

Sources of Funds	
Personal funds (capitalization)	$280,000
Net income from operations after taxes	10,840
Add depreciation	15,000
Total of Funding Sources	**305,840**
Application of Funds	
Purchase of equipment/furnishings	75,000
Inventory	23,000
Total Funds Applied	**98,000**
Net Increase in Working Capital	**207,840**
	$305,840

Figure 16.5
NEW VENTURE INC.

them in relative terms so they can be compared to ratios in other periods. This facilitates looking for important changes in the company's position. It is possible to compute ratios for virtually all the items on the financial statements, but this would be a daunting and ineffective approach. A better approach is to select financial relationships that yield useful information about important aspects of the company. The three most common groups of ratios are 1) liquidity and activity ratios, 2) debt and financial risk ratios, and 3) profitability ratios. In discussing ratio analysis, we will turn to the example statements from New Venture Inc. and use the most important ratios in each category.

Liquidity and Activity Ratios

These ratios provide information on the company's ability to meet short-term obligations over time and to maintain normal operations. The more liquid the current assets, the more easily they are converted to cash to pay off short-term obligations and maintain operations; thus, the lower the risk for creditors.

> *Current ratio = total current assets/total current liabilities*

New Venture's current ratio is $232,220/2,000 = 116.11$. This ratio means that New Venture has $116 in current assets for every $1.00 in liabilities. The higher the number, the more liquid the firm. Over time it would be important to look for increasing numbers signaling a trend toward greater liquidity, or decreasing numbers portending declining liquidity.

> **Acid test = (current assets − inventory)/current liabilities**

This is yet another way to measure a company's ability to meet its current liabilities with its current assets, but the acid test is tougher because it removes inventory, which may be difficult to convert to cash because it is obsolete or, in the case of fraudulent practices, doesn't exist. This forces the current assets to stand on their own, which is usually more difficult. For New Venture this ratio is ($232,220 − $23,000) /$2,000 = 104.61 times or 104:1. Traditionally, the rule of thumb is a minimum of 1:1, so obviously New Venture is very liquid, an enviable position for a young company.

All the liquidity ratios help the company find problems early so they can be more easily corrected.

Profitability Ratios

The most commonly used measures of profitability are the profit margin, return on assets, and return on equity.

> **Profit margin (PM) = net income/net sales**

This ratio uses net income before taxes from the income statement and net sales from the income statement to portray the amount of each dollar of sales remaining after all costs of normal operations are accounted for. The inverse of this percentage (100% − PM) equals the expense ratio or the portion of each sales dollar that is accounted for by expenses from normal operations. It is an important way to monitor costs. New Venture's profit margin = $15,250/$1,114,900 = .0137, which is far too low. It suggests that expenses may be out of line.

> **Return on assets (ROA) or Return on investment (ROI)**
> **= net income/total assets.**

This measure uses net income before taxes from the income statement and total assets from the balance sheet. It gives the percentage that represents the number of dollars of income earned per dollar of invested capital. The greater the number, the greater the return. For New Venture, this ratio is $15,250/$292,220 = .05. Five percent was earned on every dollar of invested capital.

Return on equity = net income/owners' equity

Net income before taxes from the income statement and owners' equity from the balance sheet give a measure of the amount of net income earned per dollar of paid-in capital plus retained earnings. It is a way to look at the efficiency and effectiveness of the use of investor capital. For New Venture this ratio is $15,250/$290,220 = .05, so $.05 is earned per dollar of paid-in capital plus retained earnings.

Leverage Ratio

A **leverage ratio** expresses the degree to which the company relies on debt. In most cases, a higher number signals a riskier company because whereas the firm's earnings will change, debt payments remain fixed.

Debt to asset = total debt/total assets

This is a balance sheet ratio that measures the percentage of the firm's assets that are covered by creditors versus the percentage that is covered by the owners. It is estimated that most manufacturing firms have debt to asset ratios between 0.30 and 0.70.[2] New Venture's ratio is $2,000/$292,220 = .007 which is very low for manufacturing firms.

Ratios are important tools only as they are related to comparison periods of time or when used to compare one company with another. When looking at ratios calculated by others, it is always important to verify how the ratio was calculated—what was included—and to watch for ways by which some companies improve their appearance of liquidity; for example, taking out a long-term loan just before the end of the fiscal year and repaying it at the start of the new year. The cash from the loan will strengthen the current ratio, but it doesn't reflect the true liquidity of the company.[3]

An effective financial plan should include all the elements in Table 16.1.

The financial plan represents the entrepreneur's best estimate of the condition of the business at a particular point in time. Understanding the nature of your industry and the market in which you do business will ensure that those estimates come as close to reality as possible. In the next chapter we'll look at ways to grow the business.

Table 16.1   Financial Plan Outline

Summary of Financial Plan Highlights
> Sales
> Earnings
> Cash flow
> Total cash requirements for new business

Pro Forma Cash Flow Statements
> Years 1–5, monthly years 1–2
> Notes to cash flow statements

Pro Forma Income Statements
> Years 1–5, monthly years 1–2
> Notes to cash flow statements

Pro Forma Balance Sheets
> Years 1–5
> Notes to balance sheets

Pro Forma Sources and Applications of Funds Statements
> Years 1–5
> Notes to sources and applications statements

Key Ratios

Source: Reprinted by permission, Nation's Business, February 1996. Copyright © 1996, U.S. Chamber of Commerce.

New Venture Checklist

Have you:

❑ **Collected all the operating cost data needed to construct the financial statements?**

❑ **Studied competitor products to learn about seasonality, sales volume, and market share?**

❑ **Calculated the amount of start-up capital required to start and operate the business until a positive cash flow is achieved?**

❑ **Forecasted best and worst case scenarios for the pro forma financial statements, as well as the most likely case scenario?**

❑ **Calculated a break-even analysis for the first year?**

❑ **Completed a summary of the highlights of the financial plan?**

Issues to Consider

1. Why is the cash flow statement the most important statement for the entrepreneur?
2. What kinds of information must be collected to complete the financial statements?

3. How is forecasting sales for consumer products different from forecasting sales for industrial products?

4. What three factors affect the percentage increase in sales over a three- to five-year period?

5. What are the distinct purposes of the income statement, the sources and applications of funds statement, and the balance sheet?

Experiencing Entrepreneurship

1. Interview an accountant familiar with the type of business you're interested in, to learn some of the particular issues you need to consider when doing your financial statements.

2. Interview a banker about your business to learn the key financial ratios being looked for.

Additional Sources of Information

DeThomas, A. (1991). *Financial Management Techniques for Small Business*. Grants Pass, OR: Oasis Press.

Kolb, R.W., and R.J. Rodriguez. (1996). *Financial Management*. 2nd Ed. Cambridge, MA: Blackwell Publishers.

Stickney, C.P. (1990). Financial Statement Analysis: A Strategic Perspective. New York: Harcourt Brace Jovanovich.

Internet Resources

AccountingNet
http://www.accountingnet.com
A general source of accounting information for business owners.

Glossary of Insurance and Financial Planning Terms
http://www.ucalgary.ca/MG/inrm/glossary/index.htm
A handy site that is simple to use.

Internal Revenue Service—The Digital Daily
http://www.irs.ustreas.gov/prod
This site is full of free information about the IRS and tax-related issues.

The World Bank
http://www.worldbank.org
Offers the latest news from the World Bank, including research studies and publications.

Relevant Case Studies

1. Flight Time
2. Simtek, Inc.
3. Penduline Putler

Preparing for the Future

V

17

My candle burns at both ends;
*   It will not last the night;*
But, ah, my foes, and, oh, my friends—
*   It gives a lovely light.*
Edna St. Vincent Millay

A Plan for Growth

Overview

▶ **What makes a high-growth company?**

▶ **Factors that affect growth**

▶ **Stages of growth in a new venture**

▶ **Intensive growth strategies—Growing within the current market**

▶ **Integrative growth strategies—Growing within the industry**

▶ **Diversification growth strategies—Growing outside the industry**

▶ **Growing by going global**

▶ **To grow or not to grow . . .**

Terms to Know

Profile 17.1

Finding the Best Way to Grow

Most entrepreneurs want their companies to grow; at the same time, they don't want to lose what makes a company special. Kirk Perron almost did lose what was unique about Juice Club, the company he started in San Luis Obispo, California, in 1990.

The concept came from Perron's own obsession with healthy juices. In 1993, he decided that franchising would be a good growth strategy. By 1994 he had 16 franchises but was undercapitalized, so he had to let his franchisees buy or lease the land and facilities for their stores. Consequently, he couldn't take as large a franchise fee, and he also was unable to do sufficient training or monitor quality in the stores. As a result, quality declined, and Perron began to look for another way to grow the business that would give him more control.

On a September day in 1994, Perron received an unexpected phone call from a general partner in Technology Venture Investors and Benchmark Capital of Menlo Park. Bob Kagle had noticed a long line outside the door of the Palo Alto Juice Club and had stopped to ask questions. He ended up offering to invest $3 million to grow the concept that customers were passionate about. The investors included Howard Schultz, founder of the Starbucks coffee chain. This initial investment was followed by $19 million from seven venture groups, then $44 million from another group. The infusion of capital made it possible to train managers whose compensation would be based on performance. Today every employee is trained so that quality is consistent throughout all the company-owned stores.

The company was renamed Jamba Juice Co., to distinguish itself from the knockoff companies that were quickly emerging. *Jamba* is a West African word meaning "celebration," and it gave Perron's company a multicultural aura. Its hook is the ambience: customers encounter purple and green graphics, wheat grass growing in display cases, and the persistent scent of oranges that entices them to buy some of Jamba's many specialty juices. Though the company does have a marketing plan, its primary method of acquiring and keeping customers is through referrals, and it's working: in seven years, one store grew to 59.

In August of 1997, Jamba Juice Co. took another step in its growth strategy by licensing its trademarks to Whole Foods Market for use on in-store signage, menus, advertising and promotional materials, and packaging featuring Jamba Juice's blended-to-order smoothie drinks. The relationship began with beta sites in four Whole Foods Market stores, and Whole Foods Market co-founder and Chief Executive Officer John Mackey joined the Jamba Juice Co. board of directors.

Knowing where the value of your business lies is important in determining an appropriate growth strategy. Kirk Perron was fortunate to realize early enough that control over quality was essential to distinguishing his company from other juice store wannabe's. The ability to switch growth strategies from franchising to company-owned growth is a sign of an entrepreneur who adapts to the environment and to the new information gained from listening to customers.

SOURCE: "Jamba Juice Co. Inks Licensing Agreement with Whole Foods Market Inc.," *Company Press Release*, Wednesday, August 6, 1997; "Million-Dollar Ideas—Jamba Juice," (http://entrepreneurmag.com/entmag/mdideas_jamba.hts); Hal Plotkin, "Seeking Quality, Juicer Squeezes Out Franchisees," *Inc.*, July 1997, p. 25.

Why did Perron's initial growth strategy sputter, and how did he recover? What is important to take away from this experience?

Although some entrepreneurs, for a variety of personal reasons, may ultimately choose not to grow their businesses, most founders of entrepreneurial ventures are growth-oriented. Expansion is a natural by-product of a successful start-up. It helps a new business secure or maintain its competitive advantage and establish a firm foothold in the market. The 1996 *Inc.* magazine's list of the fastest growing private companies, found that just 30 percent of the entrepreneurs had originally intended to grow rapidly or to make the *Inc. 500*. About 45 percent wanted to grow slowly, 22 percent wanted to grow enough to survive, and 3 percent expressed a desire to remain small.[1] Yet all of them showed up on the 1996 list of fastest growing companies. This can be explained to some extent by the fact that a very small company will naturally show a larger percentage of growth in the early years because it's starting from a small base, and entrepreneurs' intentions can change over time. Though an entrepreneur may have started with a business that was intended to be small, the market may have encouraged greater growth than expected. Certainly that was the case with Jamba Juice. (See Profile 17.1.) But studying the *Inc. 500* tells us that young, fast-growth companies are extremely durable. Only 57 of the 500 companies in the 1985 list have failed, while fully 238 of them are still owned by their original founders.[2]

Contrary to popular opinion, the fastest growing small companies come from a variety of industries, although the ubiquitous computer software industry does dominate the high-growth companies. The reality is that businesses in a variety of industries experience high growth, and these industries include service companies, restaurants, product manufacturing, and clothing companies. So while some industries like computers and telecommunications provide a seemingly natural environment for high growth, a similar level of growth can occur in other industries as a result of the business strategy of the entrepreneur.

What Makes a High-Growth Company?

High-growth companies display several of the following characteristics. They are:

▶ First into their niche market. In other words, each of them created the market niche in which it became the leader.

▶ Better at what they do.

▶ Leaner in their operations.

▶ Unique in what they offered.

Being first in the market with a new product or service is one of the strongest competitive advantages there is, as it presents the opportunity to establish brand recognition so that customers immediately think of your company when they think about a particular product or service. It also allows you to set the standards for those who follow you. This was certainly the strategy of Samuel Adams in the microbrewed beer industry and Microsoft in the operations and applications software industry.

Many high-growth businesses have developed innovative processes that allow them to do what they do better and to run leaner operations. For example, Papa John's Pizza, which topped the *Business Week* list of fastest growing companies in 1994, restricted its menu to pizza, breadsticks, cheesesticks, and soft drinks, while offering a small tub of garlic butter and two hot peppers with each pizza as a value-added item. Papa John's also had three centralized commissaries to make all the sauce and dough for their 485 stores, which brought costs down substantially while also producing revenue.

A fourth way these companies have achieved high growth is by offering a unique, innovative product or service. This was the strategy of Michael and Marilyn Stopka of Arlington Heights, Illinois, who founded Design Toscano Inc., which sells historical European reproductions. *Time* magazine has called them the "#1 Gargoyle-phile." In 1997 their unusual business was doing $14.5 million in revenues.[3]

Factors That Affect Growth

The degree and rate at which a new venture grows are dependent on both the market and the management strategy. Market factors that affect a firm's ability to grow include:

▶ *The size, characteristics, and buying power of the target market.* If the niche market into which the company is entering is by nature small and relatively stable as to growth, it will be more difficult to achieve the spectacular growth and size of the fastest growing companies. On the other hand, if the product or service can expand to a global market, growth and size are more likely to be attained.

▶ *The nature of the competition.* Entering a market dominated by large companies is not in and of itself an automatic deterrent to growth. A small, well-organized company is often able to produce its product or service at a very competitive price while maintaining high quality standards, as it doesn't have the enormous overhead and management salaries of the larger companies. Moreover, if an industry is an old, established one, entering with an innovative product in a niche market can produce rapid rates of growth.

▶ *The degree of product innovation in the market.* In some industries like the computer industry, innovation is a given, so merely offering an innovative product is not in itself enough. In highly innovative industries, the key to rapid growth is the ability to design and produce a product more quickly than competitors. By contrast, in an industry that is stable and offers products and services that could be considered commodities, entering with an innovative product or process will provide a significant competitive advantage.

▶ *The status of intellectual property rights like patents, copyrights, trademarks, and trade secrets.* Intellectual property rights are also a competitive advantage to a new venture as they permit a grace period in which to introduce the product or service before anyone else can copy it. However, relying on proprietary rights alone is not wise. It is important to have a comprehensive marketing plan that allows the new business to secure a strong foothold in the market before someone attempts to reproduce the product and compete with it. True, you have the right to take someone who infringes on your proprietary rights to court, but it is a time-consuming and costly process, one which the small company can ill afford to undertake at a time when it needs all its excess capital for growth.

▶ *The volatility of the industry.* Some industries are by their very nature volatile; that is, it is difficult to predict what will happen for any length of time and with any degree of accuracy. The computer industry in the 1980s was such an industry; it has lately become somewhat more predictable as the leading players in the industry have emerged. The young and dynamic telecommunications industry, however, is very volatile at this time. Consequently there are opportunities for extraordinary growth in new ventures and, at the same time, a higher risk of failure. A new entry into such an industry needs to maintain a constant awareness of potential government regulations, directions the industry is taking, and emerging competitors.

▶ *The barriers to entry.* Some industries, simply by their size and maturity, make it difficult for a new venture to enter and achieve sufficient market share to make a profit. Others by the cost of participating (plant and equipment or fees and regulations) in the industry prohibit entry by new ventures. Yet in the right industry, a new venture can erect barriers of its own to slow down the entry of competing companies. Proprietary rights on products, designs, or processes, for example, can effectively erect a temporary barrier to allow the new venture a window of opportunity to gain market share.

Management factors that affect a firm's ability to grow include:

▶ *The entrepreneur's ability to move from controlling all aspects of the company to delegating authority and responsibility for major functions.* Rapid growth requires different skills from start-up skills. In the beginning of a new venture, the entrepreneur has more time to take part in and even control all aspects of the business. But when rapid growth begins to occur, systems must be in place to handle the increased demand without sacrificing quality and service. Unless the entrepreneur is able to bring in key professional management with experience in high-growth companies, chances are the growth will falter, the window of opportunity will be lost, and the business may even fail needlessly. Many entrepreneurs have found that at some point in the business's growth, they must step down and allow experienced management to take over.

▶ *The ability to encourage entrepreneurship in the entire venture team.* Growing the business does not have to mean that the entrepreneurial spirit is lost, but the entrepreneur has to be very creative about how to maintain that sense of smallness and flexibility while growing. Subcontracting some aspects of the business is one way to keep the number of employees down and retain that team spirit. Developing self-managing teams is another way.

Stages of Growth in a New Venture

Rates and stages of growth in a new venture vary by industry and business type; however, there appear to be some common issues that arise at shared points in time. The importance of knowing when these issues will surface can-

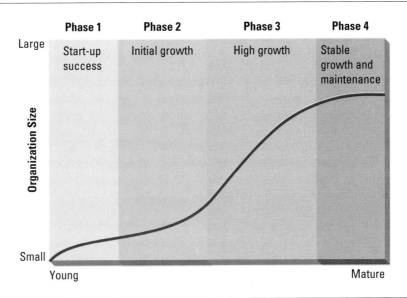

| | **Phase 1** | **Phase 2** | **Phase 3** | **Phase 4** |

Large — Start-up success | Initial growth | High growth | Stable growth and maintenance

Figure 17.1
Stages of Growth

Small — Young ... Mature

Organization Size

not be overstated, for they should become part of a well-orchestrated plan on the part of the entrepreneur to anticipate events and requirements before they occur. The stages of growth (see Figure 17.1) can be defined as four phases through which the business must pass to move to the next level of activity.

Start-Up Success

At the first level, the main concerns for the entrepreneur are to ensure sufficient start-up capital, seek customers, and design a way to deliver the product or service. At this point, the entrepreneur is a jack of all trades, doing everything that needs to be done to get the business up and running. This includes securing suppliers, distributors, facilities, equipment, and labor.

Initial Growth

If the new venture makes it through the first and most difficult phase, it enters the second level of activity with a viable business that has enough customers to keep it running. Now the concerns become more focused on the issue of cash flow. Can the business generate sufficient cash flow to pay all the expenses and support the growth of the company? At this point, the business is usually relatively small, with few employees, and the entrepreneur is still playing an integral role. This is a crucial stage for the business, for it is here that the business will either remain small or move to the next level, high growth, which entails some significant changes in organization and strategy. The owners need to decide if they are going to grow the business to a much larger revenue level or remain stable yet profitable.

High Growth

If the decision is to grow, all the resources of the business have to be gathered together to finance the growth of the company. This is a very risky stage as growth is expensive, and there are no guarantees the entrepreneur will be successful at attempting to reach the next level. Planning and control systems must be in place and professional management hired. The problems faced in this stage center on maintaining control of rapid growth. This is accomplished successfully by delegating control and accountability at various levels; failure usually is due to uncontrolled growth, running out of cash, and not having the necessary management expertise to deal with the situation. If growth is accomplished, it is in this stage that entrepreneurs often sell the company at a substantial profit, assuming it will remain successful in its growth. It is also at this stage that some entrepreneurs are displaced by their boards of directors, investors, or creditors, so many entrepreneurial ventures reach their pinnacle of growth with an entirely different management team than the one that founded the company.

Stable Growth and Maintenance

Once the business has successfully passed through the rapid growth phase and is able to effectively manage the financial gains of growth, it will have reached Phase 4, stable growth and maintenance of market share. Here the business, which usually is now large, can remain in a fairly stable condition as long as it continues to be innovative, competitive, and flexible. If it does not, sooner or later it will begin to lose market share and could ultimately fail or revert to being a much smaller business. Allowing decision making at the lowest levels in small operating units is one way to permit the company to continue to grow without losing that entrepreneurial spirit and flexibility.

High-tech companies seem to be an exception to the traditional growth patterns. Because they typically start with solid venture capital funding and a strong management team (dictated by the venture capitalists), they move out of Phases 1 and 2 very rapidly. During Phases 3 and 4, if the structure is effective, they become hugely successful. If, on the other hand, the structure is weak, they can fail rapidly.

Problems with Growth

New business growth, for the most part, is a very positive thing; however, it does bring with it some issues for which the entrepreneur must be prepared. For example, if the new venture is a retail business, and you expand by opening additional stores, you need to decide whether or not to retain control of all functions in one main store, or delegate the day-to-day management and solely control marketing, accounting, finance, and purchasing. It may be necessary to establish a computer network to keep track of sales at all locations. For a manufacturing firm, expansion may entail significant capital investment in additional plant and equipment, or developing new strategic alliances to keep production in line with demand. It may also mean locating additional distributors and even new channels of distribution. For a service business, growth may mean taking on additional associates or employees and investing in computer systems to manage information. And, of course, for the entrepreneur growth means giving up some control to others with the management skills to successfully guide the company.

This chapter looks at several strategies for growing the business:

▶ *Intensive growth strategies*, those that exploit opportunity in the current market

▶ *Integrative growth strategies,* those that involve growth within the industry as a whole

▶ *Diversification strategies*, those that exploit opportunities outside the current market or industry

▶ *Global strategies,* those that take the business into the international arena

Intensive Growth Strategies—Growing Within the Current Market

Intensive growth strategies focus on exploiting the current market fully; that is, expanding the market share to the greatest extent possible. This is accomplished by increasing the volume of sales to current customers and the number of customers in the target market. There are generally three methods for implementing an intensive growth strategy: market penetration, market development, and product development.

Market Penetration

With **market penetration**, the entrepreneur attempts to increase sales by using more effective marketing strategies within the current target market. This is a common growth strategy for entrepreneurs with new ventures because it allows them to work in familiar territory and grow while they're getting their systems and controls firmly in place. Under this strategy you would move out gradually from your initial target market, whether it is a geographic area or a customer base. For example, your initial target market for your online travel guide might be travel agencies. You would focus your efforts and resources on getting those customers solidified, then gradually move on to other target customers like hotels and convention bureaus.

Having additional uses for the product causes customers to buy more. Arm & Hammer experienced that when its customers began buying baking soda not only for cooking but for brushing their teeth and deodorizing their refrigerators. Yet another way to employ market penetration is to attract customers from your competitors by advertising product qualities, service, or price that distinguishes your product from others. A fourth way is to educate nonusers of the product or service as to its benefits, in an effort to increase the customer base.

Market Development

Market development consists of taking the product or service to a broader geographic area. For example, if you have been marketing on the East Coast, you may decide to expand across the rest of the United States. One of the most popular ways to expand a market geographically is to franchise because it is generally less costly than setting up a national distribution system.

Franchising

Franchising allows the business to grow quickly in several geographic markets at once. The franchiser sells to the franchisee the right to do business under a particular name; the right to a product, process, or service; training and assistance in setting up the business, as well as ongoing marketing and quality control support once the business is established. The franchisee pays a fee and a royalty on sales, typically three to eight percent. What the franchisee may get for the fee, depending on the business, is

▶ A product or service that has a proven market

▶ Trade names and/or trademarks

▶ A patented design, process, or formula

▶ An accounting and financial control system

▶ A marketing plan

▶ The benefit of volume purchasing and advertising

Franchises generally come in three types: dealerships, service franchises, and product franchises. **Dealerships** allow manufacturers to distribute prod-

---

Profile 17.2

Growing Whether You Want To or Not

If you're very fortunate, the customer will demand that you grow. At least that's what happened to Dave Thomas, the colorful founder of Wendy's International Inc. Thomas started out in the food business with four KFC (Kentucky Fried Chicken) franchises in Columbus, Ohio. After selling them, he started a restaurant designed to serve all his favorite foods, including made-to-order burgers. His philosophy was to serve "one customer at a time."

At that time, it was believed that the hamburger market had reached the saturation point so Thomas never expected to own more than three or four restaurants. But it wasn't long before people were literally begging him to franchise his concept. Though

he didn't want to do it, he finally relented and watched Wendy's grow to 500 units in the 1980s. Growing that fast made it difficult to maintain control over quality, so Thomas trained everyone to focus on the basics—that is, on what every customer wants from a restaurant: quality food, clean surroundings, and good service. As an entrepreneur he also learned that he had to delegate in order to expand, so he surrounded himself with good people, and Wendy's grew to 5,000 units world-wide, one customer at a time.

SOURCE: Roberta Maynard, "Building a Winner From Scratch, *Nation's Business,* October 1997, p. 65.

ucts without having to do the day-to-day work of retailing. Dealers benefit from combined marketing strength, but are often required to meet quotas. Service franchises provide customers with services such as tax preparation, temporary employees, payroll preparation, and real estate services. Often the business is already in operation before it applies to become a franchise member. The most popular type of franchise is one that offers a product, a brand name, and an operating model. Some examples are Kentucky Fried Chicken and Golf USA.

Though a popular vehicle for growth, franchising is not without its risks. It is virtually like creating a whole new business, because the entrepreneur must carefully document all processes and procedures in a manual that will be used to train the franchisees. Potential franchisees need to be scrutinized to ensure that they are qualified to assume the responsibilities of a franchise. Moreover, the cost of preparing a business to franchise is considerable and includes legal, accounting, consulting, and training expenses. Then, too, it may take quite a long time to show a profit, as many as three to five years.

The risk to franchisees who may have purchased the franchise as an entry into business ownership is also great. Franchisees will typically pay 2% to 10% of gross sales to the franchiser for monthly royalties and marketing fees, which means there is a tremendous challenge for the franchisees to control costs and get a return. Consequently, it's no surprise that one report found that only two-thirds of approximately 1,200 franchised units surveyed in 1987 survived under the same owner for four years.[4] Nearly 35 percent of franchises started between 1984 and 1987 went out of business by late 1991, as compared with 28 percent for nonfranchised businesses, according to the study by Tim Bates of Wayne State University. Another study, by Scott Shane of the Georgia Institute of Technology, corroborated the Bates study, concluding that of the 138 new franchise systems established in 1983, only 24.6 percent were still in business in 1993.[5] The reason for the failures is that franchises are typically found in retail industries, primarily eating and drinking establishments, which have a pattern of high risk and low return.[6]

Bankruptcy of the parent company, the franchiser, should be another concern for potential franchisees, and it's not uncommon. In the past decade, dozens of franchises have experienced Chapter 11 bankruptcy, including 7-Eleven, Nutri-System, American Speedy Printing, Church's Fried Chicken, and Days Inns. Most have emerged intact, but not without some harm to the franchisees. During the bankruptcy, the franchisees are left essentially in limbo, without support or information, and wondering if they'll have a viable business when it's all done. The association of the franchisee with the bankrupt parent is also a negative, since customers assume that if the parent has financial problems, so does the child. Furthermore, most franchisees have invested their life's savings in their businesses. Under the arbitration clauses in most franchise agreements, franchisees don't have the option of going to court to recoup their losses. Even if the company comes out of Chapter 11, its image is tarnished. It will have to cut back somewhere, and savvy consumers know this to be true.

Not all businesses are suitable for franchising as a growth strategy. A successful franchise system will need to have the following characteristics:

- A successful prototype store (or preferably stores) with proven profitability and a good reputation so that the potential franchisee will begin with instant recognition

- Registered trademarks and a consistent image and appearance for all outlets

- A business that can be systematized and easily replicated many times

- A product that can be sold in a variety of geographic regions

- Adequate funding, as establishing a successful franchise program can cost upwards of $150,000

- A well-documented prospectus that spells out the franchisee's rights, responsibilities, and risks

- An operations manual that details every aspect of running the business

- A training and support system for franchisees both before they start the business and on-going after start-up

- Site selection criteria and architectural standards

Developing a franchise program requires the assistance of an attorney and an accountant whose advice should be carefully considered before undertaking the effort.

Licensing

Like franchising, **licensing** is a way to grow a company without investing large amounts of capital in plant, equipment, and employees. In Chapter 7 you learned that a license agreement is a grant to someone else to use intellectual property and exploit it in the marketplace by manufacturing, distributing, or using it to create a new product. For example, you may have developed a new patented process for taking rust off machinery. You could license that process to other companies to use on their equipment and receive a royalty. Conversely, you may have an idea for a new line of promotional products and want to license a famous name and likeness to use on them, to make them more attractive to consumers. This would entail seeking a license agreement from the owner of the name and likeness to use it commercially; for example, seeking a license from Paramount Pictures Corporation to use the *Star Trek* characters on a line of products.

But licensing is much more than this, and entrepreneurs need to understand fully the value of intellectual property and how it can provide income in a variety of different ways. For the purposes of this discussion, we'll state that anything that can be patented, copyrighted, or trademarked, or that is a trade secret, has the potential for licensing. If a company has intellectual property that someone else might pay to use or commercialize in some way, there are some steps that should be taken to ensure that both parties to the transaction win. Licensor and licensee depend on each other very much for the success of the agreement, so the outcomes must be worthwhile at both ends of the deal. The following are steps licensors should take to ensure a successful transaction.

Step 1: Decide exactly what will be licensed. The license agreement can be for a product, the design for a product, a process, the right to market and distribute, the right to manufacture, or the right to use the licensed product in the production of yet another product. It will also be important to decide if the licensee may only license the product as is or may modify it.

Step 2: Understand and define the benefits the buyer (licensee) will receive from the transaction. Why should the licensee license from your company? What makes the product, process, and so forth, unique and valuable? The licensee should clearly see that dealing with your company has many advantages and will be much more profitable than dealing with someone else.

Step 3: Conduct thorough market research to make sure the potential customer base is sufficient to ensure a good profit from the effort. Of course, the licensee too will have done market research, particularly if the licensee approaches the licensor with a proposal for a licensing agreement. But the latter situation is typical only with intellectual property that is "famous" or well recognized in the marketplace: characters, for instance (Mickey Mouse, Batman). A company with new intellectual property or IP that is unproven in the marketplace may need to seek out licensing agreements to get the property commercialized.

Step 4: Conduct due diligence on potential licensees. It's important to make certain any potential licensee has the resources to fulfill the terms and conditions of the license agreement, can properly commercialize the intellectual property, and has a sound reputation in the market.

Step 5: Determine the value of the license agreement. The value of a **license agreement** is determined by several factors: 1) the economic life of the intellectual property; that is, how long it will remain viable as a marketable product, process, and so on; 2) the potential that someone could design around the intellectual property and directly compete; 3) the potential for government legislation or regulation that could damage the marketability of the IP; 4) any changes in market conditions that could render the IP valueless.

Once the monetary value of the license is determined by the licensor on the basis of these four factors, it becomes negotiable. Generally, the licensor wants some money up front as a sign of good faith, then a running royalty for the life of the license agreement. The amount of this royalty will vary by industry and by how much the licensee must invest in terms of plant, equipment, and marketing to commercialize the IP.

Step 6: Create a License Agreement. With the help of an attorney who specializes in licenses, a license agreement or contract will be drawn up that will define the terms and conditions of the agreement between licensor and licensee. The following are just some of the clauses that are typically found in such license agreements.

- A **grant clause** specifies what is being delivered to the licensee and whether or not the license is exclusive (only the licensee has the right to this IP) or nonexclusive (others also have a similar right).

- A **performance clause** specifies dates by which the licensee should achieve certain agreed-upon sales targets. This is important to prevent situations where the licensee ties up a technology through an exclusive agreement but never commercializes it, leaving the inventor without anything for his or her efforts.

- A *secrecy clause* or confidentiality clause spells out who may know the details of the intellectual property and for how long.

- A *payment clause* details the method by which payment will be made. If the license agreement deals with a foreign licensee, it will be important to designate the currency in which royalties will be paid. Normally, a U.S. licensor will definitely want to take payment in U.S. dollars, but a combination of dollars and the licensee's currency is also used. Be aware that any foreign currency will fluctuate over the life of the license agreement, so royalty payments will vary as well. This could mean more or less income for the licensor and higher or lower payments for the licensee.

- A **grantback clause**, or improvement clause, permits the licensee to improve on the product and grant back to the licensor the right to any improvements. Likewise, there may be a **grantforward clause**, which gives the licensee the right to use any improvements made by the licensor on the product.

- A *definite term* for the license agreement.

- A *sublicense clause* that specifies whether or not the licensee can sublicense the IP or assign the right to another.

Being a *licensee* is also a way to grow your company without having to incur the expense of always developing new products. From the licensee's point of view, here are a few things to remember.

1. Search for a technology, product, logo, character, or other intellectual property that you want to license.

2. Be sure to prepare a business plan to present to the licensor, showing what you're proposing to develop and market with the licensor's intellectual property. The plan should include such things as estimated sales, the target market, the plan for penetrating the market, and how you intend to finance the agreement; that is, what resources you have for carrying out the agreement.

3. Do due diligence on the licensor to ensure that the company is reputable, the IP is sound, and the company has the kind of people you want to work with over the period of the license. Remember, this is much like a partnership, so it's important to choose a partner carefully.

4. Try to negotiate favorable terms: conservative performance targets, lower royalties, little or no upfront capital, and so forth. Be aware, however, that if the intellectual property is well known—famous—or in great demand, there may not be much room to negotiate, so you'll probably pay a premium for the agreement.

Again, licensing is an excellent way to move more quickly in the marketplace with less capital investment than is needed for other forms of growth.

Product Development

The third way to exploit the current market is to develop new products and services for existing customers or offer new versions of existing products. That is the tactic of software companies, which are constantly updating software with new versions their customers must buy if they want to enjoy all the latest features. Savvy businesses get their best ideas for new products from their customers. These new ideas usually come in either of two forms: incremental changes in existing products, or totally new products. Incremental products often come about serendipitously when engineers, sales personnel, and management spend time out in the marketplace with the customers, learning more about their needs. Bringing all these team members together on a weekly basis to discuss ideas helps the business to quickly zero in on those incremental products that are possible within the current operating structure and budget. The advantage of incremental products is that since they are based on existing products, they can usually be designed and manufactured fairly quickly.

New or breakthrough products, on the other hand, have a much longer product development cycle and are therefore more costly to undertake. Breakthrough products cannot be planned for; instead, they usually come about through brainstorming, exercises in creativity, and problem-solving sessions. In other words, if the entrepreneur creates a business environment that encourages creative, "off-the-wall," thinking, the chances are greater that it will eventually come up with breakthrough products. The breakthrough environment, of necessity, has no budget or time constraints and does not run on a schedule. A combination of incremental and breakthrough products is probably the most effective way to go. The speed and cost efficiency of the incremental products keeps cash flowing into the business, cash that helps fund the more costly breakthrough products.

Branding

The most successful entrepreneurs recognize the power of a brand name; therefore, they strive to gain brand name recognition for their products and services as quickly as possible, so that they can use the recognition to create a family of related products and services under that name. A company that is able to establish brand recognition will find its marketing effort that much easier and its costs reduced. A brand name that reflects quality, service, and value is an asset that ultimately can generate huge profits for the business. One example of the value of brand name recognition is the T-shirt industry. Companies like Mossimo and Nike buy basic T-shirts from an apparel manufacturer and print their own design and logo on the shirt. Customers will pay more for a T-shirt with the Mossimo name on it than they will for the same T-shirt with an unknown company name on it—that's brand recognition.

To establish brand recognition:

▶ Know what you're good at. List the strengths your company and its products possess. For example, do you offer a higher-quality product, a wider range of accessories or models, or exciting new colors?

▶ Educate customers about your strengths. Once you have identified your core strengths, communicate them over and over again in all your marketing efforts, from brochures to signs to advertising. They should literally become a mantra for the customer. The minute customers think of your product, they should associate it with its strengths.

▶ Develop a set of rules for using the brand name. If you want your brand name to be associated only with wholesome things, you probably won't want to advertise during a television show containing violence, for example. How the brand name will be used also needs to be decided. Gentech Corporation, for instance, wanted the trade name for its product PowerSource, always to be associated with the company name, so in all its advertising and promotion, the product is referred to as the Gentech PowerSource. In this way, when additional products are developed, the common thread will be the company name, Gentech.

▶ Get feedback on brand name recognition. To make sure the brand name is achieving the recognition level you are seeking, check periodically with the target customer.

Once brand name recognition has been established, take advantage of it by developing related products under the same brand name. However, this works only when you are offering new benefits to your target market or taking the same benefits to a new market. If you take a new product to a new market, the brand recognition will not necessarily follow.

Integrative Growth Strategies—Growing Within the Industry

Traditionally, when entrepreneurs have wanted to grow their businesses within their industry, they have looked to vertical and horizontal integration strategies, but with the mantra of the 1990s being "lean and mean," entrepreneurs with growing businesses have been looking more often than not, to a modular or network strategy. This section examines all three strategies.

Vertical Integration Strategies

An entrepreneurial venture can grow by moving backward or forward within the distribution channel. This is called **vertical integration**. With a backward strategy, the company either gains control of some or all of its suppliers or becomes its own supplier by starting another business from scratch or acquiring an existing supplier that has a successful operation. This has been a common strategy for businesses that have instituted a just-in-time inventory control system. By acquiring the core supplier(s), the entrepreneur can streamline the production process and cut costs. With a forward strategy, the company attempts to control the distribution of its products by either selling directly to the customer (i.e., acquiring a retail outlet) or acquiring the distributors of its products. This strategy gives the business more control over how its products are marketed.

Horizontal Integration Strategies

Another way to grow the business within the current industry is to buy up competitors or start a competing business (i.e., sell the same product under another label). This is called **horizontal integration**. For example, suppose you own a chain of sporting goods outlets. You could purchase a business that has complementary products, such as a batting cage business, so that your customers can buy their bats, balls, helmets, and so forth from the retail store and use them at the batting cage.

Another example of growing horizontally is to agree to manufacture your product under a different label. In addition to his designer label line, New York designer Mark Eisen manufactures a line of clothes for Spiegel Catalog under a different name. This strategy has been used frequently in the major appliance and grocery industries. Whirlpool, for example, produced Sears's Kenmore washers and dryers for years. Likewise, major food producers put their brand name food items into packaging labeled with the name of a major grocery store.

Modular or Network Strategies

The latest way to grow within your own industry is to focus on what you do best and let others do the rest. If the core activities of the business include designing and developing new products for the consumer market, other companies can make the parts, assemble the products, and market and deliver them. In essence, your company with its core activities becomes the hub of the wheel, with the best suppliers and distributors as the spokes. By doing this, the business can grow more rapidly, keep unit costs down, and turn out new products more quickly. In addition, the capital saved by not having to invest in fixed assets can be directed to those activities that provide a competitive advantage. The electronics and apparel industries used this growth strategy long before it became trendy. Today many other industries are beginning to see the advantages of a modular approach. Even service businesses can benefit from outsourcing functions like accounting, payroll, and data processing, which require costly labor.

Outsourcing noncore functions can often help a company get products to market faster and in greater quantities, while at the same time spreading risk and delivering the capabilities of a much larger company without the expense. In fact, a Coopers & Lybrand survey of 400 fast-growing small companies found that two-thirds used outsourcing and that their revenues, sales prospects, and growth rates far exceeded those of companies that did not use outsourcing.[7] Outsourcing permits small, growing companies to have noncore functions completed more efficiently at a lower cost and a higher level of quality than these companies could manage on their own. Innovative Medical Systems Inc., a New Hampshire-based manufacturer, outsources the manufacture of subassemblies, product design, computer networking, payroll administration, and direct mailing and advertising placement, and handles inhouse only final assembly, quality assurance, strategic marketing, and customer service.[8] Some companies have experienced explosive growth as a result of outsourcing. This was the case with Paranet Inc., a provider of outsourced computer networking services in Houston. Founded in 1991, it now enjoys revenues of over $32 million and is projecting $75 million within the year. It employs over 400 people in 15 offices.

As with anything else, there are some negatives to outsourcing. If most functions are outsourced, it becomes difficult to develop any kind of corporate culture that will bind workers together and make them loyal to the company. When "employees" are no longer employees of the company, this presents some unique problems that must be dealt with. The key to success with a network strategy such as this is to have a good relationship with suppliers and distributors so that as the business begins to grow rapidly, they are willing to ramp up to meet demand.

Diversification Growth Strategies—Growing Outside the Industry

When entrepreneurs expand their businesses by investing in or acquiring products or businesses outside their core competencies and industry, they are employing a diversification growth strategy. Usually, but not always, this strategy is used when the entrepreneur has exhausted all growth strategies within the current market and industry and now wants to make use of excess capacity or spare resources, adapt to the needs of customers, or change the direction of the company because of impending changes in the market or economy. The latter is exemplified by the collapse of the Houston oil economy in 1984. Many entrepreneurs who saw their oil ventures drying up found they had to diversify into new product lines or services to survive and grow.

One way to diversify is to use a **synergistic strategy** where you attempt to locate new products or businesses technologically complementary to your business. For example, a food processor may acquire a restaurant chain that can serve as a showcase for the food. Another way to diversify is to employ a strategy where you acquire products or services that are unrelated to your core products or services. For example, a manufacturer of bicycle helmets may acquire an apparel manufacturer to make clothing with the company logo on it to sell to helmet customers. A final strategy for diversifying is called **conglomerate diversification** and involves acquiring businesses that are not related in any way to what you are currently doing. An entrepreneur might use this strategy to gain control of a related function of doing business—for example, purchasing the building in which the business is housed and then leasing out excess space to other businesses, to produce additional income and gain a depreciable asset. Many entrepreneurs whose work causes them to travel extensively find it advantageous to acquire a travel agency to reduce costs and provide greater convenience.

A diversification strategy for growth is not something to undertake without careful consideration of all the factors and potential outcomes, particularly when it involves an acquisition. While it is true that the entrepreneur can find consultants who are experts in mergers and acquisitions to help smooth the path financially and operationally, what is difficult to predict with any degree of certainty is how the cultures of the two businesses will merge. Acquisitions and mergers cannot be successful on the basis of financial and operational synergy alone. Organizational styles and individual personalities of key management all come into play when an acquisition or a merger takes place. As a result, the human side of the two businesses must be analyzed and a plan developed for merging two potentially distinct cultures into one that can work effectively.

Profile 17.3

The Case of a Commercial Printer*

Quick Press is a commercial printer located in Connecticut. Its owner/entrepreneur, Sam Quick, saw significant changes beginning to take place in the printing industry toward the end of the 1980s. It was obvious that traditional printing methods were being overtaken by desktop publishing via computers. Not wishing his business to become obsolete, he hired a computer consultant to determine the best way to computerize the company so it could continue to grow. The consultant informed Quick that the cost would be high and the learning curve steep, so Quick decided it might be more cost efficient to acquire a company that already had the capability he needed.

In 1991, Quick was able to buy such a company, Graphical Arts. On the surface the deal appeared to have synergy. With the capabilities of the two companies, Quick could offer customers a wider variety of services and could also do in-house some of the work that he had previously had to outsource, tasks like color-scanning. However, many of Quick's customers are large companies that also have gone to doing much of their printing in-house. The marketplace is extremely competitive, with very tight margins.

The first thing Quick found out after the acquisition had taken place was that much of the technological expertise for which he had paid, although excellent, was still in the R&D stage; this started things off badly. The next problem was the clash of cultures. There were significant differences in management style and workplace attitude: the Quick Press employees were a more laid-back group and the Graphical Arts employees much more disciplined, professional, and serious. With no preparation for the merger, it was hardly surprising that the two groups found it difficult to adjust. The bottom line is that the acquisition definitely positioned the company for future growth, but until the people issues were resolved, that growth remained stalled.

*The names in this profile have been changed to protect the principals' privacy.

Many researchers have attempted to determine the most effective growth strategy for a new venture. In general, it has been found that horizontal integration, vertical integration, and synergistic diversification have been more successful than unrelated diversification. This is true whether the entrepreneur acquires an existing company or starts another company to achieve the goal. This is not to say that unrelated diversification should never be chosen as a growth strategy. If the potential gains are by comparison extraordinarily high, the risk may be worth the taking. It is also generally true that an acquired business has a better chance of success than a start-up, for the obvious reason that it has usually already passed the crucial two stages of start-up and survival and is more likely to be poised to grow.

Growing by Going Global

Today the question for a growth-oriented company is not "Should we go global?" but "When should we go global?" There are many reasons why entrepreneurial ventures must consider the global market even as early as the development of their original business plan. Technology is hardly the sole province of the United States, and the United States can no longer ship its obsolete technology to other countries to extend its market life. Other countries now expect to receive the latest technology in the goods they purchase, and it may not always come with a United States label on it. In fact, the United States, while a huge market, represents less than half the total global market.

Furthermore, due to rapidly changing technology, product lives are increasingly shorter. With R&D so expensive, companies are forced to enter several major markets at once to gain the maximum advantage from the window of opportunity. Entrepreneurs who attend world trade shows know their strongest competition may as easily come from a country in the Pacific Rim as from the company next door. Entrepreneurs also know they may have to rely on other countries for supplies, parts, and even fabrication to keep costs down and remain competitive.

With increasing competition and saturated markets in some industries, looking to global markets can add a new dimension to the entrepreneur's business. Many entrepreneurs have found new applications for their products in other countries or complementary products that help increase the sales of their product domestically. Several events have made exporting United States products to other countries more attractive than ever before.

- Relatively low United States interest rates have made it easier for businesses to finance the exporting of their products.

- The North American Free Trade Agreement (NAFTA) eliminated trade barriers among the United States, Mexico, and Canada, which makes exporting to those countries more attractive.

- The decline of the U.S. dollar, while not good for U.S. travelers in other countries, certainly makes U.S. goods more affordable for other countries.

- The opening up and growth of untapped markets like China and Vietnam means more potential customers for U.S. products.

▶ The establishment of the first four Federal Export Assistance Centers gives businesses considering exporting a new source of help. The four centers are located in Baltimore, Long Beach, Miami, and Chicago.

▶ The Uruguay Round of GATT (the General Agreement on Tariffs and Trade) reduced or eliminated tariffs among 117 countries in 1995. It also improved patent and copyright protection, which has been a problem for businesses exporting protected products to other countries where proprietary rights may not be recognized or protected.

While you should include a global strategy in any business planning, you may not be able to export until the business is somewhat established and offering a high-quality product or service at a competitive price. Still, we are seeing more and more "global start-ups,"—companies like Logitech, the Swiss manufacturer of computer mouses—take a global strategy from the very inception of the business. Researchers have found that the number of global start-ups appears to be growing.[9] Oviatt and McDougal studied a dozen global start-ups and followed them over time. Of the dozen, four failed, for a variety of reasons, but in general, those that failed had fewer of the success characteristics that Oviatt and McDougal found in those that survived. These success characteristics include:

1. A global vision from the start

2. Internationally experienced managers

3. Strong international business networks

4. Preemptive technology

5. A unique intangible asset such as know-how

6. Closely linked product or service extensions (The company derives new and innovative products and services from its core technology.)

7. A closely coordinated organization on a world-wide basis.[10]

Whether or not you have a global start-up, exporting is a long-term commitment that may not pay off for some time. During that period you may have to adapt the product or service somewhat to meet the requirements of the importing country and develop good relationships with agents in the country. If you are dealing in consumer products, target countries that have disposable income and like American products. If, however, you are dealing in basic or industrial products, look to developing countries that need equipment and services for building infrastructures and systems. One example is Mexico, which is taking on the enormous task of building bridges and roads as it positions itself as a major player in the world market.

Finding the Best Global Market

Finding the best market for a product or service can be a daunting task, but there are some sources and tactics that help make the job easier. Start with the International Trade Statistics Yearbook of the United States, which is available in any major library. Using the SITC (United Nations Standard

Industrial Trade Classification) codes found in this reference book, you can find information on international demand for your product or service in specific countries. The SITC system is a way of classifying commodities used in international trade. You should also be familiar with the Harmonized System of classification, which is a ten-digit system that puts the United States "in harmony" with most of the world in terms of commodity tracking systems. If your international shipment exceeds $2,500, you must know your HS number for documentation.

Demand for American products is usually reflected in three areas:

Consult additional sources of information like the District Office or the Washington, D.C., office of the International Trade Administration, and the Department of Commerce (DOC). The Commerce Department's database links all the DOC International Trade Administration offices and provides a wealth of valuable research information.

The successful launch of a program of global growth should include a marketing plan and budget directed toward that goal in the business plan. You also need to bring someone onto the team who has international management experience or export experience. Depending on your budget, you may choose to hire a consultant who specializes in this area. It is also important to attend foreign trade shows to learn how businesses in the countries in which you are interested conduct business, who the major players are, and who the competition is. Finally, this chapter cannot present all the detailed information needed before beginning to export. Consulting a source dedicated to exporting, such as Jack Wolf's *Export Profits* (Upstart Publishing), is a must.

Export Financing

To make a sale in the global market, the entrepreneur must have the funds to purchase the raw materials or inventory to fill the order. Unfortunately, many

 Sources of Help for Exporting

Trade Shows and Trade Missions

The Commercial Service of the United States Department of Commerce assists U.S. companies in identifying new markets and meeting potential buyers through a variety of overseas trade events.

Matchmakers

Matchmakers are a direct approach to finding representatives or distributors for your product in selected countries. They are high-visibility trade delegations, usually concentrating in specific industries. U.S. firms are matched with potential business partners in the host country.

Catalog and Video Exhibitions

Catalog exhibitions are designed to promote the sale of U.S. products by attracting potential representatives and distributors.

entrepreneurs assume that if they have a large enough order, getting financing will be no problem. Nothing could be further from the truth. Export lenders, like traditional lending sources, want to know that the entrepreneur has a sound business plan and has the resources to fill the orders. Entrepreneurs desiring to export can look for capital from several sources:

▶ Bank financing

▶ Internal cash flow from the business

▶ Venture capital or private investor capital

▶ Prepayment, down payment, or progress payments from the foreign company making the order

A commercial bank is more interested in lending money to a small exporter if the entrepreneur has secured a guarantee of payment from a governmental agency such as the **Import-Export Bank**, which limits the risk undertaken by the commercial bank. Asking buyers to pay a deposit up front, enough to cover the purchase of raw materials, can also be a real asset to a young company with limited cash flow.

Foreign Agents, Distributors, and Trading Companies

Every country has a number of sales representatives, agents, and distributors who specialize in importing American goods. It is possible to find one agent who can handle an entire country or region, but if a country has several economic centers, it may be more effective to have a different agent for each center. Sales representatives work on commission; they do not buy and hold products. Consequently, the entrepreneur is still left with the job of collecting receivables, which, particularly when dealing with a foreign country, can be costly and time consuming.

Profile 17.4

Getting Help When Doing Business Abroad

Small companies have often had success in some countries without formal help mechanisms. Jimmy Kaplanges's chemical company had done some exporting of its industrial degreaser in Brazil, Spain, France, and Greece. Then the $3 million GP66 Chemical Corp. wanted to tap the mammoth Chinese market, and Kaplanges knew this would require a great deal of time and help. So he approached the federal export assistance center in Baltimore.

Since 1994, the Commerce Department has set up nineteen U.S. Export Assistance Centers around the country. They are essentially one-stop shops that serve as communication links to district offices and other export services. Kaplanges worked with trade specialist Nasir Abbasi. This particular service is free because it's supported by tax dollars, although there are some services that carry a fee, such as background checks of foreign companies and agents. Kaplanges also gained access to advice from Commerce Department staff members who had served in overseas business positions. The result? He closed a deal to sell his product to the Chinese government for use in factories, schools, and businesses—a deal that would increase his revenues to $12 million.

Source: Roberta Maynard, "A Simplified Route to Markets Abroad," *Nation's Business,* November 1997, p. 46.

Agents are a way to circumvent this problem. Agents purchase your product at a discount (generally very large) off list and then sell it and handle collections themselves. They solve the issue of cultural differences and the ensuing problems inherent in these transactions. Of course, with an agent you lose control over what happens to the product once it leaves your hands. You have no say over what the agent actually charges customers in his or her own country. If the agent charges too much in an effort to make more money for himself, you may lose a customer. If you are just starting to export or if you are exporting to areas not large enough to warrant an agent, consider putting an ad in American trade journals that showcase American products internationally. If you are producing a technical product, you may be able to find a manufacturer in the international region you are targeting who will let you sell your products through that company, thus giving you instant recognition in the foreign country. Ultimately, that manufacturer could also become a source of financing for your company.

Another option is to use an **export trading company** (ETC) that specializes in certain countries or regions where it has established a network of sales representatives. ETCs may also specialize in certain types of products. What often happens is that a sales rep may report to the ETC that a particular country is interested in a certain product. The ETC then locates a manufacturer, buys the product, and sells it in the foreign country. Trading companies are a particularly popular vehicle when dealing with Japan.

Choosing an Intermediary

Before deciding on an intermediary to handle the exporting of your products:

1. Check the intermediary's current listing of products to see if your company seems to fit in with that type of expertise.

2. Understand with whom you will be competing; that is, does the intermediary also handle your competitors?

3. Find out if the intermediary has enough representatives in the foreign country to adequately handle the market.

4. Look at the sales volume of the intermediary. It should show a rather consistent level of growth.

5. Make sure the intermediary has sufficient warehouse space and up-to-date communication systems.

6. Examine the marketing plan.

7. If necessary, make sure the intermediary can handle servicing your product.

Once you have decided on the intermediary, draft an agreement detailing the terms and conditions of the relationship. As it is very much like a partnership agreement, consult an attorney specializing in overseas contracts. The most important thing to remember about the contract is that it must be based on performance, so that you do not tie yourself up for many years with someone who is not moving enough product for you. Negotiate a one- or two-year contract with an option to renew should performance goals be met. This will probably not please the intermediary, as most want a five- to ten-year contract. Be firm; it is not in your best interests to have a longer-term contract until you know that the person is loyal and can perform. Other issues that should be addressed in the agreement include:

▶ Your ability to use another distributor; in other words, negotiate for a nonexclusive contract so as to have some flexibility and control over the situation.

▶ The specific products the agent or distributor will represent. This is important because as your company grows, you may add or develop additional products and not want this agent to sell those products.

▶ The specific geographic territories for which the agent or distributor will be responsible.

▶ The specific duties and responsibilities of the agent or distributor.

▶ A statement of agreed-upon sales quotas.

▶ A statement of the jurisdiction in which any dispute would be litigated. This will protect you from having to go to a foreign country to handle a dispute.

Choosing a Freight Forwarder

The **freight forwarder**'s job is to handle all aspects of delivering the product to the customer. The method by which you ship a product has a significant impact on the product's cost or the price to the customer, depending on how the deal is structured, so consider the choice of a freight forwarder carefully. The ability to fill a shipping container to capacity is crucial to reducing costs. Freight forwarders prepare the shipping documents, which include a bill of lading (the contract between the shipper and the carrier) and an exporter declaration form detailing the contents of the shipment, and they can present shipping documents to your bank for collection. The entrepreneur, however, is responsible for knowing if any items being shipped require special licenses or certificates, as in the case of hazardous materials or certain food substances.

Global Franchising

The first franchisers on the global scene were primarily the large food franchises such as McDonald's, Kentucky Fried Chicken, and Burger King. Today even smaller franchisers are going global. Franchisers are generally welcomed by foreign governments because they bring to the country not only a product but also a way of doing business, which provides jobs for the citizens of the country. Those who have chosen to try their luck in developing countries or the old Eastern Bloc countries have consistently found the cost of doing business there much higher. In addition, they may have to deal with unstable governments, volatile currencies, and a general lack of understanding of competitive market systems. Many international franchisers have discovered that having a local partner is one of the keys to a successful global effort because it allows them to acquire an understanding of the business and consumer culture in the country. They also tend to try to establish master franchise agreements, which give the franchisee the rights to the entire country or region.

One of the challenges facing international franchisers is achieving the same level of productivity and service they experience in the United States. In some countries low productivity is simply a way of life, and changing old habits can require hours of training. One source of help for potential international franchisers is the International Franchise Association (IFA) located in Washington, D.C. This organization has established a Code of Ethics and, through its Franchisee Advisory Council, provides dispute resolution for both franchisees and franchisers.

To Grow or Not to Grow . . .

Some entrepreneurs make a conscious choice to control growth even in the face of extraordinary market demand. This is not to say that growth is slowed to single digits. Instead, the entrepreneur may choose to maintain a stable growth rate of 35 to 45 percent per year rather than subject the young venture to a roller coaster ride in the triple digits. In general, entrepreneurs who restrain growth do so because they are in the business for the long term, so they don't advertise heavily or aggressively seek new customers beyond their capabilities. Instead, they diversify their product or service line from the beginning to make themselves independent of problems that may face their customers or their industries.

It is intoxicating for a new venture to realize potential demand is great and that the company could virtually fly off the scales in terms of industry averages. But "speed of light" growth has destroyed many companies that did not have the capacity, skills, or systems in place to meet demand. The growth phase of a new business can be one of the most exciting times for an entrepreneur. But if the entrepreneur has not prepared for growth with a coherent plan and budget to match, it can be instead a disastrous time for an

Profile 17.5

Domino's Goes Global

Domino's went into Japan literally against all odds. Other pizza companies had failed, which suggested that the Japanese simply didn't like pizza. Moreover, free delivery, which was the way Domino's had differentiated itself in the domestic market, was an expected service in the Japanese market. Still, after extensive research, Domino's decided to move ahead and successfully captured the Japanese market by reducing the size of their pizzas to accommodate the smaller appetites of the Japanese customers, using scooters to maneuver the crowded streets, and creating exciting packaging and brochures, which the Japanese appreciate. Today Domino's stores in Japan do twice the volume of those in the United States.

otherwise successful start-up. The keys to successful growth are, indeed, to be the best at what you do, be the first in the market where possible, operate lean and mean, offer something unique, and have a plan.

New Venture Checklist

Have you:

- ❏ Identified market factors that may affect the growth of the business?
- ❏ Determined which growth strategy is most appropriate?
- ❏ Identified potential international markets for the product or service?
- ❏ Developed a plan for globalization of the company at some point in the future?

Issues to Consider

1. What are four characteristics of high-growth companies?
2. How can both market and management factors affect the growth of a new venture?
3. What questions should you ask at each level of the new venture's growth?
4. What advantages do intensive growth strategies have over integrative and diversification strategies?
5. Why is it important to start a growth-oriented business with a plan for globalization from the beginning?
6. What are the differences among foreign agents, distributors, and export trading companies in terms of the services they provide?

Experiencing Entrepreneurship

1. Visit an export center in your area and talk to a Department of Commerce trade specialist who can advise you on how to become prepared to export.
2. Interview an entrepreneur in the early stages of his or her venture and question him or her about the growth strategy for the business. Can you identify the type of strategy being used?

Additional Sources of Information

Commerce Department. "Flash Facts," a 24-hour free fax line for information on specific international regions. Tel. for Eastern Europe, (202) 482-5745; Mexico, (202) 482-4464; Pacific Basin, (202) 482-3875; Africa, Near East, and South Asia, (202) 482-1064.

Commerce Department—District Offices. *The Export Yellow Pages.* Includes U.S. export companies, intermediaries, and freight forwarders.

Export-Import Bank, Washington, D.C. Tel. (202) 566-4490, for a list of lenders who handle international transactions.

Export-Import Bank's City/State Program. Tel. (800) 424-5201.

Rager, L. (June 1989). "How to Expand by Franchising." *Nation's Business*.

Trade Information Center. Tel. (800) USA-TRADE or (800) 872-8723. Ask for an industry desk officer who specializes in your industry.

TradeNet. An Internet electronic mailing list for international importers and exporters.
   TradeNet@cerfnet.com; TradeNet@ix.netcom.com; TACC5BA (Prodigy); TradeNetWS (America Online); 75144,3544 (CompuServe)

U.S. Small Business Administration. *Bankable Deals*. A book on export finance. Tel. (202) 205-6720. Also has lists of trade events.

Whiteley, R., and D. Hessan. (1996). *Customer-Centered Growth*. Reading, MA: Addison-Wesley.

Wolf, J.S. (1992). *Export Profits*. Dover, NH: Upstart Publishing Company, Inc.

Internet Resources

ExportNet
http://www.exporttoday.com
Tips for businesses that want to trade internationally. This is not a free service.

International Business Forum
http://www.ibf.com
Geared toward entrepreneurs who want to get into the international marketplace. Contains lists of resources in various countries, opportunities and associations.

The Internationalist
http://www.internationalist.com
An excellent source for information on a wide range of international issues including business, investment, and travel

International Trade Administration
http://www.ita.doc.gov
A division of the Department of Commerce. Offers help to companies that wish to export.

Relevant Case Studies

1. OXO (B)
2. Flight Time
3. Autopsies-to-Go

18

If you're going to play the game properly, you'd better know every rule
Barbara Jordan
U.S. Congresswoman
Ebony, February 1975

Laws and Regulations Affecting New Businesses

Overview

▶ **From idea to start-up**

▶ **Choosing a business site**

▶ **Hiring employees**

▶ **Trade issues**

▶ **Taxes**

Terms to Know

Profile 18.1

Finding a Place in the Sun

It was 1994 when Doug Mellinger ran into a seemingly insurmountable brick wall. PRT, the company he'd founded in 1989 to help other companies find technological solutions to business problems, was facing hurdles that would have thwarted even the most seasoned entrepreneur. The demand for programmers was far outstripping the supply, and the 29-year-old Mellinger had to go as far as India to find good ones. In fact, in 1993, after untangling miles of red tape, he had the beginnings of a development center in India; the problem was that his customers, Lehman Brothers, the New York City investment bankers, refused to go to India to collaborate with the programming team. He couldn't bring the programmers to the United States because of costs and immigration restrictions, and tapping other overseas talent also had its obstacles. He was at a stalemate.

The fundamental issue was that Mellinger needed a country easy to work with. Since that country didn't exist, he'd have to invent it. It would have to be a place where people wanted to live, that had everything they needed, and where they could work with people they wanted to work with. This was the ultimate solution to getting around the restrictions of the industry.

It took three years, but Mellinger built his country. It's on an island in the Caribbean, just four hours by air from New York City. In a partnership with the island nation of Barbados, and by transplanting workers, customers, capital, and infrastructure, Mellinger created his dream. And now Mellinger is becoming known for his ability to create an organization that can get things done despite regulations, laws, people, and other obstacles that can get in the way of most companies.

He has reached nearly 400 software engineers from all over the world who have come to live and work in his "company town." Here he provides housing, transportation, medical care, legal help, banking, and refrigerators stocked with their favorite foods—in essence, a turnkey lifestyle. Mellinger doesn't want his employees to think about anything but "writing killer code" and having fun. He provides the engineers with state-of-the-art workspaces and equipment, and they have the advantage of working with other engineers and managers to share ideas and try experimental projects. The reputation of his company has spread so far and so fast that he can be extra-selective as to whom he chooses to work for it.

Mellinger's customers built the complex: companies like J.P. Morgan and Chase contributed over $12 million to make it exactly what they needed. As a result, working closely with programmers in an environment conducive to innovation has produced more and better products than the customers would ever have dreamed possible. The Barbados development center has gone from zero to $19 million in revenues in two years.

Mellinger attributes his success to having a "can do" attitude. When faced with the seemingly impossible task of building a country from scratch, he didn't ask how he could do it; he asked who could help him do it. That was, in fact, essentially how PRT was started, back in 1989. Mellinger phoned CEOs of Fortune 500 companies to find out the biggest problems they were facing, then asked what he could do to solve them. They helped this young man whose primary goals were to give something back and to build an organization that served its people and its customers. PRT/Barbados development center is now a model for a great technology organization.

SOURCE: Michael Hopkins, "The Antihero's Guide to the New Economy," *Inc.*, January 1998, p. 36.

How did Mellinger use entrepreneurial creativity to overcome the regulatory challenges he faced?

You don't have to be in business very long to realize that all businesses are affected by a variety of individuals and organizations. Known as **stakeholders,** these individuals and organizations have a profound impact on the success of your business. (See Figure 18.1.) No matter how big your business is or becomes, it will be challenged on a daily basis in myriad ways by the laws, regulations, requirements, and restrictions of federal, state, and local government authorities. A number of governmental agencies write and enforce the various regulations by which businesses are bound. Probably no one would dispute the need for government regulation where it protects businesses, employees, and the general public from actions and products that would cause harm or deny people their rights. Many, however, believe that the red tape and paperwork have become so overwhelming that it now costs businesses over two billion hours per year just to fill out government forms. They are concerned that this burden and its accompanying costs appear to exceed any benefit that might be accrued from regulation. Many international business owners, such as Gordon Roddick of The Body Shop, consider the United States the most regulated country in the world. Roddick believes that compliance with regulations adds at least five percent to the cost of doing business, reducing the number of businesses that are able to start, as a new venture often must spend its scarce resources on attorneys and accountants to ensure compliance with the law.[1] You saw in the profile on PRT (Profile 18.1) that one entrepreneur decided to create his own country to overcome the highly regulated environment of the United States.

This chapter looks from a regulatory point of view at the process of starting a business, considering which regulations affect which aspects of the new venture.

From Idea to Start-Up

One of the first areas where the entrepreneur is affected by laws and regulations occurs at the idea stage before the new venture even begins. Laws determine

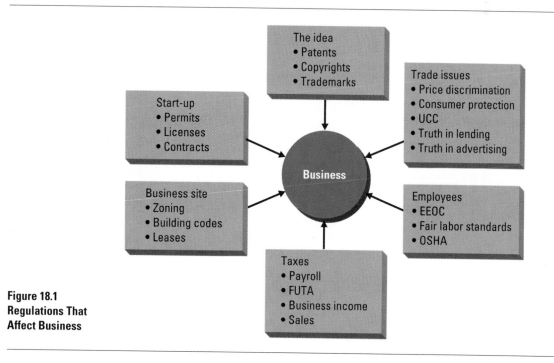

**Figure 18.1
Regulations That
Affect Business**

whether or not an invention or a design can be protected by intellectual property rights, and whether a symbol or logo that represents the business can be trademarked so no one else can use it. These legal protections can give the business a significant competitive advantage. Intellectual property rights were discussed in Chapters 7 and 17.

Contract Law

Whether or not you must deal with intellectual property rights, in all likelihood you will enter into several contracts before the business is up and running. These may include agreements with suppliers, a lease for the business site, a partnership agreement, independent contractor agreements, employment contracts, and so forth. If you have established a relationship with a business attorney, he or she will probably be able to create standard contract forms, reflecting the specific needs of your business, that can be used over and over again in similar situations. But when you are presented with a contract created by a third party (your supplier's attorney, for example), you should ask your attorney to review the document to make sure you are protected and are not agreeing to something that could ultimately harm your business. In general, contracts should be drawn in such a way as to be legally binding, so that you will have legal remedies should the other party not comply with the terms of the contract.

For a contract to be legally binding, there must be an **agreement**, which is an offer or a promise to do something or refrain from doing something.

Profile 18.2

Sub Pop Learns the Hard Way

Breaking into the multibillion-dollar recording industry as an independent label is no easy trick. But that didn't stop transplanted Midwesterners Bruce Pavitt and Jonathan Poneman from starting an independent recording company in Seattle known as Sub Pop, which featured local rock groups. Their first production, an album by a group called Soundgarden, was marginally successful. A year later Soundgarden left Sub Pop to sign with A & M Records and produce Badmotorfinger, a record that sold over 900,000 copies. Unfortunately, Sub Pop didn't receive a dime because it had never had a contract with Soundgarden.

Sub Pop quickly learned that they needed to have tough contracts that would make it difficult for a group to leave the recording company without paying something. Fortunately, Pavitt and Poneman learned that lesson early. Then another of Sub Pop's groups, Nirvana, went on to sign with David Geffen's DGC label. Because of the contract with Sub Pop, DGC had to pay a royalty of over two percent to Sub Pop on Nirvana's future record sales. Nirvana's Nevermind album alone brought over $1 million in royalties to Sub Pop, which also owns the rights to songs that Nirvana recorded before leaving. Having a valid contract in the beginning was a valuable lesson!

Source: (http://www.subpop.com) 1997.

For example, a vendor may offer to sell you a copy machine, which constitutes an offer to do something. For the agreement to be valid, however, there must also be **consideration**, which is your promise to supply or give up something in return—a check or purchase order, for example. Furthermore, the parties to the contract must have **capacity**; that is, they must be legally able to enter into a contract. Contracts cannot be entered into legally by intoxicated persons, persons who are not of sound mind, or minors. If these people do enter into an agreement, the contract may be contested and ruled to be void, as never having existed.

A lawyer's time is normally very expensive, but lawsuits can be devastating to a growing business, not to mention time-consuming. It may be possible, however, to save money by taking advantage of some of the new self-help legal software and books available. While they should not be used as a substitute for sound legal advice on complex issues, they are excellent for basic legal issues such as simple agreements. Both software and books usually provide standard forms with blanks to fill in. Some interactive programs even guide the entrepreneur through a series of questions that lead to a customized document. When using these programs, be aware that the deletion or addition of even one word can change the meaning of a sentence—with potentially disastrous consequences.

Agency Law and Small-Business Strategy

Agency law can have a significant impact on a company's competitive strategy. Employees are the agents of the company, so the company is responsible for any damages or injury an employee causes while doing the work of the company. Even a temporary worker or a delivery person can be an implied agent of the company. Domino's Pizza found that out when one of their drivers ran a red light and hit a woman in another car. A jury awarded the victim $750,000 in actual damages and $78 million in punitive damages.[2] As a result, Domino's no longer guarantees 30-minute delivery, which once was a significant aspect of its competitive strategy.

There are several types of agency authority that business owners should be familiar with.

▶ **Express Authority.** The company actually authorizes the agent to act for the company.

▶ **Incidental Authority.** The agent is given the authority to perform acts or carry out duties related to his or her job with the company.

▶ **Implied Authority.** The agent has authority based on his or her job or previous responsibilities. For example, the buyer for a retail store has the implied authority to purchase from the established list of suppliers.

▶ *Emergency Authority.* The agent has the authority to enter into contracts for the purpose of handling an emergency situation.

▶ *Apparent Authority.* The conduct of the company toward the agent implies that the agent has the authority to act for the company.

▶ **Ostensible Authority.** The company permits an agent to represent to a third party that he or she has the authority to act on behalf of the company.

In all the foregoing instances, the actions and contracts of the agent bind the company. Therefore, it is important to be clear with employees and subcontractors as to their agency relationship with the company.

Choosing a Business Site

When considering a place to locate the new business, you can't just go anywhere that seems appropriate to you. Cities and counties have laws restricting businesses from locating in areas designated for residential dwellings, agricultural development, and open land. Within areas designated for businesses, there are even more regulations, called **zoning laws**, that dictate what type of business can operate at a certain location. In general, business zoning laws fall into four categories: commercial, office/professional, light industrial, and heavy industrial. Commercial zoning includes retail stores, restaurants, and supermarkets. Office zoning permits general office uses plus some banking/financial, but no manufacturing. Light industrial zoning allows for distribution and warehousing, while heavy industrial includes major manufacturing and assembling of products. In general, as you move from commercial zoning to heavy industrial, the cost per square foot of the land declines. Consequently, manufacturing facilities that normally require considerably more square footage of buildable space enjoy less expensive land and rent costs. This is because as you move from commercial to industrial zoning, the importance of the specific location for business success decreases. Therefore, you are more likely to find commercial zoning, rather than industrial, in the vicinity of residential zoning. You can learn more about city and county zoning ordinances from the planning department or building and safety department of the city in which the business will be located. Unincorporated areas normally have their own county planning department.

The business has to abide not only by zoning ordinances, but also by building codes. Whether you build the facility or buy an existing facility, you have to ensure that the building meets local and state building standards. Such things as structural codes for earthquake safety, fire codes, and electrical codes are all mandated by these standards. If you are building, you should hire an experienced, licensed general contractor who will see that all requirements and inspections are met. If you are buying an existing building, you can hire a professional contractor or inspector to verify that the building meets all codes. If you are renting, make sure the landlord can provide proof that the building meets all code requirements, so that you won't face having to move if a building inspector condemns the building after your business is already there.

Most municipalities require that a business have a license to operate within the limits of the city or town. If the business is located within the unincorporated areas of a county, it may also be required to obtain a license. License requirements vary from city to city, but you can find out your city's requirements by going to the business license division, usually located in the city hall or planning department. Depending on the nature of the business, you may also be required to hold a permit, which can be obtained at the same location as the license. Some typical permits that may be required are building, health, electrical, fire, and sign permits.

More recent environmental regulations affect the choice of site. Most states have environmental quality regulations that protect against businesses emitting pollutants into the ground, air, or water. They also define who can handle toxic wastes and how they must be disposed of. Check with local government agencies to determine if any permits are required for your business (this is normally for manufacturing or extraction businesses). Also contact federal and state agencies like the Environmental Protection Agency, the Office of Health and Emergency Planning, and the Occupational Safety and Health Administration **(OSHA)** for information. Some states, such as California, have Environmental Business Resources Assistance Centers that provide access to the latest environmental regulatory compliance resources for small and medium-sized businesses by phone, fax, or electronic bulletin board as well as through a personal visit to the center.

Hiring Employees

Several laws exist related to hiring, firing, and compensating employees, so the entrepreneur must be aware of his or her obligations under the law before hiring anyone, to avoid future problems. An employer's obligation begins with the language used in advertising for positions in the company and extends to the interviews conducted with potential hires. The Equal Employment Opportunity Commission (EEOC) is charged with protecting the rights of employees. It mandates that you cannot refuse to hire someone on the basis of age, race, national origin, religion, gender, or physical challenge. The only time sex or race can be a valid consideration for a job is when it is a bona fide occupational qualification: for example, an acting job calling for an Asian male over the age of 40. This also means that written job descriptions must be accurate and defensible and contain clear language that differentiates essential tasks of the job from nonessential ones. It is only on the basis of the essential tasks that you can seek someone who is of a certain gender, who has no physical disability, or who can speak a certain foreign language.

If you have written a good ad, you will probably receive several résumés. When jobs are generally more difficult to find, applicants are likely to embellish their résumés somewhat to be more competitive in the marketplace. You, however, must protect yourself against hiring someone whom you may later have to fire, because firing someone is no longer as easy as it used to be. The laws protecting the employee, combined with a litigious society in general, create a very delicate situation for any employer attempting to fire an employee.

Tips for Looking at Résumés and Selecting a Qualified Candidate

1. Don't feel that just because the person has experience in only one arena, he or she is not qualified to do what you want done. Look for core skills like writing, speaking, organizing, leading, and so forth. These basic abilities can be put to use in a variety of scenarios.

2. Consider promoting from within—training current employees so that they can move up when the time comes.

3. Look for people with successful experience in the general field in which you are interested.

4. Look for people who have successfully worked in teams.

5. Look for demonstrable success, not just statements like "I was a successful salesperson for ABC," but rather statements like "Over the past five years I have increased my sales volume by 20 percent per year."

6. Look for people who have stayed with a company for a reasonable length of time.

It is, therefore, probably dangerous to take any résumé at face value. A few phone calls to references can give you a sense of the veracity of the résumé.

At the interview stage, certain questions are not permitted by the EEOC. These include questions about

- Health
- Disabilities (You may ask, "Do you have any conditions that would preclude your doing this job?")
- Age (to protect those under 21 and over 40)
- Medical history
- Living arrangements
- Religious preference
- Type of military discharge
- Pregnancy plans
- Arrest record (You may ask: "Have you ever been convicted of a felony crime?")
- Ancestry

What if You Fail to Fire an Employee?

Did you know that you can be sued not only if you fire an employee improperly, but also if you fail to fire an employee? That unusual situation occurs when an employee presents a particular hazard to other employees, and you are seen as negligent for allowing him or her to remain on the job. Here's what you should do to limit your liability.

1. Screen potential employees very carefully and check all references.

2. Watch for signs of stress, fatigue, mental illness, carelessness, aggressive behavior, and drug or alcohol use.

3. Thoroughly investigate complaints of employee misconduct.

4. Be cautious as to what you say to prospective employers about the fired employee and his or her dangerous propensity. You must walk a fine line between disclosing a potentially dangerous situation to that employer and protecting the rights of the fired employee. It's always wise in these types of situations to consult an attorney specializing in labor law.

In general, the rule is to keep all questions related to the job requirements, including skills, experience, and attitudes. One last point on this issue: It is illegal to request a photo with a job application or résumé unless the job is specifically known to be predicated on appearance, such as a modeling job.

Wage and Hour Laws

Consider the following situation: You hire an employee on salary. The employee asks if she can stay an hour late each day so that she can catch a ride home with a co-worker. A year later you fire her, and she files a federal wage-and-hour claim for back pay for the extra hour each day she spent during the year. It is likely she will win her claim. Why? Because even salaried employees are entitled to protection under the Department of Labor's Fair Labor Standards Act, which establishes minimum wage. There are a disproportionately large number of claims against small businesses, as opposed to those against large organizations. This is because small businesses rarely have personnel departments whose responsibility is to make sure the hiring and firing of employees is handled correctly so as to avoid claims.

In general, four types of job categories are exempt from minimum wage and hour laws: executive, administrative, professional, and outside sales. This is true, however, only if strict guidelines are followed. Here are the Department of Labor's basic criteria for establishing an employee as exempt:

▶ Does the employee receive a salary?

▶ Does the employee make more than $250 a week?

▶ Does the employee perform managerial duties over a unit at least 50 percent of the time?

As there are so many regulations designed to protect employees, every new business owner should become aware of federal and state laws regarding employees' hiring, firing, and working conditions. If you do not comply, you could find yourself being sued by the Department of Labor for back pay and liquidated damages, as well as attorneys' fees and costs of litigation. Some of the key laws are discussed in this chapter.

Occupation Health and Safety

Nothing strikes fear into the heart of a business owner like **workers' compensation**. Workers' compensation insurance is a no-fault system under which workers receive guaranteed compensation for injury at work and employers are protected from unlimited liability by covering the cost of the premiums. Nevertheless, the cost of worker accidents and false claims has threatened the life of many businesses. To further exacerbate the situation, premium rates, which are based on the type of business you are in and your accident history, vary from state to state, resulting in some states' having a competitive advantage over others in certain industries. Among the fastest growing and most vexing claims are those for repetitive motion injury (such as carpal tunnel syndrome) and stress-related disabilities. In 1994, companies with 11 to 49 employees reported an average of 8.4 injuries per 100 workers, two-thirds of which were repetitive-motion and stress injuries. The annual cost of these injuries is $150 billion.[3]

The high cost of workers' compensation premiums has led many small businesses to join consortiums to self-insure. While this is a complex process, there are many consultants who are able to help businesses through it. In some instances, trade associations have formed a consortium to self-insure businesses that are in the same industry and facing the same potential injury claims. Fortunately, a business can control its costs through active accident prevention and education programs. The issue of safe and healthy work environments is the purview of the Occupational Safety and Health Act of 1970 and its administrative unit, OSHA. OSHA requires that employers eliminate hazardous areas in the workplace and maintain health and safety records on all employees. OSHA inspectors regularly target businesses that have certain hazards inherent in the nature of the business, such as asbestos, and conduct rigorous inspections, liberally dispensing fines and penalties where violations have occurred (the basic fine is $7,000). All employers in all industries regardless of size must be in compliance with OSHA standards. The only exceptions are self-employed persons and farmers who employ only immediate family members. If you employ more than 11 people, you're required to maintain specific records of all occupational injuries and illnesses when they occur unless you're in retail, real estate, finance, insurance, or service industries.

Before the new business is faced with an OSHA audit, call OSHA and ask to receive some of their helpful pamphlets (see Additional Sources of Information) or ask an OSHA consultant to conduct a free, confidential, on-site test of your business and give you compliance advice. Also, local colleges usually offer seminars in safety management.

Several tips will help you avoid high premiums and the stress of OSHA audits.

▶ Develop a safety program.

▶ Increase job satisfaction. Happy employees translate into fewer claims.

▶ Pay premiums only on straight time (not overtime or vacation time).

▶ Check the rate categories for all employees carefully.

▶ Pay the smaller claims yourself.

▶ If your company has a higher safety record than average, ask for a discount in premium.

▶ Check your insurance records carefully, especially for claims from people who don't currently work for you or haven't for a long period of time.

▶ Shop around for the best rates and don't be afraid to change agents in midstream.

▶ Take care of injuries quickly.

▶ Help employees understand that high premiums mean lower profits, and therefore less money in their pockets.

Profile 18.3

Taking Care of Workers' Comp

After Portland Glass, a retail glass-installation company, instituted a five-year safety program at its Westbrook, Maine, plant, the $40 million company received a $395,000 refund on its workers' compensation premiums. The reason the company was so successful in reducing its premiums was a well-thought-out strategy to make safety part of the company culture. Here are five tips that can help reduce an entrepreneur's liability.

1. Talk about safety frequently. Dale Malcolm of Portland Glass starts every meeting with a discussion of safety.

2. Look at injuries by product category to spot potentially dangerous trends. For example, Malcolm was able to reduce auto-glass–related injuries by two-thirds by investing in special power tools and retraining employees to avoid repetitive motion injuries.

3. Have injured employees return to work quickly, to do tasks that don't aggravate their injuries. This reduces lost workdays, which in turn reduces premiums.

4. Maintain contact with injured employees to get them back to work as quickly as possible, assuming medical approval.

5. Make sure you're using the right incentives to get people to work more safely. Malcolm learned that cash incentives encouraged employees *not* to report their injuries, which could potentially lead to more serious injuries.

SOURCE: Donna Fenn, "Workers' Compensation: Safety Programs Pay Off," *Inc.,* May 1996, p. 114.

The Americans with Disabilities Act

In July of 1992 the Americans with Disabilities Act (ADA) became law and represented the most sweeping employment reform in over thirty years. Essentially, the ADA prohibits discrimination against anyone with a physical or mental impairment or disability that substantially limits one or more life activities like walking, seeing, or hearing. Other disabilities specifically mentioned in the law are diabetes, cancer, AIDS, arthritis, epilepsy, and emotional illness. The law also protects those who have had drug and alcohol dependencies in the past but have undergone treatment. It does not, however, protect those who are dependent at the time when they apply for a job. The candidate, in any case of disability, must qualify for the job in terms of skills and experience in the first place. Of the estimated 45 million Americans with disabilities, approximately 15 million are of working age.

The law applies to businesses with fifteen or more employees. For those businesses that deal with the public, the public-access provisions provide that restaurants, theaters, stores, and the like must modify their facilities to provide access to people with disabilities as long as the modification doesn't create an undue hardship on the business. These modifications might include entry ramps, Braille control panels on elevators, or wider aisles to accommodate wheelchairs. The public-access rules fall under the purview of the Department of Justice, while the employment rules are regulated by the EEOC. As the law is stated in broad terms such as "undue burden" and "reasonable accommodations," many business owners are concerned that this ambiguity translates into more litigation for them. The laws related to disability will continue to evolve over time, so it is important that the entrepreneur maintain an awareness of the status of the ADA.

Sexual Harassment

The rulings regarding unwanted attention and harassment on the job began to get very tough in the 1980s. The courts have expanded the definition of sexual harassment, and businesses are now developing policies in an effort to ward off embarrassing and expensive lawsuits. In its first ruling on the subject, the Supreme Court held that sexual harassment violates Title VII of the 1964 Civil Rights Act when the act is unwelcome and represents an abuse of power in the workplace. Generally, harassment can be divided into two categories: *quid pro quo,* where advancement on the job or a raise is conditional on certain sexual favors, and hostile working environment cases, where the employee is subjected to a sexually offensive environment against his or her will. Harassment includes but is not limited to verbal and nonverbal assaults of a sexual nature, and physical harassment. As a result, business owners should establish policies that educate employees and make clear to them what conduct is not acceptable in the workplace. In doing so, entrepreneurs can solicit guidance from the EEOC.

Trade Issues

In the United States great value is placed on the free marketplace, and generally any attempts by government to interfere in the free market process are shunned. Nevertheless, since the 1800s the government has imposed certain laws specifically designed to preserve competition and the free market. The **Sherman Antitrust Act** of 1890, one of the first, prohibited any restraint of free trade. Other regulations followed, and they are discussed in several categories.

Price Discrimination

The Clayton Act of 1914 and the even stricter Robinson-Patman Act of 1936, enforced by the Federal Trade Commission, assert that businesses cannot sell the same product to different customers at different prices without justification. In other words, they must demonstrate that the lower price was based on a quantity-sold discount, quality of the product (seconds or slightly damaged), or a cost savings on the part of the seller (the manufacturer discounted the product to the retailer beyond the normal purchase price). Therefore, the entrepreneur must be careful to be fair to all customers when setting prices.

Consumer Protection

The greatest number of laws affecting trade come under the heading of consumer protection. They include:

▶ Unscrupulous sellers

▶ Unreasonable credit terms

▶ Unsafe products

▶ Mislabeling of products

One of the largest federal agencies monitoring product safety is the Food and Drug Administration (FDA), which is responsible for research, new-product testing, and inspection of the operations of food and drug manufacturers. If your new product is a cosmetic, a drug, a food item, or anything applied to the skin, like suntan lotion, you will need FDA approval before marketing the product.

The Consumer Product Safety Commission was established in 1972 as the watchdog for consumers over products considered hazardous. Additionally, it is charged with setting standards for such things as toys for children under the age of five. If your product falls into one of these categories, you will need to be aware of the standards and requirements for marketing and producing that product.

The Fair Packaging and Labeling Act was designed to provide consumers with information so they could shop more wisely. The act mandates that manufacturers truthfully list all raw materials used in the production of the product on a clearly marked label. This is in addition to the size and weight of the packaging. If your product is a food product, the percentages of nutrients, vitamins, carbohydrates, calories, and fat contained in one normal-sized serving of the product must be displayed. By becoming aware of the regulations affecting products manufactured for public consumption, you can avoid both the possible recall of your product and potential lawsuits.

The Uniform Commercial Code

The **Uniform Commercial Code** (UCC) is a group of laws that affects everything from bank deposits and investment securities to sales. It is this latter category that impacts the entrepreneur. Any time you enter into an agreement to sell a product, you create a contract governed by the laws of contract. However, if you are a merchant, you must also abide by the laws of the UCC, which can be different. To use a simple example, suppose you have ordered some supplies from a manufacturer under a contract that contains the terms of place, delivery date, and quantity, but you have failed to ask the price. The supplies arrive and the price is higher than expected. The regulations of the UCC state that a price that is reasonable at the time of delivery should be applied, based on the fact that both you and the manufacturer are professionals who understand how the business operates. You can't claim lack of knowledge the way a layperson can; you are presumed to know the rules of the game since you are in business.

The UCC also deals with product liability issues. Historically, the philosophy of the marketplace in the United States has been *caveat emptor,* "let the buyer beware." In modern times, the burden of that philosophy has shifted to "let the seller beware," as consumer groups and advocates like Ralph Nader have forced businesses to take responsibility for the quality and safety of what they produce. Whenever you sell goods, you also sell a warrant of merchantability, which is an implied warranty that the product is of at least average quality and suitable for the purpose for which it was intended. Consequently, the shift in the burden of responsibility has resulted in numerous lawsuits by consumers and higher premiums for product liability insurance. For example, it is estimated that about 25 percent of the cost of a football helmet pays for product liability insurance. Any entrepreneur who intends to manufacture and sell a consumer product should be careful to include clear instructions on its use and warnings about the consequences of misuse.

Consumer Credit

Like consumer protection laws, the laws regulating consumer lending are pervasive in an effort to protect consumer rights. The Equal Credit Opportunity Act (ECOA) provides for fair and equitable treatment of all borrowers without regard for marital status, source of income, race, color, or national origin. It also requires prompt disclosure of the reasons for any denial of credit. It applies to all banks, credit unions, retailers, and business creditors. Before any credit granting can be completed, the Truth-in-Lending Act (**Regulation Z**) mandates detailed disclosures concerning the cost of credit. It also requires disclosures on the method of billing on open-ended contracts, personal property leases, and credit card accounts, as well as the number and amount of payments required, and the type of collateral given to secure the loan. It applies to anyone who regularly extends credit, imposes a finance charge, or permits an obligation to be repaid over more than four installments.

The Fair Credit Billing Act (FCBA) provides procedures for dispute resolution, and the Fair Credit Reporting Act (FCRA) mandates standards for reporting information on credit recipients to credit reporting agencies. If you intend to grant credit to your customers, you must make yourself aware of all of the applicable regulations. The bottom line is: merchant lender beware!

Truth in Advertising

The **Federal Trade Commission** is charged with protecting the rights of consumers against false or misleading advertising. It has come down hard on many businesses for misleading customers about what a product can do, offering a reduced (sale) price on an item that was never advertised at a higher price, using list price as a comparison if the business has never sold the item at list, and using **bait-and-switch** techniques to lure customers into the store only to switch them to a higher-priced item.

Taxes

As a business owner, you are legally responsible for paying certain taxes in a timely fashion. Since no one wants to pay more taxes than required, business owners must understand which transactions qualify as tax-free and what the tax consequences are of any transaction. For example, a $2,000 transaction is worth $2,000 to the business if it is tax-free; however, if it is taxable, it may be worth only $1,400—a sizable difference. In general, the following are tax-free receipts:

▸ Compensation from accident and health plans for injuries or illness and life insurance benefits

▸ Contributions by the employer to a qualified accident and health plan

▸ Workers' compensation benefits

▸ Meals and lodging provided for the convenience of the employer, as on business trips

Which Taxes Bother Entrepreneurs Most?

Comprehensive Business Services, a national accounting and financial-services franchise, did a study in 1995 of 400 small businesses with revenues ranging from $100,000 to $1 million to find out what these businesses' key financial concerns were. Although those doing the study expected to find searching for funding at the top of the list, the following, in rank order, were these businesses' concerns.

Insurance	73%
Federal taxes	71%
State and local taxes	59%
Coping with current economic climate	55%
Workers' compensation	53%
Current interest rates	38%
Obtaining funds	36%
Accounting systems and requirements	32%

SOURCE: Reprinted with permission of *Inc.* magazine, Goldhirsh Group, Inc., 38 Commercial Wharf, Boston, MA 02110 (http://www.inc.com). *What Taxes Bother Entrepreneurs Most,* Jill Andresky Fraser, adapted from February 1996 issue, p. 104. Reproduced by permission of the publisher via Copyright Clearance Center, Inc.

◗ Interest on municipal bonds.

◗ Income from the discharge of indebtedness if the taxpayer is insolvent or bankrupt

Beyond these items, most business transactions are taxable.

Payroll Taxes

One of the payroll taxes you will deduct from an employee's paycheck is **FICA** (social security tax) and Medicare taxes. The deduction is based on a percentage of the employee's income and as of 1997 was 15.3 percent of an employee's wage divided between employer and employee on income of up to $62,700 (includes 2.9% divided between employer and employee for Medicare). Above the $62,700, the employer must withhold another 2.9 percent divided equally between employer and employee for Medicare taxes. The employer also pays federal unemployment taxes (FUTA) for the Federal Unemployment Tax Act equal to 6.2 percent of the first $7,000 of each employee's wages. Any state unemployment tax rate you pay is subtracted from the 6.2 percent federal rate up to 5.4 percent. State and federal income taxes must also be withheld according to the current tax law and the employee's

W-4 form. This amount is a percentage of taxable gross pay after allowable deductions. It is clear that it costs more to employ a person than the mere face value of the paycheck.

In some states you may be required to pay state disability insurance. In California, for example, this amounts to 1.3% on wages not to exceed $31,767.00 and is paid by the employee.

If your business accumulates $100,000 or more of FICA and federal income tax withholdings during any pay period, you are required to deposit that amount in an approved depository by the close of the next business day or face a penalty of 2 to 15 percent of the amount. Consequently, it is very important to monitor payroll taxes carefully, particularly if you have a labor-intensive business. Don't assume that all banks have the same rules for date-of-deposit. You should deposit withholding tax either on the same day you pay employees or by the end of the bank's next business day, and deposit in a commercial bank rather than a Federal Reserve bank, which always credits deposits to the next day. A one-day error could cost your business a lot of money.

Sales and Use Taxes

Regardless of the legal form of the business, anyone who sells tangible products or services is required to collect sales tax. A **use tax** is collected from the purchaser if a sales tax has not been paid and is equivalent in amount to the sales tax. Local jurisdictions may tax occupancy, personal property, real estate property, stock transfer, real estate transfer, and alcoholic beverages, to name a few. As local governments look for additional sources of revenues, they often find them in the business community. State laws regarding sales and use taxes vary considerably, however, so the entrepreneur should discuss the business's obligations with the appropriate state authority.

Business Income Tax

The business itself must pay federal, state, or local taxes on income it earns as well, depending on the legal form of the business. A sole proprietor or a partner in a partnership pays these taxes one time as personal income from the business. If you are a self-employed business owner, you also pay an FICA tax of 15.3 percent, double that of an employee because you are both the employer and the employee. A corporation, on the other hand, pays a corporate income tax. If you receive a salary from your corporation, you also pay a personal income tax on it.

The number of regulations, taxes, and laws affecting a new business can be daunting, so you do need to consult a good attorney and accountant. In most cases, particularly in those involving the IRS, the penalties for failure to pay or failure to follow the rules are severe. Many a new business owner has discovered this too late. You must prepare in advance for the start of the business by understanding your obligations and planning to meet them.

New Venture Checklist

Have you:

❑ **Identified the types of laws and regulations that will impact your particular type of business?**

❑ **Protected aspects of your business concept that fall into the intellectual property rights categories?**

❑ **Found an attorney who can review any contracts you plan to enter into?**

❑ **Written clear and legally defensible job descriptions?**

❑ **Identified all the taxes for which you are responsible and set up a plan for meeting payment deadlines?**

Issues to Consider

1. How will you know when you have a legally binding agreement?
2. What is the purpose of zoning laws?
3. What does the Truth-in-Lending Act require of businesses, and which businesses are affected by it?
4. Which laws is the Equal Opportunity Commission charged with regulating?
5. You are about to interview a candidate for a position as bookkeeper for your business. What are some questions you can ask, and what cannot be asked of this candidate?

Experiencing Entrepreneurship

1. Interview an entrepreneur in the restaurant business and develop a list of all the laws and regulations the business must adhere to.
2. Spend an hour with a payroll clerk at a local business to find out what it actually costs to hire an employee.

Additional Sources of Information

All About OSHA and OSHA Inspections. Call OSHA: Tel. (202) 219-4667.

Job Accommodation Network, P.O. Box 6123, 809 Allen Hall, WVU, Morgantown, WV 26506-6123. Tel. (800) 232-9675.

The OSHA Handbook for Small Businesses. Tel. (202) 783-3238.

Priz, E.J. (1995) *CompControl: The Secrets of Reducing Workers' Compensation Costs.* Grants Pass, OR: Oasis Press/PSI.

U.S. Equal Employment Opportunity Commission, 1801 L Street, NW, Washington, DC 20507. ADA Helpline: Tel. (800) 669-EEOC.

What Businesses Must Know About the Americans with Disabilities Act. U.S. Chamber of Commerce. Tel. (800) 638-6582. Ask for publication No. 0320.

Internet Resources

Environmental Protection Agency
http://www.epa.gov
Much information about the EPA and its regulations.

Federal Trade Commission
http://www.ftc.gov
A large amount of information about the commission itself and the laws and regulations it administers. Good links to other business-oriented sites.

The Federal Web Locator
http://www.law.vill.edu/fedagency
Need to find government information but not sure of an agency's name or what it does? This site will help you get that information in a hurry.

FedWorld Information Network
http://www.fedworld.gov
A one-stop center for obtaining government publications and other information.

GovCon
http://www.govcon.com
This site offers free access to the Commerce Business Daily and information about an abundance of government rules and regulations.

Internal Revenue Service—The Digital Daily
http://www.irs.ustreas.gov/prod
A surprisingly flashy site, full of free information about the IRS and tax-related issues.

Patent and Trademark Office
http://www.uspto.gov
Search the patent office's database. Many links to other sites of interest.

Relevant Case Studies

1. Mrs. Gooch's Natural Food Markets
2. OXO (A)
3. Autopsies-to-Go

19

We know not yet what we have done, still less what we are doing. Wait till evening and other parts of our day's work will shine than we had thought at noon, and we shall discover the real purport of our toil.
Henry D. Thoreau

Planning for Change

Overview

▶ **The contingency plan**

▶ **The harvest plan**

▶ **Bankruptcy**

Terms to Know

Profile 19.1

Sometimes You Can't "Un-du" It

One way to get attention at a trade show with 2,000 other booths is by creating a little magic. That's what Doumar Products Inc. did at the International Housewares Show in January 1998. Mark Foley, the company's marketing director, wowed the audience by using Doumar's product *un-du* to separate duct tape from single-ply toilet paper without doing any damage to either. As if that hadn't been enough, he went on to show the audience that after a few seconds, the duct tape became sticky again.

This was not Doumar's first trade show. Actually, the company had spent the past two years in market tests, trade shows, and appearances on QVC's home shopping program and was just beginning to see some commercial success.

Doumar was founded in 1995 by a former salesman, Mark Foley (with experience in the unlikely combination of liquor, apparel, chocolate, and medical sales), and a real estate agent, Douglas Farley. It was Foley's father Charles who invented un-du. With $6,000 of start-up money, Foley and Farley started Doumar and acquired the right to distribute un-du for a period of two years. They soon realized they needed more money. A lawyer who had helped them incorporate introduced them to a Mr. Reichling, who, despite the holes he saw in the business plan, agreed to invest $75,000 in 1996 with the agreement that Doumar would acquire permanent distribution rights for un-du.

As the founders set up their network of sales reps and did the trade show route, 1996 was a busy year. In June of that year they won the "best new product" award at the Business Product Industry Association show, and later that year Reichling became the CEO. Their first year ended with $38,000 in revenues and $400,000 in expenses. The second year brought sales of $800,000 but more investment in facilities, equipment, and employees.

The founders had a sense of relief when they managed to acquire a few nation-wide retailers like Walgreen's and Staples. But that relief was short-lived; they learned that these major retailers paid in 90 days. Doumar's own suppliers were requiring payment in 60 days.

Then came the biggest challenge to date: they discovered that the Magic American Corporation, a Cleveland-based producer of specialty cleaners with $30 million in revenues, had asked the Consumer Product Safety Commission to investigate Doumar's labeling of its flammable product. Although no evidence of wrongdoing was found, the situation distracted the founders from their work. And as if to add insult to injury, Magic American announced that it would be offering a lower-priced version of un-du under the very popular GooGone brand name. When Magic American's product came out, Doumar was discouraged to find that the packaging resembled that of un-du but was different enough that Doumar had no cause for legal action. Even though the product did not have some of the benefits of un-du, Doumar now had to mount a national campaign for name recognition of its own product. Once Doumar did achieve a strong brand name, it could add other, "me-too," products and be more attractive to the big discounters like Wal-Mart and Home Depot.

SOURCE: Barnaby J. Feder, "Good Product, Sound Plans, No Sure Thing," *New York Times,* January 18, 1998.

How did Doumar handle change in its environment? What would you advise that they do to establish their brand name in the face of competition from a bigger company?

There is no crystal ball that will tell an entrepreneur what the future holds for the new venture. Many entrepreneurs have started a business with a plan in mind for where that business would go, but things changed along the way. Forces beyond the control of the entrepreneur forced the venture into new directions, and a new set of plans had to be constructed. It is a sad fact that most entrepreneurs with growing ventures do not have time for contingency planning; they are just too busy keeping the business alive. But planning is essential. In the absence of planning, the business puts itself in a reactionary mode, virtually at the whim of the environment in which it operates. Instead of dealing from a position of strength, entrepreneurs may find themselves reacting in panic and without information to situations for which they are not prepared. As a result, the quality of decision making is reduced and the business suffers.

This chapter will look at the contingency plan, alternatives for harvesting the wealth of your venture, and alternatives should your venture fail.

The Contingency Plan

By forcing entrepreneurs to consider multiple outcomes and possibilities, contingency plans help a growing business deal with the ubiquitous downturns and upturns in the economy, new regulations, changes in customer tastes and preferences, and many other events that regularly, and often without much warning, disrupt the equilibrium of the business. For example, the reason many businesses fail during a recession is that they haven't prepared for it by forecasting the potential impact on demand when signs of a recession appear and calculating how they can adjust and still maintain a positive cash position.

Recessions do not happen overnight. There are signs, even within specific industries, that signal a slowdown. Since the government began compiling indices on the economy after World War II, some consistent trends have appeared. For example, the **leading index**, which consists of such items as the Producer Price Index, the Consumer Confidence Index, and the Manufacturers' Orders for Durable Goods, typically declines for nine months prior to the onset of a recession. The coincident-lagging index, which is a ratio of the **coincident index** (employment, personal income, industrial production) to the **lagging index** (Consumer Price Index, interest rates, unemployment), declines for 13 months prior to the onset of a recession.

Being able to recognize the signs of recession before they impact the business gives the entrepreneur the chance to prepare in many ways, including maintaining a higher degree of liquidity. In recessionary times it is more difficult to raise capital from either bankers or private sources, so being liquid allows the entrepreneur to take advantage of opportunities that become available only during recessions. For example, the entrepreneur may be able to purchase a building that in good economic times was beyond reach, or he or she may be able to negotiate more favorable terms from suppliers just to keep the business moving forward.

Growing entrepreneurial ventures need to engage in both short- and long-range planning. Short-range planning involves setting quantitative goals for the coming year and developing a plan for achieving them. If a business does any planning, it is usually short-range. Long-range plans, by contrast, are based on the business's mission and focus on the direction the business will take, accounting for potential changes in the environment in which the business operates. It certainly is not possible to account for all contingencies, but there are some key crisis issues that seem to occur for all high-growth ventures.

Taxes and Regulations

Government regulations and regulatory paperwork are severe problems for growing ventures, and the cost of compliance is rising to the point that entrepreneurs are looking for a way to avoid coming under the purview of some of the regulations. The Family Leave Act now has a threshold of 50 employees, so many small businesses fight to stay below that number, because the lengthy loss of an employee in a small, growing company can impact operations severely.

The cost of hiring an employee is becoming so prohibitive that many companies are solving the problem by subcontracting work and leasing employees.

Take, the hypothetical example, a growing manufacturing company with fewer than 50 employees. On an hourly basis, per employee:

▶ Base pay is $11.

▶ Health coverage costs about $3 an hour.

▶ Social security, Medicare, and unemployment insurance are about $1.50.

▶ Workers' compensation is $1 for a total hourly cost of $16.50.

If you then factor in profit sharing, bonuses, and retirement plans, you can easily reach $20 an hour as the actual cost of hiring that employee. However, the government is cracking down on businesses that categorize people as independent contractors, so the IRS rules must be carefully followed. (See Chapter 4.)

Changes in the tax laws can place a significant burden on the business and the entrepreneur as well. The $135,000 ceiling on income subject to Medicare Tax was eliminated, which added several thousand dollars to a business's tax liability and to that of the entrepreneur in an S-corporation. Growth in state and local taxes in some states makes it more important than ever to search for states that place a smaller burden on business.

Product Liability

The chances are fairly good that if you manufacture a product, your company will at some point face a product liability suit. The states with the most industry naturally have the highest claims, with Pennsylvania, Ohio, Texas, and New York leading the list. More and more the risk of product-related injuries has been shifted to manufacturers, creating a legal minefield that could prove disastrous to a growing company.

The problem stems from the fact that even if the company carefully designs and manufactures a product, and covers it with warnings and detailed instructions, that company still is vulnerable to the misuse of and consequent injury from the product. For a company to be legally liable, the product must be defective and an injury must have occurred. But in a litigious society, those requirements don't stop people from suing. Most product liability insurance covers the costs of defense, personal injury, or property damage, but does not cover lost sales and the cost of product redesign. Moreover, if your insurance company must pay on a claim, your premiums will, no doubt, increase.

A growing company must plan for potential litigation from the very inception of the business. One proven method is to establish a formal safety panel that includes people from all the major functional areas of the business. During the start-up phase, that panel may consist of only the entrepreneur and one or two outside advisers with experience in the area. It is the job of the safety panel to review safety requirements on a regular basis, establish new ones when necessary, and document any injuries or claims made against the product. Prior to product introduction in the marketplace, the panel

Stalking the Millennium Bug

One millennium-bug prognosticator of doom has been touring the country warning business owners and non–business owners alike of the potential perils of the year 2000. He depicts a scenario, beginning at midnight of 1999, where cars will stop abruptly, banks will close, and telephone dial tones will disappear—and that's just the beginning. Computers, which have traditionally been programmed to read the last two digits of a year, will not know how to interpret the 00 in the year 2000. They may read it as 1900 or as nothing at all.

Because the world is linked via computer, which affects every aspect of our lives, no one is left untouched, from the CEO of Citibank to the farmer in the field. There are three approaches entrepreneurs will probably take to this pending catastrophe.

1. Do nothing and hope that some computer company will solve the problem with a software patch.

2. Stop making purchases around the year 2000.

3. Learn as much as they can about what to do to prepare for the change.

Naturally, the third scenario is the proactive approach. Entrepreneurs need to begin contacting everyone upstream and downstream in their industry to ask how *they* are dealing with the issue. Some large companies are foregoing some activities in favor of spending time and money on making sure their systems will work as planned when 2000 arrives. Small businesses that have accounts and dealings with larger companies need to confirm the larger company's commitment to them. The bottom line: entrepreneurs must prepare for any eventuality so that their business won't be adversely affected.

SOURCE: Leigh Buchanan, "Joined at the Chip," *Inc. Technology*, 4, 1997, p. 15.

should see that careful records of all decisions regarding final product design, testing, and evaluation procedures are maintained. Any advertising regarding the product should not contain exaggerated claims or implied promises that may give customers the impression that you are claiming more safety features than the product actually has. Implied promises can be used against you in a court of law. Instruction manuals should be easy to follow and should point out potential hazards. They should also include guidelines for when and how to service the product, which components made by other manufacturers are not covered by your warranty (unless **pass-through warranties** have been negotiated), and statements that the warranty is invalidated by misuse, misassembly, or modification, and is valid only if the specified maintenance procedures are followed. Of course, the best insurance is to keep in contact with your customers so that if a problem occurs, you will be given the opportunity to fix it before legal action is taken.

Early on in the operation of the business, identify a qualified attorney familiar with your industry to handle any potential product liability claims. This attorney should handle the first case with which the business is faced. Thereafter, if other suits arise in various parts of the country, you can save money by hiring a "local attorney" in the jurisdiction of the claim. Then let the primary attorney brief the "local attorney" on the precedent-setting cases related to the claim and assist while the local attorney carries the case to court. In this way, you do not have to send your primary attorney on the road, incurring significant travel and time expenses.

Loss of Key Employees

Today more than ever before, no one can count on having the same management team over the life of the business—or even past the start-up phase. The demand for top-notch management personnel, particularly in some industries like high-tech, means that other companies will constantly be trying to woo away the best people from the best firms. Moreover, with more CEOs traveling, the chance of a fatal accident is greater. Then, too, disease and heart attack often claim the lives of high-powered executives. This type of contingency planning is often called succession planning and involves identifying people who can take over key company positions in an emergency. Ideally that person will come from within the company, but in the case of a growing entrepreneurial company that has been operating in a "lean and mean" mode, that may not be possible, so outsiders must be found. To prepare for the eventuality that a key employee will be lost, the entrepreneur must have shared his or her vision for the company with others both inside and outside the company. It's also a good idea to purchase **"key-person insurance"** to cover the cost of suddenly having to replace someone.

Bringing in a consultant to guide the management team in succession planning is a valuable exercise for any growing venture. Often consultants are even hired temporarily to take over a vacant position for a specified period of time during which they train a permanent successor. Another solution is to cross-train people in key positions so that someone can step in, at least for the short term, in the event of an emergency. Cross training is generally an integral part of a team-based approach to organizational management.

In the case of entrepreneurs who head family-owned companies, there are special problems because they tend to look to a son or daughter to succeed them. Unfortunately, often that child will have no interest in doing so but will not have said anything to that effect to the parent/entrepreneur. One solution is to insist that the potential "successor" work for another company for several years to gain some business savvy and learn whether he or she wants to take over the family business.

Decline in Sales

When sales decline and positive cash flow starts looking like a memory, entrepreneurs often go into a period of denial. They start paying their suppliers more slowly to preserve cash; they lay off people; they stop answering the phone and insulate themselves against the demands of their creditors. Their panic often causes them to make poor decisions about how to spend the precious cash they have. They figure that if they can just hold on long enough, things will turn around. Unfortunately, this attitude only makes the problem worse, effectively propelling the business toward its ultimate demise. How can an entrepreneur lose touch with the business and the market so much that he or she puts the business at risk? What often happens is that entrepreneurs get so tied up with the day-to-day operations of the business that they don't have time to contemplate the "big picture" or stay in tune with their customers. Consequently, all too often they don't see a potential crisis coming until it's too late.

When sales decline, the solution isn't necessarily to lower prices. If you have educated your customers about the value of your product or service,

Profile 19.2

Tradition Comes of Age

Most entrepreneurs accept change as a way of life; many look forward to it—even seek it—because they know that with change comes opportunity. Still, tradition has its place as well, so when change and tradition are juxtaposed, it makes for some exciting contrasts and can breathe new life into a potentially stagnant business. Such is the case with two very old, established, respected members of the New Orleans restaurant community that have decided that change is good. Antoine's Restaurant and Galatoire's Restaurant, both highly successful family businesses, have seen the New Orleans restaurant scene change dramatically over the past twenty years. Even fifteen years ago, there were only a handful of really first-rate restaurants with very high-profile chefs. Today the market has been home to the likes of celebrities Paul Prudhomme and Emeril Lagasse, among others. The market has changed; expectations are higher and competition fiercer.

All this forced Antoine's and Galatoire's to look at themselves with a critical eye. How could they enter the 21st century, yet maintain the traditions that their customers expected? One of the first things Antoine's did was set up as another communication medium a web site where they offer an online reservation sys-

tem. This might appear in striking contrast to their 157-year historical image. Although the owners have resisted modernizing the restaurant itself because they're afraid of destroying the mystique, using electronics to advertise seems to work.

Galatoire's also uses the Internet and e-mails menus to customers who request them. To improve marketing strategy, the restaurant hired a public relations firm. At its recommendation, Galatoire's began issuing personal charge cards to customers with accounts at the restaurant, and now tracks accounts via a computer database. Even the dress code has now been relaxed. And though a few customers have complained about seeing a computer in the dining room, most find the changes positive.

Both restaurants have realized that to keep your customers coming back in the face of changing market conditions, you have to keep up with the times—while at the same time maintaining the traditions that have come to be associated with your business.

Sources: Sarah P. Jones, "Restaurants Put Change on Menu," November 10, 1997, *Inc. Online Local Business News;* James Slaton, "Technology Mingles with Tradition in Two Bastions of Fine Dining," *New Orleans CityBusiness Online,* Vol. 18, Issue 18, p. 15.

they will be confused by the sudden discounting. When there is a decline in sales, it is especially important to look at all possible sources, not just the economy. You may have been lax about checking the credit status of customers and distributors, or the inventory turnover rate may have changed. You may have failed to notice an emerging competitor offering a product or service more in line with current tastes and preferences.

When a growing business first notices a dip in sales, it is time to find the cause and make the necessary changes. This will be easier if the business has a contingency plan in place. If, however, those changes cannot be made in time to forestall a cash flow problem, it is time to consult a debt negotiation company, a crisis management consultant, or a bankruptcy attorney who is willing to work through the problem outside of court. These experts can help the entrepreneur work with creditors until the problem is resolved. To make the best effort at avoiding a cash flow crisis, the entrepreneur must be continually committed to:

▶ Producing exceptional quality products

▶ Controlling the cost of overhead, particularly where that overhead does not contribute directly to revenue generation (i.e., expensive cars, travel, excessive commissions)

▶ Controlling production costs through subcontracting and being frugal about facilities

▶ Making liquidity and positive cash flow the prime directive, so that the company can ride out temporary periods of declining demand

▶ Having a contingency plan in place

The Harvest Plan

Many beginning entrepreneurs have questioned the need for an exit plan, or **harvest plan,** since they are more concerned with launching the business and making it a success. They find it difficult to think about how to get out of the business when they have barely gotten into it. While some entrepreneurs stay with their start-ups for the rest of their lives or their business' lives, the majority of entrepreneurs enjoy the challenge of start-up and the excitement of growth, and they abhor with a passion the custodial role of manager of a stable, mature company. Exiting the business does not necessarily mean exiting the role of entrepreneur. It may in fact mean taking the financial rewards of having grown a successful business and investing them in a new venture.

There are entrepreneurs who do that very thing over and over again throughout their lives. Other entrepreneurs find that when the venture reaches a certain level, the business needs professional management skills that the entrepreneur often does not possess. In fact, the entrepreneur may actually be holding the company back without realizing it. At some point the board of directors may relegate the entrepreneur to R&D or public relations, or they may actually push the entrepreneur out of the company, as Apple Computer did with Steve Jobs. In any case, whether or not you intend to exit the business, you should have a plan for harvesting the rewards of having started the business in the first place. There are several methods by which you can achieve a rewarding harvest.

Selling the Business

Selling the business outright to another company or an individual may be the goal if you are ready to move on to something else and want to be free financially and mentally to do so. Unfortunately, however, selling a business is a life-changing event. For several years, you have probably devoted the majority of your time and attention to growing the business, and it played an important role in structuring your life. When the business is sold, you may experience a sense of loss, much like the death of a loved one. If you have not prepared for this change in your life, serious emotional problems could be the consequence. There are several alternatives to selling the business outright that will be discussed in the next section. For now, let's just say that before selling the business, you should plan for what will happen after the business is no longer part of your life.

The best way to sell a business is to know almost from the beginning that selling is what you want to do. This is so that you will make decisions for the business that will place it in the best position for a sale several years later. For one thing, you will maintain audited financial statements that give the forecasts more credibility. The tax strategy will be not to minimize taxes by showing low profits, but to show actual profits and pay the taxes on them because you will probably more than make up for the expense at the time of sale. Higher recorded profits will likely help the business be worth more. You will keep the business expenses and activity totally separate from the personal expenses and ensure that the business has value without you by preparing a successor. You will also plan for the time it will take to sell the business and wait to sell until the window of opportunity has opened.

Smaller businesses often use the services of business brokers to sell the business; however, a high-growth venture will more likely employ the services of an investment banking firm that has experience with the industry. Investment banks normally want a retainer to ensure the seriousness of your commitment, but that retainer will be applied against the final fee on the sale, which averages five percent of the purchase price. It is recommended, however, that a third party, with no vested interest in the sale, be employed to judge the fair market value of the business. This "appraiser" can also prepare financial projections based on the history of the company and the appraiser's independent market research.

When a business is sold, the entrepreneur does not have to sell all the assets. For example, the building could be held out of the sale and leased back to the business purchaser, with the original owner staying on as landlord. While the potential purchaser is conducting due diligence on the entrepreneur and the business, the entrepreneur needs to do the same with the purchaser. The purchasing firm or individual should be thoroughly checked out against a list of criteria the entrepreneur has developed. The purchaser should have the resources necessary to continue the growth of the business, be familiar with the industry and the type of business being purchased, have a good reputation in the industry, and offer synergies that will ensure that the business continues in a positive direction. It is often helpful to make a complete list of criteria and then weight them by importance to fairly compare one potential buyer with another.

Cashing Out but Staying In

Sometimes entrepreneurs reach the point where they would like to take the bulk of their investment and gain out of the business but are not yet ready to cut the cord entirely. They may want to continue to run the business or at least retain a minority interest. There are several mechanisms by which this can occur.

Selling Stock

If the company is still privately owned, the remaining shareholders may want to purchase your stock at current market rates so that control doesn't end up in other hands. In fact, the shareholders' agreement that was drafted when you set up the corporation may have specified that you must first offer the stock to the company before offering it to anyone else. If the company is publicly traded, the task is much simpler; however, if you own a substantial portion of the issued stock, you must follow strict guidelines set out by the SEC in the liquidation of your interests. If the company had a successful IPO, the entrepreneur's founders' stock will have increased substantially in value, which presents a tax liability you should not ignore. That is why many entrepreneurs in such situations cash out only what they need to support whatever

---

Profile 19.3

Making a Graceful Exit

Entrepreneurs need to think of their companies as part of an ongoing career path. So says Jerome Katz, director of the Jefferson Smurfit Center for Entrepreneurial Studies in St. Louis. He has been studying the career paths of entrepreneurs and finds that there are four major types.

1. *Growth entrepreneurs.* These are entrepreneurs who measure their success by the size of their company. They tend not to have an exit plan because they're always striving for bigger, better, faster.

2. *Habitual entrepreneurs.* These are people who love to *start* businesses and may start and run several at once. They are probably even less likely to have an exit plan because there are always new opportunities out there.

3. *Harvest entrepreneurs.* These entrepreneurs start and build a venture for the purpose of selling it. Some of these types will start, build, and harvest many companies during a career.

4. *Spiral, or helical, entrepreneurs.* Women entrepreneurs often fall into this category. These entrepreneurs are driven by what is going on in their personal lives, so their entrepreneurial tendencies occur in spurts. At times they may appear stagnant as they deal with family issues.

Katz believes it's never too early to begin to think about an endgame strategy, so that your exit will be graceful rather than "feet first."

SOURCE: Jerome A. Katz, "Which Track Are You On?," *Inc.*, October 1995, p. 27.

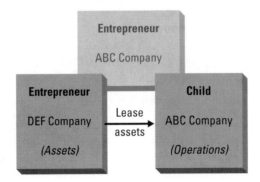

**Figure 19.1
Restructuring the
Business**

goals they have. This, of course, is based on the presumption that the company stock will continue its upward trend for the foreseeable future.

Restructuring

Entrepreneurs who want to cash out a significant portion of their investment and turn over the reins of business to a son or daughter can do so by splitting the business into two firms, with the entrepreneur owning the firm that has all of the assets (plant, equipment, vehicles) and the child owning the operating aspect of the business while leasing the assets from the parent's company. See Figure 19.1.

A Phased Sale

Some entrepreneurs want to soften the emotional blow of selling the business, not to mention the tax consequences, by agreeing with the buyer—an individual or another firm—to sell the business in two phases. During the first phase the entrepreneur sells a percentage of the company but remains in control of operations and can continue to grow the company to the point at which the buyer has agreed to complete the purchase. This approach gives the entrepreneur the ability to cash out a portion of his or her investment and still manage the business for an agreed-upon time, during which the new owner will likely be learning the business and phasing in. At the second phase, the business is sold at a price that is prearranged, usually as a multiple of earnings.

This approach is fairly complex and should always involve an attorney experienced with acquisitions and buy-sell agreements. The buy-sell agreement, which spells out the terms of the purchase, specifies the amount of control the new owner can exert over the business before the sale is completed and the amount of proprietary information that will be shared with the buyer between Phases 1 and 2.

Using an ESOP

If the business has more than 25 employees, one option for the entrepreneur is to cash out via an **Employee Stock Ownership Plan** (ESOP), but still maintain control for as long as desired. ESOPs, which are tax-qualified pension plans or defined-contribution plans governed by ERISA and IRS regulations, have long been considered viable devices for succession planning but work only where certain ingredients are present. The potential ESOP company should have revenues of at least $3 million and an annual payroll of at least $500,000, because the costs of setting up the plan can be substantial, around $100,000 for legal, bank, and accounting fees. The business also needs to have assets—inventory, accounts receivable, equipment—that can be used as collateral if a bank loan is required. Finally, the company should have excellent cash flow to repay the ESOP debt and buy back the stock of any employees who might leave the company over time.

The company sets up an ESOP trust fund into which it puts new or existing shares of stock. Another option is for the ESOP trust to take out a bank loan to buy stock and a minority interest in the company, at least 30 percent to trigger the capital gains exclusion. The shares in the trust are then allocated to individual employee accounts. The capital gains exclusion provides that the cash the owners receive from the ESOP is not taxed if it is reinvested in U.S. stocks or bonds. The banks too have an incentive to provide these ESOP loans because half the interest the company pays to the bank is tax-deductible to the bank if the ESOP owns 50 percent of the voting stock of the company. This can effectively raise the return on an 8 percent loan to 12 percent.

The ESOP company makes tax-deductible contributions of up to 25 percent of the participant payroll to the ESOP to repay the bank debt. The cash-out price for the entrepreneur is based on the company's value at the time and results from a negotiation process with the trustee for the ESOP. The ESOP procedure is not something that can be completed quickly. Normally the entrepreneur prepares for the exit several years in advance, usually the length of time to repay the bank loan. See Figure 19.2.

There are several advantages to ESOPs:

▶ The entrepreneur can reinvest the proceeds of the sale in other securities within 12 months of the stock sale and thereby defer the gain until the new securities are sold. This assumes that the entrepreneur has owned the stock for more than three years. If the securities remain in the entrepreneur's estate at death, the heirs avoid having to pay a capital gains tax.

▶ The ESOP creates a ready market for any remaining owner shares in the entrepreneur's estate upon death. The heirs can sell those shares to the ESOP.

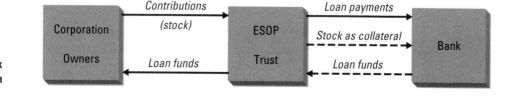

**Figure 19.2
Employee Stock
Ownership Plan**

▶ ESOP loan interest rates are much lower than normal borrowing rates because banks can deduct 50 percent of the interest income when an ESOP owns 50 percent of the company's voting stock.

▶ Assuming the ESOP owns 50 percent of the stock, it can deduct interest and principal payments on the loan, which benefits cash flow enormously.

▶ ESOPs can also fund retirement plans and health care coverage.

▶ Employees participating in the ESOP can accumulate significant amounts of money over time, once they are vested.

▶ Employee shareholders have no voting rights but are represented by the trustee.

There are also several disadvantages the entrepreneur should be aware of:

▶ A company with an ESOP cannot elect a sub-chapter S-corporation election, partnership, or professional corporation.

▶ ESOPs are expensive to set up and maintain, with annual expenses running about $10,000–$15,000.

▶ Private companies are required to repurchase the shares of employees who leave the company.

▶ New shares issued dilute the value of existing shares of stock.

In terms of information that must be shared with the ESOP participants, an ESOP creates a much more open environment than many entrepreneurs are accustomed to. Entrepreneurs often find that with an ESOP in place, employees have a vested interest in the success of the business and tend to perform accordingly. In fact, the ESOP Association reports that about 71 percent of ESOP companies surveyed experienced higher performance after the ESOP. However, the employees will also expect to be treated as partners in the venture and will want to be privy to full information on the operations of the company.

Bankruptcy

It is an unfortunate fact of life that some entrepreneurs must exit their businesses through liquidation. For whatever reasons, the business could not pay its obligations and was unable to secure capital to float the business until it could. Certainly no entrepreneur starts a high-growth venture with liquidation in mind as the exit strategy, but sometimes the forces working against the business are so great that the entrepreneur must have an exit vehicle so he or she can move on to do something else. What forces a corporation into bankruptcy is difficult to pinpoint. The immediately precipitating cause is the failure to pay debt; however, myriad other events led up to that cause. They include economic and business cycles, excessive debt, surplus overhead, shifts in demand, excessive expenses, poor dividend policies, union problems, supplier problems, and poor financial management. Of course, the common denominator for all these factors is poor management.

At this point it should be noted that not all businesses can file for bankruptcy protection. Those that are exempt include savings and loan associations, banks, insurance companies, and foreign companies. Furthermore, a bankruptcy filing cannot occur where the intent has been to defraud, and a company may file only once every six years.

Bankruptcy is normally a voluntary event; however, a company can be forced into bankruptcy by its creditors if they are:

▶ One or more creditors whose claims amount to $5,000 over the value of any assets if there are fewer than 12 claims, or

▶ Three or more creditors under the same above conditions where there are more than 12 claims, or

▶ Any number fewer than all the general partners in a limited partnership.

Involuntary bankruptcies are not common because the courts deal harshly with creditors that force a business into bankruptcy in bad faith.

The Bankruptcy Reform Act of 1978 and Public Law 95-958 provide for more than just liquidation of the business. Therefore, a clear understanding of the bankruptcy mechanisms available to the entrepreneur is essential in considering the options when a venture is faced with financial adversity.

▶ Chapter 7 discusses liquidation.

▶ Chapter 9 deals with municipal debts.

▶ Chapter 11 handles reorganization of businesses.

▶ Chapter 13 deals with the debts of an individual with a regular income.

The two chapters that are pertinent to the entrepreneur are Chapter 11 and Chapter 7.

Chapter 11

Chapter 11 reorganization under the bankruptcy code is really not a bankruptcy in the commonly used sense of the word. It is simply a reorganization of the finances of the business so it can continue to operate and begin to pay its debts. Only in the case where the creditors believe the management is unable to carry out the terms of the reorganization plan will a trustee be appointed to run the company until the debt has been repaid. Otherwise, the entrepreneur remains in control of the business while in a Chapter 11 position. After filing for reorganization, the entrepreneur and the creditors must meet within 30 days to discuss the status and organization of the business. The court then appoints a committee, which usually consists of the seven largest unsecured creditors, to develop a plan for the business with the entrepreneur. That plan must be submitted within 120 days, and acceptance of the plan must come within 60 days of submittal. Of the total number of creditors affected by the plan, representing at least two-thirds of the total dollar amount, at least one-half must accept the plan. Once the reorganization plan is approved by the court, the entrepreneur is discharged from any debts with the exception of those specified in the plan.

Chapter 7

Chapter 7 of the Bankruptcy Code is essentially the liquidation of the assets of the business and the discharging of most types of debt. This vehicle is usually chosen when the business does not have sufficient resources to pay creditors while continuing to operate. The filing of a petition under Chapter 7 constitutes an Order for Relief. A trustee is then appointed to manage the disposition of the business, the goal of which is to reduce it to cash and distribute the cash to the creditors where authorized. After exemptions, the monies derived from liquidation go first to secured creditors and then to priority claimants. Priority claimants include in order:

▸ Administrative expenses related to the bankruptcy

▸ Wages, salaries, or commissions

▸ Vacation, severance, and sick leave pay up to $2,000 per person if earned within 90 days of filing or the date of cessation of the business, whichever came first

▸ Contributions to employee benefit plans up to $2,000 per person earned within 180 days of filing or cessation

▸ Individual claims up to $900 each for services not rendered or products not received but paid for

▸ Taxes and customs duties

▸ General unsecured creditors

▸ Punitive penalties

▸ Accrued interest during the bankruptcy

Any surplus funds remaining after this distribution go to the entrepreneur. Prior to distribution, the entrepreneur has the right to certain exempt property. If the business is a corporation, those exemptions are minimal:

▸ Interest in any accrued dividends up to $4,000

▸ The right to social security benefits, unemployment compensation, public assistance, veterans' benefits, and disability benefits

▸ The right to stock bonuses, pensions, profit sharing or similar plan

If the legal form of the business is a partnership, the entrepreneur is entitled to exempt those properties specifically allowed for individuals filing bankruptcy petitions.

Lest it seem as though the entrepreneur is at the mercy of the creditors in a bankruptcy situation, it should be made clear that the entrepreneur in either type of bankruptcy petition, Chapter 7 or Chapter 11, has a great deal of power and control over the process. This power comes from the natural desire of the creditors for a quick and equitable resolution to the problem, and the protections inherent in the bankruptcy law. Often the creditors are better served by negotiating a restructuring of debt while the company is still operating and prior to a Chapter 7 liquidation, where they are not likely to receive as great a portion of what is owed them. There are, however, certain things the entrepreneur will not be permitted to do within a certain period of time before the filing of a bankruptcy petition:

◗ Hide assets or liabilities

◗ Give preferential treatment to certain creditors 90 days prior to filing the petitions

◗ Make any potentially fraudulent conveyances up to one year prior to the filing of the petition

Any of the above conveyances may be recouped by the court during the bankruptcy proceedings.

Entrepreneurs can take advantage of a relatively new vehicle under Chapter 11. Known as a "prepackaged bankruptcy," it can take from four to nine months to complete rather than the typical nine months to two years. The entrepreneur presents the creditors and equity owners with a reorganization plan *before* the bankruptcy filing actually goes to court. If the entrepreneur can achieve the required number of votes to agree to the plan (more than half the total creditors and two-thirds within each class of creditors), the prepackaged plan can then go forward expeditiously.

There is an obvious advantage to the entrepreneur using this approach. Under the traditional Chapter 11 approach, the creditors and everyone else learn of the company's problems at the filing. With a prepackaged plan, by contrast, an approved plan is in place at the point at which the public becomes aware of the problem, and the creditors thus may experience a greater

Strategies for Avoiding Bankruptcy

◗ Avoid relying on one major customer or industry for revenue generation.

◗ Keep overhead costs to essentials that directly contribute to the generation of revenues.

◗ Maintain a degree of liquidity equal to about several months of overhead expense.

◗ Maintain current and honest relationships with bankers, creditors, and suppliers.

sense of confidence in the entrepreneur. Moreover, the prepackaged plan results in far less time in legal processes. For this approach to succeed, however, the statement of disclosure for the creditors about the positive and negative aspects of the business must be carefully constructed to give the creditors all the information they need in order to consider the plan and protect their interests.

Before considering bankruptcy as an option to either exit a troubled business or restructure the business in an effort to survive, you should seek advice from your attorney and/or a specialist in turnarounds in the industry. With the aid of an accountant, you need to audit your assets and liabilities to see if the business can qualify for and benefit from a Chapter 11 reorganization. Often, seeking help before filing a bankruptcy petition can lead to alternative, less difficult solutions that are more beneficial to the entrepreneur and creditors alike.

New Venture Checklist

Have you:

❑ **Identified the issues that could potentially affect the business at various points in the future?**

❑ **Developed a contingency plan for various scenarios that may impact the business at some future date?**

❑ **Determined your goals for the business relative to an exit strategy?**

Issues to Consider

1. What is the benefit to the entrepreneur of contingency planning?
2. How can the entrepreneur prepare for potential product liability litigation both to minimize the chance of occurrence and to give the company the best chance of prevailing against a product liability claim?
3. How can the entrepreneur prepare for a potential decline in sales?
4. Which mechanisms are available to the entrepreneur when the goal is to cash out of the business but maintain some degree of involvement with the business?
5. How can bankruptcy law be a tool for the entrepreneur?

Experiencing Entrepreneurship

1. Interview an entrepreneur in an industry of your choice to learn what his or her harvest strategy is.
2. Interview a turnaround consultant about some ways to recognize problems that could lead to business failure.

Additional Sources of Information

ESOP Association, Washington, D.C. Tel. (202) 293-2971.

Freiermuth, E.P. (1988). *Life After Debt.* Homewood, IL: Dow Jones Irwin.

Friedman, R. (1993). *Small Business Legal Guide.* Chicago: Dearborn Financial Publishing, Inc.

National Center for Employee Ownership, Oakland, CA. Tel. (510) 272-9461.

Internet Resources

Entrepreneurial Edge Online
http://www.edgeonline.com
This site offers all manner of advice and help to entrepreneurs, including a forum, tips, and news of interest to those just starting out.

Essential Links to Taxes
http://www.el.com/elinks/taxes
This excellent resource has links to a remarkable number of sites with tax information, advice, and news.

NetMarquee
http://www.netmarquee.com
This handy site provides a broad range of information for entrepreneurs, plus a great deal of information geared specifically to family businesses.

Small Business Law Center
http://www.courttv.com/legalhelp/business/sites
Sponsored by CourtTV, this site has links to a number of legal resources for entrepreneurs.

Relevant Case Studies

1. Toy Tips, Inc.
2. The Penduline Putter
3. Simtek, Inc.

20

The quality of your work, in the long run, is the deciding factor on how much your services are valued by the world.
Og Mandino

Ethics, Social Responsibility, and the Start-Up Venture

Overview

▶ **Ethics**

▶ **Learning from research on ethics**

▶ **Social responsibility**

▶ **The world-class start-up venture**

▶ **Becoming successful**

Terms to Know

Profile 20.1

Acting like a Saint in the Ad Business

St. Luke's Advertising is the brainchild of one of the most revolutionary, arrogant, and successful ad agencies of all time, Chiat/Day, which pioneered the open-plan office and the virtual working environment. It was born, in 1996 in the London office of Chiat/Day, of a need to escape the bonds of corporate bureaucracy and to reinvent the image of advertising. In 1995, a Gallup poll found that advertising executives barely escaped last-place honors as lowest in honesty and ethics. (They were beaten by Congress and used-car salesmen.)

Chiat/Day was a monolithic organization with bloated overhead and inflated prices that its clients were increasingly unwilling to pay. One day Andy Law and David Abraham, account directors, walked into a meeting in the Los Angeles office, put up a picture of Aristotle, and wrote on the chalkboard the Greek word for ethics. They announced that this was what the firm had been looking for to solve its problems. Law and Abraham believed that consumers were becoming increasingly jaded by mass-market advertising. How a company interacted with its stakeholders would now become more important. In other words, ethics should become the basis of all the firm's actions.

Jay Chiat, facing huge repayments of debt from failed acquisitions, did not have the patience to implement the new philosophy and decided to sell the company to the communications conglomerate Omnicom, which in turn merged Chiat/Day with TBWA, a more conservative company. The London office and Law and Abraham were very unhappy with the merger. Eventually, concerned about the possibility of bad press, Omnicom sold the London office to Law and his associates. With no support coming from its former parent company, Law and 45 employees huddled in the London office to invent what was to become St. Luke's, a company that was based on relationships rather than on hierarchy, that was owned by its employees, and that was determined to single-handedly change the way the advertising business worked. This new philosophy started with the name for the firm, taken from the patron saint of painters, craftsmen, and healers, a much more humble title than those usually found on Madison Avenue. The new firm took as its motto the words "Profit is like health; you need it to live, but it's not what you live for."

Many in the industry were skeptical as to whether St. Luke's could maintain its ethical stance in the face of very large clients with huge advertising budgets. In one instance, the firm debated about pitching a campaign to biotechnology company Monsanto, which was involved in genetically engineered products. St. Luke's pitched it, incorporating both sides of the debate, but Monsanto chose not to buy it. St. Luke's did not go back and change its approach.

In its first year, 1996, the new firm met its growth target in just four months, and many of London's art directors and copywriters have stated that St. Luke's is where they would most like to work. It appears that St. Luke's may represent the beginning of a paradigm shift in the world of advertising. Today many advertising firms are looking for new ways to do business in a more ethical and socially responsible manner.

SOURCES: Stevan Alburty, "The Ad Agency to End All Ad Agencies," *Fast Company*, Issue 6, p. 116; Mark Espiner, "Labour's Ad Machine," *The Guardian Media*, January 19, 1998, p. 6; Linda Quigley, "Spirituality Can Pay Dividends in Big Business," *The Tennessean*, March 8, 1998.

How did the founders of St. Luke's demonstrate that they stood by their ethical values, and would you have done the same?

For a business owner, integrity is everything. It doesn't matter what type of business you own, which industry you do business in, or which part of the world you call your market. Your integrity is yours to lose only once. Today, more than at any previous time in history, it is challenging at best to maintain one's integrity and ethics in the face of business owners who will do virtually anything to get a sale. It's almost as if everything and everyone were conspiring against businesses that act on the basis of moral convictions. The global economy has juxtaposed U.S. businesses with cultures that define morality in terms of very different contexts and codes of values and ethics. And that global economy has been brought even closer through the medium of the Internet, where doing business with someone in another country can be as quick as clicking on an icon.

This chapter looks at two key issues for entrepreneurial companies, issues that will become increasingly important as the global marketplace becomes more networked: ethics and social responsibility. The profile on St. Luke's clearly demonstrates that even industries known for their lack of ethics are looking for ways to reinvent themselves. The chapter closes with a related discussion of the characteristics of a world-class start-up venture and the issue of success.

Ethics

Over the past decade, every industrial nation has experienced highly publicized incidents of business misconduct stemming from a lack of ethics.[1] **Ethics,** or the moral code by which we live and conduct business, come from the cultural, social, political, and ethnic norms with which we were raised as children. We don't often sit down to think about our value system; we merely act instinctively on the basis of it. It's only when we're faced with a situation that others might point out to us as immoral or unethical that we may consciously ask ourselves what is the correct thing to do.

Not everyone operates under the same standards of ethics. If everyone did, ethics would not be the huge issue it is today. From the employee who steals notepads, pens, and computer disks because "the employer won't miss them" to the executive who abuses his or her expense account to the business owner who avoids taxes by not reporting employee income, the lack of a clear ethical standard that is accepted by everyone is costing entrepreneurs both time and money. Entrepreneurs face special problems when it comes to ethical issues. Their small companies generally are more informal and lack systems and controls. They often don't have the resources to deal with ethical issues, and they typically don't take the time to focus on ethics during their attempts to survive as a business. These issues are not being mentioned to excuse entrepreneurs from dealing with ethics. On the contrary, an entrepreneur who deals unethically in the early stages of the business will most likely pay for it for the life of the business.

In general, ethics issues in business have been found in three broad areas: 1) the tension between ethics and profits; 2) the conflict between private gain and public good; and 3) the contrast between the results of capitalism and the intentions of the people.[2] On a practical level, these problems are described as conflicts of interest, survival tactics, peer pressure, and pushing the legal limit.

Conflicts of Interest

Conflicts of interest are one of the most universal problems in business today. One of the biggest reasons is that people have vested interests in many areas of their lives: careers, a business, family, community, and their investments, to name just a few. It is rare for all these interests to be in complete harmony with one another. For example, you might ask your employees to work late into the evening to finish a project when their families expect them at home for the evening. You may want to continue an important manufacturing process, one that provides many jobs, when your community claims that the process is not good for the environment. There are so many arenas for conflict of interest. Sometimes there is no resolution, but most often there are ways to recognize these conflicts, weigh each side of the issue and look for creative solutions.[3] For example, to help employees balance work and family obligations, you can consider alternatives such as flexible work schedules, job sharing, part-time work, and work-at-home arrangements.

Survival Tactics

Many are the stories of entrepreneurs who did whatever it took to survive, even violating their own standards. Survival is the area where most people's ethics really face a test. It's easy to be ethical when things are going your way, but what if you're facing bankruptcy or can't make payroll? What do your ethics look like then? Again, we reiterate the importance of sticking to your ethical code, because what you do today out of desperation, you will live with for the rest of your business career.

Peer Pressure

There are many stakeholders in your business, and they all want what's owed them when it's owed them. For many entrepreneurs, there are times when managing the demands of stakeholders becomes a real juggling act. For example, to grow the company to the next level, you may decide to consider an initial public offering. Once you throw that hat into the ring, you'll find lots of stakeholders pressuring you to move forward, even when you're not sure it's the best thing to do. These stakeholders include investment bankers who get a fee for doing the deal; business partners who may be able to cash out of some of their holdings in the company; and lawyers who want the additional business. All these stakeholders want to be served, and the entrepreneur must hold to his or her code of ethics and base decisions on it.

Pushing the Legal Limit

The law contains may gray areas where entrepreneurs have some leeway in their operations. Particularly in the area of income-tax compliance policies, the line between what is legal and what is not isn't always clearly defined. Some entrepreneurs spend considerable time trying to find ways around laws they don't like. If they spent more time on their businesses, they might have a better chance to survive. Generally speaking, entrepreneurs who regularly play too close to the edge of legality eventually get caught, and the price is often their businesses and their reputations. Ethical entrepreneurs don't play those games, but they're always on the alert for companies that might use quasi-legal practices against them to gain an edge in the market. These types of tactics must be dealt with strongly. For example, a large water-meter repair company that operated within the law was attacked by a competitor in collusion with a newspaper reporter. The company was accused of bribing public officials. It was a false accusation, but it caused the innocent utility company a great many problems.[4] This was clearly an unethical act by the offending competitor.

Learning from Research on Ethics

Most of the research on ethics has been in large organizations, so we have very little information about small businesses. However, work done by Longnecker et al. found that small-business owners have more stringent ethical views on such things as favoritism in promotion, acquiescence to a dangerous design flaw, misleading financial reporting, and misleading advertising. But surprisingly, they view with much greater tolerance padded expense accounts, tax evasion, collusion in bidding, insider trading, discrimination against women, and the copying of computer software.[5]

Research has also found that the ethical behavior of employees is very much influenced by the **code of ethics** of the company.[6] So it would seem to be important for a business owner to develop a formal code of ethics for the business. Cavanaugh, Moberg, and Valasquez proposed that in doing so, business owners ask three questions about any ethical decision to be made.[7]

1. Will the actions taken result in the "greatest good for all parties involved"?

2. Will the actions respect the rights of all parties?

3. Are the actions just?

In addition, the most effective code of conduct will have several characteristics:

Profile 20.2

Exporting Values with Your Products

One of the problems with doing business globally is that every country seems to have a different set of ethical values. The question becomes "Which set do you follow?" Does the old cliché "When in Rome, do as the Romans do," apply?

Levi Strauss has historically been regarded as a socially responsible company, but in 1991, a report aired on television accused the largest brand-name clothing manufacturer of treating its workers in Saipan like slaves. At the very time when the report hit the press, Levi Strauss had been drafting a new ethics code and performance guidelines for its overseas suppliers. Upon learning of the Saipan incident, Strauss sent inspectors to audit the operations of its supplier Willie Tan. The auditors determined that Tan's operation was inconsistent with the goals of Levi Strauss, and Strauss canceled its contract.

Learning from this experience, the American company conducted audits in each of the 50 countries in which it does business. Those contractors who were unwilling to comply with the new contract were terminated.

A more difficult ethical issue arose in Bangladesh, where Levi Strauss was accused of using underage children in factories. The conflict was that these children were often the sole support of their families, and their only alternative to working in a factory was prostitution or begging. Levi Strauss decided to pay the children's wages while they went to school until they reached the legal working age.

SOURCE: Richard Rapaport, "Import Jeans, Export Values, Fast Company", *Prototype Issue*, 1993, p. 19.

1. The code and its attendant policies will be clear and easy to understand and will include such areas as conflict of interest, ethics, and foreign government payments.

2. Specifics regarding special situations that need further explanation should be included (e.g., political factors in certain countries).

3. Where employee judgment may be required, descriptions and examples should be given to make it easier for the employee to make the decision.

Employers should make sure that all employees are aware of and understand the code as well as the values and culture of the company. Furthermore, employers should conduct internal audits to ensure compliance.

An entrepreneur's ethical code affects not only his or her business but also the community in which he or she does business—and the nation as well. One of the biggest reasons the U.S. economy has been so successful is that in general, business owners conduct business in ethical ways.

Ethics compliance is not a separate function of a business, nor should it be considered in a vacuum. The problems that ensue from lack of an agreed-upon code of ethics pervade every area of the business. Family businesses in particular have unique ethical issues because sometimes the generation who founded the business must make decisions that are laden with conflict of interest. How far do you go in taking into consideration the desires of the next generation? Which is more important, hiring a family member or the good of the business? The roles of business owner and family member intersect on ethics.

Two experts in family business, attorney Richard Narva and psychologist Thomas Davidow, believe that the good of the business should always come first. They tell a story about an entrepreneur whose son was not carrying his load on the job, often showing up just to collect his paycheck. One payday he was sent to meet with his father. The father was wearing a Sherlock Holmes–style hat with a button that said "Boss." Looking directly at his son, the father/entrepreneur announced that the son was fired. He immediately reversed the hat so that now a button was displayed that read "Dad." He then proceeded to put his arm around his son and say, "I hear you just lost your job. Is there anything I can do to help?"[8]

There is no way to avoid the ethical problems that businesses bring. But developing a strong ethical code and getting the cooperation of everyone in the business will go a long way toward making those problems easier to deal with.

Social Responsibility

Today it's not enough to have a successful business and make a profit. Today your business must hold itself to a higher standard of **social responsibility** by giving something back to the community or communities in which it does business and to society as a whole. This means following the laws, respecting the environment, and thinking of the impact the business has on the community, the industry, the stakeholders, and people in general. Social responsibility, therefore, is about the obligations and duties that business has to society as a whole.

Some businesses have chosen the route of defining themselves publicly as "socially responsible businesses." The Body Shop's original goal was to end Third World poverty. While that was certainly a lofty goal, it was highly unlikely that one corporation could do what entire nations had been unable to accomplish. So for all practical purposes, The Body Shop was setting itself up for failure. Furthermore, since companies like this put their social goals into all their publicity and advertising, they are held to impossibly high standards by the public and the media, who are ready and willing to remind them of their failure to achieve their goals. In the case of The Body Shop, it was accused of misleading customers in its claims, so it hired an ethicist from Stanford University, Kirk Hanson, to conduct an independent study into the claims. The findings scored the company low in 22 of 38 areas studied, and it also received the lowest marks for its reaction to criticism.[9] Still, stories like this should never discourage a company from becoming socially responsible. In fact, Paul Brainerd founded a company, the Brainerd Foundation, in Seattle, Washington, for the purpose of helping entrepreneurs to give back strategically.[10] He suggests that entrepreneurs follow two rules:

1. Don't wait until you're older to begin giving back. Start when you're young and the business is young.

2. Start at the grassroots level, where help is needed the most.

Ways to Become Socially Responsible

You don't have to be a large, multimillion-dollar company to begin to give something back to society. Even very small companies can benefit from having

---

Profile 20.3

You Can't Force Social Responsibility on Your Employees

Katharine Paine, founder and CEO of Delahay Group, a New Hampshire-based company, came back from a conference attended by successful socially responsible entrepreneurs excited about becoming a socially responsible company. She immediately told her contractors to use only "responsibly harvested wood" in their new offices and donated 5% of her company's billable hours to other organizations. She also requested that all her employees join the Literacy Volunteers.

Five years after those sweeping pronouncements, Paine reported that any responsibly harvested wood in her building probably got there by accident and that they haven't succeeded in getting anyone to read. She tells other entrepreneurs who strive to be socially responsible that you can't make people socially responsible and that it's difficult to ask people who work very long hours to give up more time on the side. She now offers paid volunteer time—16 hours a year—and the employee can choose which organization to serve. Delahay has been far more successful with this approach.

Source: Anna Muoio, "Ways to Give Back," *Fast Company,* Issue 12, p. 113.

a socially responsible mindset. There are several things you can do with your new venture that will establish positive relationships in your community and benefit both the company and the community.

Donate Your Product or Service

One of the least expensive ways to do good is by donating the products or services your company produces. Saint Louis Bread Co. gives bread, muffins, and so forth to the homeless to the annual tune of $700,000 retail.[11] Account Executive is a Philadelphia company that bridges the gap between training programs and employment for low-income women. Its founder, Abby Siegel, co-founded a nonprofit organization that provides interview clothing to help these women dress for success.[12]

Get Other Companies Involved with You

In the spirit of networking, consider putting together a group of small businesses so that your combined efforts produce results with more impact. Just Desserts, a San Francisco bakery, put together a group of 35 businesses to adopt an elementary school. With their combined financial strength, they planted trees on the school grounds, painted the school, and refurbished the classrooms, creating a positive environment for students.

Offer Your Expertise Free of Charge

Some organizations in the community needs the expertise your company has developed. Amana-Key, a Brazilian company, provided its offices for seminars

---

Profile 20.4

Social Responsibility That Improves the Quality of Your Workers

Entrepreneurs often feel that they don't have the resources for giving back to the community in the way that large corporations do. But according to General Colin Powell, who served as chairman of the Joint Chiefs of Staff under Presidents Bush and Clinton, that is simply not true. In fact, Powell goes so far as to say that the contributions of small businesses are more important because these entrepreneurs are usually an integral part of their communities. Businesses can have a significant impact on the education of our nation's youth so that future generations will be better prepared to enter the work force. Here are some ways that entrepreneurs can give back.

▶ Hire a young person in the summer or during the holiday and help him or her learn responsibility, discipline, and how to deal with customers.

▶ Allow your employees time off to be spent at a local school, mentoring a student.

▶ Partner with the school system to provide better training programs for students during high school and as they leave.

Source: "Colin Powell Tells How You Can Help," *Nation's Business*, June 1998, p. 25.

to help over 300 teenagers learn the skills they'll need to meet their future goals.[13] Doug Austin, of San Diego-based Austin Design Group, volunteered his time and expertise, along with some of his associates, to build houses for people living in shelters in Tijuana, Mexico.[14] Jay Backstrand used his technology expertise to develop a web site, Volunteer America, which merged with Impact Online in October 1996, to match nonprofit organizations with people looking for opportunities to volunteer.[15]

As you can see, there are many ways to demonstrate your social responsibility as a business. It doesn't have to cost very much or take very much time, which is an important thing for entrepreneurs with start-up ventures to know. Social responsibility and operating an ethical business are part of what's required to build a world-class venture.

The World-Class Start-Up Venture

This chapter culminates a long process that started with an opportunity and an idea in the mind of the entrepreneur. Whether or not you are an entrepreneur, by this point it should be clear that the entrepreneurial mindset is the antithesis of the bureaucratic mindset found in so many large organizations today. It is also distinctly different from the mindset of the small-business owner. Unfortunately, in much of what is written about entrepreneurs (and the term is often used loosely), these distinctions are blurred, so the reader never comes away with a clear sense of why some ventures become the Microsofts of the world and others never go beyond providing a modest income for the owner.

In this book we've emphasized several key characteristics of world-class entrepreneurial companies. In summary, these companies:

▶ Have a global vision

▶ Are innovative

▶ Put the customer at the heart of the business

▶ Develop a team philosophy

▶ Maintain absolute integrity

▶ Focus on quality and continual improvement

The defining factor for world-class ventures is not in any measure size; in fact, size may actually be a deterrent to world-class status in the new millennium. Certainly, there can be no doubt that it is much easier to start a venture with world-class intentions than it is to change the habits of years in a large organization. A new venture can set up the infrastructure and hire people who have the mindset to create a strong culture that is communicated to customers in everything the company does. While a large, bureaucratic company may have the financial resources and clout to become world-class, it may be outdistanced by the scrappy entrepreneurial venture that understands how to be world-class from the very beginning.

A Global Vision

World-class ventures are born with a global view. From sourcing materials and parts to distributing product, selling product, and setting goals for the future, these ventures know no geographic boundaries. It has often been said that new ventures should wait to go global until they are well established and have achieved a certain level of sales. Yet if Water Ventures, Inc., a resort water-sports equipment and services company in California, had listened to that advice, it might not be in business today. Water Ventures found that the best markets for its products lay overseas; in particular, in the Middle East. Consequently, the domestic market is a relatively small portion of its total sales.

Having a global vision is not just a world-class attribute—it's a matter of survival. A new venture has two choices: take the leap into the international arena or retreat within the boundaries of the United States and watch its market share being eaten up by international competitors. Of course, "taking the leap" does not necessarily mean establishing a physical presence in another country via a manufacturing or other facility. It may mean establishing a strategic alliance with a foreign company or simply exporting products internationally to gain a presence in a region before investing large amounts of capital in something more permanent. If you are an original equipment manufacturer (OEM), responding to a customer that has gone global may mean locating a distribution center in the region where the customer is selling product. In fact, in some countries, the only way to do business is through a joint venture or contract with a local company. The U.S. venture maintains control of its R&D, finance, manufacturing, and quality control, but uses locals for marketing and service functions.

Having a global vision is much more than merely recognizing an opportunity in another country, however. It entails understanding the culture and the way business is conducted in that country, learning the rules and regulations of trade, and having an awareness of global monetary markets.

Going into global markets also requires partnerships with experts in particular countries. Nowhere has this been more evident than in the former Eastern Bloc countries, including Russia. With capitalism and a market-driven economy still new concepts to the people of these countries, the local expertise that a U.S. venture intending to do business there will seek is expertise in government policy, monetary policy and exchange, and general "street smarts." Developing a relationship with a local business, no matter how small, will smooth the way into the business environment of the country.

Innovation

Innovation can often provide a competitive advantage even where legal protections are not available. An innovative marketing strategy or a unique distribution strategy, even using products or services not in and of themselves innovative, can give a new venture a niche advantage in the market. Innovation is not just about technology, or products, or processes. It is about looking at every aspect of the organization to see how things could be done better.

Innovation "is the specific tool of entrepreneurs, the means by which they exploit change as an opportunity. . . ."[16] It's about what Drucker called "creative imitation," waiting for something new to be developed and then jumping in and making it better. That is what IBM did after Apple introduced its successful personal computer. It designed a computer, based on customer needs, that became the standard in the industry, the PC. The idea was not IBM's; IBM simply exploited the success of Apple through creative imitation.

Innovation must be an ongoing process in every function of the business—not innovation for innovation's sake, but innovation that is market-driven, that will give customers what they want. New ventures have a distinct advantage over large businesses because they are used to thinking small, and it is many small experimental starts that ultimately lead to innovation. Paul Hawkin, in his book *The Next Economy*, observes that "it is one thing to start a business that becomes large and entirely another to start things on a large scale. You should imitate nature, where meaningful beginnings are almost always unnoticeable."[17] The fact that most new ventures have little capital can also be an asset because the project stays small and simple, and the pressure to succeed is much greater.

Innovation is action-oriented; it happens quickly and usually without the formality of committees, boards of directors, and strategy sessions. Innovation welcomes failure—in fact, demands it—but *quick* failures, the kind that help the company change direction and move toward success. Innovation means breaking the old rules and creating new ones. In short, innovation is the new venture constantly renewing itself.

The Customer at the Heart of the Business

The world-class venture of the new millennium lives for its customers. Customers will decide what is produced, when and how it is produced, how much is produced, how much it will cost, and where it can be purchased and serviced. Keeping the customers happy is essential to the survival and success of the business. In a market-driven business, it is not just the sales personnel who deal with the customer. Everyone from the engineers to the plant workers to the office staff knows the customers. This means that those responsible for product development spend time with customers to assess needs; those who handle billing and invoicing spend time with customers to assure that the service they provide is meeting its mark; and senior line management spends at least a third of the time with customers so as not to lose touch with the company's greatest asset. In short, all actions taken by the organization are assessed first on the basis of their impact on the customer and secondarily on the basis of their impact on the business. As we've said throughout this book, without the customer, there is no business.

The customer is an integral part of the organization and is encouraged to participate in the company through letters, newsletters, visits to the company facilities, and attendance at special meetings. Customers are given numerous opportunities to express their feelings and give their suggestions, and are regularly sampled for their degree of satisfaction with the company and its products or services. When a world-class business makes promises to a customer, those promises are kept no matter what the cost to the business to do so. The customer is always right.

A Team-Based Organization

This book has stressed the team approach to entrepreneurship because it is believed that no one person has the expertise, experience, or energy to do everything or take control of every activity of a rapidly growing venture. The classic entrepreneurial leadership style is to do all the crucial tasks yourself, hire others to do the secondary tasks, and direct and monitor everything yourself. This is, for the most part, how the majority of new ventures start out. The classic style works fine for a while, until the business outgrows the entrepreneur's ability to stay on top of everything. The classic entrepreneur, finding it difficult to delegate responsibility and authority, may hire management personnel to help but will still stay directly involved in all major decisions. This approach does not work well when you're trying to build a world-class venture; more often than not, in fact, it inhibits the growth of the business and makes it difficult to achieve excellence.

Another approach is for the entrepreneur to act as the ringmaster in a three-ring circus. The entrepreneur outsources all the tasks he or she doesn't want to do and essentially coordinates all the efforts—the ultimate virtual corporation. It is possible to build a very large business this way; however, whether or not you can achieve world-class status is arguable. What many virtual corporations find is that it is often difficult to control the quality, service, and delivery timing of other companies' resources. That lack of control is especially apparent when a member of the virtual channel suffers a loss (such as fire) that can cause a chain reaction throughout the entire channel of distribution, with potentially devastating consequences for the entrepreneur's business. To build a world-class organization under this scenario requires the complete cooperation of all members of the virtual team, a difficult achievement at best.

Complex new ventures require an **integrated, team-based approach** to management. Some examples of complex organizations are manufacturing, service organizations that provide a variety of services, and retail operations with multiple locations. These types of ventures demand that the entrepreneur delegate authority in specific areas of the business to specific people and then let those people make their own decisions. Of course, the entrepreneur retains the right to dismiss the employee if those decisions are not in line with the goals or philosophy of the company.

An integrated, team-based approach (ITB) means that key management in all the functional areas of the organization participate fully in the design, development, production, and distribution of the products or services that the business offers. This does not necessarily suggest that all members of the team are employees of the entrepreneur. They may, in fact, be virtual members of the organization, independent contractors who carry out specific functions of the entrepreneur's business within their own companies.

The advantage of the team-based approach is that it promotes skill, discipline, motivation, and learning—essential attributes of a world-class organization. It is not an approach that can be achieved overnight, however. That is where a new venture has an advantage over an established firm that is attempting to convert to a team-based approach to management. The new venture can begin with a team-based philosophy, infrastructure, and personnel prepared to take on the responsibilities inherent in this approach.

In a team-based approach, employees work in teams of perhaps six to seven people, with a supervisor who really acts as a facilitator. The team in essence has a problem-solving mandate; consequently, members of the team are paid on the basis of their skill level rather than according to the job they perform. This is a critical distinction, because in the ITB approach, problem-solving and people skills are considered as important as physical or task skills, if not more important. All teams are charged with the responsibility of finding ways to improve all aspects of the product, process, and service. A particular job is measured by the number of physical operations involved in completing a task and the number of managerial or problem-solving skills involved. This means that no longer are there assembly-line jobs that can be done without thinking. Technical and managerial competence is required for all jobs; accordingly, the people who are hired to work in a world-class business must have both skills or at least be motivated to acquire them.

It is certainly much easier to form an organization with ITB in mind than it is to decide to convert later on, after employees with a more traditional mindset have been hired. Nevertheless, even the entrepreneur with a new venture cannot simply announce to potential employees that they will have to think about their work and ways to improve it—and expect this to happen automatically. Entrepreneurs dedicated to ITB must be willing to train employees in problem-solving skills and provide incentives for continual learning. They must also be willing to educate their employees on where they fit into the big picture of the organization.

Another advantage of ITB is that less information is required to coordinate the activities of all the functions of the business because control is much further down in the organization. In the case of a manufacturing firm, however, more information is typically needed on the plant floor because of the need to coordinate the efforts of the various teams, to ensure the timely and efficient processing of the product. This information requirement can be met by the use of computer-integrated manufacturing technology (CIM), which allows those involved in the production process to manage quality control, production planning, machine setup, and problem diagnosis and resolution in real time and by interacting with staff via computer where necessary.

To balance the greater demand for information, teams are given the authority to respond to various situations as they occur. In this way, valuable production time is not lost in attempting to get approval from a higher level of authority. Of course, for teams to be able to make decisions on the spot, they must have a clear understanding of the entire production process and the impact any decision they make might have; hence, the importance of integration and continuing education. The best type of ITB is one in which all teams are cross-trained so that no one aspect of production is dependent on a single team.

Furthermore, all production teams work directly with engineering teams, marketing teams, sales teams, and finance teams, with everyone rewarded based on the performance of the business. With an integrated, team-based approach, no one team and no one person is more important than any other. Management sends a clear message that the person who solders the wires is every bit as important to the company as the person who manages the finances, or the person in sales who promotes the product. Accordingly, in an ITB organization, you will not see executive dining rooms, special parking places for certain people, or barriers of any kind to the free and open flow of communication and trust.

Of course, integrated, team-based management and process control must go hand in hand as well. Streamlining materials flow and minimizing work-in-process inventory is what allows problems and bottlenecks in the system to readily surface, so that they can be detected and solved not in a piecemeal fashion, but in a manner that allows the entire production process to continue unimpeded.

Absolute Integrity

To accomplish the successful networks of strategic alliances necessary for operating in a global economy requires integrity. The old adversarial mindset that business has traditionally held no longer works when you are striving to become a world-class venture. The environment for entrepreneurial ventures has always been volatile and uncertain. Add to that the global dimension and there aren't too many things that can be relied upon to remain constant. Hence, the one constant that must be present is the security that relationships are based on integrity, ethics, and trust. Often, in an effort to be competitive, companies promise what they can't deliver or change the terms of an agreement at the last minute when the other party is at its most vulnerable. These tactics may be successful in achieving certain ends in the short term, but the cost in loss of customers and reputation will be devastating in the long term.

Integrity is consistency in what the company says, does, and stands for. It is fair and uncompromising treatment of every supplier, every distributor, every customer, and every employee. If you are going to expect the best from these people and ask them to assume some of the risk with you, they must feel confident you will do what you promise. Integrity is confidence that the company "is who they say they are." It means knowing that you will not be shortchanged on a payment or on a quantity order, that products will meet the level of quality advertised, and that service will be provided as promised.

In a global economy the issue of business ethics often displays its formidable presence. It is common knowledge that not all countries operate under the same rules of ethics as the United States. Is it OK for an American business to accept a bribe in another country or pay a government official under the table to speed up a process? For a world-class venture the question is moot. Absolute integrity means maintaining high ethical standards in all business dealings, no matter where they take place. How can an entrepreneur expect employees to act fairly and honestly toward the business if the business is not acting that way? Honesty is still the best policy.

Continual Improvement

In their best-selling book *A Passion for Excellence,* Tom Peters and Nancy Austin said, "a passion for excellence means thinking big and starting small: excellence happens when high purpose and intense pragmatism meet." But they caution, "the adventure of excellence is not for the faint of heart."[18] Ten years later that message is probably even more relevant than it was when the authors wrote it. Like being a world-class venture, achieving excellence is not a stage in the life of a business, but rather an ongoing process of improvement that never ends. Hayes, Wheelwright, and Clark call it "continual learning."[19] They assert that wherever U.S. manufacturers have lost competitive advantage, the source can be traced to problems with cost, quality, and innovation.

For companies dealing in a global market, cost is a function of productivity and the exchange rate. If U.S. companies do not keep pace with other countries in terms of their investment in plant and equipment, any productivity gains may be lost. Moreover, while American companies strive to dispel the perception of low quality, foreign companies are also moving ahead in that arena, making it difficult for American companies to catch up.

Today savvy entrepreneurs are using continual improvement as an integral part of their competitive strategy. With customers demanding ever-increasing levels of quality, the issue of continual improvement has become a necessity, from start-up through the life of the business.

Becoming Successful

A business's success is easily measured by total revenues, earnings, return on investment and so forth, but entrepreneurs don't typically measure success in these terms. Entrepreneurs seem to take a much more personal view of what constitutes success; consequently, the definition varies from entrepreneur to entrepreneur. Wally Amos of Uncle Noname Cookies believes that success is "turning lemons into lemonade." For Sue Szymczak of Safeway Sling in Milwaukee, success is "being happy with what you're doing and feeling as though you're accomplishing something." One group of entrepreneurs decided that measuring their success in terms of the financial performance of the business did not reflect their definition of success, even at the company level. These are the entrepreneurs who started many of the so-called "socially responsible" businesses, which we discussed earlier.

Entrepreneurs who aspire to socially responsible success must understand that unless the business of the business is conducted well, there will *be* no business from which to achieve the goal of social responsibility.

No matter what your definition of success, there seem to be some constants that comprise the very essence of what is success. One of those constants is purpose. To feel successful, entrepreneurs need to know that what they are doing is taking them in the direction of a goal they wish to achieve. True success is a journey, not a destination—even the achievement of a goal will be just a step on the way to the achievement of yet another goal. Success attained serendipitously, without purpose, is usually fleeting. Entrepreneurs purposefully avoid the path of least resistance to success. An electric current will follow the line of least resistance; a light bulb will glow only when there is resistance. Entrepreneurs striving to build world-class ventures will leave the path of least resistance to those who are seeking the quick successes that usually don't endure.

The second constant is that life has its ups and downs. Failure is the other half of success, and most entrepreneurs have experienced several failures of one sort or another along the way. But entrepreneurs do not fear failure, because they know intuitively that those who obsessively avoid failure are doomed to mediocrity. To avoid failing, one has to virtually retreat from life, to never try anything that has any risk attached to it. Most entrepreneurs strive for a high batting average: in other words, for more successes than failures. To ensure this high batting average, they make sure that every time they come to bat they give it their best; then, win or lose, they strive to learn from the experience and go on. Entrepreneurs are generally optimists with great expectations.

The third constant is a sense of satisfaction with what one is doing. The most successful entrepreneurs are doing what they love, so the satisfaction level is usually very high. Does satisfaction with the work result in success, or does success bring satisfaction? Probably both are true in many instances; however, being content with how things are progressing will not always bring a successful outcome, nor will success always bring with it lasting satisfaction. For the most part, though, entrepreneurs do achieve a certain level of satisfaction when they consider themselves successful, as they usually have predetermined what success means to them, so the ultimate achievement of that success is even sweeter.

The fourth constant of success is that there is no free lunch. Success rarely comes without work. Entrepreneurs do not have the luxury of a nine-to-five workday where at five o'clock he or she goes home, leaving thoughts of the business behind. Entrepreneurs are married to their businesses twenty-four hours a day. When Microsoft co-founder Bill Gates got married, he proudly proclaimed that he now was leaving work at midnight, instead of in the middle of the night as he had done since founding the company. It is not just the number of hours of work that distinguishes entrepreneurs, of course, but how they use their time. Entrepreneurs make productive use of odd moments in their day—while they're driving, on hold on the telephone, in the shower, walking to a meeting. They make the best use of the time they have.

Success has another kind of price, however. Napoleon said that "the most dangerous moment comes with victory." Paraphrasing that statement, it can be said that the most dangerous moment comes with success. This is because people who forget that success is transitory tend to relax in their success and stop moving forward. Many entrepreneurs have suffered physical and emotional problems, divorces, financial problems, and a whole host of other maladies simply because they didn't know how to handle success. Many have seen their hugely successful ventures crumble into dust because, buoyed by their success, they didn't keep striving for continued excellence. Many have subconsciously set themselves up for failure because they weren't prepared for success. There is a tendency on the part of many to focus on how to deal with failure, but equally important is how to deal with success, for if entrepreneurs are truly striving to raise their success/failure ratio, they will potentially have more opportunities to encounter success than to encounter failure, over the long term, and must therefore be equipped for that eventuality.

The best way to illustrate how success can turn into failure is to recall a meeting that took place in 1929 at the Edgewater Beach Hotel in Chicago. Attending the meeting were eight of the world's most successful and important financiers: the presidents of the largest steel, utility, and gas companies; the president of the New York Stock Exchange; a presidential cabinet member; the most successful Wall Street investor; the chairman of the world's largest monopoly; and the president of the Bank for International Settlements. Twenty-five years later, all of them faced ruin. Charles Schwab died bankrupt; Samuel Insull was a fugitive from justice; Howard Hopson became insane; Richard Whitney served time in prison, as did Albert Fall, who was eventually pardoned so he could die at home; and Jesse Livermore, Ivan Krueger, and Leon Fraser all committed suicide.[20]

It is not within the scope of this book to fully treat the issue of the entrepreneur's inability to cope with success, but suffice it to say that those entrepreneurs who seem to have found the formula for coping with success maintain a constant state of self-renewal, a constant striving to be better at what they do and better at who they are as human beings—a constant pursuit of excellence in every aspect of their lives. Only the best is good enough for world-class entrepreneurs, these intrepid people who say not only "I can," but "I will"—and who envision their success long before it is achieved.

New Venture Checklist

Have you:

❑ **Developed a code of ethics for your business?**

❑ **Listed possible ways that your business can be socially responsible?**

❑ **Defined what success means to you?**

Issues to Consider

1. Do you believe that your code of ethics should stand firm in any situation? Why or why not?

2. Suppose you are doing business in a country like Russia where paying fees (bribes) to get through the process more quickly is standard practice. In the United States, bribery is against the law. How will you deal with this conflict in ethical standards when you're doing business in Russia?

3. In addition to the suggestions given in the chapter, name two other ways that your company can demonstrate its social responsibility.

4. Would you require your employees to give back to the community as part of their work contract with your company? Why or why not? If you would, how could you implement this policy?

5. How will you define success for your business?

Experiencing Entrepreneurship

1. Choose an industry that interests you and interview several people in that industry—suppliers, manufacturers, distributors, entrepreneurs—about the ethics in the industry.

2. What are industry organizations and trade associations doing to promote ethical standards in business dealings?

Additional Sources of Information

Bowyer, K.W. (Ed.) (1995). *Ethics and Computing: Living Responsibly in a Computerized World.* IEEE Computer Society.

Cohen, B., and J. Greenfield (1997). *Ben & Jerry's Double-Dip: Lead with Your Values and Make Money Too.* New York: Simon and Schuster.

Houck, J.W., and O.F. Williams (Eds.) (1996). *Is the Good Corporation Dead?: Social Responsibility in a Global Economy.* NJ: Rowman & Littlefield.

Reder, A. (1995). *75 Best Business Practices for Socially Responsible Companies.* New York: J.P. Tarcher/Putnam.

Rushworth, M.K. (1995). *How Good People Make Tough Choices.* New York: William Morrow and Company, Inc.

"Thoughts on the Business of Life." *Forbes*, September 25, 1995, p. 248.

Internet Resources

Business Ethics Magazine
http://condor.depaul.edu/ethics/bizethics.html
Delivers timely news, commentary, and features on social responsibility and ethics.

Corporate Conduct Quarterly
http://www.singerpubs.com/ethikos
A bi-monthly publication that examines ethical and compliance issues in business.

International Business Ethics Institute
http://www.business-ethics.org
Deals with issues of transnationalism in business ethics.

The Online Journal of Ethics
http://www.depaul.edu/ethics/ethg1.html
Contains cutting-edge research articles in the field of ethics.

Relevant Case Studies

1. Mrs. Gooch's Natural Foods Market
2. OXO (A)
3. Autopsies-to-Go

Case Studies

Flight Time

Air Charter Worldwide:
Start-Up of an Air Charter Broker

"Unfortunately, our request for the $300,000 loan has been rejected," stated Patricia Zinkowski to her two partners, Dara Zapata and Jane McBride, co-founders of Flight Time Corporation, a six-month-old air charter broker company based in Chestnut Hill, Massachusetts. It was June 1985 and the three partners were seated in the restaurant of the Suffolk Downs racetrack in East Boston, discussing Flight Time's first period of operations and future financial needs. The business had not taken off the way they had expected. Clients, and consequently cash inflows, had not been enough to support the company beyond six months, and the relevant net loss had eroded the initial investment of the three entrepreneurs. They had estimated that $300,000 was needed to continue Flight Time's operations, but their request for these funds to Shawmut Bank had been turned down, and their personal finances were not sufficient to keep the company in business.

They all agreed that their new company had potential, and the possibility of dissolving the corporation was not even considered. However, as Patti Zinkowski observed, what had started as a desire for independence and challenge "was now becoming a much more serious game."

Founders' Backgrounds

Dara A. Hoy Zapata   Dara Zapata had gained extensive experience in the airline business after graduating from Cardinal Cushing College, Chestnut Hill, an affiliate of Notre Dame, with a degree in business administration in 1971. She began her career as a tour coordinator with one of the first wholesale tour operators in Massachusetts. The firm specialized in arranging vacations in Europe, particularly in Spain, for large groups of retirees. Her job was to organize the air charter flights and the hotel sojourns for these tour groups.

In 1976, she left this company and worked for a short period of time in sales, first for a Boston-based yacht brokerage company and then for a local travel agency, selling air tickets and all-included vacation packages. In 1977, while working for this agency, Dara co-founded A.H. Zapata, Inc., with her Chilean husband. The company offered bilingual translation and interpreting services in Spanish and English, English as a Second Language program for foreign employees, and Spanish classes for U.S. personnel of Boston metropolitan service-oriented companies, such as Beth Israel Hospital, Massachusetts General Hospital, Brigham and Women's Hospital, Mass. Defenders, and the Boston Housing Authority. Dara worked alternately part-time and full-time setting up programs, marketing services, hiring and training language teachers. In 1983 Dara's husband decided to accept a full-time position at Brigham and Women's Hospital; consequently, the company ceased operations in the same year.

Case #93-32 Flight Time: Start-Up of an Air Charter Broker (A). This case was written by Alberto Bonacini, Candida Brush, and Clifton Smith. Reprinted by permission.

In 1979, while working part-time for A.H. Zapata, Dara Zapata had joined the Texas-based airline Braniff International, where she was employed as a manager of Boeing 747 flight operations, responsible for organizing time schedules of international pilots and crew. She subsequently became a manager of in-flight services in charge of catering contracts for provisions and other supplies, until she was dismissed by Braniff in 1982 due to a corporate-wide layoff.

Prior to starting Flight Time, Dara became an independent aviation consultant providing assistance to start-up airlines in meeting government regulatory requirements. She was particularly involved with the short-term leasing of aircraft and worked closely with Lusoair, a U.S. carrier that operated between Boston and Ponta Delgada in the Azores. She helped manage "wet aircraft leasing," where, along with the plane and crew, maintenance agreements were included. It was the end of 1984 when Dara, observing the business operations between this carrier and its clients—large international tour operators—began to vaguely conceive the idea of an air charter clearinghouse.

Jane F. McBride   Jane McBride, Dara's cousin, was 25 years old at the time of Flight Time's incorporation. She had graduated from Wesleyan University in 1981 with a degree in cultural anthropology, and her first job was teaching English at A.H. Zapata, Inc., Dara's enterprise. Jane also had a passion for aviation and had obtained her license as a private pilot, flying more than 200 hours on a Piper Dakota, her father's private plane.

During the summer of 1982, she left Zapata, Inc., and went to work for International Weekends, an American tour wholesaler operator that at the time moved the greatest number of passengers per year.[1] Jane was a tour escort guiding tourists to London, Amsterdam, and Paris. Because her job at International Weekends was seasonal, in 1983 she joined American Adventures, a U.S.–based travel operator, as a tour leader. In this job, Jane led ten tours of foreign tourists throughout the States, doing everything from driving the 20-seat van to coordinating the trip, arranging sightseeing, and planning overnight accommodations. A year later, Jane left American Adventures and went to work for Trans National Travel (TNT), the travel-related wholesaler division of Trans National, a financial services company based in Boston. As a tour director, her responsibilities involved organizing trips and traveling to Asia, Europe, and the Caribbean.

Jane found her job "challenging and satisfying" and stayed with TNT until the end of 1984. Then, at her sister's wedding, she had a conversation with her cousin Dara, who convinced her that joining their business knowledge and skills to start a new company would be a good idea.

Patricia A. Zinkowski   Patti Zinkowski, 27 years old, grew up in the Boston area and went to the University of Massachusetts at Amherst, planning to become a veterinarian. Before graduation Patti switched her major to the physics/astronomy department and was especially interested in climatology and aviation weather. However, due to the small number of climatology and meteorology courses, she graduated with a degree in physics and, according to her, "with no intention of using it."

---

[1] International Weekends was later bought by TWV, another U.S. wholesaler tour operator.

After graduation in January 1980, she went backpacking in Europe with a friend. She spent time in Switzerland, skiing and working as a ski instructor at camps for kids. In November 1980, the head of a Philadelphia-based company that sent American tourists overseas offered her a temporary six-month position as tour guide at a hotel in Switzerland. "I had a lot of fun organizing the stay of our clients and socializing with them. I had the best time, made a few bucks, and decided that I liked to travel." After this assignment, she came back to Boston for a visit, but ended up being hired in January 1982 by the same company Jane was working for, International Weekends, at their United Kingdom accounting office. Patti was appointed Accounts Supervisor and sent to London, where she oversaw the bookkeeping activities of related tour agencies. Here she met Jane, who was working for International Weekends as a tour escort.

In 1983, Patti left International Weekends to join Trans National Travel (TNT), where she worked as Director of European Accounting, managing all the financial aspects of tour operations in Switzerland, Italy, and Germany. In the autumn of 1984, after discussing with Jane the possibility of starting their own company, Patti decided to leave TNT in December of that year.

The Business Opportunity

The Idea

The idea for Flight Time was conceived by Dara during her consulting experience, which involved the short-term leasing of aircraft for new airlines. The leasing agreements typically required that the lessee guarantee a certain number of flight hours to the owner of the airplane.[2] Dara found that the more flight hours the operator guaranteed, the more favorable would be the lease rate. As a consultant, she tried to increase the number of guaranteed hours by making some phone calls to tour operators who she felt might need aircraft space for tour groups. One of these contacts was a tour operator whose 80 clients had been stranded in San Juan because of a last-minute flight cancelation. Scheduled flights were fully booked and the tour operator had no ideas for providing alternative air travel, so the angry tour group was unable to leave the island. After a few more phone calls, Dara "discovered that there was quite a demand for some type of a central clearinghouse, serving airline operators, who could let us know about aircraft availability, and the customer, who needed airplanes."

In September 1984, Dara, who wanted to be "independent and to do things in the [air travel] industry better," approached her cousin Jane at a wedding and over a glass of wine at the dinner party and told her about the business idea, already having selected the company's name: "Flight Time." Dara wanted Jane to be involved because she "knew her cousin had the necessary background for the tour operator component needed by the envisioned enterprise." Dara believed Jane's experience was a necessary complement to her own expertise in aircraft operations and flight contract agreements. Jane was extremely interested in the opportunity because of its "excitement, sense of adventure." She [also] "could not imagine working for anybody else."

---

[2] Flight hours are measured block to block, only when the aircraft is moving.

Dara was aware that "the third piece needed would have to be someone with a solid background in computers, accounting, and finance." Jane remembered Patti, now head of European accounting for TNT, and called her about the Flight Time idea. Patti, who in her experiences had seen travel groups getting stranded at various airports around the world, thought that the possibility of offering air charters to travel groups was very feasible and decided to join Dara and Jane in the new venture.

Getting Started

The initial business concept was to operate in the air charter industry as a pure charter broker.[3] As Dara explained: "We thought of setting up an intermediary company that would help aircraft owners to increase their utilization and assist tour operators in finding an aircraft, whatever their needs might be." From September to November of 1984, Dara and Jane met several times to explore the feasibility of the potential start-up company. Patti, who was abroad at the time, joined them in December when she returned to Boston. During that period, they called contacts they had made in the travel business over the years, to see "if the idea was really off the wall or not." Patti recalled the outcome of those phone calls and meetings:

> We asked them if we opened a business like this, "Would you use our service?" And it was an overwhelming response: "Are you in business now? Do you know of any place [that provides this type of service]?"
>
> We just couldn't see that anything was so wrong with the idea. We just thought it was a great idea since we also had personal experiences with people needing planes.

In addition to talking with potential clients, the women met with advisers from the Service Corps of Retired Executives (SCORE),[4] experienced in providing free business and technical consulting to businesses and corporate start-ups. Even though these counselors did not know very much about the industry or specific business, they concluded that if Dara, Jane, and Patti wanted to start this business, it was feasible. The three entrepreneurs felt quite reassured with this advice. Jane recollected later that excitement was growing because "at the time we did not think there was any other company doing this."

Enthusiastically they discussed the business idea with their families, but all their parents expressed reservations and thought starting a new company was risky, considering the young age of the three partners. "Why don't you get a real job?" was a recurrent suggestion. On the contrary, Jane felt, "We did not have anything to lose [because] we were between seasons with our tours," and Patti thought that "if it was not going [to work], we could have gone back to what we were doing before."

---

[3] An air charter broker is a fee-based business intermediary that links an airline having aircraft space to rent, with another entity, usually a corporation or a tour operator, needing to fly people or goods. A pure broker does not own or personally lease aircraft, but acts only as an agent for the two parties.
[4] SCORE is an affiliate of the Small Business Administration (SBA).

In December, Dara, Jane, and Patti met several more times and decided their bread and butter would be Part 135 aircraft.[5] Larger aircraft also were considered but they decided to concentrate on the smaller aircraft first. They agreed to target customers who traveled where scheduled service was lacking or when times weren't convenient. The following description characterizes Flight Time's target customer:

> If you went from Boston to Atlanta no problem: you got eight flights a day. But if you had to go from Biloxi, Mississippi, to Daphne, Alabama, there was not good service. You had to go back to Atlanta, change planes, go to Daphne, go back to Atlanta, change planes, go back to Biloxi. It was this hub-and-spoke. You just couldn't get around the wheel. You always had to come to the center where the airlines were.

Tour operators' small track programs, which involved prearranged periodical flights to and from the same destination, were also targeted as a major source of revenues. Other segments the three principals identified, in no specific order, were the leisure market (defined as "vacationers"), corporate business travel, and sports team travel. Dara stated that their target was "to have a wider client base. If one end did not pan out, the other part of the client base could pick up the slack."

In the beginning, their main objective was to get the word out, to let people know about the new service their business would provide. Jane and Dara would concentrate on contacting potential clients and operators to find out what type of aircraft they were operating and what type of utilization they would like to have.

By chance, Dara met an administrator of the U.S. Military Travel Management Command (MTMC), a federal military representation division. This official explained to her how the Military Command arranged air charter flights for its troops, how the contracts were filled out, and what kind of information was needed when dealing with air carriers. After this conversation, Dara decided to adopt this framework for Flight Time's operations.

A hired designer created a windrose high-tech logo that represented the three founders and an aircraft style design (see p. 421). Even though a formal business plan had not been written, the time had come to meet with the lawyer for the official incorporation of the company.

Business Environment

Between 1976 and 1982, the commercial airline industry was characterized worldwide by high fragmentation and intense competition. The top 15 airlines flying between the United States and Europe, the most traveled

---

[5] In 1985, Part 135 referred to a section of the U.S. Federal Aviation Regulation (FAR) governing safety and operating procedures for aircraft having, among other requirements and limitations, fewer than 20 seats and not more than a 12,500 pounds gross takeoff weight. Over these two limits, FAR Part 121 regulations applied. Aircraft operating under Part 135 and those operating under Part 121 can be generically defined as "small airplanes" and "large airplanes" respectively.

international route, had an overall passenger market share on that route of less than 70 percent in 1984. Pan Am, TWA, and British Airways, the top three international carriers, were separated by only one percentage point.[6] U.S. carriers had the largest share of world traffic in 1984 with 40 percent of the total Revenue Passenger Miles (RPMs)[7] flown, only a three percent increase from 1976.[8]

Commercial air carriers provide regularly scheduled and/or charter flights for both passenger and cargo operations. Scheduled flights serve a specific route on a regularly scheduled timetable (for instance, biweekly) and are sold to the public. For charter flights, either public charters (i.e., typically a wholesale tour operator resells the seats of the leased aircraft to the general public) or single entities (i.e., a corporation charters a flight for its employees, without reselling single seats), are purchasers of the services and negotiate their own routing and timetables. A scheduled airline may provide both scheduled and charter air service, while charter operators generally offer only the latter. Revenues from charter flights varied greatly among single airlines, ranging from less than $100,000 a year for the airline operating a single Part 135 aircraft, to nine-digit figures for nonscheduled flights of major national scheduled carriers. In 1984, scheduled air operations accounted for 89 percent of the total airline traffic measured in Revenue Ton Miles (RTMs)[9] and 90 percent of world RPMs (see Exhibit 1). The Department of Transportation (DOT) estimated that in the United States 5.5 million people—business travelers and vacationers—took air charter flights in 1984.

Before the introduction of the Airline Deregulation Act (ADA) in 1978, the competition among U.S. domestic airlines was regulated (much like public utilities) by the Civil Aeronautics Board's (CAB's) control of new entries, entries into existing markets, routes, and pricing policies. Since 1978, when President Jimmy Carter introduced the competitive aviation policy and the CAB was dissolved, airlines were allowed to voluntarily modify their route networks and marketing strategies. One of the most visible effects of the deregulation was the accelerated growth of "hubbing." Five years from the adoption of the ADA, some airlines more than doubled their hub-and-spoke operations, with an up to 10 percent increase of the load factor and a 15–20 percent increase of air travelers who flew a complete journey on a single airline.[10] Major commercial airlines began to cut regular services to and from locations considered not profitable enough, while small commuter jets, corporate jets, and charter operators blossomed. According to the *Financial Times*, in the early 1980s . . .

---

[6] Source: International Air Transport Association (IATA), 1985.

[7] Revenue Passenger Mile (RPM): As defined by the Federal Aviation Administration (FAA), "one revenue passenger transported one mile in revenue service. Revenue passenger miles are computed by summation of the products of the revenue aircraft miles flown during a flight stage, multiplied by the number of revenue passengers carried on that flight stage."

[8] Source: U.S. Department of Transportation, 1985.

[9] Revenue Ton Mile (RTM): As defined by the FAA, "one ton of revenue traffic transported one mile."

[10] Source: U.S. Department of Transportation, 1984.

. . . businessmen are increasingly taking to the air in small, light transport aircraft either owned by, or chartered on behalf of, their companies. This concept of "business aviation"—as opposed to "business travel" on scheduled airlines—has been winning favor . . . [because of] . . . the greater convenience and time savings involved, by comparison with the scheduled airlines, together with a significant saving in cost.[11]

In 1984 there were more than 12,000 airports in the United States, but only 400 were serviced by scheduled flights.[12] World-wide, there were 300 scheduled airlines, of which fewer than 30 were the U.S. scheduled carriers, accounting for more than $100 billion in revenues.[13] Approximately 4,000 carriers operated air charter flights in the United States, accounting for $2.4 billion in sales, flying more than 14,000 aircraft. Revenues from vacationers (the so-called "leisure travel") comprised more than 60 percent of the $2.4 billion dollar sales, while 20 percent of the revenues came from incentive houses[14] and corporations. The remainder was split among the U.S. government (i.e., troop movements), sports teams, and entertainment.

The largest share of the air charter market was represented by public charter flights, sold directly to the public or, more often, to tour operators. Most scheduled and nonscheduled airlines marketed their charter flights through in-house brokerage operations or through their own sales personnel. The rest was managed by wholesale and retail tour operators and by a handful of regionally dispersed and privately held independent brokers, whose revenues rarely surpassed $1 million. Tour operators, corporate incentive planners, government departments (such as the Department of Defense), and sports teams were, in order, the four main purchasers of these brokerage services.

Few charter airplanes were large jet aircraft (such as the DC-9, B737, and B757) produced by major aircraft manufacturers like Boeing and McDonnell-Douglas.[15] Instead, single-engine and two-engine piston planes, produced by specialized smaller manufacturers such as Fokker and having fewer than 20 seats, were most frequently chartered. The Part 135 aircraft made up 60 percent of the 80 seats or less segment.[16] Total shipments of general aviation aircraft to scheduled and charter carriers had been declining since 1979 (see Exhibit 2(a) on p. 433), and in 1984 experts were forecasting a steady negative trend.

This downturn in the shipment of aircraft was mainly the result of the airlines' attempt to contain fixed costs and to strive for better use of the available equipment, to be obtained partially by increasing the number of flight hours. For airline operators, the average utilization of large equipment

---

[11] Source: *Financial Times*, April 2, 1984.

[12] Source: *TravelAge East*, May 12, 1986.

[13] Source: International Civil Aviation Organization (ICAO), 1985.

[14] Incentive houses are service companies organizing the work incentive plans (such as travel bonuses) for the employees of their corporate clients.

[15] For a more detailed description of aircraft manufacturers in the 1970s and 1980s, see Professor Sushil Vachani, *The Commercial Aircraft Industry in 1987* (1990), Management Policy Department, Boston University.

[16] Source: Federal Aviation Administration 1984 Forecast, Federal Aviation Administration, 1985.

was 6 to 7 flight hours a day including scheduled flights, while for smaller airplanes utilization barely reached 2 flight hours a day. Even though fixed costs such as aircraft, maintenance, and personnel were steadily increasing, other variable costs, such as jet fuel and oil prices, after a steady increase and a sharp rise in 1979, were declining beginning in 1981 (see Exhibit 2(b) on p. 433).

The Start-Up

On January 2, 1985, Patti, Jane, and Dara went downtown to meet with their lawyer for the first step of the legal incorporation of the business.

Initial Resources

Each of the three partners was able to withdraw ten thousand dollars from personal savings without involving family funds. Flight Time, Inc., was organized so that Dara, Patti, and Jane had equal partnership in the business, each owning one-third of the three hundred shares issued at no par value. Dara described the initial financing: "We figured that $30,000 would let us go on forever. We would have enough income from our business to perpetuate the business." Then they gave one another titles, a legal condition when an incorporation occurred. Dara was named President because she had had the original idea, Patti was appointed Treasurer because she was doing the bookkeeping; and because the Commonwealth of Massachusetts required that someone be clerk, Jane was made Secretary by default.

They leased a one-room office with no windows at a travel agency in Chestnut Hill. To provide the new location with the necessary office supplies, they went to friends' basements and dug out old file cabinets; then to yard sales, other companies, and offices to obtain secondhand desks and appliances. On the first day of business, their office furnishings consisted of a few telephones, a couple of typewriters, an answering machine, a photocopier, a $4,700 Hewlett-Packard computer with dot matrix printer, and a coffee machine. They distributed various Rolodex cards with the names and the addresses of all the contacts that Dara, Jane, and Patti had made in the airline industry and the tour operator business. Besides these contacts, they subscribed to *Aviation Daily, Travel Weekly,* and other magazines and newspapers, useful for updated aviation-related news and as possible sources for their first clients. Flight Time did not have a firm commitment from anyone who prior to start-up had demonstrated interest in using the services of an air charter broker.

At Work

The first day of Flight Time's operations, Jane, Dara, and Patti went to work in business attire promptly at 8:30 A.M. According to their new business cards, Jane was Director of Operations, Dara was President and Director of Sales and Marketing, and Patti was Director of Finance. After a few weeks at the office, however, while it was clear that finance and accounting were Patti's main responsibilities, most of the other functions were managed together. Decisions other than those involving ordinary operations had to be made unanimously.

Most of their time was spent jointly, searching for clients and available airplanes. Jane recalled that "how to get the word out was our marketing plan." Sitting in the same room facing one another, they looked in the *Boston Globe* for companies that were growing. They called people they knew, from professional contacts in the tour operator business to friends and family, as well as friends of friends and other referrals. Through letters and follow-up calls, their efforts in convincing potential Part 135 clients to consider chartering a small aircraft were based on comparing charter planes to scheduled carriers: "Why change planes and why stay overnight in a hotel, when you can fly with your own plane?"

With the goal of getting the word out and reaching potential clients, Flight Time joined the National Business Aircraft Association (NBAA). Patti was able to generate a few descriptive articles about the company for the trade magazines and local newspapers. Looking for new ideas, Patti went to a public relations seminar, where she conceived the first press release of Flight Time. As she mentioned, "It was necessary to have a lot of common sense. We did not have a lot of money to spend in advertising, but we needed to get our name out there." Thus, the initial press coverage resulted in many phone inquiries that were used to build up a list of possible clients. To expand this press coverage, in April, Flight Time also started a two-page newsletter that was sent to prospective customers and air charter operators (see Exhibit 3 on p. 434). Travel people began to identify them as "the three women in Boston." In an attempt to enhance Flight Time's image and business network, Patti joined the New England Women Business Owners (NEWBO), and Jane, the National Association of Female Executives (NAFE). They were sure that being three women in a male-dominated industry would create a stronger awareness of their service.

Operationally, when a potential customer called for a price estimate, a standard client request sheet was completed and input into the computer. Information included the desired time of departure, date, place of departure and arrival, number of people traveling, and special equipment to be carried along. Flight Time then searched for the possible carriers in a computerized database they created, in the *World Aviation Directory*, and in any other publications that could provide a profile of different airlines and that included information such as contact names, types of the aircraft, and number of seats. In order to match the customer's request to an aircraft, Dara, Patti, and Jane would call various carriers and ask for a quote. Considering that the quoted price already included a 5 percent to 10 percent commission, they did not add any extra charge to the client. When a client accepted the price and aircraft type, Flight Time linked the customer and the charter airline, with only those two parties signing the final air transportation contract. A database of available Part 135 and Part 121 aircraft organized by state was set up on the computer, even though the computer was used mostly for the newsletter and business correspondence to clients and airlines. Another database, containing information about possible clients, also was developed.

On March 31, after three months of operations, they had their first official board meeting at Boston's Charles River Park, a complex housing professional offices. The three partners decided to recruit an international executive committee to assist them in searching for contacts and business advice, with no obligation or compensation for its members. Around the same time, the three founders discovered that they were not the only pioneers of the air charter brokerage industry; in fact, another company, Charter Services, had been operating in Albuquerque since 1979. This discovery reinforced Flight Time's moral: "If there is someone doing what we are doing since '79, there must be a lot of business out there."

First Clients

Dara recalled how many of Flight Time's early contacts originated from the consulting service she used to provide. "They were not a lot of contacts, but certainly enough to get going. I knew the business well enough so that I could call any airline, introduce ourselves and explain about our company." In February, the American Soy Bean Association travel planner called Flight Time because some of the members had to inspect properties located in Massachusetts and needed a Part 135 airplane for the tour. This was the first deal for the newly born clearinghouse.

In the second month of operation the phone rang again. A casino operator wanted to fly 15–20 people daily from Boston and from Providence, Rhode Island, to the casinos of Atlantic City, New Jersey.[17] The three businesswomen were speechless: it was a $1,000,000 yearly contract, one hundred thousand dollars in brokerage fees. They located a start-up airline in New Hampshire operating just the right-sized plane, a Dornier 228-201. The casino operator signed the original contract. Because this track program was a long-term commitment, he asked for a credit extension. As per Flight Time's policy, he would pay for the first flight before departure and then settle the other trips a few days later. The plane flew smoothly for two weeks; then suddenly the aircraft was not being filled, the casino operator stopped paying, and the contract failed. "But it was an eye-opener," Patti recollected later. "We had this one contract, but it got screwed up so fast. If there was one of these trips there were more of these trips."

A few weeks later, a former client of Dara's, a hardware distributor from southeastern Massachusetts, was contacted by Flight Time. The owner of the company was a pilot himself and easily understood the air charter concept. He decided that instead of picking up his clients at Boston's Logan Airport, it would be better to fly them directly to his factory. This $700 deal, paid a few days prior to departure, generated a profit of $70 to Flight Time.

By June 1985, the five-month-old clearinghouse had generated $150,000 in revenues, primarily from trips arranged at least 3–4 weeks in advance, although some flights were arranged on one-day notice. For every 10–12 price quote requests, Flight Time was able close one deal, usually settled before departure and subject to a cancelation policy of 2 to 3 weeks in advance. Most of the booked planes could carry between 10 and 50 passengers, with the 8-seater Learjet's being the most chartered aircraft. However, the time spent to shape a deal on a Learjet with 8 people was the same as for a Boeing 727, a 100-seat jet. At the end of the fifth month, the names of several potential clients had been entered into the database, and it was clear to Jane that "the only limitation to our success was creating awareness of our services."

---

[17] See Exhibit 3 on pp. 434–435.

Second Financing?

During the first week of June, Patti inspected Flight Time's financial position. The business had less than $4,000 in cash. Most of the start-up money had been used for office supplies, rent, utilities, promotional activities, and salaries to the principals. But Dara, Jane, and Patti were not ready to give up:

> The track program we had set up was not going to sustain itself, which was what the original plan was. We knew that the business we anticipated was on the books. We were waiting for the big one to come along and get us over, [but] the numbers decided for us that we needed a secondary financing.

After a quick analysis of the situation, they determined that $300,000 was needed not only to keep the business running, but also to expand it. They approached a local bank for the $300,000 loan. The bank requested that Flight Time present a business plan and disclose relevant financial information. Suggestions from SCORE helped them construct the business plan (see Exhibit 4 on pp. 436–438), and a certified public accountant was hired to produce the financial statements (see Exhibit 5 on pp. 439–441). However, because of Flight Time's lack of 2 track record and its brief business history, the bank refused to lend Flight Time the $300,000.

Dara, Patti, and Jane wondered what kind of future Flight Time could expect.

1. How did Dara Zapata, Jane McBride, and Patti Zinkowski recognize the opportunity for an air charter service?

2. Evaluate the qualifications and experience of the founding team for Flight Time.

3. What was the status of the industry at the time Flight Time was founded?

4. How did Flight Time plan to differentiate itself from other air charter services?

5. What was their financial strategy? Was it successful? Why or why not?

6. Describe their operational strategy.

7. Evaluate Flight Time's business plan according to the key questions to be answered as discussed in the book.

Exhibit 1
Flight Time

DISTRIBUTION OF WORLD AIRLINE TRAFFIC IN 1985

	International	U.S.	Total
Freight Services - Note A			
Scheduled	84%	96%	90%
Charter	16	4	10
Passenger Services - Note B			
Scheduled	81	97	89
Charter	19	3	11

Source: International Air Transport Association, *Historical Data Report*, 1985.
Note A: Measured in Revenue Ton Mile (RTM).
Note B: Measured in Revenue Passenger Mile (RPM).

SELECTED DATA FOR WORLD AIR TRANSPORT

	1981	1982	1983	1984
Scheduled Airlines				
Scheduled Services				
Passengers Carried (millions)	752	767	798	845
Freight Tons Carried (millions)	11	12	12	13
Passenger-Miles Flown (billions)	703	717	745	798
Available Seat-Miles (billions)	1,109	1,132	1,166	1,236
Ton-Miles Performed (billions)	84	86	91	99
Available Ton-Miles (billions)	145	148	152	164
Charter Services				
Passenger-Miles Flown (billions)	30	30	28	30
Ton-Miles Performed (billions)	3.9	3.6	3.5	3.7
Available Ton-Miles (billions)	6.1	5.7	5.5	5.8
Charter Airlines				
All Services				
Passenger-Miles Flown (billions)	32	37	40	43
Ton-Miles Performed (billions)	4.2	4.8	5.0	5.4
Available Ton-Miles (billions)	5.7	6.6	6.6	7.0

Source: International Air Transport Association, *Historical Data Report*, 1985.

Exhibit 2
Flight Time

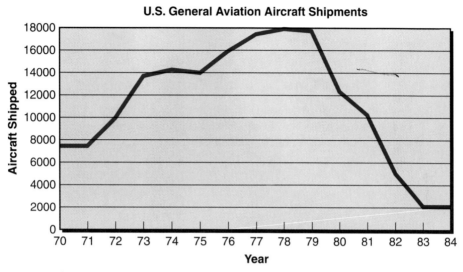

U.S. General Aviation Aircraft Shipments

Source: International Air Transport Association, *Historical Data Report,* 1985.

(a)

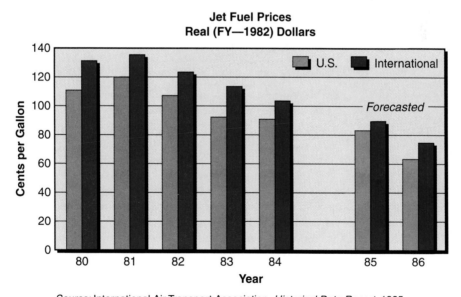

Jet Fuel Prices
Real (FY—1982) Dollars

Source: International Air Transport Association, *Historical Data Report,* 1985.

(b)

Exhibit 3
Flight Time

Flight Time's Newsletter
April/May 1985 Issue

Flight Line by Flight Time   April/May 1985

Congratulations, consider yourself an innovator in your company!

Every business needs individuals who think ahead, who are open to new ideas, and are not afraid to try new products. By showing your interest in FLIGHT TIME you are supporting a pioneer concept in the aviation industry.

This month FLIGHT TIME launches its first newsletter and introduces you to new opportunities in air travel.

Opportunity No. 1—Flight Time

FLIGHT TIME is not a travel agency. We are not an airline nor a tour operator. What we are is a resource, and an information station, dedicated to securing cost-efficient and reliable private charter air transportation for individuals, corporations, groups, and associations. FLIGHT TIME fills requests for charter aircraft for groups of all sizes, whether it be for you or your entire company.

Since you may have received some information on FLIGHT TIME prior to this newsletter, here is a brief synopsis of the services offered by FLIGHT TIME.

FLIGHT TIME: 1. HELPS you decide if private charters are your best alternative in air travel.

2. LOCATES certified aircraft that best suit your needs.

3. PROVIDES quotes and options that include aircraft descriptions, per hour costs, and technical data.

4. CONFIRMS and coordinates charter arrangements and itineraries.

Best of all, FLIGHT TIME offers these services FREE of charge.

Opportunity No. 2—Precision Airlines/Alantic City Holidays

FLIGHT TIME is pleased to announce that Atlantic City is now accessible from Boston and Providence via Precision Airlines.

Atlantic City Holidays, a New England–based tour operator, is now offering daily departures from Boston and Providence to Atlantic City, New Jersey. Round-trip air, complete overnight packages including casino transfers shall be available starting April 5, 1985.

Precision Airlines puts into service its new DORNIER 228-201 for this program. The Dornier is a new-generation commuter aircraft known for its speed, high passenger comfort, and STOL capabilities.

Further information on price and schedule may be obtained by calling: (800) 442-1162 (Mass. only) or (800) 447-2250 (outside Mass.).

Opportunity No. 3

According to the National Business Aircraft Association, the average business trip involves 4.1 people traveling 338 miles with a four-hour turnaround.

Suppose you and your team of key salespeople want to blitz a customer in Syracuse. Instead of dealing with complex schedules, two-hour layovers, and missed connections, you jump into your private plane, make a three-hour presentation, and fly back again. You get the job done fast. Your plane waits for you rather than you waiting for the plane.

Many businesses do not even consider the possibility of chartering aircraft for their business travel due to the myth that the cost is prohibitive. (Not all itineraries merit a chartered airplane.) You could be pleasantly surprised to find that on many occasions a business trip would be more cost-efficient if key employees traveled by private charter rather than scheduled carrier.

For more information call FLIGHT TIME at (617) 965-7060.

Opportunity No. 4—Eastern Charter/Nantucket

Eastern Air Charter is planning to offer first class service to Nantucket Island from Norwood, MA airport this upcoming summer season. Service is tentatively scheduled to begin May 15th.

The price of a ticket will include: First class comfort aboard executive aircraft (planes are fully air conditioned), champagne, full liquor, and soft drinks, inflight snacks, free airport parking, onboard telephone and entertainment systems.

The schedule is designed to accommodate weekend passengers with departures Friday evenings and early Saturday mornings returning on Sunday evenings. The fare for this trip will be $175.00–$180.00 per person round trip.

Exhibit 4
Flight Time

Flight Time's Business Plan
As Provided by Flight Time to Shawmut, for the Loan Request Application

Statement of Purpose

FLIGHT TIME is a service business dedicated solely to security charter air transportation for individuals, groups, associations, and corporations. FLIGHT TIME specializes in screening and locating Part 135 and Part 121 aircraft for this client base. FLIGHT TIME neither owns nor operates any aircraft.

FLIGHT TIME acts as a charter clearinghouse. The company is in the business of distributing information on aircraft prices and availability, negotiating terms of charter contracts and coordinating details of charter flight operations. Upon authority by client, FLIGHT TIME acts as agent for the client in security aircraft and arranging charter flight.

FLIGHT TIME charters aircraft (on behalf of clients) from carriers certified for charter. This means that both commercially scheduled airliners and nonscheduled airliners may be used in the selection process.

Note: FLIGHT TIME does not engage in activities such as the following, which are traditionally associated with retail travel agencies, i.e.:

- reserve and ticket airline seats on commercial or charter flights.
- arrange tours of any kind for individuals or groups.
- arrange "package deals" associated with tourism.
- reserve and confirm hotel accommodations or any other land arrangements.
- reserve or promote rental cars or ground transportation.

Business Plan—Market Section

The market for FLIGHT TIME Corporation's charter air service may be subdivided into the following segments, each with its own particular requirements.

Corporate

According to *Travel Weekly*, a trade journal, over 500 million business trips of one night or more are made each year. The report concludes that because few corporation have any organized business travel policy, millions of dollars are wasted annually.

FLIGHT TIME works, with corporations of all sizes, many of which are listed in the Fortune 1000. We recommend the following checklist to our clients as a yardstick to determine air charter feasibility:

- When 3 or more people are charter feasibility.
- When the destination or point of origin is more than 45 minutes from a major airport.
- When key personnel travel business or first class.
- When a destination does not have non-stop or direct air service.
- When the limitations of scheduled airline service mean unnecessary hotel overnights with other added expenses.

Responses to FLIGHT TIME's service have been extremely positive. Due to the wide array of available aircraft, FLIGHT TIME has been able to accommodate requests for 15 passenger turboprops, 5 passenger jets, and 80 passenger jets, just to name a few.

Tour Operators

There is a very high concentration of tour operators and wholesalers in the Northeast and for many, the key to the success of a track program is contingent upon reliable and economical chartered air space. In an industry where last-minute changes and failed contracts are commonplace, FLIGHT TIME assists tour operators in negotiating contracts with FAA certified air carriers.

FLIGHT TIME recently negotiated a contract between a Boston-based tour wholesaler and regional air carrier for daily flights from Boston and Providence to Atlantic City.

Travel Agents

Travel agents are prime targets for FLIGHT TIME's services with their corporate, leisure, and affinity markets already established. Since most travel agents, as well as the traveling public, are unfamiliar with general aviation, FLIGHT TIME's services complement those of retail and corporate agents.

FLIGHT TIME has targeted reputable agents with upscale clientele who have expressed an interest in private charter. Agents receive a percentage of FLIGHT TIME's commission.

In addition to F.I.T.s, many agencies organize their own group tour programs and frequently need larger aircraft. FLIGHT TIME has received requests from agents for groups of 15–100 passengers.

Casinos

FLIGHT TIME, sponsored by Claridge's Casino of Atlantic City, is awaiting confirmation of its vendor registration number, a license to contract directly with New Jersey casinos. FLIGHT TIME applied for the license in response to several queries from casino operators looking for charter aircraft to transport VIP clients in from the greater Northeast region.

Casinos are constantly seeking ways in which to entice "high rollers" to their establishments: flying them directly into Bader Field, located in down-town Atlantic City, is one such way. Bader Field, however, has a very short runway—only 2950 feet, and few aircraft can land there. FLIGHT TIME has located a number of high performance STOL aircraft capable of flying directly into Bader, and is actively marketing these aircraft. Several casinos have expressed interest in working with FLIGHT TIME once the vendor registration number has been assigned.

Referrals

Referrals from airlines constitute a major market segment, and these clients are usually already qualified buyers. To date, we have received referrals for trips to Cincinnati, Minneapolis, Bowling Green, Cleveland, and Atlanta.

Personal contacts and referrals have also generated considerable business.

Hotels

Deluxe hotels are constantly seeking extra amenities to offer their clients. FLIGHT TIME has contacted general managers of upscale hotels in MA to introduce our services. Executive charter, like limousine service, is considered by many as a necessity rather than a luxury. Oversized folded business cards, which include a brief description of FLIGHT TIME's services and are displayed in selected areas of a hotel, are an inexpensive yet effective way to reach the discerning business or leisure traveler.

Travel and Meeting Planners, as well as Incentive Houses, are also good sources of potential business.

Location Analysis for Business

FLIGHT TIME operates primarily via telephone, telex, and written correspondence, therefore, location is not a major factor. FLIGHT TIME is located in close proximity to the 128 belt, and is convenient to Norwood airport.

Competition Analysis

As of this writing, there exists no other company operating exactly like FLIGHT TIME. The existing competition consists of:

A. Direct Airway - New Jersey - Primary focus is corporations utilizing fleet based in Teterboro, NJ.
Charter Clearinghouse - Pennsylvania - Primary focus is on bringing clients from Pennsylvania to Atlantic City.
Charter Services - New Mexico - Concentrates on Midwest sports teams.
Netair Int'l - Colorado - Organized 12 air taxi operators in the western U.S. under the Netair name and uniform.
F. Miscellaneous Charter Operators - Charter operators who do not own or operate a particular aircraft requested, but broker it out and charge hefty commissions.

Pricing Philosophy

The difference between FLIGHT TIME and its competition lies in our pricing philosophy. FLIGHT TIME strives to offer its services free of charge to its clients. Because of the soft general aviation market, aircraft owners and operators are extremely eager to maximize aircraft utilization, and pay a sales commission to FLIGHT TIME. FLIGHT TIME receives a commission based on the overall contract value:

- 10% on Part 135 operators—i.e., aircraft with fewer than 20 seats
- 5% on Part 121 operators—i.e., aircraft with more than 20 seats

Unlike the competition, which levies 5–10% commissions on both the operator and the client, FLIGHT TIME's prices are among the lowest in the industry. We believe that by keeping prices low, we will be able to better demonstrate to our clients that private air charter can be cost-effective and competitively priced.

Credit Policy

FLIGHT TIME operates on a cash or credit card basis with the majority of sales prepaid. A 3% bank charge will be assessed on credit card sales. (Once a client has established a favorable credit history, FLIGHT TIME will extend credit on a net-10 basis, but only in situations where FLIGHT TIME has at least the same terms with the carrier.)

Exhibit 5
Flight Time

BALANCE SHEET
as of May 31, 1985
(Note A)

ASSETS

Current assets

Cash	$ 3,797
Supplies	866
Prepaid Expenses	229
Deferred Expenses - Note B	5,779
Total Current Assets	10,671

Property and Equipment

Computer	4,700
Equipment	1,853
Total Property and Equipment	6,553
Accumulated Depreciation - Note C	(175)
Total Net Property and Equipment	6,378

Other Assets

Deposits	575
Organization Expenses, Net of Amortization	596
Total Other Assets	1,171
Total Assets	$18,220

LIABILITIES AND STOCKHOLDERS' EQUITY

Current Liabilities

Accounts Payable	$ 978

Long-Term Debt

Loans Payable, Stockholders'	26,000

Commitments - Note D

Stockholders' Equity

Common Stock - Note E	3,000
Retained Earnings	(11,758)
Total Stockholders' Equity	(8,758)
Total Liabilities and Stockholders' Equity	$18,220

Note A: Balance Sheet as Prepared by Robert M. Hurst & Company, Certified Publlic Accountants.

Note B: This Amount Represents Expenses Incurred Prior to the Date Operations Commenced and, Accordingly, Are Being Amortized Over the First Twelve Years.

Note C: Property and Equipment Are Being Depreciated Using the Straight-Line Method of Depreciation Over Their Estimated Useful Lives of the Assets for Book Purposes and the Accelerated Cost Recovery System for Tax Purposes.

Note D: As of May 31, 1985, the Company Was Obligated Under a One-Year Lease Agreement Expires December 31, 1985 Covering the Premises in Chestnut Hill, Massachusetts. The Terms of the Lease Stipulate a Monthly Rental Payment of $300.

Note E: No Par Value; 15,000 Shares Authorized; 300 Shares Issued and Outstanding.

STATEMENT OF INCOME AND RETAINED EARNINGS
for the Period from January 2, 1985 (Date of Inception) to May 31, 1985
(Note A)

		% to Sales
SALES - Note B	$123,919	100%
COST OF SALES - Note C	117,356	94.7
Gross Profit	6,563	5.3
SELLING, GENERAL AND ADMINISTRATIVE EXPENSES - Note D	18,864	15.2
Net Profit (Loss) Before Other Income and (Expenses)	(12,301)	(9.9)
OTHER INCOME AND (EXPENSES)		
Gain on Sale of Stock	687	0.6
Interest Income	85	0.1
Depreciation and Amortization	(229)	(0.2)
Net Profit (Loss)	(11,758)	(9.5)

Note A: Income Statement as Prepared by Robert M. Hurst & Company, Certified Public Accountants.
Note B: Dollar Amount as from Billing to Customers.
Note C: Dollar Amount as from Billing from Aircraft Carriers.
Note D: See SCHEDULE OF SELLING, GENERAL AND ADMINISTRATIVE EXPENSES.

SCHEDULE OF SELLING, GENERAL AND ADMINISTRATIVE EXPENSES
for the Period from January 2, 1985 (Date of Inception) to May 31, 1985
(Note A)

		% to Sales
Office Supplies and Expenses	$ 4,011	3.2%
Promotion and Entertainment	3,801	3.1
Auto and Travel	3,405	2.7
Rent	1,567	1.3
Dues and Subscriptions	839	0.7
Equipment Rental	833	0.7
Telephone	715	0.6
Training	698	0.6
Postage	423	0.3
Maintenance and Repairs	418	0.3
Professional Fees	410	0.3
Insurance	383	0.3
Taxes, Other	228	0.2
Advertising	187	0.2
Organization Expense	131	0.1
Miscellaneous	815	0.7
	$18,864	15.2

Note A: Schedule of Expenses as Prepared by Robert M. Hurst & Company, Certified Public Accountants.

STATEMENT OF CHANGES IN FINANCIAL POSITION
for the Period from January 2, 1985 (Date of Inception) to May 31, 1985
(Note A)

SOURCE OF FUNDS

To Operations

Net Income (Loss)	($11,758)
Add Back Non-Cash Expenses:	
Depreciation and Amortization	229
Net to Operations	(11, 529)
Proceeds from Loans Payable, Stockholders'	26,000
Proceeds from Issuance of Capital Stock	3,000
Total Source of Funds	17,471

APPLICATIONS OF FUNDS

Acquisition of Computer	4,700
Acquisition of Equipment	1,853
Increase in Deposits	575
Acquisition of Other Assets	650
Total Applications of Funds	7,778

INCREASE (DECREASE) IN WORKING CAPITAL	$9,693

COMPONENTS OF WORKING CAPITAL

Increase (Decrease) in Current Assets

Cash	$ 3,797
Deferred Expenses	5,779
Supplies	866
Prepaid Expenses	229
Total Increase (Decrease) in Current Assets	10,671

Decrease (Increase) in Current Liabilities

Accounts Payable	(978)

INCREASE (DECREASE) IN WORKING CAPITAL	$9,693

Note A: Cash Flow Statement as Prepared by Robert M. Hurst & Company, Certified Public Accountants.

The Penduline Putter

A Case of New Product Development

Introduction

It's 1995 at the Riviera Country Club, site of the Los Angeles Open, and Paul Gurrola wants to meet professional golfer Mike Hulbert, known for his one-handed putt. An amateur golfer himself, Gurrola wants Hulbert to try out the new one-handed putter Gurrola has invented. Hulbert has just come off a second-place win in the 1995 Buick Invitational Golf Tournament in Torrey Pines, using his innovative one-handed technique. Through Hulbert's agent, Gurrola is granted a twenty-minute meeting with Hulbert prior to his round in the Los Angeles Open. That 20-minute meeting turns into an hour. Hulbert is impressed with the putter but suggests important improvements that would attract a pro to use it. For one thing, he says, the prototype putter face doesn't have loft; this means that the face is perpendicular to the ground, so when the golfer hits the ball, the ball will be pushed before it starts rolling. With loft, the face is slanted or not perpendicular to the ground, so the ball will start rolling immediately upon being struck—a distinct advantage. Hulbert also notes that the hosel, or connector between the shaft of the club and the putter head, is incorrect.

For about five years Mike Hulbert had been attempting to deliver a more fluid pendulum putting stroke by practicing with his right hand only. In this way his shoulders, arms, and club would work as one lever. So when Gurrola came back to him with the improved version of the Penduline Putter, Hulbert agreed to test it.

The Golf Merchandising Industry

The National Golf Foundation reports that in 1996 there were 25 million golfers, up from 23.5 million in 1991. More impressive is the merchandising end of the golf industry, which is a $15 billion business, up from $8.5 billion in 1991.

One-handed putting is becoming a trend, as many PGA professionals have recognized its effectiveness and large numbers of amateur golfers are experimenting with this new style of putting. There's a very good reason for this trend: the statistics of golf. Fully 67 percent of a golf score is made on shots from 75 yards and in—chipping and putting; yet most golfers spend most of their time practicing the long shots.[1]

Competition

The most popular model of putter is the heel-and-toe weighted, face-balanced putter called Pings, invented by Karsten Solheim of Scottsdale, Arizona. Prior

This case is prepared as a basis for classroom discussion rather than to illustrate effective or ineffective handling of a management situation.

[1] A.G. Pollard Jr., "Puttin' on the Hits," *Hemispheres*, December 1995.

to that were the blade putters, essentially just flat blades with no loft or just a few degrees of loft. More recently Titleist created the Bullseye putters with skinny curlicue brass heads. These are used by golfers who are fairly confident of their putting ability.

In the past couple of years, the most popular putters have been the mallet models or oversized clubs like Bobby Grace's "The Fat Lady Swings" and Callaway's "Big Bertha War Bird." Yet another innovation is the use of the face insert, a rubbery elastic insert on the putter face that gives the golfer a softer feel when the ball comes off the club. Odyssey Golf has called its model "Stronomic." It is the most popular putter on the Senior PGA Tour.[2]

The Plop putter, the Ping Pal 4, the Long John Putter, and the Stand-Up Putter each sold over 200,000 units in its first year in the market, with retail prices ranging from $65 to $100.[3] The Penduline Putter is priced between $75 and $95.

The Birth of the Penduline Putter

In 1992, having spent eight years in the financial services industry, Paul Gurrola was laid off. It seemed as good a time as any for him to go back to school to get his MBA. He chose the University of Southern California and was admitted to the Marshall School of Business. For one of his elective courses, he selected Introduction to Entrepreneurship. It was there that he began to develop the idea for his new product.

Actually, it was a bad round of golf that gave him the idea for what was to become the Penduline Putter. Gurrola was playing golf with his friends and losing badly. He just couldn't get the ball in the hole. Finally, in disgust, he swung at the ball holding the putter with only his right hand and amazingly enough, the ball glided into the hole. He tried it again, and again it worked. He began to ponder why a swing made in a moment of frustration could be so successful and finally realized that when he made the stroke with only his right hand, the pendulum arc was far better than when he tried to guide it with two hands. This was quite a revelation. Gurrola decided that he might have something that would benefit a lot of golfers who were frustrated with their short strokes.

In his entrepreneur class he began working on a market feasibility study and a prototype for the putter. His professor introduced him to a design engineer in the engineering school who helped him design the club. It took ten prototypes to reach the version that he was ready to submit for a patent and trademark. Because his resources were limited, and an attorney needed $5,000–$7,000 to handle the patent application, Gurrola decided to do the work himself. He quickly learned, though, that he would have to pay in time lost through mistakes. For example, on the first patent application, he failed to check a required box. The application came back to him four months later and he had to correct and resubmit it, having lost four months' time. One thing he did that was helpful was establishing a relationship with the patent examiner. This way he was able to find out that the patent had been approved,

---

[2] Ibid.
[3] Sporting Goods Manufacturers Association.

long before he received the actual notification in the mail, allowing him to get started on producing a mold for the club.

Establishing relationships with manufacturers and others in the industry was key to moving forward with the product. For example, Scotty Cameron, a designer of top-rated putters who had sold his company to Titleist for $12 million, met with Gurrola and gave him design suggestions that made the putter more attractive to professionals.

Gurrola and his partner, Michael Toerge, spent about $20,000 over five years to develop the putter. That is a relatively small amount in product development terms. Still, as of February 1998, they had yet to make any money on it. But for Gurrola the whole experience has been a "rush," and he wouldn't trade that experience for anything. He hasn't given up.

Because 85 percent of golfers putt right-handed, Gurrola and Toerge created only a right-handed putter, to save costs. But Toerge suspected that the more natural movement would be to use a left-handed putter in the right hand and putt backhand. The first time he tried, Toerge made a 30-foot putt with this approach. This was not surprising because when he looked at the physics of the swing, it was easier to putt backhand than forehand, with one hand. Furthermore, a two-handed putt is really overkill for short putts. The day before Christmas, 1997, they finished their first left-handed prototype. (Please refer to "The Penduline Putter" press release on pp. 445–447.)

As of February 1998, Gurrola and Toerge have focused their energy on raising money. They are writing two business plans, one for doing all the work of the business themselves and one for approaching an infomercial expert. According to Toerge, they are "scared to death." What they have, they believe, is "truly revolutionary," but there's a mountain of skepticism to overcome. Both believe that if their new product fails, it will be only because of them. Gurrola puts it best: "This is not about perfection; it's about progress."

1. What do you believe is the vital component Penduline will need to be a success in the market?

2. Can Gurrola and Toerge bring in a major investor at this point, or should they wait until they have some sales? What are the pros and cons of either course of action?

3. What should their market entry strategy be?

4. What are the unique aspects of this industry that make it difficult to enter?

PENDULINE

3810 EAST COAST HIGHWAY, SUITE 4
CORONA DEL MAR, CA 92625
949. 723-1075 TEL
949. 723-1550 FAX

THE PENDULINE PUTTER

INTRODUCING A REVOLUTIONARY NEW PUTTER AND PUTTING TECHNIQUE. THE **PENDULINE PUTTER** SIMPLIFIES PUTTING AND IMPROVES SCORING. CONSIDER THE FOLLOWING:

WHY THE PUTTER?

Thirty-five to forty-five percent of a golfer's score is the result of the use of one club, the putter. One club out of the fourteen we are allowed to carry or 7% of our clubs, is doing 35 to 45% of the work. According to Golf Magazine's subscriber survey, the typical golfer owns 4.4 putters, 3.7 fairway woods and 2.8 drivers. The typical golfer owns more putters than any other club.

WHY ONE HAND PUTTING?

If you want to hit a ball 300 yards, you need two hands on the club, however, if you are trying to roll the ball ten or twenty feet, why two hands? Putting with two hands is like throwing a dart with two hands. The "yips" are defined as the inability to coordinate several muscles and joints harmoniously into a single, pure pendulum stroke. Our one handed technique eliminates five fingers, a wrist, a forearm, an elbow, a shoulder and the upper back from the putting stroke. In this way the putting stroke is less complicated and **easier to consistently duplicate**.

WHY BACKHAND?

The muscles that give control to the backhand stroke are bigger and stronger than those that control the forehand stroke. With the backhand technique, the follow through of the putting stroke is unrestricted, allowing the putter to follow through the ball to a horizontal position. See and feel how easy it is to draw a straight line to the hole. This follow through cannot be created with conventional two handed putting. The stroke is very solid and if you miss, you'll find your misses will be better.

WHICH ARM?

Use your dominate arm, the one you use to throw or write. This requires a right handed golfer to use a left handed putter. Address the ball on the opposite side of the conventional putting address.

PUTTER DESIGN FEATURES

* **Patented and PGA Conforming, Oversized, Octagonal Grip**
  The most innovative design feature of the Penduline, the octagonal grip allows the Penduline to be held firmly without clinching and straining the hand muscles. This allows for a one piece motion initiated at the shoulder joint.

* **Oversized Putter Head**
  The Penduline is approximately 50% heavier that a standard putter head. The heavier Penduline putter head allows for greater feel and pendulum action.

* **Face Balanced Design**

* **Medium Length Shaft** (35, 37 & 39 inches)

Source: Drawn and created by Michael Lee Toerge for Penduline Putter.

PENDULINE

3810 EAST COAST HIGHWAY, SUITE 4
CORONA DEL MAR, CA 92625
949. 723-1075 TEL
949. 723-1550 FAX

PUTTING TECHNIQUE   (Assumes a right handed golfer. See accompanying diagram.)
Stand on a square stance with feet directly below the hips and toes pointing straight forward. Swing your putting arm naturally and freely. Your arm naturally swings at an angle of roughly 45 degrees to your shoulders. Since this feels most natural, it is easier to control and **easier to duplicate**.

- Grip and Stroke: Grip the Penduline at the base of the grip with your middle finger wrapped around the base of the grip and your index finger extended down along the shaft. Cock you wrist to apply pressure to your index finger which in-turn leverages the grip against the inside of your forearm. The wrist, forearm and elbow should move as one, with no break during the stroke. The Penduline putting stroke is generated in the shoulder with all other body parts still. Relax your left hand in the small of your back or your back pocket.

- Address: Identify your line. For longer putts, locate a line indicator or spot 15 feet from ball. Align the emblem of the ball with your putting line, eyes on the ball through the stroke.

- Feet Location: See accompanying diagram. From a square stance move your left foot back 6 inches and turn the toe out a few degrees. (This places the shoulders in the proper angle to swing naturally); your knees should be slightly bent. Bend at the waist and position your right shoulder over your right foot. Your right eye should be over the ball.

- Putting Angle: See accompanying diagram. Ninety degree angle from the centerline that runs through the center of your right foot from heal to middle toe.

- Ball Alignment: When in the position described above, your right arm hangs straight down over your right foot. Your back hand should be aligned with the right side of your right foot. The ball should be placed just outside the outside line of the right foot approximately 5 inches from your toe. This allows 2 inches of clearance between the heel of the Penduline and toe of your shoe

- Follow Through: The back hand putting stoke enables full extension follow through to a horizontal position. This greatly enables the golfer to draw a straight line with the putting stroke and mentally "put the putter head into the hole."

Experiment with the way in which you use the Penduline. This technique works, however, slight variations are necessary to make your Penduline putting technique as natural and **easy to duplicate** as possible.

Source: Drawn and created by Michael Lee Toerge for Penduline Putter.

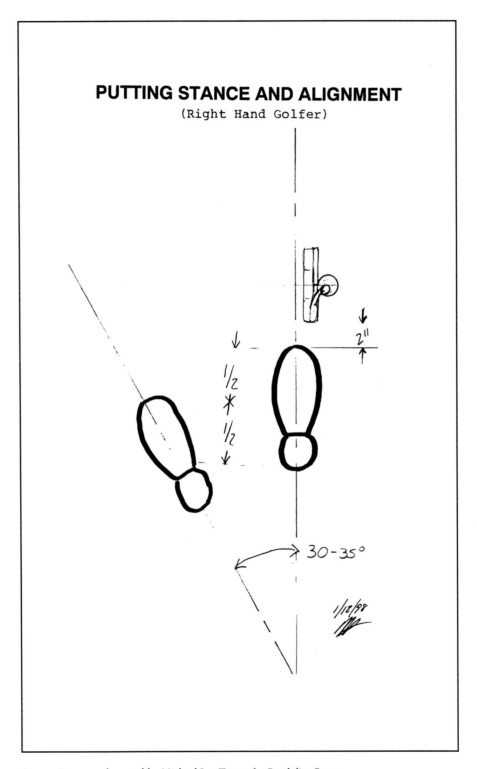

Source: Drawn and created by Michael Lee Toerge for Penduline Putter.

Autopsies-to-Go

Franchising a Dying Business

Introduction

If you had told Vidal Herrera back in the 1960s that someday he would be known as "El Muerto," king of the private autopsy business, he probably would have laughed. For in the 1960s in East Los Angeles, this self-described hippie raised in a tough environment was working in a pizza joint, just trying to keep money in his pocket. Today he presides over a rapidly growing industry that he created. Autopsy/Post-Services fills a niche in the market for private autopsies created by cutbacks in funding for hospitals and coroner's offices. In addition to providing these services to families, law enforcement, and such high-profile attorneys as Johnny Cochran, Autopsy/Post-Services also promotes and handles organ and tissue donations, does postmortem biopsy diagnosis, DNA (paternity) analysis, toxicology, and serology. Herrera has also done TV and movie production consultation.

The Birth of the Company

In 1975, Vidal Herrera decided that he had to find a career with a future. He began volunteering four days a week for two and a half years at the Los Angeles County morgue, training to become a qualified autopsy technician. He was then given a job there as a way to earn a living while going to school. It was on-the-job training all the way, from transporting bodies to assisting pathologists at autopsies. He learned about medical photography, lifting and labeling. He learned to eviscerate, to excise and dissect tissue. He also learned how to harvest tissue and clean crime scenes. He worked on such high-profile cases as the Hillside Strangler and the Nightstalker; at the crime scene of the latter, he discovered a fingerprint that ultimately led to the identification of Richard Ramirez as the Nightstalker. But in 1984, while moving a cadaver, he suffered a back injury that put him out of business for over four years. During that time he had trouble finding another job and things got tough. Finally, in 1988, his former boss, onetime Los Angeles County Coroner Thomas Noguchi, who by then was in private practice, hired Herrera to help with an autopsy and passed the word of Herrera's skills to others in the industry. As a result, the VA Medical Center in West Los Angeles hired him as an autopsy technician on a contract basis to fill the gap in the availability of trained technicians. Herrera discovered that other hospitals and mortuaries were experiencing the same problem; soon he was able to establish a network of contracts, and his business got off the ground.

It wasn't until 1993 that the business really began to take off. One day as he was watching TV, he noticed ads for 1-800-DENTIST and 1-800-LAWYER. He quickly checked with the telephone company to see if 1-800-AUTOPSY was available, and it was. He now had the hook for his business. He purchased

This case is prepared as a basis for classroom discussion rather than to illustrate effective or ineffective handling of a management situation.

a van and painted 1-800-AUTOPSY on the side panels. This attracted a lot of attention for his growing business. Soon families began calling him for second opinions on suspicious deaths or to exhume bodies for re-autopsy. The majority of his customers are attorneys seeking evidence for malpractice actions or criminal defense cases. Whereas a coroner's office would charge $2,854 for a private autopsy (if they even had the time or manpower to perform it), Herrera charges $2,000, and Herrera produces in 10 days the results that the coroner's office takes nearly 120 days to give.

Autopsies are legally required to be done by a doctor, but Herrera assists the nine doctors who work with him. In addition, he has two full-time autopsy technicians who do about 60 percent of the physical work of opening a body and dissecting and weighing the organs.

The Industry

The death care industry is an $8 billion a year industry that is expected to grow to $20 billion by the year 2010, due principally to aging baby boomers. But the reality is that the practice of autopsy is a dying science. Thirty years ago, hospitals performed autopsies on about 50% of hospital deaths. Today teaching hospitals autopsy only 10% to 20% of deaths. In most communities without teaching hospitals, the rate dips to below 5%.[1] This is a disturbing trend to medical practitioners who believe that autopsy "is the one place where truth can be sought, found, and told without conflicts of interest."[2] It is the unequivocal source of the cause of death.

Several reasons have been proposed for the current demand for private autopsy services: 1) Many hospitals don't have autopsy suites and can't provide the service; 2) city and county governments have cut budgets to coroners' offices; 3) many hospitals don't have trained technicians because there are no schools that teach them how to perform autopsies; 4) insurance companies don't cover them; 5) many doctors are concerned that autopsy results could be used against them or the hospital in malpractice suits; and 6) most hospitals will perform autopsies only for deaths under suspicious circumstances, not to determine such conditions as Alzheimer's disease, because the Joint Commission on Accreditation of Health Care organizations no longer requires hospitals to maintain a minimum autopsy rate.

Growing the Business

When Herrera was considering ways to meet the exploding demand for his services, the natural strategy was franchising. Autopsy/Post-Services can easily be duplicated, the demand is world-wide, and this franchise would probably face less competition because most franchisees "would rather open a restaurant or a yogurt shop than a dead body."[3] The typical franchisee candidates would be certified pathology assistants, autopsy technicians, embalmers, and doctors.

---

[1] "Pathologists Request Autopsy Revival," *Medical News & Perspectives, JAMA,* June 28, 1995, Vol. 273, No. 24, p. 1889.

[2] Ibid.

[3] Robert E. Howard, "Autopsy/Post-Services—A Sure Thing!" *The Stakeholder,* September 1995.

In 1995 alone, Herrera turned away 9,000 autopsy cases while doing around 900 cases a year without advertising. As of 1998, he and his team were performing five or more autopsies a day, generating more than $1 million for the business. Herrera would like to sell 72 autopsy franchises in the United States and 16 abroad. He already has 2,300 applicants for franchisee positions. He is also supplying Russia with fully equipped vans for conducting full autopsies.

Human Tissue and Organ Donation

Another way Herrera is growing the business and giving back at the same time is by promoting the donation of tissues and organs for research. He firmly believes that all human tissue can be used for transplants or research to save lives and bring the cost of medical care down. Two particular areas of interest for Herrera are AIDS research and Alzheimer's disease. This is his way of showing that death is not necessarily bad, but merely a part of the cycle of life, and that when someone dies, someone else's life can be saved or otherwise helped by organ donation or tissue research.

Herrera's concern now is not the potential for competitors, although it will be at some point, but rather how to grow the business in a way that will maintain the level of quality and service he has become known for.

1. Besides franchising, what is another way Herrera can effectively grow his business?

2. Who are Herrera's customers and what is the most effective way to reach them?

3. With no established training centers for technicians, how can Herrera ensure a sufficient supply of qualified technicians?

4. What are the barriers to entry in this industry?

Toy Tips®, Inc.

In September 1991, 23 years old and only two years out of college, Marianne Szymanski left her job and started Toy Tips, Inc., a toy research and consulting firm. For most people this would have been a very frightening thing to do, but Szymanski had no doubts her new business would succeed. Having graduated from Marquette University with a bachelor of arts degree in psychology and marketing, she had been working for a toy manufacturer selling toys to retailers and sometimes stocking shelves. Naturally, customers would come up to her and ask questions. Often they were grandparents who didn't recognize any of the new toys and consequently had no idea what to purchase.

As a result, Szymanski decided to find out if there was any information out there on the best toys to buy for kids of various ages. Consulting the major magazines related to children, she found that each seemed to have its own "top ten" list of toys. Upon closer inspection, however, she discovered that invariably, the toys on the lists were made by the manufacturers who had purchased advertising space in the magazine. Moreover, she found that the self-proclaimed "experts" in the field were being paid by the manufacturers to review their products. This was certainly not a very unbiased way to judge these toys. Szymanski, who hadn't yet decided what she wanted to do with her life, immediately saw an opportunity to provide a much-needed service and create a career opportunity for herself.

The Start-Up

Szymanski puzzled over the best way to start this business so that she could reach the most people. At the time, 900 telephone numbers were becoming a popular business venture that could be started quickly and with relatively little capital. Szymanski decided to try this avenue. So Toy Tips began as the National Toy Information Hotline, a 900 number that people could call for the latest information on toy safety, product recalls, and tips on age-appropriate toys. To start the business, Szymanski drained her savings account, then took her business plan to nearly every banker in Milwaukee. She was turned down time and time again with "This is great; this is wonderful—good luck." But no money.

Fortuitously, two days before actually starting the business, a local talk show asked her to appear. That free publicity was worth more than any bank loan. From that point on, the media picked up on what she was doing, and her business grew much more quickly than she would have expected. By the end of the first year, little town gazettes all over Wisconsin had picked up on the hotline. Then the Associated Press and *USA Today* got hold of it, and the business exploded. She started receiving phone calls from all over the United States.

This case is prepared as a basis for classroom discussion rather than to illustrate effective or ineffective handling of a management situation.

At the same time, she had also sent some information about her hotline to the Toy Manufacturers of America, New York, which is the voice of the toy industry, and they published her information in their monthly PR release to toy manufacturers. All of a sudden she was inundated with information and hundreds of samples from toy companies. Still working out of her home, testing toys on the living room floor with neighborhood children, she decided she needed to look for another site for the business because the toys were taking over. She went to a pediatrician she knew and worked out a barter arrangement that allowed her to fill four rooms of his office with toys for his patients to "test." That worked for a while, but soon she had overgrown the space and needed to move again. By now her ability to convince people of her credibility was well honed, so she went to the President of Marquette University, Father DiUilo, who helped her come up with the idea of working out of the child care center at Marquette. The arrangement was that the children would test the toys, she would observe them, and the toys would be donated to the university. And so it was that Toy Tips, Inc., moved into the child care center, a series of rooms bursting with primary colors, bustling with activity, and alive with the sounds of children.

By the end of 1991, she was working with 50 manufacturers. By the end of 1992, that number had swelled to 140, and her revenues had doubled. She had also created a magazine to carry her message and publish the notices of toy recalls. The magazine also contains Szymanski's "top ten" lists: "The Top Ten Travel Toys," "The Top Ten Educational Toys," and even "The Top Ten Environmental Toys."

Bootstrapping Genius

Even though the company was growing, Szymanski didn't have enough money to hire the employees she needed to help her handle the ever-increasing workload. But Szymanski, who is the essence of the bootstrapping entrepreneur, knew that there must be a way to get help by bartering, the way she had done for her office space. Once again she went to the university and suggested that the administration offer an internship program in which Marquette students would work for university credit in her research center. The university agreed and "Toy Tips 101" was born. Engineering students tested the toys and even designed a "toy crusher" for her. Working with one of the engineering professors, she was able to develop new tests for toys, such as tests for flammability and toxicity. Journalism students helped her do fact-checking and gather information for articles, while a public relations student helped her with her media tour. Psychology and education majors were involved in the focus groups and testing. She also used marketing students to develop questionnaires and research on the needs of parents. For quite some time, Szymanski had no "employees" in the traditional sense, but finally hired two assistants to help her carry the load.

With all the media attention she was receiving, Szymanski had to travel. She didn't have an appropriate wardrobe, and since all her money was going into the business, she didn't have enough to go out and buy one. So once again she demonstrated her bootstrapping creativity, going to the JH Collectibles clothing company and bartering for a new wardrobe for her media tour. In exchange for the wardrobe, JH Collectibles received a page of advertising in her magazine, which was handed out during the tour.

Szymanski used a similar technique to "buy" time with an attorney. She happened to attend a seminar, "Global Marketing in Europe," given by the Wisconsin trade center. Being the only woman at the seminar became an advantage, because when she later called the attorney who had led the discussion, he remembered her. She arranged for an appointment, ostensibly to talk with him about trademarks, but actually this was just an excuse to approach him about becoming the attorney for her small but growing business. She asked if he would consider working with her at a reduced rate with the understanding that when the business got bigger and she had the money, she would pay his regular rate. He laughed appreciatively at her assertiveness and agreed to work with her. He continued to do so, always charging for his time but being flexible in billing, depending on her business's financial situation.

Growing the Business

As the business grew, it became obvious that the 900 hotline was becoming a problem. Young children who had seen her on TV and knew that she worked with toys were discovering her 900 number and calling asking for "the toy tester." She imagined that their parents weren't too happy about the phone bills, so she discontinued the line. The 900 number had by then served its purpose. It gave her the resources to get her business off the ground and also gave her extraordinary media attention. Eventually she had over 850 media contacts and began appearing regularly as a "toy guest" on "Good Morning America."

Szymanski incorporated the business to protect herself and her assets from liability, but also to give the business an image of permanence and credibility. This became increasingly important as she began to do more than toy testing. She started consulting to private companies (never toy manufacturers), including McDonalds, Rayovac, HDI Engineering, and Candy & Kids Shoes. One battery manufacturer, for example, asked her to test batteries in her toys to see exactly how long they lasted. A French company wanted to learn how American children played, which gave her a chance to go to Europe and study how European children interact and play.

Toy Tips was hired by Toys 'R' Us to conduct research on toys for "differently abled" kids. The contract allowed her to set up 18 testing centers at hospitals and clinics and ask kids with special needs to test the toys. The result was a special guide to help parents of "differently abled" kids that helps them choose toys that the children can enjoy and learn from.

Growing a business means looking beyond current markets to new ones. Szymanski understood that children aren't the only people who like toys, so she organized The Annual Toy Tips "Executive Toy Test." Each year she invites 50 executives from all industries to play with toys to discover which are the best stress relievers. This event is held in a different city every year, which gives her a chance to observe differences in toy play from region to region. Szymanski also has six summer camps where kids test computer software.

The philosophy of Toy Tips has remained constant as a guide for the growth of the business: "Toy Tips does not endorse or warrant any toy that it reviews." It considers itself an independent source for informed decision-making on the purchase of toys. With this mission in mind, Szymanski must decide where to take the business next. She has considered forming a non-profit corporation for research purposes, as this would give her access to foundation grants. But establishing a nonprofit corporation is more complicated and has more rules and regulations than a C-corporation. At this point, she is not sure what the advantages and disadvantages would be.

1. What regulations will specifically impact Toy Tips?

2. Into which other markets can Szymanski take her business?

3. Are there any problems this business is likely to face?

4. Is there another corporate form that might work for this business?

Simtek, Inc.

Simtek, Inc.

In July 1985, a California corporation called Simtek, Inc., was founded to produce and market patented consumer products. The company was initially capitalized in November 1986 by selling 60 percent of its stock to two private investors. Seed capital of $500,000 was raised to develop two products—the Tapemate electric Scotch tape dispenser, and the Tapemate box sealer. Simtek, Inc., initially chose to begin development and operations with the Scotch tape dispenser, a concept that the founder, Steven Johnson,[1] had been developing since 1982.

The Product

Tapemate, a registered trademark of Simtek, Inc., is an AC electric tape dispenser that dispenses and cuts any desired length of tape when someone presses a button. The TM-100 is designed to be quick and efficient and incorporates a patented disposable tape cartridge containing Scotch brand tape. The original Scotch brand tape did not sell well when it was introduced, as there was no easy way to remove the tape from the roll. The first tape dispensers invented are those still in common usage today. They all contain a means for holding a roll of tape and a serrated blade for tearing a desired length of tape. 3M, the manufacturer of Scotch brand tape, produces an excellent adhesive product, but difficulties continue to arise when customers attempt to remove the desired length from a tape roll, even with the use of a traditional dispenser. Invariably, the tape has unwanted fingerprints, smudges, jagged edges, and so forth. The TM-100 solves this problem by pulling tape off the roll at a smooth three inches per second without fingerprints or smudges and also cutting the dispensed length of tape cleanly without serrations or jagged edges.

To further ensure the quality of the Tapemate dispenser and its intended functions, Simtek also designed a disposable tape cartridge, much like a typewriter ribbon cartridge. The cartridge helps keep the dispenser clean while ensuring that the correct type of tape is being used in the dispenser. The cartridge is easy to load into the dispenser and comes in several types of tape in a variety of widths, lengths, adhesives, thicknesses, and overall quality. Simtek felt it important to control the type of tape used in the dispenser, to guarantee the highest quality. It also planned to price the product at a price point similar to that of the electric pencil sharpener so it would sell well in major office-supply outlets. A retail price point of $79.95 was determined.

Simtek applied for and was granted a United States Patent, #4,638,696, for the electric tape dispenser. Research found that previous similar inventions suffered from a number of difficulties, including the jamming of the operative mechanisms due to the adhesive surfaces' contacting the operative

---

This case is prepared as a basis for classroom discussion rather than to illustrate effective or ineffective handling of a management situation.

[1] Steven Johnson is not the real name of the entrepreneur/inventor who founded Simtek.

mechanism of the dispensing device. Another chronic problem was the propensity for slack to form in the lead portion of the material, within the device, that would then become entangled in the operative mechanism, thereby jamming the dispenser. On the basis of this research, Simtek believed that a need existed for its Tapemate product.

The Company Philosophy

Johnson planned to begin operations with a very small staff of multiskilled individuals, subcontract for manufacturing, and use independent sales reps for a sales team. The goal was to be a "highly service-oriented company with a firm belief in quality and customer satisfaction." It would strive to maintain a very low product-defect ratio to promote customer loyalty. Furthermore, Simtek would not be a one-product company. It would continually search for new consumer products that were innovative and competitively priced.

The History of the TM-100

Johnson approached a prestigious design firm located in Palo Alto, California, to engineer the product and complete the assembly drawings, and contracted with a well-known Southern California design firm to handle the packaging design. The cost of design and development was exceptionally high. It included about $60–70,000 for injection molding tools, $30–40,000 for engineering, and $25,000 for patents. Johnson then took the drawings to a model builder to develop a prototype. At this point a total of about $150,000 had been spent in R&D. It was decided to produce the Tapemate in Korea to keep manufacturing costs down, and limited production was begun.

The initial feedback was positive; it appeared that the market for the electric tape dispenser was very large. However, it was quickly learned that the product was more price sensitive than first anticipated, and in addition, manufacturing costs were coming in higher than estimated, due in large part to overdesign of the product. In other words, the product had too many advanced features that resulted in excessive manufacturing costs.

Johnson decided to save money by acting as his own manufacturer's rep, initiating sales first in the United States, and then in Europe through a contact he had made in Switzerland. He attended trade shows and demonstrated the product in major department stores like Bloomingdale's and Macy's. Demonstrating the product resulted in greater sales, in large part because of the design of the box in which the Tapemate was packaged. While very attractive (it won several design awards), it did not, however, show what was in the box, beyond saying Simtek Tapemate. There was no picture of the dispenser on the box, so potential customers didn't recognize the product for what it was when they saw it on the shelf. Still, Johnson's efforts produced sales of approximately 7,000 units domestically and 5,000 in Europe. In 1988 gross sales totaled $16,345 with a COGS of $10,945. In 1989, gross sales totaled $28,062 with a COGS of $21,092.

At this point, the product had been on the market for three years. Simtek did additional market research and concluded that some key changes had to be made in the product—specifically, a DC battery-operated version so the product would not be geographically sensitive—and some minor design flaws had to be adjusted. For example, it was found that if a customer touched the start button too quickly and didn't hold it quite long enough, the dispensing mechanism would jam after several repetitions. Furthermore, there was the problem of the price point. Johnson's market research indicated that customers perceived the electric tape dispenser as an equivalent of an electric pencil sharpener rather than an electric stapler. This was a crucial distinction, as electric pencil sharpeners could be bought in the $15–$20 range, while the price on electric staplers was much closer to the price on the tape dispenser. At $79.95, the tape dispenser did well in gift stores because its design was very stylized and it worked well in demonstrations. However, it was not competitive in the office supply market, where margins are very small.

Back to the Drawing Boards

Having determined that the original design was probably not the most marketable, Simtek approached two major California product design firms for estimates on the development costs for the battery-operated tape dispenser. The goal of redesign was to reduce the cost of manufacturing through component optimization, part reduction, and mechanism development. The design goals included:

▶ A battery-powered product with an optional AC adapter for extended operation

▶ An improved user interface via a switch separated from the tape-dispensing area, to eliminate accidental switch activation

▶ Easy access to internal components in the event of mechanism failure

▶ Control of the minimum length of tape dispensed to avoid mechanism failure

▶ Elimination of custom cartridges. Access to the internal feeding mechanism would be provided to facilitate the tape-loading process.

▶ Replacement of the solenoid-driven cutting mechanism with a mechanically equivalent solution to reduce the overall power consumption and component cost

▶ Cost of Goods Sold held to between $5 and $6

▶ Exploration of alternative motor and drive assemblies to optimize performance and minimize cost

▶ Reduction in the number of labor-intensive processes such as electrical assembly and soldering, and provision for unidirectional assembly of all components

Estimate of Sales After Redesign

	Cost to Redesign	Unit Cost	Sales Price	Year 1 Sales	Year 2 Sales	Year 3 Sales	Year 4 Sales
Tapemate	$150,000	$6.00	$12.00	25,000 units $300,000	75,000 units $900,000	125,000 units $1,500,000	150,000 units $1,800,000

Simtek, Inc.
Pro Forma Income Statement
(Year 1 after redesign)

	Monthly	Annual
Revenues		
Sales - Tapemate	25,000	300,000
Sales - Box Sealer*	100,000	1,200,000
Gross Revenues	125,000	1,500,000
Less: Cost of Goods Sold	62,500	750,000
Gross Profit	62,500	750,000
Expenses		
1. Promotion and Advertising	250	
2. Entertainment and Travel	500	
3. Meals	100	
4. Wages	12,083	
5. Payroll Tax	483	
6. Medical/Workers' Comp	725	
7. Telephone	400	
8. Supplies	250	
9. Rent	1,500	
10. Freight	300	
11. Model making R&D	1,000	
12. Drafting R&D	2,500	
13. Materials R&D	1,000	
14. Tooling	11,000	
15. Legal	750	
Total Expenses	32,841	394,092
		355,908
Commissions		75,000
Net Profit Before Taxes		280,908

* Based on adding Box Sealer product to mix.

1. Contract PR efforts	6. 6% of payroll	11. Appearance and check models
2. Trade show travel/buyer visits	7. Average including tax	12. ME drafting to work up ideas
3. Employee travel/meals	8. Office supplies and equipment	13. Sourcing materials
4. Staff salaries	9. Office/warehouse space	14. Tapemate-$50k; Box Sealer-$75k
5. 4% of payroll	10. UPS/FedEx/US Mail	15. Patent work

It was estimated that to be competitive, the new unit must sell at a retail price of approximately $15. This translated to a manufacturing cost of $3–$4.50 per unit. The estimates from the product design firms came in at $74,000–$91,000 for concept design, breadboard design (the first stage of a design using models), documentation, prototyping, and pre-production. The entire process would take from 28 to 33 weeks to complete, with the deliverable being a production-quality prototype.

The Beginning of the End

With the design proposal and a revised financial project in hand, Johnson went in search of additional funds for redesigning and to buy out his original investors, who by 1990 were becoming frustrated. Tired of waiting any longer, though, the original stockholders finally forced a dissolution of the company and wrote off the investment on their taxes in 1991.

1. With regard to Simtek's product development process, what were the key problems with the process and how could it have been made more efficient and less costly?

2. What were the advantages and disadvantages of taking on venture partners during the product development phase?

3. With consideration to his pro forma statement for what he expects to happen after redesign, what should Steve Johnson do now that the partners have dissolved the company?

Mrs. Gooch's Natural Foods Markets

Introduction

Entrepreneurs start businesses for many reasons, but not many do it because they want to save their lives. Sandy Gooch was one such entrepreneur. In 1974, she was a wife, mother, ex-teacher, and full-time homemaker who, like millions of other Americans, often relied on convenience foods even though she knew they contained potentially harmful chemicals. One day she woke up with persistent sniffles for which the doctor prescribed tetracycline. A few days later, however, she thought she was having a heart attack. She was rushed to the hospital. The doctors could not find the cause of her symptoms. Two weeks later she developed an ear infection and was again given tetracycline. This time her "attack" lasted three days, and she nearly died. Her father, a biologist/chemist, began what was to be a year of research into food manufacturing practices. He found that Gooch was allergic to chemicals and additives commonly found in food. They affected her body in such a way that it was unable to fight off disease.

From the information her father had gathered, Gooch decided a natural diet was her best weapon, and she proceeded to get rid of everything that was not natural in her kitchen. Within a period of about three months, she was feeling better, and within nine months she was healthier than she had been for years. As she began to study nutrition and whole foods, Gooch found others who shared her problem. Like Gooch, these people had to travel from health food store to health food store, along with shopping at grocery stores, to find the natural foods they needed.

The Birth of Mrs. Gooch's

Gooch felt frustrated. Coming from a family that had always helped people in the community, it was natural that she began to explore ways to make life easier for people who wanted to eat healthy foods. There were lots of things she could do—start a newsletter, form a co-op, give seminars—but the only idea that would allow her to make a real impact on people's lives was the idea of a natural foods store that would carry only things that were good for them. Excited by the possibilities, Gooch began to consult with herbalists, chemists, biologists, cosmetologists, and physicians to gather all the information she could about diet, wholesome foods, and food allergies.

Armed with a wealth of nutritional knowledge, Gooch realized that all the knowledge in the world about food could not compensate for lack of experience in business. She would need to take on a partner. Fortunately, she had a friend who was managing a health food store in the San Fernando Valley, and she succeeded in getting him to help.

They had to find a store location that was accessible and in a good area of town. After much driving around and consulting newspapers, they found a

This case is prepared as a basis for classroom discussion rather than to illustrate effective or ineffective handling of a management situation.

market on the west side of Los Angeles that had gone out of business. It was obvious that the owners had run it into the ground, but to Gooch it couldn't have been more perfect. Using her teacher retirement money and all her savings, she opened her first natural foods market on this site in 1977. The store was an overnight success in spite of her having done no location studies or psychographic studies. She was not simply lucky, however. She had correctly determined that there were a great many people who shared her problems with unnatural foods. In other words, she had innocently and intuitively found a niche in the market. Customers lined up and kept her at the register for six hours straight without a break on the first day.

Early Problems

High demand for what you have to offer has its obvious pluses and its not-so-obvious minuses. One of the problems Gooch faced early on was a shortage of cash. Often cash flow problems are the result of poor management, but in Gooch's case, it was caused by the need to stock sufficient inventory to meet tremendous demand. That required a lot of capital, which she and her business partner didn't have. Banks were unwilling to take a chance on a woman in the grocery business, even though she could point to lines of customers extending out the door of the store. Undaunted, Gooch moved ahead by keeping overhead costs down and scrimping anywhere that didn't affect the customer. This strategy allowed her to keep up with demand fairly well.

Growing the Business

Gooch's passion for her business, her need to help people, and with the tremendous demand for what she was offering led to the opening of a second store within a year. To finance this store, Gooch offered limited partnerships to raise $125,000. From then on, through the use of internal cash flows, five more stores followed over a period of 15 years, with each store reflecting Sandy Gooch's philosophy and mission for the business.

The Nature of the Business

Mrs. Gooch's was committed to offering the highest-quality natural foods, related products, service, and information that optimize and enrich the health and well-being of the individual as well as the planet. The mission guided all the decisions she made about the stores. Accordingly, Gooch required that her suppliers guarantee the quality of their products and be able to furnish laboratory analyses or signed affidavits if requested. The products she carried could not contain chemicals, white flour, sugar, preservatives, artificial colors or flavors, caffeine, chocolate, hydrogenated vegetable oil, or irradiated food. Her mission also gave her a way to expand the product line to include, in addition to food, nutritional supplements and body care products. To increase efficiency as the company grew, she opened a produce/grocery distribution center, a food commissary for the preparation of deli and bakery foods, a design studio to create store decor, and a construction shop to build the displays.

Former teacher Sandy Gooch's love of education found its way into her business. To help achieve her mission, her 800 employees were carefully trained to be knowledgeable about the products she carried. Gooch believed strongly that their product was really knowledge and information. That belief formed the basis of her marketing strategy. She knew that an informed consumer would be an advocate for the type of nutritional lifestyle she was proposing. As advocates, her customers would return again and again to purchase her products and gain more knowledge. She promoted health awareness by offering seminars, producing a newsletter, and giving her customers free brochures on nutrition. A minibookstore in each store contained all the latest research on foods and their relationship to the body. Even the ads that appeared in newspapers were educational in nature.

Looking to the Future

Gooch incorporated the business early in its development and set up a board of directors, which included herself, her partner, a general manager, and their attorney. As this privately held company began to grow, Gooch wondered if she had made the correct decision putting only "insiders" on the board. Would they continue to share her mission for the business? Already, in the early 1990s, she was beginning to see some dissension and a desire on the part of some board members to broaden the scope of the products they offered, even introducing items like alcohol that did not fit in with the vision of Mrs. Gooch's. Would she be able to maintain her vision in the face of challenges?

1. Why is Mrs. Gooch's considered an entrepreneurial venture?

2. How did the mission of Mrs. Gooch affect the decisions she made as the business grew?

3. What intellectual property rights could she acquire?

4. What other kinds of businesses could Sandy Gooch have started, given her philosophy?

5. What potential effect could there be from using insiders on the board of directors? What can she do to remedy the situation?

6. What are some spin-off products or services Mrs. Gooch's could offer?

OXO (A)

In the summer of 1989, Sam Farber had persuaded Davin Stowell, owner of Smart Design, to develop a line of kitchen gadgets (e.g., peeler, can opener, pizza cutter, garlic press) that would be functional, comfortable, ergonomically sound, attractive, and affordable. Stowell decided to accept the challenge for a three percent royalty agreement and a small advance. Farber was expecting Smart Design to have the kitchen gadgets prototyped and ready for manufacture so that they could introduce the new line at the San Francisco Gourmet Products Show in April 1990. Before Davin Stowell would begin the process of generating prototypes, the Smart Design team needed to meet to reinforce or expand on Sam Farber's initial product criteria and help set the design goals for these new products.

The Seed of an Idea Is Planted

Sam Farber had considerable experience in the housewares industry. In 1960, he had founded COPCO, a company that produced well-designed cookware and related housewares items. COPCO's first products were enameled cast-iron cookware made in Denmark. The cookware was designed by an American, Michael Lax. Up to that time, all enameled cast-iron cookware had been traditional designs. COPCO's products were the first modern designs. The company continued to expand its sales of well-designed products in enamel and plastics and was especially known for its teakettles. At COPCO the concentration was on the shape and color of the products. The products were useful, but little thought was given to how products could be made more user-friendly.

In 1983 Sam Farber sold COPCO, but he continued to head the company under a management contract for the next five years, until he retired at age 65. Sam and his wife, Betsey, had very strong interests in the field of outsider art, and they were looking forward to spending more time writing articles and supervising art shows. They had done both in the past, but only in a limited way because of the demands of their work. They also loved to entertain and cook, and they decided they would spend at least a few months each year in the south of France, writing and cooking.

While they had never been happy with many of the tools they used in the kitchen, they didn't realize just how bad these tools actually were until they began "marathon cooking" for all of their friends who just happened to be traveling through Provençe. It became apparent that most of the kitchen tools didn't seem to meet the basics of good design: aesthetics, function, and form. Attractive products, when they found them, were a functional disaster. The bit of arthritis affecting Betsey's hands made it difficult for her to use the kitchen tools. She is one of over 20 million Americans who currently suffer

©1994, Corporate Design Foundation. This case was written by Professor William B. Gartner, San Francisco State University School of Business, with the support of the Corporate Design Foundation as a basis for class discussion rather than to illustrate either effective or ineffective handling of a business situation. Reprinted by permission.

from arthritis, so Sam and Betsey were particularly aware of how virtually none of the products considered user comfort.

They kept asking, "Why is the kitchen environment at best indifferent and at worst hostile to human use? Isn't it possible to combine form with utility in design, and combine them in such a way that it becomes accessible to the entire population? And doesn't it stand to reason that such a design would have great consumer appeal? Why can't a kitchen tool be comfortable, easy to use, of good quality, aesthetically pleasing, and easy to clean?" The seed was planted, and Sam Farber began to think about bringing this idea to market.

Market Research

Sam Farber devised a strategy to generate information on the market for kitchen gadgets with as few interviews as possible. He decided to interview buyers in different areas of distribution.

- Department stores—Bloomingdale's, Macy's
- Specialty store chains—Crate and Barrel, Williams and Sonoma
- Mass merchants—Target Stores
- Mail-order catalogs—Chefs' Catalog

These discussions centered primarily on bestselling items, price, design, packaging, display, and service. Sam was surprised (and a little disturbed) to find that buyers did not comment on the function of the product. When Sam mentioned some of his preliminary product goals, the only criteria the buyers seemed to respond to were dishwasher-safe, good quality, and design. Most buyers didn't mention the latter two. Function and user comfort didn't enter into the discussion at all.

All the buyers suggested the same bestselling items: peeler, can opener, garlic press, grater, pizza cutter, measuring spoons, and measuring cups. The mail-order catalog buyers preferred higher unit retails and therefore wanted sets that combined two or three items. All distribution areas were selling kitchen gadgets in lower price ranges than the prices Sam Farber had contemplated (e.g., peelers ranged from $.99 to $4.99). Sam was considering a peeler at a price much higher than $4.99.

Sam Farber decided to confine his interviews with consumers to five or six people he knew were good cooks. Some of these individuals were professional chefs, but the majority were very good amateur cooks. Sam reasoned that they, like him and his wife, would have thought a lot about the tools they used in the kitchen. Their answers concentrated on quality, comfort, and function.

Design Partners

Concurrently with Sam Farber's exploration of the market, he engaged the design firm, Smart Design, to undertake the design process from concept to product. Smart Design had done work for Sam previously at COPCO. Sam felt Smart Design was forward-thinking and had good technical expertise, and they were willing to take chances. The firm also had a wide variety of experience. Their client list included Corning Glass, Johnson & Johnson, Citibank, Clairol, the University of Southern California, and J.C. Penney.

Sam knew Smart Design would make a good partner, and he wanted a partner, not just hired hands. He worked out a three percent royalty agreement with Smart Design, plus a small advance. This way their success was dependent on the success of the products. In addition, Sam wanted to keep overhead costs (i.e., product design and development) minimal, as much as possible, rather than start the company with little working capital.

The Design Process

The designers discussed the product goals Sam Farber had already outlined. Most important, they attempted to identify the final customer. Was it a product for people with arthritis? Yes. Was it a product for older infirm people with weak hands? Yes. But it was really a product for everyone to use in the kitchen. Shouldn't everyone who cooks have comfortable tools? From a marketing point of view, Sam wanted to appeal to the broadest possible market, not just a very specific market for arthritics and the infirm. Sam wanted the design of these products to be of transgenerational, or universal, design.

Universal design stresses the need to make the design of any product or service fit the needs of as broad a spectrum of the populace as possible: products that make life more comfortable for everyone; products that are easy for everyone to use. Universal design acknowledges that people change over time, that their needs vary with ordinary events like pregnancy, an armful of groceries, carpal tunnel syndrome, skiing injuries, or the unavoidable changes of aging. Universal design attempts to extend the useful life of both the object and the user. Sam was hoping to push the boundaries dividing the able from the encumbered. Transgenerational design considers all these variations in strength and dexterity. It is a form of ecological thinking because it extends the life of the product and its materials by anticipating the whole life experience of the user. One of the designers put it this way: "We'd better design the stuff now because we'll need it when our abilities sag." Sam's comment was, "I think that's why I'm here."

Sam and Davin Stowell of Smart Design decided to bring in Patricia Moore as a project consultant. Trained as a designer, Moore had devoted herself to design problems addressing the older generation. For example, Procter & Gamble had asked her to help them redesign the Tide soap box to make it easier to open, so she helped them develop the snap-top box. Smart Design had collaborated with Moore on a number of universal design projects. They were eager to demonstrate that designing for a general population that included the elderly or those suffering from hand infirmities was not an excuse to make "frumpy prosthetic devices," but the opportunity to make products that are better for everybody.

Design Research

The next step was to have the design team do their own research. Information transmitted from the marketing managers to the designers can lose a lot in translation. The design team went out into the market. They talked to consumers. They examined all the competitive products. They interviewed chefs and spent many hours with volunteers from the New York arthritis group to learn the problems in hand movement. For weeks, they used products already on the market to pinpoint areas that needed improvement. This involvement as the final user brought the designers close to the project and helped them share Sam Farber's passion and belief.

It was now time to sit down and determine the product goals.

1. What are the primary product goals for these kitchen tools in terms of customer needs?

2. Once these product goals are determined, what should happen next in terms of product development?

3. What problems in the areas of product development, quality control, and pricing is this business likely to face before the introduction of these products at the San Francisco Gourmet Products Show?

4. What does Sam Farber need to do before creating a marketing plan?

OXO (B)

In the summer of 1989, Sam Farber and a design team led by Davin Stowell from Smart Design were involved in the development of a line of kitchen gadgets (e.g., peeler, can opener, pizza cutter, garlic press) that would be functional, comfortable, ergonomically sound, attractive, and affordable. Farber expected the Smart Design team to have the kitchen gadgets prototyped and ready for manufacture so that they could introduce the new line at the San Francisco Gourmet Products Show in April 1990. A number of design, marketing, and manufacturing challenges would need to be solved in the next nine months.

Determining the Product Goals

When OXO and Smart Design conducted a consumer survey about kitchen gadgets, they found users complained about rusting metal, cracking plastic, dull peeler blades, and can openers that didn't cut. Users wanted nonslip handles, easy-to-read measurements on all devices, simple directions, easy-to-clean tools, dishwasher-safe tools, a self-cleaning garlic press, and comfortable handles, especially for scissors.

The design team decided to spend most of the investigative time looking at the range of manual limitations, from serious permanent disabilities to the limited mobility and declining strength associated with aging. The team believed that by making tools that most of this group could use comfortably, they could satisfy the needs of all users.

The designers divided motions into twist (used to scoop, stir, and peel), push/pull (used with graters and knives), and squeeze (used to work scissors, garlic press, and can opener). The design team made hundreds of models and tried them all. They discovered that it was necessary to use a combination of motions to work most tools. The project would narrow down to three functional groups: gadgets and utensils with a general multi-purpose handle, squeeze tools, and measuring devices.

A general handle was to be used for the twist and push/pull motions. The handle would be large to increase leverage and oval to keep it from rotating in the hand. The short round end would fit comfortably into the palm and evenly distribute the pressure in motion.

When the group sat down to determine the product goals, they generated the following criteria:

Comfort: This was the key goal. A new product has to be able to differentiate itself from all the other ones on the market. Almost every tool they held was the wrong shape or so hard that it hurt the hands. They also experienced hand and wrist fatigue after using many of them. All the scissors on the market were a disaster. Sore fingers were a common complaint. It was actually in the conversation with one of their consumer cooks that the word *soft* appeared. They all agreed that a soft handle would be a comfortable handle and that it should be a key goal.

Easy to Use: They decided to stick to simple hand tools—ones that served one purpose and did it well.

Good Quality: This was a key recommendation from most of the consumer cooks. They complained about the inferior quality of the kitchen tools on the market. They rusted. Peeler blades became dull (or started out dull). Plastic cracked. Consumer cooks were willing to pay more for a longer-lasting tool.

Aesthetically Pleasing: There was a consensus that all the tools on the market were ugly or old-fashioned. Many people left their kitchen tools out in jugs on the counter and wanted them to be attractive.

Dishwasher Safe: A lot of people were afraid to put their kitchen tools in the dishwasher. Their previous experiences were disastrous: rusting, cracked handles. All agreed they would like tools they could just throw into the dishwasher. This was important in their search for the right soft materials for handles and led to their choice of Santoprene.

From Prototype to Product

In order to develop the general handle to be used for the different gadgets, hundreds of prototypes were constructed. Besides determining the shape of the handle, the design team also needed to specify a material to make the handle from. The design team wanted the material for the handle to be soft and flexible. However, the material had to be easy to mold and dishwasher safe. The team chose Santoprene, a material from Monsanto. Santoprene is composed of polypropylene plastic and rubber. This material has a warm nonslip feel to it. Since Santoprene is used for dishwasher gaskets, there was no doubt that it was dishwasher safe. By using Santoprene, it was also possible for the designers to incorporate another feature of the handle, "fingerprints softspots," which are flexible fin sections. These resilient fins help the handle to bend to an individual finger grip, thereby giving the user more cushion and control, even when hands are wet or soapy. The flexible fin feature was subsequently patented. The "fingerprints softspots" were added to the handle because Sam Farber saw a need to make an innovative feature of the general handle (soft spots) visible.

In conducting their research on the usability of different handle prototypes, the Smart Design team had identified the need for "soft spots," a portion of the handle that was softer than the rest of the handle in order to make the handle easier to grip and maneuver. The Smart Design team had originally designed, in many of the prototypes, the soft spots to be "invisible"; that is, the handle looked the same from tip to end, but when grasped, a portion of the handle, where the finger gripped the tool, "gave" more and therefore provided a better grip. Sam Farber felt that this feature needed to be visible to the customer: "The handle should invite involvement." Creating flexible fin sections for the soft spots on the handle gave it a distinctive and visually descriptive design. Much like an elegant sneaker built for the hands, the flexible fins on the handle were a sign to prospective customers that this was not another "me too" product.

In order to achieve the necessary rigid inner structure in the handle to support the tool end of a particular gadget as well as provide a base for the soft flexible outer handle, the metal part of the tool was molded to an inner core of in-expensive ABS plastic. The injection-molded Santoprene handle was then slipped over the ABS core.

The squeeze tools were designed with wide flat handles, so that in the clenching motion of the whole fist, the pressure on the hand was evenly distributed to alleviate sore spots and finger cramps. In designing the scissors, the team added a hidden spring in the hinge, which opens the blades automatically. The user does not have to use the tender back part of the thumb to pull the blades apart. The scissors were designed to use the strength of the whole hand for cutting. They were designed so that the bottom of the handle was flat, so that a user could press the scissors down on a table or countertop and, therefore, put the weight of one's shoulder into cutting through tough items like poultry joints or tree branches. The scissors were also designed to be used in either the right or the left hand. A pair also latches shut for safe storage in a drawer or on a hook.

The measuring cups and measuring spoons were designed with wide handles for extra control and big easy-to-read size markings that were color coded. This feature helps the eye perform better, as well as the hand. Finally, big holes on the gadgets and big rings for the measuring items enhance ease in hanging.

Manufacturing

The key group of items that would be Sam Farber's focus of attention when selecting a factory for production involved the peeler group of gadgets. Peelers are the biggest selling item in a line of kitchen gadgets. A factory was required that could manufacture a high-quality peeler, and OXO peelers would require a factory that had expertise in both metal parts production and plastic production. Because of Sam Farber's prior experience at COPCO in manufacturing kitchen products abroad and in selling kitchen wares in the United States market, he knew that OXO's products would have to be made in the Far East to be price competitive. Sam knew that the cost of tooling in the Far East would be lower and that he could get factories to share in the costs of making the tooling. Yet Sam did attempt to coax American manufacturers to bid. When Sam approached a factory in the United States that was making bicycle grips with a material similar to Santoprene, the factory manager looked at the Santoprene/ABS composite prototype handle and said, "It can't be done." When Sam visited a Japanese factory, the factory manager looked at the prototype handle and said. "Very interesting—why not?" Sam selected a Japanese factory to make the peelers. He had used this factory before to make knives for COPCO.

Sam turned to other factories in the Far East to manufacture the scissors, garlic press, measuring cups, and measuring spoons. He researched many factories in Taiwan and found three quality producers offering competitive prices. For manufacturing the large stainless steel tools, such as spoons and turners, Sam sought out factories in China. These large tools require a great deal of hand labor for a polished finish, and labor for this type of work is cheaper in China. Sam worked with a Hong Kong company that would ensure quality control in China. Sam sought companies that had experience selling to the German market. German consumers demanded higher quality than American consumers. The Hong Kong company was producing products for a number of quality German importers.

In summary, all the factories that Sam Farber chose met the following criteria:

1. They were producing similar products, so that they were familiar with the production problems that could arise and could consult effectively with the designers during the final stages of design.

2. They were quality-conscious.

3. They understood the process of exporting to the U.S. market.

4. They were willing to help pay for the cost of tooling as well as accept low minimum quantities on the original order.

Developing a Timetable

After selecting the factories to produce the products, Sam Farber established a time schedule with each factory, laying out a time frame from the day final drawings would be received to the shipping date of the gadgets. When he returned to the United States from this trip, Sam Farber met with the design team to map out a design and production schedule. Sam planned to show the line at the Gourmet Products Show in San Francisco in April 1990. Working back from this date, the following activities would have to be accomplished:

1. The preliminary conceptual designs would be ready on October 15. A design direction would be chosen. If none of the designs were accepted, the design team would try again.

2. The final designs would be presented for approval on November 15.

3. Prototypes would be made by Smart Design or their model maker on December 15.

4. Final drawings and prototypes would be sent to the factories on January 1, 1990.

5. The lead designer and Sam Farber would visit the factories and finalize all designs and give approval to start the tooling.

6. In order to show something at the Gourmet Products Show by April, temporary molds of the gadgets made at the Japanese factory would be made, and prototypes of the items made at the Taiwanese and Chinese factories would be shown.

7. Stock would be in the warehouse by July 1 for shipment.

Though this schedule was ambitious, Sam felt it could be achieved. In bringing the kitchen gadgets into production, Sam never went to the Far

East without someone from the design team. He believed that the designer needed to be familiar with the factories and their production capabilities, what a factory can and cannot do. Sam felt that "factory guys" are notorious for saying "It can't be done." Sam found that the design team couldn't just work in the studio, but had to be actively involved in the early marketing studies and in the production techniques and manufacturing: "You can't accomplish design innovation in a vacuum. All the players have to participate and feel they are partners all along the way."

Other Considerations

All the distribution areas (e.g., department stores, specialty kitchen shops, mail-order catalogs, discount retailers) suggested the same bestselling items: peeler, can opener, garlic press, grater, pizza cutter, measuring spoons, and measuring cups. The mail-order catalogs preferred higher unit retails and were therefore interested in selling sets that combined two or three items.

All distribution areas were used to selling kitchen gadgets in lower price ranges than OXO had contemplated: e.g., most peelers were selling from $.99 to $4.99, while the OXO peeler would be sold from $5.99 to $7.99. The mass market companies were interested in the lower end of the price range. This was an important factor in the decision to produce a second line for this distribution area, which would be lower-priced. This line, labeled "Prima," would sell peelers for $3.99, which is at the higher end for mass merchants. In order to manufacture gadgets at this lower price, tradeoffs in the quality of the product would have to be made. While the handle would be user-friendly, it would be made of hard plastic and in one piece, rather than made from Santoprene, and in two pieces. Farber also decided he was willing to take a lower gross margin on the Prima line in order to sell the product for a lower price.

Department stores and mass merchants wanted items packaged on cards in a traditional manner. Farber and the design team realized that their "story" was in the handle, so they designed cards so that the handle swung free. Customers could actually grab the handle and feel it. OXO also realized that many specialty stores didn't like cards, so gadgets were also sold uncarded, or with small countertop displays. The demands from the mail-order catalogs were mixed. Some wanted cards for customer information and some didn't.

The accepted display technique in all stores was to hang the items on the "gadget wall." The team's marketing observations were that these walls were unsightly—it was difficult to find a product, and none of the lines were presented together as one package. Since OXO had a story to tell, they wanted to keep their line separate from the others. The department stores and specialty stores were receptive to the idea of a freestanding display. The mass merchants used only the wall. The design team created a large display at first, subsequently created a smaller revolving display, and finally, created a display, holding six items, that could be placed near the cash register.

Most department stores wanted service, either complete service such as inventory counting and display maintenance, or display maintenance. Some mass merchants were not interested in service because they had sophisticated scanning devices for quick reordering through EDI setups as well as trained stock people in the stores. Other retailers wanted merchandise sold to a distributor who would handle stocking and service. For example, Target stores wanted merchandise sold directly to them, while Caldor wanted merchandise to be sold to Federal Wholesale, which maintains Caldor inventories and displays.

Because the handle was the key to the whole line, the design team realized the gadgets needed a name that told the customer what was special about these products. "Good Grips" proved to be a perfect name. This name communicated the major advantage of the line to the customer quickly: these products were comfortable kitchen tools.

Expanding the Team

Sam Farber had invested his own money in the venture during these initial stages of development, but he realized that as the company began manufacturing the product, he would likely need more capital for inventory expansion and working capital. He approached a few of his friends, explained his idea, and received assurances from them that they would like to participate as investors. When Sam talked about OXO to his son John, a Prudential Bache vice president in mergers and acquisitions, John agreed to become Sam's business partner but not actually work full-time for the company. However, a few months later, John changed his mind and decided to become an active participant. Sam and John decided to form OXO as a limited partnership with four of Sam's friends as the other partners. Through the assistance of Sam's accountant, the partners arranged for a line of credit with Chemical Bank. Surprisingly, because of strong initial sales and inventory purchases on a just-in-time basis, OXO had a healthy positive cash flow and never did borrow any money from the bank.

Sam's wife Betsey had shared the same passionate beliefs about the products from the very beginning. Her experience in the kitchen and her arthritis were key factors in the original concept. She decided to join the company rather than return to the practice of architecture. She came to be in charge of all publicity, trade shows, brochures, copywriting, and in-house graphic design.

Though Sam had many contacts with buyers, he knew he needed to focus his own efforts on developing new products. OXO would need a sales force and someone to manage this sales force. One of his former sales vice-presidents from COPCO, Ed Beren, was working as a sales consultant to two or three companies in the housewares field. When Sam explained the idea of "Good Grips" to Ed and showed him some of the initial models, Sam had another passionate believer. Ed agreed to work as OXO's sales manager and as a consultant to the company for a percentage of the sales and a small advance. Though OXO would not get all Ed's time, it would only have to share in paying for his expenses, thereby turning what is often a fixed overhead expense into a variable cost.

The meeting with Ed took place in February. It was agreed that Ed would find a sales force of manufacturer's representatives and bring them together for the first time at a sales meeting during the San Francisco Gourmet Products Show in April. The manufacturer's representatives would all work on commission.

A three-year marketing plan was developed. The initial line of kitchen gadgets would be sold to upscale distribution outlets, to establish the concept and the name. The design team targeted January 1992 as the time to introduce a second line of kitchen gadgets geared to mass merchants, like Wal-Mart, Kmart, and Target. By the end of 1993, they would produce a third line, aimed at the supermarkets and lower-priced kitchen stores. Although the lines would be different from one another, they would adhere to the same basic principles of universal design: all the tools would be easier to hold and use.

Last-Minute Details

Right before the San Francisco Gourmet Products Show, Sam and Betsey contacted many of the trade magazines about the story of OXO and Good Grips. Trade magazines look for news of new products. The editors of these magazines jumped at the opportunity to write feature stories on the company and the concept. Magazine editors and writers were introduced to the Smart Design office. The entire design process was explained. Sam wanted them to become believers too. They did. A number of articles were written that celebrated the revolutionary qualities of the new designs for these kitchen gadgets.

In building a display booth for the Gourmet Products Show, the team realized they didn't have much product to display, and the products themselves were small. In order to catch the buyer's eye quickly and communicate the features of these unique products, the booth was constructed of photo murals of the products.

A week before the Gourmet Products Show, the Japanese factory sent the initial samples for the show. But the grade of material chosen for the handles was noticeably harder than what the design team had wanted. The Japanese worked around the clock and through the weekend to produce another set of samples in time for the show. Sam's view of this burst of cooperation was:

> They too had become believers. They felt involved as partners. Making the supplier a part of the team in the early stages is one of the keys to success of a project. In any innovative design project, you're probably pushing way beyond the boundaries of present products and present techniques—and in many cases present technology too. Those land mines hide all over the road. It is hard to imagine this statement in relation to a fairly prosaic item like the potato peeler. But we were using a material unfamiliar to our factories, and one never before used in kitchen tools. We were asking them to mold very thin uniform sections in the material. We were *convinced* it could be done and Monsanto felt it could be done.
>
> Naysayers are a serious impediment in the process of design innovation. They can be outside suppliers, technical people, or people within your own

company who always follow the safe path. Safety and self-doubt don't flourish along the pathway of the entrepreneur. It's not the way of someone trying to push through a revolutionary design project. That's why it is so important to have the suppliers involved. When they believe, they will continually try to help you prove that it can be done.

The Good Grips line was an instant success when it was presented at the San Francisco Gourmet Products Show in April 1990. Everyone wanted the merchandise. While the product had been promised for delivery in July, shipments did not begin until September. OXO was able to place the products in all the major department stores and specialty stores. Sales did meet initial projections.

Expansion and Growth

In Spring 1991, OXO introduced a line of knives using the Santoprene handle. The handle has a slightly different shape, since knives are held differently than other kitchen gadgets. In July 1991, OXO introduced the "Prima" line for mass merchants in the 500-store western chain Target. The Prima line has the same finger grip, but uses less of the Santoprene, that is an expensive material. Other products that were introduced include a hand-held jar opener that easily twists off stubborn jar lids and bottle caps and a "flying nun" corkscrew with a large easy-to-turn knob, and wide wings contoured to the curve of the hand to facilitate the downward push that lifts out the cork. (The screw is coated with zylon, a nonstick material that enables it to glide easily into the cork without tearing it.)

OXO has also introduced a line of tools designed for the garden. The handle uses a soft material similar to the Santoprene. It has the patented fingerprint fins, but the shape of the handle has been altered slightly to conform to the different ways the hand moves when using a garden tool. OXO signed a licensing agreement with the Sierra Club to market the tools as "Good Grips Sierra Club Garden Tools." Part of the proceeds from the sale of these tools goes to the Sierra Club to help preserve and protect the environment.

The company is developing nonskid mixing bowls. It is also conducting extensive studies on the arm and wrist movements involved in lifting a pot filled with food, in order to design a line of cookware using a version of the patented handle. In terms of the future, Sam commented:

> We think there is still much more we can do in designing innovative items for the kitchen and related home areas. We also realize that our patented handle and our work in promoting universal design has potential even beyond that. At the present time we are licensing our knife handle to a major medical supply company. They are using it to produce a set of tableware— rocker knife, fork, and various spoons—for use by people who have physical difficulty holding ordinary silverware. Our factories manufacture the implements exclusively for them and we receive a royalty. We are also in the process of discussing licensing the patented handle to a paint tool company

and to a hair brush company. Our scissors are about to be introduced in a number of poultry processing plants where relief of hand and wrist fatigue in repetitive motion is very important. We feel that we are just at the beginning, both in developing our own new products and in licensing our handles in other markets.

In the four years since the first showing, these products have won a number of design awards:

▸ *International Design Magazine* Annual Design Review, 1991. Selection for consumer products category out of 1,300 submissions.

▸ Industrial Design Excellence Awards. Gold Medal, 1992. A contest conducted by the Industrial Designers Society of America and sponsored by *Business Week*.

▸ Design Leadership Award for Growing Companies, 1993. Winner for product design. A contest sponsored by *Inc.* magazine and the Corporate Design Foundation.

On October 20, 1992, General Housewares Corporation (GHW) announced the acquisition of OXO International L.P. In making the announcement, Paul A. Saxton, Chairman, President, and CEO of General Housewares, said:

> The acquisition of OXO and its exceptional portfolio of distinctive products strengthens General Housewares' position as the leading domestic supplier to the highly involved, discriminating kitchen consumer. We are especially pleased to become associated with Sam Farber and John Farber, the principals of OXO. Sam and John will be joining the GHC executive team, continuing their direct management roles in OXO. They will also play a key contributory role in our sourcing and new product development programs. With the addition of kitchen tools, we provide to our customers a more comprehensive product assortment, as well as create for GHC new and exciting cross-merchandising opportunities building upon our existing products.
>
> OXO is an acquisition that fits very well with GHC's strategy. As with the Chicago Cutlery acquisition, OXO embodies a truly superior product line and an emerging brand franchise that we believe will add important value to GHC in the years to come.

Sam Farber commented,

> We are extremely excited about the combination with General Housewares. As our business continues to grow dramatically, we have become increasingly aware of the need to bring top-quality service as well as products to our customers. General Housewares is known in the industry for the superior quality of its marketing and customer service and I believe those capabilities, combined with our product development work, create a unique force in the housewares industry. Finally, we have been very impressed by the character and depth of the General Housewares management team and believe that our compatibility with them will ensure a very successful future.

Plans for the Future

With OXO now part of a company with substantial resources for product development and marketing, Sam Farber felt that OXO needed to direct its energies to new opportunities. But in order to do that, Sam needed to determine the company's direction:

> What should we do next? Are we a kitchen company or are we a company developing comfortable universal design products for any place in the home or office or outside the home? I have posed this question to everyone at OXO and to our designers. We are in the middle of discussions.

1. How were OXO's philosophy and mission used to develop the product line?

2. Was it necessary for OXO to join forces with General Housewares Corporation to grow? If so, why?

3. Is OXO a kitchen company or is it a company developing comfortable universal design products for any place in the home, the office, or outside the home? Why is it important for Sam Farber to answer this question.

References

Chapter 1

[1] R.H. Brockhaus, "Risk-taking Propensity of Entrepreneurs," *Academy of Management Journal*, 23 (1980), pp. 509–520; P.F. Drucker, *Innovation and Entrepreneurship* (New York: Harper & Row, 1985).

[2] D.C. McClelland, "N-achievement and Entrepreneurship: A Longitudinal Study," *Journal of Personality and Social Psychology*, 1 (1965), pp. 389–392.

[3] D.B. Greenberger and D.L. Sexton, "An Interactive Model of New Venture Initiation," *Journal of Small Business Management* (1988), pp. 1–7.

[4] W.B. Gartner, "Who Is an Entrepreneur Is the Wrong Question," *American Journal of Small Business* (1988), pp. 11–31; K.H. Vesper, *New Venture Strategies* (Englewood Cliffs, N.J.: Prentice-Hall, 1990).

[5] William B. Gartner and Candida B. Brush, "Entrepreneurship: Emergence, Newness, and Transformation" (Paper presented at the Academy of Management Entrepreneurship Division Doctoral Consortium, Boston, August 1997).

[6] K.G. Shaver and L.R. Scott, "Person, Process, Choice: The Psychology of New Venture Creation," *Entrepreneurship: Theory and Practice,* 16(2) (1991), pp. 23–47.

[7] S.W. Becker and G. Gordon, "An Entrepreneurial Theory of Formal Organizations, Part I: Patterns of Formal Organizations," *Administrative Science Quarterly*, XX (1966), pp. 315–344.

[8] J.E. Pfeffer, *Organizations and Organization Theory* (Cambridge, Mass.: Ballinger, 1982).

[9] H. Liebenstein, "Entrepreneurship and Development," *American Economic Review,* 58(2) (1968), pp. 72–83; R. Nelson and S. Winter, *An Evolutionary Theory of Economic Change* (New York: Belknap Press, 1982).

[10] J. Case, *From the Ground Up* (New York: Simon and Schuster, 1992).

[11] P.F. Drucker, *Innovation and Entrepreneurship* (New York: Harper & Row, 1985).

[12] Elyse M. Friedman, ed., "New Economy Almanac," *Inc.: The State of Small Business* (1997), pp. 108–121.

[13] Heather R. McLeod, "Crossover," *Inc.: The State of Small Business* (1997), pp. 100–105.

Chapter 2

[1] Charles Thompson, *What a Great Idea!* (New York: HarperPerennial, 1992).

Chapter 3

[1] Zenas Block and Ian C. Macmillan, "Milestones for Successful Venture Planning," In *The Entrepreneurial Venture* (Boston, Mass.: Harvard Business School Publications, 1992), pp. 138–148.

[2] Joseph R. Mancuso, *How to Write a Winning Business Plan* (Englewood Cliffs, N.J.: Prentice-Hall, 1985).

[3] Fred L. Fry and Charles R. Stoner, "Business Plans: Two Major Types," *Journal of Small Business Management* (January 1985), pp. 1–6.

[4] Stanley R. Rich and David E. Gumpert, "How to Write a Winning Business Plan," In *The Entrepreneurial Venture* (Boston, Mass.: Harvard Business School Publications, 1992).

[5] Gerald E. Hills, "Market Analysis in the Business Plan: Venture Capitalists' Perceptions," *Journal of Small Business Management* (January 1985), pp. 38–46.

Chapter 4

[1] A.H. Van de Ven, R. Hudson, and D.M. Schroeder, "Designing New Business Start-ups," *Journal of Management*, 10 (1984).

[2] Grant Thornton, *Changing Roles for Boards of Directors in Entrepreneurial Companies*, GT Online: Assurance and Governance (*http://www.gt.com/gtonline/assuranc/changec.html*, 1996).

[3] Donald J. Jonovic, Ph.D., "Professionalizing: The Key to Long-term Shareholder Value, Part 1" (*http://hsb.baylor.edu/html/cel/ifb/legacies/jonovic.htm*).

[4] Ibid.

Chapter 5

[1] K.E. Knight, M.J. Dowling, and J.B. Brown, "Venture Survivability: An Analysis of the Automobile, Semiconductor, Vacuum Tube and Airline Industries," In *Frontiers of Entrepreneurship Research* (Wellesley, Mass.: Babson Center for Entrepreneurial Studies, 1987), pp. 138–153.

[2] W.H. Starbuck, "Organizations and Their Environments," In *Handbook of Industrial and Organization Psychology* (Chicago: Rand McNally, 1976); J. Pfeffer and G.R. Salancik, *The External Control of Organizations* (New York: Random House, 1978).

[3] Michael E. Porter, *Competitive Strategy: Techniques for Analyzing Industries and Competitors* (New York: The Free Press, 1980), p. 3.

[4] Amir Bhide, "How Entrepreneurs Craft Strategies That Work," *Harvard Business Review*, Vol. 72, No. 2 (March–April 1994), p. 154.

Chapter 6

[1] G.E. Hills, "Market Analysis and Marketing in New Ventures: Venture Capitalist Perceptions," In *Frontiers of Entrepreneurship Research* (Babson Center for Entrepreneurial Studies, 1984), p. 43.

[2] Holly Celeste Fisk, "Business Beat: Friendlier Skies," *Entrepreneur* (November 1996), p. 24.

[3] J.A. Hall, *Bringing New Products to Market* (New York: AMACOM, 1991).

Chapter 7

[1] K. and T. Fujimoto Clark, *Product Development Performance* (Boston: Harvard Business School Press, 1991).

[2] B. Joseph Pine, II, *Mass Customization* (Boston: Harvard Business School Press, 1993).

[3] Christoph von Braun, "The Acceleration Trap," *Sloan Management Review*, 32(1) (Fall 1990), p. 49.

[4] Pine, op. cit. p. 21.

[5] U.S. Patent and Trademark Office, Design Patents (*http://www.uspto.gov/web/offices/pac/doc/general/design.html*).

[6] U.S. Patent and Trademark Office, Disclosure Document Program (*http://www.uspto.gov/web/offices/com/sol/notices/disdo.html*).

Chapter 9

[1] Tom Williams, "Selected Topics on Internet Law" (Unpublished paper, University of Southern California Law Center, May 1996).

[2] Ibid. p. 10.

[3] Ibid. p. 17.

[4] Raymond Nimmer, *Law of Computer Technology*, 55 (1996); Edward Cavanos and Gavino Morin, *Cyberspace and the Law*, 44 (Boston: Warren, Gorham, and Lamont).

[5] Baum, *EDI and the Law*, 129, ed. Ian Walden (1989).

Chapter 10

[1] Randy Myers, "Temporary Tenant," *Nation's Business* (August 1995), p. 39.

Chapter 11

[1] E.J. Hay, *The Just-in-Time Breakthrough* (New York: John Wiley and Sons, 1988).

[2] "Feigenbaum's 40 Steps to Quality Improvement" (*http://deming.eng.clemson.edu/pub/tqmbbs/prin-pract/feig40.txt*).

[3] Ibid.

[4] Kenneth Hopper, "Creating Japan's New Industrial Management: The Americans as Teachers," *Human Resource Management* (1982), pp. 13–34.

[5] Feigenbaum, op. cit. p.1.

[6] Warren H. Schmidt and Jerome P. Finnigan, "The Race Without a Finish Line," *Small Business Reports*, 18(2) (February 1993).

Chapter 12

[1] Adrian J. Slywotzky, *Value Migration* (Cambridge, Mass.: Harvard Business School Press, 1996).

[2] Teri Lammers Prior, "Channel Surfers," *Inc.* (February 1995), p. 65.

[3] "Surrogate Distribution," The Virtual Consultant, Inc. Online (*http://www.inc.com/301/ideas/1078.html*).

Chapter 13

[1] D. Krackhardt and J.R. Hanson, "Informal networks: The company behind the chart," *Harvard Business Review*, 71(4) (1993), p. 105.

[2] *Inc.* (October 1993), p. 86.

[3] J.R. Katzenbach and D.K. Smith, *The Wisdom of Teams* (Boston, Mass.: Harvard Business School Press, 1993).

[4] R.M. Grant, R. Shani, and R. Krishnan, "TQM's Challenge to Management Theory and Practice," *Sloan Management Review*, 35(2) (1994), pp. 25–35.

5 Liz Fisher, "Total Quality: Hit or Myth?" *Accountancy*, 113(1208) (1994), p. 50.

6 Bill Creech, *The Five Pillars of TQM* (New York: Truman Talley Books/Plume, 1994).

7 R.L. Osborne, "Minority Ownership for Key Employees: Dividend or Disaster?" *Business Horizons*, 3(1) (1992), p. 76.

Chapter 14

1 Don Peppers and Martha Rogers, *The One to One Future: Building Relationships One Customer at a Time* (New York: Currency/Doubleday, 1993).

2 Ibid. p. 36.

3 "Ask the Marketing Doctors," *Inc.* (October 1995), p. 68.

4 Donna Fenn, "Leader of the Pack," *Inc.* (February 1996).

5 Peppers and Rogers, op. cit. p. 83.

6 J.C. Levinson, *Guerrilla Marketing* (Boston, Mass.: Houghton Mifflin, 1993).

7 J.C. Levinson, *Guerrilla Marketing* (Boston, Mass.: Houghton Mifflin, 1993).

8 "Firms Now Spend More on Old, Not New, Customer," *Los Angeles Times* (November 1, 1994).

Chapter 15

1 A. Bhide, "Bootstrapping Finance: The Art of Start-Ups," *Harvard Business Review*, 70(6) (1992), pp. 109–117.

2 Robert A. Mamis, "Power of Poverty," *Inc.* (August 1997), p. 40.

3 Ibid.

4 Jeffry Timmons, *The Entrepreneurial Mind* (Acton, Mass.: Brickhouse Publishing, 1989).

5 L. Brokau and S. Cook, "The Ethics of Bootstrapping," *Inc.* (September 1992), p. 87.

6 John Freear and William Wetzel, Jr., "Who Bankrolls High-Tech Entrepreneurs?" *Journal of Business Venturing* (March 1990), pp. 77–89.

7 "SBA Loans Spur Start-Up Growth," *Inc.* (November 1992), p. 66.

8 *The State of Small Business: A Report of the President* (Washington, D.C.: Government Printing Office, 1995), p. 287.

9 W.D. Bygrave and J.A. Timmons, *Venture Capital at the Crossroads* (Cambridge, Mass.: Harvard Business School Press, 1992).

10 *Venture Capital Journal*, Special Report (April 1990), p. 1.

11 Gary D. Zeune, "Ducks in a Row: Orchestrating the Flawless Stock Offering," *Corporate Cashflow* (February 1993).

12 Donald E. Vaughn, *Financial Planning for the Entrepreneur* (Englewood Cliffs, N.J.: Prentice-Hall, 1997), p. 67.

13 Ibid. p. 68.

14 James H. Schilt, "A rational approach to capitalization rates for discounting the future income stream of closely held companies," *The Financial Planner* (1982).

15 Thomas W. Zimmerer and Norman M. Scarborough, *Essentials of Entrepreneurship and Small Business Management*, 2nd ed. (Englewood Cliffs, N.J.: Prentice-Hall, 1998).

Chapter 16

1 J.M. Stancill, "How Much Money Does Your New Venture Need?" In *The Entrepreneurial Venture* (Boston, Mass.: Harvard Business School Publications, 1992).

2 Robert W. Kolb and Ricardo J. Rodriguez, *Financial Management*, 2nd ed. (Cambridge, Mass.: Blackwell Business, 1996).

3 Ibid.

Chapter 17

1 "The 1996 Inc. 500 List," *Inc. 500* (1996), p. 24.

2 Martha E. Mangelsdorf, "The Class of '85," *Inc. 500* (1995), p. 76.

3 Hal Plotkin, "What They Do (and Don't) Teach You in Business School," *Inc.* (December 1997), p. 88.

4 Jay Finegan, "The Smartest Franchisees in America," *Inc.* (November 1995), p. 48.

5 Janean Huber, "Thrill Seekers," *Entrepreneur* (May 1995), p. 128.

6 Timothy Bates, "Look Before You Leap," *Inc.* (July 1995), p. 23.

7 Dale D. Buss, "Growing More by Doing Less," *Nation's Business* (December 1995), p. 18.

[8] Ibid.

[9] Benjamin M. Oviatt and Patricia McDougall, "Global Start-ups: Entrepreneurs on a Worldwide Stage," *The Academy of Management Executive* (May 1995), p. 30.

[10] Ibid.

Chapter 18
[1] George Gendron, "Regulation Time: 60 Seconds with . . . Gordon Roddick," *Inc.* (June 1993), p. 16.

[2] "Liabilities, Awards, Settlements," *The Financial Times Limited World Insurance Report* (January 14, 1994).

[3] Robin A. Gagemi, "Ergonomics: Reducing Workplace Injuries," *Inc.* (July 1996), p. 92.

Chapter 20
[1] D. Vogel, "The Globalization of Business Ethics: Why America Remains Distinctive," *California Management Review*, 35(19) (1992), pp. 30–49.

[2] S. Vyakarnam, A. Bailey, A. Myers, and D. Burnett, "Towards an Understanding of Ethical Behaviour in Small Firms," *Journal of Business Ethics*, 16(15) (November 1997), pp. 1625–1636.

[3] Courtney Price and Kathleen Allen, *Tips and Traps for Entrepreneurs* (New York: McGraw-Hill, 1998).

[4] Ibid. p. 270.

[5] J.G. Longenecker, J.A. McKinney, and C.W. Moore, "Ethics in Small Business," *Journal of Small Business*, 27 (1989), pp. 27–31.

[6] G.M. McDonald and R.A. Zepp, "Business Ethics: Practical Proposals," *Journal of Business Ethics*, 81 (1989), pp. 55–56.

[7] G.F. Cavanaugh, D.J. Moberg, and M. Valasquez, "The Ethics of Organizational Politics," *Academy of Management Review*, 6 (1981), pp. 363–374.

[8] Richard Narva and Thomas Davidow, "Six Questions for Growing Family Businesses," Umass Family Business Center *Related Matters Newsletter* (Summer 1995) (*http://nmq.com/fambiznc/cntprovs/orgs/umasscfb/Newslttr/Summer95/*).

[9] "Front Line Articles: Be Careful What You Wish For," *Business Ethics Magazine* (*http://condor.depaul.edu/ethics/biz_aug1.html*), © 1996.

[10] Anna Muoio, "Ways to Give Back," *Fast Company*, 12 (December 1997–June 1998), p. 113.

[11] Ellyn E. Spragins, "Making Good," *Inc.* (May 1993), p. 114.

[12] Muoio, op. cit. p. 113.

[13] Ibid.

[14] Ibid.

[15] Ibid.

[16] Peter F. Drucker, *Innovation and Entrepreneurship* (New York: Harper and Row, 1985).

[17] Paul Hawkin, *The Next Economy* (New York: Holt, Rinehart and Winston, 1983), pp. 172–173.

[18] Tom Peters and Nancy Austin, *A Passion for Excellence* (New York: Warner Books, 1985).

[19] R.H. Hayes, S.C. Wheelwright, and K.B. Clark, *Dynamic Manufacturing* (New York: The Free Press, 1988).

[20] O.G. Mandino, *University of Success* (New York: Bantam Books, 1982).

Index